Carole Naggar
David 'Chim' Seymour

Appearances – Studies in Visual Research

Edited by
Tim Allender, Inés Dussel, Ian Grosvenor,
and Karin Priem

Vol. 4

Carole Naggar

David 'Chim' Seymour

Searching for the Light
1911–1956

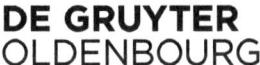

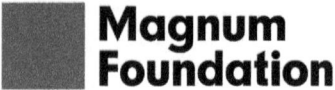

ISBN 978-3-11-070416-7
e-ISBN (PDF) 978-3-11-070634-5
e-ISBN (EPUB) 978-3-11-070637-6
ISSN 2628-1740

Library of Congress Control Number: 2022930309
Bibliographic information published by the Deutsche Nationalbibliothek
The Deutsche Nationalbibliothek lists this publication in the Deutsche Nationalbibliografie; detailed bibliographic data are available on the Internet at http://dnb.dnb.de.

© 2022 Walter de Gruyter GmbH, Berlin/Boston.
Cover image: Chim in Paris, early 1930s. Photographer unknown.
© David Seymour-Magnum Photos.
Typesetting: bsix information exchange GmbH, Braunschweig
Printing and binding: CPI books GmbH, Leck

www.degruyter.com

To Fred, Ariel, and Ezra, my family.
To Ben Shneiderman and Helen Sarid, Chim's family,
In memory of Richard Whelan, who introduced me to Chim's family.

Table of Contents

Abbreviations —— 1

Prologue: Something Like an Owl… and Something Like a Buddha —— 3

Chapter 1: Peace and War. 1911–1929 —— 9

Chapter 2: The City of Books. 1929–1931 —— 15

Chapter 3: Becoming Chim. 1932–1933 —— 27

Chapter 4: Front Populaire. 1934–1936 —— 41

Chapter 5: The Good Cause. Spring 1936–February 1939 —— 61

Chapter 6: From Chim to David Seymour. 1939–1945 —— 95

Chapter 7: Welcome to the Time Inc. Stink Club. 1947–1948 —— 111

Chapter 8: Children of Europe. 1948 —— 135

Chapter 9: Return to Poland: An Obliterated Past. 1948 —— 149

Chapter 10: I am a Mediterranean —— 163

Chapter 11: Tracing the Letters. 1950 —— 177

Chapter 12: Generation X: This is our Character, this is our Strength. 1952 —— 185

Chapter 13: Of Saints, Snakes, and Angels. 1951–1955 —— 193

Chapter 14: Under Greek Skies. 1951–1954 —— 203

Chapter 15: Pinups, Snails, Pigeons, and Spaghetti. 1950–1955 —— 213

Chapter 16: I Found a Home: Israel. 1951–1955 —— 237

Chapter 17: I Want to be into Things. November 10, 1956 —— 255

Epilogue: His Name Opened Doors. Chim's Legacy —— 265

Table of Contents

Timeline —— 273

Appendix —— 276

Selected Bibliography —— 278
Books by Chim or containing his photographs —— 278
Books and Periodicals —— 279
Periodicals Consulted —— 284
Archives and Collections Consulted —— 284

Acknowledgements —— 286

Also by Carole Naggar (selection) —— 288

Index —— 289

"It should not be said that the past illuminates the present or that the present illuminates the past. On the contrary, an image is where *Then* meets *Now* in a flash to form a constellation. In other words, the image is dialectic at a standstill."

Walter Benjamin

"Every war is a war against the child."

Eglantyne Jebb, Founder of the *Save the Children* Fund

Abbreviations

Throughout the notes, the following abbreviations have been used:

MPNYA	Magnum Photos New York Archive
MPPA	Magnum Photos Paris Archive
MP	Magnum Photos online database
ADSS	Album David Seymour Stories, (followed by a date and number).
AJGMUC	John G. Morris Archive, University of Chicago
JFAP	James Fox Archive, Paris
MFNY	Magnum Foundation, New York
DST	Text by Chim for a story.
DSC	Caption by Chim for a story
CNA	Carole Naggar Archive
ICPADS	International Center of Photography, David Seymour Archive
ICPARC	International Center of Photography, Robert Capa Archive
DAS	www.davidseymour.com online Archive
UMA	University of Maryland Archive
BSA	Archive of Ben Shneiderman, Bethesda, Maryland
GRA	Archive of George and Jinx Rodger, Smarden, Kent
UNESDOC	UNESCO Digital Library

In the New York and Paris Magnum Photos offices, Chim's contact sheets are organized with the following reference system: year, placement of the story in the year, number of the contact sheet within the story. Each 35mm image is numbered. Images made with Rollei are sometimes unnumbered.

#54-2-1, for instance, designates the first contact sheet in a 1954 story, the second story covered by Chim that year.

In the *Magnum Photos* online database (MPPA or MPNYA), the photographs follow a double numbering system:

Ex: SED1951004W00001/18: 1951. Chim's name (Seymour, David) & year when the story was shot; 004 is placement of the story in the year (fourth story); W00001 refers to the number of the contact sheet in the story, and 18 is the picture number on the contact sheet, when known—some negatives have been lost.

Ex: PAR116249: additionally, pictures have in parenthesis an inventory number with a reference to either New York (NYC) or Paris (PAR) archives.

At the time of this writing, due to the archive review process, access to the Magnum Pro site/database is limited to image licensing and assignment professionals. It's closed for browsing by students and enthusiasts though there are discussions about opening access back up in the future. See more about this in the Appendix.

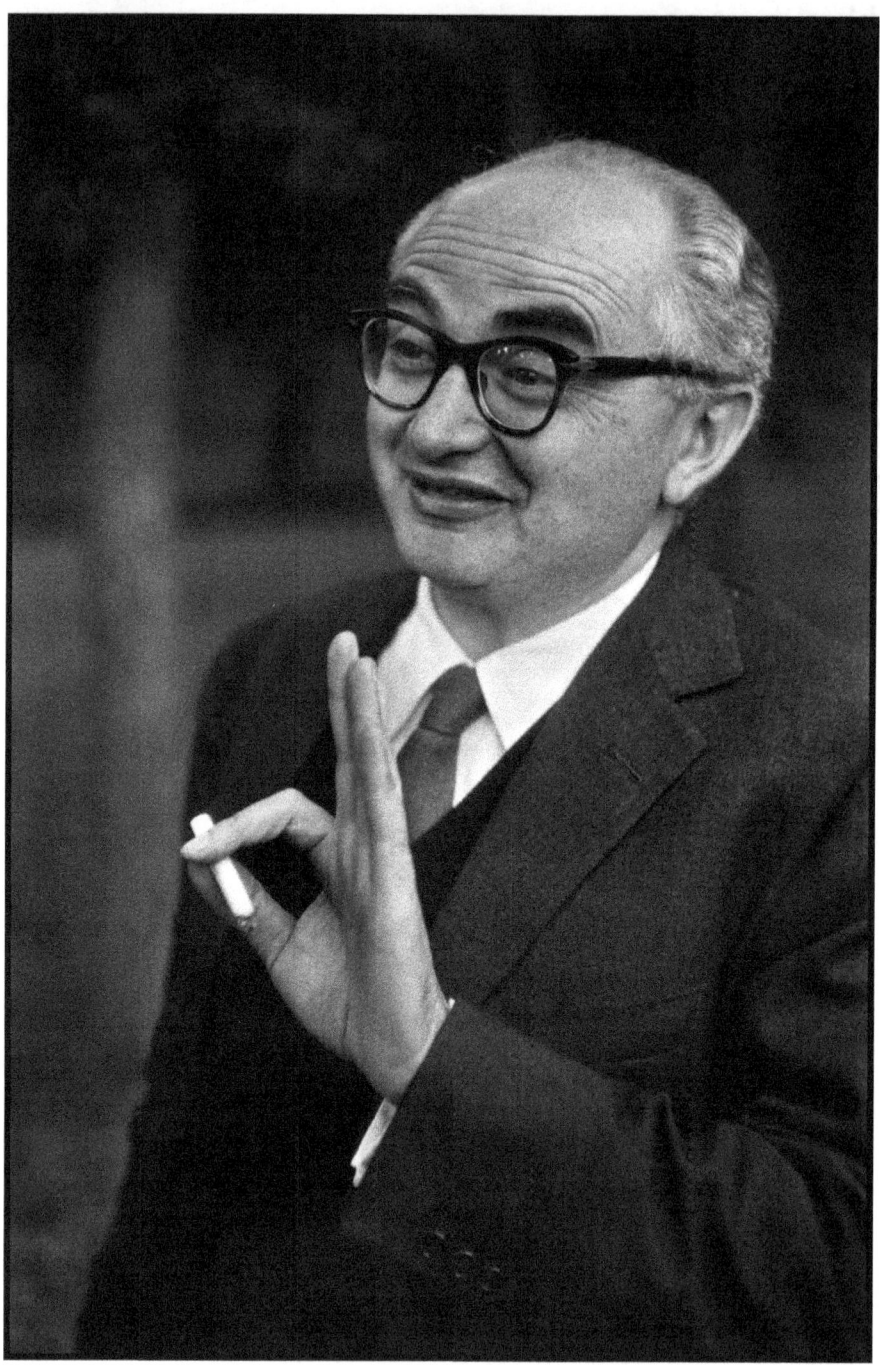

Fig. 2: David "Chim" Seymour near Magnum Photos office, 125 rue du Faubourg St Honoré, Paris, 1956. © Elliott Erwitt-Magnum Photos.

Prologue: Something Like an Owl... and Something Like a Buddha

Dawid Szymin was born in Warsaw in 1911, when no independent Polish state existed. Always vulnerable to land grabs from its neighbors—the Russian Empire, the Kingdom of Prussia and the Habsburg Monarchy –, the country would gain only fragile independence at the end of World War I. And when Dawid died in Egypt in November 1956, his coffin was draped in the American flag, a country whose nationality he had chosen in 1943 but where he almost never took pictures.

Between these two dates, his life traversed a revolution, a civil war, and two world wars; he lost his family to the Holocaust, moved to Italy and explored Greece, fell in love with Israel, and died an absurd death in the Suez War three days after the ceasefire. Through his many lives, David Robert Seymour, as he was known in America, constantly reinvented himself, a citizen of the world who nevertheless remained a European.

He never answered to Dawid, seeming to invite pet names: Dick, Dik, Didek, as a child and youth, Chim, Chimou, Chim-Chim or Chimsky later, before settling on Chim. He had a plethora of nicknames too: his colleague Elliott Erwitt called him "The Unflamboyant", and journalist Horace Sutton wrote that "he avoided ostentation as if it were the Automat."[1] His fascination with the rituals of Italian Catholicism prompted Trudy Feliu, a Paris editor at Magnum in the 1950s, and his Roman friends, to call him "Il Papabile."[2] Because of his bookish looks, many called him "Il Professore."

Born into a cultured community of Yiddish and Polish speakers, Chim was attached to his Jewish roots, to the specificity of his family's milieu, and to their craft of bookmaking and publishing. As a child in World War I, when his family fled to Russia in 1915 as the German advance on Poland began, he made the first of his many linguistic journeys, from Yiddish, Hebrew, and Polish to Russian. Later on, he brushed up on his high-school German and learned French in Paris, where he had followed the trail of many Eastern European artists and writers of his generation.

When he arrived in New York in 1939, he did not speak the language but soon, in the words of his friend Judy Friedberg, "added eloquent, if ungrammatical, English to the clutch of languages he commanded."[3] In the early 1950s, Italian followed. Through his travels and exiles, Chim remained profoundly shaped by his early interests in music, literature, design, and politics, and his left-wing convictions gave him an important connection to the future members of Magnum Photos.

---

1 Horace Sutton, "Magnum Opus", *The Saturday Review*, December 1, 1956, 54.
2 Interview of Trudy Feliu by the author. Morristown, N.J., June 23, 2005.
3 Judy Friedberg, *Chim: A Man of Peace*, 3/28/66, MPNYA, ADSS, 1956.

Chim did not possess a striking physique. He was neither tall nor muscular, with delicate features that seemed a bit lost in his round, owlish face. His most expressive aspect—moody, hazelnut eyes—was hidden behind thick eyeglasses, and his dark blond hair soon receded. He usually had a cigarette held between index finger and thumb or dangling from his lower lip.

His unassuming appearance was paired with a deliberately neutral elegance: silk tie and gray three-piece suit, white bespoke silk shirt, shoes shined to a mirror, and black camera bag. He might have taken off the jacket in a Magnum meeting, but he would never, ever roll up his sleeves. From the 1930s to the mid-1950s, successive photographs show surprisingly little change in his looks or the way he presented himself, except for the graying of his hair and his increasing chubbiness, the inevitable consequence of the convivial, gourmet dinners that were his joy.

This self-contained, somewhat mysterious man resembled the main character of a detective movie: John Morris, a long-time Magnum editor, thought that he looked like Peter Lorre. He wrote[4] "Seymour was the most enigmatic of the founders. (...) For months I thought he was a spy, which in a way he became when he worked for Allied Intelligence in London as a photo interpreter." Marc Riboud, who joined Magnum in 1955, told me, "There are men who, without being good looking, possess a great beauty. Chim was not handsome, but his face reflected his wit and obvious intelligence."[5]

Martha Gellhorn, a war correspondent, and writer who was Ernest Hemingway's companion in the Spanish Civil War and future wife, wrote a short story[6] where she changed Chim's name to Lep. This is how she describes him:

> Lep looked something like an owl and something like a panda, and something like a head of Buddha, quiet to the verge of invisibility, a man who smiled slowly and rarely laughed, a serious man, given to, serious obscure friends like archaeologists and doctors and musicians in Philharmonic orchestras, a small gentle man with a domed forehead over his vast spectacles (...).

Chim's colleague Jean Marquis remembers: "He had a very soft voice and a certain elegance in his way of expressing himself. His gaze was very expressive. It was like an interior laugh, not nasty. He was not aggressive, but his remarks could be very pointed. Bob [Capa] paid a lot of attention to his remarks and would frequently ask his opinion." Marquis's wife Susie, who worked for several years at the Magnum office in Paris, added: "He was very accessible work wise but not personally. He did

---

4 [4] John Godfrey Morris in *International Herald Tribune*, November 18, 1989. John Morris Archives, Paris, consulted June 2005, and interview of John Morris by the author, Paris, June 10, 2005.
5 CNA, Interview of Marc Riboud by the author, Paris, May 4, 2005.
6 Martha Gellhorn, *Till Death Us Do Part* (New York: Simon & Schuster, 1958 and New York: Vintage Books, 1994), 171.

not let on anything about his personal life. There was a distance and he wanted to keep it that way."[7]

Professionally, Chim was an attentive reader of his colleagues' work and his own contact sheets, one of the very few people, for instance, to whom, Cartier-Bresson showed his layout and text for *Images à la Sauvette* (The Decisive Moment,1952). His colleague Jean Marquis remembers:

> He is the one who taught me editing. He was interested in both the composition and the technical aspect of photography. He taught me how to tell a story in pictures. He let me choose and then he looked and made suggestions, but he never imposed. Contrary to Henri, it was about storytelling rather than aesthetics. I never saw him irritated or angry. In meetings, he tried to be persuasive. Sometimes he would get a little more heated with Bob when it was necessary.[8]

Never cruel, always attentive, Chim was the voice of reason in heated group discussions. He rarely laughed aloud but smiled often, and, when surprised, lifted a thin eyebrow. He was also a shrewd businessman who in 1955 wrote the Magnum bylaws that gave the agency its foundation and are still in effect today. Marc Riboud noted: "After Capa and Bischof's deaths in 1954, he was an efficient president."[9] His colleague Elliott Erwitt added: "Chim made a great contribution on the business side. Henri [Cartier-Bresson] had no understanding of money. Capa had no sense of business: he was a good promoter and salesman but a terrible administrator."[10]

Trying to describe Chim's personality, colleagues and friends give contradictory opinions. Distant, withdrawn, silent, some say. Plaintive, even: "Please, please, don't feel neglected," his colleague Maria Eisner admonished him.[11] "Like the wandering Jew, he seemed to carry the world upon his shoulders, but I suspect he was hiding his pleasure at going out on the job," Jinx Rodger says.[12] No—warm, smiling, generous, charming, others retort. They stress his lack of ego and his generosity in suggesting assignments to younger photographers as well as helping them financially, by taking them out to dinner, or socially, by introducing them to influential people. He taught his niece Helen how to drink gin and brought her to a tailor for her first Italian silk shirt. He never forgot his nephews', nieces' and colleagues' friends' birthdays and would appear with armfuls of presents, often bought at FAO Schwarz, the famous New York toy store, during his visits.

Among his multiple faces are that of a quiet seducer (as certain letters reveal), benevolent brother and uncle, formidable businessman and negotiator, king of pub-

---

[7] Interview of Jean and Susie Marquis by the author. Rambouillet, May 11, 2005, https://davidseymour.com/writings-on-cn-friends-and-colleagues/, accessed February 23, 2022.
[8] Ibid.
[9] CNA, Interview of Marc Riboud by the author, Paris, May 4, 2005, ibid.
[10] CNA, Interview of Elliott Erwitt by the author, New York, May 20, 2008.
[11] Maria Eisner, letter to Chim, December 22, 1947. JGMA, Paris.
[12] Interview of Jinx Rodger by the author, Smarden, Kent, January 6, 1998, davidseymour.com/writingson-cn-friends-and-colleagues/.

lic relations, friend of princes and prelates, secretaries, and bartenders. He remained secretive about his personal life—especially his girlfriends—and had many friends who often did not know each other. One of them remembered wistfully: "When I went to announce his death to his friend Dave Schoenbrun, he said to me in the conversation that followed: 'You and I know each other very little. And yet Chim was a friend of both of us. He was a man of secret compartments and he forgot to make them communicate.'"[13]

Chim was definitely an eccentric. A people collector, he had friends in the most varied milieus, and from their acquaintance or the many books he read, liked to acquire arcane knowledge about all sorts of fields, knowledge that he would drop unexpectedly into conversations. "You never knew what he would come up with—striptease or the history of the Franciscan order," his friend and colleague Burt Glinn recalled.[14] A wine connoisseur, he would drink not to get drunk but to savor the wines' varied flavors as if they were books to read. A gourmet, he loved to find new, out-of-the way restaurants to taste obscure dishes such as the ortolan, a minuscule stuffed bird soaked in cognac and eaten whole, bones and all. But in difficult circumstances, such as the Spanish Civil War, he was content to share with his comrades a simple meal of beans or lentils, stale bread, and sardines with cheap red wine.

Socially adept, he could easily project himself into any role that the situation required and connect with just about anyone—from street children to communist militants, Spanish Civil War fighters to Vatican priests, world-renowned artists to Hollywood stars, and kibbutz dwellers to Egyptian civilians. Seamlessly slipping from country to country and milieu to milieu, he seemed, like a cat, to be living nine lives.

Old or young, poor or famous, colleagues or strangers, people loved him. To each, he would reveal only a fragment of himself, but in such a way that, warmed by his welcoming kindness, each would feel for an instant that he was the best, the closest friend. As Cartier-Bresson once told me, "Capa was a pal, but Chim was a friend."[15]

Bill Pepper, a *Newsweek* editor in Rome, gives a beautifully nuanced description of him: "Chim came in and out of our lives unexpectedly like a sunrise. He extended our inner lives with his feelings. He was so like an inner voice in our lives, it is strange how he came along. This correlates with his affinity with children in his photography. We all have children inside us, the residual element of wonder that is never extinguished, and this is the part he was talking to."[16]

---

13 Horace Sutton, "Magnum Opus," *The Saturday Review*, December 1, 1956, 55.
14 Interview of Burt Glinn by the author, East Hampton, New York, November 10, 2005, https://davidseymour.com/writings-on-cn-friends-and-colleagues/.
15 Interview of Henri Cartier-Bresson by the author, Paris, January 4, 1998 in Carole Naggar Archive, New York.
16 Interview of Bill and Beverly Pepper by the author, New York, April 17, 2005.

A peace correspondent who died at war, Chim was, behind his smile, a man haunted by the Holocaust that destroyed the Jews of Europe, including most of his family. And if sometimes he withdrew with his pile of unanswered letters, letting the phone ring, maybe it was because he was overcome by the great wave of a sadness that would not end.

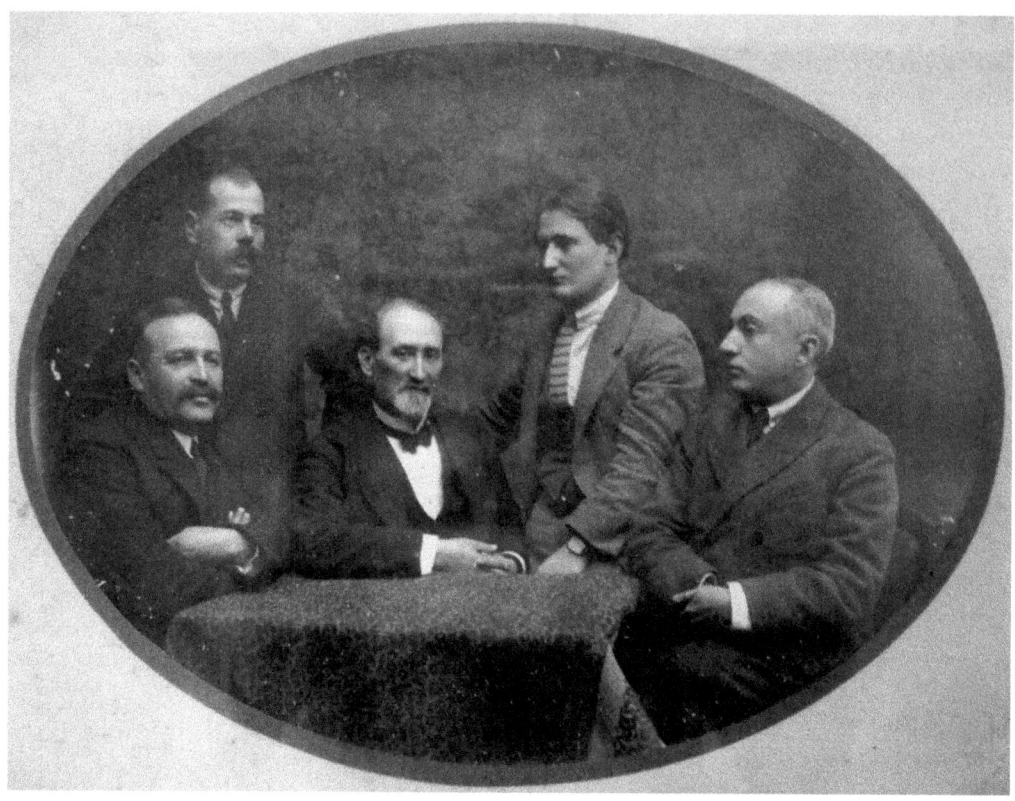

Fig. 3: Group photograph of the Partners of Warsaw "Central" Publishing Company. R-L: Benjamin Szymin (Binyomin Shimin), Yakov Lidsky, Ben-Avigdor (Avraham Leib Shalkovich), Mordechai Kaplan, Shloyme (Shlomo) Sreberk. Photographer unknown, courtesy of Professor Shlomo Izre'el (grandson of Shlomo Sreberk).

Chapter 1: Peace and War. 1911–1929

Dawid Szymin was born in Warsaw on November 20, 1911, to a cultivated, intellectual couple, Regina (Rivka), née Segal, born circa 1881 in Maków, and Benjamin Szymin, born circa 1880 in Otwock. His sister, Chaja-Halina (she would later become known as Hala), was three years older than him, and he would keep close ties with her throughout his life. Because of World War II and the subsequent destruction of Warsaw and, therefore, of the Polish Jews' archives, very little is known about Dawid's family and early life.

As part of the Russian Empire before World War I, Warsaw had been flooded with Jewish refugees from the late nineteenth-century pogroms, and as a result, it had the largest Jewish population in Europe—340,000 of Poland's three-and-a-half million Jews. With its thriving intellectual life, the city became the center of publishing in Poland and Russia. The daily and weekly press, the many literary magazines, and other periodicals in Hebrew and Yiddish provided a lively venue for elite writers, poets, scholars, and journalists.

Dawid's father was one of several noted Yiddish and Hebrew publishers who, in 1911, cooperated to form a publishing syndicate named Central (צענטראל, *Tsentral*; also named in Hebrew: מרכז, "Merkaz"). In addition to Lidski's Progress, Kaplan's HaShakhar, and Sreberk's S. Sreberk (ש. שרעבערק) the syndicate incorporated A. L. Ben Avigdor's (A. L. Shalkovich) pioneering Hebrew publishing company Tushiva (תושיה) and Benjamin Szymin's (ב. שימין) company (figure 3).

Located at Nowolipki 7 in Warsaw, Central was influential, the first Jewish publishing house to establish ties with Jewish communities outside of Russia, including the United States, and distribute its books worldwide. It also owned a bookstore, and the publisher and the store became a magnet for young Polish and Yiddish writers from smaller towns, including Sholem Asch, whose book *The Shtetl* Szymin published. It published works of the greatest Yiddish and Hebrew writers, historians, and intellectuals; children and young adults' books; textbooks, primers, and manuals, as well as popular calendars depicting paintings of biblical scenes, famous figures, and photographs of Israel; and Passover *Haggadot* and *Shana Tova* (Happy New Year) greeting cards. In 1912, Central's subsidiary, *Ahisefer*, released the literary collection *Netivot* ('Paths': *Free Stage for Matters of Life and Literature*), featuring Yiddish translations of European authors such as Jean-Jacques Rousseau, Victor Hugo, Tolstoy, Mark Twain, and Guy de Maupassant.[1]

---

[1] See "Lidsky, Yakov," in Hirsz Abramowicz, Zalman Reisen, *Leksikon fun der yidisher literatur, prese, un filologye*, 2nd ed., vol. 2, (Vilnius: B. Kletskin, 1927), 128–129. Translated as Hirsz Abramowicz, "Zalmen Reyzen," in *Profiles of a Lost World: Memoirs of East European Jewish Life before World War II*, 313–320 (Detroit: Wayne State University Press, 1999), and Avraham Novershtern's article *Reizen, Zalmen*, The Yvo Encyclopedia of Jews in Eastern Europe, https://yivoencyclopedia.org/article.aspx/Reyzen_Zalmen, accessed March 30, 2019; Zeev Gries, "The Revolution in the

Passionate about literature, and encouraged by his writer friends such as Sholem Asch, Isaac Bashevis Singer, Sholeim Aleichem, Leon Feiberg, Moshe Mandelman, Oskar Rosenfeld, and Barukh Glazman, Benjamin Szymin dedicated most of his time to Central. A friend of the family remembered: "The Szymin's home was a place where the best Jewish and Hebrew writers of our time met (...) David and his sister Hala were brought up in this atmosphere of idealism and quest for beauty and cultural values."[2] (figure 23 & figure 24)

In the book-lined rooms of the Syzmin's Art Nouveau apartment on Nowolipki Street 23, there were constant comings and goings of visitors, a hubbub of music—the family owned a phonograph and classical records—and literary and political discussion in Yiddish, Polish, or Russian. The family knew Hebrew too. On Shabbat, the fragrant smells of *cholent*, a stew of meat and barley that had been slow cooking since the previous afternoon, *kasha* with mushrooms, cinnamon, and chocolate, drifted out of the kitchen while Dawid, who loved to eat and was always hungry, tried to practice scales on the piano.

He loved this bustling family life but what he looked most forward to was the visit of the traveling cinema man who periodically arrived in their yard with his machine. Dawid would spend a few *grosze* of his pocket money to watch the adventures of the dog Rin Tin Tin who saved a baby left on the rails just before the locomotive arrived, or of Tom Mix chasing bandits on his white wonder horse, Tony. These early images and his frequent visits to the local movie theaters may have triggered his love for images.

On June 28, 1914, the assassination of Archduke Ferdinand of Austria and his wife in Sarajevo sparked a series of upheavals that rocked Polish Jewry. On August 1, Germany declared war with Russia and World War I began. Warsaw was bombed, and with the rumble of war, Dawid's warm, secure world was to be shattered. Like thousands of Polish Jews, Benjamin and Rivka fled, moving their family to Minsk, in Ukraine, which was linked to Warsaw by the Warsaw-Moscow railway. Benjamin had relatives in Minsk, a flourishing and cosmopolitan city of almost 100,000 people, mostly Jews, but also Poles and Russians, and a smaller group of Belarussians. Minsk had a wealth of theaters, cinemas, newspapers, schools, and colleges, as well as Jewish institutions, societies, and philanthropic organizations, synagogues (almost a hundred, as well as smaller prayer houses), churches, monasteries, and a mosque. A cultural and spiritual hub, it was the cradle of the Litvak (Lithuanian) culture, a tradition that favored rationalist interpretations of Jewish lore over the mystical ones endorsed by Hasidic rabbis. Together with Vilnius, "The Jerusalem of the North," Minsk was considered a protected place for Jews, and later on was home to exceptional artists, writers, and philosophers such as Jacques Lipchitz, Chaim

---

World of Hebrew Books at the Start of the Twentieth Century," *The Book in the Jewish World, 1700–1900*, 181–190 (Oxford: Littman Library of Jewish Civilization, 2007), 181–190.
2 DSA, Unsigned document describing the ceremony that followed Dawid's death.

Soutine, Marc Chagall, and Sergei Eisenstein. Minsk was also an important center for modern Jewish political movements and labor groups such as the Bund, but the political situation was unstable, and in 1916, the Szymin family, like many others, escaped to Odessa, where Szymin had many ties to the business community and where his publishing house was already known. (According to family lore, he left Minsk like a peddler, pushing a cart full of books). "The first winter in Russia was hard and David caught rheumatism, which he suffered from all his life. His legs were very weak," his sister Hala remembered.[3]

Chim's brother-in-law Samuel Leib Shneiderman, (later, Emil), Yiddishist, poet, journalist, and writer five years older than Chim, who as a child lived in the small town of Kazimerz Dolny, Poland, vividly remembers the World War I period:

> At the time, events of historic significance were taking place in the outside world: the Russian Revolution, February 1917; the British Balfour Declaration, November 1917, with the promise of a Jewish homeland in Palestine; and the rebirth of independent Poland at the close of World War I. These three turning points in modern European history are superimposed upon each other on the screen of my memory as if they had taken place at the same instant.[4]

He writes about the immediate effect of the Balfour Declaration on the religious community:

> The messianic age seemed close at hand (...). He [the poet Chaim Szendorowicz, speaking during *Hanukah* services at a local synagogue] said the dream of the return to Zion was about to be realized; it was the duty of every Jew to contribute generously towards this effort. Gold brooches, chains and diamond rings were promptly dropped from the women's gallery, and the men surrendered their gold and silver watches. The large bowls, used on the eve of the Day of Atonement for charitable collections, were quickly filled.[5]

With the subsequent coming of the Russian Revolution, Odessa was engulfed by civil war. Different factions—Bolsheviks, the Ukrainian Army, and finally the White Russians—fought for control of the city until April 29, 1918, when Odessa became the capital of the Odessa Soviet Republic. The advent of the Soviet regime and the end of World War I marked the end of Odessa as a Jewish cultural center and the home of the *Hibbat Zion* Zionism movement.

On November 11, 1918, when Dawid was about to turn seven, Poland regained its independence after 123 years of partitions by Austria-Hungary, Germany, and Russia, The Szymins were finally able to return home, to Warsaw; Central became one of the largest Yiddish language presses in Warsaw as well as a leader in Yiddish translations of prominent European writers such as Mark Twain, Victor Hugo, Maupas-

---

3 Robert E. Hood, *12 at War* (New York: G. P. Putnam, 1967), 130.
4 S. L. Shneiderman, *The River Remembers* (New York: Horizon Press, 1978), 83–84.
5 Yom Kippur is the holiest day in the Jewish calendar when the faithful must repent from their sins towards the community.

sant, Heinrich Heine, aimed at the more cosmopolitan readers of the Jewish community. However, in the words of S. L. Shneiderman, "no sooner had the dream of independence been realized in 1918, when abuse of the newly won liberty was resumed at the expense of the Jews (...) The Jewish storekeeper or worker quickly sensed that he was degraded to the rank of second-class citizen."

Small for his age, and quiet, Dawid was a gifted child. "At eight years of age he already spoke a second language, Russian (...) and was reading such Russian classics as Tolstoy and Dostoyevsky."[6] He hoped to become a professional musician, embracing his piano practice, and he loved to play chess. On January 5, 1920, he was accepted at the Boys Gymnasium of the Ascolah Society. However, his last year's school report of May 1929, suggested he was a mediocre student.[7] Though very bright, he had worked only hard enough to pass his "maturity" examinations.

When he played truant from school, he would spend time in the Krasinski Gardens with his friends. Under the auspices of the Maccabi, a Jewish sports association, he learned to swim in the Vistula at a covered swimming pool—and hated it. Although he did not play soccer, he followed the local Jewish teams and in winter he rode improvised sleds made of cardboard down the steep slope of Mostowa Street or on the iced waterfall at the Krasinsky public gardens.

Dawid would probably go to the market with Hala and their mother, a scene that has been described by his contemporaries:

> You did shopping at Swietojerska Street, there was a covered market there (...) My mother bought giblets, goose stomachs and other stuff. I often accompanied her there. (...) There was a vegetable section, there were stalls selling poultry, fish. There was also a ritual slaughterhouse, where they ritually slaughtered the chicken right on the spot. That was quite an experience—you brought a live chicken and the *shochet*, praying, slaughtered it.[8]

Sometimes Dawid would pluck up the courage to explore by himself, all the way to Nalewki Street, a more traditional neighborhood than his own. It was like traveling in a time-machine: impassioned conversations in Yiddish; arguments that went from one balcony to the next; women who did laundry or beat carpets on frames. There were no cars, only bicycles. He would push his way through the jostling crowd, between the women in black kerchiefs. The little gourmand loved looking at the stands of smoked herrings and breathing in the sour smell of gherkins in their jars or the scent of cinnamon and honey pastries. A city within the city, this was a dense and densely populated world, a labyrinth of dead ends, winding passages

---

6 Robert Hood, *12 at War* (New York: G. P. Putnam, 1967), 130.
7 School transcripts communicated by Ben Shneiderman, Bethesda,MD.
8 November 2005 Interview of Feliks Nieznawoski by Joanna Fikus, Centropa.org. The Koszyki market was a major brick covered market at Koszykowa Street in downtown Warsaw. https://www.centropa.org/biography/feliks-nieznanowski, accessed February 23, 2022. In Chim's work, street markets and explorations of out-of-the way neighborhoods will be recurring motifs.

and courtyards that overlooked other courtyards. The narrow streets and passages were lined with high, slender buildings with shops on the ground floor that sold just about anything, from corsets and dresses to cooked meals, from razors and knives to furs, umbrellas to shoes to chairs.[9]

Like many other Jewish families, the Szymins spent summer vacations and some weekends in Otwock, a small resort 15 miles southeast of Warsaw, with a Jewish community of 14,000. They stayed at the Pensjonat Zachęta, a whitewashed building with high windows, patio doors, and a cobblestone yard on Basia Street, at the corner of Mlądzka and Konopnickiej Streets. It was a bed and breakfast run by Dawid's aunt, Malka Flint, in partnership with his parents.[10]

Those times in Otwock were idyllic. The surrounding countryside was dotted with farms and the farmers drove their carts into town to sell their milk. For breakfast, Dawid and Hala ate seeded rolls with fresh milk and in the evenings, they helped their mother and aunt set the table with white tablecloths and pitchers of lemonade and wine. When it was sunny, the French windows were opened onto the paved yard and the warmth of summer evenings.

Never very physical, Dawid was more interested in his piano, chess, and books than in sports, but with cousins and friends, he and Hala swam in the Swider River or the lake, rode their bikes, or played cowboys and Indians in the black oak and red pine forest where the sandy ground was covered in pink pine needles and pinecones. They saw movies at the Oasis and the Capitol theaters where Dawid developed a passion for adventure films such as *Zorro's Mark*, *Robin Hood*, and *The Thief of Bagdad*, then fell for Chaplin and Buster Keaton, and, finally, for Greta Garbo. Their parents attended lectures organized by the Tabrut association at the People's Home.

Benjamin Szymin wanted his children to acquire the tools that would enable them to take over the business when the time came. To that end, 1929, Dawid was enrolled at the *Staatliche Akademie für Graphische Kunst und Buchgewerbe* (Academy of Graphic and Book Arts) in Leipzig to study the art of the book from design to the newest printing technologies. It was only an hour away by train, but still, to Dawid, his first time away from his family, and from his country.

---

9 Barbara Kirshenblatt-Gimblet and Lucian Dobroczyski, *Image Before my Eyes, a photographic history of Jewish life in Poland 1864–1939* (New York: Knopf Doubleday, 1987), 84–89; and Basil Blackwell, *The Jews in Warsaw* (Institute for Polish Jewish Studies, Cambridge, Mass., Oxford, 1991), 54–55.
10 Email messages to the author from Helen Sarid, Chim's niece, May 21 and June 2, 2021.

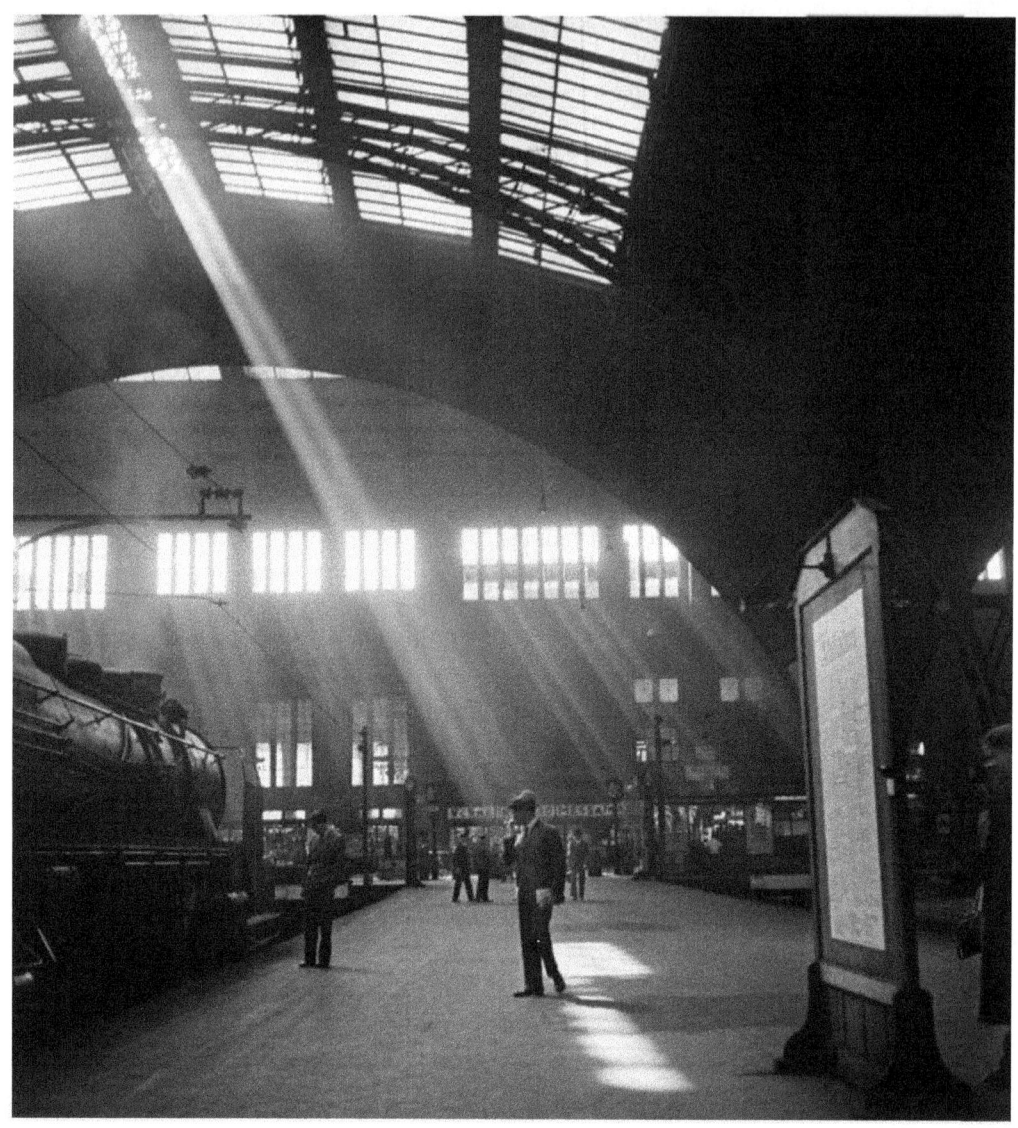

Fig. 4: Sunlight streaming into Leipzig Central Station, Leipzig, Germany. 1929-early 1930. © Roman Vishniac-Magnes Collection, U.C. Berkeley.

Chapter 2: The City of Books. 1929–1931

In early October 1929, the 18-year-old Dawid stepped off the train in Leipzig. He would be able to come home during school breaks–but still, he was on his own for the first time, and he was feeling both exhilarated and frightened. He would miss home, his mother's cooking, his cousins and friends, and, most of all perhaps, the lively conversations with his sister, Hala. It is at her high school, the Warsaw School for Journalism, that she met her future husband, Samuel Leib Shneiderman. In his autobiography, S. L. Shneiderman wrote:

> At the Warsaw School for Journalism, I met my future lifelong companion, Halina Szymin, the daughter of the eminent Yiddish-Hebrew publisher, Benjamin Szymin, co-owner of the prominent publishing house *Central*. She has played an active role in my literary life since our student days. At the time she was translating Yiddish literature into Polish and reviewing books for the literary annual published by the Jewish students' union.[1] I edited the annual, which appeared in three languages: Polish, Yiddish and Hebrew (…) Halina Szymin, my colleague from journalism school, also collaborated on the anthology by translating short stories by two Jewish-American writers, Jonah Rosenfeld and Barukh Glazman, who happened to be visiting Warsaw just at that time and were guests at her family home.[2]

After her studies in Warsaw, Hala took off for Berlin to study economics, (what we would call today economics and business management, but at the time also social work) at the prestigious Technische Universität Berlin (Berlin Institute of Technology). In a city thriving with scientific, political, and cultural discoveries, she was one of the 'New Women', exceptional at the time, obtaining a university-level education as well as practical skills that complemented her journalism studies. With Berlin only a 90-minute train ride from Leipzig, she and Dawid would be able to stay in contact.

Leipzig Hauptbahnhof, where Dawid arrived, was then, and still is, the largest and most modern station in Europe, a monumental modernist structure of stone, concrete, glass, and steel, with glazed skylights and 26 platforms. (figure 4).[3] Carrying only small luggage, mostly books and a travel chess set, and aware that the

---

[1] *Almanach Literatcki*, 1931, an anthology of modern Hebrew and Yiddish literature in Polish translation.
[2] S. L. Shneiderman, *Notes for an Autobiography*, translated by Fannie Peczenik, August 1, 2001. University of Maryland Library, https://www.lib.umd.edu/slses/donors/autobio, accessed March 3, 2020.
[3] Eva Maria Kido, "Historical and Modern Structures at Railway Stations", https://pdfs.semanticscholar.org/e10d/ccf37631bb2838a9d57de59c3380b7ba972d.pdf.Accessed, accessed September 12, 2020. The station was designed by William Lossow and Max Hans Kühne, who had won a disputed national competition. Started in 1902, construction had taken 13 years. The 300-yard-long façade had three identical domed entrance halls facing the street.

school grounds on Wächterstraße were only about 25 minutes away, he decided to walk and get acquainted with the city.

He started out along Preußenseite and Am Hallischen Tor, wide streets that were more animated than he was used to, as tramways, cars, and bicycles competed with horse-drawn carriages. Further on, the buildings became smaller, more intimate, the streets linked by courtyards and passages that teemed with *flâneurs*, browsing at small bookstores, crowding the shops, bars, and cafés in the Vienna style. Passing the famous Riquet restaurant, he admired its façade adorned with Asian motifs and two enormous bronze elephant heads.

Dawid had missed by just a few days the huge September 22,1929 demonstrations against fascism. In Leipzig as in the rest of Germany, the political atmosphere under the Weimar Republic was rife with conflict: on the right, nationalists associated the republic with the crushing defeat in World War I, which they attributed to a betrayal by "Jewish-socialist" civilian politicians rather than battlefield failure. They resented having to pay what they considered to be excessive war reparations dictated by the Treaty of Versailles and longed for a return to traditionalist authority. And the National Socialist Party wanted to replace the republic with an authoritarian regime. On the left, the Communist Party (KPD), sought to topple the republic and institute a proletarian power– what is called, in Marxist philosophy, " a dictatorship of the proletariat".

The onset of the Great Depression in 1929 shattered many Germans' faith in the ability of the government to solve their problems. Unemployment was soaring, welfare insufficient. As the Nazi party, Hitler's NSDAP, grew to more than 60,000 members, communists were finally forced to take the Nazis into account, even though they were still a minority.

At the time of his arrival, Dawid probably had little awareness of the political situation; but over the two years he was there, Leipzig, like much of Germany, was in the throes of economics depression and political unrest. It was impossible to ignore societal problems such as massive firings and unemployment, which soon reached six million. The extreme right, with the Brownshirts of the National Socialist Party, roamed the streets, spouting antisemitic slogans and promising a solution to all ills; massive political rallies were broken up by armed police. Strikes, massive political rallies, street violence, and riots were increasingly met with fierce police attacks (figure 26).

The Communist Party was active and instrumental in politicizing the students, many of whom—especially Jewish émigrés from Hungary or Poland—were either already politicized, or would soon become members of the KJVJD, the Union of Communist Youth. At Easter 1930, tens of thousands of young communists marched into the city for the Vth Congress of the Union of Communist Youths. Ernst Thälmann, leader of the German Communist Party, arrived from Berlin to speak in front of a crowd that would be estimated at 100,000 people.

On Leipzig's Karl Friedrich-Strasse, in an attic room over his parents' apartment, a few miles from Dawid's attic lodgings at Taübenchweg 89, lived the young George Kuritzkes, a member of the KJVD, the Youth section of the KPD, the Communist Party of Germany (figure 25). The same age as Dawid and probably much more politically active, he held important responsibilities in the KJVD and had been tasked with finding cheap lodgings for the crowds of young people who flocked into Leipzig for the rally. Since they both moved in Leipzig's intellectual and cultivated circles, it's more than likely, but so far impossible to prove, that he and Dawid crossed paths.

Kuritzkes's girlfriend was the charismatic Gerta Pohorylle, known among her friends as Poho. The favorite daughter of Polish Jewish immigrants, she had, like Dawid and Kutitzkes, grown up in a culturally but not deeply religious Jewish tradition. She had studied at least seven European languages as well as accounting skills in the commercial school she attended in Stuttgart. A flamboyant, boisterous, and spirited young woman, she quickly became the center of attention. She was beautiful, with auburn hair, delicate features, and natural grace, and she loved to dress up, swim, dance and listen to jazz.

Like Dawid and many Central European Jews, Poho had known a childhood of fear, poverty, insecurity, cold, and hunger during the "beetroot and potato" years of World War I. These memories and her relationship with Kuritzkes undoubtedly helped her forge a new political awareness that, just a few years later, led to activism. It's tempting to think that maybe, at a party attended by Kuritzkes's communist mother's friends or a political rally, or even during Mardi Gras, young Dawid and Gerta Pohorylle met for the first time.[4]

In 1933, after one more exile, this time to Paris, Poho renamed herself Gerda Taro. She became Capa's great love and in 1936 she would join Capa, Henri Cartier-Bresson, and Dawid, now renamed Chim, at the front of the Spanish Civil War.

After checking in with the administration, Dawid found lodgings and settled in about three kilometers from Wächterstrasse 11 where the school was located.

Founded in 1764, the prestigious Staatliche Akademie für Graphische Kunst und Buchgewerbe (State Academy of Graphic Arts and Book Trade) was the oldest in Leipzig and one of the oldest and most prestigious in the Weimar Republic (figure 29). The curriculum originally centered on drawing and painting, but photography had been introduced as early as 1893, with Germany's first professional chair for artistic photography. As at the Bauhaus, the program stressed the connection between arts and crafts and in 1929, under the direction of Walter Tiemann, a famous typographer, illustrator, and book designer, the syllabus was chiefly geared to bookmaking of the highest quality in terms of design and workmanship.

---

4 For all facts regarding Leipzig's political atmosphere during Chim's studies as well Gerda Taro's early days I relied heavily on Irme Schaber's excellent biography, *Gerda Taro: with Robert Capa as Photojournalist in the Spanish Civil War* (Berlin: Axel Menges, 2019).

The academy had an international reputation and many prestigious alumni, including photographers Walter Peterhans and Lucia Schulz (who would become Laszlo Moholy-Nagy's first wife), Jan Tschichold, a prominent typographer whose *Die neue Typographie* (1928) became a standard textbook, and René Zuber, who later in Paris became a well-known photographer and a friend of Andre Kertész and Ergy Landau.[5]

Since 1913, the academy had accepted women, one of the rare programs to do so. When Dawid started his studies, 73 out of the 224-strong student body were from abroad, from Switzerland, Austria, Poland, Russia, Czechoslovakia, Romania, France, Turkey—and as far away as China, Japan, and the United States. This was his first exposure to an international community of peers. He studied with Professor Tiemann, the director, who taught cliché-making for letterpress and Carl Blecher, a specialist in printing techniques whose classic book *Lehrbuch der Reproduktionstechnik* (Textbook of Reproduction Technology) analyzed the methods of reproduction of originals in the printed press.[6]

Beyond the specialized studies in printing that occupied Dawid's curious, precise, and mathematical mind, the school had much to offer. It encouraged the students not only in learning printing and photographic techniques, but in their own production, and in 1930, students' and teachers' work were included in the *Ausstellung für Deutsche Lichtbildkunst* in Munich.[7]

This was the environment in which Dawid's interest in photography developed and began to flourish. Hugo Erfurth taught a course in photographic techniques for publicity that Dawid attended. A famous portrait photographer whose favorite subjects were artists like Man Ray and Moholy-Nagy, he created photograms, shadow-like photographs made by placing an object between a light source and light-sensitive paper, as well as industrial images. He had co-founded the exhibiting group *Gesellschaft Deutscher Lichtbildner*, the Society of German Photographers. On the ground floor, the academy's large exhibition space displayed Erfurth's photographs and in 1929, Dawid, who knew little about contemporary architecture, could see photographs of recent buildings by Swiss modernist architect Le Corbusier, including the controversial Villa Savoye, built in France.[8]

---

[5] Christian Bouqueret, "Les années de formation: Leipzig" in René Zuber, *La Nouvelle Objectivité* (Paris: Marval, 2003), 2.

[6] Sächsisches Staatarchiv Leipzig. Students files 1929/1930, signature 136 (arch.sig.56/1).

[7] Initiated by Gusta Stotz and part of the Fifo (Film und Fotografie) exhibition, the show opened in Stuttgart in May 1929 and presented an overview of contemporary photography. It is widely recognized as one of the most important photographic exhibitions of its time. Lazlo Moholy-Nagy was responsible for the German section. After Stuttgart, the exhibition toured to Berlin, Wroclaw, Munich, Essen and Dessau before traveling abroad as far as Japan. For a detailed study, see Jonathan Long, *Film und Fotografie*, https://www.rem.routledge.com/articles/film-und-fotografie, accessed January 10, 2022.

[8] All references to books as well as list of teachers come from the Library archives of the Staatliche Akademie für Graphische Kunst and Buchgewerbe, Leipzig, and the Archives of the Museum für

Non-technical classes and seminars were led by photographers with an international reputation, among them Walter Peterhans, who had himself studied photographic reproduction and printing processes at the academy from 1925 to 1926. He had just been appointed as a photography teacher and director of the photography department at the Dessau Bauhaus, just an hour or so away, where photography was a central part of a new foundation course that was compulsory for all Bauhaus students and, from 1923 to 1928, was taught by Moholy-Nagy.

Lotte Collein, who studied at the Dessau Bauhaus from 1927 and, like many of her fellow students, took up photography, said: "With a touch of self-irony we said that 'photographitis' had broken out at the Bauhaus."[9] It was all about the small, hand-held 35 mm camera that Leica had put on the market in 1925. The easy-to-carry camera would revolutionize the field of photojournalism and photography in general. Bauhaus teachers and students started a diary-like practice, documenting the buildings and the classes, making portraits of themselves and their colleagues and photographing each other doing sports, swimming, or in playful moments.

Leipzig itself had much to offer the fledgling photographer. With more than 200 printing firms, the city was the book capital of Germany, nicknamed "the city of books". Increasingly, photography in all its forms thrived there. Many professional studios specialized in architecture or portraits, one of them run by the pictorialist photographer Arnold Genthe. Photography was an important part of everyday life. Reporters such as Johannes Mühler covered parades, festivals, and political events; Albert Hennig (figure 26) photographed tradesmen, street workers, and children; while portraitists Hans Gehler, E. Hoenisch, and Ursula Richter sometimes collaborated in ateliers such as the *Helinovum*. Hermann Walter, Eugen Ravenstein, and Alfons Trapp specialized in architecture.

The year 1929 has been called "the second birth of photography" and this new art emerged in two ways. One was the New Objectivity; the other was photojournalism and the illustrated press, with magazines such as *AIZ*. It was a year of paradox, both promise and menace, as National Socialism tightened its grip. Some could proclaim that the world was beautiful while others—including John Heartfield, known for his politically-driven photomontage contributions for *AIZ*—saw it in a much cruder, crueler light: in one of his montages, a German helmet, floating in the sky, hides the sun like a monstrous eclipse.

Geschichte der Stadlt Leipzig (Historical Museum of the City of Leipzig), years 1929–1930 (no file number). With thanks to Christoph Kaufmann for his welcome and guidance in the collections, and to the school archivist, Julia Blume.

9 Cornelia Jeske, "The Discovery of Photography", Bauhaus-Dessau Foundation, https://artsandculture.google.com/culturalinstitute/beta/exhibit/the-discovery-of-photography/2wIimKc6rx6wJA, accessed July 28, 2020.

Although the city did not have its own photo magazines, during this chaotic but fertile period, photojournalism flourished, as it had in Berlin.[10] Magazines such as *AIZ* (*Arbeiter Illustrierte Zeitung*, The Workers' Illustrated Newspaper), established in 1924, became successful. With a circulation of almost half a million, *AIZ* dealt with social conditions and the growing forces of National Socialism. Armed with portable cameras such as the Leica, which gave photography edge, speed, and immediacy, professional photojournalists constructed stories in which the articulation of the sequence gave added meaning to their images, while in Germany, France and the USSR amateur "worker-photographers", often photo-club members, started sending photographs to the illustrated press which solicited their contributions.[11] And during the summer holidays, Dawid interned for four weeks at the daily newpaper *Leipziger Neuesten Nachrichten*, an important first experience with the press. A conservative newspaper, *LNN*, as it was known, was nonetheless a logical choice for Dawid (maybe organized by his school)—because it was known for its use of modern printing technology.[12]

After Moholy-Nagy left the Bauhaus in 1928, he was active as a freelance teacher and designer and commuted to the academy to teach students the techniques of photo collage. His newly published book *Malerei, Photographie, Film* (Painting, Photography, Film, 1925) was on their reading list[13] (figure 28). Predicting photography's growing role in the years to come, he stressed the importance of sequence in articulating the photographic message and wrote that "the Illiterate of the future will be the person ignorant of camera and pen alike."[14]

Moholy-Nagy's influence on Dawid was profound and showed itself two years later, in the first photographs he took in Paris, where the dynamic geometric patterns, the exploration of different perspectives, the opposition of strong light and

---

10 Herbert Molderings, *La seconde découverte de la photographie*. Paris-Berlin catalogue (Paris: Centre Georges Pompidou, 1978); and Arthur Lubow, "The New Leipzig School," *The New York Times*, January 8, 2006.
11 For an in-depth study of these "documents of social life", see Damarice Amao, Florian Ebner & Christian Joschke, *Photographie, arme de classe*, (Paris: Centre Pompidou-Textuel, 2018).
12 School historian Julia Blume found a mention of Chim's summer internship in the school papers. It is not known if he worked with text, photographs, or both. For further details on the press in Leipzig, see Michael Meyen, *Leipzig's Bourgeois Press in the Weimar Republic: Interrelationships between Social Change and Newspaper Development* (Rosa-Luxemburg-Verein, Leipzig 1996); see also his dissertation, University of Leipzig, 1995, 111.
13 Brochure *Ausstellung Moderner Französisch Architekturbilder von le Corbusier*, Library Archives of the Staatliche Akademie für Graphische Kunst und Buchgewerbe, Leipzig, and the Archives of the Museum für Geschichte der Stadt Leipzig (Historical Museum of the City of Leipzig), 1929–1930.
14 Lazlo Moholy-Nagy, quoted by Louis Kaplan in *Moholy-Nagy: Biographical Writings* (Duke University Press, 1995), 36.

shadows, bird's-eye views and close-ups all reflected Moholy's teachings, as did his fascination with the posters of Cassandre, Colin, and other French masters.[15]

While strolling the streets and browsing the small bookshops that reminded him of his father and his days in Warsaw, Dawid must have seen a recently published album with a light-blue linen cover. Unlike any other book of the time, it was purely photographic, with full-page pictures; the terse captions were relegated to the end of the book so that the reader had to study the photographs for themselves, not in relationship to text. The goal of the author, Albert Renger-Patzsch, was to record the exact appearance of objects, their essence, rendering it with a sober, unsentimental vision. "The secret of a good photograph," he had written two years earlier in the magazine *Das Deutsche Lichtbild*, "which can possess artistic qualities just as a work of visual art can, resides in its realism."[16]

Titled *Die Welt ist Schön* (The World is Beautiful)—the photographer had wanted his book to be called simply *Things*—the album came to symbolize the school of the *Neue Sachlichkeit*, the New Objectivity. Reacting against the painterly pretensions of pictorialism, it stated that photography was independent from painting and should be dedicated to the observation of the world as it is.

1929 was the year of the *Film und Foto* show in Stuttgart (figure 27), the largest and most influential international photography and cinematography exhibition of the time. Moholy-Nagy, who was one of its curators, must have recommended the trip to Stuttgart to his students. The exhibition had been organized by Gustav Stotz, but, reflecting a new European fascination with America and its technological advances, Edward Weston and Edward Steichen had also been invited as curators. Moholy-Nagy (representing the Bauhaus aesthetics), Piet Zwart, and El Lissitsky organized some of its sections. Containing about 1,000 photographs, it was the biggest concentration of new research in photography ever organized.

In his presentation text, Stotz stressed the difference between painting and photography and announced the beginnings of a new photography:

> Today's photographer only uses the technical means provided by the camera to do his work. Thus he obtains results that man's hand cannot attain (...). He can get extremely close to his object, seize it from the side, from up, from down, revealing entirely new aspects of what he photographs. Therefore, it is not surprising that new domains are opening to photographic activity. Without the extraordinary success in the realm of reportage, the numerous illustrated magazines would not be possible. Their exactitude and the integrity of their representations made them indispensable to science and technique. Progressively, photography conquers all

---

[15] Their commercial and cultural posters were notable for their strong primary colors, spare elegance and innovative graphic solutions and were exhibited at the 1925 Exposition Internationale des Arts Décoratifs and in many other venues.

[16] *Das Deutsche Lichtbild, Jahresschau* (The German Annual of Photography, Verlag Robert & Bruno Schultz Berlin, 1926).

of the publicity sector. All these realizations are shown for the first time in this Stuttgart exhibition, thanks to the best works coming from the whole world.[17]

Film und Foto encompassed reportage, illustration, publicity, and still life, and for a young student like Dawid there was much to discover, including photographers based in Paris such as Atget, Man Ray, Berenice Abbott, Florence Henri, George Hoyningen-Huene, Andre Kertész, Germaine Krull, Eli Lotar, and Maurice Tabard. Man Ray's work demonstrated abstract research and techniques such as solarization and photogram; the Bauhaus was well represented, and Rodtchenko and other Russian photographers explored unusual perspectives and daring geometric effects.[18]

That same year, another important show opened in Berlin: Franz Roh and Jan Tschichold's *Foto-Auge*.[19] Tschichold, a Leipzig academy alumnus, was the most famous typographer and book designer in Germany. He had created hundreds of fonts and designs, and any academy student would have used his creations. Two-thirds of the selected German photographers, including Herbert Bayer, Aenne Biermann, Max Burchartz, Hans Finsler, Albert Renger-Patzsch, Willy Zielke, and Herbert List, were pioneers, open to all kinds of experiments.

Maybe, Dawid wondered, he could do more than reproduce photographs in books. Maybe he too could create photographs and express his own vision. It is possible that while attending classes with Erfurth and Tiemann he had begun to do practical exercises with his own camera. The academy possessed an excellent photography lab where he could have developed and printed his first images.

Meanwhile, he was experiencing another form of culture. In 1928–29, Bertolt Brecht's *Threepenny Opera* was a huge success, playing all over Germany.[20] Laced with irony and propelled by Kurt Weill's jazz score, the play relates the story of the villain "Mack the Knife" as he dodges the authorities and attempts to cheat the hangman's noose. Dawid's brother-in-law-to-be, S. L. Shneiderman, recalled in his memoir that Dawid had attended the play at the Dessau Bauhaus, which had its own theater and stage, designed by Gropius.[21]

On March 9, 1930, Brecht's next play, *The Rise and Fall of the City of Mahagonny*, opened at the Leipzig Opera, with music by Kurt Weill and Gustav Brecher and with the great Lotte Lenya in the starring role. Brecht imagined Mahagonny as a city created by criminals for the purpose of extracting money from people by pandering to their most basic desires: food, sex, fighting, and drink. The opera explores scenarios

---

17 Gustav Stotz, 1929 preface to *Film Und Foto* catalogue (New York: Arno Press, 1979).
18 Ibid.
19 Franz Roh and Jan Tschichold, *Foto Auge, 76 fotos der zeit zusammengestellt* (Tübingen: Verlag Ernst Wagmuth, and Paris: Editions du Chêne, 1973 for the French edition).
20 S. L. Shneiderman, *Notes for an Autobiography*, translated by Fannie Peczenik, August 1, 2001. University of Maryland Library, https://www.lib.umd.edu/slses/donors/autobio, accessed March 3, 2020.
21 Ibid.

of greed, gluttony, lust, and a justice system where a murderer can buy his way to freedom. The heroine, Jenny, is a prostitute.

Was Dawid in the audience again? If so, he would have had had to fight his way through a picket mounted by the Nazi youth. Perhaps they disliked Brecht's analysis of capitalism, or perhaps they simply rejected the opera as "degenerate music," as they would later reject modern art as "Degenerate Art" (*Entartete Kunst*). After one Berlin performance, Mahagonny was banned and would not be produced again in Germany until the 1950s.

Dawid did not know that a few years later, in June 1935, in Paris, he would be making Brecht's portrait. In his memoir Dawid's brother-in-law remembers that 1935 encounter: "While photographing the tall and lean Bertolt Brecht, Chim was able to draw him into conversation about their earlier meeting at the Bauhaus Academy in Dessau, pre-Nazi Germany's center of daring experimentation in architecture, art and the theater. Chim had once attended there a performance of Brecht's Threepenny Opera."[22]

As his good grades show, Dawid did well in both intellectual seminars and hands-on courses. In his practical training, he worked on stereotyping machines. Studying the new color printing techniques would prepare him to use the most up-to-date lithographic presses his father had acquired for his publishing house. By the time he received his diploma on March 9, 1931, he had mastered the whole cycle of book production from beginning to end in terms of paper choice, typography, design, and image reproduction in black and white and color.

Each year, just before graduation, the students organized a great feast: The *Mummenschanz, Maskenfest der Akademie* was a masked party with music, drinks, and food. Liberated by the masks they created and wore, the students could let go of restraint and behave without inhibitions or fear of being recognized. Playing musical instruments, they frolicked in the streets of Leipzig, pushing a cardboard sharp toothed whale on wheels, and to commemorate the event designed and printed an illustrated prospectus.

Just 16 months after he had arrived in Leipzig, strolling around in his mask on February 12, 1931, was Dawid's last experience of the city before returning to Warsaw. He had expected to settle there, into the ready-made place that awaited him at his father's business. But during the short period away, he had changed from a provincial, although cultured boy, to a thoughtful, open-minded young man, aware of the larger world of photography, music, theater, and culture beyond the confines of the Polish-Jewish world of his childhood.

The world was changing, too. In September 1930, with the Reichstag elections, the National Socialists had become the second most powerful party in Germany. For European Jews, politically aware or not, it was the beginning of the end. And for

---

22 Ibid.

Dawid, Warsaw would turn out to be just a short stop before he launched himself into another life, another city, and the unknown.

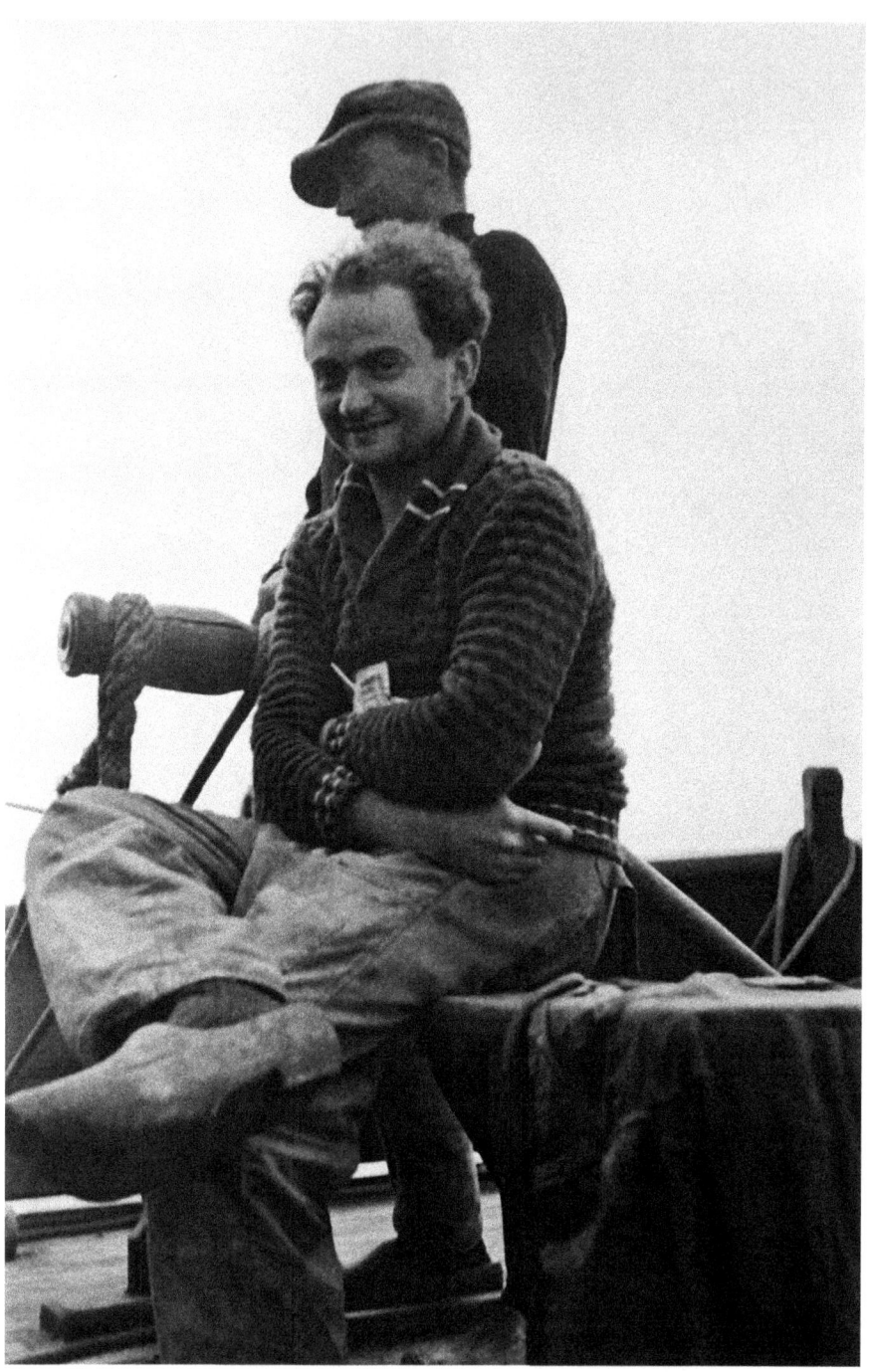

Fig. 5: David Seymour during reportage on tuna fishermen. Concarneau, Brittany, France, 1935. © David Seymour-Magnum Photos.

Chapter 3: Becoming Chim. 1932–1933

Back in Warsaw, Dawid was expecting to apply to the printed page the most recent modernist trends in typography and layout that he had learned in Leipzig (figure 30). However, since his departure, economic and political conditions had taken a turn for the worse. The future he had envisioned for himself no longer made sense, with fascism and anti-Semitism on the rise in Polish politics. Following the watchword *Nie kupuj u Zyda*[1] (Do not buy from the Jew), commando actions, boycotts, and attacks against Jewish businesses multiplied. Priests and practicing members of the Catholic Church propagated hatred against Jews and when a Jewish delegation visited the interior minister to ask for help, its members were told: "Today, everyone in Poland is an anti-Semite. We cannot assign a policeman to every Jew, and we have no intention of hanging our youth because they are anti-Semites."[2]

At the university, students of the National Democracy right-wing groups organized against Jewish students, expelling them from learning establishments or confining them to "ghetto benches." In many Polish universities, a *numerus clausus* was unofficially established and in 1928–29 the proportion of Jewish students decreased from 20 % to 8.2 %.[3] Some of them left to study in other countries. Dawid's community, numbering 340,000 and representing 38 % of the Warsaw population, had once a cultural impact comparable to that of New York's Jews today, but now people felt frightened, vulnerable, powerless. Their world had become precarious, vulnerable to social upheaval, and split between modernity and tradition.[4]

In the face of this rejection, some Jews found Zionism a replacement for their sense of identity. Many of Dawid's contemporaries wanted to emigrate but the possibilities were scant: the US had instigated a strict quota, and so had Great Britain, the gateway to Palestine. In France, too, few were accepted. Dawid was one of the lucky few young people who were able to leave when they wanted, escaping the fate of their peers, who have been called "the generation without a future".

With his family's help—they had promised him a monthly allowance—Dawid decided to enroll at the Sorbonne in Paris: Arriving in the spring of 1932, he got his German diploma translated and he registered for a B. A. in science with a major in advanced chemistry and physics. His student card bears his portrait—delicate features in a round, owlish face; moody, hazel eyes hidden behind thick eyeglasses. He wore a striped shirt, a sweater, a tweed jacket, and a striped tie, even then quite a formal attire for a student.

---

1 Jean-Charles Szurek, *Juifs et Polonais (1918–1939)*, in *Les Cahiers de la Shoah* #1 (Paris: Liana Levi, 1994), 3, http://www.anti-rev.org/textes/Szurek94a, accessed April 4 2020.
2 Jean-Charles Szurek, ibid., 2.
3 Ibid., 4.
4 Ibid., 4.

Perhaps for residency purposes, he kept his student registration until 1935, even though he had by then completed his courses.[5] Emma, Dawid's girlfriend in Warsaw, had also been able to leave and she enrolled in a nursing program in Nancy. When they could not get together, mostly because she did not have the money to come to Paris, they would correspond, and did so through 1932 and 1933. She called him Dick, not surprisingly, because he had never liked his given name, and seemed to invite nicknames. In one of her letters, dated January 29, 1932, Emma writes:

> Dear Dick!
> Despite your request, I could not come to Paris this week. The very serious reason—a total lack of money. The last few days (the end of the month) all of Nancy, or rather, of "the student world" feel a total depletion of liquidity. Of course I am no exception. However in all probability I will try to see you next week. It looks like we will have two days off, and I would use them to visit your honorable person. Are you satisfied? (...)
> For my part it is the same old story—I study a lot, I already have an exam in March. Aside from that at the institute, they really make us toil. (...) Dick, I would love, despite the difficult times you're going through in Paris now, that you don't lose your spirits. I know it's not going well, but don't hang your head, it isn't like you after all. Try to think of the pleasant things that happen to you enough to "sweeten" the more unpleasant ones. Besides, I'm sure you won't give in to "whining". You have to be strong, you can't if you don't survive this "vale of tears and ills."
> PS: Dick, maybe you need tea, cocoa. I received a package from home yesterday when I already have enough supplies for ten years. In Nancy everyone has good reserves in these products, so I could supply Paris. What do you think? Write me absolutely.[6]

Clearly, Dawid was having trouble adapting to his new life. As he matured, he was to become adept at projecting himself into a variety of situations and roles and connect with just about anyone, but when it came to his personal life, girlfriends especially, he would always remain elusive. In November 1933, after completing her studies, Emma returned to Warsaw, and their relationship seems to have petered out.

More than most of his young contemporaries, Dawid had been exposed to different European cultures since childhood, but he had never known anything like Paris in the early 1930s. The city of that period has since become the stuff of myth, as evidenced by the number of books dedicated to it, from Hemingway's *The Sun Also Rises* to Janet Flanner's *Paris Journal*, written under the pseudonym *Genêt*. The ebullience of the arts—literature, theater, dance, film—was extraordinary and thrilling. Jean Arp and Theo Van Doesburg had just founded the group Abstraction-Création; Picasso and Toulouse-Lautrec had their first retrospective and Serge Lifar authored his first choreographies; André Malraux published *La Condition Humaine*. Jean Renoir, Pabst, Alexander Korda, Julien Duvivier, and René Clair were the most prominent filmmakers and the Venice Biennale recognized cinema as an art form with its first cinema festival. The Pierre Colle Gallery exhibited the surrealists; Le Corbusier inaugurated his Swiss Pavilion at the Cité Universitaire de Paris; painter

---

5 DSA Diploma Papers and student card.
6 DSA, Document #324–325, translated from Polish.

Balthus and sculptor Germaine Richier made their public début in Paris; The Institute of Psychoanalysis was created on the initiative of Marie Bonaparte the same year as Louis Armstrong gave a triumphant concert at Salle Pleyel.

Photography was a vibrant part of the scene, with landmark exhibitions such as the 1928 *Salon de l'Escalier* on the stairway of the Théâtre des Champs-Elysées, featuring a mix of French and American photographers and a group of Eugene Atget's photographs, and, later, the huge *Exposition Internationale de la Photographie Contemporaine* at the Musée des Arts Décoratifs (1936). As of the early 1930s, photography was featured in magazines such as Jérôme Peignot's prestigious *Arts et Métiers Graphiques*. A large number of photography books came out, documentary or surrealism inspired, including Germaine Krull's *Métal*, which provided an abstract perspective on modern engineering, and, most importantly, Brassai's *Paris de nuit* (1933).

Dawid's father's business had declined to the point where it was now on the verge of bankruptcy and, because he did not want to impose on his family, Dawid decided to support himself while studying. He probably took up photography as early as 1932, when he possessed a Polish journalist's card, the result of an occasional collaboration with Ruan, a photo agency in Warsaw dedicated to press and publicity.[7]

It was the perfect moment to embark on a career in photojournalism. The 1930s were roiled by upheaval, severe economic hardship, massive political action, and sit-down strikes, and intellectuals from all over the world gathered in Paris to make common cause against a common enemy. Even funerals became demonstrations.

The invention of the indispensable Leica, and of film more sensitive to light, was a major factor in the creation of photo-reportage. New rotogravure techniques made it possible to mount image and text simultaneously on a transparent sheet, so that layout and printing were easier and faster than they used to be. As a result, the 1930s became a golden age for illustrated magazines such as *AIZ* and *BIZ* in Germany, *Picture Post* and *The Illustrated London News* (known as *Illustrated*) in London, and *Vu*, *Ce Soir*, *Voilà*, and *Regards* in Paris.

Since it used sequencing to build stories, the new kind of reportage relied on a close collaboration between writers and photographers. At the time, there was no real demarcation between literature and journalism. Writers such as Joseph Kessel, Egon Erwin Kisch, Pierre Mac Orlan, Pierre Bochot, Ilya Ehrenburg, Philippe Soupault, André Viollis, and many others, most of whom Dawid collaborated with, published novels or poems as well as articles in the press. Ehrenburg, for instance, had lengthy excerpts from his 1930 book *Mon Paris* (мой париж) published in *Regards*, with a layout designed by El Lissitzky. In 1929, the writer Georges Pillement observed: "There is no more strong distinction between writer and journalist. You can easily see that at a press conference. Half the journalists that attend are also

---

[7] Journalist card in Ben Shneiderman Archive, Bethesda, Maryland.

writers, and as the journalists in turn publish their articles and reportages in book form when they are worth (...) the two professions are mixed, confused."[8]

Since the early 1930s, more than 30 French or foreign agencies had controlled the system of collection and distribution of photos to the press and photojournalism was considered a job rather than a profession: "Photographers played little part in the captioning of the images (...) Their names were not mentioned, and their work was credited only to the agency. They did not even own their own negatives."[9]

In 1933 Dawid found work with an agency owned by a friend of the family named David Rappaport. A Russian Jew, Rappaport was a member of the Socialist Party and the Russian Revolutionary Party and at its office in the fifth arrondissement, his small agency, Agence Rap, received and distributed news photographs from foreign agencies to the publishing industry, magazines, and newspapers, in France and abroad [59] (figure 36). Since Dawid could not afford a Leica, he borrowed a 35mm camera with a Vidom viewfinder from Rappaport. The practical knowledge he had acquired in Leipzig, and his precise, mathematical mind, must have helped him in mastering the technical aspects of photography. "Chim was an excellent technician thanks to his German formation" said Jean Marquis, a future colleague.[10]

In Magnum's New York office, a black album titled *Misc images no numbers* holds Dawid's very first Paris photographs, taken before he was given assignments, and it gives a sense of his interests. Interspersed with personal photographs, such as a portrait of his girlfriend Emma (figure 33) are images of workers pushing wine barrels, probably at Les Halles; of a child in a poor neighborhood, taken right after a huge publicity shot for Cadum soap featuring a "perfect" baby. Leaving the center of the city, he shot bird's-eye views of workers exiting the Renault car factories in Boulogne-Billancourt and of a gypsies' caravan. Walking near the Seine, he photographed homeless people sleeping under the bridges and two rag-pickers, themselves in rags, standing in front of a towering pile of old scraps of fabric, an image similar to that taken by his future colleague Henri Cartier-Bresson in the same location, *Quai de Javel* (1932). He avoided the tourist spots: there are no shots of Montmartre or Notre Dame on his early contact sheets, and only a few modernist studies of the Eiffel Tower, towering over tiny passers-by.

---

8 "Il n'y a plus de distinction tranchée entre l'écrivain et le journaliste. On peut s'en rendre compte à un congrès de presse. La moitié des journalistes qui y prennent part sont en même temps des écrivains et comme les journalistes publient à leur tour leurs articles, leurs reportages en volumes, quand ils en valent la peine, (...) les deux professions sont mêlées, confondues." Georges Pillement in "Les générations d'après-guerre et la presse", magazine *Les Marges*, Paris, Summer 1929, 37, https://books.openedition.org/septentrion/81403?lang=en, accessed February 23, 2022, translated from French by the author.

9 Michel Frizot and Cédric de Veigy, *Vu: The Story of a Magazine* (London: Thames & Hudson, 2009), 15–16.

10 Carole Naggar, "Magnum Photos & Picto, Entwined Histories", in *Picto & Magnum Photos, 70 Years of Correspondences* (New York: Richard Taittinger Gallery, 2020), 111.

Meanwhile in Germany, Hitler was rising to power. In Dessau, the Bauhaus had been dissolved on the "advice" of Nazi authorities, and on May 10, 1933, in Berlin and all major university towns, Goebbels ordered a public *auto-da-fe* of books considered "decadent, corruptive and foreign to German spirit."[11] It would not be long before a slew of artists, filmmakers, and photographers started leaving for Paris, New York, and Chicago.

Fearing the mounting popularity of fascist and Nazi ideologies, European writers and intellectuals had decided to unite in their work and in public demonstrations against these rising forms of nationalism. They felt that European culture was in danger and that it was up to them to save it. Prominent French intellectuals and politicians, some officially affiliated to the Communist Party, some not, including Paul Vaillant-Couturier, Henri Barbusse, Romain Rolland, and Frantz Jourdain, founded the AEAR (Association des Ecrivains et Artistes Révolutionnaires) in March 1932. It had a photography section organized by Louis Aragon with photographer Eli Lotar as secretary, and 22 members or sympathizers, among whom were Robert Capa, a Hungarian emigre who had changed his name from Endre Friedmann in the hope of selling more pictures, Dawid, and Cartier-Bresson and it promoted a militant photography, intended to document society, denounce its social problems, and fight fascism.

Cartier-Bresson, who at the time was signing his pictures "Henri Cartier," was already well known in European circles, and his work had been exhibited regularly, for instance in the group show *Modern European Photography* and at the Gallery Julian Levy in New York in 1933. He came from an affluent family of thread manufacturers, had been influenced by Surrealism, and before taking to photography had studied painting under traditionalist André Lhôte.

With the passage of time, witnesses' accounts have varied as to the first meeting between Dawid and Cartier-Bresson. Was it on a bus on Boulevard Montparnasse, because Cartier-Bresson was carrying a Leica (the too-shiny brand-name taped over) strapped around his neck with an old belt, and that attracted Dawid's attention? Or at the offices of *Ce Soir*, a communist newspaper to which both sometimes sold pictures? (figure 47)

It is more likely that they met in 1933 during AEAR meetings. Dawid, who had already developed strong left-wing leanings, was getting more formally politicized. Together with Cartier-Bresson and Pierre Gassmann, a German-born photographer and printer, he attended theory classes on Marxism-Leninism given by German émigré Johannes Schmidt,[12] and as a member of AEAR, he participated in his first group

---

11 Joseph Goebbels, Public Address, Opernplaz, Berlin, May 10, 1933, https://encyclopedia.ushmm.org/content/en/article/book-burning, accessed January 10, 2022.

12 Christian Bouqueret, *René Zuber, la Nouvelle Objectivité* (Paris: Marval, 2003), 37.

show in November-December 1933 at the gallery of the bookstore and publishing house ESI, in the Quartier Latin[13] (figure 35).

In March 1935, Cartier-Bresson, Capa, and Dawid exhibited their work together in *La photo qui accuse*, and two months later they exhibited again at the Librairie de la Pléiade, in *Documents de la Vie Sociale: Exposition de l'AEAR*, with an accompanying pamphlet of black-and-white reproductions.[13]

Dawid was still staying at a remove from his subjects, except for some portraits of friends, and his family when they occasionally visited Paris. He was drawn not to glamor but to the vulnerable and the dispossessed: an older woman in a ratty black coat, begging because she had lost her pension; a group of Parisian *clochards* under a bridge at night, warming their hands at a small fire; scrap metal workers; street kids, standing in a doorway or rooting for food in garbage cans; shantytowns on the outskirts of Paris. In one of those early pictures, a woman, her feet planted in the mud, a large bundle on her head, turns her back on the viewer.

Attracted to the more traditional trades, he also photographed welders, carpenters, butchers at Les Halles (figure 31), flea markets, and shipyard workers. In the Marais, the fourth arrondissement, home to kosher shops and a newly erected Art Nouveau synagogue by Hector Guimard (who had recently designed the gracious welded iron entrances to the Metro), he found scenes reminiscent of traditional Warsaw neighborhoods, as in his portrait of a bearded Jew in a long coat and black hat in his secondhand clothing store, in front of a mountain of rags. He photographed his brother-in-law's brother Moishe Sznajderman in his tiny cobbler's shop in the Marais, repairing shoe uppers.[14] At the Jewish Social Services, he documented the wounded and maimed, and newborns.

Unlike Brassai and André Kertész, Dawid did not seem interested in nudes—except for a 1935 series of pictures of friends lying naked on the grass during a picnic. As for erotic photographs, there are only two from his Paris years, and perhaps his entire career. One, shot in a music hall, focuses on a Black dancer, gesticulating, blurred, backlit, with gigantic shadows emphasizing her movements. Another, much more intimate, is of a woman whose face, tilted back, remains mostly hidden, while her transparent, filmy black voile dress showcases her breasts and sex. The photograph has a mysterious, almost surreal quality. There is a woman with exactly such a dress in Brassai's book *Secret Paris of the 1930s*. Brassai's woman was shot at Suzy's, a small brothel in the Latin Quarter; in Brassai's words, "one of the discreet houses that guaranteed the anonymity of the guests. Even priests got in and out

---

13 *Une exposition de photographies*, Gallery of the E. S. I. bookshop, Paris, November 18–December 2, 1933. With Barna, Denise Bellon, Jacques-André Boiffard, Henri Cartier-Bresson, Nora Dumas, Janer, André Kertész, Germaine Krull, Ergy Landau, Jacques Lemare, Eli Lotar, Man Ray, Makovska, Moïssi, Roni Ney, Tracol, René Zuber, Ylla, and six photographers from the Groupe "Travail" in Budapest, http://archive.davidseymour.com/section5_fs.html.

14 Photograph given by Nelly Leonhardt, a Paris cousin of Chim.

without being seen or recognized." [15] The madam was a music lover, and it would have amused Dawid—who hated opera—that she adored all the great arias from famous operas.

In 1933, Dawid was already doing well financially: he had earned 10,000 francs in picture sales—of which Rap took 50 percent. But he was still undecided: should he stay in Paris or go back to Warsaw? A letter that he wrote to his Polish friend Ewa on the letterhead paper of Bar-Café-Brasserie Roblin, close to his studio, mentions his earnings but shows his doubts:

> My situation is complicated since I am alone in having to make a decision about my next years—I am forced to go back to Poland in July to straighten out my military situation one way or another. I know that when I go back to Poland I will not leave again; I will stay and take root—after all there are many things and people that hold me in 'that' Warsaw. I could stay in Paris, get acclimated here, after all I am on the way, with a job, I have connections (...) Ewa! Write me a little about that Warsaw—Would I be well there? How do you live there?[16]

The AEAR's first public demonstration against fascism took place on March 21, 1933, under the presidency of writers André Gide and with help of André Malraux and Jean Guéhenno. The AEAR founded a choir with a militant repertory that participated in all public occasions, an important factor in drawing crowds. One of their hits was *The Song of the Unemployed*:[17]

> Work and Bread
> It is our war cry.
> Enough! Enough of misery
> As an eternal friend (...)
>
> We are hungry but wheat is plentiful -
> Our masters prefer to burn it.
> We are cold, but coal is piled
> On the tiles of deserted wells.

---

15 Brassai, *Secret Paris of the 1930s* (London: Thames & Hudson, 2001), 23.
16 Undated letter from Chim to Ewa in Polish, 1931–1932. The Ben Shneiderman Archive, Bethesda, Maryland.
17 Composed by Sylvain Itkine, of the Mars group, the song was sung again during the great November 18–December 2, 1933, Hunger Demonstrations.
"Du travail et du pain
C'est notre cri de guerre
Assez, assez de la misère
Comme éternel copain.
Du travail et du pain!
Les bourgeois font bonn'chère
Chez nous les femmes, les vieux, les gosses ont faim...
Du travail et du pain, du travail et du pain."
Translated from French by the author.

In Paris, Dawid now had a new girlfriend, Bianka (figure 34), who also belonged to AEAR, and whom he was seeing frequently. A letter from her, which mentions Madeleine Braun, a prominent publisher, and Communist Party deputy, reads in part:

> Would you like to meet on Monday evening? The best would be for you to come home; I come home from work (oh well) around seven, so be there around seven. Try to let me know if you couldn't or didn't want to come. Telephone or write (...). I am tired now and I want to go to the meeting—I was hoping that you would stop by, but too bad Madeleine [Braun] is sympathetic and 'friendly'.[18]

Capa was an habitué of Le Dôme, a brasserie in Montparnasse where Hungarian emigres liked to congregate. Dawid too, frequented the place, which may be where the two had first met, and they became fast friends. Dawid, who had lived at first in a small studio apartment in the twentieth arrondissement in the north of Paris, had by then moved to a better one on Boulevard Jourdan, in the fourteenth arrondissement, near the Cité Universitaire.[19] He introduced Cartier-Bresson to Capa who, outspoken and decisive, became a major influence on him, persuading him that keeping the label "surrealist" would isolate him: he should call himself a photojournalist.[20]

As a group, the friends were in sharp physical contrast: Capa's dark hair and eyes, his tanned complexion, and heavy eyebrows, lent him an exotic air; Cartier-Bresson, tall and thin with light hair that he combed back, had an unobtrusive, very French physique that allowed him to blend into a crowd and photograph without being spotted. His only remarkable trait was his piercing blue eyes. As for Dawid Szymin, short and somewhat rotund, he was already balding a bit and wearing glasses—but his style was impeccable. The three soon shared Dawid's place and converted the bathroom into a darkroom.

These men shared a gift to relate to anyone, from the very poor to the wealthy. Besides their passion for photography, they also had in common their left-wing convictions, and their love of women and a good time—from cafés and pinballs to restaurants and, especially for Capa, the races. It is in Paris that Dawid acquired his taste, almost an obsession, for gourmet food and, little by little, as his finances improved, he got to know all the best places to eat, even in the most out-of-the way neighborhoods.

According to Gerda Taro's biographer, Irme Schaber, "Chim (...) was for Endre [Friedmann aka Capa] both friend and mentor. Like Friedmann or Henri Cartier-Bresson, he collaborated with Alliance Photo. An introvert, soft-spoken and quiet, his

---

[18] DSA, letter from Bianka, Paris, circa 1933–1934, http://archive.davidseymour.com/section1_fs.html.
[19] DSA, letter to Emma, 1933, http://archive.davidseymour.com/section1_fs.html.
[20] Fred Ritchin, "What is Magnum," essay in *In Our Time, The World Seen by Magnum Photographers* (New York: Norton, 1989), 424.

discretion was in striking contrast with Gerta's manner and a society-lover like Endre Friedmann, who did not go unnoticed."[21]

Dawid's developing closeness with *Regards* and the AEAR made him aware of a new group of anonymous worker-photographers, grouped under the label APO (*Amateurs photographes ouvriers*, or Amateur worker photographers) which became an inspiration. The new group was inspired by the Soviet *rabcor* (worker correspondents) and the German group *Arbeiter-Fotografen Vereine* (Workers-Photographers Clubs) and had obtained the backup of the AEAR journalists. In a seminal text he wrote to define the activity of the AEAR, one of its members, Henri Tracol, defined "Photography as a class weapon".[22]

The idea behind the APO was to create a new kind of photographic imagery to fight the "bourgeois" image present in most illustrated magazines of the time. According to the APO, information must not be a specialist's privilege, it should be created by the protagonists themselves. The APO's photographers sent their work to newspapers and magazines such as *Regards*, *Vu*, and *L'Humanité*, where the editors coordinated the information.

Little by little, social photography became a new visual, esthetic, and ethical genre which would develop during the Spanish Civil War. Historians Damarice Amao and Christian Jochske explained, "Alongside amateurs or workers whom they accompany in their photography practice, the latter [AEAR affiliated photographers such as Szymin] have experienced a language at the crossroads of critical discourse, militant action and the aesthetics of documentaries. They drew on the Soviet and German examples while pursuing a path specific to the French social and political context."[23]

In a different vein from this straightforward and documentarian approach, some of Dawid's photographs from these Paris days show attention to geometric planes and contrasts of light and shadow and denote the influence of Bauhaus and Constructivism, which had been a strong component in the program at the Leipzig academy. A 1935 picture of the Medrano Circus, for instance, exhibits a flattened perspective, strong geometrical composition, and contrasts between the dark mass of a horse and the white-clad body of the trainer; the taut horizontal rope in his left hand closes the triangle opened by the outstretched legs of a clown lying in the foreground, his arms parallel to the picture's frame. In the background, the faces of an attentive crowd are blurred, gray dots as if in a charcoal sketch.[24]

---

21 Irme Schaber, *Gerda Taro: With Robert Capa as Photojournalist in the Spanish Civil War* (Göttingen: Steidl, 2007), 135.
22 Henri Tracol, *Photographie, arme de classe* (Paris: Centre Pompidou, 2018), 271. Originally published in L'Humanité, 26 mai 1933, 4.
23 Damarice Amao and Christian Jochske, in *Photographie, arme de classe* (Paris: Centre Pompidou-Textuel, 2018), 2–3.
24 MPNYA, PAR116023.

The rest of the series is focused on a juggler, dancing horses, and the white bodies of the trapeze artists emerging dramatically on a black background; an especially good image is a tilted close-up of two clowns holding each other's shoulders, their whitened made-up faces almost dwarfed by their huge, interlaced boxing gloves (figure 6). In a whimsical story shot at the Vincennes Zoo, two giraffes' necks draw geometrical curves against the sky.

Dawid also started to use tilted perspectives, close-ups, and bird's-eye views: a queue of people waiting in front of an open-air food display are shot from above, capturing the geometric patterns of the bodies and their projected shadows. Another picture, shot in the Bercy warehouses, where wine was stocked before being sent to stores and restaurants, focuses on the accumulation of the barrels and their geometric patterns.

He was already fascinated by the strong geometric and graphic quality of posters by Cassandre, Colin, and other masters that would soon be a strong component of his photographs of the Front Populaire: on Paris walls he sought giant-sized posters such as a publicity for Rasurel swimsuits, for Scandale corsets or for the Navigation Aérienne aircraft company, which he contrasted with the hurried, blurred form of passers-by.

A portrait of a woman, certainly a friend, wearing a white muslin collar adorned with a rose, is remarkable by its use of light and shadow dividing her face. Another woman's portrait, backlit in a small room, is an image partly bathed in shadows, head tilted in front of the strong shape of a knotted curtain. Another yet, a severe beauty, is seen from above so that her very white face assumes a triangular form. With her hair pulled back from her face and her collar drawn against it, it evokes Moholy-Nagy's portrait of his wife Lucia that Dawid might have seen at the *Film und Foto* exhibition two years earlier.

In 1933 Dawid had started selling his pictures to *Paris Soir*, *Ce Soir*, *Voilà*, and *Regards*, and to match his new life he chose a new name, "Chim" for his byline. Shorter and easier to pronounce—in French it is pronounced "Shim"—"Chim" also evokes his former name while erasing his Jewishness. It symbolized the distance he was taking from his youth in Warsaw and his family, and his identification with a new milieu, international and secular, turned towards the values of socialism and humanism. "No one called him David," photographer Burt Glinn recalls. "We called him Chim, Chimou, Chimsky."[25]

Chim's collaboration with *Regards* was becoming essential to his career. While he published in other magazines, *Regards*' editors little by little gave him the opportunity to expand his talent by using sequences of photographs rather than individual images.

The magazine, originally titled *Nos Regards, Illustré Mondial du Travail*, had been founded in 1928 by Lilly Corpus, the editor-in-chief of AIZ, and Babette Gross,

---

25 DSA, interview of Burt Glinn by the author, East Hampton, NY, November 10, 2005.

the editor-in-chief of *Neuer Deutscher Verlag*, both closely linked to the Secours Ouvrier International founded by Willi Münzenberg in 1921. These two women spent several months in Paris to set up the new French monthly illustrated magazine on the model of *AIZ*.[26]

In 1932, the magazine became a weekly, *Regards*, under the direction of Henri Barbusse, with a prestigious editorial committee that included André Gide, Romain Rolland, and Maxime Gorki. The large-format magazine considered itself a platform whose mission was to educate and instruct French workers. Among the contributing writers were Louis Aragon, Ilya Ehrenburg, Arthur Koestler, André Malraux, Paul Nizan, and Vladimir Pozner. The photographers included Brassai, who when he was not earning a living with journalism was working on his seminal book *Paris By Night*, Cartier-Bresson, Capa, and Taro.

Another illustrated magazine, *Vu*, shared *Regards*' ideology and methods. In 1932, *Vu* published a 68-page satirical brochure by designer Maximilien Vox and *Vu*'s editor-in-chief Carlo Rim. "It is a pessimistic and ironic vision of world disorder, political violence and the brewing war" says historian Christian Joschke. "We see the abuses perpetrated against Chinese opponents, the arms race, the repression of the social movement (...). The cover illustrates both the feeling of disorder and the rise of perils in Europe. The Palais-Bourbon flickers, Hitler's face is pressed against a body whose two arms are machine guns, two cannons cross the page diagonally."[27]

Following the Soviet and German example, photomontage became a powerful tool of the illustrated press, appearing on many covers of *Regards*, some by John Heartfield, some montaged from unsigned photographs, probably by APO photographers. Aragon enthusiastically reviewed Heartfield's 1935 Paris exhibition. His Christmas tree with angled branches ending in swastikas was also shown at the 1935 *Documents de la Vie Sociale* exhibition in which Chim participated.

The *Regards* contributors' goal of fighting for the interests of the workers, for truth, for the picture propaganda of socialism, echoed the views of Egon Erwin Kisch, one of the magazine's collaborators, who had defined photo-reportage as a form of literary art in which accuracy of observation and fidelity to facts combine with creative narrative: "Nothing is more amazing than the simple truth, nothing more exotic than the world around us, nothing more fantastic than actuality. And there is nothing more sensational than the time in which one lives!"[28] This desire to present contemporary life in its immediacy and to clarify our understanding of it seems to have animated both journalists and photojournalists of the 1930s.

---

26 Christian Jochske, "Presse communiste et correspondants ouvriers: Allemagne, France, URSS," in *Photographie, arme de classe* (Paris: Centre Pompidou, 2018), 71.
27 Maximilien Vox and Carlo Rim, *Tout est foutu*, in *Photographie, arme de classe* (Paris: Centre Pompidou-Textuel, 2018), 188.
28 Harold B. Segel, *Egon Erwin Kisch, the Raging Reporter* (West Lafayette, In.:Purdue University Press, 1997), 211.

Chim's first story for *Regards* appeared on June 1, 1933. It was fully credited to him and not *Rap*. Until then, he had mostly sold individual images through *Rap*, but now he was becoming more ambitious, working with journalists, and constructing photo stories to fulfill the magazine's assignments. The first such story is *Puits 14 avec les mineurs de Paris* (Pit #14 with Paris's miners) with a text by Mars.[29] A July 6 one-page piece, *Pain de contrebande* (Contraband Bread), was accompanied by a text by André Seigneur, a communist writer who collaborated with the *Cahiers du bolchevisme*. In August (issue #23), an essay, also on the miners, is entitled *Pays noir, vie noire* (Black country, black life). This time the photographs are credited to Rap-Chim.[30]

---

29 Photographs signed Chim, *Regards*, June 1, 1933, 19. International Center of Photography's online collections, https://www.icp.org/browse/archive/objects/regards, accessed February 23, 2022.
30 Photographs signed Rap-Chim, *Regards*, n° 23, August 1933, 12, 15. International Center of Photography's online collections, https://www.icp.org/browse/archive/objects/regards, accessed February 23, 2022.

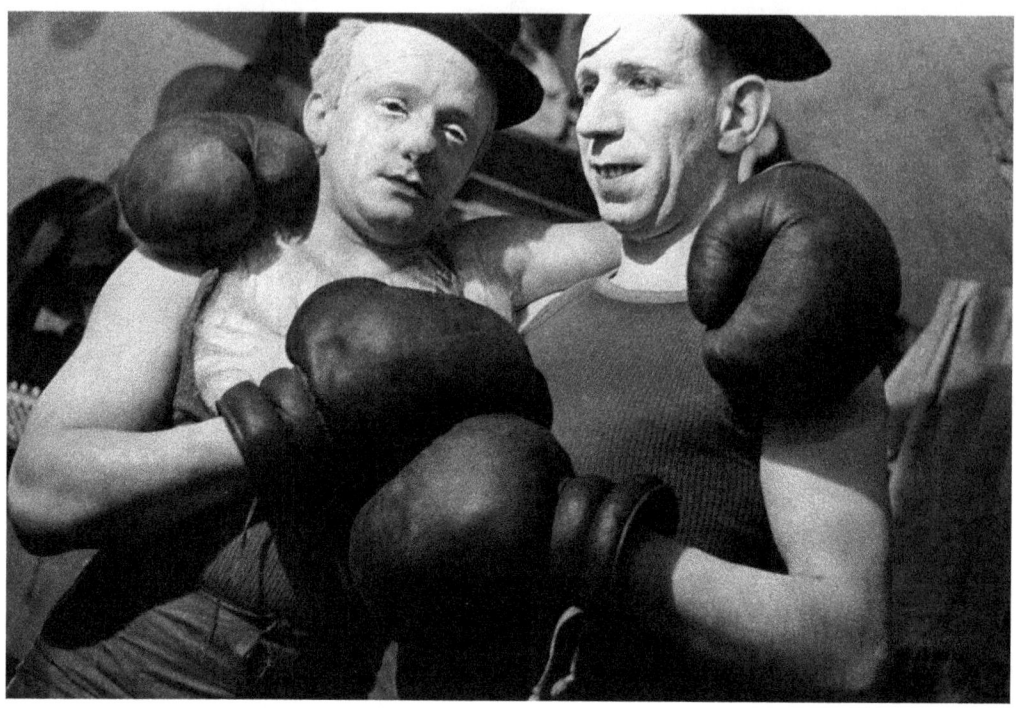

Fig. 6: Boxing Clowns at Medrano Circus, Paris, circa 1933. © David Seymour-Magnum Photos.

Chapter 4: Front Populaire. 1934–1936

In the spring of 1934, Chim's career took off in earnest when *Regards* hired him as a full-time contributor. He produced 19 photo-essays for the magazine in 1934 and 27 the following year.

Regards strongly propounded the idea that, while photography may be truthful, it is not neutral. Most photojournalists at that time saw their work as a way of expressing their feelings and their point of view, which was to redress social inequality. They were driven by the immense hope of winning readers to their perspective, changing the world even as they recorded it. This was the conviction that Chim adopted, and his time in Paris was essential in consolidating his values as well as refining his photographic abilities.

Even though Chim's work for *Regards* would from now on be copyrighted to him, the idea of the integrity of a photograph as we know it now did not exist. In *Regards*, as in many magazines of the time, pictures were seen not as a language of their own but as pieces of a story. They were casually reframed, cut up in circles or trapezes, superimposed, partly obscured by titles or columns of text, mounted together as in a scrambled visual puzzle.[1] An early example is Chim's first back cover of *Regards* from November 1933, which featured a story on a Catholic pilgrimage city, *Lourdes ou le triomphe de la Maison Soubirous et Cie* with a text by Aragon. Chim had probably met Aragon at an AEAR meeting, since he, besides working at the communist daily *L'Humanité*, was editor of AEAR's journal *Commune*. In that surreal-looking double page on Lourdes, Chim's photographs have been cut up and fitted (as a contact sheet or stills from a film) into a large drawn diagonal cross, with other cut-outs on the side: a statue of the Virgin and a pilgrim kneeling.

The layouts in these issues often evoke Moholy-Nagy's "Where is Typography Going?" panels from the *Film und Foto* exhibition, which had featured montages of typography and news photographs[2] and straddled fixed and moving image, reportage, and publicity. Inspired by this work, art director Edouard Pignon sought an effect of visual dynamism in his layout and often used photomontage on the covers. On the double pages, photo shoots were followed by counter-shots, high- then low-angle shots, closeups segued into bird's-eye views, all inspired by cinema.

Because of the social unrest and constant demonstrations in France, Chim had his hands full. Just three years after the American Depression, the economic climate

---

1 Some issues of *Regards* magazine 1934–1939 featuring Chim's and other photographer's contributions can be consulted on the site of the Bnf (Source gallica.bnf.fr / BnF) or in the International Center of Photography's online collections, https://www.icp.org/browse/archive/objects/regards, accessed February 23, 2022.
2 Images of the panels in Karl Steinhorth, ed., *Film und Foto. Internationale Ausstellung des Deutschland Werkbund* (Stuttgart: Deutsche Verlags-Anstalt, 1979) and the exhibition *Lazlo Moholy-Nagy and new typography: A reconstruction of a Berlin exhibition from 1929*. Staatliche Museen zu Berlin, August–September 2019.

was deteriorating. Unemployment was on the rise. The Daladier and Boncourt government gave its resignation. Aggressive demonstrations by the right-wing, Nazi-inspired group Croix de Feu led to more social unrest, culminating in the February 6, 1934 demonstrations in which workers and the police clashed head on. Police violence rose to extreme levels as police cars deliberately ran over workers and groups of communists and fascists battled each other.

A report spread over two *Regards* issues stated: "At two o'clock [in the morning] at the Beaujon hospital, a male nurse, his blouse drenched in blood, tells me: 'I am not allowed to tell you how many dead there are. Only here, there have been 200 wounded.'"

The writer described the street atmosphere:

> The rue de Rivoli as it leads into the Hôtel de Ville has a formidably tragic aspect: the emptiness of the street, and the night pierced by the flashes of projectiles, limned by the flames that furiously leap from the roots of the broken lamp posts that block the street, and, from time to time, a van approaches, full of police bodies where the truncheons throw their white stain; at times, a squad of guards on horseback shatters the silence.[3]

These battles soon evolved into even larger street demonstrations across the country. There were 150,000 demonstrators just in Paris, and large numbers also in Marseille, Lyon, Bordeaux, and other major cities. A popular front was called together to stop the homegrown fascists. First known as the "Comité National du Rassemblement Populaire," its professed goals were expressed in the slogan "Le Pain, la Paix, la Liberté" (Bread, Peace, and Freedom).[4] Under their leader, Maurice Thorez, the communists for the first time worked openly in alliance with the socialist parties.

By then, *Regards*' scope was not limited to France: reporters such as Kyochi Souzouki, P. L. Forster, and Vladimir Pozner sent articles from Africa, Japan, Mexico, the USSR, the U.S., Germany, Czechoslovakia, Austria—where Pozner enthusiastically describes the fight of the Left against Hitler and Mussolini, the red flags suspended from telegraphic cables, the chalked slogans on house walls.

The magazine's political emphasis was strongly pro-USSR, describing the Soviet Union as "the only country in the world where millions of proletarians and

---

3 "A deux heures à l'hôpital Beaujon un infirmier, la blouse trempée de sang, me dit: je n'ai pas le droit de vous dire combien il y a de morts. Il y a eu au moins 200 blessés rien qu'ici. La rue de Rivoli jusqu'à l'Hôtel de Ville est d'un tragique formidable; dans le vide de la rue et de la nuit sabrée d'éclairs de projecteurs, bordée par les flammes qui s'échappent furieusement de la racine des lampadaires fauchés qui obstruent la rue, de temps en temps passe un car bondé de viande policière où les matraques jettent leurs taches blanches ou bien un peloton de gardes à cheval trouent le silence" (unsigned article, translated from the French by the author. The French text uses the scornful term 'police meat'.

4 The electoral slogan of the Popular Front, inspired by Maurice Thorez's watchword.

kolkhozians are masters and creators."[5] It is a paradox that Chim, who had to suffer in Russia as a child, first while Poland was under Russian control, then when his family was forced to immigrate to Ukraine and to Odessa, would subscribe to such an ideology. But, though he never formally joined the Communist Party, he was a sympathizer. Maybe the idea of intellectual and manual workers joining forces resonated with him because of his strongly technical, hands-on background, while the enthusiasm *Regards* collaborators felt for culture and the arts must have reminded him of the atmosphere at his father's publishing house. The fact that *Regards* espoused humanistic values grounded in peace and egalitarianism that would bring together people from different backgrounds and countries surely appealed to him, to the point where most of his 1934–35 reportages were centered on workers.

Chim's first full story for *Regards*, *Chômeurs sans secours* ("Unemployed Without Help"), ran over two issues, February 23 and March 2, 1934, with a text by Pierre Bochot, *Journal d'un chômeur*.[6] Chim worked in 35mm to photograph the men queueing in front of the Théâtre du Chatelet, hoping for small parts as extras: "Four francs to be an idiot between nine o'clock and midnight" says one of them. In one image, a young man sells books of matches. Another, in stark contrast, is a night shot of the Place du Châtelet with its beautiful soft lights and a sculpted stone fountain. In the morning, the jobless men are seen at Les Halles, jostling for small jobs as porters. They live in dark, 40-francs-a-week rooms in shabby hotels. "Oh, how dark is the room!" exclaims one of them. "But there is electricity," answers the concierge. Chim's images show the scaly, moldy facade of the hotel and a jobless man bringing his mattress on a cart, while in the second issue he photographs women selling small rolls of fabric or second-hand irons, and unemployed men selling matches or ties on the sly. Some of them, weary of the police, hold modest bouquets or strings of garlic and mingle with legitimate open-air market vendors. Pierre Bochot describes the scene featuring the tie salesmen:

> 'Two francs each, your choice all colors!' He whistles through his fingers. Suitcases are closed and fly away. In the blink of an eye all the peddlers have disappeared and the *bête noire* of the street, the man that they have a thousand reasons to hate, the guardian of established disorder, the enemy, kepi tilted on the eye, enters the scene: the street is his![7]

---

5 "L'unique pays au monde où les millions de prolétaires et de kolkhoziens sont les maîtres et les créateurs." January 1934 editorial page of *Regards* stating its mission. Translated from French by the author.

6 *Regards*, February 23, 1934, 4–5, https://gallica.bnf.fr/ark:/12148/bpt6k76358178/f4.item; *Regards*, March 2, 1934, 6–7, https://gallica.bnf.fr/ark:/12148/bpt6k7635818p/f6.item.

7 Meaning the bane, literally the "black beast," "Deux francs au choix, toutes les teintes! Il siffle dans ses doigts. Des valises se ferment et s'envolent, en un clin d'oeil tous les camelots ont disparu, et la bête noire de la rue, l'homme qu'on a mille raisons de hair, le gardien du désordre établi, l'ennemi, képi sur l'oeil, entre en scène: la rue est à lui!" Translated from the French by the author.

While the inexperienced Chim did not yet possess a deep knowledge of Paris and its people, Bochot did. A strong and interesting character, his life experiences made him an ideal teammate. He had lost his mother at a young age, and although he dreamed of becoming a painter, without financial means he had had to work at menial jobs: carter, butcher boy, farmhand, precious stone etcher, employee at a fabrics store, restaurant worker, insurance agent, newspaper seller, and so on.[8] As a result, his texts strongly demonstrate empathy with the jobless and the very poor. He had shared their fate.

Bochot and Chim continued to work as a team and their byline often appeared together. On April 6,1934, Chim's photographs illustrated Bochot's article on the Renault factory, *Dans l'engrenage de Billancourt* (Caught in Billancourt's mesh). As if to show the objectification of the factory worker, Chim's photos, cut into round shapes, are fitted into the contour of a wheel's gear, and the dynamic typography, inserted on the outside, seems to rotate with the wheels (figure 32). In the follow-up issue[9], a title runs diagonally across a picture of the workers leaving the factory, taken from above and horizontally, over a close-up portrait of two men with wrinkled, exhausted faces: "They get out of the factory at full speed. It looks like lava flowing because they are all the same, mute, depressed, gray! They come out—twenty thousand workers! It is like a terrible explosion of gaunt faces with haggard eyes. They have crushed shoulders, hollow chests, ponderous arms and enormous hands, heavy like tools,"[10] Bochot writes in his vivid, dramatic style. A third part of the story was published on May 27, 1934.

In May of the same year, Chim and Bochot's work was featured in an international report that *Regards* published on working conditions. The American novelist and journalist Theodore Dreiser wrote about workers and unemployment in the United States; the Austrian journalist Egon Erwin Kisch reported on coal workers, illustrated with stills from a just-released documentary by Joris Ivens and Henry Storck, *Misère au Borinage* (Poverty in the Borinage); and Japanese journalist Kyochi Souzouki wrote a two-part series on the lives of poor Japanese peasants.

Between the wars, socialist and communist municipalities financed avant-garde architectural constructions such as schools in a number of Paris suburbs such as the Karl-Marx school in Villejuif, built by André Lurçat, and *Octobre* in Alfortville: they wanted to demonstrate that the left-wing, when in power, was able to build struc-

---

8 Complete biography of Pierre Bochot in Le Maitron, https://maitron.fr/spip.php?article73337, notice BOCHOT Pierre by Jean Prugnot, posted online on August 15, 2009, edited last on March 18, 2018, accessed April 3, 2020.
9 *Regards*, April 13, 1934, 11–12, https://gallica.bnf.fr/ark:/12148/bpt6k7635824d/f10.item.
10 "Ils sortent de l'usine à toute vitesse. On dirait de la lave qui coule, tant ils sont tous pareils, muets, déprimés, gris! Ils sortent (...) Vingt mille ouvriers! C'est comme une terrible explosion de visages blêmes aux yeux hagards. Ils ont des épaules écrasées, des poitrines creuses, des bras pesants, des mains énormes, lourdes comme des outils." Translated from the French by the author.

tures corresponding to the needs of workers and their children.[11] A month earlier,[12] Chim had photographed one of these new schools, the Groupe Scolaire *Octobre*, a pilot project that had just been built in the Parisian suburb of Alfortville. Built out of concrete with an angled façade that looked like an ocean liner, the modern building, conceived by Georges Gautier, featured three different buildings: a kindergarten; a structure for boys and one for girls; and a professional school for boys, as well as a nursing room, a sports field, resting rooms, and a solarium. The editor laid out Chim's photographs in a vertical strip, like a film, featuring "back to school" after the vacation, study in a well-lit classroom, recess, and a parade in the streets to celebrate the school's opening.

Chim also produced a feature on the assassination of Joseph Fontaine, a communist militant, by the right-wing *Action Française* group, in the northern town of Hénin-Lietard (Pas de Calais)[13]. Bochot's text ended in bold letters: "We will avenge you." Chim has the cover, a powerful portrait of a miner with a grim expression, the background photographed in a low-angle shot; Chim and Bochot are both credited as "envoyés spéciaux"—special correspondents—a definite rise in status for Chim who, by now, through his contact with a wide variety of social topics, had polished his style. Always methodical, he improvised very little. He believed in background checking, in careful preparation, and it was often only after following the writer and listening to the interviews that he started taking pictures. He thought his stories through, and, although he was aware that the editors would intervene, saw them as sequences that were both conceptual and pictorial, that would convey the story while engaging the reader's emotions.

The careful construction and sequencing of these stories, even the very first ones, indicates that Chim wanted to control his publications and may well have come to the editor with a prepared sequence of photographs, or at least an edit, an unusual step at a time when photography was still considered secondary to text, more an illustration than a language of its own. But Chim's Leipzig experience of modernism, especially his knowledge of Moholy-Nagy's work on sequences, must have been a strong influence as he tried to balance meaning and graphic strength in this early work.

As the year 1934 continued, Chim's assignments for *Regards* steadily became more substantial. A piece entitled *Le fascisme ne passera pas* (Fascism will not prevail)[14] features his uncredited cover showing a speaker, the socialist politician Léon Blum, in close-up as he faces the 3,000-strong crowd at the Cirque d'Hiver Congress.

---

11 Gabrielle de la Saelle, *La photographie militante en action: l'imauguration du groupe scolaire Karl-Marx de Villejuif en 1933*. https://arip.hypotheses.org/3609#identifier_25_3609, accessed January 12, 2022.
12 *Regards*, April 13, 1934, 7, https://gallica.bnf.fr/ark:/12148/bpt6k7635824d/f7.item.
13 *Regards*, April 20, 1934, 8–9, https://gallica.bnf.fr/ark:/12148/bpt6k7635825t/f8.item.
14 *Regards*, May 15, 1934. Cover and 6–7. This issue is not available on the Bibliothèque Nationale website.

Several portraits inside are credited to him: André Malraux, Léo Vannes, the Anti-Imperialism League, Marcel Cachin, and Professor Langevin, a celebrity from the scientific world, as well as an aerial view of the crowd.

In the June 1, 1934 issue of *Regards*, "100.000" is a collage of images: A picture of a group of demonstrators is collaged on the lower right corner while the background is occupied by a placard and "a flag with a swastika seized from the Nazis last Friday: 'Do not tolerate this emblem'." The main image is a dynamic view of a famous communist singing group, Groupe Mars. In the Front Populaire period, the group participated in numerous workers' demonstrations and festivals, and during the May 1936 strikes, they acted and sang in the occupied factories.

Continuing Chim's in-depth study of French society, in the summer of 1934 he and Bochot worked on a three-part story on taxi drivers and mechanics in the Levallois suburb of Paris: *Levallois, Ville des taxis*. This was an analysis of the lives of people who work 10-hour days and often make less than 30 francs daily. Other drivers, the "nuiteux," (night workers) work all night, sometimes 20 hours in a row. Chim, too, worked through the night until dawn, focusing on the taxi drivers and the mechanics. His photographs are credited only in the third part of the piece, but his style is easily recognizable. While the photographs remain elegant and well-composed, they possess a stark quality that matches their subject matter and Chim's deepening political commitment. In his text, Bochot underlines their harsh working conditions and low salaries.

Chim's cover for the first issue is uncredited,[15] while Bochot receives credit. The cover features a close-up of a mechanic in work overalls lying under his car's chassis to make repairs. The image is anchored by the strong crossed diagonals of the metal bars, forming a triangle that looms over the subject's face. As Chim crouches on the garage floor, he captures the mechanic's attentive expression and his hand grimy with sludge. Inside the magazine, a double page is devoted to the activity in the garage, with mechanics making repairs, brushing, and spraying the cars, repainting the license plates. Chim and Bochot followed one driver, Mimile, through his 12-hour day and on one page featured a portrait of him in his gray blouse and cap with a union badge, his expression melancholy. He is displaying his taxi meter, showing that he only made 1franc 50 that day.

Photography was opening and changing Chim's world: he had found a purpose. In the fall of 1934, he wrote to his friend Ewa in Warsaw:

> Today it is one year since I came to Paris—an important anniversary that puts me in the mood for reflections and memories. I am not working today. It is raining, no weather for photographing (...). I am sitting at my desk, with a globe of the world on it, in my new apartment (...). Yes, I don't live anymore in that hole on the ground floor of rue de l'Ermitage [in the 20th ar-

---

15 *Regards*, June 8, 1934, cover and 8–9, https://gallica.bnf.fr/ark:/12148/bpt6k7635832z/f7.item, *Regards*, June 15, 1934, 11–12, https://gallica.bnf.fr/ark:/12148/bpt6k7635833c/f9.item.*Regards*, June 22, 1934, 7. https://gallica.bnf.fr/ark:/12148/bpt6k7635834s/f6.item.

rondissement Belleville-Ménilmontant], but in a real apartment on the first floor with modern conveniences and a lab (...). And so many things have changed. I am working, running, seeing fascinating things. I am getting to know Paris; I am becoming a part of it.
As you know, I am not working anymore at reproduction (photolithography). I am a reporter, or more exactly a photo reporter. Lately I was photographing a very interesting reportage—people working at night. I have been busy with it for the past two weeks, it requires a lot of preparation: to get the information, to look for contacts with all sorts of people in different occupations. I did a story about taxi drivers at night, about a garage, construction workers in the Metro, in a bakery, in a printing plant.
Last night I spent at Les Halles. I took two friends with me (It is unpleasant to work alone at night and there are always people willing to join in such an adventure). We were roaming around all night until three in the morning. In the meat packing section, we had a triumphant reception with wine. They let us into the huge freezer-chambers. Then I photographed the vegetables (...). But I am too tired now, after the sleepless nights, to describe to you the flavor of this unique experience.
In two weeks, I am going to the North for a few days. I have an assignment for a reportage on the life of the miners. All expenses paid![16]

A month later, Chim writes another long letter to Ewa, describing his accomplishments and aspirations:

My stories appeared lately in *Paris Soir* (about the Metro). I got 300 francs. *Voilà* printed a couple of my pictures. *Regards* will publish my two big stories on Strasbourg and my stories about the *clochards*. Things are moving. I shouldn't complain, but I am not in a good mood (...). I am trying to analyze what the reason is. It will probably go away shortly. Basically, I am satisfied with myself because I am working well. I know what I want at the moment, and I am making progress in that direction. But I want to do something bigger and have no possibility. That would be point number one. Point number two, I am moving in new circles, away from the Polish gang. I am more around photographers, thinking people, interested in the same problems as myself. However, I feel a foreigner and I am missing the 'togetherness' of our Polish bunch. I met a German girl who became quite prominent in the French press, and she feels as I do. We are trying to organize some kind of association of revolutionary-minded photographers. Maybe that will create a circle of good people.[17]

The "German girl" was Maria Eisner, who started the agency *Alliance Photo* in 1934, buying and distributing photographs. Born in Milan in 1909, Eisner had moved to Germany at the beginning of World War I and, in 1929, started working for photography magazines in Berlin. In 1933 she had had to leave because of the rise of the Nazi party and moved to Paris. Like all immigrants working in the press, Eisner put her international contacts to good use: she worked with the German refugees who founded Black Star in New York, and ABC Press Service in Amsterdam (directed by Capa's Hungarian friend, Imre Rona). They all distributed Alliance's images and sent Eisner their own, so that her agency started to function as an international business.

---

16 DSA, http://archive.davidseymour.com/section1_fs.html.
17 Ibid.

Chim was not a formal member of the agency but, like Cartier-Bresson, he sometimes gave Eisner his reportages for distribution. Among Alliance's French clients were substantial magazines: *Le Document*, *Match*, *Regards*, *Voilà*, *Vu*, and *Visages du Monde*, Jérome Peignot's elegantly illustrated journal, *Arts et Métiers Graphiques*, and also more commercial outlets in fashion and tourism.

In 1947, Eisner would become head of the Magnum Photos Paris office. Chim's letter, with his mention of "some kind of association of revolutionary-minded photographers," gives the strong impression that as early as 1934 the two already had the germ of the idea that Capa would later take up, and that would become Magnum. Eisner knew perfectly well Capa's real identity. According to Irme Schaber, "Gerta (...) who was working for Maria Eisner (...) introduced Endre to Maria as 'Robert Capa, a famous international photographer.' Maria saw through the ruse but played along, offering to sell Endre's pictures as those of 'Capa.'"[18]

On July 13, Chim and Pierre Bochot published a new "grand reportage": "Paris Taudis" (*Paris Slums*). They visited the slums that remained in the twisted, ancient, streets of the Marais, right in the heart of Paris: rue la Reynie, rue de Venise, rue Simon Lefranc, and rue Saint-Martin in the third and fourth arrondissements on the right bank of the Seine, close to chic neighborhoods, as well as the slums of the thirteenth arrondissement, where living conditions were medieval. Their focus was on a man named Paulin, recording his struggles to buy furniture on credit and procure food for his family.[19]. Inside, the bold, dynamic typography contrasts with a sober layout, with photographs in two columns framing the text. Chim also authored the magazine's back cover, the long perspective of a narrow street, lined with barracks with disjointed roofs made of discarded materials, unemployed men and women waiting, a lone child at play. Dispassionate, yet empathetic, this image strongly evokes those taken by Chim's colleague Eli Lotar in Paris's poor suburbs.

Chim's photographs are a faithful reflection of the worsening social situation in France. Raging unemployment had spread to all social classes, even intellectuals, engineers, students, and doctors; some medical students, after completing their studies, had to work in hospitals for just eight francs a day because they could find no other jobs.

In two September, 1934 issues of *Regards*, Chim published a story about the ways in which the economic crisis was affecting the small craftsmen of Paris, "Les Petits Artisans de Paris"[20]. This time he was associated with journalist Etienne Constant. Constant was the pseudonym of a Rumanian woman writer, Sofia Jancu, who had arrived in Paris in 1931. She became a member of the AEAR (Association des

---

18 Irme Schaber, *Gerta Taro: With Robert Capa as Photojournalist in the Spanish Civil War* (Fellbach: Axel Menges ed., 2019), 116.
19 *Regards*, July 13, 1934, 3–4, https://gallica.bnf.fr/ark:/12148/bpt6k76358371/f4.item.Regards.
20 *Regards*, September 7, 1934, 4–5, https://gallica.bnf.fr/ark:/12148/bpt6k76358371/f4.item; *Regards*, September 14, 1934, 4–5, https://gallica.bnf.fr/ark:/12148/bpt6k76358460/f4.item/ https://gallica.bnf.fr/ark:/12148/bpt6k7635847d/f1.image.

Ecrivains et Artistes Révolutionnaires) in 1932 and started working for *Vu*, *Ce Soir*, and *Regards*.[21]

The two journalists documented shoemakers, embroiders, milliners, upholsterers, carpenters, hatters, cabinetmakers, none of whom could make ends meet. They worked mainly in the southeast of Paris, in the nineteenth and twentieth arrondissements, which were then the center of artisanal life. Walking small, winding streets where narrow stores huddled close to each other, they climbed to insalubrious apartments that served as both residence and workplace. For once, the design for the series was very sober, with few juxtapositions, to accommodate Chim's beautiful full-frame portraits of artisans at work. In these striking portraits the artisans, who are paid by the piece, do not pause to look at the photographer and the journalist but keep working as they talk: "The woman, with a young face, keeps her back hunched even as she is talking to me," Constant writes about a seamstress.

"It is August, and the heat is unbearable," she continues: "The poorly ventilated rooms are submerged with fetid odors rising from the uncollected trash. For economic reasons, thousands of artisans work from home: the same room does triple duty as bedroom, kitchen, and atelier."

For the last installment of the story, Chim and Constant worked mainly in the fourth arrondissement, once an aristocratic neighborhood, now inhabited by Jewish artisans. "In front of shops where live carps and chicken killed according to ritual are sold, buyers are haggling, and you could not say if they come from Poland or Spain, Rumania or Germany," Constant writes. "Rue des Rosiers, rue Charlemagne, rue de la Verrerie, rue Vieille-du-Temple, rue Fauconnier, rue Ave Maria, those are teaming with life: it seems as if everyone lives in the street."[22]

Maybe because Chim could easily relate to such scenes, similar to those he saw as a child when he must have ventured into traditional Jewish neighborhoods full of such craftsmen, this part of the reportage is not as grim as the previous installments. Constant writes:

> 'You work even on Saturdays?' I ask my old Polish friend, a hatter.
> 'But I eat on Saturdays like on other days!(...) Our line line of work is intensive only for one or two weeks before the holidays. You have to take advantage of these occasions to make a small profit.'[23]

---

21 For a biography of Etienne Constant, see Le Maitron (https://maitron.fr/spip.php?article20536), notice CONSTANT by Claude Pennetier, accessed May 3, 2020.
22 "Devant les boutiques ou l'on vend des carpes vivantes et des poulets tués suivant le rite, lorsque les acheteurs marchandent, on ne pourrait dire s'ils viennent de Pologne ou d'Espagne; s'ils sont de Roumanie ou d'Allemagne. Rue de la Verrerie, rue du Temple, rue Fauconnier, Rue Ave Maria sont grouillantes de vie, il semble que tout le monde vive dans la rue." Translated from the French by the author.
23 "Vous travaillez même le samedi? Dis-je à mon vieil ami polonais, le casquetier-Mais je mange le samedi, comme les autres jours." Translated from the French by the author.

Even without an assignment, Chim continued photographing on the streets. One striking image is of a woman, a beggar, in ragged clothing. Seated on a small chair in front of indifferent passers-by, she clutches what looks like a wooden drawer. Suspended from her bicycle's handlebars is a homemade sign, "Grande victime du travail sans pension" (Serious work victim without a pension).

After completing the story, Chim continued to focus on French working life and the social and economic problems of the times. In three consecutive issues of *Regards*, he photographed an in-depth reportage: *"Marius, fils de Marseille"* (Marius, a son of Marseille).[24] Rather than studying a group of people, he focused on a single symbolic character: Marius, a fisherman's son, whose family lived in the Panier, a popular neighborhood close to the harbor, and who dropped out of school at 13. Marius was looking for a job and, for the moment, he was working at the open-air market in Grand' Rue in the mornings and selling newspapers in the evenings. Sometimes he worked aboard a large trawler, a *chalutier*, but his dream was to become a mechanic. Thanks to a friend of his father, he landed a job as an apprentice in a garage, but his luck did not last: with small businesses in crisis, he found himself jobless and had to join the cabin crew on a transatlantic ship. While he got to see China, Indochina, Singapore, and Djibouti, he would have preferred *"le plancher des vaches"*[25] (solid ground).

In the last part of the reportage, Chim focused on the lives of the dockers who hauled bags of coal or sulfur. Exploited by bosses who did not respect contracts, they worked for seven francs a day. Walking on the quays among large sheds that smelled of vanilla beans or rose essence, Chim and Gazagnaire easily connected with the workers and struck up conversations with them, giving their piece a direct style reminiscent of the work of legendary investigative journalist Albert Londres:

> "I would like to know," says one of the workers, quoted by Gazagnaire, "if we are dockers or if they are confusing us with tractors."
> "As a matter of fact," another replies, "they are confusing us with slaves."[26]

In the Panier neighborhood where he had met Marius, Chim photographed children, who, left to their own devices, mainly lived on the street. They were everywhere: sitting on steps, playing cards, or fishing on the quays among prostitutes and sailors. For the first time, he had chosen disenfranchised children as his subjects, and it is immediately apparent how well he related to them. We see here the seeds of qualities that will be so marked 14 years later in his famous work on post-war European

---

[24] *Regards*, October 19, 1934, 8–9, https://gallica.bnf.fr/ark:/12148/bpt6k76358519/f7.item; *Regards*, October 26, 1934, cover & 6–7, https://gallica.bnf.fr/ark:/12148/bpt6k7635852q/f6.item; *Regards*, November 2, 1934, 10–11, https://gallica.bnf.fr/ark:/12148/bpt6k76358534/f9.item.
[25] Cows' floor, meaning dry land.
[26] "Il faudrait savoir si on est des dockers ou si on nous prend plutôt pour des tracteurs. Le fait est qu'on nous prend plutôt pour des esclaves." Translated from the French by the author.

children who, like the children of Marseille, have become detached from adult help or rules, and rely only on other children in a society of their own.

Maybe remembering his early excursions to the market with his mother, Chim would always favor open-air markets as a subject, as evidenced, for instance, by his 1950 series on Venice's Rialto fish market, and he had photographed les Halles, which Victor Hugo called "The Belly of Paris," when newly arrived in Paris. He revisited the market in the spring of 1935[27] for a *Regards* cover story, *Les Féodaux des Halles* (Feudal Lords of Les Halles), with text by Bochot, who described it as a medieval miracle court where all social classes mix:

> The poor, porters and prostitutes, the salesmen and policemen, butchers, wholesalers, strongmen, farmers, restaurant owners, the unemployed, the four seasons' sellers, the grocers, and the snitches, shout, insult and fight each other in a setting made of the most beautiful, tastiest, and sweetest-smelling produce on earth![28]

Taken at dawn, suffused with a light mist, these new pictures focus on the expressive pantomime of the sellers and buyers and capture the arrival of the carts and trucks of the produce providers. His most impressive pictures portray the "*forts des Halles*" (strongmen of Les Halles), hunched under the weight of the vegetables. One of them rests his back against a pile of jute bags and from under his cap's visor looks indifferently at the photographer. Butchers pose under hooked carcasses. Two women haggle for cauliflowers. The photographs have an immediate yet poetic feel that often recall Brassai's study on the same subject. Chim might not have been familiar with Brassai's photographs at the time, but he would certainly have met him at Le Dôme with other recent émigrés.

In April 1935, Chim continued his study of working-class neighborhoods with a piece on the Faubourg St Antoine, home to carpenters, cabinetmakers, and wood sculptors.[29] A photograph of a deliveryman pulling a heavily loaded cart has a strong Eastern European feeling, evoking a portrait by Toso Dabac, a noted photographer from Yugoslavia, taken in Zagreb a decade before. As before, these craftsmen had very little work. Their only order lately had been the furniture for the liner "Normandie." "The Faubourg St Antoine is dying," says the caption. In France, the dark times are getting darker, with bankruptcies multiplying, salaries cut by as much as 25 percent, and unemployment skyrocketing to 810,000.

---

27 *Regards*, March 21, 1935, back cover and 6–7, https://gallica.bnf.fr/ark:/12148/bpt6k7635873w/f13.item.
28 "Gueux, porteurs, employés, camelots, policiers, marchands des quatre saisons, chômeurs, restaurateurs, chauffeurs, épiciers, mouchards, cultivateurs, bouchers, approvisionneurs, forts, mandataires, prostituées, s'agitent comme des damnés, crient, s'injurient, se battent, dans un cadre formé par les produits les plus beaux, les plus savoureux, les plus odorants de la terre!". Translated from French by the author.
29 *Regards*, April 18, 1935, 6–7, https://gallica.bnf.fr/ark:/12148/bpt6k7635877j/f5.item.

Chim also photographed a women's meeting of a fascist group influenced by Mussolini and Hitler: Marcel Bucards' *Francistes*. The emblem of the movement, created in 1933, was the *francisque*, a double-headed axe, which would later become the emblem of the Vichy regime. The previous year, the fascists had taken part in violent rallies alongside other right-wing groups such as *Action Française* and *Croix de Feu* and attempted to topple the government. Chim, who maybe thought he had left antisemitism behind when he left Poland, now confronted the very public and growing manifestation of its appearance in France: posters and slogans at election campaigns and rallies. A series of chilling photographs features the headlines for this dark story of his, the titles screaming hate: "The Jew, he is the enemy," "Jews everywhere!", "Die for the homeland? Yes, always. Croak for the *Internationale*? No, never."

Next, Chim covered the June 21–25 Writers Congress for the Defense of Culture, held to "discuss the means of defending culture against the dangers that menace her in a certain number of countries," as written in a public declaration with signatures of André Gide, Jean-Richard Bloch, Romain Rolland, Malraux, André Chamson, and Henri Barbusse, editor of the influential journal *Monde*.[30]

Prestigious delegates from the US, Great Britain, Hungary, the Netherlands, Czechoslovakia, Spain, and the Soviet Union arrived, including Brecht, Karel Capek, Ehrenburg, Waldo Frank, Valle Inclan, Heinrich Mann, Robert Musil and others. Gide opened the proceedings with these words: "Literature has never been more alive (…) but the intellectual impoverishment of some countries lets us see that culture is under menace. Country to country solidarity and danger of contagion are such nowadays that the examples from our neighbors instruct us, and we all feel more or less under the gun."[31] For four days, the writers held intense discussions about the concept of humanism, the problems of creation, dignity of the spirit. The proceedings ended on June 25 with the launching of a permanent Paris-based international association for the defense of culture against fascism and war.

Chim's sister Hala and her husband Emil accompanied Chim to the congress.

According to Chim's nephew Ben Shneiderman, his family's archive and Chim's early contact sheets show that that Hala and Emil married in Warsaw, on March 25, 1933. Then, in 1934 or 1935, they moved permanently to Paris. Helen Sarid, Chim's niece, recalls that "they did not return to Warsaw till my mother took me for my first birthday—Dec 1938—to meet both sets of grandparents that are immortalized in Chim's photos." (figure 23).

---

30 *Regards*, June 27, 1935, cover and 11–12, https://gallica.bnf.fr/ark:/12148/bpt6k7635887x/f8.item.
31 "La littérature n'a jamais été plus vivante. Que la littérature soit menacée, l'appauvrissement intellectuel de certains pays nous le laisse tristement entendre. Mais la solidarité de pays à pays est telle aujourd'hui, les possibilités de contagion, que les exemples voisins nous instruisent, et tous nous nous sentons plus ou moins menacés." Translated from French by the author.

Chim's parents visited their children in Paris (figure 40). Helen Sarid adds: "I know that my father went back and forth from Paris to Warsaw—but I don't know if it was 1933 or 34. Regina [her grandmother] came to visit in Paris—it was before I was born Dec 1937—and from the photo—my mother [Hala, later Eileen] looks much younger than she does in Chim's photos in the hospital when I was born."

Judging by the contact sheets, Hala and her husband had moved to Paris in 1934. The following year, Chim's parents visited, and his personal contact sheets show many portraits of them, alone, together or with the Shneidermans[32]. Observing Chim while he worked, Emil commented: "Chim's native intellectual curiosity was stimulated by his face to face with leading writers of West Europe, America and the Soviet Union as he covered the deliberations of the First International Congress in Defense of Culture held in Paris in June 1935. At such a gathering his command of the German, Russian and other languages made it easier to establish friendly relationships with authors he already knew. An especially close affinity sprang up between the young photographer and the shy, withdrawn Isaac Babel, the great Russian writer who was to be murdered by Stalin's politics. The tie between them grew out of the stories Chim told of his childhood years during the Russian Revolution in Odessa, Babel's hometown, to which Chim's family had come as war refugees from Warsaw."[33]

Despite the difficult working conditions—he was on the floor in a crowded hall, and the light was very poor—Chim managed beautiful individual portraits of Gide, Malraux, who had just become famous for his book *La Condition Humaine* (Man's Fate), Aldous Huxley, and Alexis Tolstoy. Later, in Barbusse's office, Chim made a group portrait of intellectuals. It's a lively and engaging image that captures the individual expressions of each sitter, quite a feat considering that Chim was given only a short time to shoot.

Meanwhile public unrest was surging, and a few days later, on Bastille Day, Paris saw its largest and most organized demonstration, estimated at half a million people, as major political groups came together in the streets. Chim published four pages on the topic in the June 26, 1935, issue of *Vu*, where his work seldom appeared, to illustrate an article, "*Défense de la Culture*." A tragic coda to the Congress came with the death of Barbusse, and his funeral at the Père Lachaise cemetery, with its strong symbolic value and connection to the Paris Commune.

With Rolland, Barbusse had founded the International Antifascist Committee and was a hugely popular figure. His interment (he had died in Moscow on August 30,1935, and received an elaborate funeral in the USSR before his body was repatriated) turned into an anti-war demonstration attended by over 300,000 people (fig-

---

[32] MPNYA, ADS, Paris Life, 1A-70, # 55A and 71-130,#74B,75, and email message to the author from Ben Shneiderman & Helen Sarid, July 8, 2021.
[33] See Chapter Two "Peace and War".

ure 38). Moving around constantly, Chim was able to alternate group shots—of the crowd, of Barbusse's close friends standing at his grave—with individual close-up shots of subdued, sad demonstrators, including three schoolgirls in matching berets, fanned in a semi-circle, in front of their father, who holds a flower garland. Photographing the crowd from a high perspective, he must have been touched that the portrait of Barbusse he had shot in June had been used as a model for a painted banner held at the head of the rally.

In two consecutive issues of *Regards* (September 12 and 19), Chim teamed up with writer Philippe Deval (one of Georges Soria's pseudonyms)[34] who would become one of his most frequent colleagues to report a photo-essay on the lives of tuna fishermen in Concarneau, Brittany [35]. The story, *"14 jours en mer avec les thoniers Bretons"* (14 days at sea aboard a trawler) shows him looking at the sea, wearing the (for him) unusual attire of wooden clogs, loose chinos, and a heavy knitted sweater. (figure 5). Aboard the ship, he made beautiful portraits of the fishermen, often tilted in a New Objectivity style, and one looking up from the deck to show a sailor climbing the mast. Back in the harbor, he focused on a long perspective of silvery tuna fish stacked up on the paving stones, dwarfing the two small boats in the background as they neared the quay with their catch. A close-up on a fisherman focuses on his calloused hands holding a tuna hook, while the photo's background remains blurred.

In January of the following year, Chim photographed a crowded birthday party in honor of Romain Rolland at the Palais de la Mutualité. In Rolland's absence—he was in Moscow, serving as an unofficial ambassador of French artists to the Soviet Union—Chim made portraits of politicians such as Paul Vaillant-Couturier and Marcel Cachin, and the writers Aragon, Malraux, and Bloch, whom he had already photographed at the Writers' Congress.[36]

After a serious February 13 attack against politician Leon Blum, shortly before he became prime minister, when he was seized from his car and brutally wounded, the Front Populaire organized a huge, peaceful demonstration, attended by half a million participants: "La réplique magistrale du people de Paris" (*The magnificent response of the people of Paris)*. [37]Chim first shot bird's-eye pictures of the crowd before coming down from his perch and photographing at street level a compact mass

---

34 André Carmaux (*Regards*) A. C. (*Regards*, 12.XII.35), Vlad Dekabrev, André Géry, V. Krylov, Louis Le François, Jacques Maréchal (*Regards*) Mr Terry (letter from Maxim Lieber September 4, 1942), André Vaillant ("I thought I knew my France", *The American Mercury*, NY, III.37), Commandant Z. (*Regards*), Capitaine Zeno (*Regards*, 19.XII.35). Information communicated by his son: Email message to the author from André Pozner, September 15, 2019.
35 *Regards*, September 12, 1935, 10–11, https://gallica.bnf.fr/ark:/12148/bpt6k7635898q/f6.item; *Regards*, September 19, 1935, 10–11, https://gallica.bnf.fr/ark:/12148/bpt6k76358994/f7.item.
36 *Regards*, January 30, 1936. Cover and 4–5, https://gallica.bnf.fr/ark:/12148/bpt6k76546632/f4.item.
37 *Regards*, February 20,1936, 4–5, https://gallica.bnf.fr/ark:/12148/bpt6k76546669/f4.item.

of flag-wielding demonstrators, workers wearing caps, and middle-class demonstrators with hats.

The Front Populaire, a broad coalition of the left, center-left, and major trade unions, had come to power amid the intense social and economic turbulence that Chim had been documenting over a couple of years. On April 23 and May 3, Chim photographed the French votes that led to its victory [38]: first, the posters in the street, studied by passers-by young and old, then the voting booths, and, finally, huge placards held by groups coming from Marseille, Lyon, the Nord-Pas de Calais, and the Seine departments, showing the left-wing delegates who had just been elected.

Even before Blum had moved into his official residence as prime minister, violent strikes had began. Simone Weil commented, "This is about finally daring to stand tall after having suffered everything, taken blows in silence for months and years finally daring to stand up tall. Take the floor for once. Feel like men for a few days."[39] A number of factors had led to this moment: economic crises, the internal threat from the far Right, and the international fascist menace and threat of war, particularly in a bitterly divided Spain. The scale of the unrest and strikes helped Blum persuade employers to give workers important new rights, including the right to unionize, the right to a 40-hour work week and a paid vacation (the Congés payés), as well as government subsidies for families with several children. Fascist organizations were banned. These concessions, the Matignon Agreements of June 7, 1936, have been described as the beginning of a new era.

Throughout the spring of 1936, Chim was busy covering the turmoil in Paris. In May, he shot a large demonstration for "Unity of action against the fascist war" for the cover of *Regards*, featuring the strong back of a worker with raised fist seen in closeup on a background of flowering trees.[40] He returned to Père Lachaise cemetery on May 24, for a homage that the Front Populaire organized in front of the Mur de Fédérés (*Communards' Wall*),commemorating the last survivors of the 1871 Paris Commune who were executed there.[41]. Chim's cover juxtaposes a closeup of a man carrying his small daughter on his shoulders, her fist raised, with a bird's eye view of the parade. The back cover, also by Chim, features a group of smiling politicians in front of the Wall.

The homage lasted for hours, sowing the seeds of an alliance between socialists and communists that was solidified on July 14, the official birthdate of the Front Populaire. The ceremony attracted 35,000 people, many of them carrying striking serigraphic posters with portraits of Zola, Signac, and Vallès. It was here that Chim

---

38 *Regards*, April 23, 1936, 8, https://gallica.bnf.fr/ark:/12148/bpt6k76546758/f7.item; *Regards*, May 7, 4–5, https://gallica.bnf.fr/ark:/12148/bpt6k76546773/f5.item.
39 Simone Weil, article in the Communist monthly *Révolution Prolétarienne*, June 10, 1936.
40 *Regards*, May 7, 1936. Cover, 2, 4–5, https://gallica.bnf.fr/ark:/12148/bpt6k76546773/f1.image.
41 *Regards*, May 28, 1936. Cover, back cover and 4–5, https://gallica.bnf.fr/ark:/12148/bpt6k7654680k/f1.image.

shot his famous picture of a little girl with half-closed eyes, an intense expression on her face and a raised fist, sitting on her father's shoulders, while a long crowd snaked behind them. He stayed all day, until the last group entered the cemetery by the light of torches and lanterns.

Chim photographed Blum against the Communards' Wall and, with a spectacular perspective from the ground up in the Moholy-Nagy style, the famous communist choir, the *Groupe Mars*. The actor-singers, dressed in black, had climbed up on a small chapel and, bellowing into their loudspeakers, sang for the crowd to wild applause. The six choir members were Jewish: Simon Lichtenstein, Sarah Rochwarger, Henry Fush, Michel Rochvarger, Charles Dinerstein, who later died in a concentration camp, and Nathan Korb, who survived the war and became famous for his lyrics under the name Francis Lemarque which he had adopted while fighting in the French Resistance.

One of Chim's photographs was published in *Life*. Willy Ronis, a French photographer in the humanist tradition who was starting out at the time and had just met Chim, remembers:

> I have known Chim shortly after he came from Poland to Paris. He developed his photos in a maid's room. He had learned that I was working with my father who had a photography studio. He asked if he could glaze his photographs on our glazing machine. At times, we were working on identical political subjects. There is a photograph he made at the Mur des Fédérés of a famous singing choir of four young men. When I saw this photograph in the jubilee issue of *Life*, I thought that it was mine, but in fact we were one behind the other when we were shooting.[42]

Ronis, a gifted photographer but a loner, seems to have become somewhat jealous of his friend's rising fame and as a result started spending less time with him, on the pretext that Chim was spending time with a group of emigrés who were, he said, "bitter and self-promoting." He preferred to hang out with Capa, whom he found "more optimistic and less tormented" than Chim.[43] Capa was always gregarious, the life of the party, downplaying his growing reputation. and happy to engage with just about anyone.[43]

The aloof and private Ronis was wrong about Chim, who had become gifted at public relations. His physique was not seductive; at 23, he was already balding, and his melancholy eyes were hidden behind horn-rimmed glasses, but probably because of his capacity for listening and his empathy, he was increasingly able to make friends in every walk of life and persuade people in authority to give him access where other photographers were denied.

Chim's photographs of the Bastille Day demonstration and the parade at Père Lachaise show scenes familiar from the accounts of other participants: the paint-

---

[42] Willy Ronis's father photography shop was in Belleville, not far from Chim's first basement studio.

[43] Interview of Willy Ronis by the author, Paris, May 23, 2005.

ings, statues, and triumphal floats, most of them anonymous and ephemeral. The crowds carried painted banners with portraits of revolutionary heroes such as Marat, Robespierre, Saint Just, or the painters of war's horrors, such as Goya, Daumier, and Courbet, who were considered ancestors of *art engagé*.

Writer and painter Boris Taslitzky describes the workers dancing when he visited the Renault factories during the 1936 strikes and remembers the popular parade of July 14: "The Bastille square had been our decoration motif. Leaning against the July column, the gigantic portraits of Robespierre, Marat, Saint Just. Mirabeau had been painted by us (…). In the parade we advanced, cheered on by a whole people celebrating; in our lead were Aragon, Gromaire, Lurcat, Moussinac, Lipchitz, J. Richard-Bloch, Sauveplane, hundreds of writers, musicians, painters, scientists, singers, actors (…). We, the young ones, carried the portraits of the greatest thinkers or artists of our time. I carried a Jacques Callot painted in a camaieu by Gruber, and he carried a Daumier painted by myself. Soon in the streets of French towns and villages shouts of 'Blum in power!' followed by 'Planes, Canons for Spain!' went up."[44]

The same banners feature prominently in Chim's reportage, held by a massive crowd that snakes around the cemetery's monuments. Chim focused on the rally's leaders, Blum and his team, and the communist leaders, the jowly Maurice Thorez and self-satisfied André Marty, but he also singled out individual participants, such as a worker in his Sunday clothes whose small daughter, perched on his shoulders, raised her fist in a salute.

Chim's eloquent photographs, often taken from above with the tilted perspective that he liked, show rows of workers in their round helmets raising a fist, their expressions serious, lined up on a tall crane with a factory chimney in the background, or in a triangular arrangement inside a factory during a strike. Workers dressed up as women, or maybe actors from a troupe, dance in a circle of laughing compatriots (figure 39). More intimate images show them raising their glasses at a table or at a bar, or distributing baguettes, tins of sardines, and cigarettes to the strikers.

In June, Chim photographed a meeting for disarmament in Saint-Cloud.[45] His most spectacular image is that of people in a crowd raising their fists under a gigantic *Disarm* poster with the image of a man breaking a gun on his knee (figure 37). Other posters claim, "War is Insanity!" or "Pour le désarmement" (*For the disarmament*). In a vertical close-up, Chim focuses on two men holding their children on their shoulders. As in a photomontage, the children's raised fists seem to reach for the image of the gun, breaking it. However, pacifist slogans were soon to be drowned out by the cry "Planes for Spain!" as many on the left pressed Blum to bring French help to the beleaguered Spanish government. But Blum, afraid of losing support, de-

---

[44] Boris Taslitzky, *La Nouvelle Critique*, (Paris: Editions du Parti Communiste français, December 1955), no page #.
[45] *Regards*, June 11, 1936, 2–7, https://gallica.bnf.fr/ark:/12148/bpt6k7654682d/f2.item.

cided on non-intervention. His ill-inspired move would reassure Mussolini and Hitler in their belief that democracies were incapable of resisting them.

Over these two years in Paris, Chim had matured fast. *Regards* was the place of his apprenticeship, the place where he developed his specific style and learned journalistic techniques: how to make background checks; use existing lighting, however poor; tell a concise story in pictures; and collaborate successfully with a writer. In contrast with Cartier-Bresson, Chim was never a "decisive moment" proponent, and his style best asserts itself in sequences of photographs rather than in individual images. However, both men demonstrated tough, self-critical judgment when it came to assessing their own photographs.

A decade later, Chim would often choose to write his own text and captions for his stories. Rodger, one of the other co-founders of Magnum Photos, and sometimes, too, Cartier-Bresson (for his 1948 reportage in China, for instance) shared this new approach to reportage, which was termed a "package story."

Even though Chim often sold individual pictures to other magazines such as *Ce Soir*, *Vu*, and *Voilà*, it is *Regards* that became Chim's home in France, the first group where he belonged emotionally and intellectually before he became part of Magnum a decade or so later. *Regards* had made him, as much as he made the magazine, but soon he would expand his territory beyond Paris and France to tackle the biggest story in Europe. As an *envoyé special* (special correspondent) for *Regards*, he was on his way to Spain to cover the Spanish Civil War.

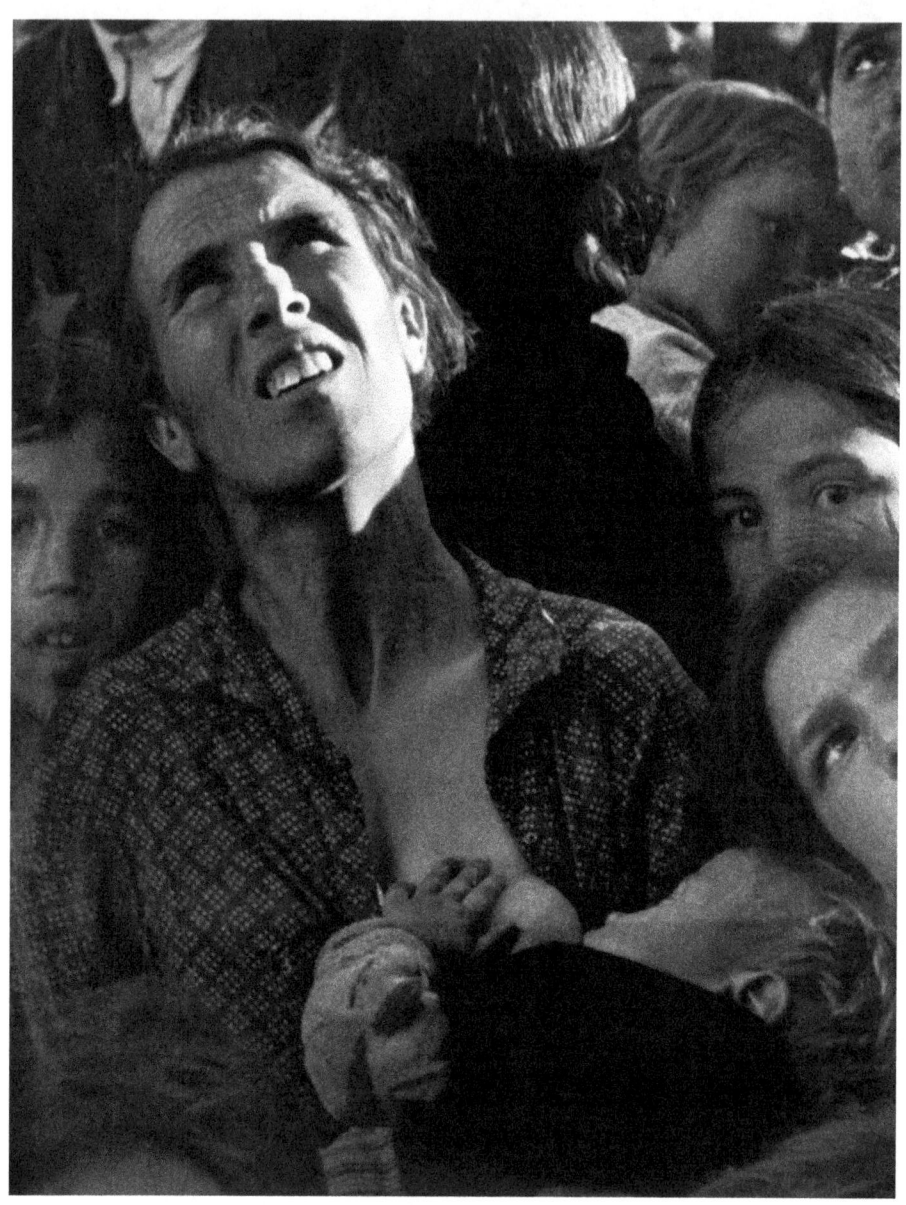

Fig. 7: Woman nursing a baby at a land reform meeting near Badajoz, Extremadura, Spain, May 1936. © David Seymour-Magnum Photos.

Chapter 5: The Good Cause. Spring 1936–February 1939

To this day, the Spanish Civil War remains a unique episode in history: the first battle of World War II, and the last manifestation of fierce idealism, a symbolic battle between fascism and democracy. It polarized the nations of the world. While the Nationalists received military support from Nazi Germany and Fascist Italy, the Republicans were not helped by Britain, which stood aloof from the Republican cause, nor much by France, which was badly divided. However, this policy of "non-intervention" adopted by Britain, and soon by France, led a number of progressive artists and intellectuals from many countries to embrace the Republican cause. A sense of solidarity with Spain propelled some 35,000 courageous people into the International Brigades willing to put their lives on the line for the new Spanish republic. To them, it was a matter of defeating the forces of evil that sought to drag Spain back into an unjust and unequal past.

The war took place after a long period of political turbulence which had created deep divisions in the country. In a worldwide depression, it was hard for the reforming Republican government to alleviate the terrible poverty in which millions of citizens lived. Landless Spanish peasants subsisted by harvesting vast and wealthy agricultural estates. The Catholic Church identified with the landowners and saw universal literacy as a danger rather than a goal. The republic had made some progress, especially in primary education, in introducing co-education, and also in introducing a divorce law, and these kinds of changes enraged conservative Spain, especially the army or, more specifically, certain sectors of its officer corps who saw themselves as embodying the conservative values that they identified with the "true" and "patriotic" Spain. Their military coup against the democratizing republic triggered the conflict that would escalate to full-scale war.

As Susan Sontag wrote, this was "the first war to be witnessed (covered) in a modern sense: by a corps of professional photographers at the lines of military engagement and in the towns under bombardment, whose work was immediately seen in newspapers and magazines in Spain and abroad."[1]

They came in droves. Coverage of the war was possibly greater even than the coverage of World War II would be. It was also far from neutral: many photographers took an enthusiastic stand for the Republican side and saw their art as a tool to publicize the cause and facilitate its victory. In those days, photography was still thought of as something that could help change the world. As war correspondent Martha Gellhorn noted, the photojournalists felt that "the Western democracies had two commanding obligations: they must save their honor by assisting a young, at-

---

[1] Susan Sontag, "Looking at War," *The New Yorker*, December 9, 2002, https://www.newyorker.com/magazine/2002/12/09/looking-at-war, accessed February 23, 2022.

tacked fellow democracy, and they must save their skin by fighting Hitler and Mussolini at once in Spain instead of waiting until later, when the cost in human suffering would be unimaginably greater."[2]

In the crowd were individual photographers such as Chim, Capa, and Taro; the Germans Hans Namuth and Georg Reisner; the Americans Sam Walters and Erwin Rolfe; the Spaniards Antonio Camparia, Agusti Centelles, and the Mayo Brothers, and, from 1937, the Hungarian Kati Horna, who published mainly in anarchist newspapers. Many international news photography agencies were also present. All these photographs appeared in *Vu*, *L'Illustration*, *Daily Mail*, *Illustrated*, *Photo History*, and, as of May 1936, reached the 1.6 million readers of the newly launched *Life*.[3]

Photographs by amateurs—especially group photos of combatant units—were also widely published in Brigade books and newspapers and displayed on bulletin boards, and they played a major role in constructing a collective memory during the war. The Brigades had photographic departments and a mobile photographic lab that followed the moving fronts, and they kept one or two photographers with the units at all times (figure 110). Thousands of Brigade photographs have survived the war; the Abraham Lincoln Brigade Archives owns 400 photos by a Yugoslavian volunteer, Major Vladimir Stefanovich.[4] James Noguez, a poet who drove an ambulance in the war, remembers the "Leica Maniacs" he met there: Capa, Chim, Taro, and Cartier-Bresson, who, between October 1937 and March or April 1938, would shoot a 16mm film, "With the Abraham Lincoln Brigades," to be used for raising funds from the American public.

The professionals' essential tools were the new portable 35mm cameras such as the Leica, which could take 36 photographs before being reloaded and which allowed them to get closer to the action than ever before. Meanwhile, with picture magazines on the rise, photography became increasingly viewed as a professional practice. Image and text, published together, were regarded as truthful, objective reports on current events. However, like the posters both Nationalists and Republicans would soon use to recruit people to their cause, they were used as propaganda.

At the beginning of 1936, Chim was still in Paris to photograph the solidarity demonstrations for Spain. He was going to war, as well as his brother-in-law, jour-

---

[2] Martha Gellhorn, *The Face of War*, 5th ed. (London: Granta Books, 1993), 17.

[3] Paul Preston, "We Saw Spain Die-Foreign Correspondents in the Spanish Civil War" (London: Constable, 2008), 15. A long list of correspondents for four magazines can be found in Francois Fontaine, *La Guerre d'Espagne: un déluge de feu et d'images* (Paris: BDIC, 2003), 101–107.

[4] For a detailed history of the Brigades, see William Lorentz and Marc Crawford, "The Lincoln Brigade—A Picture History" (Westborough, MA:The Apex Press, 2013); to consult the Stefanovich archive, or the ALBA photographs: The Tamiment Library, N.Y.U., New York, Guide to *International Brigade Archive, Moscow: Selected Images*, ALBA.PHOTO.177 (approximately 1,276 negatives), as well as http://dlib.nyu.edu/findingaids/html/tamwag/alba_photo_015/, accessed February 23, 2022. The Photobrigade had four members—Harry Randell, Mayer Levine, Herbert Klein, and Jacques Lemarre—who worked in photography and in film. Their photographs can be consulted at the library.

nalist S. L. Shneiderman, and this is most probably when his entire family visited from Poland, a visit commemorated by several group photographs taken in the hotel room where they stayed[5] (figure 40).

On February 16, the *Frente Popular* won the Spanish elections with 273 seats out of 473 and an agenda that included the hope of re-activating the land reforms that had begun in 1932. As soon as the writer and political leader Manuel Azana took power, he dismissed General Francisco Franco from his post as Chief of Army Staff, sending him off to the Canary Islands. But the popular mood was desperate and impatient; there were some seizures of land, and on the streets the left clashed with the right.

The cause of the Spanish Republic was close to Chim's heart. He had followed it since 1934, and as soon as he knew the results of the election, he left for Spain, excited by his promotion to special correspondent for *Regards*, and inspired by what he saw as more than a reportage (figure 49): a mission. His magazine had featured Spain on its covers two years earlier, on October 12, 1934, with a reportage by George Sadoul, "Revolution in Spain," and the following week with a story on the Oviedo commune, but now it was time for intense coverage.

Chim arrived at the height of the post-election tension when clashes were occurring across the country between proponents of the newly elected Popular Front and right-wing supporters. In an attempt to calm the situation, in March the government banned the fascist party *Falange*, and its leader Jose Antonio de Rivera was arrested. However, the fascists continued to foment a climate that could justify military intervention with a succession of bombings and murders. On July 11, *pistoleros* killed an officer of the newly created Republican police and in retaliation José Calvo Sotelo, a right-wing leader, was shot.

It was probably the murder of Calvo Sotelo that precipitated the military coup. General Franco left the Canary Islands for Morocco where he issued a manifesto calling on all Spaniards to revolt: "Spaniards! Whoever feels a holy love for Spain, whoever among the Army and the Navy has made profession of faith in the service of his country, whoever has sworn to defend her from her enemies, the Nation calls you to her defense (...)."[6] Franco had under his command Spain's colonial "Army of Africa," consisting of Spanish career officers in charge of Moroccan troops, or "Moors" as they were popularly called at the time.

During the thousand days of the Spanish Civil War, Chim traveled across Spain to produce almost 30 stories, primarily for *Regards*, but also for *Vu*, *Voilà*, and *Vendredi*, and the evening paper *Ce Soir*. Maria Eisner of Alliance Photo often resold his pictures to magazines outside France, such as the *Illustrated* and *Life*. It was through

---

5 Photograph discovered in her archive and communicated by Helen Sarid, Chim's niece, October 2021.
6 Manifest by General Francisco Franco, July 17, 1936, as transcribed in Kenwood Alun, *The Spanish Civil War: A Cultural and Historical Reader* (Providence, RI: Berg Press, 1993), 56–58.

Chim's strong recommendation to *Regards* editors that Capa and Taro also went to Spain, where Taro would die on the Brunete front and Capa would shoot his photo, the Falling Soldier, that became an international symbol of war photography, "widely hailed as the most exciting and immediate shot of battle action ever taken," as Capa's biographer Richard Whelan wrote.[7]

Chim was the first photographer of the war to achieve public recognition. His name was showcased on the cover of *Regards*, and his work described in glowing terms as "*sensationnel reportage photographique*" (sensational photographic reportage) and "*un reportage unique*" (a unique reportage).[8] Constantly on the move, unlike many war correspondents, he not only photographed war and moments of action but also tried to understand its causes and repercussions, intent on capturing the nuances and differences between the various cities involved.

In April, he was in Tetuan for a story that appeared on the back cover of *Regards* with the title, "With the Spanish people, A Reportage of our Special Correspondents Soria and Chim."[9] The following week, his focus was the workers at a closed-down trolley system that they had seized and collectivized, salvaging old cars, dismantling, and reassembling more than 20 that were out of use and rusted, and then repainting the locomotive bright red. Titled "Ciudad lineal: le tram collectivisé" (*Linear city: the collectivized tramway*) the story, credited to "our special correspondents", runs on two pages. A joyful image shows the tramway workers proudly standing on top of their newly repainted tram, fists raised. Chim's photographs bear a large credit in capital letters.[10]

Tunisian-born Georges Soria, who worked with Chim all through the war, had arrived in Paris in 1934 and become a successful special correspondent for several newspapers. A virulent anti-Trotskyist, he worked in close cooperation with the Soviet Security Services and had links with the Central Committee of the Spanish Communist Party and with the Soviet representatives in Spain of the intelligence services and the NKVD, the Soviet's secret police. As for Chim, as far as we know, he never joined the Communist Party, but he was definitely a sympathizer with socialist causes and had been since his beginnings with *Regards*.

In early May 1936, in a small town in the province of Extremadura, more than 2,000 peasants (over 200 of them women) assembled in the Plaza de la Republica, representing the 60,000 who had occupied the land.[11] Land distribution was a key issue for peasants who had to give most of their crop to the landowners: owning

---

7 Richard Whelan, "Robert Capa: A Biography" (University of Nebraska Press, 1994), 115.
8 For instance *Regards* cover, September 10, 1936, "Dans les arsenaux espagnols: sensationnel reportage photographique de Chim" (*In the Spanish arsenals*, sensational photographic reportage by Chim). https://gallica.bnf.fr/ark:/12148/bpt6k76546951/f1.image.
9 *Regards*, April 23, 1936, back cover, https://gallica.bnf.fr/ark:/12148/bpt6k76546758/f1.item.
10 *Regards*, April 30, 1936, 14–15, https://gallica.bnf.fr/ark:/12148/bpt6k7654676p/f11.item.
11 *Regards*, May 14, 1936, back cover and 8–9, https://gallica.bnf.fr/ark:/12148/bpt6k7654678h/f7.item.

their share of the land could entirely change their circumstances. "Thinking that Azana's reforms were implemented too slowly," Soria wrote, "peasants and *junteros* have taken their affairs in their own hands."[12] He and Chim were there to attend a meeting organized by the workers of the *Humanitaria*, a 2,000-acre piece of land whose owner had been obliged to rent part of it out to 526 laborers. It was at this gathering, as a socialist deputy addressed the crowd, that Chim created his iconic image of a woman listening to the speech while breastfeeding her child.

A drastic editor of his own work, Chim took scissors to his contact sheet, leaving us only the beginning and end of this film: frames 2, 3, and 4 and frames 31, 32, and 33. However, because his reportage was published in *Regards*, we know that he had spent some time before the meeting photographing peasants in the fields, and then the village militia that escorted the Socialist deputy to the meeting where he was to speak. *Regards*' editors' choice also included a frame, probably the first in the film, that focused on a group within the crowd, shot from a low vantage point. At the bottom of this horizontal image, the nursing woman on whom Chim will later focus is frowning, full of expectation.

Chim moves swiftly. In frame 2, he photographs from a medium vantage point, perhaps a wall of the enclosed plaza, then he moves up onto the town-hall balcony beside the speaker and focuses on the people who pack the vertical frame (that frame was published in Soviet writer Ilya Ehrenburg's 1936 book on Spain, *Ispanya*). By the end of the contact sheet, he is mixing with the crowd and shooting from much closer, once with a tilted frame (frame 32) that reminds us of his interest in modernism.

In frame 33, Chim switches to a vertical format and focuses on the woman he has selected as his main subject. Her face is serious, caught up in concentration. The sun is in her eyes and she blinks. The last rays of the sun fall on the left side of her face, stressing both her tired features and the intensity of her gaze, directed upwards and out of the frame to the public speaker we cannot see. Her rapt expression is echoed in the eyes of two children crowded in on her left.

Absorbed in her listening, the woman pays no attention to the photographer. Nor does the older woman in frame 31, with three men in caps aligned in a diagonal behind her. The faces fill the frame to capacity, a spatial density that evokes the rest of the crowd and conveys the key role of public speeches throughout the war. George Soria commented: "I think that there is no country in Europe except for Spain where an orator is listened to with so much fervor."[13]

This image is a snapshot because the photographer has seized a moment; but it also manages to become an in-depth portrait, focusing on the tender, intent expres-

---

12 Georges Soria in *Regards*, May 14, 1936, "Les paysans et les *junteros* ont pris leurs propres affaires en main."
13 Ibid., "Je ne pense pas qu'il y ait de pays en Europe où l'on écoute avec tant de ferveur un orateur qu'en Espagne." Translated from French by the author.

sion of the subject's face while she is absorbed in listening. In emotional moments like this, the subject is unaware of the photographer, but it is as if her whole soul is revealed to the attentive observer.

Like Capa's Falling Soldier image, Chim's picture became emblematic of the war. Editors often tightened the shot into a Madonna-like, cinematic, more generic portrait, for instance in *AIZ* (July 29, 1936) and *Nova Iberia* (January 1937) republications. In the first volume of Ehrenburg's book, *Ispaniya*, however, the picture was used in its entirety, as a frontispiece, full frame.

Cropped and reframed into a square, the image also appeared on the cover of *Madrid*, a 1937 booklet, as part of a symbolic montage, with airplanes flying above the woman in combat formation and a bomb, marked with a swastika, falling down from blue skies, as if the picture had been taken during an air-raid.[14] The style resembles that of Soviet publications such as *Itogi Pervoi piatiletki* (Results of the Five-Year Plan), the 1932 booklet skillfully designed by Varvara Stepanova, which features planes flying high over women's heads.[15] The *Madrid* appropriation changes the meaning of the woman's upturned gaze from fervor and rapt attention to fear. What had been a picture of empowerment thus became a public appeal to save victimized civilians.

The negative was later lost, and as of 1947 and for many years afterward, Magnum distributed the photograph in a close-up version made from a copy negative, as if editors were adding a zoom lens that Chim had not owned at the time. A book on Chim that the International Center of Photography (ICP)[16] published in 1974 again shows the cropped version of the photograph, with a caption that has the wrong location and a wrong date: "Air Raid Over Barcelona, 1938." This illustrates the way that the reading of an image can be changed throughout history and acquire new meanings in the process.

The surviving frames demonstrate Chim's intuition and his capacity to relate to unknown people, especially women, and children. By excluding the speaker and preferring to photograph an event as reflected in the faces of the onlookers, he seems to suggest that it is not a single leader but the people themselves who are the real agents of their own history.

The so-called Mexican Suitcase was an important cache of negatives from Capa, Chim, and Taro. These three cardboard boxes, which held 4,500 images, or about 120 rolls of film, arranged in compartments with captions inside the lid, had been lost for 70 years. In 1939, as he was fleeing the Nazis in France, Capa handed the boxes to Ciki Weiss, his dark-room manager, who carried them to Bordeaux on his

---

14 *Madrid* (Barcelona, Generalitat de Catalunya, 1937). The image is reproduced in the ICP catalogue *We Went Back*, 2013 (Figure 16, 37.)
15 Alexander Lavrentiev, *Varvara Stepanova: The Complete Works* (Boston: MIT Press, 1991), 131.
16 David Seymour, "Chim," 1911–1956, ICP Library of Photographers (New York: Grossman Publishers, 1974), 43.

bicycle and entrusted them to General Francisco Aguilar, the Mexican ambassador to the Vichy government. Carrying the boxes in his luggage, Aguilar left France for Mexico in the Spring of 1942.

There were persistent rumors that a cache of negatives existed and in 1979, Cornell Capa, Robert Capa's brother, who had become the director of the ICP in New York, started to search for them, hoping to find the lost negative of his brother's Falling Soldier photograph. In 2007, the boxes were finally located in the possession of a Mexican filmmaker, Benjamin Tarver, whose mother had been a friend of the general. Trisha Ziff, a Mexico City-based documentary filmmaker, established contact with Tarver and eventually brought back the boxes to New York.

The fragile celluloid negatives were unspooled with a special mechanism, the Planer Film Duplicating Device, built in 2008 by conservators of the George Eastman House in Rochester, and then each frame was scanned in high resolution so that the scanned films could be reviewed on a computer.[17] They span the duration of the war, beginning with Chim's photographs of marching Republican dignitaries, pre-war, in April 1936, and ending with Capa's portraits of Republican refugees in concentration camps in southern France in March 1939. The Falling Soldier, however, was not included.

It is only with the 2007 rediscovery of the Mexican Suitcase and the ICP curators' thorough analysis of it that it has become possible to do a rigorous examination of Chim's contact sheets, fully understand. and assess the scope of this work and correct some mistaken attributions to Capa.

The 27 stories that Chim published before and during the Spanish Civil War represent just a small portion of his vigorous output during these three years. Many of his pictures remained unpublished. By contemporary standards, the number of photographs Chim took seems small, but in the 1930s, cameras did not have motors like those that photojournalists once used to multiply their shots– now replaced by digital cameras that take multiple shots electronically. And Chim's spirit in his 35mm work, as in his medium-format images, was one of conciseness, economy. Even during the fast action of war, he took the time to carefully reflect and compose his photographs, a characteristic that endured throughout his career.

Still in May, Chim and Soria visited Triana, one of the poorest neighborhoods of Seville, for a reportage entitled Grève des loyers à Triana (*Rent Strike in Triana*)[18]. In that suburb, a family of seven lived in a building without water or electricity on a few pesetas a month. To feed his family, the father picked up overripe fruit from the market at 4 a. m. and then went fishing. The families in this building were on strike because they wanted their rent to be cut by half. When Soria asked them if they ever

---

[17] The two-volume *The Mexican Suitcase*, published by Steidl, Göttingen, 2010 for the ICP, New York exhibition, contains reproductions of all of Chim's contact sheets as well as detailed analysis by several curators and photography historians.

[18] *Regards*, May 28, 1936, 6–7, https://gallica.bnf.fr/ark:/12148/bpt6k7654680k/f5.item.

ate meat, they repeated incredulously, "*Carne! Carne!*" and laughed at him for this extraordinary idea.[19]

In early July 1936, Chim and Soria were off to Barcelona. The city had until now seemed immune from the conflict, with everyone busy making final arrangements for the Olympiad. These Olympic Games had been conceived as a reply to the ones being held in Germany. All over Europe, athletes were eager to take part in games held in a spirit of freedom and racial equality, without the swastika banner floating overhead, and many journalists were coming to cover this symbolic event. Among them were representatives of several Spanish press agencies and freelance photographers, as well as foreign photojournalists, including the two young progressive Germans Hans Namuth and Georg Reisner who had come to cover the Olympics but, when the fascist generals staged their revolt in Barcelona, stayed to photograph the war. "We did not stay in Spain because we were press photographers," Namuth later wrote. "We stayed because Franco was our enemy and because it was also our war."[20]

The war began in earnest with the army's coup attempt against the government. On July 16, secret orders from the military conspirators went out to sympathetic army commanders to strike the following night, in the hope that all over Spain, the army would be in full command by the next morning. But the fascists had not anticipated the determination of Spanish civilians, and instead of a swift takeover, they had to contend with a general population that was called upon to break into the barracks and take up arms. By the next day there was a stand-off. While the military coup against the Republic initially succeeded in Seville, Jerez de la Frontera, Cordoba, Saragossa, and Oviedo, it failed in the major urban areas of Madrid, Barcelona, and Valencia.

The resistance against the military insurgents and their fascist (Falangist) allies was led by radical trade unions that seized arms for the occasion. Soon, because the militia had few professionals, common folks from the party and union organizations also enlisted. On July 19, in the soft early morning light, the Barcelona uprising started and Chim was ready to cover it.

All the fascist regiments quartered in town marched out of their barracks and converged into a full-fledged rebellion. Their goal: some would capture the government buildings and City Hall while other groups would simultaneously take over the palace of the civil governor. Caught in the increasing crossfire between soldiers and antifascists, one-horse garbage carts galloped down Avenida Diagonal while sparrows, chased out of the trees by the racket, spiraled wildly in the summer sky. Soon pandemonium erupted as machine-guns opened up, their cold crackle resounding through the air.

---

19 George Soria, "De la viande! De la viande!" *Regards*, May 28, 1936.
20 Hans Namuth & Georg Reisner, *Spanische Tagebuch 1936* (Berlin: Nishen Verlag, 1986), no p.#

Chim covered the combat, alternating 35mm and square format. For a piece entitled "In Barcelona with the antifascist heroes," he photographed fighters armed with sub-machine guns and cannons seized from the fascists in front of the Central Powders Warehouse.[21] Leaning against their horses, assault guards were firing back. Soria describes people screaming into microphones at street corners, firefighters racing to burning churches, cars speeding through the streets. Chim recorded the mix of violence and excitement that made up the city's atmosphere. He did so without idealizing the Republicans' actions, many of which were violent and extreme: churches burned, artwork and religious statues destroyed. Captured fascist officers who were held on a freighter anchored outside Barcelona's harbor were hastily tried and executed.

Working in the roar of mortars and the rattle of machine guns, Chim photographed civilians passing barricades of rubble that had been piled up on the streets to block the tanks and army trucks. An eyewitness, Lawrence Fernworth, described the scene in the streets during a lull in the fighting: "Over by the monument I saw dead horses lying about and splotches of blood drying on the pavement where the wounded had been taken away. The stone walls of many buildings were broken and chipped by bullets. Empty cartridges and bandoliers were lying about everywhere."[22]

After four days of merciless fighting, on July 22, 1936, the Canadian government announced, "The battle for Barcelona has been won by the armed people." Realizing that they faced a long struggle, the right-wing generals appealed to fascist dictatorships in Italy, Germany, and Portugal and began to receive men and supplies from Mussolini, Hitler, and Salazar. The Republic in turn received aid from the Comintern, an international organization that advocated world Communism, but it was always too little too late. The cards were stacked against the Republicans: Mussolini sent tens of thousands of regular troops to Spain and Hitler sent the elite Condor legions, planes, and high-tech hardware.[23]

It has been mistakenly said that Chim never went to the front. Unlike Capa and Taro, he tended to avoid images of dead bodies and the wounded, but over the months and years of the war, he took several action shots at great risk and in the heat of battle. One image published in *Regards* in September,1937 is a full-page close-up of militiamen firing guns. Other shots taken a month later near Madrid show a cannon, firing, drenched in the smoke of combat. At an unidentified location, he shot close-ups of Republican soldiers in combat with a cannon and antiquated guns. The cover of *Regards* from February 1937 showcased the risks he was taking: "An exceptional document: a few meters from a short 155-cannon, a 77-shell

---

21 *Regards*, July 30, 1936, 6–7, https://gallica.bnf.fr/ark:/12148/bpt6k76546899/f6.item.
22 Gabriel Jackson, *A Concise History of the Spanish Civil War* (New York: John Day, 1974), 116. Fernworth was an American journalist and writer.
23 *The Civil War in Spain*, ed. Robert Payne (New York: Putnam & Sons, 1962), 129.

exploded. Our photographer Chim was exactly ten meters from the drop point marked by a haze of smoke on the image."[24] Another February cover states: "Our photographer Chim in the trenches under besieged Oviedo."[25] Inside, his series of close-up shots shows the *dinamiteros* ready to set fire to their charges with a cigarette (figure 41).

In 1938, at the battle of the Ebro River, he composed panoramic close-ups of soldiers running and throwing hand grenades in a cinematic style resembling Capa's, the figures blurred by movement (figure 42). These photographs were taken close to ground level, with the photographer clearly crouching, and we feel immersed in the action, as if the smoke and dirt of the battle were exploding in our faces. Again, in a series shot during a fierce September battle near Irun, Chim's pictures of the front resemble some of Capa's work in their urgency and closeness. Chim has renounced the niceties of composition. Instead, his blurry images, shot at ground level, bring us into the middle of the action, the smoke, and the mud.

At the end of October 1936, Chim would return to Barcelona, to photograph the refugees sheltered at the Monjuich Arena in Barcelona. His image of a woman writing a letter, using a suitcase as a table, was featured on the cover of *Regards*.[26] In a maternity ward, a woman held her newborn and read the *Vanguardia* newspaper; nurses held four newborn babies. He photographed 15,000 refugees from Catalonia and the Basque country—parents, children, and grandchildren sleeping in dormitories and eating at long refectory tables in the stadium, and he later shot them again, for the December 31 issue.

Even in the middle of war, Chim took time to capture the scenes of everyday life that always fascinated him—soldiers at the amusement park, for instance, or, more bizarrely, lying on the ground in a shelter while wearing their weapons and gas masks for a toxic gas bombing drill, in an image both menacing and surreal.

Children had been an early focus of Chim's photographs, as in his early reportage on Marseille's Panier neighborhood, and were a particular focus for Chim throughout the war, an interest he would later develop in his famous 1948 UNESCO series, "Children of Europe." He photographed small children eating soup and taking showers in a daycare center in Madrid in August and September 1936 as well as young scouts in Madrid's El Capricho park near the Palacio de los Duques de Osuna. Seemingly oblivious to war, they read Mickey Mouse cartoons and ride a sphinx statue. The following month, he photographed kids receiving milk and food, or writing their lessons on the blackboard in a Barcelona public school.[27] Months later, in a more

---

24 "Un document exceptionnel: à quelques mètres d'un canon de 155 court, un obus de 77 explose. Notre photographe Chim se trouvait exactement à dix mètres du point de chute que marque, sur l'épreuve, une brume de fumée." Translated from French by the author.
25 "Notre photographe Chim dans les tranchées sous Oviedo assiégée."
26 *Regards*, November 19, 1936, cover, https://gallica.bnf.fr/ark:/12148/bpt6k7654705z/f1.image.
27 MPNYA, for instance, SED1936008W414 & SED1936004W00032/X14C.

somber mood, an image from February 1937 centered on children playing with a helmet found in the ruins of the town of Gijón in Asturias, with mountains in the background.[28]

Chim first visited Gijon in the summer of 1936. Although it was a pro-Republican city, the previous summer it had housed a bastion of insurgents. In July and August 1936, the workers assaulted the Simancas barracks, where 180 members of the insurgent contingent resisted. The Francoist cruiser Almirante Cervera bombed the city for two weeks, destroying entire districts, including the library of the Institute of Asturias with its magnificent drawings by Dürer and Velasquez.

Apart from his portraits of children playing in the ruins, Chim photographed buildings ripped open with gaping windows, and "still lives": a table loaded with abandoned cartridges, like a funereal picnic, and the melted and charred remains of a typewriter in the rubble of the *Regimento Simencas* headquarters.[29] The subtlety and strength of these images lie in the indirect way they describe the effects of violence on civilians, places, or, as here, objects. The photograph of the typewriter was never published during his lifetime, but since it was discovered in the Mexican Suitcase, it has attracted attention.

Chim had a strong emotional connection to the typewriter as an object (figure 20). As we know, his father was a renowned publisher, and during Chim's childhood, he invited writers to their home and published books in Yiddish and Hebrew as well as classical texts. For Chim the typewriter was also, like the camera, an extension of his hand: he always wrote the captions, and often the texts, for his reportages, and almost all his correspondence (except that with family) was typed.

In this image, there is no sky. The foreground and background of rubble, pulverized bricks, and cartridges combine to form a kind of photomontage. Like the last sentences of a dying man, the machine's keys seem to have ejected fragments and debris instead of words. The concrete pedestal that differentiates this photo from similar images taken by Lee Miller during the London Blitz or Bischoff in Lindau in Germany in 1945 gives it the appearance of a modernist sculpture, evoking Picasso's absinthe glass or John Chamberlain's assemblages and, like many of Chim's images, this one retains its ambiguity: should we read it as a symbol of the human spirit, which resists war even when gravely wounded? Or as a cenotaph, an homage to a journalist, a colleague killed during combat? The possibility of differing interpretations adds to the strength of the image.

For us today this photograph of a disappeared object has become nostalgic, a relic, like the objects that Shomei Tomatsu would photograph in Nagasaki after the nuclear explosion, including a distorted and melted beer bottle, similar to a Soutine painting of skinned beef. In 1948, during his reportage on Europe's children, Chim would roam and document the destroyed landscapes of Europe, and visit the ruins

---

28 MPNYA, SED1937001W0000X/25-035 & SED1936008WMS025/34. From the "Mexican Suitcase".
29 MPNYA, SED1937001W0000X/021-013.

of the ghetto in Warsaw, his birthplace. After the concentration camps, after Hiroshima and Nagasaki, war acquired dimensions that Chim could not have predicted. But like Tomatsu, Chim demonstrates in this image the eloquence of objects, silent witnesses to our life, imbued with our gestures and our emotions. On October 21, 1937, Gijon would be taken over by the Francoists.

On August 6,1936 Chim published his famous series of photographs of Dolores Ibarruri, "La Passionaria." The *Regards* back cover features an understated portrait; all in black, she has her hair severely pulled back in a bun. Clutching a handkerchief in her right hand, she looks down with a thoughtful expression. In his accompanying text *"Une femme, une militante, un chef"* (A Woman, a Militant, a Leader), Elie Faure, a renowned intellectual who later became an art historian, described her as a sort of Joan of Arc of the Spanish Republicans. "You need to hear," he wrote, "this broken voice punctuated by the dance of the hands around the still torso, the handkerchief that she clutches in her bony fist as if to cling to herself, while her thought springs from word to burning word."[30]

Of peasant origins, this miner's wife had been elected deputy from Oviedo. She was a fiery orator and became the symbol of the Republican cause, responsible for many of the slogans that summed it up: "Better die standing than live on your knees"; "Better to be a hero's widow than a coward's wife." She gave new life to an old slogan that the *poilus*, the French soldiers of World War I, had used. *"No Pasaran!"* (They shall not pass!) became the leitmotiv of the Battle of Madrid. In the magazine, a sober series of four oblique portraits of her forms a cinematic sequence. On July 25, *Voilà* used the portrait that was on the *Regards* cover as a cut-out, showing only her head and shoulders, as one of the illustrations for "Carmen de la Révolution," a reportage on the women leaders of the insurrection.

In early August 1936, in Saragossa, Chim photographed a crowd surrounding a Republican plane that the fascists had taken down. For a piece in the August 13 issue of *Regards* using that picture, the journalist J. E. Pouterman chose the title "Spain fights for the world's freedom," demonstrating the extent to which the Spanish War was seen in France and in antifascist Europe as the symbol of a common struggle. On August 12, Chim photographed the first International Brigades volunteers arriving in Spain. That first unit was comprised of German antifascists, refugees who had come from France, and escapees straight from Germany. They named their outfit after Ernst Thaelmann, the communist leader who was already a prisoner of the Nazis and would die at Buchenwald, and they were soon joined by Italians, mainly escapees from fascism, who organized themselves into the Gastone-Sozzi Battalion and the *Giustizia e Libertà* column. Chim's photographs of these fighters are very

---

[30] "l faut entendre cette voix cassée que ponctue la danse des mains autour du torse immobile, le mouchoir serré dans son poing maigre comme pour s'accrocher à elle-même, tandis que la pensée bondit sur les mots brûlant." Translated from the French by the author.

personal. Even when he chooses a group like the Thaelmann Brigades for symbolic content, he usually zooms in on one main character, such as the young soldier in his metal helmet, slightly turning toward the viewer as he marches by.[31]

By early September, 1936, Chim and Pouterman were at the front, in the hills near Irun. This Basque town was key because its road and rail links sat at the border with southwestern France. Fascist forces had been ordered to take Irun and the nearby resort town of San Sebastian. South of Irun, on the Puntza ridge, Chim photographed the insurgent forces, including newly arrived foreign legion troops, the Bandera of the Tarcio. It was an uneven contest: the Republican side consisted only of elements of the Basque army, some Asturians and anarchist militias, part of a volunteer Paris battalion, and a few French machine guns. As we see in Chim's pictures, the soldiers' machine guns and rifles were old, and for the most part the men did not even have helmets, let alone uniforms. On the other hand, the insurgents were supported by artillery and by Italian planes.[32]

The fascists advanced and despite heavy casualties were able to clear the ridge, but they met fierce resistance and hand-to-hand combat from the Basques and their allies, and the ridge changed hands more than three times. Inevitably, however, the Republicans, outmanned and outgunned, lost the battle for Irun, but not before they had burned or dynamited most of the town's government buildings to prevent the fascists from using them.

Two days after Chim's action-packed coverage was published in *Regards* on September 3, Irun fell, and its defenders had to flee across the Bidasoa River into France. A victory march, complete with fascist salutes, took place on the city streets just a day after Prime Minister Francisco Largo Caballero had presented his new government, a coalition of socialists, communists, and left Republicans. Irun was a major victory for the fascists, who could now isolate Basque country from the French border and the rest of the Republican territory.

While Capa and Taro returned to Paris in mid-September 1936, Chim embarked on a series of secret missions to document munitions and aircraft factories, focusing often on the role of women in the war effort. In the Basque country, he photographed women at work, replacing the male factory workers who had gone to fight.[33] Some were working in armaments factories, others were busy in assembly workshops, putting together airplanes sent in parts by the USSR, painting bombs, or manufacturing shells in an armament's factory. Months later, in February 1937 in Langreo, he would photograph women in the mines as, surrounded by towering piles of coal, they shoveled the fuel into wagons. These women are shown as independent and strong, able to sustain the war effort. The first of his reports on the women workers

---

31 Elie Faure, "Portrait of the Passionaria," *Regards*, August 6, 1936. Chim, back cover and 9, https://gallica.bnf.fr/ark:/12148/bpt6k7654690z/f9.item.
32 *Regards*, September 3, 1936, 8–11, https://gallica.bnf.fr/ark:/12148/bpt6k7654694m/f8.item.
33 *Regards*, September 10, 1936, 9, https://gallica.bnf.fr/ark:/12148/bpt6k76546951/f8.item.

was published in *Regards* on September 10: "In Spanish Warehouses: Cannons for Spain, Aircraft for Spain."

Along with the poet and writer José Bergamin, Chim was the only journalist authorized to board the Jaime I, the largest destroyer of the Spanish fleet, which Franco's forces claimed to have sunk.[34] In July, the Jaime I had played an important role in resisting the military coup when the crew revolted against their mutinous officers, killing some of them, and put themselves under the command of a petty officer sympathetic to the Republic. Thereafter the Jaime I became the government's chief weapon against Franco. The *Regards* cover is a close-up portrait of a sailor. An impressive full-page image in Modernist style shows the whole crew assembled in a triangular formation on the battleship deck, followed by an eight-picture sequence showcasing the sailors' life aboard. Chim gets a large credit line. Through Eisner's good offices, his reportage was also published in *Illustrated* after its appearance in *Regards*.

By mid-October,1936 Chim was working in Madrid as tensions mounted and Franco's army threatened.[35] He photographed La Passionaria's speech on the defense of Madrid to the combatants of the militia's Fifth Regiment, a key militia in the capital. Lina Odena, one of the directors of the Unified Youth movement, had been killed on the Cordoba front, and Chim photographed a parade of young people holding a banner with her name and the inscription "*Vinceremos*," soliciting donations for hospitals from the passers-by. The photographs are scattered on the page, their corners overlapping, as if dropped by chance

Among Chim's most intriguing and detailed photo essays (four rolls of film) are the October 1936 portraits he made of the *Regulares Indigenas*, Moroccan troops who had been recruited to fight on Franco's side against the Republicans. Found in the Mexican Suitcase, these images are part of the rediscovery of an obscure history. These were unacknowledged soldiers, fighting for a cause that was not theirs, and they died by the thousands.

While Franco's forces were photographed by several Spanish photographers and by foreigners such as the Frenchman Jean Clair Guyot, working for *L'Illustration*, these Moroccans constituted a rarity in Chim's work. As far as we know, only one of the images was published in *Regards* during his lifetime, with text by Ehrenburg. Dubbed by Franco's propaganda "volunteers of the heart," fighting for "a good cause under the eye of God," the Moroccans described themselves somewhat differently: "They took us as if we were cows," recalled one veteran interviewed in the film *The Moroccan Labyrinth*. "We knew nothing." And again: "When you're hungry, you can't see".[36]

---

34 *Regards*, October 1, 1936, cover and 11–13. https://gallica.bnf.fr/ark:/12148/bpt6k76546988/f11.item.
35 *Regards*, October 22, 1936, 6, https://gallica.bnf.fr/ark:/12148/bpt6k76547019/f6.item.
36 Film by Julio Sánchez Veiga, 2007. See also Driss Deibach, *Los Perdedores*, 2006.

The promise of regular food, a salary, and the *muna* or small wage for their family was enough to lure them, pushed into desperation as they were by drought and famine. Serving in the army was a chance to save themselves and their families. Moreover, these Moroccan soldiers, enlisted with the help of local chiefs, were led to believe that they would be fighting a *Jihad* against infidels, helping the people of the book, Christians and Muslims, against the godless Reds. They were promised land in Spain, but after Franco's victory in 1939 they were instead expelled *en masse* and sent back with a meager pension.

Flown to Seville on Italian and German planes, the *Regulares* first arrived in the south of Spain at the end of July 1936. By November 6, they were at Madrid's doors. The city had been under siege for several weeks but now the battle to take it from its Republican defenders was beginning. On November 8, General Mola launched an attack with 20,000 men. The Moroccans who formed most of his troops, together with Italians and Germans, became cannon fodder in the siege of the city. Sent to the front lines, they died at the rate of 1,000 a month. In a second attack launched on November 9, they fought house to house and, again, they died in large numbers.

While the intense fighting lasted for 10 days, the battle for control of the city would last, on and off, until March 1937. As the fighting progressed, the *Regulares*—killing, raiding, and looting—gained a well-earned reputation for violence. In small villages, posters showed them with a horn and tails or with long teeth, devouring babies. In this context, it is very probable that Chim's reportage on the Moroccans was assigned as propaganda, to demonstrate that the Republicans treated their prisoners well. It would serve the same function as his reportage from the Basque front, or his well-known series, also shot in November, on Republicans who saved works of art from the bombings, both of which helped counter the anti-Republican tenor of much mainstream news reporting.

Chim's photographs fit the bill. With its rectangular paved yard, airy rooms, stone walls, large windows, high ceilings and vaults, a Madrid prison for *Regulares* —probably a soldier's barracks—has no cells but a refectory equipped with long benches and wood tables, and clean dormitories with cots and striped sheets. We follow the prisoners: in white shirts and pantaloons, some wearing the fez, some a small white turban, some with a shaved head and a thin braid, they are led inside. In just one image out of more than 100, guns are pointed at them.

Chim's photographs linger on groups of Republicans and Moroccans who share the same activities. They eat bread and stew together; wash up at the stone sinks; relax in the dorms. One Republican reads the newspaper *Ahora*, in which the headline ("Oviedo: Children in the line of Fire") dates the photographs to mid-October 1936. Then Chim focuses on smaller groups of three, four, or five soldiers: Republicans lighting a cigarette for a prisoner; prisoners and Republicans in conversation. One prisoner playfully raises his fist in a salute as the Republican soldiers watch. Will he cross over to the other side?

Chim moves closer for a beautiful series of individual portraits, often showing three-quarters of the face in deep shadows, a Bauhaus-like style learned during his studies in Leipzig and previously used in his portraits of the Jaime 1 battleship, especially the shot of the sailor that made the cover of *Regards*. The prisoners' faces are serious rather than sad, their body language is relaxed. Are they relieved to be spared battles like those where so many of their friends have already died?

These sober and moving photographs go beyond his assignment, beyond propaganda. They do not pass judgment but have a quality of tenderness and mystery. Looking the "other" in the eye, he photographs with humanity and the same respect he shows for the Republicans.

The photographs were never published. Did the editors and the public, perhaps fueled by inherent racism, prefer to see the enemy as cruel and inhuman, the *Regulares* as torturers and baby-killers? The question remains.

In November 1936, Chim published a story on the palace of the Duke of Alba in Avila.[37] Built in the eighteenth century, it housed an art collection reportedly second only to that of the National Palace and had been used as HQ by the Spanish Communist Party and its militia, the Fifth Regiment, since the beginning of the war. It had been damaged by Nationalist aircraft earlier in the month: "German airmen dropped incendiary bombs on his palace—not just one but many (…). Now all these treasures would be burning, if the workers-guards, risking their lives, had not rescued them from the flames and laid them out in the grass: ancient weapons, paintings, medieval armors, costly folios from the Duke's library. What an image for those who really want to determine which class is defending culture and which class is destroying it!" wrote a *Regards* editor.[38]

In sharp contrast with his earlier photographs of Republicans destroying statues of saints, Chim here shows the Republicans—uniformed soldiers and armed men and women—caring for the palace treasures. The title reads: "Are the Barbarians those who destroy national art, or those who preserve it with love?" Some carry a wooden Christ on their shoulders as in a religious parade; others are waxing the floors to a shine. Elsewhere, Republicans work hard to salvage works of art at the Monastery of the Descalzas or in Madrid's Palacio de Liria, where Chim documented the process of cataloguing and staging shipments of art so that they could be swiftly removed to the new capital, Valencia, away from the rebels' bombing raids. The July 29 issue of *Vu* featured an unsigned Chim photograph of a soldier guarding a museum (several of his images were reused in *Illustrated*, a pro-Franco magazine, with ambiguous captions that do not clarify the Republicans' role in salvaging art).

In the same issue of *Regards*, Chim published a reportage with a text by Albert Soulillou on the Monjuich stadium in Barcelona, which housed a number of refugees

---

37 *Regards*, November 26, 1936, 11, https://gallica.bnf.fr/ark:/12148/bpt6k7654706c/f11.item.
38 Quote from Mikhail Koltzov's text *Madrid in November*, *Regards*, July 14, 1937, https://gallica.bnf.fr/ark:/12148/bpt6k7635914c/f12.item.

who had fled Seville, Irun and other cities. In a photograph taken from above, Chim captured hundreds of families eating a long makeshift tables. He also made empathetic close-ups on children and their mother, bearing an anguished expression.[39]

As the war continued into 1937, Chim's coverage intensified, and he published in seven consecutive issues of *Regards*.

For the January 14 issue of *Regards*, Chim, again working with Albert Soulillou, did seven photographs and the cover for a story on miners in Das, in the Catalan Pyrenees.[40] He went 30 meters down into the coal, mine, with the elderly peasants who had replaced the young miners deployed on the Aragón front. Once mined, the coal was carried on small hand-held, primitive plows drawn by oxen.

Chim joined the miners for the outdoor picnic lunch that women and children had brought, and he made several haunting portraits. "A ray of sun comes out. We take advantage of it and they align against the shed, sheltered from the north. They agree with simplicity to the demands of the photographer, who is delirious with the beauty of certain types," writes the reporter, Albert Soulillou. "There is a nice old guy who is all moved to know that his portrait will be published in the paper, just like that of a brave revolutionary fighter. He cannot stop shaking our hands. He has tears coming to his eyes."[41] One of these close-up portraits, the sunny wall serving as improvised background, made the back cover of *Regards*.

By mid-January 1937, Chim and Pouterman were aboard the ship Aya Mendi that left Bordeaux for Bilbao, the Basque capital, following an indirect route to avoid Franco's pirates and Hitler's battleships.[42] What was usually a 15-hour trip took them four days and nights, with Chim photographing war cargo seized on the German contraband ship Palos, the Basque ship Soton, and the British ship Blackhill. After his trip, he traveled all over the Basque Republic on the Aya Mendi, focusing on Bilbao and Vallejo after their recent battles, and photographed three armed fishing boats (*bous*) that protected the coast against the forays of Franco's fleet, creating beautiful portraits of their captains. One of them had captained a boat that captured the German ship Palos, loaded with supplies for Franco's forces. Chim's reportage of the Palos was republished in *Illustrated*.

While most of the Catholic church in Spain supported Franco, Basque country was exceptional: The Catholic Basque separatists strongly supported the Basques' own autonomous government in Bilbao. Chim's photographs stress this unusual alliance of Catholics, socialists, and anarchists against fascism. One of his most striking pictures for *Regards* shows a group of women walking Bilbao's streets, clutching

---

39 *Regards*, November 1936, 12–13, https://gallica.bnf.fr/ark:/12148/bpt6k7654706c/f12.item.
40 *Regards*, January 14, 1937, cover and 12–13, https://gallica.bnf.fr/ark:/12148/bpt6k7635914c/f12.item.
41 Albert Soulillou, "Mineurs des cîmes," *Regards*, January 14, 1937, https://gallica.bnf.fr/ark:/12148/bpt6k7635914c/f12.item.
42 *Regards*, January 21, 1937, 8–9, https://gallica.bnf.fr/ark:/12148/bpt6k7635915s/f7.item.

Bibles tight against their chests as they would children.[43]. Again Chim, like the journalist J-E. Pouterman, gets a big credit.

In the February 4 issue, Chim continued his coverage of Catholics mobilized against the fascists with a cover story on the 18th-century Amorebieta cloister, about 20 kilometers from Bilbao: The magazine's editors write: "Basques clerics and militiamen fraternize, the cover announces, a moving reportage of our special correspondents Pouterman and Chim". It is one of the most striking aspects of this Basque republic, where the Catholics, a majority of the population, fight as brothers with the communists, the socialists and the anarchists against fascist barbary.[44] The cloister's brothers had given their old refectory to the militias from the Transmission Battalion.

Rather than confirming stereotypes, these photographs unsettled ready-made assumptions, as one of Chim's most powerful reportages shows.[45] It was intended to counter the Francoist claim that Republicans were godless. "In Spain's Basque country," the reporter wrote, "there is no conflict between the people's Republican aspirations and the Church." Also shot in the winter of 1936–1937, this story, "Country Mass on the Basque Front", published in *Regards* and subsequently in several European magazines, showed an outdoor mass celebrated for the soldiers before combat in the village of Lequeisto, on a hill near the Berriatua front. Most of the village had been destroyed by Insurgent raids.

Looking at Chim's contact sheets, we can follow his systematic movements all around and above the priest and the crowd, creating multiple angles: ground-level perspectives from the front and the sides and a very effective bird's-eye view that includes the priest and his open Bible, the table with his implements, the crowd of standing, contemplative men, and a huge Basque flag floating on the right. In another reverse bird's-eye view, he photographed the crowd from the back and the farm's façade. To capture one image of a man approaching the table to take communion, Chim went down from his high vantage point and his picture is framed in part by the oval stone arch of the house. Since there is no organ, a Basque musician plays the flute and the tambourine during the ceremony.

These images are a testimony to Chim's early interest in religion and Catholicism, which he would later build on in his 1949 reportage on the Vatican, and his 1950s series on religious festivals in Southern Italy and Sicily. Before the mass, Chim's attentive eye had seized a modest still-life on a straw chair: a candleholder, a bell, a cup of wine. Ever conscious of details, he often composed eloquent still-lives like these.

---

43 *Regards*, January 28, 1937, 6–7, https://gallica.bnf.fr/ark:/12148/bpt6k76359166/f6.item.
44 "A travers la République Basque: religieux et miliciens basques fraternisent," *Regards*, February 4, 1937, cover and 6–8, https://gallica.bnf.fr/ark:/12148/bpt6k7635917m/f5.item.
45 Regards, March 4, 1937, 6–7, https://gallica.bnf.fr/ark:/12148/bpt6k7635921h/f5.item.

In Oviedo, Chim shot two of his best reportages, on the miners of Asturias, with whom he had already spent time before the war.[46] Early in February, 1937, fighting had erupted there as the miners, supporters of the Republican cause, sought to recapture Oviedo from Franco's troops. Basque troops—the famous *dinamiteros*—under the command of General Aranda joined the miners. Working in the trenches from up close, Chim photographed all the aspects of the miners' lives, from their assaults against the fascists to a break taken inside an old barrel or under a makeshift tent. The opening picture in the *Regards* spread is a close-up on a *dinamitero*. He has approached the enemy lines, dynamite charge in hand, and is about to light it with his cigarette—there was a shortage of matches—taking the risk that the charge can explode in his hands (figure 41). Other action photographs show the miners shooting through a breach they have just created with dynamite. Chim's story, a classic that made the miners heroes, was republished on March 6 in *Illustrated*. With a total of ten photographs, it was one of his longest pieces.

Back in Paris at the end of May 1937, Chim collaborated with Cartier-Bresson for a June *Regards* issue on a Paris art fair, *Exposition Internationale: Arts et techniques dans la vie moderne*. In February, colleagues, and representatives of the Spanish Republican government, including Josep Renau, then the Republic's director of fine arts and its most influential architect of new wartime cultural policies, had come to Picasso's home to ask him to paint a mural for the fair. Picasso had always supported the Spanish Republicans financially and he agreed, but he did not feel inspired. The concept of political art did not appeal to him. Then several things happened to drastically change his mind and catalyze his artistic engagement. First he read a collection of Louis Delaprée dispatches on the massive bombings of Madrid on January 8, 1937, *Le Martyre de Madrid* (The Martyrdom of Madrid), published in the Communist newspaper *L'Humanité*.[47]

Then, at Franco's request, on the afternoon of April 26, 1937, Guernica, the sacred city of the Basque people, was systematically destroyed by the Nazi Condor Legion and by planes from Mussolini's air force. For over three hours, the town was pounded by high explosive and incendiary bombs. Guernica burned for three days. Hundreds of people, perhaps thousands, were killed or wounded. It was the first time a civilian center had suffered such a fate on such a scale.

On April 30, eyewitness reports filled the front pages of *Ce Soir* and all major newspapers in Europe. More than one million protesters filled the Paris streets to voice their outrage in the largest ever May Day demonstration. Picasso, stunned by what he had seen in the papers, rushed through the crowded streets to his studio and immediately started preparatory drawings on "Guernica." In a week, the drawings took on their final scale and design, with the predominant bull, the frenzied

---

46 *Regards*, February 18, 1937, cover and 12–14. https://gallica.bnf.fr/ark:/12148/bpt6k7635919f/f11.item and *Regards*, February 25, 1937, 6–7, https://gallica.bnf.fr/ark:/12148/bpt6k76359203/f5.item.
47 Martin Minchom, *Morir en Madrid*, Collected Essays of Louis Delaprée, (Madrid: Raices, 2009)

horse, and the weeping woman. Picasso worked with surprising speed and on May 11, Dora Maar photographed him drawing the full design on canvas. "In the picture I am now painting," said Picasso, "which I shall call 'Guernica,' and in all my recent work, I am expressing my horror of the military caste that is now plunging Spain into an ocean of misery and death."[48]

In Chim's photograph, an intense, fiery-eyed Picasso stands with arms crossed, unsmiling. This is no official portrait. Chim was making a personal statement about his admiration of Picasso and his painting at a time when "Guernica" was rarely understood and came under a barrage of partisan, utilitarian criticism. The German guide to the fair called it "a hodgepodge of body parts that any four-year old could have painted."[49] The Soviets reacted coolly: they favored realistic imagery. The Left, and especially the communists, the very people who should have understood and supported it, attacked the painting: It did not illustrate a political agenda, and it expressed suffering rather than optimism. There were even those in the Spanish Republic's Culture Ministry who wanted to remove it from the Spanish Pavilion and declared it "antisocial, ridiculous and entirely foreign to a healthy proletarian outlook."[50] *Regards* featured Picasso's portrait, and two views of the devastated city.[51]

The Spanish Pavilion was one of the hits of the fair. It had been conceived to show the world the country's identity but also to mobilize the public by informing them about Spain's tragic situation, and maybe convince some of them to support the Republican cause. Pierre Gassmann, a photographer, and printer who would later become a friend and collaborator of Magnum and was already close to Capa, Taro, and Chim, together with François Duffort, a printer he had just hired, were commissioned to make giant prints of Capa's and Chim's Spanish Civil War images to show there.

Renau, who had secured "Guernica" for the Pavilion, was Spain's Director of Fine Arts and the most prominent Spanish exponent of the use of photography, typography, and avant-garde graphic design. As of 1929, he had been one of the first artists to use the technique of photomontage in Spain and from 1937 he would be the key figure implementing such techniques as part of a mass cultural mobilization policy in support of the Republican war effort.

Under his management, the pavilion's images were deployed to enhance the whole political agenda, with photographs on government projects concerning heritage, education, and popular tradition. As a propaganda support and medium, the photomurals juxtaposed an image of traditional Spain before the Republic with one depicting its subsequent achievements. References to the bombing of Guernica were

---

48 Pierre Daix, *Picasso the creator*, (New York: Somogy, 1964), 143.
49 German brochure for the *Exposition Internationale Universelle* (Paris, 1937).
50 Quoted in *Guernica versus El Guernica*, https://cronicaglobal.elespanol.com/letra-global/cronicas/guernica_75287_102.html, accessed August 5, 2020.
51 *Regards*, June 3, 1937, 11–13, https://gallica.bnf.fr/ark:/12148/bpt6k76359344/f11.item.

also present, in order to support an understanding of Picasso's painting, which was widely considered the pre-eminent work at the pavilion.

From the photographs that French photographer François Kollar made of the pavilion's walls,[52] we can see that Renau also used photographers' cut-up images to create the photomontage murals both inside and outside the building: for instance, Chim's portrait of poet Federico Garcia Lorca and a picture of an armed Republican soldier protecting artworks at Palacio de Liria in Valencia where they had been moved from Madrid.

On July 14, 1937, *Regards* published a special issue on one year of civil war in Spain and it contained some of Chim's images, republishing his pictures of the Palacio de Liria in Madrid and some action pictures.[53] The following week, a second special issue featured the Second Congress for the Defense of Culture, attended by 200 writers from 26 countries.[54] Both Capa and Chim covered the congress and Chim did beautiful portraits of Alexis Tolstoy, Egon Erwin Kisch, and Jose Bergamin. Even though they were shot in public situations, the portraits do not look official; it feels as if the photographer and his models had established an intimate rapport. Chim subsequently reported a story on France's first *Congés Payés* (paid vacation): the two-week paid vacations for all salaried workers had been unanimously voted by the Front Populaire. "In the small beaches of the north, our photographer Chim went to surprise the vacationers, in those small beaches, simple ones without insolent luxury or casinos."[55]

Meanwhile, Capa and Taro, who had become Capa's fiancée, had also been working all over Spain. They had photographed street scenes, and, at the railroad station in Bilbao, soldiers bound for Aragon, the Huesca front, and Saragossa. After spending a week or so on the front they had proceeded to Madrid, then to Cerro Muriano, on the Cordoba front, where Capa made beautiful pictures of the civilian population and created his iconic image of the Falling Soldier. The two were in Paris when Taro decided to return to Spain, to the Brunete front, near Madrid. With the war in Basque territory over and the battle lines in the rest of Spain relatively stable, the Republicans, determined to make a frontal attack on the enemy lines at Brunete, embarked on a brutal battle that lasted through most of July 1937, in intense heat, with positions changing hands many times over. In the end, the Republicans gained a small advantage but suffered shattering losses. Working the front lines, Taro shot

---

52 Noted French photographer François Kollar was assigned by the French Ministry of Culture to make a detailed reportage on the exhibition. His photographs can be seen online: https://www.culture.gouv.fr/collections_locales/Search?xsl=ac_kollar&f.b=&f.ou=&rv=mosaic&f.eb=false&text2=%2B(Kollar)&text=exposition+internationale+1937, accessed July 18, 2021.
53 *Regards*, July 14, 1937, 6, 7, 11, 16, https://gallica.bnf.fr/ark:/12148/bpt6k7635940v/f21.item.
54 *Regards*, July 22, 1937, 6–7, https://gallica.bnf.fr/ark:/12148/bpt6k76359418/f5.item.
55 "Dans les petites plages du nord, notre photographe Chim est allé les surprendre, dans les petites plages simples, sans luxe insolent, sans casino." Translated from French by the author. *Regards*, July 29, 1937, cover and 12–13, https://gallica.bnf.fr/ark:/12148/bpt6k7635942p/f11.item.

pictures for *Regards*, which published them on July 22: "In Brunete and Villanueva de la Cañada: a sensational photographic reportage by Taro."

On her last day at Brunete, Sunday July 25, Taro decided she wanted to shoot the action one more time, and she set out for the front with her colleague Ted Allan. When they arrived, they were warned to leave immediately, since heavy combat was expected. Although Allen was prepared to obey, Taro persuaded him to stay on with her as she shot dramatic close-ups of insurgent planes raining bombs on the dugouts.

Putting herself in extreme danger, she shot images of the fighting, and then she and Allan came across a jeep that was transporting the wounded. The driver let them stand on the running-boards as he drove away. Suddenly Italian bombers swooped overhead and as they did, a tank ahead of them swerved out of control. The jeep's driver tried to pass it, but the tank, sideswiping the car, knocked Taro off the running-board and ran over her stomach and legs, crushing her. Lightly wounded, Allan fell on the other side. The two were rushed by ambulance to a hospital where Taro was operated on. She died early the next morning.

That same day in Paris, Capa read in the communist daily *L'Humanité* a short report: "A French journalist, Mlle Taro, is reported to have been killed in a combat near Brunete." That night Capa, Ruth Cerf, and *Ce Soir* editor Paul Nizan left for Toulouse, then for Perpignan where Taro's body had been taken, and then they took a train back to Paris. Richard Whelan wrote, "Capa was absolutely devastated by grief. Until the funeral he remained in his studio, weeping and refusing all the food and drink that Inouye [a colleague] brought him."[56]

Thousands of mourners attended the funeral procession that went from the Maison de la Culture to the Père Lachaise cemetery. Pieces dedicated to Taro appeared in *Ce Soir*, *Life*, then *Regards* on August 5 under the title "Accident in Brunete": "Our readers may have remarked the talent of Gerda Taro for her audacity, sometimes her contempt for death, on the fronts of Andalusia, Aragon, Madrid, from where, with our reporters Capa and Chim, she brought back a documentation that *Regards* since last August had been alone in presenting and that contributed to make vivid the terrible realities of the fight of the Spanish Republic for the world's freedom," wrote journalist Léon Moussinac in a heartfelt homage.[57]

In a welcome break from covering the war and its tragedies, Chim traveled to Brittany to cover the Pardon de Sainte Anne La Palud, an important annual religious festival and celebration in honor of Sainte Anne, the Virgin Mary's mother. [58]It took

---

56 Richard Whelan, *Robert Capa: A Biography* (University of Nebraska Press, 1994), 115.
57 "Nos lecteurs avaient peut-être remarqué le talent de Gerda Taro, que son audace, parfois son mépris de la mort, sur les fronts d'Andalousie, d'Aragon, de Madrid, d'où, avec nos reporters Capa et Chim, elle nous apporta une documentation que, dès le mois d'août de l'an dernier, Regards était seul à pouvoir présenter et qui contribua tant à rendre sensibles les terribles réalités de la lutte de l'Espagne républicaine pour la liberté du monde." Translated from French by the author.
58 *Regards*, September 16, 1937, 12–13, https://gallica.bnf.fr/ark:/12148/bpt6k7635949k/f9.item.

place on the beach at Plonevez-Porzay, with an open-air mass and procession on the dunes.

Chim had always loved religious festivals—he would cover many of them in Italy in the 1950s—and he relished photographing the 5,000 pilgrims converging, most on foot, some carrying banners to the saint's chapel or wooden sculptures of ships in homage. His photographs show the participants in regional costumes, men with the black round Breton hat, women with the high Bigouden cylindrical headdress, and several of them carrying an ornate statue of the Virgin. Chim made individual close-up portraits of the best-looking women, one of whom made the cover of *Regards*, which announced "un beau reportage de Chim" (a beautiful reportage by Chim).

In September, still deeply grieving Taro's death, Capa was in New York, where he conceived, maybe with his friend André Kertész, the idea of a homage to her with a book. *Death in the Making* came out in February 1938, with a layout by Kertész and a moving dedication: "For Gerda Taro, who spent one year at the Spanish Front, and who stayed on."

The book contains more than 100 photographs and writings from Capa and paints a lively chronicle of the Spaniards' lives and their resistance, but the publication is in some ways disappointing, with grayish reproductions and cheap paper that do not do justice to the photographs. And for reasons unclear, Taro and Chim, who had, respectively, 24 and 13 images in the book, are not credited.

The same problem dogged a companion exhibition, *Life in the Making*, which opened that same month at the New School of Social Research in New York, a progressive institution favoring the Republican cause. The 200-print show included pictures from the book, plus a group of others from Chim which had not been included in the book, notably his 1936 iconic portrait of a woman nursing her baby at a land reform meeting in Badajoz (figure 7). The pictures in the book had been attributed to Capa and Taro, but not to Chim. This was the beginning of a 70-year story of misattributions of Chim's work to Capa, which was only recently corrected with the rediscovery of the Mexican Suitcase. At the time of this writing, Capa curator Cynthia Young has republished *Death in the Making* in a new version, with correct attributions to Capa, Chim, and Taro and a deeply researched, eloquent preface.[59]

Staying on in France in the autumn of 1937, Chim went south to Antibes and Pegomas for a reportage on *La Marseillaise*, a film shot by noted director Jean Renoir with whom Cartier-Bresson would also collaborate. [60]Through the history of a group of Marseillais, the film narrated an episode from the early days of the French Revolution. Historically correct, the film was based on research by the Sorbonne's newly founded *Institut d'histoire de la Révolution française*, and it was hoped that it would

---

[59] Cynthia Young, ed., *Death in the Making* (New York: Damiani and ICP, 2020; original edition: New York: Covioci-Friede, 1938).
[60] *Regards*, October 1, 1937, 13, https://gallica.bnf.fr/ark:/12148/bpt6k7635949k/f9.item.

cement enthusiasm for the Popular Front by celebrating the birth of the French Republic, but when it was released the following year, it was not a success.

Over the next few months, Chim worked in both France and Spain. In December 1937 he was in Paris, where he rushed to the hospital as soon as he got the news from Hala and Emil. Once in the room, he made a series of tender photographs of his sister Hala and her newborn daughter, Lenka[61] (figure 43).

But in Spain the war was taking a turn for the worse. Although fighting would rage for another 18 months, the Francoist troops, better armed and better organized, were making steady progress. At the French-Spanish frontier in Le Perthus, he photographed the arrival of the first Spanish refugees, their anxious faces showing in the train's windows.[62] In France, he photographed several consecutive stories on factories, the Navy, music halls, miners, and the hobos of Marseille. And by early August 1938, he was back in Spain, documenting the action at Teruel, on the Ebro front lines, for a *Regards* piece, "La Victoire de l'Ebre" (*Victory in Ebro*).[63]

Perched on the top of a low hill, isolated in desolate terrain, Teruel, although only 60 miles from Valencia and its orange groves, had the lowest temperatures of any Spanish town in winter. While Franco planned simultaneous offensives towards Guadalajara and Madrid and the Mediterranean coast, the Republicans had their eyes on Teruel, and they managed to bring 40 or 50 thousand troops under the command of Colonel Sarabia to the front without the insurgents finding out.

The battle of Teruel was the turning point of the war. The fighting in these treacherous chalk hills took place over two months in the dead of winter, the worst Spain had endured in 20 years. Blizzards raged; the snowdrifts were six feet deep. Men died of the cold. The Republicans attacked on December 15 and by New Year's Day most of the town was in their hands, although it would not remain so for long.

Chim joined Capa and they photographed as Republicans and Nationalists vied for control of the city, a strategic point of entry to the north and east of the country. Premier Negrin sought to succeed in a military action that would show the great powers that the Republican army was a force to be reckoned with, one that could mount a military offensive rather than just react to Franco's attacks. Planning to strike at the communications between Franco's troops, he placed the fighting in hill country, to minimize the enemy's material superiority and allow the Republic to protect its scarce reserves and supplies. He chose the bend of the Ebro River, between Fayon and Benifollet, an area where Franco's troops were thinly spread. North of this bend, the Republic concentrated about 100,000 men, 100 planes, over 100 heavy guns, and several dozen light anti-aircraft pieces.

---

61 Photos from her archive communicated by Helen Sarid, October 2021.
62 MPNYA, SED1939001W00195/X05C.
63 MPNYA, SED1936002W00195B/35A, SED1936002W00195B/XX1 and *Regards*, August 4, 1938, cover and 10, https://gallica.bnf.fr/ark:/12148/bpt6k7636490b/f9.item.

On the night of July 24, 1938, the soldiers started to cross the Ebro River on pontoons. The maneuver achieved complete surprise and in the course of a week, 50,000 men were able to occupy the hills north of the river. In response, the Francoists opened the dams along the tributaries of the river, and the floodwaters destroyed the pontoons. Franco rushed reinforcements to the area and by August 1 the Republican advance had been stopped. The performance of the Republican army at the Ebro reminded the world of Verdun and Madrid. The losses were incredibly heavy, and many Republicans who had not died in battle were executed point-blank by the Nationalists.

In photographing war, Chim's approach was thoughtful and analytical. While his friends Capa and Taro were most at ease in action shots, Chim's range was perhaps wider. His interest included life behind the scenes, focusing on the means by which the war was fought. He made a unique contribution to the imagery of war, in part because of the sheer variety of topics and styles he presented and his concentration on civilian life. Journalist Martha Gellhorn, describing Chim as Lep, and Capa as Bara in one of her short stories, describes the two photographers' styles, and their relationship:

"Bara said that Lep was the finest photographer alive, an artist, not a hit-and-run man with a camera like himself. Bara's pictures were the famous ones; everyone wanted Bara's work if they could get it; yet Bara only valued his pictures if Lep did; Lep was his final judge. His final judge in everything, she thought, for if Bara made the decisions in his final way, Lep had the right of veto, which he exerted quietly, hardly bothering to explain himself…. If Lep did not want to do something, then it should not be done; if Lep did not like something, then it was not to be liked."[64]

Free from editors, Chim was able to self-assign stories and be confident of their publication. While he favored carefully constructed, well-sequenced, in-depth stories, many of his single images are striking on their own. Some were used with his captions, but others were taken out of context, especially by the editors of *Ce Soir*, who seem to have been less respectful than his colleagues at *Regards*.

Carefully cross-referencing Chim's vintage prints with his negatives, contact notebooks, and publications, and especially his only surviving notebook, which is kept at the Archives Nationales in Paris and contains stories from Asturias and the Basque country, Cynthia Young has written: "Every roll is stringently edited that way, with many frames and architectural details eliminated. Dark, blurry or inessential images are edited out; not one roll is included in full (…). Chim sees his work through subjects rather than events. This notebook (and only in relation with the negatives) shows us a very different photographer than Capa and Taro, perhaps one more secretive, more critical, more demanding of his own work."[65] This attitude im-

---

64 Martha Gellhorn, "Till Death Do Us Part," in *Two by Two* (New York: Simon & Schuster, 1958), 171.
65 Cynthia Young, *The Mexican suitcase* (Göttingen: Steidl, 2010), Tome 1, 111.

mediately calls to mind Cartier-Bresson's methods, the way he had of selecting only rare images from contact sheets that he considered drafts, not worthy of being looked at.

In 1970, the Spanish researcher Carlos Serrano uncovered eight notebooks of contact sheets and negatives by Capa, Chim, and Taro in the *Archives Nationales* in Paris. It is not known when Chim singled out these portraits from the Republican soldiers at Asturias and, cutting them off his contact sheets, glued them to the pages of his notebook. Cynthia Young wrote that "they were produced to show the full coverage of stories to potential editors and to keep track of which images had been used in publications."[66] He may have conceived of the portraits as a thematic story to be run on its own, but if so, no publication followed up on that idea.

At the end of August 1938, Chim made a quick trip back to France: he returned to Marseille, where he had worked in the Fall of 1934 for his story on the *Panier* neighborhood and made a reportage on the dockers who worked on the quays, discharging merchandise and carrying incredibly heavy loads. His reportage made the cover of *Regards*: in front of the massive hull of an ocean liner, a worker walks towards us, face down, weighed by an enormous load. [67]

The image parallels those of workers by his colleague André Steiner, published earlier in *Regards*.

Following the *Anschluss* of Austria to Nazi Germany in March 1938, the conquest and breakup of Czechoslovakia became Hitler's next ambition, which he would obtain with the Munich Agreement in September 1938, unopposed by France and Great Britain. Hitler justified the invasion as a way of relieving the supposed suffering of the ethnic German population living in these regions. By October, the Sudetenland began to be annexed into Germany.

With his usual sharp political intuition, Chim was already in the region by Spring 1938, accompanied by Andrée Viollis, one of the most famous and prolific women journalists of the interwar period. She was a devoted socialist, feminist, and freethinker, and, like Chim, she covered the Spanish conflict in depth. From the 1920s to the '40s she would also cover the Irish conflict, the Bolshevik and Indian rebellions, civil war in Afghanistan, colonialism in Indochina, Nazi Germany, and racist tensions in South Africa. Her texts were accompanied by Chim's photographs in *Vendredi* and *Ce Soir*, while *Regards* often used Capa and Taro's images with her articles.

On April 26, 1938, *Ce Soir* announced a series on the Sudetenland, "*Coeur d'Europe*" (Heart of Europe), that would run in several issues until May 12. On the last page of that late April issue, Chim, cited as "Our special envoy in Sudentenland"

---

66 Ibid.
67 *Regards*, September 8, 1938, cover and 12–13, https://gallica.bnf.fr/ark:/12148/bpt6k7636495d/f11.item.

shows people marching with arms outstretched in a Nazi salute, some wearing a military outfit and high boots, and people from diverse ethnic backgrounds, evidence that ethnic Germans were not the only inhabitants of the region and that Hitler's claim was spurious.[68]

For two weeks Chim and Viollis produced stories from Czechoslovakia: on the Czech air force—Chim's closeup, sympathetic portraits of officers and pilots are in the same spirit as his Spanish Civil War portraits of Republicans—on Bratislava and its open-air markets, and on the parliament in Prague.[69]

On May 7, in Eger, the residence of Konrad Henlein, chief of the pro-Nazi party in Sudetenland, the subtitle of Viollis' piece is a quote from people she interviewed: "Germans do not scare us." Viollis also notes: "I find our good photographer Chim coming to a stop in front of an array of boots in every shape and type of leather.— Triumph and symbol of the hour! says Chim. And with a fast click, he adds them to his collection."[70] On May 12, during an interview Viollis was conducting, Chim made a beautiful series of portraits of Edvard Bénès, the country's president, who opposed Nazi Germany's claim to the Sudentenland. *Ce Soir* published the portraits in a vertical sequence like a film strip.[71]

Toward the end of the Spanish Civil War, on August 3, 10, and 17, 1938, Chim published a little-known reportage in *Ce Soir* called "*Les mystères de la Tunisie*," with a text by Viollis.[72] Chim and Viollis had arrived in Tunisia at a time of transition —after April's bloody demonstrations for independence and the violent repression that followed—and before France's Vichy government delivered the country to Mussolini. Their investigation took the form of a political travel account, set in Tunis, the countryside, and a few other towns.

That summer, the situation in Tunisia was confused and violent, riven with sectarian conflict. As Franco had done with the Moroccans during the Spanish Civil War, Mussolini made false promises to the Tunisians. Meanwhile, the hopes raised by the Popular Front had been sorely disappointed. In sum: Nothing seemed to have changed and Tunisian society remained unjust.

Viollis' reporting for this story is characterized by her richness of description, her dramatization of interviews, detailed reconstruction of historical and socio-economic backgrounds, and analysis and interpretation of the international importance

---

68 *Ce Soir*, April 26, 1938, 8, https://gallica.bnf.fr/ark:/12148/bpt6k76334690/f8.item.
69 *Ce Soir*, May 1, 1938, 4, https://gallica.bnf.fr/ark:/12148/bpt6k76334749/f4.item; *Ce Soir*, May 8, 1938, 6, https://gallica.bnf.fr/ark:/12148/bpt6k76334801/f6.item.
70 Andrée Viollis, *Ce Soir*, April 26, 1938, 8, https://gallica.bnf.fr/ark:/12148/bpt6k76334690/f8.item.
71 *Ce Soir*, May 12, 1938, 2, https://gallica.bnf.fr/ark:/12148/bpt6k7633484p/f2.item.
72 *Ce Soir*, August 3, 1938, 6, https://gallica.bnf.fr/ark:/12148/bpt6k7633567h/f6.item.zoom; *Ce Soir*, August 10, 1938, 6, https://gallica.bnf.fr/ark:/12148/bpt6k7633574n/f6.item.zoom; *Ce Soir*, August 17, 1938, 6, https://gallica.bnf.fr/ark:/12148/bpt6k7633581s/f6.item.zoom.

of the events she covers. From her text (and the book she published later)[73] it is obvious that she wanted to demonstrate the fascistic character of the colonial bourgeoisie.

"But suddenly, again" Viollis wrote, "it was the Neo-Destour [the independence movement] who protested violently, it was the unrest, the bloody riots of April 1938, the state of siege. Now the operetta has turned into a tragedy. Why? How? 'Or' What? African truth is a woman with a veiled face, said my friend Louis Roubaud. Will I be able to lift the veil?"[74]

The two reporters met French trade unionists and Tunisian nationalists, but no prominent citizens or large-estate owners. They interviewed several people who had been arrested after the April 8 demonstrations, among them the leader Habib Bourguiba—the future President of Tunisia—whom they met in a military prison where he was detained. They also talked to several young educated but unemployed Tunisians, who could not find work appropriate to their level of studies and complained bitterly about racism in the workplace: Not only in France, where they had studied, but in Tunisia as well, they were made to feel like foreigners.

In her text, Viollis hints at the difficulty of photographing in Tunisia:

> Standing on a stool, draped in a burnous jacket like a toga, a man with large noble features speaks in a guttural voice, chanting his sentences with the eloquent gesture of his thin brown hands with long reddened nails. A fascinated circle surrounds him. I look at these tense and fascinated faces, these half-open lips on the white teeth, these fiery pupils under the red chechia of the townspeople or the immense straw hat of the *fellahs*.—What's he saying?—It is undoubtedly some marabout who comments on the verses of the Koran. The scene is so curious that one of us unconsciously lifts his camera. Immediately, the storyteller stops, stares at us harshly. And all the glowing eyes turn to us, also disapproving. Better not to insist.[75]

Chim photographed bird's-eye views of the whitewashed, cube-shaped houses of Tunis and, even though people were resistant to being photographed, he was able to shoot several beautiful close-up portraits, including a lively snapshot of Mr. Kastally, a refined intellectual wearing a gold-threaded turban, during an interview. Several full-face portraits taken outside Tunis recall those he had done of the Basque combatants in Spain a few months earlier. One is of a traditional, half-veiled very young girl, with whom they could not communicate; several are of *fellahin*, one of them wearily smiling.

Chim also photographed street scenes, including a discussion among a group of workers being hired to load wood and fighting for union hourly wages. A stone's throw from Tunis' most beautiful palaces, they discover a poor neighborhood where a group of women invite them in: "They insist on offering us tea, lemonade, and we

---

73 Andrée Viollis, *Notre Tunisie* (Paris: Gallimard, 1939)
74 Viollis, *Ce Soir*, August 11, 1938, 6, https://gallica.bnf.fr/ark:/12148/bpt6k76335752.r=1938August%2010%2C1938%20August%2010%2C1938?rk=128756;0.
75 Ibid.

accept this hospitality of the poor while Chim takes pictures," Viollis writes.[76] Chim also photographed the place where an unarmed and innocent man, Micelli, had been assassinated a few months earlier by a trio of fascists, as well as young fascists of the Dopo Lavoro nationalist movement who were traveling back to Italy.

From Tunis, Chim sailed to Minorca, off the Catalan coast, where he shot one of his last reportages from the Spanish Civil War: Minorca was the only island that had declared itself against Franco. The photographs were widely published, in *La Voz de Menorca*, *Regards*, *Illustrated*, and *Ce Soir* (figure 46). For *Ce Soir*, he teamed up again with Andrée Viollis, who wrote: "In Minorca, a few thousand men have defended for more than two years the roads of the Mediterranean"[77]

As was his custom, Chim focused on people trying to conduct their daily lives in wartime, demonstrating the inhabitants' courage as they persist in their activities even while being menaced by Franco's bombers. Housewives shop at the fish market, careful with their ration coupons. Two fishermen caulk their boats on the beach while others repair their nets. "Refusing to be deprived of their concerts," a caption reads, "music-loving people of Minorca listen to orchestra." The concert takes place in a casino in the capital, Mahon, with famous Catalan musicians: the cellist, Maria Teresa Muntadas, and pianist, Llorenç Galmès. Children still attend school, but shelters have been constructed under the school building. Football games still attract an enthusiastic public. Chim photographs a crowd declaring its solidarity with the Republicans in a large meeting at the Mahon theater, a previous target of the Francoist raids. He also photographs the ruins of the Trianon theater after a bombing.

In Chim's reporting, Minorca took on the romantic role of the Republic's last bastion against fascism (in reality, the town of Alicante resisted longer than Minorca, until March 1939). To that end, he covered the island's military life: army parades; sailors at the naval base; young recruits attending a military college; a radio transmitting station where the radio operator communicates with Republicans in Barcelona. At a new hospital that had been carved out of the Mahon cliffs to protect patients from shrapnel, Chim photographed nurses in white uniforms, lined up as in a family picture. The cover of *Regards* featured a portrait of a young, resolute, helmeted soldier holding a rifle and was titled *L'héroïque résistance espagnole à l'offensive italienne* (Heroic Spanish Resistance to Italian Offensive). In another image, taken on the coast at sunset, a sentinel surveilled the sea. More relaxed shots feature a group of three soldiers on a low wall reading a newspaper, and a sailor reading *Justicia Social*, a militant broadsheet.

The most famous image of the series shows school children massed in an underground shelter, at the end of a tunnel carved in the soft rock(figure 45). Their teacher

---

76 Viollis in *Ce Soir*, August 18, 1938, 6, https://gallica.bnf.fr/ark:/12148/bpt6k76335826/f1.image.
77 Viollis in *Ce Soir*, August 18, 1938, 6, https://gallica.bnf.fr/ark:/12148/bpt6k76335752.r=1938August%2010%2C1938%20August%2010%2C1938?rk=128756;0.

behind them, the children are standing close to each other during an attack, stock-still and terrified. The group is illuminated only by the single bulb in the ceiling, which draws a circle of light around them and creates drama. The image's symbolism is strong, reminding us that the Spanish war was the first time that a European civilian population was targeted *en masse* through the aerial bombardment of big cities.[78]

On November 1, Chim met again with La Passionaria in Barcelona, and her melancholy farewell speech to the International Brigades felt like an acknowledgement that the war had been lost. As Viollis wrote, "A feeling of sorrow, an infinite grief catches in our throat—sorrow for those who are going away, for the soldiers of the highest ideal of human redemption, exiles from their countries, persecuted by the tyrants of all people—grief for those who will stay here forever mingled with the Spanish soil, in the very depth of our heart hallowed by our feeling of eternal gratitude (...). Those men reached our country as crusaders for freedom, to fight and die for Spain's liberty and independence threatened by German and Italian fascism."[79]

Chim's next-to-last story from the war was published early in 1939 when he photographed the Spanish refugees crossing the border at Le Perthus, in the Pyrenees mountains.[80] (figure 48). Even though the French régime had supported the Civil War, the French attitude to the refugees was dismal. They had offered refuge but were unprepared for such numbers and did not want to complicate their future relations with the victors – Franco would be in power for the next forty years.

By February 5, the French had counted 170,000 refugees and decided to allow only the civilians to cross, even though staying in Spain amounted to a death sentence for Republicans. From February 5 to 9th, the French allowed 300,000 soldiers on condition of surrendering their weapons at the border- these weapons were then turned back to the Franquists.

In February 1939, after photographing at the French side of the border, Chim decided to go back to Madrid. It was a very dangerous destination. The city's siege had lasted for two and a half years. By the time he arrived, the situation was dire. The population was suffering from a lack of warm clothes, arms, and ammunition. Their food supply would last only a few weeks more; there was no hot water, heating, or medical supplies. Bitter fighting continued until March 8, while Franco tightened

---

78 MPNYA, SED1938003W00XX1/XX1C.
79 "Un sentiment d'angoisse, d'infinie douleur vous monte à la gorge vous la serrant comme des tenailles (...). Angoisse pour ceux qui s'en vont, soldats de l'idéal le plus élevé de la Rédemption humaine, déracinés de leur patrie, poursuivis par la tyrannie de tous les peuples (...). Douleur pour ceux qui restent ici pour toujours, se confondant avec notre terre et vivant dans le plus profond de notre cœur, auréolés par le sentiment de notre gratitude éternelle (...). Ils sont arrivés dans notre patrie comme des croisés de la liberté, pour combattre et mourir pour la liberté et l'indépendance d'Espagne, menacée par le fascisme allemand et italien." Translated from French by the author.
80 *Regards*, February 2, 1939, cover and 2, https://gallica.bnf.fr/ark:/12148/bpt6k7639187r/f2.item; *Ce Soir*, January 30, 1939, 1, 5, https://gallica.bnf.fr/ark:/12148/bpt6k7636399q/f6.item.

the vise and continued to bomb the city relentlessly. Chim's photographs, published in *Life* (February 20), *Ce Soir* (February 28), and *Match* (March 2), together with those of the Mayo brothers, are a testimony to the total devastation Franco had caused. The images published in *Ce Soir* also appeared with some variations in *Regards* no 269 (*Le Visage de Madrid*, March 9, 1939).[81] With its lighthearted cover of a group of smiling children, the issue is a study in contrasts: photographs evoking war such as an image of two children on a balcony looking at a panorama of Madrid and pointing to the smoke rising from a shrapnel attack, a barricade separating the city from zones of combat, a group of soldiers talking a break in a building of the Faculty of Medicine...are interspersed with much more optimistic images of the people's resilience under fire and of Madrid's reconstruction: a group of women knitting for the soldiers, a meeting between a wounded soldier and his friends, gardeners replanting in front of the Prado, a factory where objects are repaired and repurposed, a book fair...At the Spanish Theater, a choir performs a cantata by Rafael Alberti, Cantata to the Heroes, dedicated to the International Brigades.

On February 28, Manuel Azana had resigned from the post of president of the Republic. On April 1, General Franco announced that the war was over. With the Francoist victory, Republicans were herded into overcrowded prisons and camps where repression was fierce. Hundreds of thousands perished. It has been calculated that the loss of life, including deaths from malnutrition and those shot after the war, was close to half a million.

Why had Chim gone back into Spain when it was clear that the Republicans had lost the war? A caption on page 7 of *Ce Soir* and p. 5 of *Regards* gives us at least a partial explanation: Chim was accompanying an express visit by President Juan Negrin who, despite bombardments, had traveled from Madrid or Barcelona. During the last days of the war, he had put together an important reserve of money, artworks, and treasures that he hoped to use for helping the Republicans in exile. But because of strong opposition by Indalecio Prieto, ex Minister of Defense and leader of the Socialist Party, his project failed.

While censorship precluded a more direct denunciation of the Francoists, Chim's photographs of the calm heroism of Madrid's people were meant to encourage moral and financial help from the readers to a wounded, defeated Spain.

Early in 1939, probably right before his last trip to Madrid, Chim had started planning his exit. Like Capa, he knew that he had to leave: Franco had won the war, Hitler's shadow was growing over Europe, and they both were internationally-known Jews and communist sympathizers, whose lives were now in danger.

Chim "obtained three letters of recommendation, from *Life, The March of Time* Paris bureau, *Black Star*, and Mrs. Muir, an independent agent in London, who sold pictures by Capa and Chim to the British press, and who wrote that it would be 'im-

---

81 *Ce Soir*, February 28, 1939, 8. https://gallica.bnf.fr/ark:/12148/bpt6k76364280/f8.item.

possible to replace him'.[82] Chim and Capa packed up many of their best negatives from the Spanish Civil War [83] and planned to meet in New York, joining Capa's mother, brother and friends."

Finally, the Republican government in exile arranged for the transfer of 150,000 refugees to Mexico and South America. The new French weekly *Match* would assign Chim and George Soria to cover the trip of 1,600 Republicans aboard the S. S. Sinaia, the first of three ships bound for Mexico: this convenience assignment was their passport. Chim did not know that World War II was soon to start, or that he would not be back in Europe for more than a year. Nor did he know that his reportage on the S.S Sinaia and a subsequent story on Mexico would be his last until the war was over.

---

[82] Letters in the ICP Chim archive, quoted by Cynthia Young in *We Went Back: Photographs from Europe 1933- 1956 by Chim*, (New York: Prestel and ICP, 2013), 38.

[83] For a detailed analysis, see Cynthia Young, *The Mexican Suitcase*.

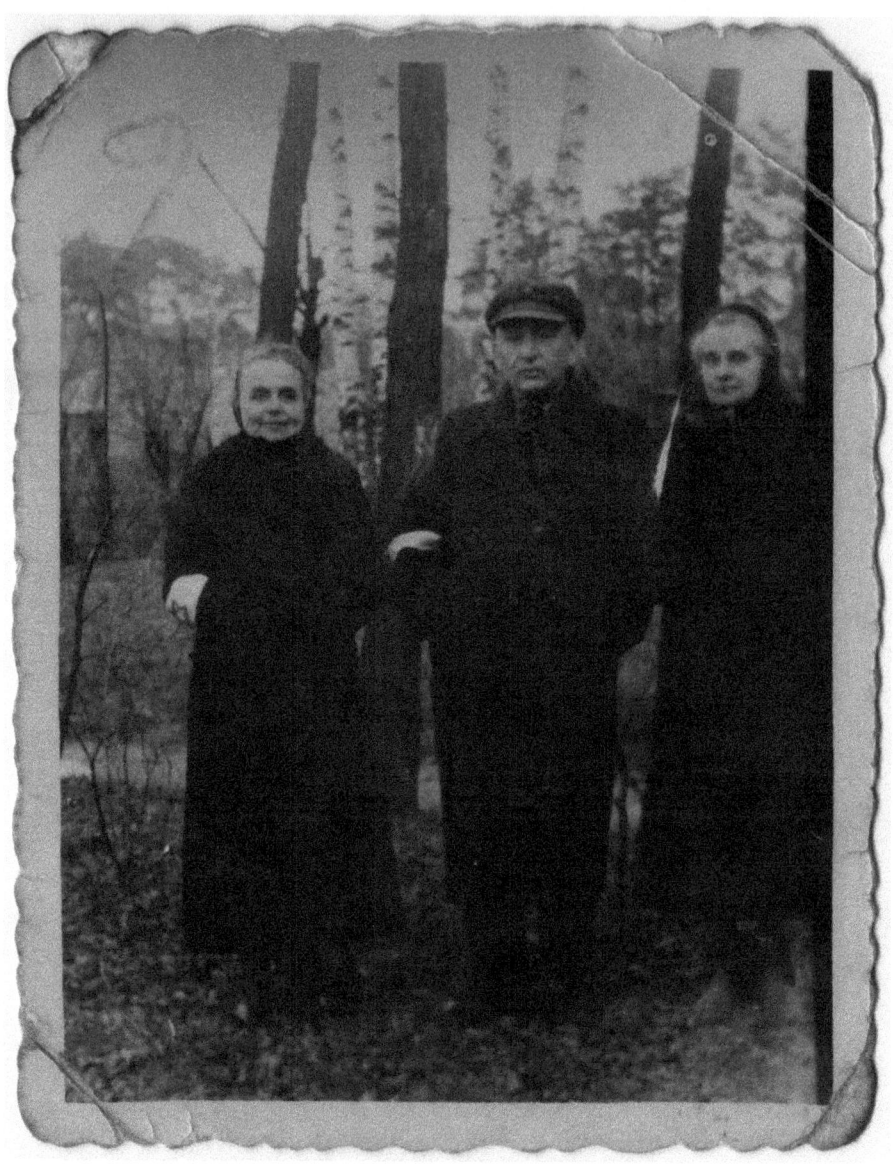

Fig. 8: Regina and Benjamin Szymin and Regina's sister, Malka Flint, behind the Pensjonat Zachęta, wearing the yellow star band. Photographer unknown, Otwock, Poland 1939-1941. © United States Holocaust Memorial Museum Collection, gift of Ben Schneidermann.

Chapter 6: From Chim to David Seymour. 1939–1945

The news from Poland were disastrous. Hala and Emil had been in Paris for five years, and despite their efforts and their contacts as journalists, the three of them had been unable to extract their parents and extended family from Poland. No news or letters were filtering out from there.

Germany had been rallying behind Hitler. On January 30, 1939, he appeared in front of the Nazi *Reichstag* (Parliament) and issued a public threat against the Jews:

> In the course of my life, I have very often been a prophet and have usually been ridiculed for it. During the time of my struggle for power it was in the first instance only the Jewish race that received my prophecies with laughter when I said that I would one day take over the leadership of the State, and with it that of the whole nation, and that I would then among other things settle the Jewish problem. Their laughter was uproarious, but I think that for some time now they have been laughing on the other side of their face. Today I will once more be a prophet: if the international Jewish financiers in and outside Europe should succeed in plunging the nations once more into a world war, then the result will not be the Bolshevizing of the earth, and thus the victory of Jewry, but the annihilation of the Jewish race in Europe![1]

The Jews of Europe were in mortal danger. On March 15, Hitler annexed Czechoslovakia into the Third Reich. The country surrendered and Nazi troops entered Prague while the Czechs stood in silent despair. As for the Spanish Republicans, with whom Chim had passionately sided, they had lost the war to the Francoists, and France, which had been an ally of the Republic, proved unprepared and overwhelmed by the sheer number of Spaniards fleeing Franco's murderous reprisals. In *Ce Soir*, journalist Simone Théry shared her deep anxiety about their fate: "At this moment when Madrid is handed over to Franco (…) 25,000 people in the prisons are doomed to the execution squad. I just arrived from Spain, and I am shouting out my horror, my anguish."[2]

Between January 27 and February 10, more than half a million refugees crossed into France. Loaded with cardboard suitcases or heavy bundles, wrapped up in covers against the bitter cold, the families, the wounded, and many unaccompanied children formed pitiful columns that snaked towards the border crossings of Le Perthus and Cerbère in the Eastern Pyrenees. Chim's last story on the Spanish war, a melancholy one, had been published early in 1939, and it showed long lines of grim refugees snaking through the Perthus pass, their figures blurred by the fog. Chim's deep sadness and disenchantment are almost palpable in these images.

---

[1] N. H. Baynes ed., *The Speeches of Adolf Hitler*, I (London, 1942), 737–741. Quoted in https://www.yadvashem.org/docs/extract-from-hitler-speech.html, accessed August 7, 2020.

[2] "Au moment où Madrid est livrée à Franco (…) 25000 personnes dans les prisons sont vouées au peloton d'exécution. J'arrive à l'instant d'Espagne et je viens vous crier mon horreur, mon angoisse." Translated from French by the author.

The Republicans had expected a warm welcome and they were indignant when the gendarmes frisked them like criminals. As we know from writers and journalists who tried to sound the alarm and alert public opinion,[3] France's unpreparedness immediately turned into cowardice and hostility. Some peasants at Le Perthus watched the refugees with tears in their eyes, but others muttered *sales Rouges* (dirty Reds) under their breath. Not only were the weapons of the refugees confiscated, but the policemen often appropriated the few worldly goods—watches, jewelry, or battered typewriters—that they had managed to bring with them.

Policemen corralled and marched the men, women, and children of the Republican *Retirada* to a dozen bleak internment camps that had been hastily opened in Agde, Argelès, Barcarès, Bram, Banyuls, Elne, Gurs, Rivesaltes, Saint Cyprien, and Septfonds. Officially named *centres d'hébergement* (housing centers), some had wooden barracks but for the most part they were just deserted spaces, battered by the cold winds of the *tramontane*, enclosed in three-meter-high coils of barbed wire. It has been suggested that the French government, unwilling to receive the Spanish refugees, purposely created these horrendous living conditions in order to force them back to Spain.

From planks, reeds, bits of fabric, and pieces of sheet metal, the refugees improvised tattered tents over holes they had dug in the sand of the beaches. They tried to warm themselves around small fires. They received dismal food rations—50 grams of lentils or chickpeas a day with a piece of day-old bread—and almost no water, so that they often had to filter sea water. There were no showers. Pneumonia, scurvy, dysentery, typhoid, and diarrhea were rampant; the internees were attacked by vermin and mosquitoes, and the few improvised infirmaries had almost no medication. After 1940, these same camps would host Jews and Romas, many of whom would be sent on to the Drancy concentration camp. Capa visited two of these infamous places, Bram and Argelès-sur-Mer, where he photographed heartbreaking scenes of fear, disenchantment, and loneliness. Those images were later found in the Mexican Suitcase.[4] Several other photographers also photographed there, including the Franco-Colombian Manuel Moros and Paul Senn, who has been called "the Swiss Capa."[5] One of the photographers, the Catalan Agusti Centelles, even photographed Bram from the inside while he was interned.

As for Chim, two months later he and his frequent collaborator Soria would be taking up their *Match* assignment to accompany refugees aboard the SS Sinaia to

---

[3] See for instance André Carmaux [aka Vladimir Pozner] "L'action se passe en France," *Les Volontaires* #8, (July 1939), 627–639.

[4] Cziki Weiss, Capa's friend and assistant, entrusted the 4,500 negatives by Chim, Capa, and Taro to Aguilar, who took them with him to Mexico. After their rediscovery in 2008 the three cardboard boxes containing the negatives were dubbed "The Mexican Suitcase". See previous chapter.

[5] Michel Lefebvre, *Paul Senn, Un photographe Suisse dans la Guerre d'Espagne et dans les camps français* (Rivesaltes: Tohu-Bohu, 2019); Gregory Tuban, *La Retirada dans l'objectf de Manuel Moros* (Perpignan: Mare Nostrum, 2009) and *Agusti Centelles 1909–1985* (Arles: Actes Sud, 2009), 212–224.

Veracruz. The two reporters had probably received this access through the intervention of Mexican activist Fernando Gamboa. Chim had known Gamboa since the November 8, 1936 Valencia Congress, when Valencia became the center of the Spanish resistance and, during the siege of Madrid, the home base of the legitimate government of the Second Republic. Mexican President Lazaro Cardenas and the Spanish republican government in exile had asked Gamboa to execute Cardenas's plan to provide asylum for Republican refugees by arranging for the safe arrival of this first group. British radicals, including the Duchess of Atholl, also gave financial support to this humanitarian endeavor, and the duchess sailed aboard the Sinaia, along with Gamboa's wife, Susana.

The Spaniards aboard the Sinaia had been previously interned at the camp "Mexique" in Le Barcarès and in a horse farm, the Haras of Perpignan, then brought to Sète by train. The names of those who would be leaving were announced by megaphone during the night, after they had spent ten days waiting for an embarkation that they thought would never happen. A bedraggled crowd of people with torn blankets around their shoulders, cardboard suitcases, and knots of dirty laundry in bundles waited anxiously from dawn on Quai d'Alger, the children sleeping on piles of sacks. Finally, families who had been separated in different camps after crossing the border were reunited. Friends who had fought together in the Ebro trenches and then lost each other hugged and cried.[6]

On May 24, around nine in the morning, the crowd began to board, and the Mexican flag was hoisted amid applause. As the departure siren sounded, the frightened children huddled in the corners, waiting for a bomb to fall. The ship left Sète harbor with Chim and Soria among the few non-Spaniards aboard.

Chim first photographed the chaos on the quay, then the last glimpses of Europe receding behind the ship, as many refugees stood in silence, not knowing if they would ever return. Among their number were workers, farmers, and 575 intellectuals: cultural activists, politicians, teachers, painters, engineers, doctors, and members of the political intelligentsia whose lives were most at risk, including 83-year-old Antonio Zozaya, a newspaper editor, the oldest passenger.

Chim captured everyday life on the ship in a series of simple, diary-like scenes. Matching his subjects' feelings, the images are suffused with a mixture of relief and melancholy. A woman who has managed to hold on to her little dog looks at the horizon; two men shave their friends and cut their hair in an improvised barber's shop; men and women write letters on their knees or on cobbled-up tables and play chess, the board set up on a crate. One woman, tucked in the infirmary bed, awaits the birth of her daughter, the first child to be born aboard, who will be named Susana Sinaia del Mar, after Gamboa's wife. Another woman plays with her baby. A sailor reads a newspaper article aloud to a group of men; a small boy plays with his

---

[6] The scene is described in *Vladimir Pozner, Un Pays de barbelés dans les camps de réfugiés espagnols en France, 1939.* Alexis Buffet ed. (Paris: Claire Paulhan, 2020), 173–186.

wooden toy car. Near the ship's guardrail, a group of men, their underwear serving as improvised bathing suits, enjoy the sun while others sunbathe on the upper deck.

Along with daily dance parties and concerts, the event that helped break the journey's monotony was the distribution of *Sinaia*, the on-board roneotyped newspaper. Professionals produced its 800 copies under Susana Gamboa's direction, and its eight pages contained texts and drawings, caricatures, and world news transcribed from radio broadcasts. One of the pages featured caricatures of Chim and journalist "Ribécourt",[7] a pseudonym for Soria (figure 53). While *Match* did not publish an article about the voyage, several articles signed by Ribécourt and illustrated with photographs by Chim appeared in the *Ce Soir* on August 13 and 15. Chim's pictures also appeared in Life, *Regards, Illustrated*, and *Billed-Bladet*, among other publications.[8]

On June 12, 1939, the *Sinaia* docked in Veracruz and the refugees received a hero's welcome with banners and an orchestra. President Cárdenas, who was in the process of implementing his land reforms, commissioned Chim to cover their progress and some aspects of traditional life. The reform was the most sweeping ever undertaken in Latin America. Its two showcases were in the cotton-growing region of La Laguna. These land redistributions, including the expropriation of large-scale commercial estates, were carried through at breakneck speed and have often been criticized as haphazard and politically motivated, doing little to improve the condition of the *campesinos*. After the reforms, 60 percent of the peasants were still landless. In his 1948 short story *They Have Given Us the Land*, Mexican writer Juan Rulfo describes the reaction of a group of men who were given a patch of barren wasteland. As they walk through, they discuss how completely worthless it is, impossible for farming.[9]

Czech journalist Egon Erwin Kisch, who arrived in Mexico in 1940, a year after Chim, and visited many of the same sites, was told by an interviewee: "You don't understand Mexico. They never show visitors anything more than what will impress outsiders (...) they [the peasants] are well coached. They don't tell anything except what suits the unions. Pity the man who tells the truth! And you, sir, were so naive that you believed them?"[10]

---

7 See *Sinaia: diario e la primera expedicion de republicanos españoles à México*, presented by Adolfo Sanchez Vasquez, Mexico, *Coordinacion de difusion cultural*, UNAM, 1989, http//cervantesvirtual.com/obra/num-5-30-de-mayo-de-1939, accessed September 10, 2020.
8 *Ce Soir*, August 13, 1939, 1, 6, https://gallica.bnf.fr/ark:/12148/bpt6k7636191q/f6.item; *Ce Soir*, August 15, 1939, 1, 3. https://gallica.bnf.fr/ark:/12148/bpt6k7636193j/f3.item; *Regards*, August 17, 1939, 21–22, https://gallica.bnf.fr/ark:/12148/bpt6k7639215m/f21.item; *LIFE*, July 17, 1939, 64–69; *Le Courrier de la Presse*, June 1939, 10.
9 Juan Rulfo in *The Mexico Reader: History, Culture, Politics* (Duke University Press, 2003), 465–469.
10 Egon Erwin Kisch, "The Agrarian Reform in La Laguna," *The Mexico Reader: History, Culture, Politics*, Gilbert M. Joseph, Timothy J. Henderson, Orin Starn, and Robin Kirk eds. (Durham, N.C.: Duke University Press, 2003), 449.

During this short visit, Chim could not transcend his outsider's perspective, and, except for a few scenes of urban misery, his pictures are mostly optimistic— maybe because, after the Spanish debacle, he was eager to find a cause he could believe in. He photographed peasants eating under a large mural by Siqueiros; a model school; groups of peasants and their families at a farmer's cooperative in La Laguna; a mother and her child in front of a giant agave plant; somewhat triumphalist pictures of gleaming machines in a factory; a street festival with family scenes and musicians garbed in traditional Aztec costumes; spectators at a bullfight. In a picture of workers at a cooperative, sitting on a tractor, the men are posed as in his Popular Front images, arranged in a triangle with a strong receding perspective. His best images are the more intimate ones: a serious child standing stiffly in front of a fruit shop, framed by clusters of pineapples that hang in the doorway; and a closeup portrait of a serious, sad woman. He shows only three-quarters of her face, lending mystery to her handsome features.[11]

His assignment completed, Chim was ready to return to Europe. But on September 3, 1939, World War II was declared. As a well-known Eastern European Jew and a socialist, he was all too aware that going back to Europe would mean risking his life and endangering his family. Instead, he took a bus to the border and, some time in November, crossed into the United States at Laredo, Texas, and went on to New York. Arriving without papers or a job, he was now an exile, like the half-million Spanish Republicans he had supported.

At first, he lived with a friend of the family in the East Village. In the New Year, he would be joined in New York by Hala and Emil and it was largely due to their imminent arrival that he decided to stay in the city. However, life was difficult for him, and worry over his parents' whereabouts added to the strain of his precarious legal and financial situation. On November 1, 1939, Hala wrote: "I have absolutely no news from our parents and who knows how long we'll have to wait to get some. Write a few words to the Kazimierz, maybe that's where an answer will come from and they know more about the parents. Try also to write to the Goldwassers in Warsaw, Nowolipki 25. If you have other ideas, let me know right away. Don't be stingy with your news (....)."[12]

---

[11] Chim's 1937–1938 photographs of Barcelona and Minorca were sent to Gamboa who meant to use them as part of a campaign for the Spanish Republic. They were rediscovered in Mexico after having been lost for more than 70 years and exhibited, together with his 1939 photographs from Mexico, in the exhibition "Chim-Gamboa-The Mexican Connection", at Centro de la Imagen, Mexico, December 9, 2010-March 6, 2011. Curated by Trisha Ziff with Patricia Gamboa (Mexico), Carole Naggar (USA), and Pedro Corral (Spain).

[12] DSA Letter from Hala, November 1, 1939.

Then there is a glimmer of hope. Again from Hala, writing from Paris:

> Today I have many things to write you, and before everything—I have a hello from Father! A few weeks ago, Dr. Szoszkies [journalist, traveler, director of the Cooperative Union of Polish Jews] has arrived from Warsaw. Two weeks ago, he met father in the street in Warsaw by chance. He was in a hurry to catch the tram (trains are not working). Father does not look too bad, the bed-and-breakfast is still open (!), full of clients like all the pensions in Otwock. For the moment, they are not touching the Jews there, and Otwock has suffered little from the bombings.
>
> I am happy for this hello, even if all the rest he tells about Warsaw is terrifying.[13]

Hala's optimism about Otwock was due to the town being 15 miles away from Warsaw which, ravaged by German bombers and artillery, had been captured on September 30. Persecution of the Jews followed. But her optimism was not warranted. In Otwock, where the Szymin family had their pension, just a year later, all the Jews in town would be forced into a ghetto, then either executed in the nearby pine woods or deported to Treblinka in cattle cars, to be massacred two hours after arriving.

However, in 1944, Chim, in full denial, would still be hoping that they were safe, as evidenced by what he wrote in a letter to Hala: "I hope with all my heart that nothing will happen to our parents."[14]

Chim was far from being the only European photographer to have landed in New York, which was already home to many established photographers. In spite of his high recommendations, he could not find work as a photojournalist. With his money running low, he received a stern letter from the US Department of Labor: "Your continued presence in the country after November 1939, is unauthorized and illegal. Therefore you will arrange to depart from the US immediately."[15] Unhappy and lonely, he fell ill. Hala wrote to him, "Our paperwork is nearing the end and if everything goes according to plan, we will leave on January 4th on the Rex (...) I am happy that we will see each other soon. Maybe you will feel little more serene when we will be together. (...) I can only tell you that many people would exchange their fate with yours with pleasure."[16] Finally, after a delayed departure, Hala, Emil, and their two-year old daughter Lenka announced their imminent arrival in New York: "We are leaving in a week from now and on February 12 we will be boarding in Genova on the ship *Manhattan*."[17]

Two years after he arrived in New York with his wife and Lenka, Emil wrote a poem: "My Child, You Are a Refugee," that reads in part:

---

13 DSA Letter from Hala, December 13, 1939.
14 DSA, letter to Hala, August 20, 1944.
15 DSA, letter from the US Department of Labor, December 1939.
16 DSA, undated letter from Hala, early 1940.
17 DSA, letter from Hala in Polish, January 30, 1940.

And now, my child, is the time
To tell you your story:
You were born in Paris in a small street by the Pantheon
And on the day of your birth, your father, the reporter,
Flew in from bombarded Barcelona.

I cried
When from your eyes, for the first time,
Their blueness struck me, so bright.
I thought then of the Spanish children
At night. In the cellars of Guernica and Teruel.

And your father, like a fool,
Prophesied and warned (I knew so well)
Spain's war will reach all your borders
And neither will the children of Paris and Warsaw
Escape Nazi shrapnel.

And that was true for you as well, my child.
In December 1939 – on your second birthday -
The first sirens woke you in Paris by the Seine.
And late at night, your father carried you
Down to the crowded cellar by Porte Saint-Martin.[18]

That feeling of being a refugee in an unknown land would never leave Hala, Emil, and Chim, even after they became American citizens.

After a few weeks of uncertainty, Chim's lawyers, Oliphant & Lerman, succeeded in extending his residence in New York for two months. The Hebrew Sheltering and Immigrant Aid Society arranged for another four-month extension.[19] With a new sense of stability, Chim rented an apartment at 61 Riverside Drive and began casting about for work, shelving his career ambitions for the time. He contacted Leo Cohn, the owner of Leco Service, a developing and retouching photo lab based on 42nd Street with a client list of eminent photographers, including André Kertész and Eliot Elisofon (figures 56, 57).

Chim started working for Cohn in early 1940 and became his associate on August 22, 1942.[20] He was relieved but unsatisfied. True, he was making a living, but the cameras he had left behind in Paris were constant reminders of the profession he could not practice. All he had with him were one or maybe two Leicas, which he had used on the SS Sinaia. Although he had asked Hala to bring his two Rollei cameras to New York, she had said it would be impossible, because they would "have to show documentation proving that they belong to us" and pay customs duties.[21]

Lucy Frucht, who worked at Leco as a secretary, remembers Chim's moodiness, probably born of frustration:

---

18 Email message from Helen Sarid to the author, September 12, 2021.
19 DSA.
20 DSA.
21 DSA letter from Hala, January 30, 1940.

> I came to America in 1942 and Leco was my first job. There were three people who worked at Leco. I did a little of everything. We alternated tasks so we wouldn't always do the same thing. Leco was quite well known.
> Chim was very personable, très bien. But one day he was, ah ma chérie, everything wonderful, the next he was grumpy (...). Sometimes he talked a lot, mostly about himself but we didn't mind, and other times he was perfectly serious and did not talk at all. We liked him well enough.[22]

After Pearl Harbor, Chim tried to join the Office of Strategic Services, then the American Air Force, as a photographer, but he was rejected from active service because of his poor eyesight. The Army, however, accepted him. We know the dates of his various transfers and occupations in the Army because of the chronology that his sister made, based on their correspondence. But due to war censorship, we do not know his exact locations.[23]

On October 26, 1942, Chim was inducted into the Army and sent first to Fort Dix, then to Camp Edison in New Jersey:

> Today is the first free day of my military career! (...) Tomorrow I am starting what is called basic training school, which will last four weeks. During that period, I will be instructed, trained, I will have to walk 10, 15, 20 kilometers, run, jump, climb obstacles, crawl, shoot, wear a mask, etc. All this is 4 weeks of condensed training. If I 'survive' until the end, I will—if all goes well —be sent to the photography school near New York. There is a lot of work here and they push us terribly. My little tummy will disappear, I am sure of it. It is colder and colder, and I have to spend the night in a one-person tent (...).[24]

In May 1943, Chim became an American citizen, with the new name David Robert Seymour. He was hoping that this change in his identity might protect his family in Europe from Nazi reprisals. [25] It seems likely that his naturalization happened so quickly because he was due to be assigned to sensitive work in intelligence, where his photography skills would be put to use. Six months later, he arrived at a secret base, Camp Ritchie, Maryland, to be trained as a photography instructor interpreting aerial photographs.

Chim was part of a group, The Ritchie Boys, 15,200 servicemen who had been drafted, or volunteered to join, the U. S. Army, and, because they could speak the language of an enemy, had been sent to Camp Ritchie on secret orders. About 2,200 of them were Jewish refugees born in Germany, Austria, or Poland. Most were fluent in German, French, Italian, Polish, or other languages that the US Army needed. They would become an important weapon for the Allies. A classified post-

---

22 Interview of Lucie Frucht by the author, Riverdale, New York, June 22, 2005.
23 DSA. His letter headings read "Somewhere in the East" (Spring 1944), London (April 16,1944), London (end of May 1944), "Somewhere in France" (end of July 1944), somewhere in Luxemburg (March 1945), Austria (June 1945), Germany, London, and Paris (August 1945).
24 DSA, letter to Hala, November 18, 1942 (in Polish).
25 DSA, David Robert Seymour's naturalization documents.

war report found that nearly 60 percent of the credible intelligence gathered in Europe came from the Ritchie Boys.[26]

A fellow trainee, Earl Prebezac, wrote about the new arrival:

> Chim and I were partners in all field exercises in our training. I also worked with him in the photo lab there. I even have a single 35mm print he took of me (…) Chim was about 11 years older than I, wiser and certainly more intelligent, whereas I was so very young (18) and eager (…) always eager, impetuous, anxious, naïve. He always held me back during field exercises (…) admonishing me to take care, be very cautious, slow down. He warned me not to take chances. (…) Dave was a mature, intelligent, worldly, well educated, multilingual intellectual and a skilled photographer. He did NOT like the Army.
>
> He got tied up with me, an 18-year-old who dropped out of school at age 15. How were disparate personalities such as Dave and I selected and thrown together for this Military adventure? By punch cards, a forerunner of the modern-day computer. The US Army was looking for people with special language skills. Education and experience which matched the needs of Military Intelligence. They ran punch cards with army personnel data (…) looking for any soldier who might have indicated any of these skills.[27]

Chim was promoted to the rank of sergeant, and after a year of training, on March 25, 1944, he left Camp Ritchie for Europe. His language skills had improved to the point where he could write to his family in English. "It is not without emotion to come back to the old country," he wrote to Hala, "to old little houses and so close to Europe, I mean [the] continent. I met already some of my old friends. Capa is here—and we had quite a lot of old things to remember."[28] After completing a further six-week training in identification of military equipment, airplanes, tanks, artillery, ships, and the like, he was appointed a photography interpreter at the Allied Central Interpretation Unit (ACIU) in Danesfield House, Medmenham, in Buckinghamshire, 35 miles from London. This was the main interpretation center for photographic reconnaissance operations in the European and Mediterranean war theaters (figure 51).

In April, Chim happily reunited with his friends Capa and Rodger in London.[29] At work he had been sleeping in a tent and often felt the cold, but in London he was able to use Capa's guest room. In May, he "was on a big party—with Hemingway and all the war correspondents and my friends, photographers. I was drunk, but so was

---

[26] Bruce Henderson: *Son & Soldiers, the Untold Story of the Jews Who Escaped the Nazis and Returned with the U. S. Army to fight Hitler* (New York: William Morrow, 2017), and David Frey's interview, https://www.cbsnews.com/news/world-war-ii-jews-escape-nazi-germany-hitler-60-minutes-2021-05-09/, accessed February 23, 2022.
[27] DSA, Earl Prebezac, Remembrances of Chim from Camp Ritchie, May 2008. DSA. https://davidseymour.com/writings-on-earl-prebezac/, accessed February 23, 2022.
[28] DSA, letter to Hala, April 16, 1944.
[29] DSA, letter to Hala, May 16, 1944.

everybody. Hemingway had an accident that night and is in hospital as you read probably in the papers. I had only a long hangover."[30]

John Godfrey Morris, who at the time was picture editor at *Life*'s London office, recalls that party, which he describes as

> memorable even by wartime West End standards (...) Papa [Hemingway] left the party in the care of Dr Peter Gorer, a friend of Dave Sherman's, and unfortunately for all involved, the owner of a car. Dr Gorer promptly drove headlong into a water storage tank, sending Hemingway into the windshield and then a hospital bed. (...) With his head bandaged in a turban and his thick beard stuck out over the sheet, Hemingway resembled an Arab potentate (...) Pinky [Capa's girlfriend] playfully tugged on his hospital gown, revealing his wide rump. Capa thoughtfully recorded the moment on film.[31]

Photographic interpreters played a key role in the Allied victory. They could observe enemy activity in three dimensions and no attack could take place without their preparatory work. They also made detailed analyses of tactical and strategic targets. It was a thankless, difficult, and exhausting task: for 24 hours a day, teams alternated work shifts, using stereoscopes with lenses that could magnify the original images by four and tube magnifiers that could magnify them by seven. They worked from contact paper prints, about 60,000 of which would land every day in the hands of specialists like Chim.

Chim's detailed-oriented, methodical, and perfectionist mind served him well in the job. His years as a photojournalist and then developing negatives at Leco had reinforced his observational skills and powers of intuition. In the texture and grayscale of a photograph, he could decipher much more detail than an ordinary observer could. It is paradoxical that this man who had been rejected for active service because of nearsightedness should have made his greatest contribution to the war effort via his visual acuity.[32]

In 1943 and 1944, the obscure interpreters from Medmenham played a crucial role in the planning of landings in Normandy and the south of France. However, after the D-Day landings, Chim was greatly disappointed to find that his sector—the Brittany coast—had been one of the decoy areas.[33] Dino Brugioni, a photography intelligence specialist, wrote:

> These organizations (...) were heavily involved in the planning of the Normandy and Southern France landings. Support to the Normandy landings alone required an estimated half-million photo interpretation man-hours. The stepped-up Allied bombing offensive of German strategic industries in 1944, which included synthetic fuel plants, also involved extensive photographic

---

30 DSA, letter to Hala, May 26, 1944.
31 John Godfrey Morris, *Get the Picture* (New York: Random House, 1998), 75–76.
32 For a detailed analysis of photo intelligence during World War II, see Constance Babington Smith, *Evidence in Camera: The Story of Photographic Intelligence in the Second World War* (London: Chatto & Windus, 1957, republished Phoenix Mill: Sutton Publishers, 2004).
33 Inge Bondi, *Chim: The Photographs of David Seymour* (New York: Bullfinch, 1996), 73.

analysis and assessments. Other high priority projects included the searching for and destruction of V–1 and V–2 rocket sites, jet aircraft plants, and submarine production facilities. Photo interpreters were also employed in the planning and execution of special bombing missions against critical targets. The volume of materials being received for photo interpretation must also be considered (…). By V-E Day, over five million prints were in storage. More than 40,000 reports had been prepared from these prints.[34]

During these war years, Chim picked up his camera again and shot many individual portraits of the soldiers, some in eloquent closeups, as well as group portraits or medium-range photos showing the soldiers during their breaks, drinking coffee, or eating. A portrait made by one of his fellow soldiers shows him pointing his Leica; several photographs show him in company of friends or a girlfriend, also in uniform (figures 54, 55). She may be the "Lucy" to whom he dedicated a 1944 photograph.[35] In another picture he wears a helmet while standing in front of a bunker, looking awkward in a military coat, uniform, and boots that bulk up his small frame.[36] Because of lack of time or army censorship, Chim rarely wrote captions for those photographs; we sometimes know the names of the people he photographed, but not the dates and places.

A handmade album, the sheets of images punched with two holes, then tied with a shoelace under a thick paper cover signed David Seymour, tell a wartime photo story. Most probably compiled in 1945—but maybe shot before– it is the only document we have from that period in his life (figure 58).

As he had done during the Spanish Civil War with his photograph of the destroyed typewriter, Chim photographed war indirectly, with melancholy images that show the effects of the conflict on places and objects. He constructed a sequence of landscapes whose locations remain unknown: probably England after bombing raids; a demolished bunker; a bird's-eye view of a village in ruins; a cathedral's portal pocked with holes; barbed wire half-obscuring a landscape, probably a view from a concentration camp. This is followed by close-ups of a group of wheeled cannons; rolls of ammunition; the fallen medieval stone head of a saint over a mound of debris. There is only one image with a human being in it, a soldier walking between mud trenches on a deserted road.[37]

Another short series, with pictures sequenced two to a page, reflects Chim's sense of humor: at the entrance to a small building, a panel that reads "Herman Goering's Art Collection, through the courtesy of the 101st Airborne Division" documents a series of artworks stolen by Goering and seized by the Allies.[38] (figure 59). With a bespectacled soldier sitting, legs crossed, as a museum guard, the images

---

34 Dino Brugioni, *Military Intelligence 9*, #1 (Jan.-Mar. 1983), 50–55.
35 DSA, http://archive.davidseymour.com/section5_fs.html, accessed February 23, 2022.
36 MPNYA, DSA, "Misc.images no numbers," Contact sheet #1, 4, 7, 9.
37 DSA, see figure #58 showing cover and a few photographs from the handmade war album.
38 DSA, see figure #59 showing part of Goering's "art collection".

document groups of religious sculptures and paintings by Holbein, Renoir, and other famous names piled up in a tiled hallway and a large kitchen or bathroom with a sink.

On August 18, 1944, Capa, Rodger and Charles Wertenbaker—*Time-Life*'s chief correspondent— in a Packard 'requisitioned' from the German army, entered Paris just behind the tanks of General Leclerc, followed by a unit of the U.S. Fourth Division. Cartier-Bresson had arrived months earlier to join an informal group of photographers (Brassai, Robert Doisneau, Willy Ronis, René Zuber and others) to cover the Liberation of Paris. When General de Gaulle entered the capital, German snipers were still being flushed out of the Hotel de Ville, and Capa photographed the terrified crowds trying to escape, as a few German snipers were still hiding, while Rodger joined De Gaulle's victory parade on the Champs Elysées. He was standing in the Packard adorned with an American star on the front door, his Leica around his neck, when Cartier-Bresson, posted near the Rond-Point, clicked the shutter on his camera: he did not know yet who the tall, good-looking British soldier with a black beret was.

Rodger and Capa spent the following week roaming the liberated capital and taking in the giddy atmosphere: balconies draped with flags, men, women, and children throwing flowers, hugging their liberators. At London's Time-Life office, John Morris edited the 1,300 frames shot by Life photographers on the liberation of Paris and sent them to New York. Meanwhile, Rodger got drunk on Pernod, which may explain why his pictures of the city's liberation did not reach the office in time for publication.

After D-Day, Chim worked with General Bradley's twelfth army group, briefing the Supreme Headquarters Allied Expeditionary Force (SHAEF) command in London on the results of American bombing raids over Europe, and he was awarded the US Bronze Star for his work.[39] (figure 52). Ecstatic about his promotion to lieutenant and his Bronze Star, he wrote to Hala and Emil from "somewhere in Germany.": "What a week! Last Monday I got my commission as 2nd Lieutenant in the U.S. Army—I was waiting for it for a long time already. Next day I was flying to Paris and had the great joy to be at 1500 hours close to the Arc de Triomphe—when the whistles and the sirens and the horns start blowing and peace was officially in (…). I just came back—my head is still buzzing from the trip—but have to write you these lines—just to tell you (…)."[40]

But worries about their parents were gnawing at him: "Everything is going fantastically, and the end is very near (…). We all hope that it is true. Now my thoughts are often turned towards the East and I hope with all my heart that nothing happened to

---

39 DSA, Bronze Star diploma.
40 DSA, letter to family, October 20, 1944.

our parents. Try to make contact with them—as much as possible—I don't need to tell you how anxious I am to get news from them."[41]

In October 1944, Chim made a brief visit to Paris to check on his old apartment at 152 boulevard Brune. The Gestapo seal was still on the door:

> The concierge recognized me immediately—and it was a great greeting (...). The apartment was closed down [sic] by Gestapo (...). It was really a motion picture scene. When I turned the key and opened the door, here was my old room and everything intact since 5 years. Scraps of old letters and old photographs and old books and old junk. And the old couch & the mirror & the fireplace—and even the Mona Lisa in Pola's room. And a postcard on the shelves—from vacations 1938 saying I am well and enjoy it.[42]

His landlady had saved his possessions from being confiscated by the Germans, including his books, which his sister later catalogued.[43]

Chim may not have had a striking appearance, but he was thoughtful, attentive, tender and a great listener, qualities that attracted many women. While in Paris the following summer, taking a break from his intelligence job, he embarked on a short liaison with Denise, a theater student, who wrote him long, beseeching letters that were found with the personal papers that his sister Hala would later put together; these letters are unique: it seems probable that Hala censored that aspect of her brother's correspondence. A paragraph from Denise's first letter reads: "Come back to me soon, David. I feel that all of my thoughts during these few days will have but one goal, to see you soon again. You made me yours and I am proud, you made me deeply happy, and still I feel your caresses on me, so enveloping, so sweet, my dear lover—it is so sweet to call you by that name."[44] Although he was billeted just outside Paris until the fall, he did not answer: to him, it was a short-lived affair.

The war was finally over, but Chim was back on the job; this period of his life remains obscure, only documented by a few letters or V-mails to his family, which had to pass censorship, and were dated "somewhere in Luxembourg", "somewhere

---

41 DSA, Letter dated *Somewhere in Germany*, May 13, 1945.
42 DSA, Undated, Fall 1945.
43 DSA. The list compiled by Hala includes Photokina catalogue, 1956—Robert Doisneau, *Banlieue de Paris* -Inge Morath, *Guerre à la tistesse*, with a dedication by Inge—Henri Cartier-Bresson, *Images à la Sauvette*, with a dedication by Henri—Henri Cartier-Bresson, *Les Européens* with a dedication by Henri and Eli—Andrée Viollis, *L'Afrique du sud*, with a dedication—Dave Schoenbrun, *Men who make your World* with a dedication Czeslaw Milosz,- *The Captive Mind*—Irving Howe, *Adversary in the House*—Alison Cooke, *A Generation on Trial*—Thomas Mann, *Stories of Three decades*—Felix Krull, *Confessions*—John Steinbeck, *East of Eden* Stendhal, *Amitié amoureuse*—Le Forum Romanum and l'Amérique du sud (brochures)—André Lhote, *Traité du paysage*.
44 DSA, letter from Denise, July 16, 1945. "Reviens-moi vite, David, je pense que toutes mes pensées durant ces quelques jours vont n'avoir qu'un but, le prochain revoir. Tu m'as faite tienne et j'en suis fière, tu m'as rendue parfaitement heureuse et je sens encore tes caresses sur moi, si enveloppantes, si douces, mon amant chéri, qu'il est doux de te donner ce nom." Translated from French by the author.

in Germany". Then it's Wiesbaden, Salzburg (where he enjoyed a Mozart opera *Die Entführung aus dem Serail* (*The Abduction from the Seraglio*) with the Vienna Symphony orchestra, starring Elizabeth Schwartzkopf as the heroine, Konstanze. His correspondence places him in several other cities including Munich, Nuremberg, Frankfurt, until mid-September 1945, when he is told that he will soon be shipped back to New York.

The American entry into World War II had brought a high level of cooperation and overlap between diplomatic and military couriers, with military personnel frequently assigned to support the Department of State. Thanks to that longstanding cooperation, Chim returned to New York as a courier, carrying a classified pouch with 2,000 negatives to the Pentagon.[45]

In a letter from Ober Ursel, he announces: "Hala, will you look over my suits and ties and give them to the cleaners...I'm coming back...and now it's official. I'll be flying to London tomorrow... early next week I'm flying to Paris... then I'll be on my way home."[46]

---

45 Inge Bondi, *Chim: The Photographs of David Seymour* (New York: Bullfinch Press, 1996), 74.
46 DSA, Letter to Hala, September 13, 1945.

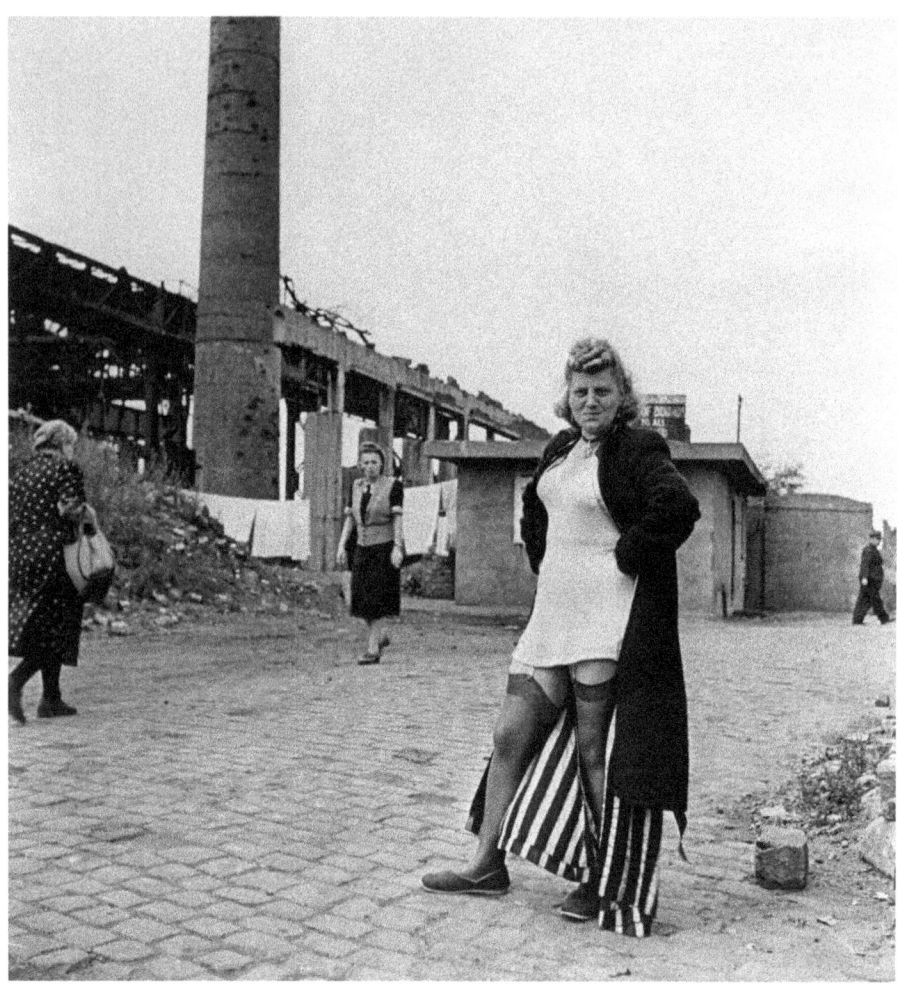

Fig. 9: Prostitute in front of partly demolished Krupp Factories, Essen, West Germany, 1947. © David Seymour-Magnum Photos.

Chapter 7: Welcome to the Time Inc. Stink Club. 1947–1948

After the war, Chim was happy to be back in New York, less so about returning to work at Leco. But finally, in April 1947, he received an important assignment from *This Week*: to photograph the progress of the U. S. Army in Europe as the war wound down, and to document living conditions in England, France, Belgium, Holland, and Germany two years after the end of the conflict. In the context of the Marshall Plan for the Reconstruction of Europe that President Truman would propose that June, Chim's photographs were intended to be a plea for help, to make Americans conscious of European suffering, while also showcasing Europe's resilience, courage, and strong work ethic. The reportage would be called "We Went Back."

According to Bill Downs, the CBS correspondent who would be traveling with Chim, Capa had originally been offered the work, but he had decided to travel to the Soviet Union with John Steinbeck and recommended his friend for the project.[1]

Leaving Leco, Chim remained on good enough terms with Cohn that he was able to borrow a Rollei from him. He never encumbered himself with as much paraphernalia as many of his colleagues did, usually carrying only one or two cameras and the odd lens or two.

He had his Leica, and probably a second Rollei—maybe the one he had left in Paris before the war—that he would use for color only. Most of the photographs for this assignment, both black and white and color, would be shot in medium format, with the 35mm shots mostly repeating the square images.

Chim and Downs left for Europe on April 25 on a military transport, with a crew of sound technicians. Chim started taking pictures during the flight, photographing U. S. Army officers asleep among piles of luggage.

This story was a new experience for Chim, who was used to working alone or with one journalist, taking his time to cover subjects in depth, and proposing his own subjects rather than following a script developed by an editor on a tight deadline—in this case, June, because CBS planned to produce a show in time for the second anniversary of the war's end. Another added difficulty was that Chim was required to shoot at least part of the story in color, something he had not done before. In 1937, the Eastman Kodak Company had released Kodachrome, a new color transparency film for still cameras. It had previously been used only in the motion picture industry but was now accessible to professionals and, by the late 1940s, developments in printing technology allowed weekly and monthly publications to take advantage of color photographs, which they eagerly did.

---

1 Cynthia Young, *We Went Back: Photographs from Europe 1933–1956 by Chim* (New York: Prestel & ICP, 2013), 40. She refers to an undated interview with Bill Downs, ICPARC.

A few months later, on August 27, 1947, Rita Vandivert, an administrator for the newly-formed Magnum Photos, Inc., in a letter to Maria Eisner, had encouraged Magnum photographers to use color.[2] Some resisted; they had a low opinion of it and believed that black and white was the more appropriate medium for serious reportage. Even before Vandivert's letter, Chim had been one of the first founding Magnum members to demonstrate the possibilities of color used in a serious context.

Part of a team of war correspondents known as "the Murrow boys" whom Edward R. Murrow had hired to cover World War II for CBS (the nascent news division of Columbia Broadcasting), Downs was returning to Europe after his wartime work from the Eastern Front, where he had delivered eyewitness reports. He had been the first journalist to broadcast live from Normandy after D-Day, and from Hamburg after the city's surrender on May 3, 1945.

This new piece would be published in *This Week* on August 10. Chim had the cover, and the article, 22 pages long, featured 26 color and black-and-white images credited to "War Veteran David Seymour." Four days later, CBS radio broadcast an audio version of the trip "narrated by Robert Montgomery with the voices of Downs, Hurlbutt, Costello and the people they interviewed."[3]

While some of Chim's photographs have an agenda, showing, for instance, crowds receiving food distribution packages, or farmers working with new American harvesting equipment, they are not mere propaganda.[4] Carefully framed, they are soulful and lyrical in their description of people and places. This is, after all, Chim's return to a Europe he had longed to see again when he was in New York, and his return to photography after an unwanted hiatus.

He was on the track of the still-fresh memory of the war. As in many of his photographs, the past flows into the present with a strong current. In impeccably composed images, he succeeded in telling a story in an indirect way through its effect on faces and landscapes; a bittersweet story, where remains and ruins were interwoven with beginnings and hopes. It was a subtle business. As Downs perceptively wrote, "it is my observation that reporting the peace is a much more difficult job than reporting the war."[5]

Chim began the series in Britain, in East Anglia, at an airfield in Steeple Morden near Cambridge, which was a place heavy in symbolism: at the time of their last mission from that base, on April 25, 1945, the U.S. Air Force had scored 868 victories. In Chim's photographs, a sheet-metal hangar stands under a gray sky and mountains of steel cylinders—surplus wing tanks—form a still life, as do ammunition boxes

---

2 MF011-001-001/2.
3 Cynthia Young, *We Went Back: Photographs from Europe 1933–1956 by Chim* (New York: Prestel & ICP, 2013), 40. *This Week*, August 10, 1947. Cover and 1, 4, 5, 7, 9–15, 17, 19–28.
4 MPNYA, ADS, *We Went Back*, 1947001- Rolls 81–120 and 121–147.
5 *America at the Dawn of the Cold War*, script of a speech given by Bill Downs in Oklahoma City on January 14, 1949, https://www.billdownscbs.com/2015/06/1947-america-at-dawn-of-cold-war.html, accessed June 22, 2020.

piled up on a carpet of grass. The site he photographed seems suffused with the presence of ghosts. Novelist W. G. Sebald gave a vivid description of a similar airfield at Seething near his Norfolk home: "Grass has run over the runways, and the dilapidated control towers, bunkers and corrugated iron huts stand in the often eerie landscape where you sense the dead souls of the men who never came back from their missions, and of those who perished in the vast fires."[6]

Chim photographed a family improvising in dire circumstances. Their house destroyed, they squatted at the abandoned base. He was impressed by the resilience of a village coming back to life after liberation: in her sitting room, Mrs. Doris Dixon had improvised a lampshade by pleating a sheet; the local baker proudly carried piles of freshly baked loaves in his arms. Chim noted that the dignified and very British baker, Mr. Albert Johnson, wore a tweed jacket, shirt, and tie under his apron. At a pub in the village of Odsey, Chim made informal portraits of the regulars, industrial workers, contrasting them with a tuxedo-wearing waiter; shot in the soft light that filters in from the high windows, the images are reminiscent of a Marcel Carné film. In Bassingbourn-Royston, Chim shot starker portraits of German prisoners in a P. O. W. camp, working in the fields and in construction jobs.[7]

Back in London, Chim photographed a group of dockers resembling those he had portrayed in Marseille in 1934 and 1938 for *Regards*, and a cabby, Arthur Barnes. In Southampton, he documented Operation Pluto ("Pipelines Under the Ocean"): as of 1944, huge pipelines had been laid in the English Channel between Southern England and France so that fuel could safely be transported to the troops in Europe. This engineering feat was key to the success of the Allied invasion of Europe.

One of Chim's best Operation Pluto contact sheets is a prime example of his working method. The sheet is sparer in these straitened post-war circumstances, he was frugal with his film and carefully observed a situation before taking pictures. He started with general views of the harbor: the delicate partitioned structure of the cranes standing out against a cloudy sky in front of piled buoys; gigantic heaps of rubber pipelines looking like Mayan pyramids. Then he focused on a group of six workers carrying a heavy pipeline. Aligned and stepping in turn, they look as if they're dancing.[8]

Thoughtful contacts like these reflect Chim's early interest in chess and in music. As in a game of chess, he anticipates the changes in light and his subjects' movements and places himself accordingly; as a musician, he composes images in harmony, with leitmotivs and parallels, far and near, light and shadow, shapes resonating together like clusters of notes, while the whole sequence develops through time and space as a piece of music does, or a mathematical equation. Though some images do stand out and become the natural lead of his stories, he

---

6 W. G. Sebald, *On the natural history of destruction* (New York: Random House, 2003), 70.
7 MPNYA, ADS, *We Went Back, England*, 1947001- Rolls 1–40 and 41–80
8 MPNYA, ADS, *We Went Back, England*, rolls 1–40, contact #47-1-19.

usually does not, unlike Cartier-Bresson, focus on a "decisive moment," but rather on developing careful sequences that build his narrative. Raw slashes of the instant, like those in Capa's action photographs, are not his style either. Cartier-Bresson wrote: "He had the intelligence of a chess player with the look of a math teacher. He used his camera like a doctor would use a stethoscope to diagnose the state of the heart. His own was vulnerable."

Writers and colleagues who worked alongside Chim have described how gifted he was at walking into a public space and making himself forgettable, almost invisible. His unremarkable appearance helped. He could get from one point to another in plain sight and yet it seemed as if no one saw him. They would look through him and go about their lives without changing a thing. That is the gift he used in a workplace, a demonstration, a street festival, on a movie set.

However, when he worked one on one, making portraits for instance, or an in-depth feature on a particular character, he seemed to undergo a complete transformation. No more neutrality or self-effacement. He wove an intense connection between himself and his subject. The people he photographed felt his empathy. They felt that he cared. It was if they were, for him and in that moment, the only people in the world.

In Normandy, Chim photographed the town of Saint-Lô, which had been almost entirely razed in July 1944. Samuel Beckett called it "the capital of ruins."[9] In one image, a couple, seemingly dazed, walks away from the camera through the aftermath of the rampage, and a large iron bell remains hanging from the remains of the bell tower's fragile structure, the only thing intact. In another heartbreaking image, a woman, on her knees, persists in washing and scrubbing the floor of her house even though the walls are pulverized, and the ground is covered in debris.

At Omaha Beach, the site of D-Day, where Capa made his pictures, Chim followed a group of small children playing on the beach, then focused on four of them wearing white underwear instead of swimsuits, squatting in the wet sand and digging in the shadow of an enormous assault pontoon, stranded like a whale, obliquely pointing to the sky. His striking color image would be the cover of *This Week* (figure 63).

Further on, a child sits on a rusted rocket-launcher as if on a swing. On the ruins of a concrete bunker, someone has painted the picture of a mini-skirted pinup with the words "Dream Girl." The sea, which in Capa's famous photographs of the D-Day landing was stormy and darkened by blood, is now smooth and shiny, like a mirror without a memory. As in Gijon ten years earlier when he photographed the destroyed

---

[9] *The Complete Short Prose of Samuel Beckett* (New York: Grove Press, 2020). His text is dated June 10, 1946. The title derives from a booklet of photographs of the bombed-out city entitled *St. Lô, Capitale des Ruines, 5 et 7 juin 1944* and describes the functioning of the Irish Red Cross hospital for which the author worked in Saint-Lô.

typewriter, Chim has captured an eloquent still life: this time around, it's a handful of ammunition left in the sand like strange seashells, a grim reminder of the battle.[10]

This was an emotional visit for Downs, whose words echo Chim's photographs:

> I'm on Omaha Beach, where not very many months ago, I saw bodies stacked like cord wood—American bodies. Behind me lie the remains of the Mulberry Docks, the improvised harbor that meant so much on D-Day. The sea is very quiet today. Battered ghost ships ride low in the surf. This morning—when the sun was just coming out—the moisture on the beach came up in small clouds of steam. I'm standing at the entrance of an American assault boat. There are about 50 here—some holed by shells, some by collisions. They're old and rusted, down at the stern, half-buried in sand.[11]

Chim had gained the "We Went Back" assignment thanks to his friend Capa, and as he photographed the children playing on the beach under the shadow of a looming concrete shape, the under-portion of a pontoon nicknamed 'Beetle'[12], his thoughts must have been for his friend who was there three years earlier.

On that day in 1944, Robert Capa had landed at Colleville-sur-Mer on a stretch that represented a breach in the German defenses and shot the 11 D-Day pictures that brought him much glory and became, many years later, the stuff of a bitter controversy. The scene was awful. A seasoned correspondent for the *Boston Globe* and the BBC, Iris Carpenter recorded the Omaha Beach landing as eyewitnesses reported it to her:

> Feet slipping in the shifting sand, men stumbled through grey wave caps which raced over them to slap them down with their too-heavy equipment, toss them on the beach, suck them back, toss them again among the nightmare of jumbled equipment, smashed boats, drowned and broken bodies ( ) From the sea the view was as unmenacing-looking as the Normandy landscape.... Only later it became visible— visible as a wall of fire so withering it cut down men in drifts which will forever haunt the memories of those who had to fight their way in over the. (...) When, eventually, the first tanks debarked the drivers cried and vomited as they had to drive over the bodies of their buddies.[13]

For Capa, who was an experienced war photographer, there was little time to take pictures if he was to survive. He ran for his life and took shelter in a landing craft,

---

10 MPNYA, ADS, *We Went Back, England*, 1947001 Rolls 1–40, contact sheet #47-1-30, picture #1-359.
11 Bill Downs, *This Week*, August 10, 1947, special issue: *A Report to America Two Years After V-Day*, 20–21.
12 "Each section of pontoon ('Whale') was supported at each end by 'Beetles'. The 'Beetles' were slipped under the pontoons. By stringing scores of these together they created floating causeways out to deeper water". Email message from military historian Charles 'Chuck' Herrick to the author, October 11, 2021.
13 Nancy Caldwell Sorel, *The Women Who Wrote the War* (New York: Arcade, 1999), 227.

then left and sent his films via courier to editor John Morris at LIFE's London office so he could meet the magazine's June 8 deadline.¹⁴

Just above the beach, the white crosses of the St. Laurent U. S. military cemetery, stretching back to the horizon, composed a grim landscape. Chim photographed several Jewish graves adorned with a wooden star of David.¹⁵ He continued to the commune of Sainte-Mère-Église where, against the backdrop of the devastated Montebourg cathedral, three children read the inscription to the dead on the town's monument; then, sitting on the chains that surround it, they swing slowly, caught in the moment, oblivious to the destruction around them.

At the end of May, Chim made a quick detour to Paris to photograph several small stories: an award ceremony for the underground fighter, Suzanne Berthillon; street scenes, such as a first communion in Montmartre; workers shoveling gravel and laying railroad tracks in the Juvisy suburb. Since his 1930s Paris days, he had been fascinated by poster design, and this time he photographed the poster for the new movie *Bataillons du ciel*, which tells the story of Free France parachutists, a *Moulin de la Galette* poster by Paul Sescau in Montmartre, and a giant poster of *Scandale* girdles on the Champs-Elysées, dwarfing a hatted passer-by (figure 60). In front of a Rasurel swimsuits poster that covers an entire façade, Chim built a powerful triangle of figures: the couple in the Paradise Garden on the poster, a smaller silhouette of a woman under it. In the foreground, the massive, darkened figure of a man turns away, a newspaper under his arm, bringing movement to the image.¹⁶

As Chim continued his "We Went Back" reportage, relaunching his interrupted career, he retraced in Germany some of the routes that Cartier-Bresson had followed from April to November 1945 with Allied troops: Dessau, Villingen, Schwenning, and finally, Belsen which George Rodger had been the first photographer to enter.

On a detour to Paris, he received a telegram from Maria Eisner in New York: "You are Vice President of Magnum Photos. Detailed letter sent to Paris on May 22nd. I will soon have interesting assignments for you. Advise you against coming back now. Wait for me in Paris."¹⁷ Soon afterwards, Chim received the letter where Rita Vandivert described the venture. She repeated the words: "Welcome to the Time, Inc. Stink Club!" That term, "stink club," was a private joke between the photographers, thumbing their nose at *Time-Life* publications, and especially *Life*, which they thought had treated them poorly. Magnum Photos was being created to give them the independence and control that they felt they deserved. As many have com-

---

14 For a detailed account of the landing as well as an argument against Robert Capa, John Morris and Cornell Capa's version of the D-Day facts, see A. D. Coleman's lecture, *SPE's (Society for Photographic Education) 55th Annual Conference*, Philadelphia, March 2, 2018. https://medium.com/exposure-magazine/alternate-history-robert-capa-on-d-day-2657f9af914, accessed February 23, 2022. For Robert Capa's first publication on D-Day, see *Beachheads of Normandy*, LIFE, June 19, 1944, 25.
15 MPNYA, ADS, *We Went Back, England*, 1947001 Rolls 1–40, contact #47-1-24.
16 MPNYA, ADS, *We Went Back*, 1947001 Rolls 41–80, picture #47-1-56.
17 AJGMUC, consulted in Morris's Paris office, unnumbered.

mented, the term Magnum referred to the glamour of the giant bottle of champagne; but it may also be an allusion to the famous Smith & Wesson Magnum revolver, used in all the "Cowboy and Indian" movies that Robert Capa, a Hollywood fan, loved.

The idea of a cooperative did not spring up fully formed one day in 1947, but matured slowly over the years, nurtured by friendship, networks, life experience and common political beliefs. The initial vision belonged to Robert Capa and George Rodger.

Several years older than Capa, Rodger was a war veteran and reluctant hero who had fought on 17 war fronts and traveled 17,000 miles. The two men had struck up a friendship in Algiers in 1943, and then met again on the Italian front in September 1943 where they lived at the Villa Lucia in Vomero with another correspondent, Will Lang.

In several, often boozy conversations in October, Capa and Rodger hashed out some of the principles that would result in Magnum's foundation four years later. They dreamed of controlling the publication of their photographs as well as their growing archive; owning their copyrights; and plotting their own stories rather than catering to editors' whims. As Rodger recalled their discussions,

> We spoke about it all over the Middle East and Africa and especially in Vomero. Capa thought that photographers should be authors, a revolutionary thought in the 1940s when they were mostly seen as secondary to writers, in charge of illustrating and reinforcing text... Capa and I both very definitely had the same idea of an eventual brotherhood...that would be free of all sorts of editorial bias, and that we could work on the stories that we knew were valid, and have a staff or even just a single person who could handle the material when it came back so that we would didn't have to go through all the sweat of processing and editing and dispatching and talking to editors.[18]

The photographers were particularly angry at *Life*'s editors, and at Margaret Bourke-White, their hard-nosed competitor, who, as a staffer there, was often given the best assignments. They were particularly frustrated with the fact that they did not own their copyrights. Capa's 'Falling Soldier' had made him famous but not rich; neither had Rodger's photographs, since he was officially on *Life*'s masthead.

Years later, Rodger would still remember Capa's Hungarian-accented exhortation: "Listen, old goat: today does not matter and tomorrow doesn't matter, but it's the end of the game that counts, and what counts is...how many chips you've got in your pocket. And that is, if you are still playing." [19]

---

18 GRA, Transcript of George Rodger's interview by Patricia Wheatley in the BBC television series *The Magnum Story*, 1985, no page#.
19 GRA, Transcript of George Rodger's interview by Patricia Wheatley in the BBC television series *The Magnum Story*, 1985, no page #. The nickname derived from the fact that showers were rare on the front.

Chim, Cartier-Bresson and Capa had known each other since their Paris days. They had put their beliefs to a hard test during their three years in the Spanish Civil War. Then, while Cartier-Bresson worked for the Résistance and Chim for the Allies in England, Capa had sailed for New York in October 1939 on the ship *Manhattan* (the ship that a year later transported Hala, Emil, and their two-year-old daughter Lenka to New York); then, frustrated at being away from action, he returned to Europe, got himself accredited, and spent the war on the Sicilian and Italian fronts and in the Middle East.

Now, two years after the end of the war, Chim, Capa and Cartier-Bresson, along with Rodger, could take a breather and make plans for their creative and financial future. Capa was the one to take the initiative, confirming a final agreement at New York's Museum of Modern Art (MoMA). Cartier-Bresson's "posthumous" exhibition opened there early in 1947 (he was thought to have died in a German prisoner-of-war camp but escaped on his third attempt) and some time in May—the exact date is unknown—at the museum's cafeteria, or maybe on the roof terrace, Robert Capa, Maria Eisner, William Vandivert, a *Holiday* magazine staffer, and his wife Rita, a shrewd businesswoman, met and drew up an outline for the "photographic community" of their dreams. Thus Cartier-Bresson, Chim, and Rodger, all of them traveling, were absent from the meeting where their future was decided.

In order to wrest independence from the big publishers that had controlled their work, Magnum Photos was designed to be an international cooperative run by its seven members: Capa, Chim, Cartier-Bresson, Rodger, and Vandivert as photographers, with Eisner and Rita Vandivert as administrators. Members would own their copyrights and negatives and insist on writing their own captions for their magazine pieces. Each member would have to put up $400 and agree to work only through the agency, which would take a portion of the fees: 40 percent for assignments set up by the agency, 30 percent for those arranged by the photographers themselves, and 50 percent for reprints.[20] Rita Vandivert would head the New York office and Eisner would direct the Paris office.

Capa divided the world along the lines of the photographers' interests: He would be a correspondent at large ("roving reporter"); Chim would continue in Europe; Cartier-Bresson would travel to the Far East and China (figure 64); and Rodger would work in the Middle East and Africa. As for Bill Vandivert, who was already working for *Holiday* and *Fortune*, he would pursue his arrangement with the magazines and photograph in the United States. However, the Vandiverts were starting a family, and weary of the risks and financial insecurity involved in a start-up business, left the following year.

In her letter to Chim, Rita Vandivert further outlined the details:

---

20 DSA, letter from Rita Vandivert, New York, May 19, 1947.

> The tentative title for the company is MAGNUM PHOTOS INC., it will be incorporated here [in New York] with all seven members as directors, myself as President, the rest of you all Vice-Presidents, & Maria treasurer and secretary.
> We are keeping our investment as low as possible, planning to get running expenses, which will be kept very low, out of returns pretty soon (...). The idea is that from the start of the agency each photographer puts in all his photographic assignments which are magazine or newspaper work, e. g., Capa puts in his Russian deal, Bill puts in his *Fortune* or whatever other magazine deals he has pending or makes from then on (...).
> [The *Illustrated*'s] Lens Spooner is over here now, has been sitting in our discussions, is going to have a special contract with the agency (...) whereby he gets first look from England at all our photographers' pictures (...). The way Capa sees it working for himself and some of the others is this: he makes a deal with a publication to send him somewhere, gets expense money, etc. & does the agreed number of pages for them. Then he shoots as much material as he can on the side, keeping closely in touch with both Paris and New York offices so that we know what he can get, just where he will be and how long he thinks it worthwhile to stay. Only by this close cooperation however can we hope to save waste of time, energy & material—the photographer must know what the magazines are interested in, and the agency girls must know at all times what the photographers are up to (except on their evenings off).[21]

The common dream had come true, and Magnum Photos was born. A few years later, in 1955, Chim would draw up the cooperative's charter, which, remarkably, is still in effect today.

Magnum may have chosen a big, glitzy name for itself, but its tiny Paris office at 125 rue du Faubourg St Honoré was, at its beginnings, a messy, disorganized, noisy affair that Ernst Haas described as a "pigeon coop." Lois Witherspoon, a researcher who was a friend of the photographers and often stopped by (she would become Rodger's second wife), remembers that "the office was crowded—camera equipment, shoulder bags, old coats, books and maps lying anywhere, telephones ringing, empty coffee cups littering tabletops. And photographers cleaning cameras, bending over light box boxes, gazing at contact sheets—talk, talk, talk in French and Dutch and German and Italian." [22]

Historian and curator Clara Bouveresse, who has written extensively about Magnum's inner workings, explains how the agency planned to distribute and sell work:

> Magnum gradually devised a system to circulate and sell distributions. During its first year in 1947, the New York office set up a log to register and number each story with its arrival date, the number of prints and the clients to which they were sent: this formed the first "distribution" system. On Mondays, the log was analyzed to determine which clients were next in line for a particular set of pictures. Distributions were indeed to be sent to clients in a strategic order, as their value decreased over time, and the agency sought to attract the highest bidders.[23]

---

21 DSA, letter from Rita Vandivert, New York, May 19, 1947.
22 Inge Bondi, *Ernst Haas: Letters & Stories*. (New York.: Delmonico, 2021), 33.
23 See Clara Bouveresse, "Magnum Distributions,1947–1960: Photographers'Emancipations and Concessions", Photography and Culture, Volume 14,2021, Issue 1. https://www.tandfonline.com/

Chim was delighted by the whole idea and immediately accepted the offer. To him, Magnum was more than a professional endeavor: it constituted a family of sorts, a symbol of solidarity and cooperation, common goals, and humanistic values. It offered a way of working independently while still feeling connected to others, and maybe a way of healing, which was much needed in the aftermath of the war.

"Very early on," said Inge Bondi, Chim's first biographer, then an editor at Magnum New York since 1950 (later a general manager of that office)

> Chim and Capa both had the idea that they needed a community of like-minded people to flourish. After having braved the war years, they got together and said, we are forty, we need to do what is really important to us (...) They were very close, very intimate, also very protective of each other, probably because they were two young men, refugees in a different country. Chim had come from a much more settled, solid, intellectual family than Capa. Capa was wild, untamed and passionate. But in their political and ideological goals they had the same ideas (...) They were like branches of the same tree.[24]

Richard Whelan, Capa's first biographer, also describes their close friendship:

> Their friends spoke of them as the sun and the moon. But Endré [Capa] did not dominate the friendship; on the contrary, the two young men saw themselves as very different but equal. Endré had unbounded respect for Chim's intellect, for his moral judgement, and for his eye. He always said that Chim was the better photographer, and took Chim's advice and criticism very seriously (...) From Chim, Endré learned that although a photojournalist has to be aggressive, and even callous, in order to get into position to take the most dramatic photographs, all his efforts will be wasted unless, at the actual moment of taking the picture, he can replace his boldness with sensitivity and tenderness.[25]

On June 15, 1947, a written legal agreement drawn up by New York lawyers listed the photographers' rights and obligations. The document reads in part:

> The Agency will act as the exclusive agent for the photographer, selling and distributing all his photographs, including both moving pictures and still pictures (...). The Agency will use its best efforts to sell the pictures of the photographer to periodicals and to obtain the best possible prices for the photographer's pictures (...). All negatives and transparencies shall remain the property of the photographer but shall remain in custody of the Agency (...). All photographs will be stamped by the Agency with the name of the photographer followed by the name of the Agency, separated by a hyphen, and the Agency will request periodicals to publish such credit line and will use its best efforts to insure the use of such credit line whenever possible.[26]

---

eprint/5VCEJ84ZMTXCAMJPGSBU/full?target=10.1080/17514517.2020.18159, accessed November 9, 2020.
24 Interview of Inge Bondi by the author, Princeton, New Jersey, March 11, 2005.
25 Richard Whelan, *Robert Capa, a Biography* (New York: Alfred A. Knopf, 1985), 56–57.
26 In MPNYA, no number. The lawyers were listed as Poser, Katcher, and Driesen, 295 Madison Avenue, New York.

Pursuing his reportage with Bill Downs, Chim traveled from Paris to Reims, where he photographed the room in which the Germans had surrendered to the Allies almost two years before, on June 7, 1945. Between Aachen and Liège, he photographed the Henri-Chapelle Cemetery and the grim inscription on its Wall of the Missing: "To the Memory of the soldiers of the United States Army who while prisoners of war were massacred by Nazi troops on this spot, on December 17, 1944".

At the German-Belgian border, near Aachen, the Huertgen forest was burnt to cinders. In black and white and color, Chim made one of his most powerful war still lifes: a German tomb decorated with a simple birch cross and three iron helmets hanging from its branches (figure 65). In another image, a young frontier guard, his face dreamy under his cap, guards the former Siegfried Line.[27]

In Belgium and the Netherlands, again working in both black and white and color, he photographed a destroyed German tank in a field, and people who, for lack of new clothes, wear discarded US Army clothing. At the Bastogne town entrance in Belgium, a temporary memorial lists the war dead. In the market, Chim made images that feature contrasting views of the ruins and an abundance of food, as well as a playful image of Downs wearing his usual white fedora hat and holding a squirming piglet. He photographed POWS working on the Red Ball highway that linked Bastogne to Germany, some of the many German civilians and captured soldiers whom the Allied Forces had forced into labor.

In Nijmegen, Holland, Chim photographed the bridge that had been the site of a fierce battle. As an eyewitness to that battle, Downs, on September 24, 1944, had described the attack as "a single, isolated battle that ranks in magnificence and courage with Guam, Tarawa, Omaha Beach (…). Today the Nijmegen bridge is in our hands intact a monument to the gallantry of the Americans who crossed the river and the British and airborne troops who stormed it from the south."[28]

Still in Nijmegen, Chim photographed the mayor and scenes at a market and a flea-market. There are just a few things for sale: coins and random items of clothing. Only flowers seem plentiful. A modest building bearing the inscription "American Bar-Manhattan Special Dancing" stands in front of a field of ruins. By a gutted church, people have started small plots for vegetable gardens. In the Jonkerbos military cemetery with its rows and rows of white crosses, a girl kneels to place a small bunch of flowers on a tomb. Resourceful locals have reused discarded metal munitions crates to store grain.

Chim went on to cover the dismantling of the Krupp war factories in Essen, where the Allies were tearing apart the remnants of German industries—plants, machinery, and the railroad system—and transporting steel, coal, and other components of industrial production out of the country. In his pictures, we see German

---

27 MPNYA, ADS, *We Went Back*, Rolls 121–147, pictures #1-1036 to 1-1040.
28 "The Battle of Nijmegen Bridge," *The Listener*, BBC, September 28, 1944, https://www.billdownscbs.com/2013/10/1944-battle-of-arnhem.html, accessed June 22, 2020.

steelworkers laboring under the muted light generated by acetylene lamps and molten metal (figure 79). Cavernous halls are littered with gigantic, destroyed metal tubes and debris. The portraits of the workers are sober. Even with his own painful memories of the Nazis, the photographs clearly show that Chim was able to sympathize with the forlorn workers—to him, they belonged to the same class as those he had met in Extremadura and Asturias.[29]

Later that year, Downs described the sadness of the scenes the two witnessed, in the article Chim's portraits illustrated: "Today these workmen are as confused, as hopeless, and as demoralized a group of people as there is in all of Germany. Walking through the ruined Krupp gun shops, the dirty, ragged laborers seldom speak, even among themselves. Only the occasional hissing of an acetylene torch chopping up gun barrels breaks the almost cathedral-like silence."[30] In the Ruhr mines, where the steel furnaces were still producing railroad lines, Chim's beautiful portraits of the miners in darkness (including portraits of communist labor miners Wilhelm Marcianak and Karl Dakowski) are punctured by the sparks from their torches.

Essen, almost entirely bombed by the Allies, was a ghost city with destroyed iron bridges plunging into the Ruhr River, fragmented highways, and shells of buildings; residents were living in caves, bunkers, cellars. From Chim's contact sheet, we know that, attracted by the eloquent background, he first included a child in his pictures before moving in and focusing on a young woman and her baby. Backed by Piranesi-like ruins, she pushes a baby carriage in which her newborn, the son of a British soldier, sleeps peacefully, wrapped in white blankets; the contrast is so striking that the picture looks like a photomontage. In front of the Krupp factories, a not-so-young sex worker stands, showing off her stockinged legs (figure 9). Chim built his photograph along a diagonal line that joins the factory chimney to the foreground character, the sex worker, with a woman passing in-between, conservatively dressed, eyeing the other woman with disdain. With his eye for detail, he has noticed the sex worker's coarse stockings and slouchy, tattered slippers that speak of her awkward effort to attract customers in reduced post-war circumstances.[31]

In Essen, the main actors are children. They fill the frame, vying for his attention. Holding enameled cups, they queue at the soup kitchen and sit at long wooden tables, their faces expressing destitution and loss. With good reason, Chim sees them as the real victims of the war. In another striking image, a white-faced, disoriented-looking boy comes up the stairs of the cellar that serves as a home for his family. Many images from this reportage would turn out to be a dress rehearsal for the series on children of Europe that Chim made for UNICEF the following year.

Berlin, too, was in utter ruins, and on the verge of inflation. Neither cars nor petrol could be found. On the Kurfürstendamm, Chim photographed Baroque statues

---

29 MPNYA, ADS, *We Went Back*, 1947001 Rolls #121–147, picture #1-135.
30 Bill Downs, "The Men in Germany's Future," *This Week* (October 5, 1947), 5.
31 MPNYA, ADS, *We Went Back*, 1947001, contact #102, picture #193C and PAR114625.

of Titans supporting a stone arch as if swimming up from a mound of rubble. A synagogue stood, wrecked. Advertisements for a photographic portrait studio contrasted sharply with a ruined façade featuring an ad for corsets. The Krupp's Villa Huegel had been spared and featured three stories, an imposing façade with columns and a sphinx statue at the entrance. The Rainbow Snack Bar had been established next door to Hitler's home at the Reich's Chancellery. A gaunt woman tried to make a living by selling flower bouquets on a rickety table placed in front of a ruined building even as a newly reopened luxury shop sold jewelry and accessories.

In one of Chim's most haunting photographs, a man has assembled a makeshift baby carriage and from cartwheels, a handle, and a crib, in which his daughter seems encaged. His older boy walks in front of the cart (figure 61). Their three parallel shadows line the ground, tenuous oblique lines that echo the six massive Greek pillars of the Brandenburg Gate. The destroyed chariot from the gate's statue stands just west of the section where, in November of the following year, East and West Germany would part ways. The bronze Victory goddess has lost her wings. Here is Chim, a lonely witness, standing on the border between the East where he was born and the West where he's made his name. On the ground, his projected shadow has a ghostly presence.[32]

In many of the cities Chim visited, food was scarce for the survivors of the Allied bombings and the black market was thriving. In Frankfurt, Chim photographed the vegetable market crowd while Downs interviewed the buyers and sellers.

Next, Chim worked with journalist Dena Burger on another aspect of the civilians' survival, a story entitled "Germany's Bucket Economy."[33] Residents had cultivated small patches of land between the ruined buildings, brought in earth and manure, and created fruit, vegetable, and flower gardens. Every inch of available land was cultivated, even right in the center of town: one of his photographs shows such a garden dug in front of the Reichstag.

His story centered on Frau Wanderer, who grew tomatoes, cabbages, beets, lettuce, and geraniums on a patch of land that used to be her home on Neue Kraeme Strasse, in the center of Frankfurt. "Green leaves show through the broken walls. Geranium blossoms are brilliant against crumbled stone and flaking plaster (...). Climb the shattered rock, scale the jagged wall, step gingerly over the powdered marble that was once a fireplace—and you are in Frau Wanderer's tomato farm,"[34] Burger wrote, in an exact description of Chim's color photographs.

The story found interested readers in Britain, where people remembered a similar phenomenon, the World War II Victory Gardens. But the German gardens were

---
32 MPNYA, ADS, *We Went Back*, story #47-001, rolls 148–170, picture #157 and MPPA, PAR133278.
33 *Illustrated*, October 4, 1947, pp. 13-15 & MPNYA Text by Dena Burger, *Germany's Bucket Economy*, story #47-3.
34 Text by Dena Burger, see previous note and MPNYA, NYC131483.

those of defeat, of a broken and humiliated people. Rather than mourning and dwelling on their misery and the family members they had lost, they threw themselves into work. A janitor, Peter Mietke, went into the tobacco business: he planted it in a patch near his ground floor apartment, collected the ripened leaves, dried them, and turned them into cigarettes. When Dena Burger asked him why, he gave a revealing answer: "We the Germans are a defeated nation, and we know it all the time. A man feels like a man again when he has a cigarette in his mouth."[35]

All in all, Chim's story strikes an uneasy chord. The brilliance of the garden's colors is set against a stark background of ruins, reminding us of the relentless, massive Allied bombing of German cities, which killed more than 400,000 civilians.[36] It is as if there is a fissure, a divide, within the images. Their backdrop of ruins lends them a strident, bitter-sweet tonality. Cultivation may be a sign of optimism, but it is also a way of avoiding grief: the earth where these beautiful fruits and vegetables grow is full of corpses. They are this crop's fertilizers.

Sober but perhaps most chilling in their stark, austere style, unique in Chim's oeuvre, are the photographs he took at Dachau (figure 50): the gas chambers and the trials that the War Crimes Group of Buchenwald's staff held there. In the portrait of the high-ranking Nazi Otto Skorzeny in the Dachau military prison, the man's ironic, taunting, expression is striking as, facing the photographer, he calmly lights a cigarette.[37] Meanwhile, German POWs outside are watching a soccer game.

Chim completed his reportage in mid-June, and he quickly sent off his film without seeing the results. Unsure of the job he had done, he wrote to Capa and Eisner: "You must have gotten my letters and seen my contact sheets. I am extremely curious about the results of my work and impatient to know what you think of it. The reportage was hard to handle, and I felt rushed by the speed of our journey on the Continent. Look carefully at the contact sheets—especially the 35mm. And as I have asked before—send me a telegram as soon as you have seen them. It will take a weight off my shoulders."[38] His worries were unfounded. On June 26, he received a telegram from Jerry Mason, editor of *This Week*: "Sensational photos congratulations."[39]

Because he had not worked as a photographer during the war, unlike Capa, Cartier-Bresson, and Rodger, Chim had lost some of his pre-war reputation and now needed to take financial risks and accept most assignments. Magnum needed to sell its photographers' work in the U.S. if it were to survive and the American public, which had little interest in looking at the past (no more refugee stories), wanted

---

35 Text by Dena Burger, see note 28.
36 For detailed commentaries on the Allied Bombings, see W. G. Sebald, *On the natural history of destruction* (New York: Random House, 2003), and Heinrich Böll, *The Silent Angel* (London: Cassell Military Paperback, 2002).
37 MPNYA, ADS, *We Went Back*, 1947001, Contacts #47-1-62 & 47-1-63.
38 DSA, letter to Robert Capa and Maria Eisner, July 17, 1947.
39 DSA,

more optimistic, future-oriented reportages. Reluctant to conform to the new climate, Chim sought guidance from his editors as to how to orient himself. In a 1947 letter, Rita Vandivert explained the situation: "Lots of magazines seem to be thinking in terms of a two page spread on any simple but lively subject—preferably something where the idea is familiar to the American reader but the setting strange and interesting (...) stories showing how people live, their family life, their work, recreation, hobbies, etc."[40] As for Capa, he was much more blunt; according to him, Chim had to find new ideas that were easier to sell. "Get your little fat legs in motion (...). France is overcrowded with good photographers. If you need a kicking, this is it."[41]

In September 1947, Chim covered "Architects of a New World," a first postwar congress of modernist architects that took place in Bridgewater, England. About 70 delegates attended, including Le Corbusier—then engaged in his Marseille project—Walter Gropius, Sigfried Giedion, Wilhelm Schutter, and Jose Luis Sert. If the assignment was lackluster—basically, a series of portraits which he hoped to sell to *Fortune* and *Illustrated* as a story on Europe's reconstruction—it proved fortuitous for Chim, because this is where he met Julian Huxley's secretary and subsequently connected with Huxley, UNESCO's first director-general. Huxley was interested in learning from photojournalists ways to develop his organization's mass communications strategy through print media, radio, and television campaigns and he approached Chim about a reportage on post-war Europe's reconstruction. A few months later, Chim wrote to Vandivert and Eisner: "Huxley is excited over the reconstruction story. John Grierson (?) wants me to give him the project, well presented and the amount of money I need." He asked Eisner and Vandivert to decide if a trip to Europe—under the auspices of UNESCO—would be worthwhile.[42]

His next assignment was for a global group project. Conceived by Morris, now the picture editor of *Ladies Home Journal*, it was a comparative essay on ways of life around the world, to be produced by a group of photojournalists over one year, covering all four continents. To the owners of the magazine, the Goulds, Morris pitched the story as "People Are People The World Over," writing,

> If people will only stop to consider the fundamental natures of those whom they often consider 'foreign', they will soon realize that there are really no foreigners—anymore. And if there are no foreigners there are no people to fight, for you don't fight 'your own kind.' So the editorial job is to explain peoples to peoples in intimate, vivid terms, taking them not country by country but trait by trait, problem by problem.[43]

Morris wanted to run the reportage in 12 consecutive issues of the magazine. To cut costs, he decided to capitalize on some of the photographers' existing assignments

---

40 Letter from Rita Vandivert, MFNY, no number.
41 November 12, 1947 radiogram from Robert Capa, MFNY, #011-001-001/2.
42 Chim, *Letter to Magnum*, January 29, 1948, MFNY.
43 JGMAUC, letter from John Morris to Bruce and Beatrice Gould, no date.

and he wrote to Rodger, suggesting that while in the Middle East and Africa, he shoot two or three stories on families of farmers. Capa already had his well-paid assignment to travel in Russia with John Steinbeck, so Morris contacted him, too, and Capa immediately wanted to make the project a Magnum story. Cartier-Bresson was planning trips to China and Japan, but Morris, worried that the Frenchman was too independent to stick to a shooting schedule, assigned instead a *Life* photographer, Horace Bristol, who was based in Tokyo. Chim was to photograph a rural French family in the Cher department, near Bourges, and a German farming family.

The Goulds asked Morris and Capa to do a week-long test story in Glidden, Iowa, a hundred miles from Des Moines, and after seeing Capa's photographs of the Pratts, a family of farmers, the Goulds approved the project, agreeing on a $15,000 budget —about $2,000 per assignment. The photographers would have to follow a strict shooting script focusing on 12 families around the world; shooting would begin by the summer of 1947 and be done by the fall. In what would today be considered politically incorrect terms, John Morris explained the project's focus: "How people cook, bathe, go to school, worship, travel. It showed that people confront the same problems everywhere (...). We had naked African children learning the alphabet next to well-clothed American children in school."[44]

Chim was not a fan of the shooting script framework, but he really needed the work and the money. He shadowed his two farming families from morning to night, emphasizing in his photos and captions the restrictions in food and supplies they were experiencing after the war. In France, his subject was the Bédouin family ("Madame Bédouin fixes a meat stew and washes with rationed soap"), and in Germany, the Stieglitz family ("Frau Stieglitz lights her coal stove at 5.30am to prepare morning 'coffee' (made of sugar beets)"). One image that stands out is that of German children at their desks, writing their assignments—a theme that Chim would return to, first in his 1948 *Children of Europe* series, then two years later in his illiteracy series shot in Southern Italy.

On August 22, 1947, Morris wrote: "Dear Chim, I am still awaiting the French family story, but I just want to send a note of congratulations on your pictures in *This Week*. They are really good, and I am beginning to understand why Capa has always bragged about you (he admits you are even better than he is)."[45]

Capa ended up photographing families in Czechoslovakia and sold his Russian Journal project as a separate series to the *Journal*. As for Rodger, he worked in Egypt and with a Pakistani family. In 1949, under the title *Magnum Reports the World*, the *People Are People* project was exhibited at the prestigious Photo League Gallery in New York.[46]

---

44 *Ladies' Home Journal*, Editorial, January 1948.
45 DSA, letter from John Morris, August 22, 1947.
46 Photo League Gallery, New York, *Magnum Reports the World*, no date found.

Morris and many commentators have credited the *People Are People the World Over* project as the main inspiration behind Edward Steichen's *Family of Man* exhibition, which would open in 1955 at MoMA in New York. That may well be the case. However, the project as published is disappointing, with the look of a drab school assignment. The images were displayed in a small format, in horizontal and vertical rows that formed a rectangle on a double page around Morris' central text and an image of the world's globe with arrows pointing at the countries the photographers had covered (figure 86). The presentation makes it look as if the photographs were mere illustrations for the text and captions, and many of the images feel stilted and staged.[47]

The project was also drowned by its environment. Built on the editors' premise that "the family is still the basic building block of society," *Ladies Home Journal* was heavily centered on a traditional ideal of women at home, dedicated to making things work (if possible, on a shoestring). Glamor came from fashion pages in color, and romance from a serialized novel. For the magazine's editors, the perfect woman was the one who knew how to remedy dry skin or childhood constipation and give indoor laundry 'spring-breeze freshness'.

Despite his growing success, Chim was always prone to self-doubt. In the summer, when everything in France ground to a halt, he had trouble setting up an exclusive story on French nuclear plants and on a couple he had already photographed in 1934: Irène and Frédéric Joliot-Curie, joint recipients of a Nobel Prize in Physics. In a letter to Vandivert,[48] he presented his reportage with exclusive photographs of the couple as a "real first." He complained to Eisner about his difficulties, and on July 15, she wrote him a long letter:

> Chim, My Old, Please come to earth for a few minutes (...). The agency can only sell and promote those who can, to a marked extent, help themselves, can think clearly in an editorial sense, can profitably shoot marketable stories without assignments as well as those assigned, can help promote themselves. (...) Magnum cannot be a wailing wall. It can and will sell what photographic and editorial energy you put into it (...). Buy yourself a bottle of good Cognac, get a little high—find a dark, voluptuous girl—go swimming—anything. (...) This is a new venture and a high adventure. It calls for the best we are capable of.[49]

Chim persisted in his efforts and assisted by David Schoenbrun of CBS, he finally arrived at the end of July at Le Bouchet, a pilot factory dedicated to the concentration and refinement of uranium, with Frédéric Joliot-Curie giving him a guided tour and detailed caption material. Chim also met Dr. Bertrand Goldschmidt, Head of the French Atomic Energy Commission. In a series taken in the Joliot-Curie's Antony garden, south of Paris, where they entertained friends and family, gardened and played

---

47 *Ladies Home Journal*, June, July, August, September, October, November, December 1948, January, February, March, April 1949, all with presentations by John Godfrey Morris.
48 Letter to Rita Vandivert dated July 8, 1947, MFNY, 011-001-001/2.
49 Letter from Rita Vandivert dated July 15, 1947, MFNY, 011-001-002.

tennis, the couple look relaxed. "I had the fright of my life," Chim wrote Magnum, "when after photographing the graphite pile, Dr. Goldschmidt very seriously announced that he thought I had come too close to the pile and that all my films would get black from exposure to radiation. I had all my rolls in my pockets, and I bid adieu to my reportage. Naturally, nothing happened. Something else: I beat Irène Joliot-Curie at ping-pong. 21–17. That's all."[50] As for his colleague David Schoenbrun, in his companion piece "Can France Make an Atom Bomb," he reported "22–20 in an overtime battle".[51]

However, the story was not a success. *This Week* thought it dull. Usually politically savvy, Chim had failed to predict the lack of response from American magazines: in the McCarthy era, the fact that the Joliot-Curies were communists made them untouchable as subjects. The couple were ardent partisans of world peace but at the height of the Cold War, Joliot-Curie was dismissed from his position at the French Atomic Energy Commission. A few months later Irène also lost her post as commissioner. In 1953, the ACS (American Chemical Society), one of the largest scientific organizations in the world, which claimed to be working for the advancement of chemistry and not using political tests for its membership, rejected Irene Joliot-Curie's application because of her political reputation. The case became a cause célèbre, *l'Affaire Curie*. In the end, only *Science Illustrated* published the reportage, with a text by Schoenbrun who quoted Frédéric Joliot-Curie saying, "We are in the same historic phase as was the primitive man before the conquest of fire."[52]

Eager to take the pulse of the post-war political landscape, Chim accepted an assignment to cover the French municipal elections of October 1947.[53] He was intrigued by the socialist and communist parties, and De Gaulle's new political party, *le Rassemblement du Peuple Français*. Although de Gaulle was a Résistance hero who had worked with communists during the Résistance, his new party excluded supporters of Pétain's Vichy regime, but also communists.

At the Vincennes racetrack—as he had done in Extremadura in May 1936—Chim did not focus on De Gaulle, who was giving a speech, but, as he always preferred to do, on the outskirts of the event, with the crowd listening, their faces tilted in rapt attention and protected from the sun with folded newspapers, visors, caps, or hats.

Chim covered the voting in two schools in Parisian suburbs and two other Paris locations: the Ecole des Beaux-Arts and Passy, a quiet residential neighborhood where he photographed nuns casting their ballots. In a municipal election center, he photographed a mother with her two children, preparing to vote inside a curtained booth. In another image, Chim has moved closer to make a portrait of a man holding a baby in the crook of his left arm while voting with his right hand. In Armentières, a

---

50 DSA.
51 *No Atom Bomb for France*, in *Science Illustrated*, 1948, 19–23.
52 *Science Illustrated*, 1948, 19–23, no exact publication date known.
53 MPNYA, ADS, 1947-002-1947-009, Story #47-5.

poor town in the north of France, political posters for De Gaulle's party show his face and the French flag defaced with crude swastikas[54] (figure 62). In Paris's Place des Vosges, right in the center of town, an exhausted man falls asleep on a bench, his body leaning over, his cap fallen to the ground.

In February 1947, the United Nations Council established the Free Territory of Trieste between Northern Italy and Yugoslavia. Trieste had strategic importance for trade with Central Europe, and the intention was to end the competing territorial claims of Italy and Yugoslavia and create a neutral independent country. Six months later, the free state came into official existence and Chim traveled there from Italy.[55] He photographed soldiers from the American, British, and Yugoslav forces of occupation, and acknowledged the dissenting forces at work in the city: "The war of signs was one of the weapons used by the pro-Yugoslav elements. Stenciled portraits of Tito and Stalin, Yugoslav flags and slogans, are literally covering the countryside."[56] Some of his strongest images show a stenciled portrait of Stalin on a wall. Near the Yugoslavia border, another shot depicts women peasants crouching in a field and the inscription, "We Want Freedom, We Want Yugoslavia" painted on a wall in the background that looks like a stage set.[57] In the harbor's waters, he photographed sunken ships that had not been retrieved.

As a result of the conflict, Trieste had six different newspapers, all in bitter opposition to each other, including the Communist *Lavatore* and the right-wing *La Voce Libera*. Since they had to share the same printing plant, they made an agreement that the newspapers would be printed one after the other but released at the same time. Conscious of the ironies of the situation, Chim photographed the workers at the plant, "a unique place in Europe, where communists and rightists [sic] newspapermen work together in a communal setting room, sometimes looking over each other's shoulders to find out what a competitor is doing."[58]

When Chim was on assignment and covering the topics that were relevant to the story, he always kept his mind open to chance and life's strange quirks. In Trieste, he met, standing against a sunny stone wall, a family group coming from a party: two women, one in a fur collar, and a girl. The girl stared at him. She was wearing a plaid dress and a long, white fairy hat with painted disks on it, and she was blowing into a whistle as its paper tail trailed in the breeze.[59]

On assignment from *Fortune*, Chim reported a piece on the distribution of aid packages in Avron, Pas-de-Calais, a small, drab town in the northern French mining district[60] characterized by its *corons*—identical one-story brick houses that the min-

---

54 MPPA, PAR168376.
55 MPNYA, ADS, 1947-002 to 1947-009, Story #47-6.
56 MPNYA, DST, for *Trieste*, Story #47-007.
57 MPNYA, NYC131484.
58 MPNYA, Story #47-07, no image number visible on contact sheet.
59 MPNYA, Story #47-07, no image number visible on contact sheet.
60 MPNYA, ADS, 1947-002 to 1947-009, Story #47-9.

ing-companies built for their workers. Formed two years earlier, the non-profit organization CARE (Cooperative for American Remittances to Europe) had made the decision to send these food rations to European populations suffering from hunger in the wake of the war. CARE worked with the U.S. Army to acquire its surplus food rations that had been stockpiled but never used and Americans were offered the opportunity to purchase a CARE package for $10 to send to friends or relatives in Europe. Even when a donor did not have the recipient's address, CARE would find that person. As a result, the packages became a vital missing-person service in the postwar chaos.

Chim photographed a ceremony held to distribute 50 CARE parcels to widows and mothers of large families as they queued up for their rations. The setting was modest, the outside of a small café near the railroad tracks, operated by a husband and wife who had been leading members of the Résistance. Demonstrating how distant European recovery still was two years after the end of the war, his story is a follow-up of sorts on his earlier "We Went Back" reportage. So is his photo-essay called "Monte Cassino rises again," which would be published in the *New York Herald Tribune* on September 3, 1948.[61]

In 1944, when they were in Italy together, Capa and Rodger had photographed part of the brutal six months long battle for Monte Cassino which had culminated on March 15 and led to complete destruction. With the town too ruined for reconstruction, a new town had been started in the valley, a few hundred feet from the old one. The monastery was being rebuilt, even though its third-century frescoes were beyond repair.

In the same spirit, Chim did a story on the rehabilitation of the Corinth Canal that connects the Gulf of Corinth with the Aegean Sea. This reconstruction was part of a program to rehabilitate Greek infrastructure that had been damaged during the war; German forces had sabotaged the canal by dumping rocks, railcars, mines, and bridges into the water—about one million cubic yards of debris. By the time Chim made his reportage in September 1948, the engineers' cleaning efforts had led to the canal's reopening to traffic.[62]

The spring of 1948 marked Chim's first experience of Italy as he covered the run-up to the Italian elections. It was a momentous time in Italian politics: women had just been given the right to vote in national elections and hold government positions. The 1948 election would be the first since Mussolini's "march on Rome" in 1922 and the Italians were going to the ballot box not just to elect a government but to determine the political orientation of their country. The United States provided backing for the Christian Democrats, who would win 48 percent of the vote, while the Communist-Socialist Alliance won 31 percent.

---

61 MPNYA, ADS 1948-001-1948-003, Story #48-5-2.
62 MPNYA, NYC27273.

On March 14, 1948, 30,000 women, the "*Donne della Resistenza*," arrived from all over Italy for a peace march and demonstration. Chim followed the peace parade from Piazza Venezia to Foro Italico. He made close-up portraits of politicians, such as the socialists from the group *Giustizia e Libertà*, and Carlos Sforza, a foreign minister who supported the settlement of Trieste and the European recovery program. In the large forum of the ancient Basilica di Massenzio in Rome, Chim photographed the crowd listening to a speech by socialist Pietro Nenni (figure 80). His beautifully lit image takes in one of the Basilica's three large archways under which a crowd of 100,000 is massed. On the right, sunlight lingers on the large, coffered stone vaults and the upheld faces, while shadows darken the other side and mist rises in the back of the image. After focusing on the crowd, Chim brought his attention to a group of young men: perched in an alcove that held statues of emperors in Roman times, they hold communist and Italian flags as they listen.

As he always did, Chim also followed his instincts to capture the atmosphere of the time and ordinary people's hardships. Far from the crowds, he explored the peripheries of events, roaming the streets of Rome to photograph children's games; men gluing political posters to the walls; and poor street vendors selling pots and pans or luggage and shoes from tables set on the street.

During his work in Rome, Chim met the writer Carlo Levi, whom he knew by reputation and whose book *Cristo si è fermato a Eboli* (*Christ Stopped at Eboli*), published right after the war, he had read with admiration. A member of the group *Giustizia e Liberta*, Levi was a young doctor who was harassed because he was an artist, a Jew, and an antifascist activist. He had been arrested several times, incarcerated in Turin, then in Rome, and finally exiled by Mussolini's government to one of the poorest regions of Italy, the Basilicata, deep in the south. He spent a year in Grassano and Aliano, which he called Gagliano in the novel that he published immediately after the war with his "dear editor," Luigi Einaudi.

The publication of Levi's book had tremendous repercussions beyond literary circles. Thanks to Levi, the privations of southern Italy (the *Mezzogiorno*) were finally becoming a key issue in the public debate. The photographer and the writer-painter shared political convictions and became good friends. Chim made a portrait of a relaxed and smiling Carlo Levi wearing his customary rumpled corduroy suit and sitting in front of a Roman pizzeria.[63]

It is most probably during this time that Rome started to replace Paris in Chim's affections, and he pondered the idea of relocating there. It would be easy—he mostly lived out of suitcases.

He traveled to Naples and the surrounding area and saw firsthand the poverty of the south that Levi had described. Naples was still a city of misery, with children playing in its debris. Modest street markets sold bulbs, cheese, kitchenware, and Italian tobacco. Chim visited poor neighborhoods where the rows of rickety houses

---

63 MPNY, NYC119313.

had no running water—he photographed a woman filling her jug at a public fountain and took both his Leica and his Rollei to document the families who, their houses bombed out, had moved into small shacks constructed in the grottoes of Megellin, a Naples suburb.

One of his images shows the enormous rock cave where children play beneath hanging laundry, while a photograph taken from further away, and from a higher perspective, displays, like a stage set, the large triangle of the cave's opening with the group of shacks that nest there, joined by lines of laundry. Inside the caves, Chim took more intimate pictures of the families. One depicts a family playing cards on a rickety table inside a cave where they have built a wooden shack with wood they've collected. Another from the same series shows a young man resoling a pair of worn-out shoes, helped by his son, while two younger children, half-dressed, sit in the dirt. A beautiful Rollei portrait shows a young woman smiling, head tilted in the sunshine, against a mass of laundry that surrounds her like floating sails, while a starker 35mm photograph portrays two children that seem lost, standing in the dark recess of the cave where they live.[64]

Less than two years later, Chim would travel again to the Mezzogiorno, and, taking up the same cause as his friend Levi, document the glaring inequality between north and south and the peasants' and teachers' fight against one of Italy's worst evils: illiteracy.

---

64 MPPA, PAR218575, PAR188504, PAR 191230, MPNYA, NYC119313.

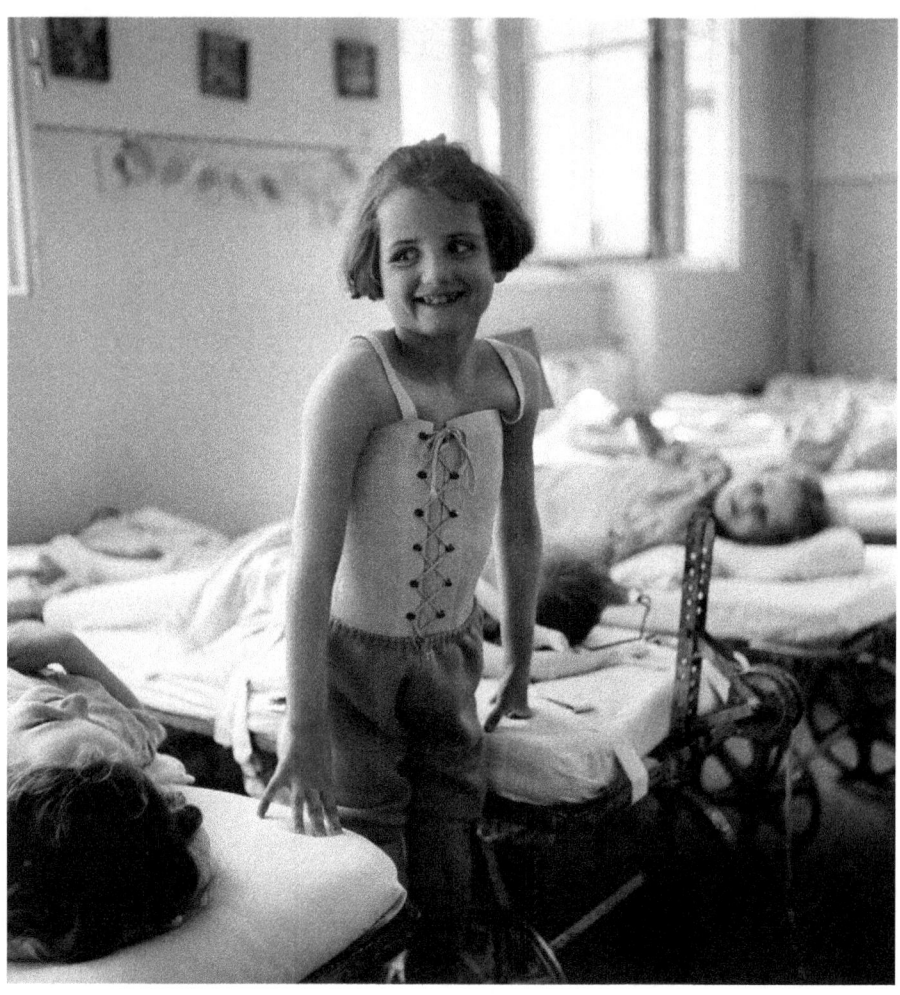

Fig. 10: This little girl, suffering from spinal tuberculosis, must wear a special stiff body jacket. Bellevue Hospital for Children, Vienna, Austria, 1948. © David Seymour-Magnum Photos.

Chapter 8: Children of Europe. 1948

After the war ended, the plight of children, its innocent victims, became Europe's priority. There were 13 million children in Europe whose lives had been affected by the war. Maimed, orphaned, homeless, sometimes imprisoned, they lived their lives in war-shattered landscapes, in orphanages or in care facilities. In that context, many had been reduced to begging, stealing or prostitution. Assessing their needs and coming to their aid was an urgent task. On December 11, 1946, the newly created United Nations established UNICEF to address and alleviate the desperate needs of these children. Its relief effort was aided by UNESCO which, in the preamble to its constitution, declared that "since wars begin in the minds of men, it is in the minds of men that the defenses of peace must be constructed."[1]

In this postwar period, organizations such as Magnum and UNESCO became instrumental in defining photography as a universal language that would help to construct those defenses. Believing that photography was a language everyone could understand, UNESCO decided to communicate its message through exhibitions, photobooks, and magazines. From today's perspective, the humanistic idea of a universal photographic language capable of building peace seems somewhat naive, overly optimistic, and Western-centric, but it was certainly welcome in a world still reeling from World War II's destruction and chaos.

On March 10, 1948, Chim received a telegram from John Grierson, then deputy director of UNICEF: "when are you returning paris. Most anxious discuss immediate photographic journey to eastern European countries Grierson."[2] Immediately he was assigned as a "special consultant" to photograph the condition of European children who had survived the war, and to show UNICEF in action as it provided 13 million children with necessities such as powdered milk, soup, and shoes, as well as vaccinations against tuberculosis and other diseases.

Other photographers, such as Werner Bischof, and, most notably, Thérèse Bonney, had covered the topic of children during the war. Bonney's book *Europe's Children* (1943), the precursor of Chim's *Children of Europe*, was geared to an American audience, and had been shot in Western and Northern Europe during the war. Through its stark images and urgent captions, the book made a strong emotional appeal to viewers. Chim's photographs, though also humanitarian in spirit, have a different, more hopeful feeling because they were shot in the post-war reconstruction

---

[1] UNESCO Constitution, http://portal.unesco.org/en/ev.php-URL_ID=15244&URL_DO=DO_TOPIC&URL_SECTION=201.html, accessed July 18, 2021.
[2] DSA.

period, and also because he worked in Eastern Europe, where he had strong emotional ties.³

Just before Chim left Paris on his UNESCO trip, Dita Camacho, an editor at *Life*, sent him a letter she had received from Bill Churchill, *Life*'s editor-in-chief:

> Re UNESCO children story: that is an idea we have been kicking around here for quite a while, but never have been able to find a photographer with enough time to even attempt it. Can you assure UNESCO and Seymour that we're definitely interested in it and would like to have first look (…) I am sure that if Dave has the time and can travel sufficiently, he is bound to get a good story.⁴

Chim was the ideal candidate for such a mission. He had always possessed a special empathy for the most vulnerable, which he had first shown during the Spanish Civil War when he photographed the conflict's impact on the civilian population, women, and children.

The UNESCO assignment became a labor of love. Instead of his usual $100 a day fee, Chim accepted $2,600 for a job that would end up taking him over six months, bringing him to five countries (Greece, Italy, Austria, Hungary, and Poland). Not only did he shoot 257 rolls of film⁵—considerably more than the assignment required—but he went well beyond illustrating UNICEF's work and succeeded in creating a deeper, broader portrait of the children living through the chaos of post-war Europe.

As always, the children were the most vulnerable victims of a conflict that had raged for six years. Many of them had known nothing in their lives but war. In 1946, UNESCO had estimated that 8 million children in Germany, 6.5 million children in the Soviet Union, and 1.3 million children in France remained homeless. The numbers were staggering: 1,700,000 orphans in Poland, with 100,000 in Warsaw alone; 50,000 in Czechoslovakia; 200,000 in Hungary with an additional 100,000 homeless. In Greece, one out of every eight children was an orphan. In Italy also, the numbers were enormous: 40,000 *scuscia* or street children in Milan; 65,000 in Rome; and 75,000 in Naples, part of the three million homeless children in Italy.⁶

These abandoned children had spent their first years in underground shelters, bombed streets, ghettos on fire, refugee trains, and concentration camps. They had grown up in a world of fear. Living in groups, many were active in the black market and pilfered so they could live. The girls frequently had no other choice than to sell

---

3 For a detailed comparison between Chim and Thérèse Bonney's respective books, see the excellent 2019 analysis by Jane H. Pierce *A Humanitarian Lens: The World War II Era Photobooks of Thérèse Bonney and David Seymour*, https://academicworks.cuny.edu/hc_sas_etds/421/, accessed August 20, 2021, retrieved October 5, 2020.
4 DSA, letter from Bill Churchill to Dita Camacho, March 4, 1948.
5 Numbers from https://www.magnumphotos.com/newsroom/society/david-seymour-children-of-europe/, accessed August 11, 2021.
6 "Somewhere in Europe: A Photographer Highlights the Drama of Post-War Youngsters," *UNESCO Courier* 2, no. 1 (February 1949), 5–9.

cigarettes or turn to prostitution. The "Letter to a Grown-up", the short introduction to the book Chim published with UNESCO in French and English versions,[7] was written in the voice of a child but most probably by a UNESCO employee. It reminds us that we should not pass judgement: "The day-to-day struggle for individual survival was our book of morals. Do not be surprised, then, by what we are today."

In black and white close-ups or group pictures, most taken with his Rollei but some with the Leica, Chim photographed children as young as four or five years old, and as old as 17, in a variety of settings: hospitals and orphanages, prisons and camps, schools and farms, dormitories, workshops, factories, and fields. He did not avoid the tragic side of their lives, showing the horrific wounds they had suffered in the war. He showed their vulnerability as they slept on rubber tires, in jute sugar bags, behind fragile partitions fashioned out of blankets. Yet he did not idealize them: he showed their involvement in petty crimes, in begging, selling cigarettes on the black market and their bodies on the street. He witnessed their arrest and sentencing in juvenile courts, their detention in reformatories.

In Chim's photographs, the violence is subtle, but it is unmistakably there—inscribed in the children's expressions and in the physical appearance of the cities in ruins: Monte Cassino's gaping arches, Warsaw's destroyed ghetto, the broken-winged horse statue at Berlin's Brandenburg Gate. It is a world where the paucity of material possessions is supplemented by ingeniousness. It is still a world where a measure of harmony can be brought through games, music, study, and social experiments such as the new factories' kindergartens or children's towns.

Chim first visited Greece, which had been occupied first by the Italians and then by the Germans, and where a fierce partisan resistance had occurred.[8] In 1946, while the rest of Europe was starting to rebuild itself, Greece entered this second war, more vicious than the one against the Axis powers. It tore Greece apart. Out of a population of a little over seven million, close to 150,000 perished. One million became homeless (figure 72). In a controversial decision that the Communist Provisional Democratic Government of Greece adopted in the name of "saving the children from the horrors of war,"[9] around 28,000 Macedonian and Greek children were evacuated from the areas affected by military actions. The original plan was for them to stay in Eastern European countries for a short time, but they were exiled for a decade.

Greek public opinion turned against the communist leadership because of that controversial evacuation. When a vehemently right-wing, anti-communist military

---

7 *Children of Europe* (Paris: Unesco, 1949), 60 p., with unsigned text (probably written by a UNESCO staff member following Chim's notes) and 55 photographs by Chim.
8 MPNYA, ADS UNESCO, 1948, contacts #48-22-2 to 48-23-74 (story has 23 Leica contacts and 43 Rollei contacts).
9 Katerina Mirčevska, "The Children evacuated from Greece in 1948: to the Eastern European countries and Yugoslavia," *Politeja* #30, (Krakow: Księgarnia Akademicka, 2014), 79–88. https://www.jstor.org/stable/24919715, accessed August 11, 2020.

establishment won the war, Greece became the only country in the Balkans and Eastern Europe where communism had attempted to take power and failed.

Chim covered the evacuation of children who were being sent either to the island of Leros or to Eastern Europe[10] in a dramatic sequence of pictures. He showed children crying as they were separated from their families and loaded onto trucks, then queueing, supervised by nurses, to board an enormous ship, the Samos. In the dim light of the ship's hull, he photographed the crowd resting or sleeping on the floor; then he went up to the deck and made a sweeping view of hundreds of children standing in rows.[11] Later on, he focused on a group looking on as one girl reads a letter from home. The frame is packed to the brim with the children's anxious or hopeful faces. Further on, a young boy props his head on his elbows as he looks up, expectant, dazed, or simply dreaming.[12]

He traveled through the country, photographing in black and white. In the village of Promahi in Macedonia, near the Yugoslavian border, Chim portrayed a family sharing a modest meal in their home. While the mother ladles food to the children who sit on the floor, the father sits on a low stool, holding a gun.[13] In Igoumenitza, a port southwest of Saloniki, he made a series of photographs of a woman holding her baby in a wooden crib as she breastfeeds him. In another tender image, taken from above in the village of Andartikon, an Orthodox priest bathes a baby in a small bucket. Chim caught his hands in movement as they hovered over the baby's wet head.[14]

In the preface of the book that Chim published the following year, it is noted that "In Greece nine-tenths of the schools were destroyed and 200,000 children are unable to attend primary school. In classrooms that are much too small, there is only one textbook or desk for three or four pupils."[15]

Chim made it a priority to document the efforts that were being made to reestablish education. In Dionata, the school was too small to host the 250 children at the same time and they had to attend classes in two shifts. Chim photographed classes improvised in a village house with hastily assembled tables and benches. In the nursery, babies were sleeping, two in each crib. In a village near Odessa, the children's desks had been thrown out into the yard. In Chortiatis, a mountain village burned down by the Germans in retaliation for partisan acts, school was held in a church and children did their gymnastics outdoors: lined up in rows, their feet

---

10 MPNYA, ADS UNESCO, 48-23-1, # 2-1.
11 MPNYA, for instance NYC119551, NYC119310.
12 MPNYA, NYC100972, PAR152477.
13 MPNYA, ADS UNESCO, 48-23-11, #2-11 to 2-27 and MPNYA, NYC100971.
14 MPNYA, ADS UNESCO, 48-22-19, #G 19 and MPPA, PAR116251.
15 *Children of Europe* (Paris: UNESCO, 1949), 60 p., with unsigned text and 55 photographs by Chim.

planted apart, they lift their arms while in the background their burned-out school stands like a theater set, with rows of empty windows open to the sky.[16]

During his long visit to Ioannina, Chim shot 24 rolls of medium-format and several rolls of 35mm pictures in a large refugee camp made of tattered tents. There he recorded the everyday life of the adults and children who were refugees from the civil war zones. The families seemed discouraged and apathetic, filled with anxiety for their future; scores of children had already died from malnutrition, disease, and injuries. Conditions improved somewhat when UNICEF sent a team of ten scoutmasters from Athens to help clean up and reorganize the camp, where hygiene had been a major problem.[17]

Chim made emotional close-up portraits of mothers and children in the camp, including one showing a tiny toddler, nestled in his mother's arms, with a metal bowl in his grip. In one family's tent he shot a family in their tent and made close-ups of a mother ladling food into her baby's expectant mouth. As groups of older children played, another mother bathed her young son in a wooden tub. Documenting a distribution of food packets, he photographed a UNICEF employee who ladled condensed milk powder mixed with water into children's cups, as some of them watched hesitantly before deciding to drink. Further on, sugar jute sacks dried on a line before being used as improvised bedding.[18]

Back in Athens, Chim photographed a team of nurses giving outdoor vaccinations to fearful children and some adults, while further away on a hill, a group of girls danced in a circle and a large group of other children organized a parade and held a gymnastics contest. These joyous and energetic scenes were a welcome antidote to the sadness he had witnessed in the camp.[19]

In the preface to his 1949 book *Children of Europe* published by UNESCO (figure 76), the unidentified writer, maybe Chim, wrote several commentaries about the social experiments involving children that he witnessed, such as this one:

> Everywhere abandoned children are gradually ceasing to live in isolation and are preparing themselves to enter the true social community among men, among their compatriots. Before leaving the Village, we must have made good the years of schooling which we have lost, learned a trade, and even begun to practice it. Everything has been tried, all methods have been applied, every kind of experiment made.[20]

---

16 MPNYA, ADS UNESCO, 48-23-29, # 2-39.
17 MPNYA, for instance PAR190984, PAR158681, PAR190988.
18 MPNYA, ADS UNESCO, 48-23-45, #2-45, 2-46, 2-47; 48-23-50, 2-50 to 2-53.
19 MPNYA, ADS UNESCO, 48-23-66, #2-66.
20 *Children of Europe* (Paris: UNESCO, 1949), 60 p., with unsigned text and 55 photographs by Chim.

Italy was his next destination.[21] In Naples[22] where about 75,000 street children struggled to survive, he photographed a pathetic children's orchestra playing at a café in Galleria Umberto, while a small child on crutches collected a few coins from the public. [23] A little girl named Angela, no more than eight years old, peddled black-market American soap and cigarettes to sailors. A boy, acting as a pimp for his sister, discussed arrangements with them. [24] At a crowded beach, a Neapolitan *mamma* posed happily, hand on hip, feet in the waves, surrounded by her children. Naked children played with improvised toys or beer bottle caps in the narrow, humid streets. In a happier image, Chim photographed the portrait of a young boy apprenticed to an open-air shoemaker's shop. While he hammers at a sole, he gives the photographer a wistful look, a small smile. Meanwhile, a bunch of small kids hangs off the back of a streetcar, as in a scene reminiscent of Rossellini's film *Rome, Open City*, which had been released in 1946.[25]

Some of Chim's best Naples photographs were taken at the Albergo dei Pobre,[26] a big complex in the center of town containing several orphanages, a reformatory, and a juvenile tribunal. At the end of the war, the Albergo, a palatial building built in 1752 by King Charles III of Naples and Sicily, had been turned into a reformatory where young vagrants, prostitutes, and thieves were placed by order of the juvenile court. More than 400 boys worked in a variety of workshops and attended school there.

For this story, Chim used both his Leica and Rollei. In the court, he focused on a nine-year-old boy who had been raped by an 18-year-old and was listening to the reading of the deposition he had made at the police station. Another girl, an 18-year-old who had been accused of poisoning her father and already spent time in prison, was pleading not guilty. Working with the Leica, he followed the girls at recess in the yard, where they joined in a ring, then sat in a circle under the care of a nun wearing a full habit. With his Rollei, he photographed the boys' orchestra and gymnastics session, and the children in gray uniforms lined up in rows as if—somewhat ironically—for a family portrait (figure 66).

Boys and girls were kept in separate buildings and the girls were taught embroidery by Catholic nuns who saw this type of work as both educational and redemptive. In the room where the girls were sewing, Chim was drawn towards the oldest, an adolescent. According to the caption she had been raped, but subsequent captions often identify her mistakenly as a young prostitute. Her beautiful face bears a haunted expression; a patch of light rests on her body as well as her embroidery and

---

21 MPNYA, ADS UNESCO, 48-25-22 to 48-35-37 (Rollei) and 48-24-3 to 48-24-13 (Leica).
22 MPNYA, ADS UNESCO, for instance 48-24-1, 48-25-2, 48-25-5.
23 MPNYA, NYC131491.
24 MPPA, PAR114458.
25 MPPA, PAR114516, PAR191229.
26 MPNYA, ADS UNESCO, for instance 48-25-6, 48-25-7, 48-25-8, 48-25-9, 48-25-10. Girl sewing: 48-25-8, picture #86.

briefly illuminates her left cheek. Behind her, a soiled wall marked with scratches speaks of the palace's lost splendor. The shot's slight blurriness lends it a dreamlike quality, giving it a power beyond literal documentation (figure 67).

Looking at Chim's contact sheet, from each image to the next, we can follow him around the room as slowly, silently, with cat-like movement, he explores one face after another in tight frames. Though he was far from tall, the contacts indicate that he must have crouched to be at the children's height. In the text he wrote for his story, Chim regretfully noted the unwanted sad effect his presence had on the children: "For the photographer's benefit, toys were handed to the children by the sister in charge. But there were too few toys or too many children, and in the fight to possess them some were broken. The toys were then collected—by force—and given to another group whose turn it was to be photographed, and finally, once all the photos had been taken, the toys were taken back again, despite the children's piercing protests."

One photograph shows the girls seated in a row as if in a classroom, wearing loose, drab uniforms. It's the only group shot in the series: Except for that frame, Chim preferred to isolate his subjects, as if to echo their own solitude and alienation. While none of them smile, the girls return the photographer's attentive gaze with seriousness and maybe a hint of hope, perhaps feeling that they have been seen apart from the rigid penal system that controls them, recognized and respectfully singled out as individuals. We feel that Chim is questioning the punitive aspect of the institution that judges the children without understanding them, fails to take their needs into account, and finally hardens them rather than helping them to integrate into society.

Each photographic square in the contact sheet carves a hole into the scene and draws the viewer into the mystery of these young faces, as if Chim the photographer had somehow managed to open a brief window of light into the post-war darkness of the room, and of their souls.

In Matera, in the Lucania province, Chim explored the troglodyte village where 400 homeless families had tunneled holes into the soft chalk rock and erected primitive wood shacks where they lived in abject poverty. An inner room, behind the main room, was reserved for their animals. Even though their conditions were harsh, they told Chim that they liked living in the grottos because they were warm in winter and cool in summer.[27] Chim made a beautiful portrait of a girl leading her family's horse from the fields to the cave. With the knotted rope of the rein thrown over her shoulder, she tilts her head back and laughs in happiness.

In Rome Chim shot some of his most poignant pictures at the Villa Savoia,[28] an institution sheltering children maimed by war and by accidents resulting from caused by mines and left-over surplus ammunition. In his remarkable pictures, a

---

27 MPNYA, DSC, "Europe's Children, Italy," #19-4.
28 MPNYA, ADS UNESCO, 48-25-13 to 48-25-15.

group of boys who have lost limbs happily play ball in the sunshine. Chim chose to depict their zest for life rather than their handicap, attentive to the way they seem to forget their wounds and get lost in the moment, in their game. In a striking close-up, a blind boy without arms shows extreme concentration as he reads a Braille book with his lips. Without the caption, we would not know that he has no arms. Chim has kept them out of the image and focused on the act of reading as restorative. It is typical of him to suggest rather than demonstrate, and to focus on the positive aspects of the children's lives, on the fact that they are trying to take charge, rather than simply showing them as victims.

In Bari, on the Adriatic coast, Chim did a story on an orphanage where the children were well cared for, clad in nice white outfits and sun hats. He made beautiful group shots of the children in an outside structure with the straw threads of its roof throwing parallel shadows on their heads.[29]

On his way back to Rome, Chim stopped at Monte Cassino, where street kids made a living by collecting shrapnel and mortar shells that they resold to scrap metal buyers, sometimes losing limbs in the process (figure 70). The destroyed abbey and black silhouettes of bombed buildings make a striking background to these scenes. In one of the images, three boys proudly pose with the result of their daily scavenging: shells piled at their feet like monstrous vegetables. Further on, a nun in full habit plays ball with a group of girls in the ruins of their former orphanage.[30]

After photographing a group of boys singing, he wrote one of their favorite songs in his notebook, calling it "a rather frightening commentary of the young generation":

> I went to the market, and I bought a little flute-flu-flu-flu, I bought a little flute.
> I went to the market and bought a tambourine-rat-rat-rat, I bought a tambourine (...)

And so on, through a trombone, which goes tra-tra-tra, to a pistol, which goes pouf-pouf-pouf, and then a rifle, and then a cannon. The last verse ran:

> I went to the market and bought a bomba atomica -boom-boom-boom-a bomba atomica![31]

His last Italian story, a more hopeful one, was shot in Civitavecchia, not far from Rome. A priest named Don Antonio Rivolta had founded Santa Marinella, a village for gangs of vagrant children living off plunder, to help them find a kind of normalcy. They had their own houses and lived there in self-sufficiency, electing their own mayor and deputies. Artisans taught them a craft in various workshops. After the war, a number of similar experiences in independent living took place all over Europe.[32]

---

29 MPNYA, ADS UNESCO, 48-24-10 to 48-25-33.
30 MPNYA, PAR116038 and ADS UNESCO, 48-25-26 to 48-25-31.
31 MPNYA, DST, text for UNESCO Story.
32 For instance, in Moulin-Vieux in France, in Torino, in Pestalozzi's village in Florence, in Hungary, in Marcellino and Trogen in Switzerland, in Apeldoorn in Holland. See David Niget "Pieds nus

Chim's reportage on Italy shares its vivid style and stark but tender view of humanity with the Italian neorealist films of the time, such as *Bicycle Thief* by Vittorio de Sica, and Roberto Rossellini's *Germany Year Zero* and *Rome, Open City*. He was familiar with these films since he had started photographing actors and producers such as Roberto Rossellini and Ingrid Bergman from the Cinecittà studios, which had emerged as a major location for filmmaking and had been nicknamed Hollywood on the Tiber.

Moving on to Austria,[33] Chim visited a prison for juvenile delinquents in Vienna, where he learned that the increase in juvenile crime was huge. More than 4,000 cases a year were brought to the court, the most common involving petty theft, prostitution, and robbery. "Living conditions have turned normal children into thieves," Chim comments. "Most of the cases in this prison were concerned with stealing food."[34]

He photographed the court in session, with the judging of a 12-year-old boy who had been sentenced to three months in prison for theft, and then the inside of the cells. Under a large window, three older prisoners are absorbed in a game of chess; a younger boy lies on a narrow bed or sits on the window sill, looking outside, gripping the bars. In all of these portraits, shot in medium format, Chim photographed the children and teens from the back, or left their faces in shadows, keeping them anonymous so that he would not re-victimize them, and the images are permeated by a sense of hopelessness, endless waiting, time standing still.[35]

Next he visited an old, half-destroyed arsenal that was housing displaced persons from the Sudentenland.[36] The adults in the community had started to rebuild it and they had created a nursery that they ran themselves. The conditions were harsh: children sleeping in lines of crude wooden beds that look like troughs; five children sleeping on the ground under a single blanket. In the nursery, he focused on a group of small girls who sat on the wooden floor under high windows, their faces and the floor flooded with light. They hold rudimentary dolls made of rags, but rather than simply holding the toys, they seem to be clinging to them. Either because of the harsh light or her deep sadness, the face of one little girl is etched in a mute grimace.[37]

In that same orphanage Chim made one of his most famous images: leaning on a wooden table, a girl holds a chunk of bread in her left hand.[38] Behind her, in the

---

dans les ruines: le regard de Chim sur les enfants de la guerre," *Rhei, Revue d'histoire de l'enfance irrégulière (2013)*.https://journals.openedition.org/rhei/3504, 2013, 143–145, I-IV.
33 He shot 40 rolls with Rollei and 14 rolls with Leica.
34 MPNYA, DSC, "Europe's Children- Austria, Delinquency", #1-40.
35 MPNYA, NN11469811, NYC100956, NYC100957.
36 A province in northern Czechoslovakia, bordering Germany, that Germany wanted to include in its territory during the war. See MPNY archive, ADS, UNESCO.
37 MPPA, PAR114509.
38 MPPA, PAR152481.

shadows, other faces are crowded. Her forlorn expression tells us that this chunk of bread cannot sate her hunger. It is that deep-seated need that Chim depicts through the faces he photographs, a need so great that it goes beyond words. The emotions he captures shine through the children's faces from one picture to the next, revealing lives pared down to the necessities of survival.[39]

In his text for the book, the writer comments: "UNICEF prepares 100,000 hot lunches every day that are distributed in Viennese schools. The meat and vegetable soup is given by UNICEF and the bread by the Austrian government. 400,000 Austrian children receive food from UNICEF- all kids under six."[40]

Chim visited a camp for parentless children, Russian, English, French, and American, often the result of rapes. A private institution, it was run by the Vienna community, which received UNICEF food and other Allied relief, and it was well maintained, with 15 nurses caring for 93 children under three. In Chim's photographs, the children seem well-dressed and well cared for by the affectionate nurses who hold them in their arms or supervise play time.[41]

Chim also worked in hospitals and clinics. In Vienna, where tuberculosis cases had grown by 50 per cent after the war, he photographed a hospital for tubercular children in the Bellevue neighborhood, documenting the doctor as he made his rounds with a stethoscope, as well as children getting ready for tuberculosis vaccinations. One remarkable portrait shows a young girl with tuberculosis of the spine (figure 10). Standing between two beds and supporting herself with the tips of her fingers, she wears a laced surgical corset. But what Chim has caught is her luminous smile, her improbable joy.[42]

After photographing the banners and crowds at a May 1 demonstration, Chim documented food distribution in a school; in his text he says that he was aiming for "symbolic pictures."[43] Doctors examining the children there divided them into three categories: healthy, not so healthy, and six kilos underweight. A third of Vienna's children, severely undernourished, were classified in that third category. In a photograph taken from a bird's-eye view, a crowd of children waiting for their food seems to overflow the frame, as each child holds an empty enameled cup towards the viewer. The repetition of the gesture and the worried expressions on the children's faces have a claustrophobic intensity.[44]

As he walked around the ruined city, Chim spotted a group of children playing in the destroyed former Gestapo HQ, climbing up heaps of debris and ruined stairways, and perching on columns (figure 69). In Favoriten, a working-class neighborhood, he focused on a boy who, with pieces of wood and cardboard, had built an

---

39 DSC: Austria-Sudeten DPs 1-53 and 1-90. # 48-21-5, 48-21-6, 48-21-8.
40 MPNYA, DST, "Europe's Children, Austria."
41 MPNYA, ADS UNESCO, 48-29-9, 48-29-10, 48-9-11.
42 MPNYA, ADS UNESCO, 48-29-12 & 48-29-17.
43 MPNYA, ADS UNESCO 1948, text by Chim, "Europe's Children, Austria."
44 MPNYA, ADS UNESCO, 48-21-20 to 48-21-23 and NYC100961.

Indian village on top of the large rubble of a destroyed wall.[45] Werner Bischof, who would become Chim's colleague at Magnum, had photographed a very similar scene three years earlier in Freibourg-en-Brisgau, Germany.[46]

At a shoe repair depot organized by Swedish Aid, the Swedes imported machines and paste to repair a daily total of 200 pairs of second-hand shoes sent from Switzerland and Sweden to ensure that children would not go barefoot during the winter.[47] As he had done with the destroyed typewriter in Gijon ten years earlier, Chim composed a still life of a pile of donated shoes full of holes.[48] Then he photographed a family: a mother and eight children, with only one pair of shoes between them. Sometimes it is the indirect view that works best.

In early August, back in Rome for a short breather, Chim was weary. Still, he found the time to write his family before starting out on the last leg of his UNESCO assignment: "This evening I am leaving for Zürich and from there am flying to Prague, from there I will go on to Poland and Hungary. So as you see, there is no end of moving around (...) It is still 2 months to run around and somehow I am not very happy about it."[49]

Despite these doubts, Hungary would turn out to be the country where Chim showed the most optimistic spirit. Rather than depicting the children's sufferings, he chose to focus on situations where they showed self-reliance, strength, and initiative.

In early September he arrived in Hajduhadhaz,[50] a town that had undertaken a remarkable experiment in autonomy: 350 boys and girls, orphans who were vagabond or delinquent, were being trained to live in a self-sufficient way in a camp that they considered home. They elected their own government, mayor, and municipal council, cultivated the land, took care of their animals, went to school, and learned a trade with professional instructors. Again, Chim's images showed the joyful energy of children in their workplaces, such as carpentry or shoemaking workshops; in a printing workshop where they learned to print books; doing agricultural work; attending open-air classes; or sewing their own clothes.

He focused especially on social experiments involving children and on the teachers' ingenuity. In a Szeged high school, the teachers without lab equipment for their physics and chemistry classes devised substitutes for beakers, such as old light bulbs or empty ink bottles. Weights for a homemade scale were fashioned from pieces of wire; and bottles replaced Bunsen burners. With teachers using the Swiss model of *école du travail* that relied on practical experiments, the children collected plants for natural history lessons, constructed a teaching aid showing different types

---

45 MPNYA, PAR190922.
46 See Carole Naggar, *Werner Bischof, Carnets de Route 1932–1954* (Paris: Delpire, 2008), 57.
47 MPNYA, ADS UNESCO, 48-21-34.
48 MPNYA, NYC131490.
49 DSA, letter dated Rome, August 21, 1948.
50 MPNYA, ADS UNESCO, 1948. See for instance NYC119567 & NYC119566.

of cereals and even assembled a home-made phonograph. One image shows a pupil making a model of his home farm using wool, cotton, and matches in a sand tray. A teacher demonstrated different types of village layouts using models made of wood. Chim photographed the intensity of concentration on the children's faces. Eager to make up for the years they had lost, they were completely focused on their studies.[51]

In a Budapest suburb, Chim visited a kindergarten that received UNICEF milk supplies and photographed a nurse who was walking and playing the violin as the children, fascinated, followed her in a line, as in the Pied Piper story. The airy, dreamlike image feels as if it was drawn from a children's fairy tale.[52]. Working from an elevated point of view, he shot a dramatic image of the destroyed Elizabeth bridge, its deck submerged in the river (figure 68).

In the little village of Pilis, 40 kilometers from Budapest, with a population of 9,000, Chim recorded the first day of school. The villagers have built a small paddling pool connected to a well where a few children paddle and splash while others in the background play with boats built by the village carpenter (figure 73). The whole scene has the feel of a country fair: a merry-go-round adorned with wooden horses; crude swings shaped like boats. For this first day, most of the children are dressed in their Sunday best and Chim focuses on a little blond girl in pigtails who, beset by separation anxiety, clings to her mother's arms. Another child uses chalk for the first time to write on a blackboard, the teacher's hand guiding her while the mothers look on.[53]

Pursuing his work on schools, Chim stopped next in a summer camp that had been set up in a palace on the former estate of the Karolyi family in Foth. Children played football on the palace's grounds and others danced in a circle on a hill over Budapest, with a view of the Margareten Bridge and the river in the background. In another school, in Debrecen, children helped construct a school and a playground. In Fono, a textile factory had started a kindergarten where working mothers could leave their children. In black and white and in color, Chim photographed the kids clambering over climbing bars or bathing in a swimming pool.[54]

In the hills of Buda, Chim did a story in 35mm on a red and white narrow-gauge electric railway that had just been constructed. "The unique thing about this railroad," he wrote, "is that only the engine-driver is an adult; every other function is taken over by children between the ages of 12 and 14."[55] A thousand children, drawn from Budapest schools, had been trained in each aspect of the train's operation. On Sundays, as many as 25,000 people would come to see and visit the station and ride the train. Chim photographed the different parts of the experiment: the station mas-

---

51 MPNYA, ADS UNESCO, 48-27-39 to 48-27-44. NYC119317, NYC119318. MPPA, PAR191337.
52 MPNYA, ADS UNESCO, 48-27-1 to 48-27-6.
53 MPNYA, ADS UNESCO, 48-27 31 to 48-27-33.
54 MPNYA, ADS UNESCO, 48-27-24 to 48-27-30.
55 MPNYA, ADS UNESCO, 48-27-45, 48-27-46.

ter, proudly wearing a gray uniform with red epaulettes and gold buttons, a worker operating a signal switch, a cashier counting money at the ticket office, children operating a miniature telegraph and telephone services or traffic switchboards.[56] "The authorities believe that this practical work has great educational value and the time spent working—which is also play to the children—is profitable for their development."[57]

Back in Budapest, Chim met with his friend Capa who was staying in town for six weeks on assignment for a *Holiday* story for which he would both write the text and take the pictures. The two reported together on an anti-communist demonstration on the Kossuth bridge, across from the Parliament. Capa photographed in medium format and in color and Chim used his Leica for black and white images. The crowd's banner said, "Thanks to the Soviets, you are in peace," an irony not lost on Chim. He later made a portrait of Capa talking to Giörgy Markos, a young painter and journalist who directed the press service for the National Office of the Hungarian Republic.[58] While in Budapest, Chim also photographed Gyula Kacze's gypsy orchestra; Katalin Karady, a Hungarian actress; and Joszi Bencze, one of the last great shoemakers "who talks about shoes as poets talk about women"[59] in his store in Vaci Licca.

The Hungary trip would be the next to last for Capa, who published a long piece in *Holiday*, and Chim was headed to Poland, the country of his birth. It would be the last time that the two friends worked side by side.

---

56 MPPA, PAR159267, PAR159270.MPNYA, NYC119570, NYC119565, NYC119322.
57 MPNYA, DST *Europe's Children, Hungary*.
58 MPPA, PAR347045. For an analysis of Chim's portrait of Robert Capa and Markos, see Bernard Lebrun's unfinished text in his personal archive, *Une rencontre à Budapest*, 1948 (*An encounter in Budapest*). With thanks to Bernard Lebrun.
59 MPNYA, DST, Budapest, no page number.

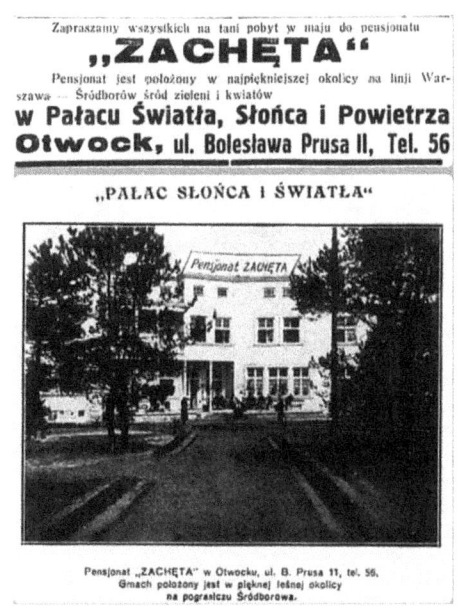

Fig. 21: 1920s newspaper ad for Pensjonat Zachęta, Chim's family's bed and breakfast in Otwock, Poland. Source unknown.

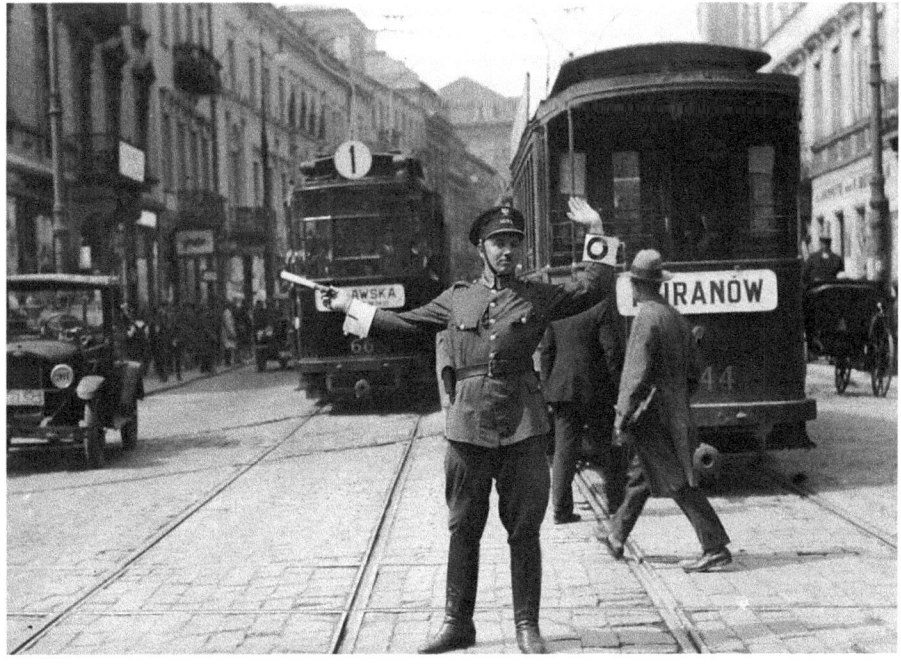

Fig. 22: Street life in Warsaw, 1920s. Photographer unknown.

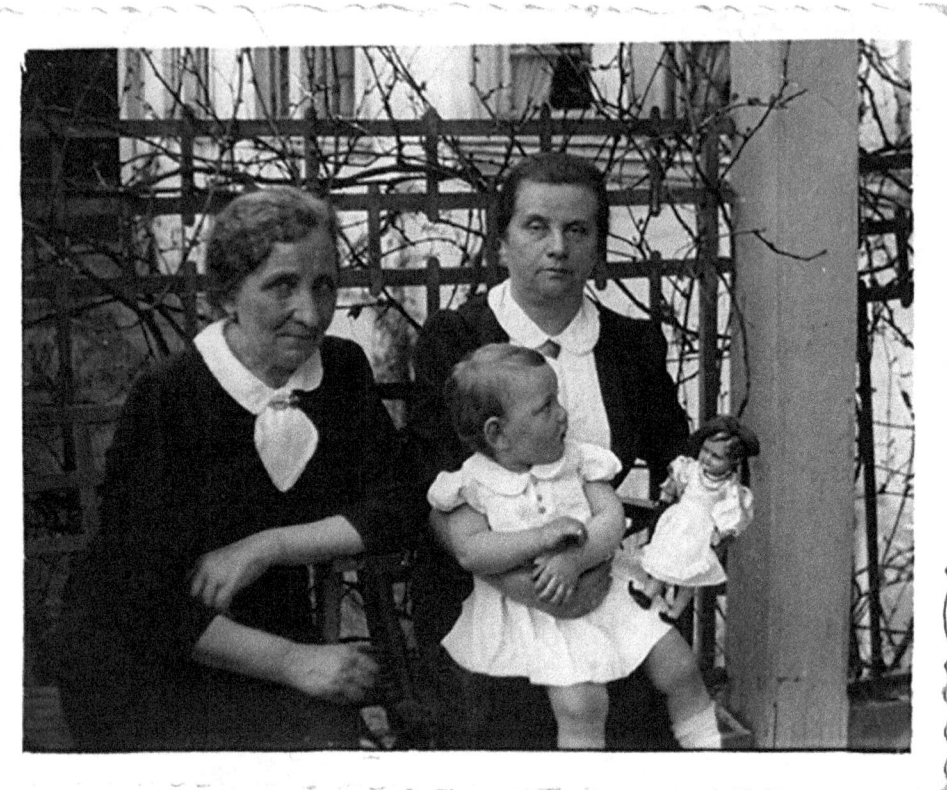

Fig. 23: Chim's sister Hala and her grandmothers, Otwock or Warsaw, Poland, circa 1910. © United States Holocaust Memorial Museum, courtesy of Ben Shneiderman.

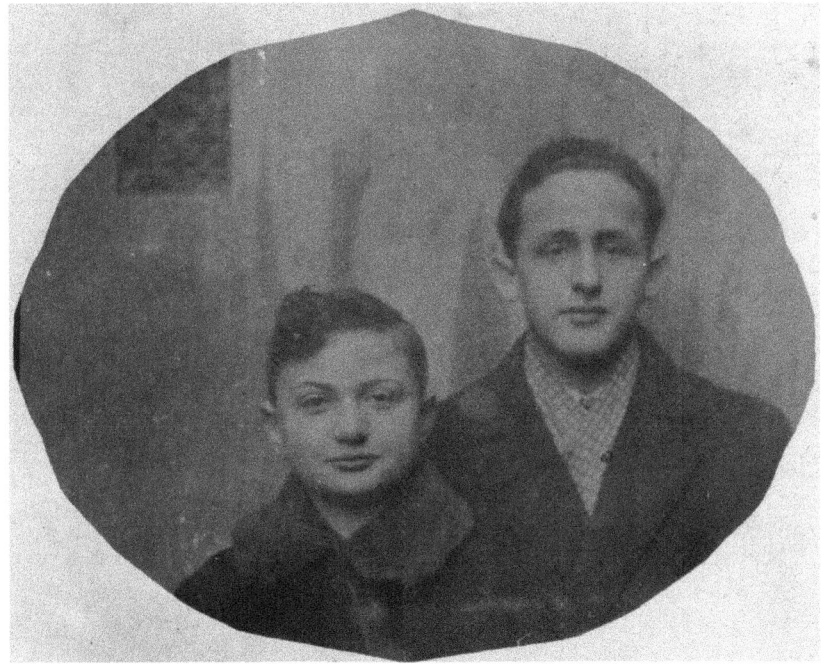

Fig. 24: Portrait of Dawid with his cousin Mendele Segal circa 1919. Collection Ben Shneiderman and Helen Sarid.

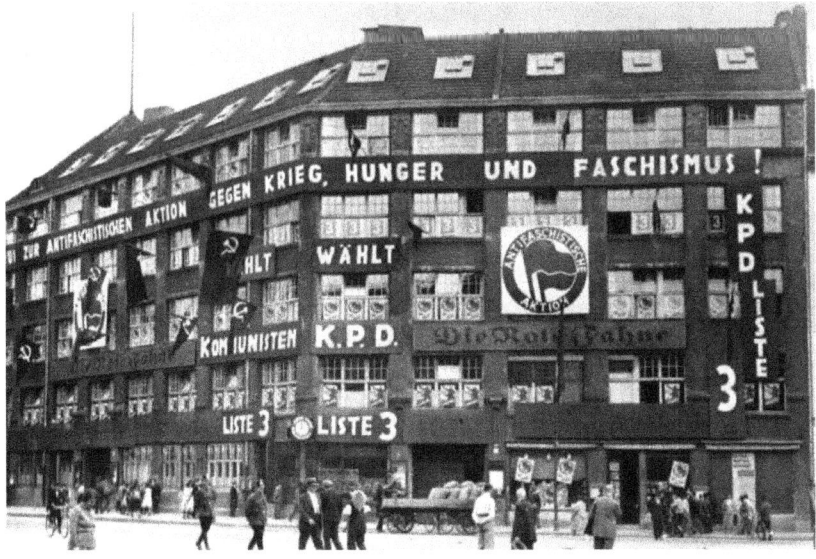

Fig. 25: Headquarters of KPD (Communist Party of Germany) from 1926 to 1933. © Carl Weinrother, 1932.

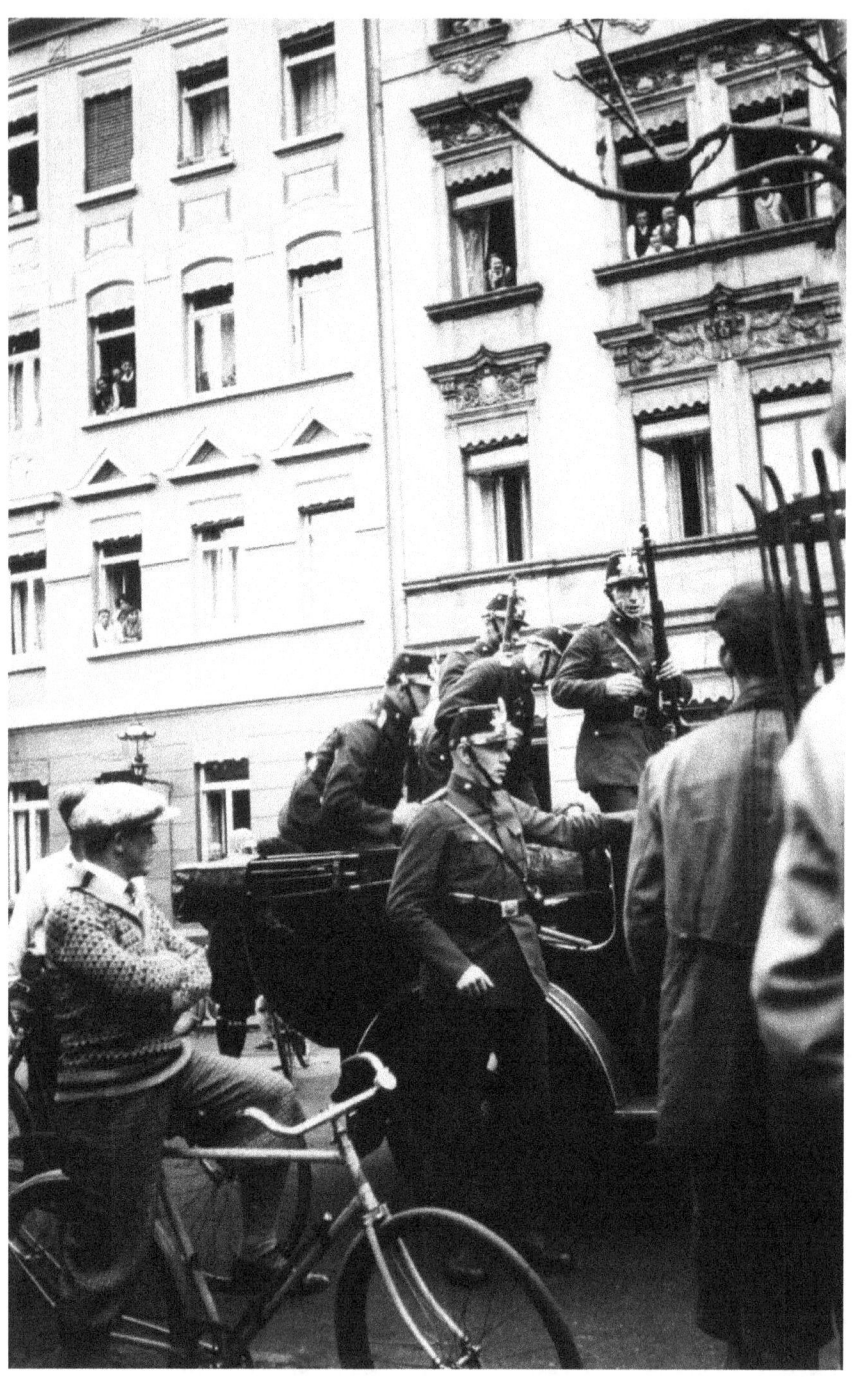

Fig. 26: Units of the Security Forces Deploying for a Speech by Ernst Thälmann in the Congress Hall in Leipzig, Germany. © Albert Hennig, 1929.

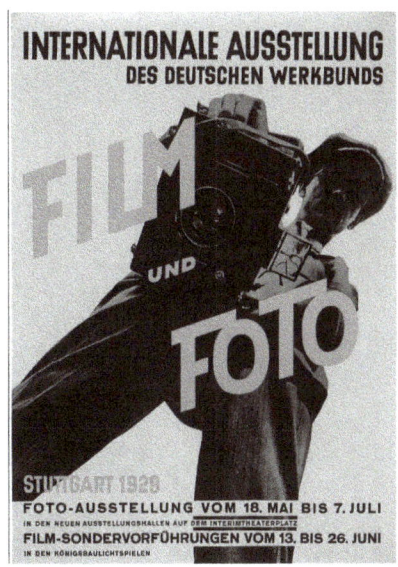

Fig. 27: Poster for Werkbund International Photography Exhibition, Stuttgart, Germany, 1929.

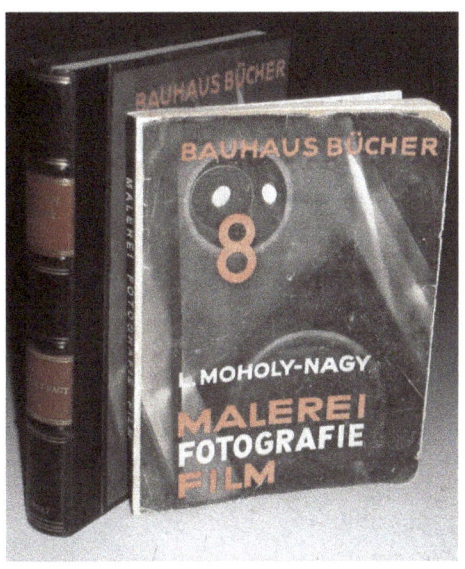

Fig. 28: Original edition of Lazlo Moholy-Nagy's 1925 classic book "Painting, Photography, Film." Photo courtesy Josef Schladek, Vienna.

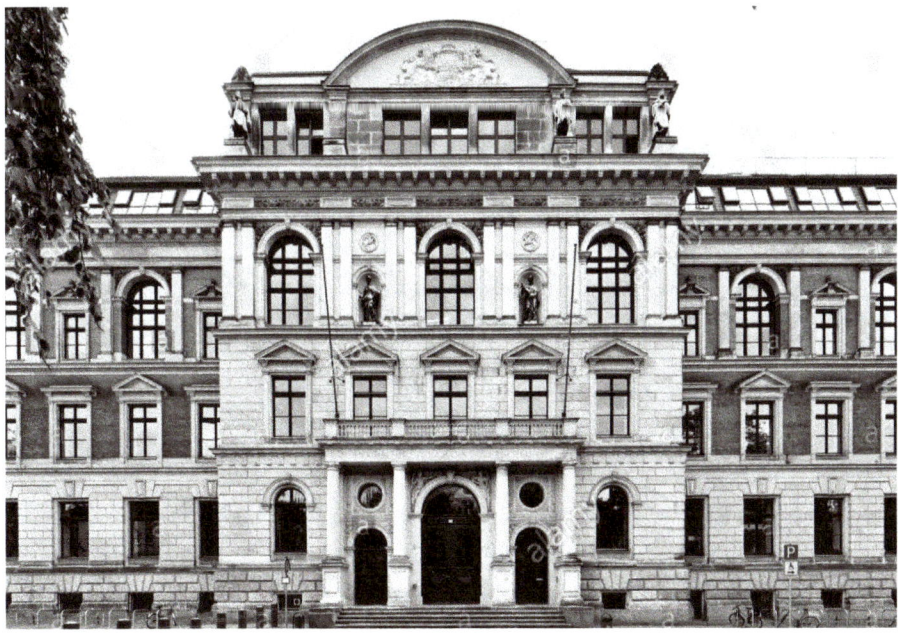

Fig. 29: The Stäatl Akademie für Graphische Kunst und Buchgewerbe (State Academy of Graphic Arts and Book Trade) in Leipzig where Chim studied. © the author, 2009.

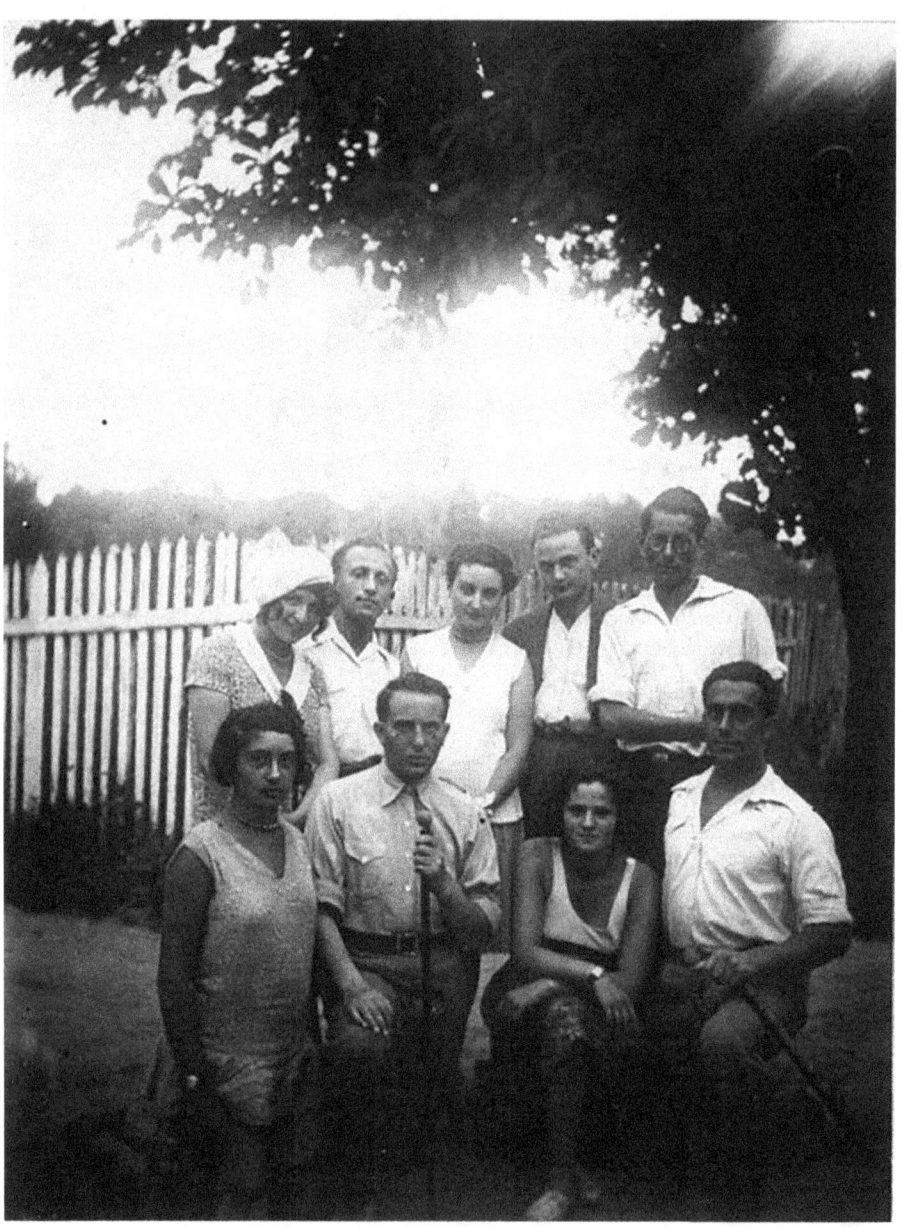

Fig. 30: Chim with friends in Poland (upper row, second from right), 1931-1932. Helen Sarid Archive, Tel Aviv.

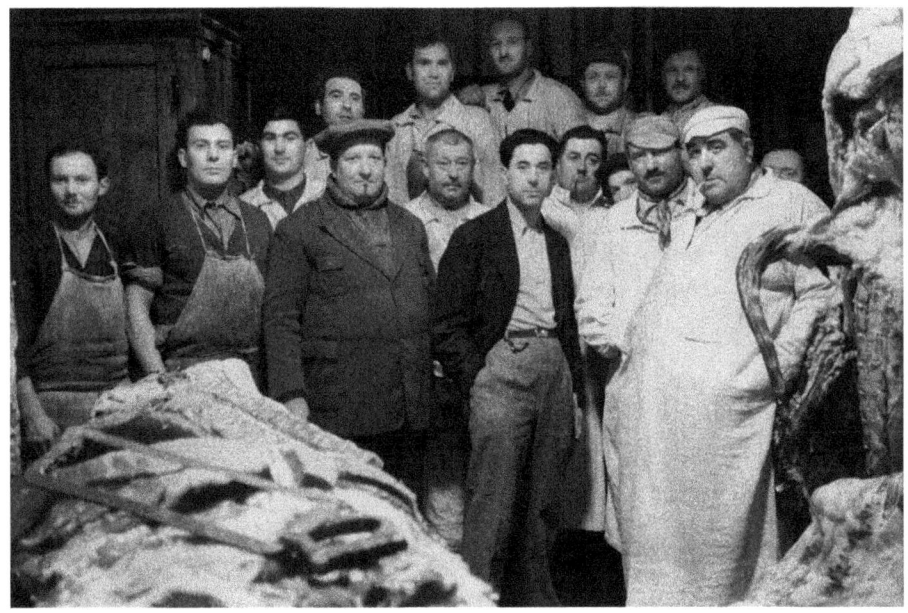

Fig. 31: Butchers. Paris, Les Halles, 1933. © David Seymour-Magnum Photos.

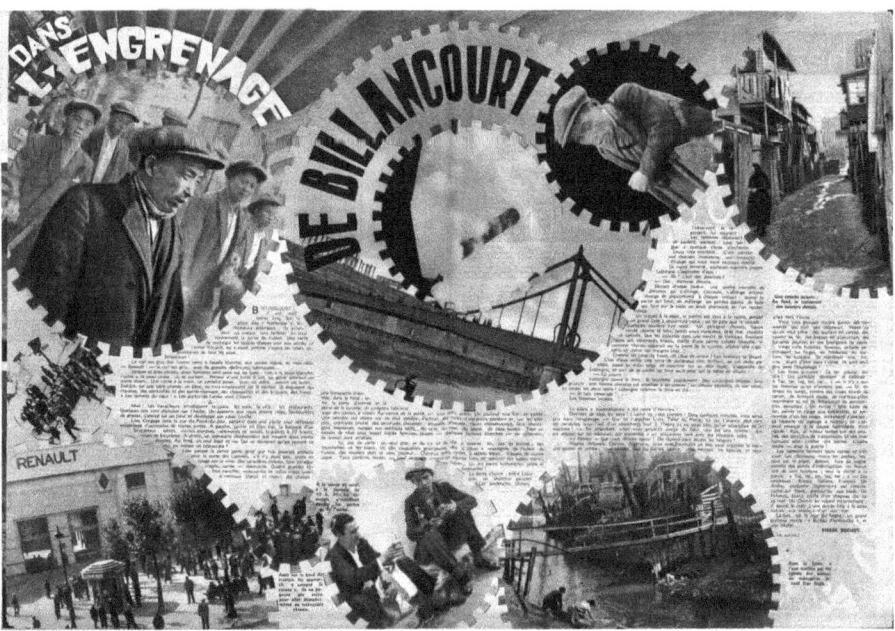

Fig. 32: Double page of Chim's reportage *Dans l'engrenage de Billancourt* (in Billancourt's Mesh). Regards, April 6, 1934. © Bibliothèque Nationale de France (gallica.bnf.fr).

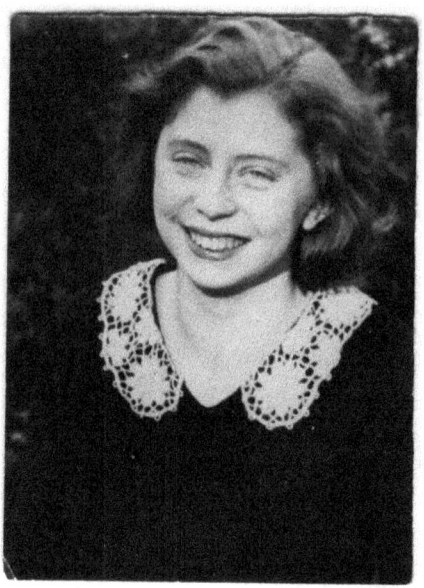

Fig. 33: Portrait of Emma, stamped Paris 1934. © davidseymour.com online archive.

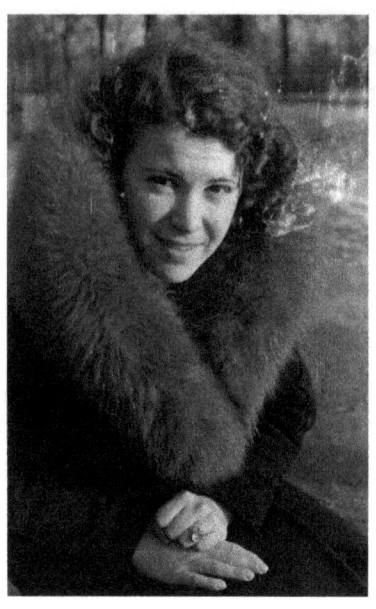

Fig. 34: Portrait of Bianka, 1932. © davidseymour.com online archive.

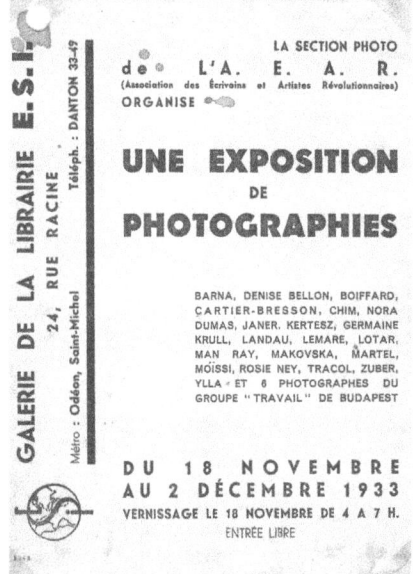

Fig. 35: Brochure for AEAR group exhibition, Paris, 1933. © davidseymour.com online archive.

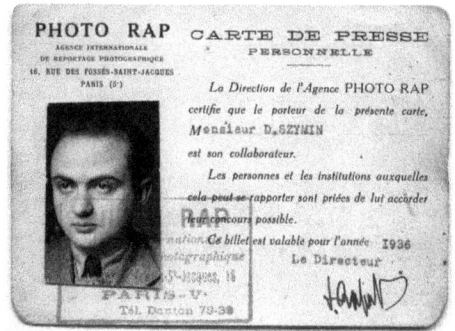

Fig. 36: Chim's press card with Photo Rap agency, Paris, 1936. © davidseymour.com online archive.

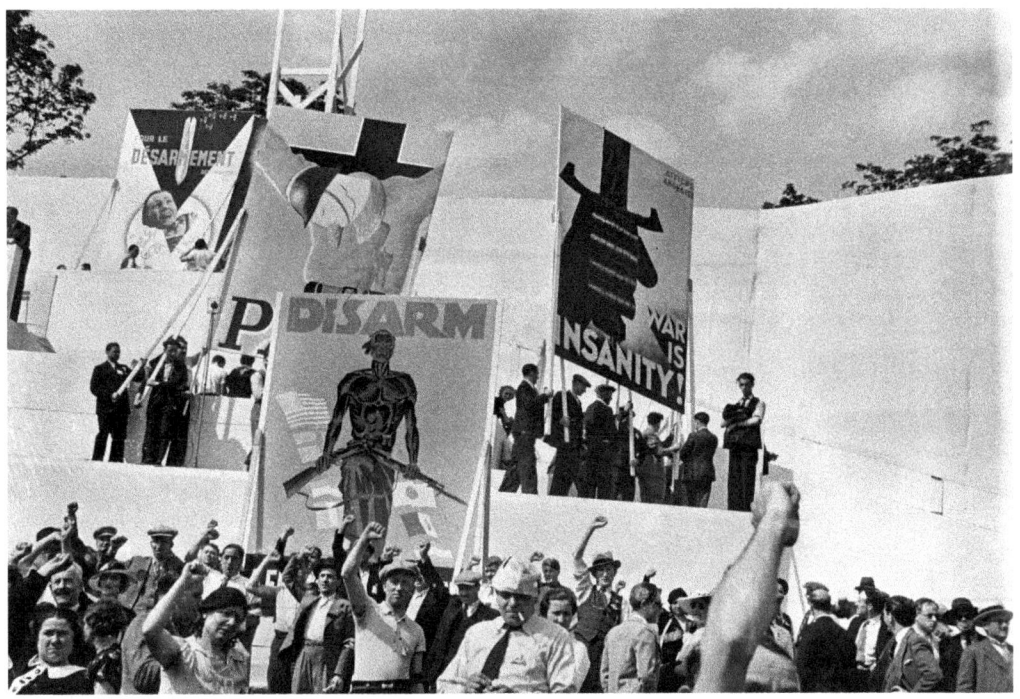

Fig. 37: Pacifist meeting for the disarmament of nations. Saint-Cloud near Paris, August 9, 1936. © David Seymour-Magnum Photos.

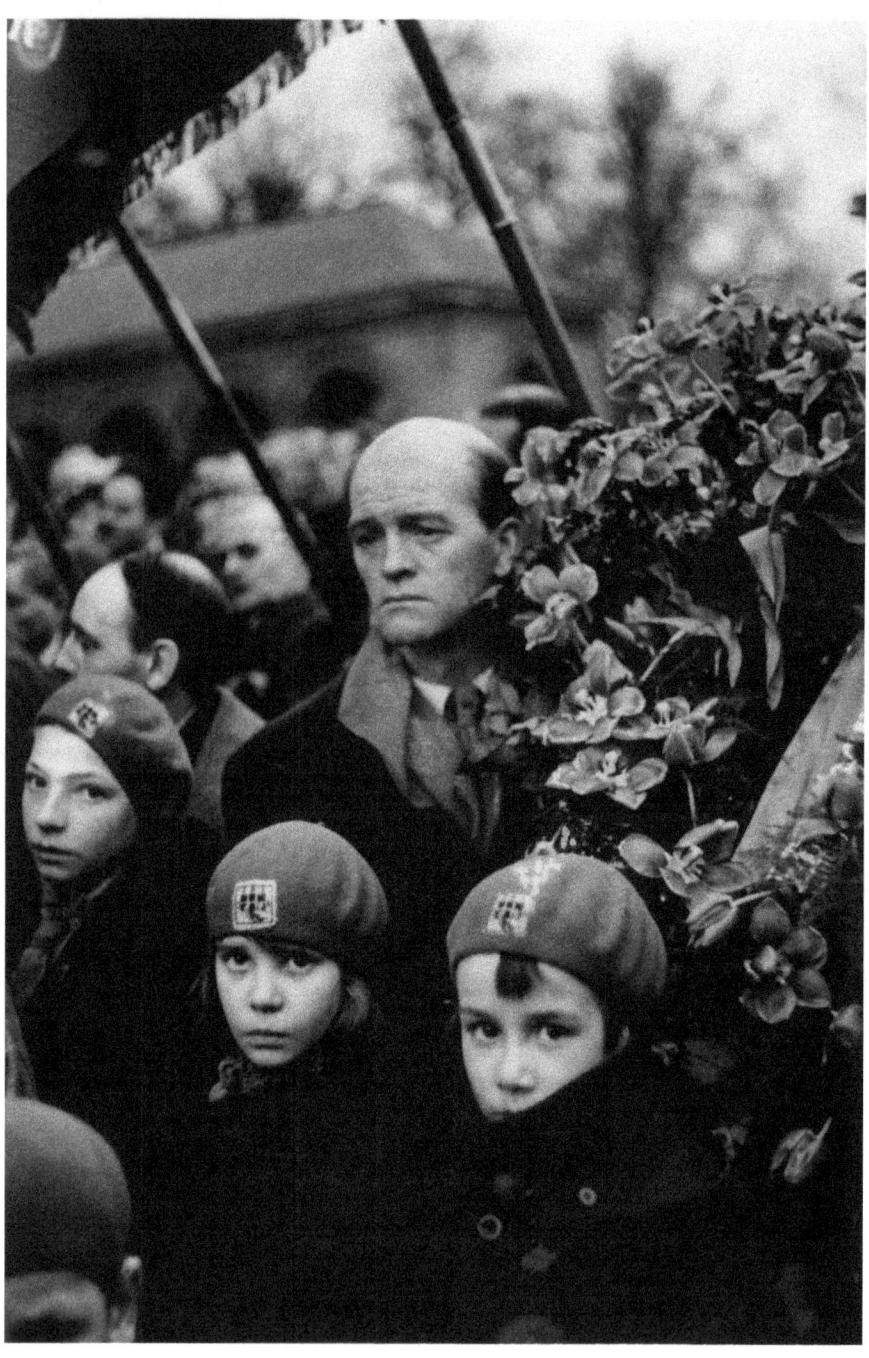

Fig. 38: A large crowd pays tribute to French writer Henri Barbusse at his funeral. He was a war veteran from the war of 14-18, the author of "Under Fire" (Le Feu) and an anti-fascist intellectual. Paris, September 7, 1935. © David Seymour-Magnum Photos.

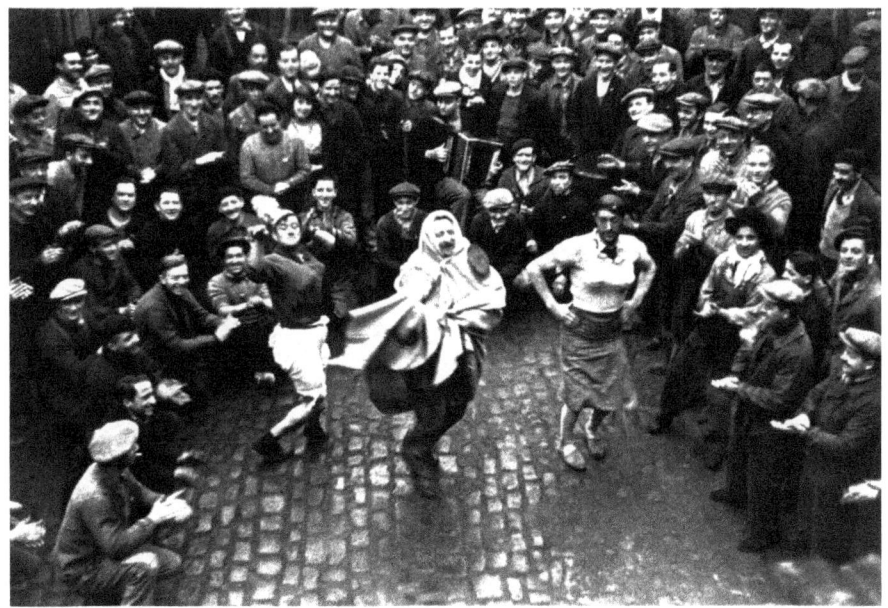

Fig. 39: Striking workers in the courtyard of the Jacquenet and Mesnet factory, Paris, June 1936.
© David Seymour-Magnum Photos.

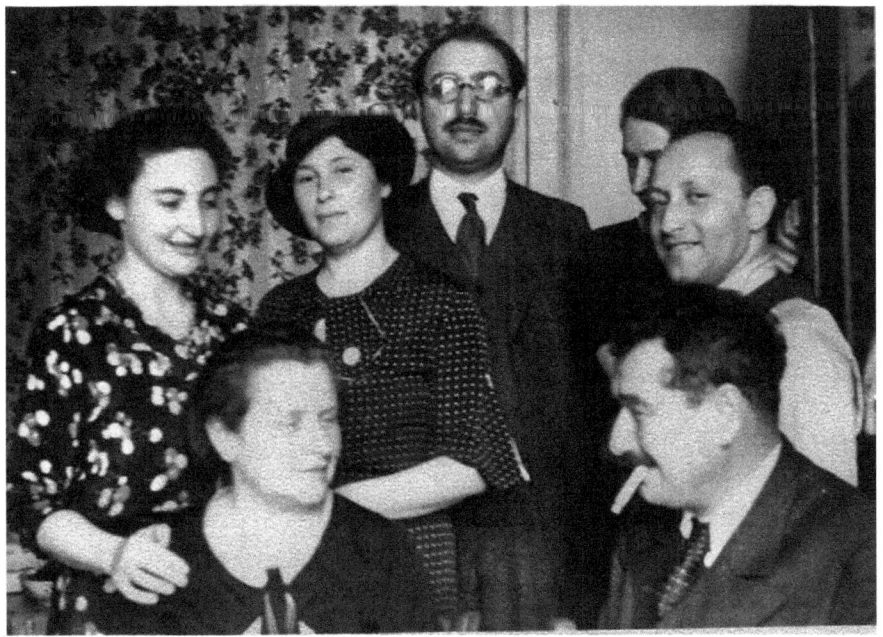

Fig. 40: Family reunion in Paris, 1936. Helen Sarid Archive, Tel Aviv.

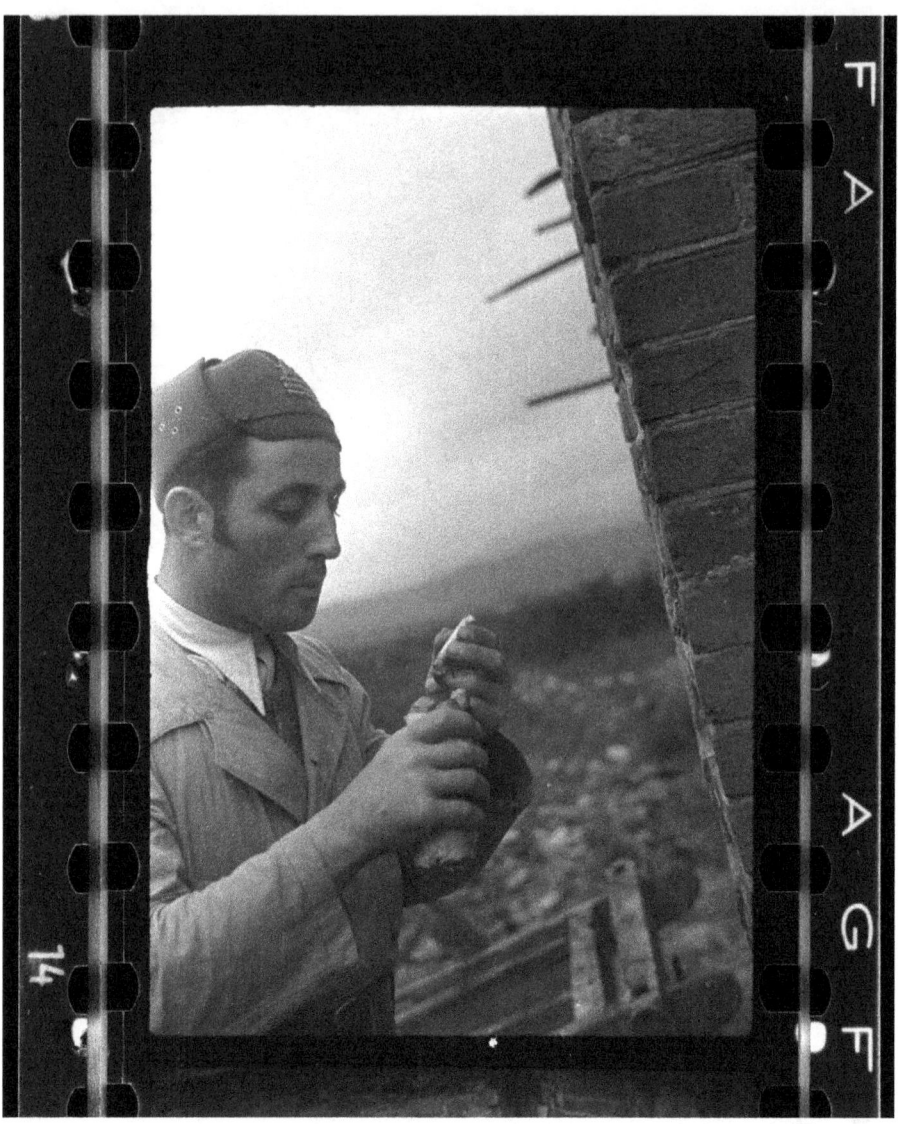

Fig. 41: Dinamitero setting his charge. Oviedo, Spain, February 1937. © David Seymour-Magnum Photos. From the Mexican Suitcase.

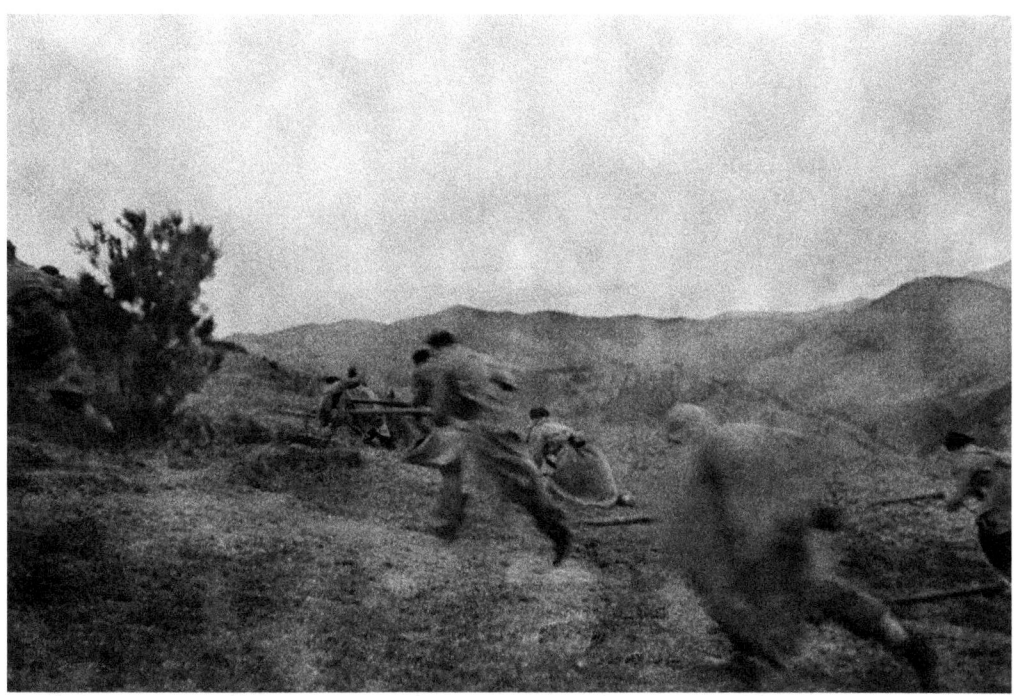

Fig. 42: Basque region. Republican soldiers running. Amorebieta, 1937. © David Seymour-Magnum Photos. From the Mexican Suitcase.

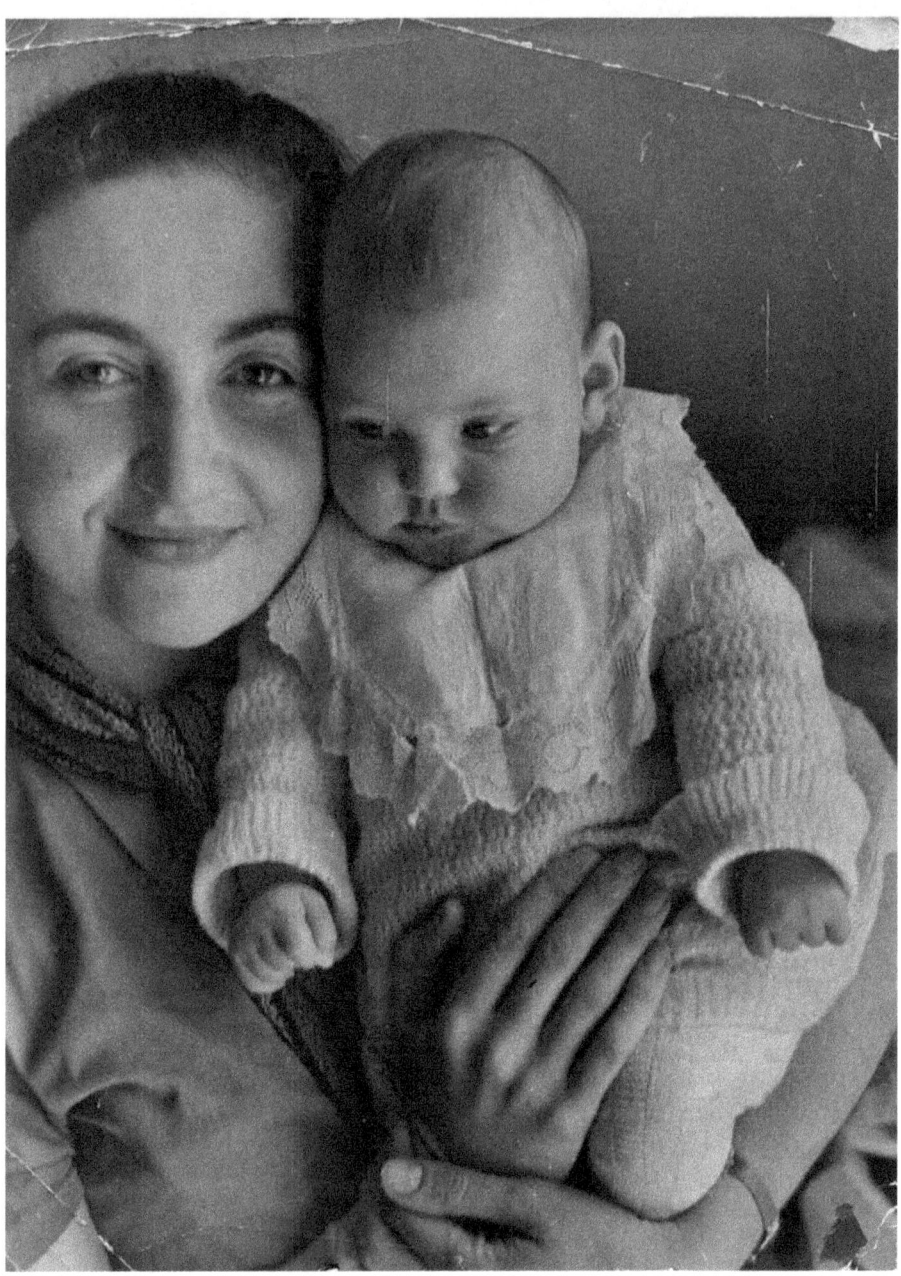

Fig. 43: Hala, Chim's sister, holding her newborn daughter Helen 'Lenka' in hospital, Paris, December 1937. Helen Sarid Achive, Tel Aviv.

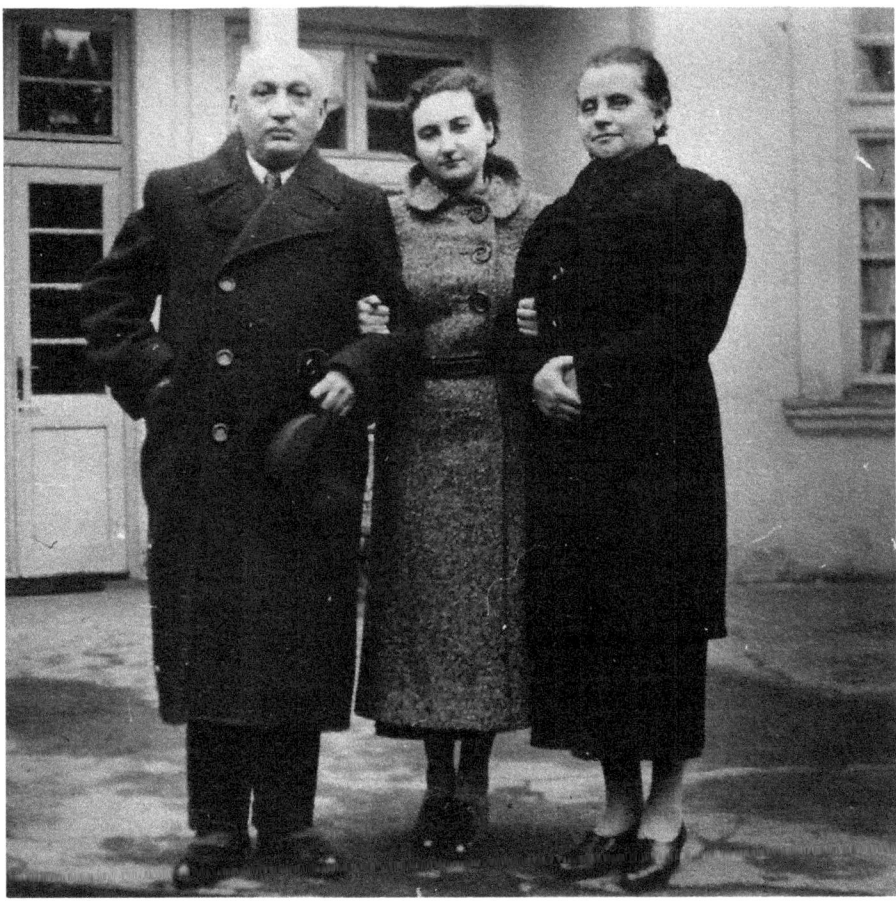

Fig. 44: Benjamin Szymin, his wife Regina and their daughter Hala at the family bed and breakfast, Pensjonat Zachęta. Otwock, Poland, 1937. © United States Holocaust Memorial Museum, courtesy of Ben Shneiderman.

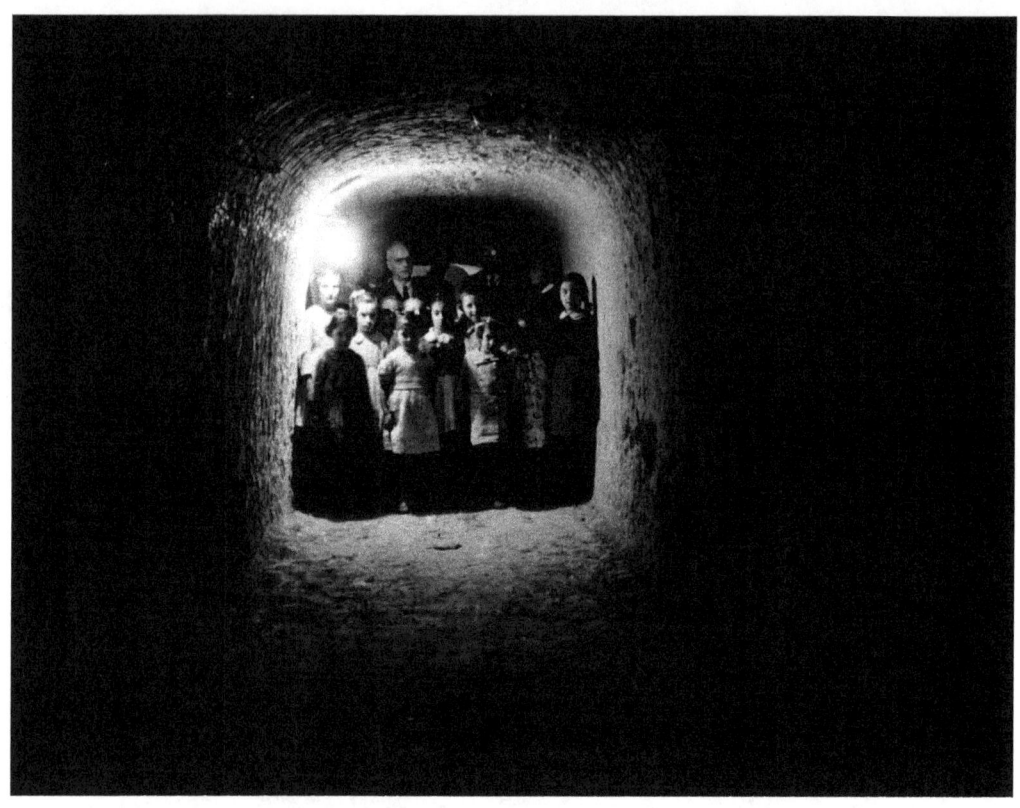

Fig. 45: Children take refuge in an underground shelter to escape the bombings. Minorca was the only island to remain loyal to the Republic. Island of Minorca, Spain, 1938. © David Seymour-Magnum Photos.

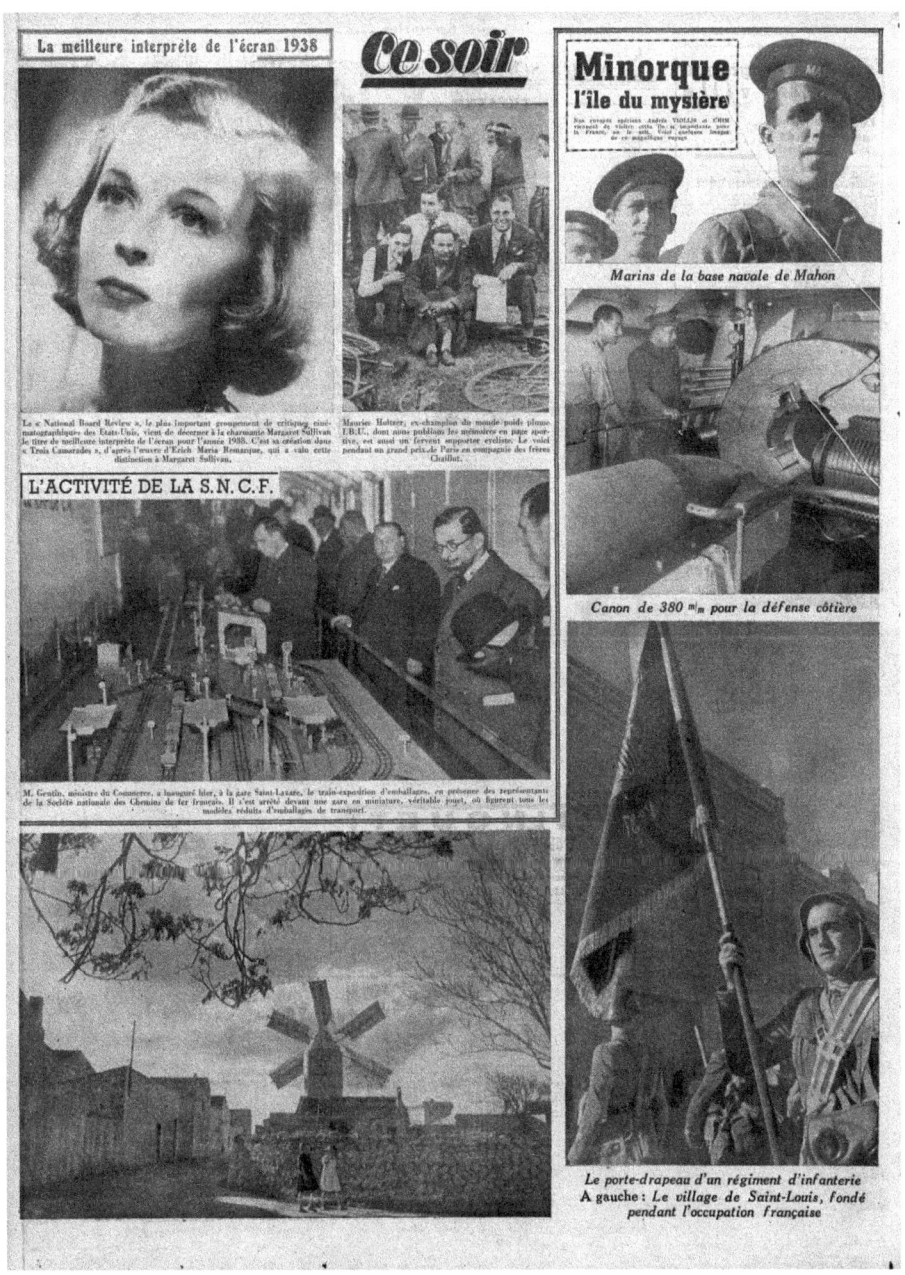

Fig. 46: *Minorque, l'île du mystère* (Minorca, island of mystery), reportage by Chim in *Ce Soir*, January 1939. © Bibliothèque Nationale de France (gallica.bnf.fr).

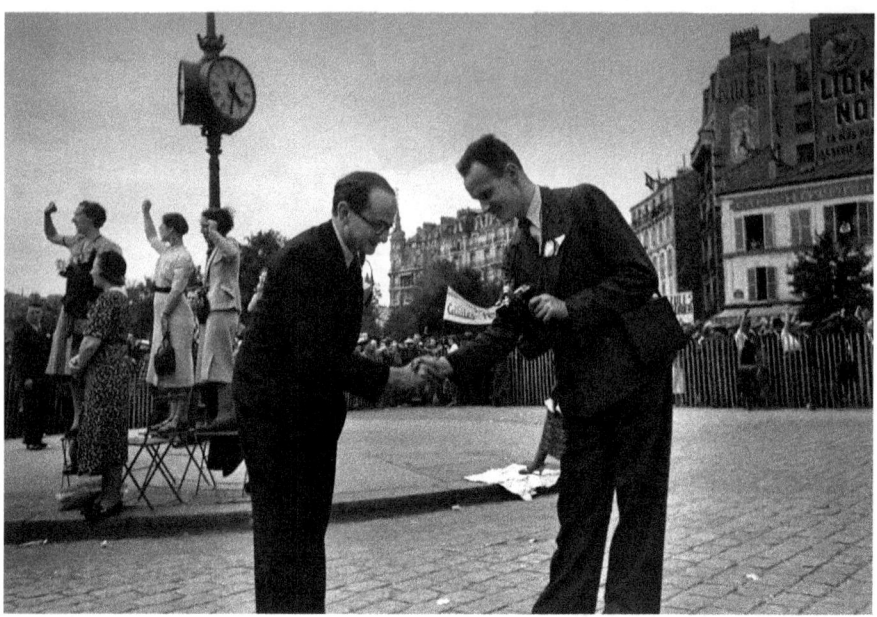

Fig. 47: Chim greeting Henri Cartier-Bresson, Paris, Bastille Day, July 14, 1938.© David Seymour-Magnum Photos.

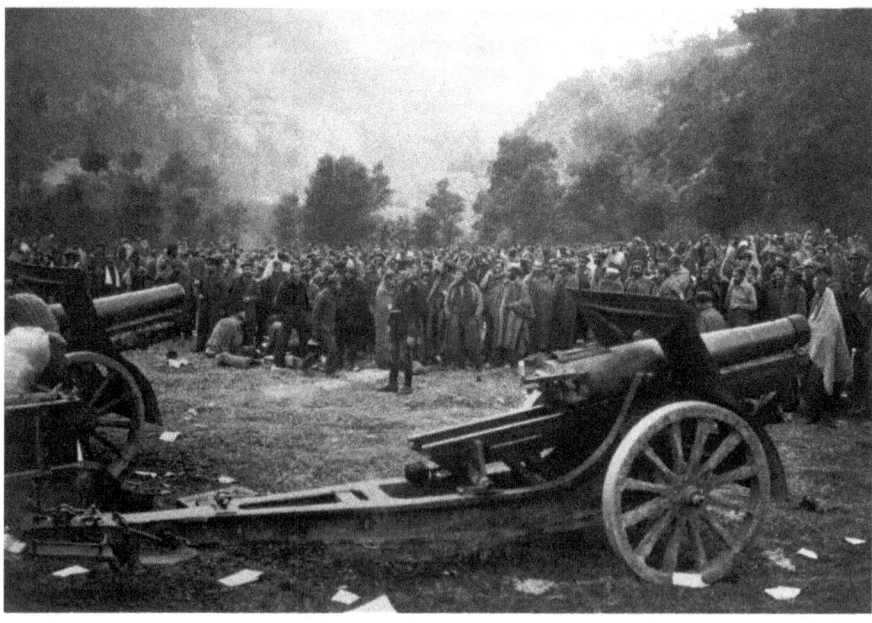

Fig. 48: Spanish Republican troops are disarmed as they cross the border. Pyrenees, Pass of Le Perthus, February 1939. © David Seymour-Magnum Photos.

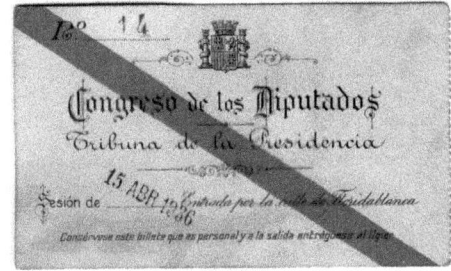

Fig. 49: Chim's press pass in Spain, 1936. © davidseymour.com archive.

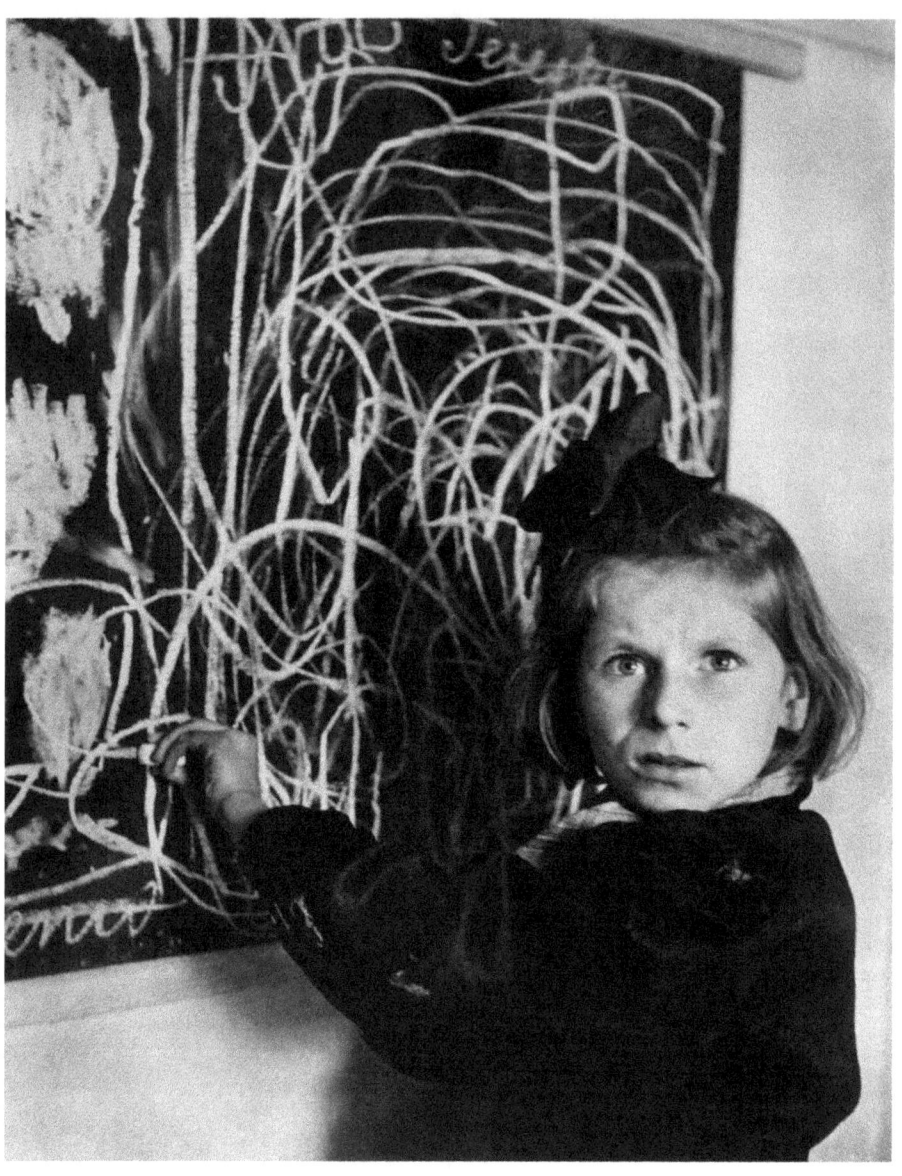

Fig. 11: Tereska, a child in a school for traumatized children, is asked to draw a home. Warsaw, 1948. © David Seymour-Magnum Photos.

Chapter 9: Return to Poland: An Obliterated Past. 1948

In 1943, Isaac Bashevis Singer wrote a famous article for *Di Tsukunft* advising his fellow writers not to go back to Poland. There was nothing left to see there, he wrote. They should just keep memories of a happier time:

"For the Yiddish writer coming from Poland, along with Jewish Poland, the soil from which he derived his sustenance is destroyed. His heroes are dead. Their language has been silenced. There is nothing left for him to draw on other than memories."[1]

However, like a good number of community activists and journalists who made the pilgrimage to their homeland, Chim thought differently: He *had to* go back, and not only to fulfill his UNICEF assignment: he wanted to see for himself. He had lost any hope of finding his family alive: a year earlier, his brother-in-law S. L. Shneiderman had traveled to Warsaw and Otwock and confirmed their death.

The first leg of Chim's trip was a 12-hour train ride to the Polish border town of Bartoszyce where he was planning to photograph an orphanage.

The country Chim had grown up in, and left 16 years earlier, was gone. Borders had changed dramatically. As of May 1945, the Soviet Union had annexed the German territories east of the Oder-Neisse and expelled 12 million people. As part of the politics of reparations, the southern region of former East Prussia was incorporated into Poland as Masuria (Mazursky), a "recovered territory," and resettled with Polish citizens. Within its new borders, Poland now had a population of 24 million, mostly Catholics, as compared to 36 million before the war. For the first time in its history, the nation-state had become ethnically homogeneous, without prominent minorities.

The war had completely devastated Chim's country. Much of the industry and infrastructure was very badly damaged. Wrocław and Gdańsk lay in ruins, and social conditions bordered on chaos. Warsaw, the scene of two uprisings, was affected the most: 85 to 90 percent of the city had been razed to the ground.

In the spring of 1940, the Soviet secret police had killed 4,443 Polish army officers and thrown their bodies into a mass grave in Katyn Forest on the Soviet side of the border with Belarus. The killings were sanctioned by Stalin, whose wider plan was to eradicate any potential resistance to the Soviet occupation or communist ideology. An estimated 22,000 members of Poland's elite—officers, doctors, teachers, engineers, and students—were also massacred at various locations in the region. In total, six million Poles were killed during the war, including three and a half million Jews: more than half of the six million killed in the Holocaust. Six major concentra-

---

[1] Isaac Bashevis Singer, *Di Tsukunft (The Future)* 48, no. 8, (August 1943), 475.

tion camps had been established in German-occupied Polish territory: Chelmno, Belzec, Sobibor, Auschwitz-Birkenau, Majdanek and Treblinka. Poland had lost most of the prewar Polish-Jewish citizens who had once formed 11 percent of its population.

Within this newly redrawn Poland, a committee was at work reorganizing a care network of 35 care centers and 2,611 pupils. The Bartoszyce orphanage that Chim had come to visit had been set up in a huge former German barracks where, ironically, officers had planned the destruction of Warsaw.[2] With more than 500 children, it was the largest in Poland. Surrounding a very large courtyard, the orphanage consisted of several four-story buildings. Inside, the walls were decorated with frescoes and children's drawings.

As in Hungary, the children had formed a "children's town" with their own government. They elected their own representatives and practiced self-discipline, a tenet of Janusz Korczak's teachings.[3] In one of Chim's photographs, we see high-school-age children standing under a gigantic portrait of Dr Korczak, who was a well-known writer of children's books and educational works and the director of a large Jewish orphanage in Warsaw. When the Germans demanded that he send the children to a concentration camp, he refused. Threatened with force, he led the orphans off to Treblinka where he was murdered with them.

On Sunday mornings, the children, who had their own theater troupe and orchestra, gave concerts and, as he had done at the Albergo dei Pobre in Naples, Chim photographed them playing their saxophones and trumpets.[4] The barracks was surrounded by almost 2,500 acres of land where the children were growing vegetables and fruit in the hope that they could become completely self-sufficient. They were also studying hard to make up for the time lost in the war years when learning had been impossible. Chim captured the tender gesture of a student putting his hand on a friend's shoulder while they study from the same manual. A blond student with a tired, serious face is dreaming, his hand on a page of his book. From a tall window, light falls on his face.[5] All in all, the impression we get from these photographs is that the orphanage was a symbol of resistance and optimism in the face of hardship.

---

[2] MPNYA, DSC, #P7-7, "Europe's Children: Poland, Children's Town."
[3] Janus Korczak, a pen name for Henryk Goldszmit, was an author, pediatrician, and pedagogue. In 1911–1912 he became director of an orphanage for Jewish children in Warsaw where he established a "Republic for Children" with its own parliament, law-court, and newspaper. During the war he was forced to move his orphanage into the ghetto. He went with the children though he had been offered shelter on the "Aryan side" and he died with 200 children at Treblinka in 1942. For a more detailed biography, see https://www.yadvashem.org/education/educational-materials/learning-environment/janusz-korczak/korczak-bio.html, accessed August 11, 2020.
[4] MPNYA, ADS UNESCO, 48-29-26, 48-29-27.
[5] MPNYA, ADS UNESCO, 48-29-30. "These serious children are preoccupied with the need to make up for their lost years of schooling" (caption by Chim, Europe's Children: Poland, Children's Twon, #5-264).

Leaving the orphanage, Chim made his way to Warsaw where he probably stayed at the Hotel Polonia (which still exists at Jerozolimskie 45, in the city center).

Chim's brother-in-law S. L. Shneiderman had traveled to Warsaw the year before, to report to his New York paper *Forverts*, bring whatever help he could, and generally, like many activists, to assess the need of remaining Polish Jews, most of whom wanted to immigrate. It was the only one in Warsaw still standing and equipped to welcome travelers, but the rooms were shared, the mattresses were made of straw and some travelers found themselves sleeping in a bathtub.[6]

He was driven, through a landscape of ashes and ruins where undernourished war or camp survivors roamed the destroyed streets like ghosts, begging. The ruins resonated with sporadic gunfire and soldiers armed with automatic rifles stood everywhere at the ready.

It was only when his driver pointed out streetcar tracks embedded in the soil of the former Nalewki street that Shneiderman was able to recognize the neighborhood where he had once lived.

> Then, following a narrow footpath between bricks and stones on one rubble-strewn street, the writer made a surprising find: In front of me lay a four-sided piece of metal with a large, engraved number "23" and the name Nowolipki. I apparently found myself standing next to the house where I had lived. I picked up the piece of metal and held onto it like a trophy. The metal, which must have been in place while the ghetto was in flames, had the color of ash, but the letters and the number that would at night be lit by the lantern above the house, remained legible.[7]

Just as his brother-in-law had done, Chim roamed the ravaged city from east to west, looking for the places of his childhood and youth, photographing the devastation and the survivors. As he did so, Chim was methodically composing what amounted to a eulogy for Polish Jewry and Yiddish culture.

It was an afternoon in late September when he started walking. He knew that his childhood home on Nowolipki Street had been swallowed up by the Warsaw ghetto. Officially called the "Jewish Residential District in Warsaw" (*Jüdischer Wohnbezirk in Warschau*) the ghetto was established in November 1940. It was circled by three-meter-high walls topped with barbed wire and enclosed a 3.4-square-kilometer area of the city that had been inhabited predominantly by Jews. Within these walls, 460,000 Jews were imprisoned.

---

6 For the above description of Hotel Polonia and Shneiderman's discovery, I have relied on Jack Kugelmass excellent study: *Sifting the Ruins: Émigré Jewish Journalists' Return Visits to the Old Country, 1946–1948*. David W. Belin Lecture, American Jewish Affairs, Volume 23 (2013). See also S. L. Shneiderman's memoirs, *Tsvishn shrek un hofenung: a rayze iber dem nayem Poyln*. (Buenos Aires: Tsentral farband fun poylishn, 1947), 8. Translated into English as *Between fear and hope* (New York: Arco, 1947).

7 S. L. Shneiderman, *The River Remembers* (New York: Horizon Press, 1978), 84: an English translation of his 1947 book *Ven di Weisl Hot Geredt* ('The Vistula Speaks Yiddish').

The population steadily decreased because of starvation (by 1942, almost 100,000 had already died from hunger), outbreaks of infectious diseases, such as typhus, and regular executions. Escapees were shot on sight. In the summer of 1942, the so-called Resettlement to the East program sent a quarter-million residents by cattle trucks to the Treblinka extermination camp. In May 1943, after the Ghetto Uprising had succeeded in temporarily halting the deportations, the Germans razed the ghetto.[8]

As Chim made his way to his old neighborhood, the sky was a pale blue, and a soft wind was blowing. He might have been thinking of the chilling message Reichsführer SS Heinrich Himmler had given to German commanders of military districts at the beginning of the uprising: "We will finish with them within five to six weeks, and then Warsaw will be liquidated, and that city, capital of the nation that for seven hundred years has hindered our push towards the East, will cease to exist. Every city resident will be killed, we will take no prisoners. Warsaw will be razed to the ground and will thus show the whole of Europe a terrifying example."[9]

In the text for his story, Chim wrote about what he saw:

> All the buildings have been completely wiped out, blown up by dynamite, and the streets were completely covered with rubble. A few main thoroughfares have been cleaned through the rubble. At the edge of the ghetto on Stawki street stands a school which was just beyond the ghetto boundaries and escaped destruction. The children attending this secondary school have to pass through the ghetto.[10]

He climbed on a mound of debris to get a better perspective (figure 75). Rubble crunched under his feet and with each pace he raised small clouds of dust. He looked around: he was on the edge of a gigantic lot filled with ruins. Even though he had known his neighborhood like the back of his hand, he could not orient himself because the layout of the streets had been erased. As far as he could see, there were only two buildings left standing: the school on Stawki Street and, further on the horizon, the St. Augustine church.

Chim saw a troop of children filing out of the school and he approached them, first photographing them from afar in their dark uniforms as they walked home after classes. Then he lined them up for a group portrait. Some climbed up the columns of former buildings.[11]

Chim knew from his sister and brother-in-law that his family had died in the Holocaust. He may have visited the Jewish cemetery in Warsaw, but did not write

---

[8] For a history of the Warsaw Ghetto, see for instance: http://www.deutschlandundeuropa.de/37_98/due371.htm, accessed August 11, 2020.

[9] Speech of August 1, 1944. *Zbrodnie okupanta w czasie Powstania Warszawskiego w 1944 roku (w dokumentach)*, ed. S. Datner and K. Leszczyński (Warsaw 1969), 306, https://warsawinstitute.org/warsaw-city-no/, accessed August 11, 2020.

[10] MPNYA, ADS UNESCO, captions "Europe's Children/Poland: Ruins," #5-27 & 5-23.

[11] MPNYA, NN11546485, NYC135863, NYC122327, NYC119573, NYC100986.

about it or photograph it, even for himself, maintaining the silence that was characteristic of survivors. Still, he wanted to do his job. What did it take to walk around the destroyed landscape of his youth, all too aware that his family had been obliterated, to push away his despair, and still compose beautiful images with a classical perspective? The immense sky, the church's bell tower silhouetted in the back, the elegant curve of the narrow road snaking among the piled debris, the children filing in the front?

When his friend and colleague Rodger entered Bergen-Belsen three years earlier, on April 20, 1945, the first photographer to do so, he had berated himself for looking for "good composition" with the corpses.[12] Chim, wiser perhaps, somehow knew that framing beautiful images was the only way he could respond to such massive trauma. Only then could he stand it. Only then, pulled into the scene by beauty, could witnesses understand the chaos and horror. His bittersweet images of the ghetto are poised between melancholy and the hope that the children represent: of learning, of playing. To them, the ghetto was an immense playground.[13]

The St. Augustine church—visible at the back of several of Chim's photographs—was on Nowolipki Street,18, the very street where Chim and his family had lived and where his father worked at the Central publishing house. Chim had been told that during the uprising, the bell tower had served as a base for German sub-machine guns. He walked down his street, or what he thought was his street, but nothing was left of his family home or the building where his father's business had been.

Only two years earlier, on September 18, 1946, at Nowolipki 68, two milk cans had been unearthed. They held part of the secret archives of Emmanuel Ringelblum and his group, who with dark irony called themselves *Oyneg Shabbos*, "Joy of the Shabbat." Daily, they had written their diaries, thus becoming historians of the life that the Nazis were extinguishing, and had enclosed testimonies of their everyday life, from family pictures to chocolate wrappings, concert programs, milk coupons, tram tickets.[14] Now, Chim too was bearing witness.

With the advent of digital cameras, contact sheets have become disappearing artifacts. They were, and still are, essential tools for the historian, helping us understand how a photographer worked, his physical and mental changes of perspective, his choices. In Chim's case, many contacts (except those he cut up himself) and negatives (except those sent to magazines before 1936) have survived intact. By looking

---

12 "The natural instinct as a photographer is always to take good pictures, at the right exposure, with a good composition. But it shocked me that I was still trying to do that when my subjects were dead bodies. I realized there must be something wrong with me." In Carole Naggar, *George Rodger, An Adventure in Photography* (Syracuse University Press, 2005), 140. In interview with George Rodger, *The Guardian*, February 1995.
13 MPNYA, ADS UNESCO, 48-29-3 and 48-29-4.
14 Emmanuel Ringelblum, *Notes from the Warsaw Ghetto* (New York: Ibooks Inc., 2006).

at the captions he wrote and his contact sheets,[15] we can retrace some of his Warsaw wanderings.

After leaving the ghetto, Chim first took pictures at the Legia Warszawa soccer stadium, where he had watched games with his favorite cousin when he was a kid. Then he walked among Warsaw's ruins, seeking subjects and photographing on the way. Most of the neighborhoods were destroyed, and classes with no access to proper school buildings had been improvised in army barracks or in abandoned apartment buildings. In front of Publiczna Szkola Poszechna 181 (Public Primary School No. 181), in the Praga neighborhood, he photographed children entering the repurposed building with their school bags.[16] In other pictures, he photographed another school under construction; with the ground floor still unfinished, children were going to class upstairs.

In a high school, he captured an image of young girls carrying spades, like so many young *Komsomols* in a Russian propaganda photograph, to clear rubble.[17]

> Wherever I went, in any of the five countries, the first new buildings I saw, white and cheerful amidst the desolation of war-blinded cities, were schools. Everywhere I saw overworked teachers fighting with enthusiasm and resource against shortages of school supplies—making old electric bulbs into chemistry retorts, corned-beef cans into calorimeters, or building optical instruments with raw macaroni.[18]

Chim seems to have found the children's seriousness and concentration very moving. Absorbed in their studies, they paid almost no attention to him as he photographed them in close-up. As the son of a publisher, his childhood had been spent around books and music, and he was deeply touched by the teachers' dedication and the children's thirst for knowledge.[19]

During his reportages, Chim liked to follow the children, who would almost always lead him to some place of interest. In Warsaw, he chanced upon a group of schoolchildren pushing wheelbarrows full of rubble and a small girl enthusiastically digging with her shovel in a garden plot. He went into the school that stood behind the garden.[20] And in this school for "backward and psychologically upset children" (the expression that was used at the time), as Chim states in his story's captions, he photographed a row of children standing in front of a blackboard, and made por-

---

15 *Magnum Photos* New York office (MPNYA) where Chim's contact sheets, captions, and texts are kept.
16 MPNYA, #48-29-5.
17 MPNYA, #48-29-6.
18 "Somewhere in Europe: A Photographer Highlights the Drama of Post-War Youngsters," *UNESCO Courier* 2, no. 1 (February 1949), cover, 5–9.
19 MPNYA, #48-29-11.
20 MPNYA, #48-29-8 and 48-29-9.

traits of Wojtek and Genia,[21] who like most of the children had drawn cheerful scenes of houses with tiled roofs and smoking chimneys, happy mothers preparing food, a sun in a cloudless sky. Only one child, remembering a recent raid, had drawn airplanes in the sky above houses. The teachers' assignment, pinned on top of the board, was "To jest dom"—"This is a home".

At the end of the row, Chim focused on a seven- or eight-year-old girl, Tereska (figure 11). What she had traced in chalk was a tangle of frantic lines. Her haunted eyes reflected her confusion and anguish. Dressed in his usual attire of dark suit and tie, drawn by the child's expression, Chim stopped in front of her.

Over the years, many people have come to believe that Tereska was a concentration camp survivor. This interpretation may have begun as early as 1957 in an exhibition that Peter Pollack organized at the Art Institute in Chicago. The wall caption to the photograph reads: "A little girl produces this extraordinary drawing of entangled lines showing the confusion of her mind. She suffered nervous shock during the war, growing up in a concentration camp." (figure 77). From then on, this interpretation became the accepted one, and is still frequently found in diverse media, especially websites.[22]

However, in 2017, with the help of the Tereska Foundation,[23] Polish researcher Patryk Grazewicz, from the nonprofit group *Warszawska Identyfikacja* and a human rights journalist, Aneta Wawrzynczak, embarked on a quest: to identify Tereska. They were able to name the building toward which the wheelbarrow-pushing children were walking, the school where Chim had photographed Tereska, on Okopowa Street, in the Muranów district. The school was the topic of a 1948 short film[24] where features of the classroom that were visible in Chim's photographs were clearly recognizable: wooden floors, similar wall painting, a black trim painted on the wall, and a big round black metal buzzer placed near the door. The school, no longer a special-needs institute, has now become Primary School No. 177 and has relocated on Tarczynska Street, in the Stara Ochota district.

The institute's archives have been moved to this new location, where the principal readily granted the researchers access to papers pertaining to the 1948–1957

---

21 MPNYA, ADS UNESCO, Captions Europe's Children/Poland-Backward Children, #P3-20 and 5-111.
22 The Art Institute exhibition, "Chim's Children," took place at the Art Institute of Chicago in 1957 and traveled in the United States (MPNYA, DSA, 1957 wall texts). For websites, see for instance Art Institute of Chicago (artic.edu/artworks/5817/) and sites such as Aphelis.net or https://rarehistoricalphotos.com/girl-concentration-camp-disturbed-children-1948/ and numerous writers such as *New York Times* critic Michael Kimmelman, "Images Engraved I History's Heart", 1996, in his otherwise excellent text.
23 The Tereska Foundation, headed by Gregor Siebenkotten, was inspired by Chim's Tereska picture. It provides help for children in need through local and international charitable institutions, https://www.tereska.de/en/about/about-the-foundation/.
24 A 32-second document from the Polish Film Chronicle No. 38/48 entitled "The First Day of the New School". Such shorts were shown at the movie theaters before the main film.

years. There were three possible "Tereskas" on the 1948 class list. One of them was too old to be the girl in the image. When the researchers saw family pictures of the second Tereska, it became obvious that she was not the girl they were seeking. The third girl was seven or eight, which tallied with the picture, and she had left the school after a year. The archive still held a few notes made by her teachers, such as this one: "She is talkative, keen on schoolwork, and actively contributes to reading and counting classes."[25]

The research team was able to find Tereska's brother and sister-in-law and piece together a few elements of her life. Teresa Adwentowska came from a Catholic family. She was one of two daughters of Jan Klemens, who was an activist in the "Polish Underground State", the Resistance. During the Warsaw Uprising (August-October 1944), he was badly beaten, and the Gestapo broke all his teeth at their Warsaw headquarters and in prison. During the war, Tereska's mother Franciszka did her best to make ends meet, visiting the Jewish ghetto to trade goods.

When the German Luftwaffe bombed Warsaw, Tereska's home was destroyed, and her grandmother was most likely shot by Ukrainian soldiers who were helping the Germans. Tereska was struck by a piece of shrapnel that left her brain damaged. Fleeing Warsaw after the bombings, four-year old Tereska and her 14-year-old sister Jadwiga spent three weeks trying to reach a village 64 kilometers from Warsaw—on foot, in a war-ravaged country. They were starving.

That episode left Tereska with an insatiable hunger, and her physical and mental condition steadily deteriorated. Since her early childhood she had loved drawing, mainly flowers and animals. As a teenager she became addicted to cigarettes and alcohol and became violent toward a younger brother that she never accepted. During the 1954/1955 school year, she had to be sent to a psychiatric asylum in Świecie (about 300 kilometers from Warsaw).

From the mid-60s she spent the rest of her life at the Tworki Mental Asylum near Warsaw.[26] The only things that still meant anything to her were cigarettes, food, and her drawings. In 1978, at the age of 37, she met with a tragic death, accidentally choking on a piece of food that she had stolen from another patient, perhaps still feeling the unquenchable pangs of her war-time hunger.

Apart from some pictures in Tereska's family's private album, Chim's photograph remains a singular portrait of Tereska as a child. Caught in the tangled web of her own chalk lines, she remained frozen in time: for Tereska, the war never ended.

Before the war, Poland had had 13,500 doctors but by the late 1940s only about half that number were left, and the country was facing the highest tuberculosis mortality rate in Europe: 15 out of 10,000 annually. In May 1948, the Polish Government

---

[25] Institute's Archive at Primary School #177, Warsaw, years 1948–1957.
[26] The Psychiatric Hospital is still functioning and has been the topic of a recent novel by Marek Bienczyk, *Tworki, writings from an Unbound Europe* (Evanston, Ill.: Northwestern University Press, 2008).

signed a treaty with the Red Cross authorizing it to form three teams, two Polish and one Scandinavian, in each of Poland's 14 administrative districts to examine and vaccinate children against tuberculosis. Danish Red Cross teams had already started work a year before, and between May 1947 and July 1948, 90,000 people had already been examined and 250,000 vaccinated.

UNICEF took part in this new campaign, and Chim photographed it in progress in the town of Garwolin. His story strikes a lighter, more positive note than some of his earlier work. The sequence of images shows, first, children in a horse cart *en route* to a vaccination center; then, a group of children waiting for their turn while, full of curiosity, they watch a Red Cross ambulance. Two nurses, one Danish and the other Polish, working together, vaccinate the children while another nurse keeps the register. Several mothers accompany their children, who are afraid of being vaccinated—the subsequent images show the children's relief once the procedure is over.[27]

It was probably at the Polonia in Warsaw that he met the social worker who told him about an orphanage that had recently opened in Otwock. This was the little town in which his mother and aunt Malka had run the bed-and-breakfast where he had spent his summer holidays as a boy. He decided to go there, taking the short ride on the narrow-gauge electric train from Warsaw.

This is how Singer, one of the writers Chim's father published at Central (he would later win the Nobel Prize) described the town:

> There is a small town of Otwock located a dozen or so kilometers from Warsaw. It was famous all over Poland for its crystal-clear air and sanitariums for those suffering from lung illnesses. (...) Kilometers of pine woods, air filled with the smell of resin; this was the place where Jews constructed their houses also called villas. They were wooden, painted brown, had to have a veranda; almost all of them looked the same. (...) In the summer Otwock and neighboring villages were destinations of thousands of families. (...) It is hard to imagine that there are no Jews anymore. The only thing left is sand.[28]

In the 1920s, Otwock had four synagogues and it had become a popular vacation spot. On the east side of the tracks was a district of pension houses, restaurants, and residences for wealthy, assimilated Jews—the villas that Singer described—where Chim's family maintained their bed and breakfast, Pensjonat Zachęta (figure 21, figure 44). On the other side of the tracks, the less well-off Jews lived in small wooden houses clustered around the bazaar.

In the Fall of 1939, Chim's sister Hala had sent him a photograph of his father, his mother, and his aunt Malka standing in the forest near Pensjonat Zachęta, wearing on the sleeves of their winter coats the yellow star band that was required to indi-

---

27 MPNYA, # 48-29-15, 48-29-16, and 48-29-17.
28 Isaac Bashevis Singer, *Lost in America*, part one, *The London Review of Books* 4, no. 5, (March 18, 1982). rb.co.uk/the-paper/v04/n05/isaac-bashevis-singer/lost-in-america-part-one-of-a-memoir-by-isaac-bashevis-singer, accessed January 15, 2022.

cate that they were Jews.[29] (figure 8). After that, just one mention of news from his father in December 1939, in a letter from Hala. Then, silence.

His parents and aunt had been shot on August 19, 1942, under the red pine trees of the forest abutting their house; most of the Jewish population of Otwock, about 8,000 people, had been herded to the train station and transported inside crowded, locked wagons to the Treblinka concentration camp to be gassed a few hours after they arrived.

In Otwock, Chim first photographed the Zofiowka Sanatorium, home to orphaned children, a place with a dark, complicated history. Founded in the 1900s by the Society for the Protection of Mentally Ill Jews under the directorship of Samuel Goldflam, an eminent Polish psychiatrist, it was built on 75 acres of land with funds donated by benefactress Zofia Endelman. The four buildings of the sanitarium housed almost 400 children and adults and employed 994 staff who used innovative methods of psychological treatment, such as insulin therapy for schizophrenic patients.

In September 1939, when Germany invaded Poland, the picture changed drastically. Bent on creating a "master race" of so-called superior beings, the German government in collaboration with many physicians began to exterminate all those judged to be defective: the physically and mentally disabled, vagrants, homosexuals, and Jews. The process of killing the mentally ill started in German-occupied Poland.

Established on January 15, 1941, the Jewish ghetto of Otwock was sealed on May 28, which meant that no patients could be discharged from Zofiówka to their families.[30] Most of the original staff had fled toward the East at the outbreak of the war; food, medical supplies, and coal were becoming scarce. Because of crowding, cold, deprivation, and unsanitary conditions, more than half of the residents died between June and November. German health authorities nevertheless continued to send more and more mentally ill Jewish patients to Zofiówka.

In August 1942, the staff were warned that the next day the ghetto was to be liquidated. Some patients and many of the doctors and nurses committed suicide by ingesting potassium cyanide. The few who managed to escape to the countryside were betrayed later by the local population. On the hospital grounds, the SS machine-gunned 140 children and adults. The patients who had not been murdered that day were deported with the other residents of the ghetto to Treblinka.

By the end of 1942, the only people left at Zofiówka were two SS men and 20 Jewish policemen who were tasked with renovating the buildings, readying them for

---

[29] Holocaust Museum Archive, New York, courtesy of Ben Shneiderman and Helen Sarid.
[30] A complete history of the Sofiowka Sanatorium can be found in Mary Seeman, "The Sofiowka Sanatorium", https://doi.org/10.1176/appi.ajp.2013.13081114-, and T. Nasierowski, "The extermination of the mentally ill in Poland during the Second World War," *International Journal of Mental Health* 35 (2006), 50–61.

their new occupants: "racially pure" unmarried and pregnant Aryan women carrying "racially pure" fetuses: the *Lebensborn Ostland*.

Lebensborn, literally, "Fount of Life", was an SS-initiated, state-supported, registered association with the goal of raising the birthrate of "Aryan" children via extramarital relations between anonymous people classified as "racially pure and healthy" as set out in the Nazi ideology of racial hygiene and health. These children were adopted by similarly "racially pure and healthy" parents, particularly the families of SS members such as those who had killed Zofiówka's children.

In January 1945, after Otwock was liberated, Zofiówka became a sanatorium for Jewish children suffering from tuberculosis. When Chim visited, there were about 70 of them under the care of the TOZ (*Towarzystwo Ochrony Zdrowia Ludnosci Zydowskiej*) Society to Protect the Health of the Jewish Population). Some of his photographs show the small patients lying in rows on the terraces, swaddled in blankets and coats, soaking up the sunshine and looking at the photographer with questioning eyes. In other shots taken from above in a Bauhaus-like style reminiscent of Moholy-Nagy, Chim photographed a gymnastics session where the patients' arms are extended parallel to the ground and their shadows are projected onto the black-and-white tiled floor, as if in a geometric ballet (figure 74). Another series, taken at lunchtime, shows the children in close-up, eating stew at a long table. These images strongly evoke the portraits of refugee children that Chim took in 1936 at the Montjuic stadium during the Spanish Civil War, showing the continuity of his work over a decade.[31]

As a survivor and an orphan, Chim must have seen himself in the children he photographed. They must have felt it, too. Photographer and subjects connected. Feelings of loss and healing coursed through some of his portraits.

In Otwock, Chim had one more place to document, an orphanage called Dom Diecka (Children's House), which had its own remarkable history. In January 1945, just after the Soviets liberated Otwock, Franciszka Oliwa, a Jewish resident who had survived the 1943 liquidation of the ghetto by traveling to Warsaw with Aryan papers, returned to her hometown to search for surviving relatives. She found none. The Germans had burned the ghetto to the ground, and Poles from the town had pillaged the remains, stealing from their dead neighbors anything that could be of use, from kitchen utensils to the wood that remained from the elaborately sculpted verandahs and balconies of the houses where 14,000 Jews used to live.

Oliwa happened to encounter a Soviet soldier who was walking with a group of ten starving children in rags. He told her that they were Jewish orphans who had survived the massacre and asked her to take care of them. She told him she had no home, and he led her to an abandoned, white-washed building at 11 Bolewslawa Prusa Street. The large bay windows were blown out and the house had no running water or furniture.

---

31 MPNYA, #48-19-18 to 48-19-22.

Oliwa turned for help to Colonel Ovochowski, in charge of a nearby Soviet field hospital, and he provided paper mattresses and blankets from his supplies, helped replace the glass on the windows, and donated hospital striped aprons, which became the children's first item of new clothing. In March 1945, the CKZP (*Central Committee of Jews in Poland*) stepped in to help improve the children's living conditions and three months later appointed Luba Bielicka Blum as a director. By June 1945 *Dom Diecka* (Children's House), as it was called by then, housed 130 children. Most of the educators and staff were also Holocaust survivors.

Chim's friend Judy Friedberg remembers: "A social worker invited the American photographer to come to see a marvelous orphanage that had been established in Otwock for little war victims. When they arrived at the house, Chim found himself staring at the country home in the pine forest where he had gone so often with his parents. The emotional shock was great." The building where Dom Dziecka was housed was his family's Pensjonat Zacheta, where Franciszka Oliwa was still working as a teacher.[32]

Chim's Otwock contact sheets contain no pictures of Dom Diecka. He never wrote or talked about it. Sometimes, the absence of an image is just as telling as its presence, and trauma can only express itself in silence.

If he had walked a bit further, to Swiderskiej 6, he could have found on the plaster of a doorframe the faint imprint of a *mezuza*, the hollow metal tube that contained a protective prayer in Hebrew, one of the last surviving traces of the Jews of Otwock.[33]

Many years later, in 1975, Chim's sister Hala and Shneiderman visited the old Gęsia cemetery on Okopowa street in Warsaw's Wola neighborhood. It had been the site of mass executions by the Germans during the ghetto uprising. Part of it was deteriorated, and many tombstones were broken and covered with ivy and weed, but some inscriptions were still visible on intact monuments.

> "There are mass graves of Jews executed during deportations", Shneiderman wrote in a book he dedicated to their children Ben and Helen, "as well as the heroes of the ghetto uprising, who were buried on the spot where they fell". Their remains were transferred to the Gęsia cemetery after the Liberation.
>
> "My wife broke down at the site of a monument, erected in 1947, with an inscription stating that here are buried the remains of a few Jews from the suburban ghetto of Otwock, victims of

---

32 MPNYA DSA, Judy Friedberg, *"Chim- A Man of Peace, 3/28/66."*
33 When Oliwa left in 1949, she took with her the children's monthly newspaper, children's memoirs, and a number of photographs by William Bein, a photographer for the Joint Distribution Committee, as well as a film he had shot, later giving all the material to the Yad Vashem Archives. For Oliwa's story, a detailed story of Dom Diecka, the children's home in Otwock, numerous portraits of children, and the film of a theatrical play mounted by children and staff in the mid or late 1940s (no date), see https://www.yadvashem.org/yv/en/exhibitions/otwock/francziska-oliwa.asp, accessed February 28, 2022.

the mass execution on August 17, 1942. My wife's parents were among those who perished on that day in Otwock. (...) The graves of some of them are in the cemetery, others died in the ghetto with no trace."[34]

The following year, UNESCO published 55 of Chim's images in book form in three languages—French, English, and Spanish—with the title *Children of Europe*.[35] From 1949 to 1951, 10,000 copies would be printed. The reportage was distributed by both UNESCO and Magnum more widely than any of his assignments to date. Pierre Gassmann, the owner of Picto, a Paris photo lab that printed for the agency, remembers spending a year with François Duffort, producing 23 sets of 60 prints for exhibitions and distribution.[36] In addition to appearing in the UNESCO *Courier*, Chim's images were widely published in weekly magazines such as *Life* (December 27, 1948), *Illustrated*, *Sie und Er*, *France Illustration*, and *Harper's Bazaar*.[37] They were also used in other UNESCO publications, including Theodore Besterman's *UNESCO: Peace in the Minds of Men* (1951) and in UNESCO-sponsored exhibitions such as the traveling *UNESCO Human Rights Exhibition* (1949), centered on children as symbols of the future, and meant to illustrate the tenets of the "Universal Declaration of Human Rights," which had been adopted in 1948. The photographs were also used in UN conference reports such as *Homeless Children* (1949), and in UN-sponsored exhibitions until the late 1950s.

Chim had now regained the reputation he had before World War II, but his personality had undergone a profound change. Hala wrote: "He had the look of a man prematurely aged under the burden of the stormy events of his time, saddened by disillusionment in the ideals and causes for which men of his generation sacrificed themselves."[38]

---

34 S. L. Shneiderman, *The River Remembers* (New York: Horizon Press, 1978), a translation of his 1947 book *Ven di Weisl Hot Geredt ('The Vistula Speaks Yiddish')*, 84.
35 "The children of Europe: a UNESCO photo story," *UNESCO Courier* 2, no. 1 (February 1949), 1, 5–9, https://en.unesco.org/courier/children-europe-unesco-photo-story, accessed February 23, 2022.
36 Interview of Pierre Gassmann by the author, Paris, May 1994.
37 Among the publications: *LIFE*, December 27, 1948, 13–19, "Children of Europe," *UNESCO Courier*, February 1949, cover and 5–9; "The Children of Europe: A Unesco Photo Story," *This Week*, November 27, 1948, 6–7, "Hitler's Orphans."
[341] Transcript of Eileen Shneiderman interview, 1994, in ICP Archive, now Mana Contemporary, New Jersey. Unnumbered.
38

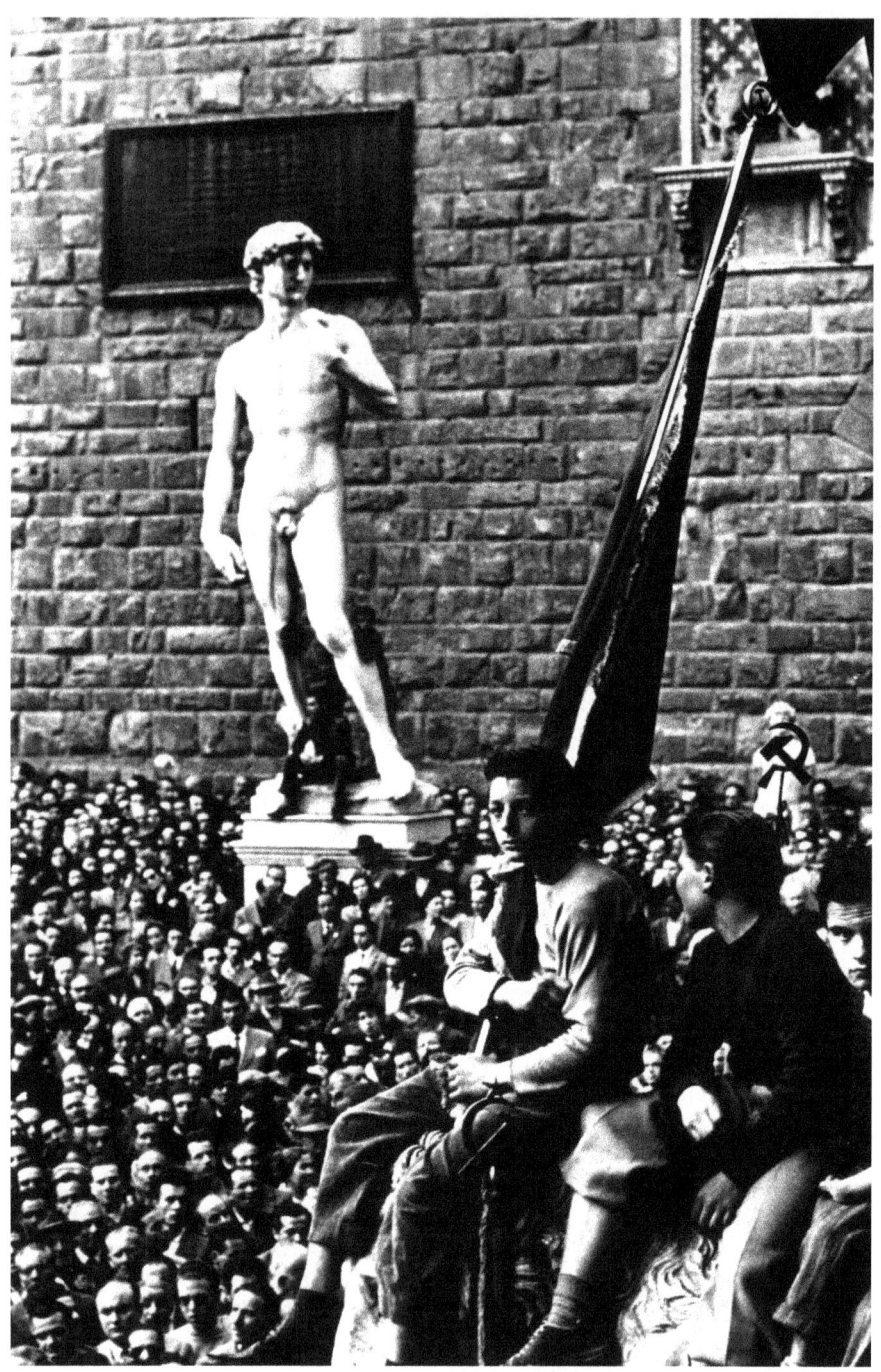

Fig. 12: Communist meeting, Piazza della Signoria, Florence, Italy, 1953. © David Seymour-Magnum Photos.

Chapter 10: I am a Mediterranean

Chim was mourning his family, and probably experiencing survivor's guilt. It was obvious to his friends and colleagues that the traumatic events of war had deeply changed him: he became more secretive, less outgoing, smiled less. He never talked about the Holocaust and never mentioned it in his letters, even when he confided in Hala.

This kind of silence should not surprise us: it is shared by the whole generation of people who lost someone in the camps, such as Susie Marquis, Capa's cousin, who worked at Magnum in Paris after the war. "At that time, the Holocaust, we did not talk about it," she wrote. "We looked at each other, we cried. It is only much later that we started talking about it."[1]

In Chim's case, reluctance to talk about the Holocaust added to his customary reticence to reveal his inner life and emotions. This reserve would extend to most of his personal relationships, particularly with women. Though almost all letters pertaining to Chim's sexual life have been either destroyed by himself—except letters from his youth girlfriends from Warsaw and three 1945 gushing, passionate letters from Denise, a young theatre student– or were censored by his sister Eileen Shneiderman when she originally organized his archive, his very silence and secrecy—he did not talk about his personal life to his family, friends or colleagues—and this compartmentalizing habit hints at a man who led several lives. I believe that Chim conducted several relationships, some short-lived, other deeper, especially during his years in Paris and during his years covering Cinecittà in Rome. During his Cinecittà assignments, Chim met many young starlets and movie stars with whom he had close relationships that may have been physical. All the women saw him as a confidant, career and wardrobe adviser and comforter during career hardships. He encouraged the most gifted to read, study music, educate themselves. Irène Papas, whom he photographed early on as she was modelling ancient Greek jewelry, wrote him several tender letters: "Shim [sic] I know you are my friend and I know also you are my first one".[2]

An intimate relationship would explain the abandon and ease with which all the starlets posed for their portraits.

Judy Friedberg, who grieved deeply when Chim died, acted—according to a disparaging comment from one of Chim's friends– as if she was his widow: But maybe she was. In any case, it was to her that he confided in his letters.

---

[1] Interview of Jean and Susie Marquis by the author, Rambouillet, May 23, 2005.
[2] Letter to Chim, July 1955 ww.davidseymour.com, http://archive.davidseymour.com/friends_page17a.html, accessed February 23, 2022.

Henri Cartier-Bresson, who was his close friend, told me: "After Chim died, I had to go ring the bell of all his girlfriends in Paris. He had promised marriage to every one of them"[3]

That claim is vigorously denied by Chim's family; but Cartier-Bresson, whom I frequented for many years, did not make up stories and had no reason to invent such an episode about one of his closest friends.

In 1949, leaving the weight of the Holocaust behind him, Chim set up his home base in Italy, where he immediately felt at ease. He settled in Rome, at the Hotel Inghilterra near the Piazza di Spagna, in a tiny room that contained little more than a bed, a chest of drawer, a small mirror, a table to type up stories and a chair. His colleague Burt Glinn recalled: "Hotel Inghilterra was not the chic place it is now. It was not completely well known in the great circles of Rome, it was a discovery, and it became Magnum's office in Rome."[4]

Chim's curiosity and thirst for knowledge, often arcane, was vast, and Rome was an ideal place to satisfy it. Located at the heart of social and political power, the hotel was a perfect spot for meetings and networking. Without strolling far away from Piazza di Spagna, he could meet editors, journalists, or the specialists he needed to acquire information about any topic, from Catholicism to current politics, ancient rituals to 16th -century painting. Attuned to Italian and world politics and always on the lookout for interesting stories, Chim read a dozen newspapers every day, but also Stendhal, a particular favorite. He would sit for hours at a café on the Piazza del Popolo, Bar Rosati or Bar Canova, often discussing world affairs with his good friend the writer-painter Carlo Levi whom he had known since working with him the previous year in Italy. He went out drinking and eating with the many friends and colleagues who lived in Rome, such as Bill and Beverly Pepper, or visited and Henri Cartier-Bresson, who, during one of his stays in Rome in 1951, made a reportage on the Trastevere and a portrait of Carlo Levi.

Chim's small table was piled high with letters and telegrams from Robert Capa, John Morris, Inge Bondi; from editors or agents like Jerry Mason, Vincento Carrese, Dave Schoenbrun, Ross Anderson, Andy Anderson, Mike Todd, Corbin Gwaltney, Norton Wood, …. And from magazines such as Life, *Holiday, Newsweek, l'Europeo, Epoca, Stampa, Harper's Bazaar, This Week*, and a score of others. As if this was not enough, he was an unofficial guide for a series of visitors to Rome, among them his friends Henri Cartier-Bresson, and Krishna and Jean Riboud, Marc Riboud's brother.

He met several writers through Levi's circle and that of his friend Giulio Einaudi, the "red editor" and most brilliant publisher of his time, whose catalogue included, among many others, Cesare Pavese, Italo Calvino, Alberto Moravia, Elsa Morante, and Natalia Ginzburg. Recently discovered in the newly digitized Photography Archive of the Fondazione Carlo Levi, a photograph copyrighted "Tiro Foto Roma"

---

3 Interview of Henri Cartier-Bresson by the author, Paris, May 11, 1998.
4 Interview of Burt Glinn by the author, East Hampton, NY, November 10, 2005.

shows Chim next to Linuccia Saba, Carlo Levi's lover, shooting clay pigeons (*piatello*) at a street fair.⁵

In Chim's new circle, intellectuals, artists, ex partisans or previous members of the Resistance were trying to cope with their feelings of loss and confusion, and channel them into creative and political action, while those who had supported Mussolini felt the bitterness of defeat. Levi perfectly caught the flavor of the times in his book, *L'Orologio*, published in Italy the year Chim arrived in Rome: "Now, after seven years of pain and slaughter, the wind had fallen, but the old leaves still could not return to their branches and the cities looked like naked woods, waiting under a modest sun for the haphazard flowering of new buds."⁶

Unlike the Eastern European countries where Chim had worked for UNICEF, Rome had good food and abundant sunshine. And the creative world was blooming. Soaking up the sun, the atmosphere, and all that Italy had to offer, Chim mixed the deadline demands of the assignments he took on to boost Magnum's finances with self-assigned stories on the topics that suited him; and he blended work and leisure in an almost seamless way.

Throughout his time in the city, Chim kept in close touch with the Magnum Paris office and after Capa's May 1954 death at Thai Binh, Indochina, as he shouldered financial and organizational responsibilities, he spent more time in Paris as needed.

Kimura Ihei, a well-known Japanese photographer who visited Rome and other European cities at a time when Japan was becoming interested in Western photography, wrote his impressions about the Magnum members with whom he struck up friendships. He would meet Cartier-Bresson, Chim and Riboud at Picto lab, which Pierre and France Gassman had recently founded. Kimura wrote, "When the weather forecast is good, he [IICD] comes to fetch me on his bike, saying 'La *Lumière* [in French in the Japanese text] is good, let's go take pictures.'" Their jaunts often took them to the Seine banks or to Blois.

Kimura notes that the three Magnum photographers also met at Deyrolles, a shop that sold cameras and lenses, where Chim, always interested in the newest technical advances, would be eager to discuss the latest Japanese lenses. Next to a photograph of Chim and Marc Riboud, Kimura's text reads: "David Seymour (see my article in the February issue on the art of Bresson) is one of the founders of Magnum and a renowned journalist, but alongside his photographic activity, he is now responsible for the financial side of Magnum. He is an impressive and impeccable figure who oversees the agency's dossiers."⁷

---

5 See https://carlolevifondazione.it/archivio-fotografico fotografi/?archID=fotografico&vocabulary-Value=Seymour,%20David%20(Magnum%20Photos), accessed February 23, 2022. With thanks to Giovanna Hendel.
6 *The Watch*, (New York: Farrar, Straus & Giroux, 1951), 85.
7 Kimura Ihei "Authors, all passionate," *Asahi Camera*, Tokyo: April 1955. Translated from the Japanese by Kinuko Asano and Tsuyoshi Takemori. Kimura's book on Paris was published in

During the fall of 1948, Chim traveled in Europe and did several light stories, including one for *Holiday* called "Fat Man in Marienbad." [8] He found his subject in a Prague film studio and followed him through his cure, as he walked; sadly consumed his solitary, spare meals; drank mineral water; and took mud baths. Chim wrote, "He was the fattest extra they had and weighed 120 kilos (254 pounds). Thanks to *Holiday*, the gentleman got a free reducing cure and as a result will probably lose his movie job as fattest extra on the lot."[9]

However, despite an intense social life—as far as can be told from letters to and from colleagues and postcards and letters to his family, he was rarely alone—Chim remained morose and dispirited, plagued by painful memories of the war. The rheumatism he had had in his knee since childhood was flaring up. On January 23, just before leaving for Rome, he wrote to Hala, apologizing about not having spent more time with her when he went to New York, and alluding to unexplained personal problems: "You know, darling, how sensitive I am—and how sometimes not very actually important things can put me in a 'stew'. I cannot somehow arrive to simplicity in my personal life and everything gets so terribly involved and unhappy (…). Please understand me—my life is not a very easy one and I am struggling emotionally as hard as I can to make sense of it."[10]

Returning to Germany, he made an extended reportage,[11] "Germany Today," parts of which would be published in the fall in several European newspapers and magazines: *Stern*, *Illustrated*, and *This Week*, and in the U.S., *The New York Times* and *Time*.

He started with the elections and from inside a building in Königsplatz, Munich, made a striking image of a rally, with two people addressing the crowd from a balcony. An apron-wearing woman and a one-legged man on crutches occupy the front of his photograph, their silhouettes back-lit, while a shoulder-to-shoulder crowd fills the square to capacity.[12] In a second image, Chim focused directly on the crowd. But in a stark contrast to his May 1936 image of a political rally in Spain, this shot conveys no sense of shared enthusiasm. The men's faces (there are few women) are not hopeful and attentive but grave and sad.[13]

1974 after his death as *Afterimage of Paris 1950s* (Tokyo: Nora Sha, 1974), republished Tokyo: Clavis, 2016. It remains one of the rare books of the period to have been shot entirely in color.
8 MPPAA, PAR289838.
9 MPNYA, DST, Story #48-10, "Fat Man in Marienbad".
10 DSA, Letter to Hala, January 23, 1949.
11 MPNYA, ADSS 1949, contacts #49-1 to 49-102. Publications in LIFE "Konrad Adenauer," "We Are of the West" (August 29, 1949), 24; Thomas Mann, "Germany Today," *The New York Times* (September 25, 1949), 14–33; "Prof Dr Theodor Heuß," *Heute* (September 28, 1949), 2; Willi Frischauer, "Germany's Year of Destiny," *Illustrated*, (October 15, 1949), 9–17; Willi Frischauer "Fraulein in Search of Happiness," *Illustrated*, (October 22, 1949), 23–25, 37.
12 MP, image #PAR122874 (SED1949001W00029/18).
13 Cynthia Young ed. *We Went Back, Photographs from Europe 1934–1956 by Chim*, (New York: Prestel & ICP, 2013), figure #60, 140.

During the same period, Chim made a stark portrait of Former Nazi General Otto Ernst Remer, who in July 1944 had played a key role in putting down Colonel von Stauffenberg's conspiracy to murder Hitler and seize control of the government. Captured by the U. S. army toward the end of the war, Remer remained a prisoner of war until 1947 but was then released from Allied captivity and took an active part in post-war German politics. In 1950 he would establish the Socialist Reich Party, campaigning on the claim that the Holocaust had been an Allied propaganda invention, and the United States had been building fake gas chambers and producing bogus news-film footage about concentration camps. Facing criminal charges, Remer would flee to Egypt and become a consultant to Egypt's President Nasser.

Bremer's portrait is one of Chim's very few images where antipathy, even hatred, are visible in the way he chose to photograph (Figure 81). The ex-General unrepentantly and proudly holds a framed portrait of himself in full Nazi regalia, wearing a knight's cross. Chim emphasized his tilted chin, disdainful and taunting expression, and brought in a deep shadow so that his dull, lifeless eyes looked like black holes in an almost skeletal face.[14] In another photograph of a German count and baron sharing a chair in a decrepit small flat they now share in Hamburg, the photographer's feeling hovers between pity and irony.[15]

By contrast, some of Chim's other images underline the sense of a transition and hope in new beginnings: a fashion parade in Berlin, a famous brewery, a zoo, and a pageant of town history in Munich; smiling young people at a table at "12 Penguins"[16]; a nightclub in Hamburg[17]; a peace meeting in Munich[18]; a woman bending over her balcony in Hamburg with a sign advertising free rooms[19]; a bookstore advertising American books in a building still surrounded by ruins[20]; team athletes lacing their shoes at a well-attended track event in Cologne.[21] For a story on youth in Germany, he chose to photograph a young seamstress.

Other photographs are grimmer: the trial of Erich von Manstein, a Nazi financial wizard, with his counsel; Hjalmar Schacht, a Nazi financial counselor who had been acquitted by the Nuremberg trials,[22] relaxing in shorts in an idyllic forest landscape; and former Navy Admiral Conrad Albrecht.

Chim shows dark irony in an image of an American soldier playing tourist at Dachau and taking a picture of his girlfriend near a sign that reads "Old Gallows

---

14 MPNYA, NYC128490.
15 MPNYA, NYC131506.
16 MPPA, PAR133350.
17 MPPA, PAR133329.
18 MPPA, PAR82613.
19 MPNYA, NYC131507.
20 MPNYA, NYC131505.
21 MPPA, PAR133354.
22 MPPA, PAR122858.

Stand."[23] Germany's postwar misery does not escape him: he notes a listless worker dismantling machinery at the Krupp factories in Essen[24] and street views of Cologne's ruined houses. While swimmers sunbathe on the sand, a guard and his dog pace the beach at Travermünde, on the Baltic coast. The juxtaposition of the two groups feels surreal.[25] In the background, barbed wire and a minefield mark the East-West border, established on May 23, that cleaved Germany into two for the next 40 years.

Chim's "Heil Adenauer!" is a feature on West Germany's new chancellor, Konrad Adenauer, in *Illustrated*, with a text by Willi Frischauer,[26] an Austrian-British journalist whose parents had been murdered in the Theresienstadt camp. The reason for the provocative title is that Adenauer's outlook was fiercely anti-British. The article displays several spreads of Chim's work, but not his best photograph, which was an informal portrait of Adenauer at home in Rhöndorf with his pet sheep. That image would have clashed with the more serious image of the chancellor that the editors wished to convey.

The piece opens with a dour portrait of Adenauer, cropped from the full image that Chim had taken at a political rally. Communist leader Max Reimann, whose party had lost the election, gets a fierce portrait on the next page, coupled with the crippled man and the woman on the Munich balcony. The spread is followed by a portrait of one-armed and one-legged Social Democrat Kurt Schumacher, and a close-up on the crowd attending that same Munich meeting. The next page features four vignette-sized photographs taken in Frankfurt, Bonn, Hesse, and Munich, while a larger image focuses on people working in a city's ruins, salvaging construction materials. The last page is a full-bleed image of a worker dismantling the Krupp factory in Essen, an undertaking that all German parties abhorred and that became one of the main reasons (apart from the massive bombings of civilians) for their deep resentment of the Allies. Chim's strong picture of a prostitute in front of the factory's site was not included.[27]

Chim's photographs of Vienna are mostly joyful, because he focused on the Prater, an amusement park.[28] In a backlit image, two soldiers are silhouetted against the sky and near a merry-go-round with a big wheel behind it. He captured scenes of a balloon vendor, Soviet soldiers going around in flying gondolas, a girl riding a pig on a merry-go-round, children at a marionette theater.

Once back in Rome, Chim's spirits improved. In contrast to his work from Germany, the Rome photographs are suffused with promise, energy, and optimism. For him, Rome had some of the warm, close spirit he had found in Spain in the 1930s.

---

23 MPPA, PAR133318.
24 MPPA, PAR133351.
25 MPPA, PAR47210.
26 *Illustrated*, September 3, 1949.
27 See figure 79 in book.
28 *Illustrated*, September 3, 1949.

The street was like a theater where people loved to pose for him, and he would happily engage in conversations with just about anyone, the subjects of his stories or passers-by. As he explored Rome and other Italian cities, he would quiz artisans about their work: gondola-building or glass blowing, furniture gold-leafing, espresso-making, sausage curing. Some of what he learned came from observing Italians' expressive faces and hand gestures, and how they varied from Rome to Naples. Now he liked to tell his friends, "I am a Mediterranean." Even though he was an American citizen, he felt more attuned to a humanism that the New World could not provide. With history ever-present, the centuries seemed to coalesce around him in a way that felt immediate and deeply personal.

In the Spring of 1949, Chim launched into a major project: taking photographs for a book that journalist and writer Ann Carnahan, the first female journalist allowed into Vatican City, planned to write about it. The Vatican was a paradoxical subject for a Polish-Jewish photographer, given that many of its priests and cardinals were anti-Semites who had most probably failed to protect the Jews during the Shoah. Still, it was the center of power in Rome, and Chim, who always had a deep curiosity about unknown worlds, must have been curious about its secretive, exclusive, and ritualized aspect; he looked at it as a key to understanding his new home city, introducing him to a world that he knew nothing about. His friend and colleague Burt Glinn told me: "He was intrigued by the Catholic Church because it was steeped in tradition. He loved that kind of intrigue that goes on in the Church. I am sure Cardinal Richelieu would have been a favorite of his!"[29]

Chim had already shown strong interest in, even reverence for, Catholic subjects during the Spanish Civil War, when he photographed life at the Amorebieta convent, where the monks had hidden Republicans and held an outdoor mass for Basque Republican fighters. His colleague René Burri explained: "He wanted to go past all nationalisms and religions and confront paradoxical topics such as the Vatican."[30]

In a letter to Hala and family, Chim mentions that he has started on the project:

> I am doing much better—but the knee is not completely ok (...). But I can walk by now and am working. Fortunately the Vatican is slow too (...). It is a strange story with continuous resistance to be broken. [They] always want permissions, always want explanations—every movement is checked and rechecked by so many authorities. There is always a cardinal that has to be consulted—and it takes time.[31]

Although he had originally intended for the reporting to take three weeks, the team worked intensively for ten weeks, seven days a week, starting in the early morning when the gates were unlocked to admit the first workmen and provisions and ending

---

29 Interview of Burt Glinn by the author, East Hampton, New York, November 10, 2005.
30 Interview of René Burri by the author, Paris, May 15, 2005.
31 DSA, letter to Hala, March 20, 1949.

late at night when the gates were barred again. He took some 2,500 photographs,[32] including an official portrait of the pope, Pius XII, which he made during a private audience, so short that few words were exchanged between photographer and subject.[33]

Chim was certainly aware of the controversy surrounding Pius XII, a future candidate for sainthood, about his response to Nazism and the Holocaust. Even now, when the papers in the Vatican archive have finally been opened to scholars, the controversy rages between those who believe that the pontiff remained shamefully silent while Jews were massacred, and those who claim that he acted behind the scenes, encouraging the Catholic Church to help shelter Jews and other victims of the Nazis.

Trudy Feliu, a Magnum editor who was close to Chim, recalls, "We started calling Chim 'Il Papabile' because he loved the pomp and ceremony of the Catholic Church and became so steeped into it. He did not mind at all."[34] As Carnahan remembers it, they were given open access to every aspect of life in 'the city within the city'.

> We talked to workmen, cooks and plasterers working three floors and seventeen centuries below the basilica. Repair artists doctoring the famous Raphael frescoes, lawyers of the Sacra Rota, carpet cleaners in the Sistine Chapel and plainclothesmen of the Pontifical Guard became our friends (...). We ate our lunch in the workers' canteen, cheered a soccer game at the Ethiopian College [It was in fact handball].[35]

The New York publisher Farrar, Straus & Giroux published text and Chim's photos as a book, *The Vatican-Behind the Scenes in the Holy City*. As his *Children of Europe* had been, Chim's reportage became a major success, and was featured in numerous magazines in Europe and the U. S.[36]

However, the story remains a mixed success. While Chim was adept at making portraits of the main characters—the Pope blessing pilgrims or being carried in his ceremonial chair on porters' shoulders, and other dignitaries as well as the interior architecture, the tourists admiring Michelangelo's frescoes, the Pinacoteca galleries and their paintings, the library, the Sistine Chapel, the Vatican's formal gardens and fountains, and the set of marble stairs leading to St Peter's from the square—these images fail to surprise. They feel conventional, as if shot from a script. One exception

---

[32] MPNYA, ADSS1949. The story numbers 110 contact sheets in Leica and Rollei.
[33] MPNYA, PAR218552.
[34] Interview of Trudi Feliu by the author, Morristown, N.J., June 23, 2005. Trudy Feliu was the editor at Magnum Photos Paris from 1954 to 1956 and was close to Chim.
[35] Ann Carnahan, preface to *The Vatican: Behind the Scenes in the Holy City* (New York: Farrar, Straus 1949).
[36] *Leica Magazine, Look, Heute, This Week* (November 20, 1949), 14–17, *Chicago Tribune, Harper's Bazar, Illustrated* (December 10, 1949), 18–25, 43, 45; (December 17, 1949), 26–29; *Katholieke Illustratie* (December 22, 1949), 1680–84.

is his series of portraits of Cardinal Montini, the future Pope Paul VI, then Archbishop of Milan.[37] A much more liberal figure, Paul VI became the instigator of a document produced by the Second Vatican Council, *Nostra Aetate*, a declaration on the relation of the Church to non-Christian religions which radically redefined the church's relationship to the Jews: "In her rejection of every persecution against any man, the Church, mindful of the patrimony she shares with the Jews and moved not by political reasons but by the Gospel's spiritual love, decries hatred, persecutions, displays of anti-Semitism, directed against Jews at any time and by anyone."[38]

The Council would take place on October 28, 1965, almost exactly nine years after Chim's death.

Chim was at his best, and his photographs were livelier, more intimate and whimsical, when he captured aspects of everyday life without and within the Vatican, the marginal aspects of the big story: workers queuing at the canteen, each with a different expression, each holding a tin container for his food, and a close-up on the tired, watchful[39] faces of the destitute at the soup kitchen[40]; the two sisters in stained aprons and white wimples ladling out rations from a gigantic pot from which they feed 600 workers every day[41]; a vendor outside the Vatican walls holding a cluster of balloons, with Saint Peter's cupola in the background[42] (Figure 93); a classic perspective of workers getting ready for the pilgrims, hosing, widening and repaving the Via della Conciliazone leading to St Peter's; a branch of the Banco Santo Spirito, plastered with Communist posters; a monk reading an old manuscript from the Vatican collections; a laborer, body relaxed in sleep, napping against one of the Bernini columns that encircle St Peter's Square; a gaggle of round-hatted, black-robed priests wandering on St Peter's roof among the cupolas; black seminarians from the Ethiopian College playing ball in an interior courtyard [43] (Figure 94); the Swiss Guards' laundry drying on the line in early-morning sun.

A few years later, when Chim showed Morris and his wife around the Vatican, everyone still remembered him: "[it was] a visit conducted by Chim, our very own Roman emperor. Chim (...) seemed to know everyone: the pope's chauffeur, shoemaker, and pharmacist, the gardeners and plainclothesmen, the scholars of the Vat-

---

37 MPNYA, PAR328139.
38 Nostra Aetate, Declaration on the Relation of the Church to Non-Christian Religions, Proclaimed by His Holiness Pope Paul VI on October 28, 1965. https://www.vatican.va/archive/hist_councils/ii_vatican_council/documents/vat-ii_decl_19651028_nostra-aetate_en.html, accessed February 28, 2022.
39 MPNYA, NYC131508.
40 MPPA, PAR328141.
41 MPNYA, PAR286101.
42 MPNYA, PAR153617.
43 MPPA, PAR153612.

ican library, the cleaners of the carpets in the Sistine Chapel. Pope Pius XII had given him a private photographic audience."[44]

A photograph of people queuing at the Vatican grocery store under lines of hanging salami seems like the best introduction to Chim's next reportage. Morris had assigned him to photograph a piece about Rome and its neighborhoods for the *Ladies Home Journal*. This time, he was invited to write the script himself, and he seemed excited at the possibility of deepening his knowledge of the city he had come to love. In a letter to his American editor, Corbin Gwaltney, he explained his desire to link past and present in the project:

> What I am trying is to get a few photographic visions of places and tell a story related to them. I am searching for light stories which have some human appeal. The ones which move you and fill you with wisdom derived from the feeling that people were always human and that passions are similar and that traces of that remain in stone (…). Today I took my camera and my books and was sitting in the sun and reading and photographing. It was a joy. And the book was Stendhal's *Promenades romaines*, and how alive it is![45]

In a letter to Morris,[46] he acknowledged the complexity involved in shooting a story on a city, as opposed to earlier, simpler reportages on the farming world. He made detailed comments on the photographs he was sending in and wrote lengthy captions, explaining the logic behind his choices of subjects, how he got to know and interview them so that he could be accepted when he photographed, and why he had alternated color and black and white, striking a compromise between the color editors now wanted, and his personal preference for black and white.

Hesitant about including views of Rome's nightlife ("Capa considered there is a need in my story for elements of luxury and nightlife; I personally do not agree, but to be on the safe side, I asked Carl Perutz, who is now in Rome, to take a shot of one of the luxury nightclubs and one of the exclusive shops along Via Condotti"[47]) and deciding "against the obvious and well-known views," he chose to focus instead on different aspects of the city.

For his color lead, he decided on the beautiful stone sculpted Trevi Fountain, where Neptune rides a shell-shaped chariot. The fountain is the terminal point of the aqueduct that has supplied water for the city since Roman times where tossing a coin in the water with the right hand over the left shoulder is supposed to bring good luck. "I thought this corner has it—the color of Rome, the fountain, the legend, the church, and the human element of people sitting around and children playing," Chim wrote to Morris.[48] Throughout his reportage, he tried to associate ancient, his-

---

44 John Godfrey Morris, *Get the Picture: A Personal History of Photojournalism* (Chicago: University of Chicago Press, 2002), 115.
45 DSA, April 16, 1949.
46 DSA, May 20, 1949, JGMAUC, unnumbered.
47 DSA, May 20, 1949, JGMAUC, unnumbered.
48 See previous note.

torical elements with the present, showcasing the layers of history that Rome represents. One photograph, for instance, focused on a giant poster for Coca Cola, the bright letters a stark contrast with the Coliseum's weathered walls.

With this idea established, he focused on street life. Looking for a flavor of everyday Rome, he found a small, cobbled street, the Via dei Lavatori, running from the fountain to the marketplace.

He followed his usual method, getting to know local people who in turn introduced him to others, forming a chain of personal contacts.[49] Through a doctor, Francesco Lilli, who was beloved in the neighborhood, he gained access to the Pirazzoli family. Through Mrs. Pirazzoli he met the baker, the pasta and egg salesman (*Pasta e Uova*), the butcher, the poultry and lamb seller, and the owner of the *salumeria* (the pork and sausage shop). At the produce market, he photographed the vegetable stand owner, then the wine shop manager, before visiting the local priest, who in turn phoned the schoolteacher, the postman, and the policeman.

This motley crew recovered at the local café, the Aurora Bar, where Chim learned the technique of espresso-making and photographed the manager, who served up to 1,000 cups of coffee a day.

Enlarging the frame for his story, he photographed the busy buses and trams, and finally visited the Royal Theatre, where operas were staged; then he started worrying that there would not be enough room in the *Ladies Home Journal* to fit all these images.

Throughout this story, Chim used the Rollei, which allowed him to include a lot of background in his frame (as in several sun-and-shade treatments of the Via dei Lavatori, some shot from a bird's-eye perspective; intimate interior views of the Pirazolli's apartment during a meal; or a portrait of the butcher, Mario Ricci, under the suspended calf heads and skinned rabbits that hang at his shop's entrance) or, alternatively, to focus on close-up portraits. One of his best is a tender photograph of the young Doctor Lilli, his head on a small girl's chest, tracking her heartbeat while he gently probes her stomach. In full uniform, Vittellio Lucantoni, the policeman, poses in front of the Palazzo Poli, near the fountain he is guarding. Giuseppe Fortù, the baker, bends over, sliding bread into the oven with his large wooden peel.[50]

All through the story, the choice of modest subjects and the sense of empathy displayed in the portraits evoke stills from neorealist films such as De Sica's *Bicycle Thieves*, which Chim might have seen when it came out in the previous year, taking his inspiration from the street and market scenes of the movie, or *Rome, Open City* by Roberto Rossellini, whose portrait Chim would make many times.

The fields of photography and films were, at the time, following parallel aesthetics, and photographers were often hired to publish photo-documentaries, coming up with plots, ideas, and storylines expressed in sequenced photographs that could in-

---

49 See DST on Rome, 7–10. MPNYA ADSS 1949.
50 MPNYA, ADSS 1949, contacts 49-8-1 and seq.

spire new movies. Chim's Rome images could easily have been the basis for such a film.

A photograph of Chim riding a donkey in a mountain village, wearing a suit and tie with two laughing villagers looking on,[51] documents a trip he took to Macedonia in October or November. In a letter to his family, he wrote:

> Just came back from a fascinating trip to the Yugoslavia-Albania borders in Northern Macedonia. It is an amazing country, high mountains—bad roads—winds and rain—and the wonderful clear days—with the mountain tops white with snow. I feel a little tired but it was fun. We went to villages where there is no road, on donkeys, and rowed the mountain lakes on motorboats. By the end of this week I will be in Rome then Paris.[52]

It was probably during this trip that, in contrast to the sadness of his earlier 1948 reportage on the refugees of the Greek civil war, he shot a more optimistic story in Oxia, a remote mountain village. Little Elefteria was the only child who had not been evacuated during the war. Dressed in an oversize, ragged sweater, her hair cut in a bowl shape, Elefteria tried on her first pair of shoes, distributed by UNICEF: "For a long time four-year old Elefteria just stared at the new shoes. Finally, her grandmother was allowed to put them on her feet. Then the ice was broken. Elefteria ran through the village, laughing with delight. Her happiness was absolutely perfect," Chim wrote. The lively, compassionate image sequence, reflecting Elefteria's puzzlement when her grandmother fits the shoes on her feet, then her unbounded joy, seems like a set of stills for a short film and the story was widely published.[53] (figure 16)

After a birthday celebration at the house of the UN representative in Salonica ("even a cake with 21 candles—evidently in my age the number stops on that") he traveled on to Finland and the Arctic Circle. From Hotel Torni in Helsinki. Aware of his own prudishness and distaste for outdoors activity, he wrote:

> Just spent [a] few wonderful days 400 km above the Arctic circle. It took [a]twenty-four hours train ride from Helsinki. Then ten hours car ride up north to arrive to a nice little village lost in the snow. The sky was getting reddish around ten o'clock in the morning— then two-three hours grey daylight—more of a twilight—then eve and [a] little red again to dignify sunset— and darkness back again. It was exceptionally warm, only 15 degrees below—but inside the houses an open fireplace was burning all the time to make life nice and pleasant. The people were charming to us. I seldom was received with more kindness. So we sat around the fire, played cards, drank coffee all the time and every night around eleven went to the traditional steam bath (sauna) to sweat it out. Naturally, I was not running naked in the snow like most of them did. I just watched them to find out to my amazement that such things really exist.[54]

---

51 DSA, November 22, 1949.
52 MPNYA, ADSS 1949.
53 MPNYA and MPPA, see image sequence: NYC131512, PAR116261, PAR210055, PAR231764, PAR116262, NYC70110.
54 DSA, letter to family, November 22, 1949.

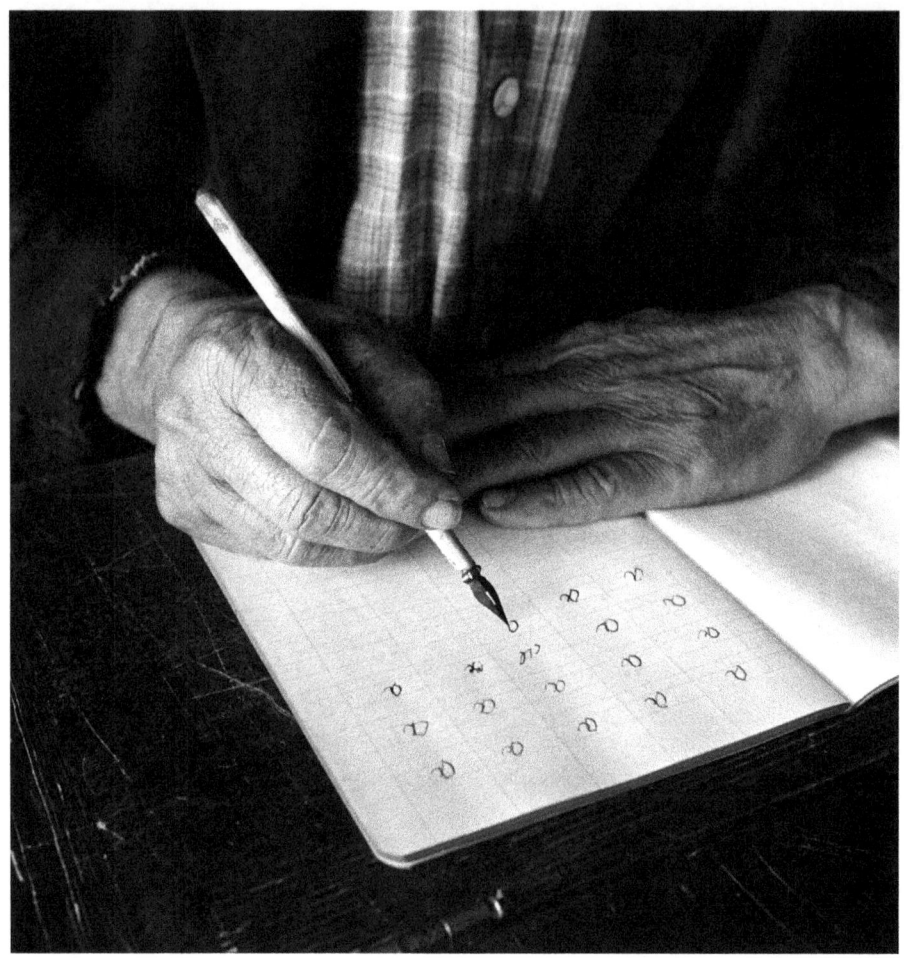

Fig. 13: Peasant during a writing class. Roggiano Gravina, Calabria, Italy, 1950. © David Seymour-Magnum Photos.

Chapter 11: Tracing the Letters. 1950

In the Spring of 1950, UNESCO commissioned Chim again, this time to document the state of the Italian south, the *Mezzogiorno*, in its continuing fight against illiteracy.

This part of the country was very different from Milan, Rome, and Venice—the places he knew best. His previous experience of the south had been limited to the short trip he had taken two years earlier to Naples, Basilicata, Bari, and the troglodyte village of Matera. Nothing had prepared him for the poverty and isolation he would meet in the *Mezziogiorno*.

Lucania, as it was called then, was a harsh countryside, too hot in summer, too cold in winter, where poor peasants etched a living in isolated villages, with heavy winter snow often making roads impassable. In contrast to northern Italy, which was experiencing rapid progress, the *Mezzogiorno* had not undergone an industrial revolution and it had all the characteristics of an underdeveloped region: misery, subsistence agriculture, "*latifundia*" (landed estates), underemployment, illiteracy. The contrast between north and south was strikingly unfair at a human level—and politically dangerous.

UNESCO was very active in the region, working in cooperation with the main Italian organization operating in the field at the time: the *Unione Nazionale per la Lotta contro l'Analfabetismo* or UNLA (National League for the Struggle against illiteracy). At the time illiteracy affected as much as 35 percent of Italy's rural population and the UNLA was part of an effort to open a large number of schools. By 1950, that initiative had reached 300,000 adults and children, creating People's Cultural Centers where adults who had benefited from the literacy classes could pursue their education. Also that year, the Cassa per il Mezzogiorno, a government effort to stimulate growth in southern Italy, started coordinating a basic program of public investment in the south, and UNESCO was continuing its efforts by sending an envoy, the education expert Paul Lengrand, to various centers in Calabria and Lucania.

In his decision to accept the UNESCO assignment, Chim was undoubtedly influenced by his friendship with Carlo Levi. In the two years since Chim and Levi had first met and befriended each other, Chim's vision had been deeply influenced by Levi's work.

Levi's relationship to the region went way back. As an antifascist and a Jew, he had been arrested several times, incarcerated in Turin and Rome, and finally exiled by Mussolini's government to one of the poorest regions in the south, the Basilicata. *Christ Stopped at Eboli*, the famous memoir he wrote after his year there, had repercussions far beyond literary circles. Thanks to him, the *Mezzogiorno* question was finally an issue for public debate. Chim, an avid reader, had read the book as well as a 1949 *New York Times* piece Levi wrote on illiteracy, which was illustrated by his paintings,[1] and had visited Levi's studio in 1948.

For Levi, art was a form of active resistance to the rise of fascism and its cultural politics, and the condition of southern Italy was both a fundamental tenet of his political work and a magnet for his creativity as a writer and a painter. Throughout his life, he would pursue his political and social activism in defense of the peasants he had come to love when he lived among them. He became an informal ambassador of the *civiltà contadine*, the civilization of the poor, excluded, landless peasants who could be found anywhere on the planet, translating their life and culture for an urban, metropolitan civilization:

> They [the peasants] live in an immobile and timeless world circumscribed by ancient rites and customs and the tasks imposed by the changing seasons; yet, a world that is rich in human values and a culture all its own (...) a peasant art and a peasant philosophy that have been handed down without benefit of the written word in the heritage of legends, folk-tales, popular dramas and songs (...).[2]

There are striking similarities between Levi's paintings and Chim's photographs from the south—the faces and everyday gestures, the arid landscapes and steep mountain paths, the small, dark houses that seem to huddle together, and the ubiquitous animals. Chim visited Levi's studio once more after his trip, as is documented in the contact sheets kept in Magnum's New York office, and when he saw Levi's paintings, he must have been struck by how little things had changed in the *Mezzogiorno* between Levi's exile there and his own trip 14 years later.

Chim's reportage functions as a classic series, telling a story sequentially. But if we focus on individual pictures, it becomes a very different matter. He worked with close-ups inside peasants' homes, old mills, disused barns, and cellars that served as classrooms. He used the poor lighting to create strong, dramatic, chiaroscuro effects. The individual photographs seem to expand into contemplative moments. It seems as if Chim, like Levi, had been able to leave behind the accelerated rhythm of urban life and started to share in the slow, almost immobile sense of time that was part of his subjects' lives (figure 13).

Back in Rome after his reportage, Chim photographed Levi in his studio (figure 84) and made wonderful portraits of his owl, Graziadio, often portrayed by Levi. [3]The

---

1 Carlo Levi, "Eboli Revisited: New Life Stirs," *The New York Times*, March 13, 1949; Levi, "Italy Fights the Battle of Illiteracy"; and his other articles: "Peasants Stir in Groping Italy," *The New York Times*, September 14, 1947; "Is Europe Through? A Decided 'No'," *The New York Times*, December 7, 1947; "For Freedom We Must Conquer Fear," *The New York Times*, October 3, 1948; and "Italy's Peasants Look at Land Reform," *The New York Times*, May 17, 1953.
2 Carlo Levi in *Christ Stopped at Eboli*, 1945.
3 MPNYA, PAR291996.

Gufo story, as they called it, would be published together with Chim's photographs in the UNESCO *Courier* in 1957.[4] The owl, an ancient animal that plays a role in peasant animistic cults, was connected to the question of time and crucial for the construction of Levi's novel *The Watch* published the same year.[5] In the novel, the vision of an archaic temporality, embodied by the owl, merges with the clock, a symbol of a modern time. In Chim's photographs as in Levi's novel, time was definitely on the side of the owl.

Chim's reportage on illiteracy bears an extraordinary similarity in style and point of view to his 1948 photographs of children in Hungary, Poland, and Austria. Those children were victims of war, but when Chim visited them at school, he captured them hard at work, trying to catch up on the learning they had missed during the war years. In this new reportage, the children's postures as they hunched over their text- or notebooks or pored over maps, the paucity of learning materials, the improvised surroundings, furniture—child-sized tables, chairs, and benches—and the improvised classroom materials all recall those postwar photographs. Chim gathered the information he needed on site, from the devoted doctors and teachers in the region. But, more importantly, his vision was nourished by his constant observations: he noted the way people walked in the street, how the women carried furniture, vegetables, or hay on their heads, how the men tilled and watered their fields, cared for their flocks, cobbled up furniture from spare wood, how the women knitted and sewed...[6]

In his photographs, he seemed to be suggesting that the people in the *Mezzogiorno* were also oppressed victims of a war of sorts, waged not through weapons but through politics, that had created a huge disparity between north and south. The people of southern Italy had been forgotten by progress. They seemed to live in an enclave where time had stopped, while the rest of the country advanced in big strides in the 1950s and 1960s—a period that has been called the "Italian economic miracle."

---

4 "As yet, I have no news from New York about publication of our 'Gufo' story. I only know that Mrs. Snow couldn't publish it because they are filled up with the Raadkais [sic] Italian material. HOLIDAY is considering it, but I have no final decisions. You know that Mondadori will use it in EPOCA, and also it will appear in ILLUSTRATED in London." Chim to Carlo Levi, October 2, 1950, Archivio dello Stato, Archivio Carlo Levi, Correspondence 1924–1975, envelope 37, dossier 1306. The story was eventually published in a special issue of the *UNESCO Courier* entitled "Famous Authors as Artists." Introduced by a brief essay on Carlo Levi illustrated with his own paintings, "The Owl" was illustrated with photographs by David Seymour. See "Carlo Levi: Artist by Day, Author by Night," *UNESCO Courier* 10, no. 8 (August 1957), 25; and Carlo Levi, "The Owl," ibid., 26–27.
5 Carlo Levi, *L'orologio* (Milan: Einaudi, 1950). An English translation, *The Watch*, was published by Farrar Straus & Young in 1951.
6 For a detailed analysis, see Karin Priem in-depth study: "Visual presence and Interpretation: Two dimensions of the Fights Against Illiteracy in Texts by Carlo Levi and Photographs by David Seymour", in *Appearances: Studies in Visual Research* 3, (Berlin: DeGruyter, 2021), 189–202.

Chim did not limit himself to the fight against illiteracy. Just as he had done in *Children of Europe*, he went beyond the assignment, to paint a broader picture of the peasants' life. Exploring the streets, he made portraits of girls walking barefoot or in makeshift shoes along the village's muddy paths, wrapped in wool shawls against the cold, sitting in a door-frame, doing homework; of women and even children carrying huge loads of furniture or firewood on their heads (Figure 83); of a young boy with his dog and a young shepherd (Figure 82); of a woman crowned with a nest of dried flowers or vegetables; of a village teacher on his motorcycle; of farm-workers, the *braccianti*, occupying the land and tilling the dry fields—just as in his reportages on the Spanish Civil War.

He expanded his view to include the unforgiving landscape of steep mountains and narrow, twisting paths, and the barren fields dotted with few trees. This journey into nature depicts the humble objects of everyday life, light, shadows, and animals, as if he was traveling into the mind and consciousness of the people he photographed. His photographs are not merely anthropological, they have a sense of depth and radiate poetry. They are deeply personal and imbued with empathy and emotion. All in all, Chim created a lyrical portrait of a fragile society on the brink of change.[7]

In a letter to Levi dated December 26, 1951, Chim wrote: "The Italian Government finally authorized the distribution of my story about analphabetism [illiteracy]in Calabria and I am getting ready to distribute it in the magazines. As you remember, you authorized me to distribute your *New York Times* article with the story so I will proceed in this direction."[8] Chim's photographs and one of Levi's articles would be distributed together by Magnum and published in March 1952 by the UNESCO *Courier* and the Dutch magazines *Panorama* and *Katholieke Illustratie*.[9]

While especially powerful, the pairing of Chim's photographs and Levi's text was in no way unique. As of the early 1940s, the relationship between writers and photographers or filmmakers had undergone a profound change. Still and moving images were no longer considered a simple illustration of words. In 1942, Elio Vittorini, influenced by Walker Evans's *American Photographs* (1939), edited the anthology *Americana*, a collection of short stories illustrated by photographs.[10] In 1950, he and the photographer Luigi Crocenzi made a trip to Sicily where Crocenzi took 1,600

---

7 For a detailed look at Chim's illiteracy reportage, see the book *They did not stop at Eboli* (Unesco/De Gruyter, 2019), 183. The book contains all Chim contact sheets for the illiteracy story, a large number of photographs, and studies by Giovanna Hendel, Juri Meda, Carole Naggar, and Karin Priem. For a selection of Chim's *Children of Europe* photographs, see Carole Naggar, *Chim's Children of War* (New York: Umbrage Editions, 2013).
8 Letter from Chim to Carlo Levi, December 26, 1951, Archivio Centrale dello Stato, Archivio Carlo Levi, Corrispondenza 1924–1975, envelope 37, dossier 1306.
9 "Zuid Italië leert het ABC," *Panorama* (March 21, 1952), 5–7; "Van zes tot zestig," *Katholieke Illustratie*, (March 21, 1952), cover, 2-3.
10 *Americana*, first published in 1942, was reissued in July 2015 by Bompiani, Milan.

photographs for a new edition of Vittorini's 1941 *Conversazione in Sicilia* (*Conversations in Sicily*), which Bompiani would publish in 1953.

As previously noted, Chim's work has a lot in common with the photographs of the post-war Italian neorealists.[11] In the words of writer Martina Caruso,[12] the photographs that Chim's colleagues Haas and Bischof took in southern Italy, or the work of the American Marjorie Collins, all commissioned by the US State Department, "corresponded to a dry, straightforward documentary style, at time accompanied with anthropological or *National Geographic*-style descriptions."

A much more lyrical style often called "lyrical realism," and akin to Chim's, was visible in Enzo Sellerio, Mario de Biasi, and Fulvio Roiter's 1950s work in Sicily, Ando Gilardi's photographs of the land strikes of Emilia Romagna peasants, and Aldo Beltrame's stories on Friuli peasants, among others. Foreign photographers, such as Paul Strand with his famous series *Un Paese*, also worked in that style and, like Chim, used a medium-format camera.[13] The magazine *Cinema Nuovo* published these photographic reportages on specific people or regions as potential storylines or inspiration for films.

At the time, the discovery of the south was also the leitmotif of ethnographic missions. Noted anthropologist and communist Ernesto de Martino documented his journeys into the underdeveloped regions of Italy and during a period of intense engagement with the rural populations of the south, he met Levi and discovered the universe of the peasantry. In his research on the world of magic and religious rituals, he stressed the dialectics between archaic elements and the peasants' resistance to cultural colonization from the industrial north. Demonstrating a point of view strikingly similar to that of Levi and Chim, he once said:

> I have personal experience of the Lucania peasants, I know many of them by name and surname, and I know their life stories; I stayed with them for a long time, I visited their homes, I ate and drank with them (...). Society had thrown them into misery, had denied them the two most important means of culture, reading and writing, but as whole persons they had never resigned to recite the role of the uncultured in the world, and through the pressure of the critical events of life, birth, food, fatigue, love, and death, they had built a system of responses, that is, a cultural life, thus building, against the written tradition of hegemonic culture, the oral tradition of their knowledge (...). Nobody has written this dramatic history of the oppressed, but someone must do it.[14]

---

11 The Italian Neorealists were recently featured in an exhibition and a book: Enrica Vigano, ed., *NeoRealismo: The New Image in Italy 1932–1960* (Milan: Admira Edizioni; Munich: Prestel; London and New York: Delmonico Books, 2018). The exhibition took place at the Grey Art Gallery, New York, from September 6 to December 8, 2018.
12 Martina Caruso, *Italian Humanist Photography from Fascism to the Cold War* (London: Bloomsbury, 2016), 91–92.
13 Paul Strand and Cesare Zavattini, *Un Paese* (Milan: Einaudi, 1955). An American edition, *Un Paese: Portrait of an Italian Village*, was published in 1997 by Aperture.
14 Ernesto de Martino, *Panorama e spedizioni: le trasmissioni radiofoniche 1953–1954* (Torino: Bollati Borighieri, 2002), 34. Unless otherwise noted, all translations are by the author.

While fascist propaganda had used photography and words as tools to show the "New Italy," Chim and Levi turned those weapons around to reveal the Italy that had been denied by fascism: the poor, archaic Italy that did not trust, or care about, governmental promises. They illuminated the poverty and hunger, the lack of access to land and education—the daily life of the peasants—that propaganda photographs never showed.

A Polish Jew, Chim, whose world approach was close to the Italian sensibility, liked to call himself "a Mediterranean." As for Levi, his biographers dubbed him "*un torinese del Sud*."[15] Both men managed to penetrate, appreciate, and do justice to a civilization and a people to which they did not belong. They did not keep their distance but sought, successfully, to be witnesses and protagonists at the same time.

For Chim, most probably guided by Levi's writings, the journey provided both a way to reconnect with his political past and a creative direction for the future. Over the next six years, the photo essays and texts he would create depicting religious and pagan rituals in the Italian south—in Caltanissetta, Piana dei Greci, Cagliari, Isnello, Capobasso, San Fratello, and Cocullo...—were a follow-up to that first illiteracy reportage.

The two men answered to a Jewish tradition of ethics embodied in the concept of "*tikkun olam*"—repairing the world—a phrase that has come to embody the concept of social justice. Both of their lives had been deeply affected by the Holocaust, and with their ethical values informing their life's work, they shared a hunger for political engagement and a belief in the value of the individual over the system, recognizing the immense importance of each lived experience. Making human beings the center and subjects of their stories and of history, they sided with the most vulnerable members of society. Their meeting was truly a meeting of minds.

In 1961, Hala and her husband Emil contacted Levi and asked him to write an introduction for an illustrated monograph on Chim that they were planning. Levi accepted but the book was never published,[16] and I have not found any draft in his Rome papers.

Levi kept the promise he had made to the Basilicata peasants that he would be back. He was buried in Aliano, Lucania, where he had spent one of the most important years of his life.

---

15 Gigliola de Donato and Sergio d'Amaro, *Un torinese del Sud, Carlo Levi: Una biografia* (Milan: Baldini & Castoldi, 2001).

16 DSA, letter from Hala and Emil to Carlo Levi, January 1961.

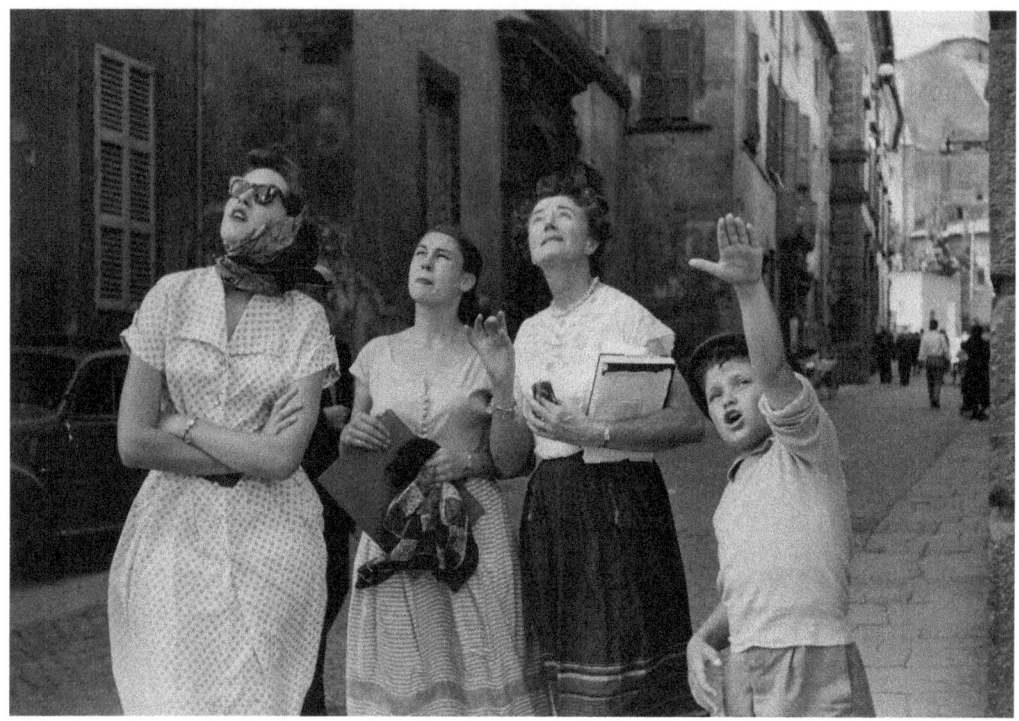

Fig. 14: Young Roberto Moncelsi shows tourists architectural details of Orvieto's Duomo, 1954. From the series *The World of Children*. © David Seymour-Magnum Photos.

Chapter 12: Generation X: This is our Character, this is our Strength. 1952

The early 1950s were a time of reflection for Magnum. Its members were sobered by the difficulties they faced in keeping their fledgling cooperative financially afloat. They needed to expand their list of clients beyond *This Week*, *Illustrated*, *Heute*, *Panorama*, *Epoca*, and *Holiday*.

Chim's role at Magnum was very much that of a peacemaker, as evidenced by several private letters he exchanged in April and May with Maria Eisner, who was in strong disagreement with Capa's leadership, which she found too autocratic. One thing she especially disagreed with was Capa's idea to join forces with a New York agency, Scope. Always the diplomat, Chim acknowledged Eisner's important contribution to the agency over the years and tried to minimize the problems:

> I hoped we would avoid the present open conflict. I wrote to you trying to impress on you the need of not destroying the 4-year old unity of the 'old timers' group. My suggestion to appoint Capa acting president for the interim period was made in view of our present emergency. And I hoped that you would accept it—even welcome it (...) Leadership is not always element of 'führership'. There is a great deal of coordination and decisions to be taken in Magnum and some person has to take them. I feel that Capa's position in Magnum in the past make[s] it logical that, with you unable to attend to, he should be entrusted officially. (...) Capa is planning to fly to NY next week and I encourage him to do so. A personal conversation with you is more than needed and I hope that you will arrive jointly to the best solution. Please, Maria, talk with Capa without any prejudice or hurt feelings. Magnum is so important to our future that we cannot treat it lightly. Give Capa all the benefit of your experience and impress on him the need of serious attitude toward the responsibility he freely accepts during the interim period. I plead with you—accept the majority desire and do everything to overcome the present crisis. (...) In January we all get together and on the basis of all, our experience will decide about the future

Robert Capa remained as an interim president, and in one of his reports to the stockholders, he reviewed the agency's first five years, listing some stringent problems but also showing optimism about the future:

> As I said above, the basic policy was rather childish and mystic. We had been babbling about the pictures we wanted to take and insisted that the magazines respect our artistic and reporting integrity (...). We are not as good as we think we are. Our pretensions are enormous. Our working methods are idiotic and wasteful. And we are existing. (...) We have a very valuable outfit which very soon can give its members security and at the same time artistic and moral independence, which certainly no agency or even staff can offer. (...) We can succeed in making a fair and not unpleasant living in a not too fair or too pleasant a world.[2]

---

[1] DSA, letter to Maria Eisner, date Rome, May 11, 1951.
[2] Robert Capa, Report to the Magnum Stockholders, February 15, 1952, MFNY, 010-004-001.

He also reiterated that photographers should pay attention to what editors were looking for: "human interest" stories, yes, but "stories with guts, drama, and timely journalistic angles."[3] To achieve these goals, Capa worked both as a photographer and as a packager of stories that would reinforce unity in the group by creating joint assignments.

It is often thought that Capa, capitalizing on the success of the "People Are People" project, came up with a new idea on a similar template: "Generation X," a story about children coming of age after World War II. And he is credited with coining the term: "We named this unknown generation, the Generation X, and even in our first enthusiasm we realized that we had something far bigger than our talents and pockets could cope with."[4] However, Burt Glinn, then a young Magnum photographer, remembered it differently: "Chim was responsible for a lot of things that Magnum was able to do. After the war, *Holiday* was starting out. Chim came up with the idea that we ought to do stories on Generation X, people born after the atomic bomb. It was the kind of idea that Chim's mind would form."[5]

At the beginning of 1949, Magnum sent a short proposal to several magazines, pitching the project as an ambitious international survey that would combine pictures and interviews: "The purpose of the project is to explore the problems and aspirations of youth—Generation X—the generation which is now coming of age and on whose shoulders lie the burden of history during the coming half-century."[6]

Capa initially sold the idea to *McCalls*, but as the finished stories came in, both *McCalls* and Magnum felt, probably justifiably, that the profiles were "too documentary, lacking mobility, excitement, and interest", as Pat Hogan stated in a forceful letter addressed to the photographers.[7] Gael Mayo, a writer-researcher who worked with Cartier-Bresson and Chim at the time, has still another version of the story:

> Unexpectedly disaster struck 'Generation X.' Thousands of dollars and months of shooting and research had been invested in it, but according to John G. Morris, in an article published in 1974, the child of Capa almost died, killing with it Magnum's future. The reason was that the magazine that had originally agreed to back it wanted to make radical cuts. Capa did not agree and since he was not one to be pushed around, he withdrew it from them. It was not until six months later that disaster was averted, when Capa sold it to *Holiday*, and Magnum's momentary fragility was overcome. It grew its true strength from then on. *Holiday* called it 'Youth of the World.' Our story was the lead in three issues.[8]

---

3 Robert Capa, Report to the Magnum Stockholders, February 15, 1952, MFNY, 010-004-001.
4 I was unable to source this quote. It is repeated on several sites, such as for instance https://www.thevintagenews.com/2017/07/05/robert-capa-called-the-greatest-war-photographer-in-the-world/ Retrieved August 12, 2020.5
5 Interview of Burt Glinn by the author, East Hampton, New York, November 10, 2005.
6 JGMAUC, *Magnum Generation X*, October 20, 1950.
7 CNA Robert Capa to Pat Hogan, May 29, 1951, communicated 2005 by John Godfrey Morris from his Paris Archive, Paris, then unnumbered, later moved to University of Chicago.
8 Gael Mayo, *The Mad Mosaic, a Life Story* (London: Quartet Books, 1983).

In a letter to George Rodger, Robert Capa bluntly summed up his ordeal: "I sold GX ['Generation X']. All this meant lots of hustling because New York editors are stupid and scared and it takes [several] people to be seen at the same magazine before you can straighten out the smaller matter, for which finally they pay a ridiculously low sum."[9]

Determined that Magnum should handle the entire project, Capa hired new stringers: Eve Arnold, Dennis Stock, and Erich Hartmann. Chim recruited Erich Lessing, an Austrian who was a photographer with the Associated Press. The ten photographers were working under Capa's direction, and Roger Angell wrote the text. With the addition of this new generation of photographers, "Generation X" provided the impetus for Magnum to grow. Ten members of the agency fanned out to 14 countries to meet and photograph two dozen young people coming into adulthood in a war-scarred but freshly hopeful world: Cartier-Bresson (Great Britain), Chim (Italy, Germany, Israel), Werner Bischof (Japan), Capa (Germany, Norway), Fenno Jacobs, a *Fortune* photographer who occasionally worked on Magnum projects (Yugoslavia, Brazil), George Rodger (Kenya, Syria), Kryn Taconis (France), Homer Page (South Africa, Liberia), Ernst Haas (United States), Eve Arnold (United States). The series was a success, serialized in magazines such as *Point de Vue–Images du Monde*, and reprinted in others, among them, *Heute* and *Picture Post* as well as *Katholieke Illustratie*, *Panorama*, and *Epoca*.[10]

Among the best photos in that story are Capa's images of a troubled and apathetic German youth, Rudolf Kesslau, a coal miner and former member of a Nazi youth organization; compassionate photographs of street children in Chile that brought Sergio Larraín's work to attention; Leonard Freed's strong images of the civil rights movement; Arnold's work with migrant potato pickers on Long Island, one of her very first reportages; and stunning images of the life of a child on Daufuskie Island, South Carolina, that Constantine Manos made in 1952, when he was only 18 years old. Bischof contributed two stories, one on a young communist in Japan and one on a young Indian dancer; and Ernst Haas, a story on an American Marine lieutenant.

But Capa still felt unhappy with the final choice of subjects, finding them too watered down and apolitical. The Magnum proposal to include a French communist and an Egyptian prostitute had not met with favor by editors... "I felt that as much as the major problem of this generation is war, we certainly should have had a Western European conscript or at least a British sailor in it [the story]" he wrote.[11]

More telling perhaps was the absence of photographs from the Eastern bloc, except for Yugoslavia, which, under Tito, had split with Stalin in 1948. "Due to the Iron

---

9 GRA, Letter from Robert Capa to George Rodger, January 16, 1952.
10 *Aktuell* (Norway), *Femina* (Denmark), *Famillie Journal* (Denmark and Sweden), *Zondagsvriend* and *Soir Illustré* (Belgium), *De Spaarnestad* (Netherland), *Das Ufer* (Germany), *Du* (Switzerland).
11 Robert Capa, in *Report to the stockholders*, 2-15-52, MFNY, 010-004-00

Curtain, there are no young people in this story from the nations of the Soviet bloc," the editors wrote. "Because they are not here, it is difficult to speak with confidence about the chances of peace."[12]

Four years after it was originally pitched, *Holiday* finally published the story in three parts (January, February, and March 1953), with each issue devoting 10 to 15 pages to the story, and each young subject featured on three pages. The presentation was much livelier than the "People Are People" story; its mix of color and black-and-white gave it an up-to-date lifestyle and tourism feel.

The layout awarded the photographs a big play, with well-reproduced, single or double-page groupings of images, sometimes even full-bleed—without a white margin. The series was a success and led to two subsequent Magnum assignments for stories along the same lines: "Generation Women" and "Generation Children."

Ultimately, despite the concessions that Magnum had to make, Capa cited the collective project as an exemplar for the agency's future and wrote: "Its prestige value cannot be overestimated. We are the only outfit which has people on the same level of human and photographic quality, and while singly we may be replaced by other photographers from other agencies, no other outfit can produce collective jobs with such variations. This is our character. This is our strength." [12]

In choosing his Italian subjects, Chim had proceeded differently from many of his colleagues in trying to find a common thread that linked them. His theme was "the desire to escape from surroundings (...). Both of my characters—the girl and the boy—have left or would like to leave their homes and their families. Both of them have ambitions and they are looking for their own way (...). They feel that to get what they want from life they have to leave their homes and fight for what they believe is important for them. My story caught them in the early stage of this endeavor".[13] According to Chim, leaving home was common in Italy, where overpopulation often led to emigration, seen as a way to escape poverty. However, his choice was also an echo of his own life and the circumstances that pushed him towards Paris, then Rome, finding his own way to free himself from his family's traditions.

His first subject was Anita, an educated 20-year-old Sicilian from Messina who wanted to become an actress. Like many girls, she had the naive hope that a director in search of authenticity would pick her out from the street—it had happened a few times. After a protracted fight with her father who did not want her to leave, she finally was allowed to leave for Rome, where she would live with an aunt and attend a movie-acting school. When Chim met her, she had only been in Rome four months but swore to him she would not return to Sicily until she had appeared on the big screen. Thinking that Italy was not big enough for her ambitions, she had hopes of marrying an American and moving to the US.[14] Chim's story depicts Anita's efforts at

---

12 Robert Capa, in *Report to the stockholders*, 2-15-52, MFNY, 010-004-001.
13 "Youth and the World: Conclusion," *Holiday*, March 1953, 59.
14 MPNYA, ADS GX 1951024, DSC *Generation X Girl-Italy*.

self-transformation at the school: she takes lessons to lose her Sicilian accent; studies makeup; tries to learn to ride a horse; attends physical culture and dancing sessions. Two of the high points of her new life are the chance to wear expensive gowns while she models in a fashion show and going to a ball where she meets a young actor, Aldo Fabrizzi, who played the priest in Rossellini's recent film *Roma, Città Aperta* and might help her get a part.[15]

His other subject, 20-year-old Ubaldo ("Baldo") was from a more modest family in Umbria. Musically talented, he had won a prize in a national competition for accordionists. He worked on his father's farm and as an apprentice in a garage in Gubbio, while earning pocket money playing the accordion at Sunday dance halls.

Chim wrote: "Anita and Baldo, on different levels, represent the youth of Italy, who dream of a better life and a better future. They are both talented; they both have the love of music; the fascination of [sic] pageantry and a certain sense of theatre." About Baldo, he added: "His father made an effort to give him a good education, above the minimum prescribed by the law, and encouraged him to learn how to play the accordion. A year ago, there was the National Competition for accordionists in the city of Ancona. Baldo's father made it possible for him to attend and he won a prize." [16]Anita and Baldo both cite the return of relatives from prison camp—their father in one case, uncle in the other—as the happiest day of their lives.

The Baldo story,[17] shot in both Leica and Rollei, color and black and white, depicts private and public moments in his life. He practises the accordion in front of a fire at his house, which has no electricity: the scene is in chiaroscuro, with part of Baldo's face illuminated by an acetylene lamp and part of it in shadow (Figure 85) Then we see him playing in an open-air dance ball and participating in a parade of the San Antonio fraternity, the *Festa dei Ceri* (Race of the Candles) where he carries an enormous candle, then is rewarded with a free drink of wine at the fountain in the pouring rain. At the garage where he works as an unpaid mechanic to learn the trade, he is shown washing a car and crouching under a chassis. On the farm, he helps with harvesting the wheat. He spends his time off with his girlfriend Marietta, and they lie together in the ruins of the Roman theater in Gubbio while geese strut in the grass.

In Germany, Chim's subject is Rosemary, a refugee who came from Breslau to Freiburg, where she lives in an attic room with a small stove and no running water. For a "Generation X" questionnaire, Rosemary, who now studies history of art and philosophy, wrote: "I can say that I have not enough to eat. When I go to my parents' house during my vacation, I have a chance to eat more and immediately I can see a

---

15 MPNYA, ADS GX 195001-1951-004, DSC *Generation X Italy-Boy*.
16 Ibid.
17 MPNYA, ADS GX 1951001-GX1951004. Also see *Points de Vue: Images du Monde*, December 18, 1952, cover, 2.

difference in the way I feel." [18] Rosemary, who joined the Hitler Youth at ten, has had a change of heart; now, her greatest desire is the reunion of Germany's two parts.

For some time, Chim had wanted to go to Israel: to him, because of his family's story, it was homecoming. He seized the occasion that the Generation X project gave him for his long-delayed trip. He selected as his subject Cari, age 21, a "wife, mother, nurse, and border patrolman[sic]," whose main job was to care for the children of the kibbutz Jezreel near the Jordan border where she lived with 60 other people. "There is little to say about Cari's personal life," Chim writes, "because it is so impersonal, so shared with others. All her energies and her efforts are spent for and with the entire community." Diffident, Cari would not share her personal opinions: "I have a political conviction of my own, as all of us have," she wrote, "but I decline to talk about it (…) my political view is nothing to be discussed or argued with strangers."[19]

Back in Italy, Chim, who loved to act as a guide to his new home, showed Morris around Milan, then the mecca of Italian publishing, introducing him to editors—and to the Italian lifestyle. Morris described them "first calling on Arnoldo Mondadori", head of the house that published the picture weekly *Epoca*. Mondadori thought of himself as the Henry Luce of Italy and revered *Life*, which produced many a "copycat" sale for Magnum. "Chim and I lunched with Vincenzo Carrese, our new Italian agent—a previous one had absconded with Magnum money. That evening, sitting with Chim in the choicest seats of La Scala, I reflected that working with Magnum had rewards, even if not financial."[20]

There was an important editorial difference between "People Are People" and "Generation X." In the first series, Morris was looking for a unified vision, attempting to demonstrate the similarities of life in different countries. "Generation X" makes no such claims. Instead, the project describes lives that are singular, each with its own approach to the world and its own problems. The first post-was generation to come of age, most of the youngsters share very modest economic circumstances, with homes without hot water, electricity, or heat. But, also recognizing the diversity of their personal experiences, Roger Angell wrote in his accompanying text that this generation "did not speak with a single voice," and consisted of many individuals and "few recognizable types."[21]

The only thread linking the 23 youths from France, Germany, India, Israel, Japan, Italy, Liberia, and Yugoslavia was that they did not linger on memories of war, instead looking towards freedom from the past and the hope of a better life. By

---

18 MPNYA, ADS GX 1951, Rosemary's questionnaire.
19 MPNYA, ADS GX 1951, Cari from Kibbutz Jezreel, Israel's questionnaire, May 1952.
20 In John Godfrey Morris, *Get the Picture* (NY: Random House 2002), 150.
21 Roger Engell, *Holiday*, 1953, Part III, 59.

calling these young people Generation X, Capa had understood and acknowledged their singularity and the many dark threads of the unknown that wove their life stories.

On February 5, 1953, John Morris left *Ladies Home Journal* to become Magnum's editorial director. Historian Clara Bouveresse writes:

> He advised photographers, promoted their work and selected pictures with or without them—a process described as 'boiling down' stories. In the mid-fifties, there were two stages of selection: a first choice of thirty to fifty pictures, and then a set of six to eight pictures distributed internationally (...). In 1955, the New York office also started to sort stories according to their progress, marking each of the 200 topics being processed simultaneously: S, for Suggestion, the development of an idea; A, for Assignment, when the shooting took place; and P, for Pictures, at the post-production and sales stage.[22]

In this editorial role, Morris would oversee a new series of projects, which would entail being an intermediary between photographers and editors as both parties jostled for control of the story, and also ensuring that distribution would not be the overlarge selection of pictures that editors (such as *Life*'s Wilson Hicks, for instance) often demanded, but, rather, an organized, sequenced narrative reflecting the photographer's intentions, in line with the four founders' concept of a package story. Magnum's members were not satisfied with the promise of a copyright and a no-cropping policy; they also wanted to be sure that the captions editors affixed to their images would be faithful to their intentions. In a series of meetings in 1954, they wrote: "This photograph can be reproduced only with accompanying caption or with text strictly in the spirit of its caption."[23]

---

[22] Clara Bouveresse, https://www.tandfonline.com/eprint/5VCEJ84ZMTXCAMJPGSBU/full?target=10.1080/17514517.2020.1815967, accessed September 2, 2021; and John Morris, "Memo on the European Distribution System," June 19, 1956, MF011-001-001/2.

[23] Summary of Magnum meetings in Paris, June 29–July 3, 1954. MF010-004-001.

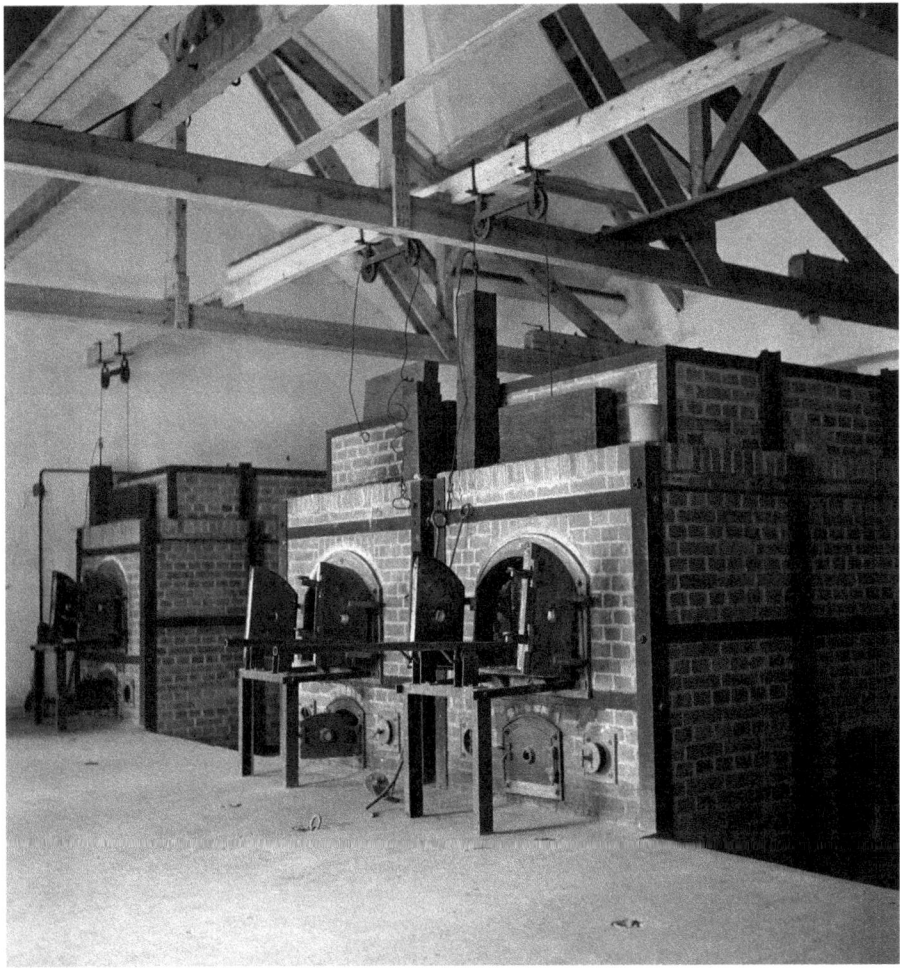

Fig. 50: Crematorium ovens at Dachau concentration camp, Spring 1947. © David Seymour-Magnum Photos.

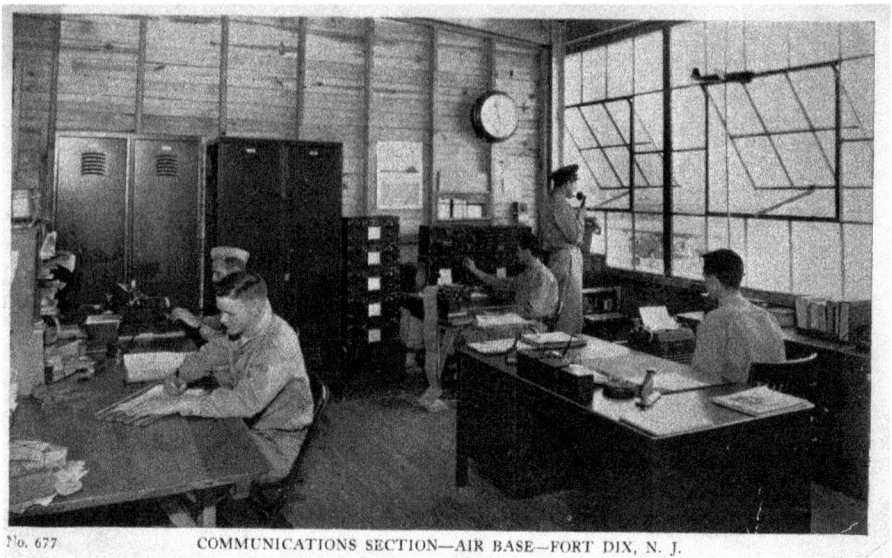

Fig. 51: Office where Chim worked as a communications specialist during World War II, Fort Dix, New Jersey, 1940. © davidseymour.com online archive.

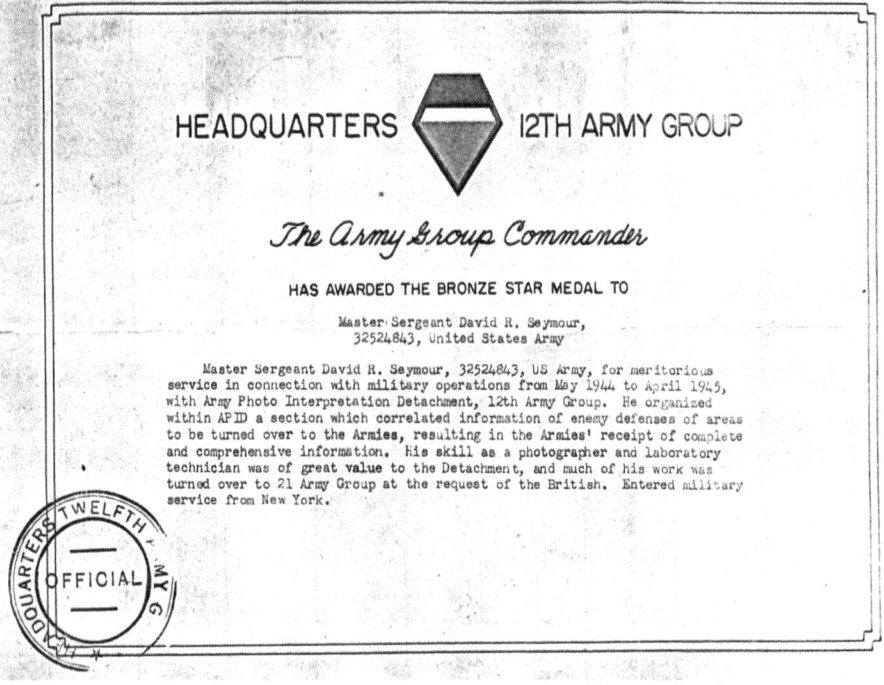

Fig. 52: Chim's Bronze Star Diploma, 1945. © davidseymour.com online archive.

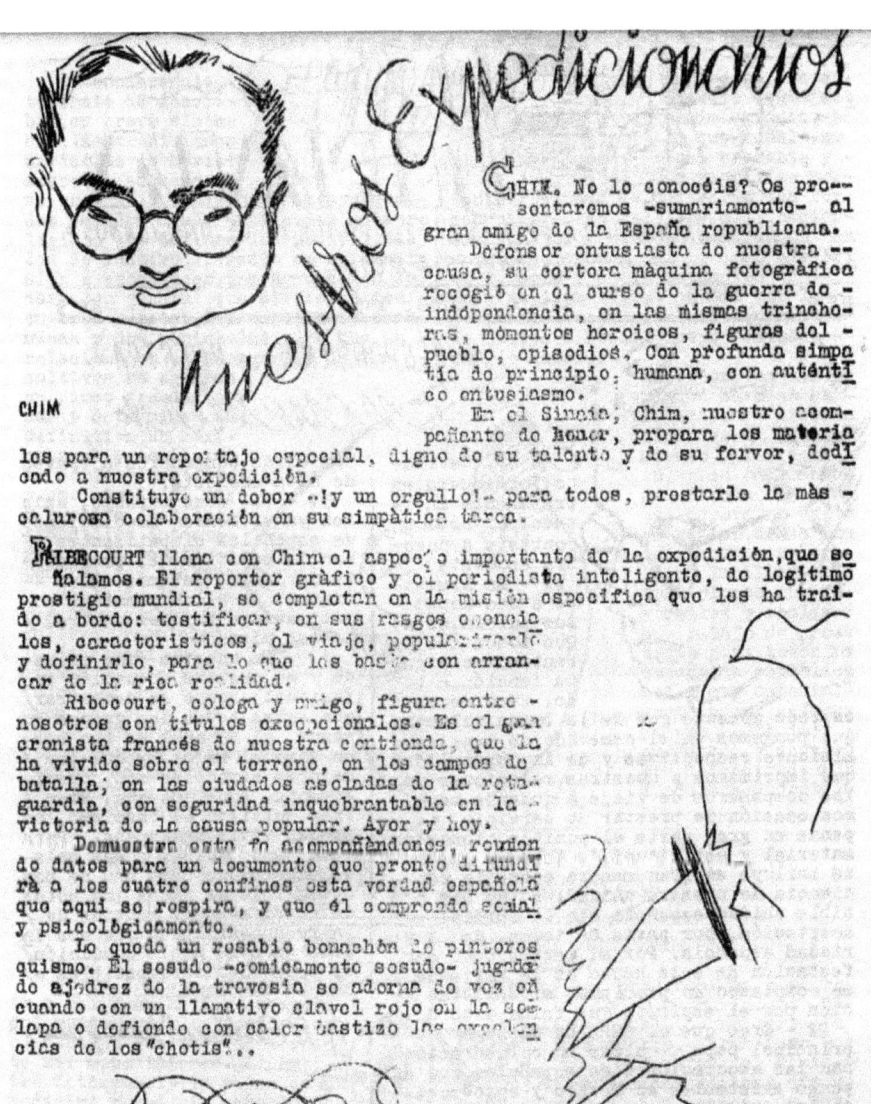

Nuestros Expedicionarios

CHIM

CHIM. No lo conocéis? Os presentaremos -sumariamente- al gran amigo de la España republicana.

Defensor entusiasta de nuestra causa, su certera máquina fotográfica recogió en el curso de la guerra de independencia, en las mismas trincheras, momentos heroicos, figuras del pueblo, episodios. Con profunda simpatía de principio, humana, con auténtico entusiasmo.

En el Sinaia, Chim, nuestro acompañante de honor, prepara los materiales para un reportaje especial, digno de su talento y de su fervor, dedicado a nuestra expedición.

Constituye un deber -¡y un orgullo!- para todos, prestarle la más calurosa colaboración en su simpática tarea.

RIBECOURT llena con Chim el aspecto importante de la expedición, que señalamos. El reportero gráfico y el periodista inteligente, de legítimo prestigio mundial, se completan en la misión específica que les ha traído a bordo: testificar, en sus rasgos esenciales, característicos, el viaje, popularizarle y definirlo, para lo que las bases con arrancar de la rica realidad.

Ribecourt, colega y amigo, figura entre nosotros con títulos excepcionales. Es el gran cronista francés de nuestra contienda, que la ha vivido sobre el terreno, en los campos de batalla; en las ciudades asoladas de la retaguardia, con seguridad inquebrantable en la victoria de la causa popular. Ayer y hoy.

Demuestra esta fe acompañándonos, reuniendo datos para un documento que pronto difundirá a los cuatro confines esta verdad española que aquí se respira, y que él comprende social y psicológicamente.

Le queda un resabio bonachón de pintoresquismo. El sesudo -comicamente sesudo- jugador de ajedrez de la travesía se adorna de vez en cuando con un llamativo clavel rojo en la solapa o defiende con calor castizo las excelencias de los "chotis"...

RIBECOURT

Fig. 53: Caricatures of Chim and journalist George Soria ["Ribécourt"] in roneotyped paper, published during the SS crossing to Mexico, Spring 1939. © davidseymour.com online archive.

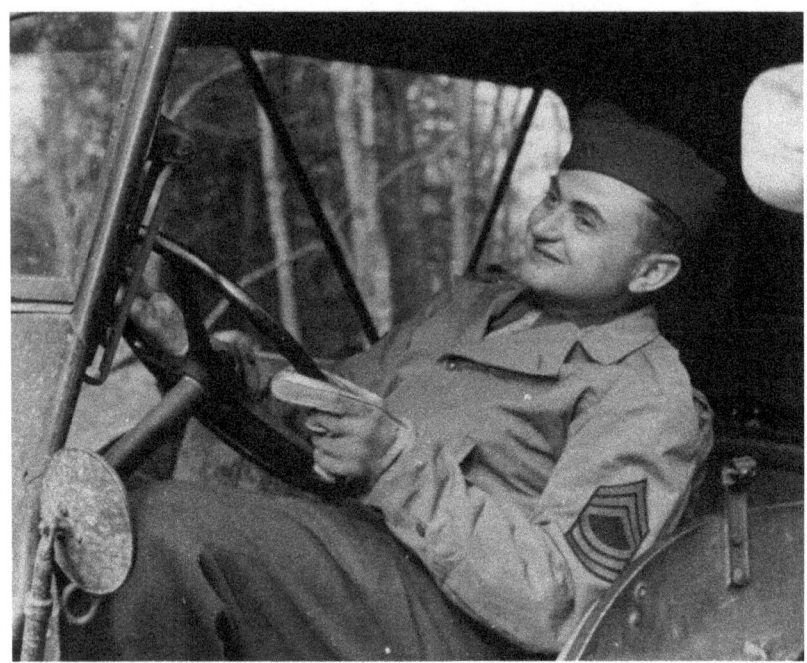

Fig. 54: Portrait of Chim as a soldier in the U.S. Army, location unknown. Dedicated on back "To Lucy, starting a ride in the future, Chim, 18 March 44." © davidseymour.com online archive.

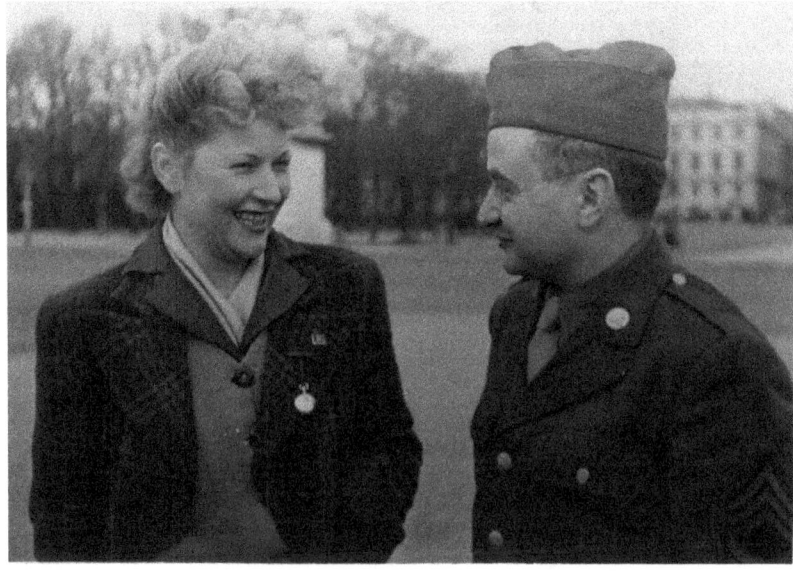

Fig. 55: Chim with friend in the U.S. Army, location unknown, circa 1944. © davidseymour.com online archive.

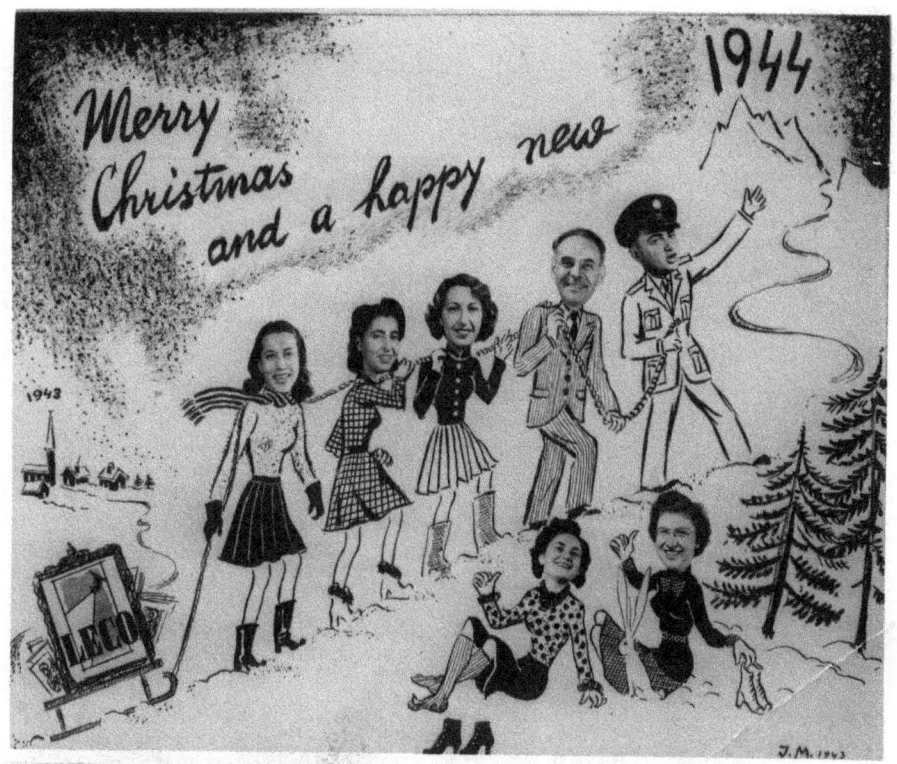

Fig. 56: New Year card sent from New York by Leco Photolab, 1944. © davidseymour.com online archive

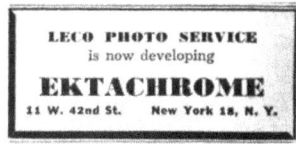

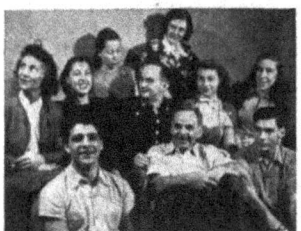

Fig. 57: Chim with Leco staff, New York, 1945. Photography published in unknown U.S. newspaper. © davidseymour.com online archive.

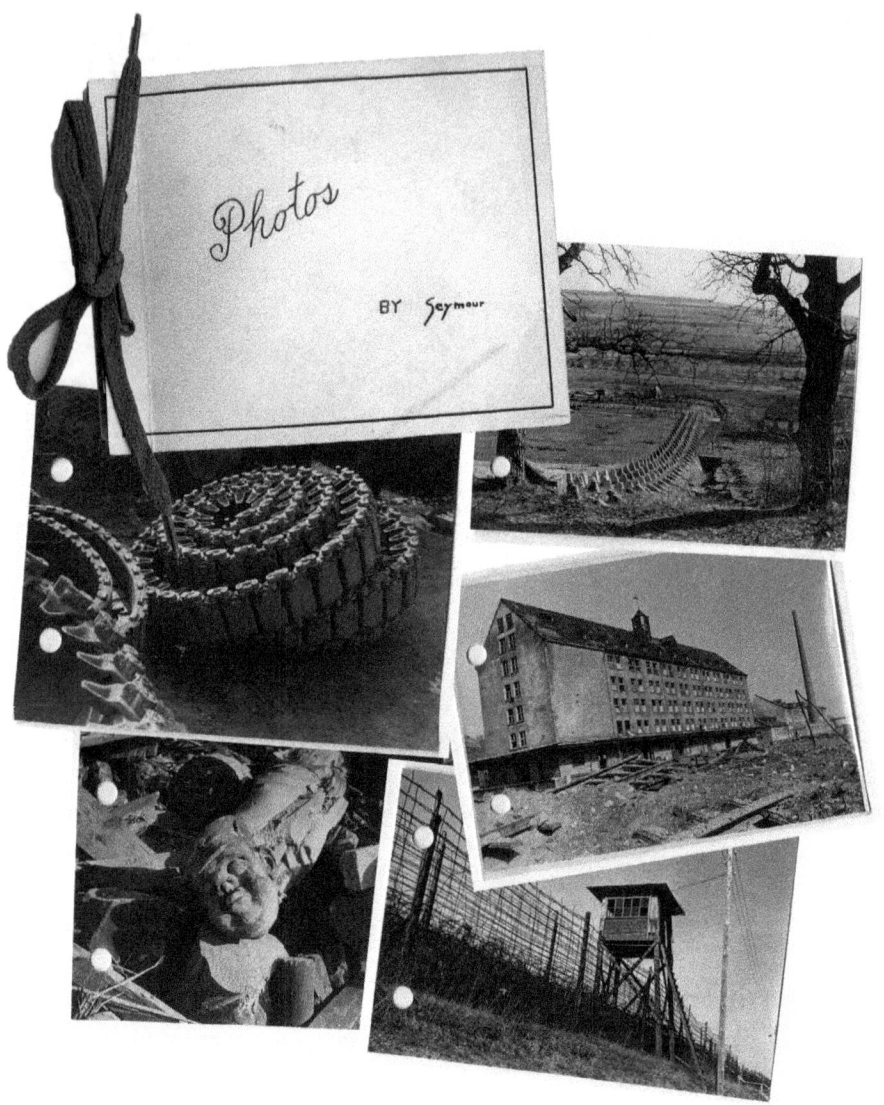

Fig. 58: Cover and photographs from Chim's private World War II photo album containing 22 photos, 1941-1945, © davidseymour.com online archive. Montage by Zoe Freilich.

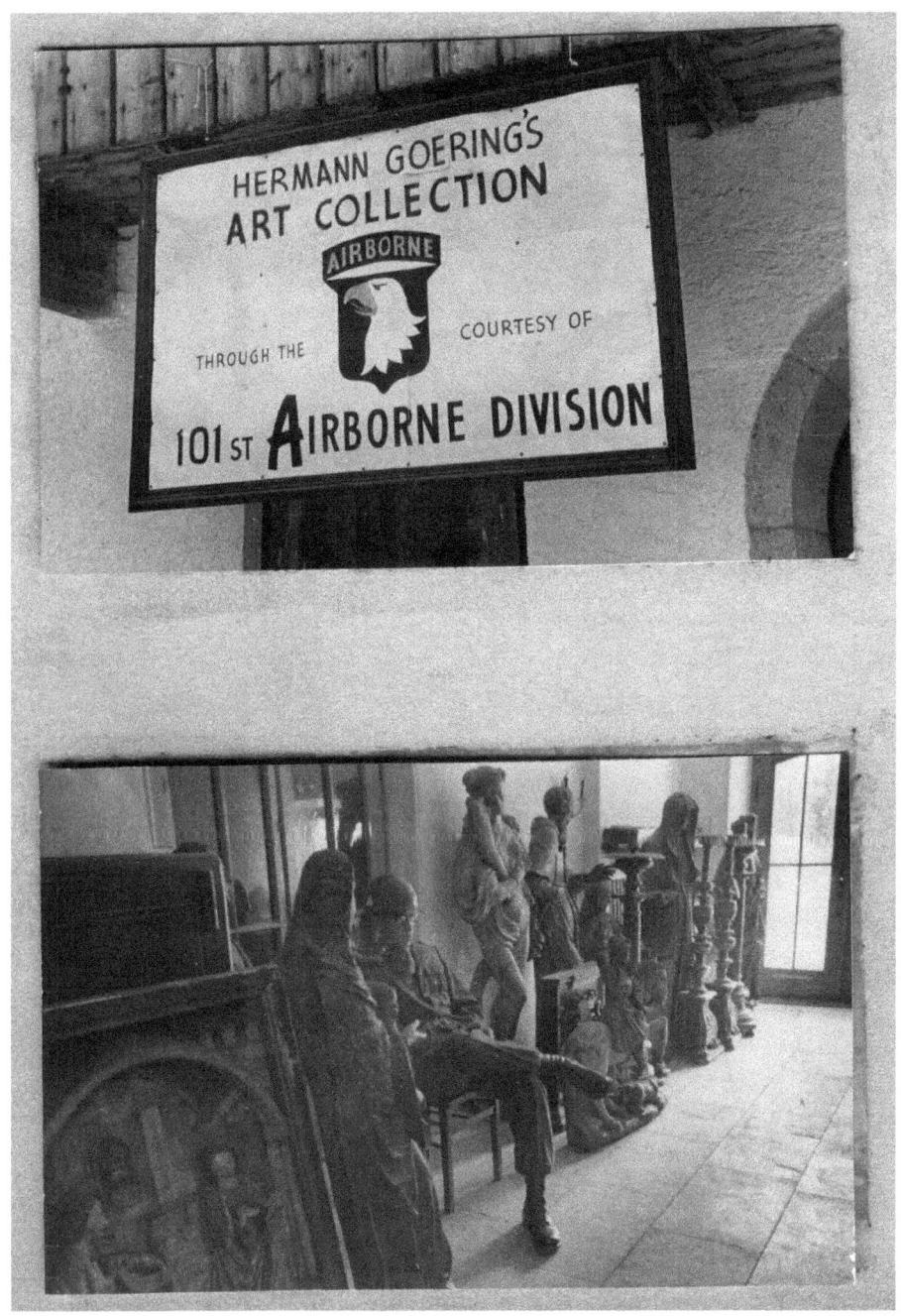

Fig. 59: Herman's Goering's Art Collection, photos mounted on carton, circa 1944. © davidseymour.com online archive.

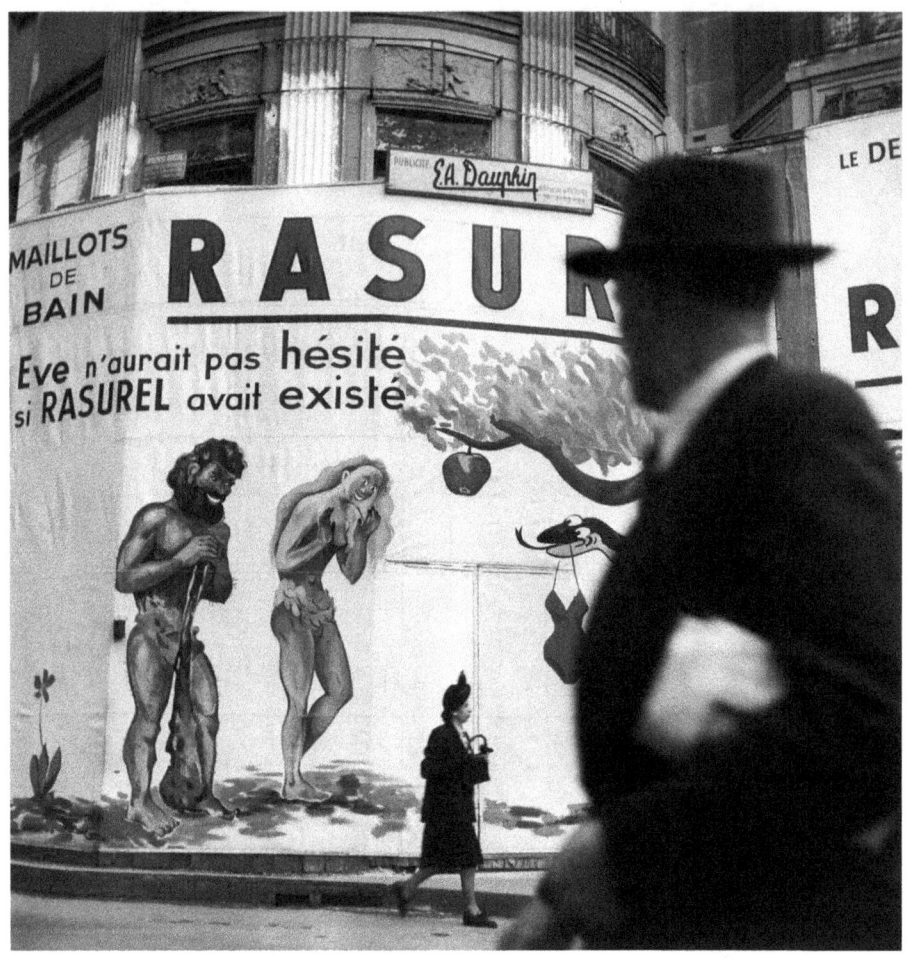

Fig. 60: Paris, 1947. © David Seymour-Magnum Photos.

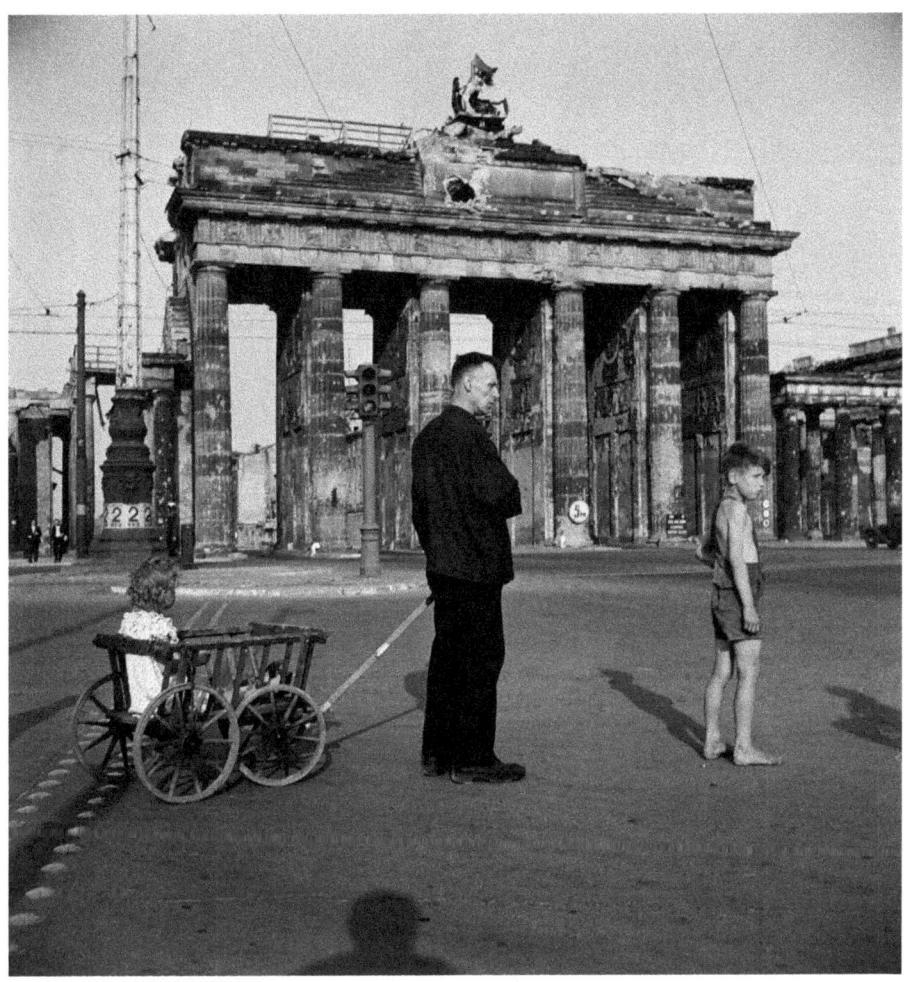

Fig. 61: In Front of Brandenburg Gate, Berlin, 1947. © David Seymour-Magnum Photos.

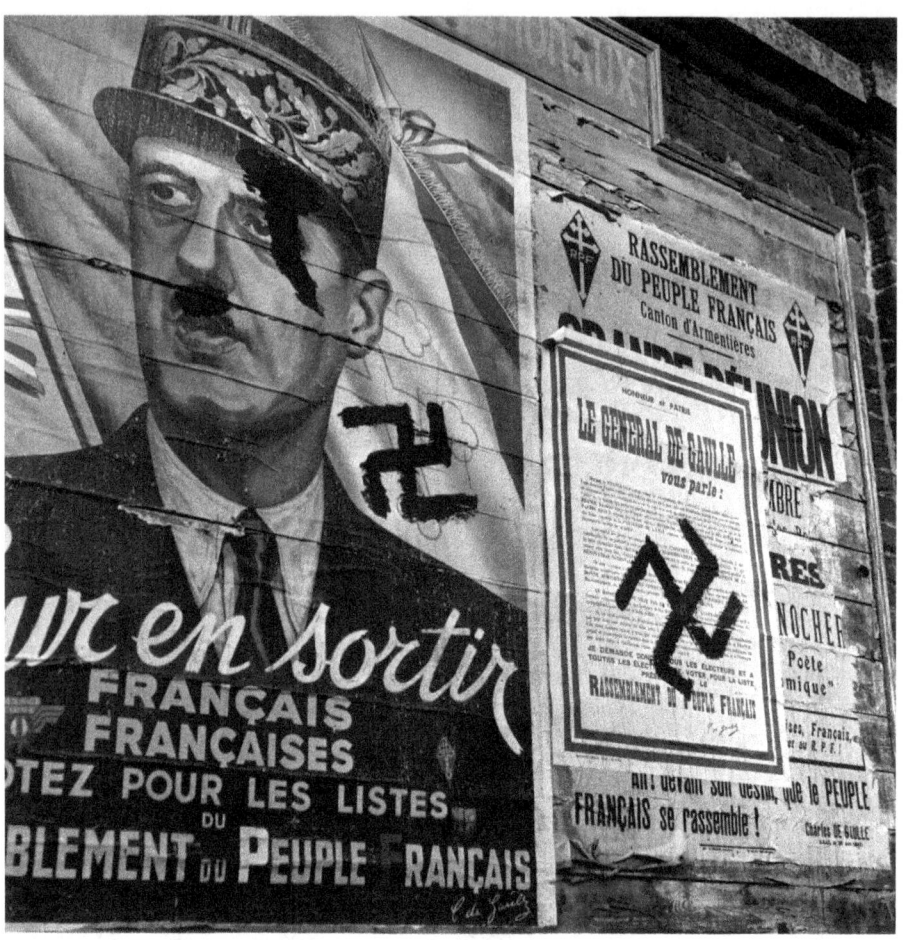

Fig. 62: Political posters, one with an image of Charles de Gaulle covered with swastikas. Armentières, France, 1947. © David Seymour-Magnum Photos.

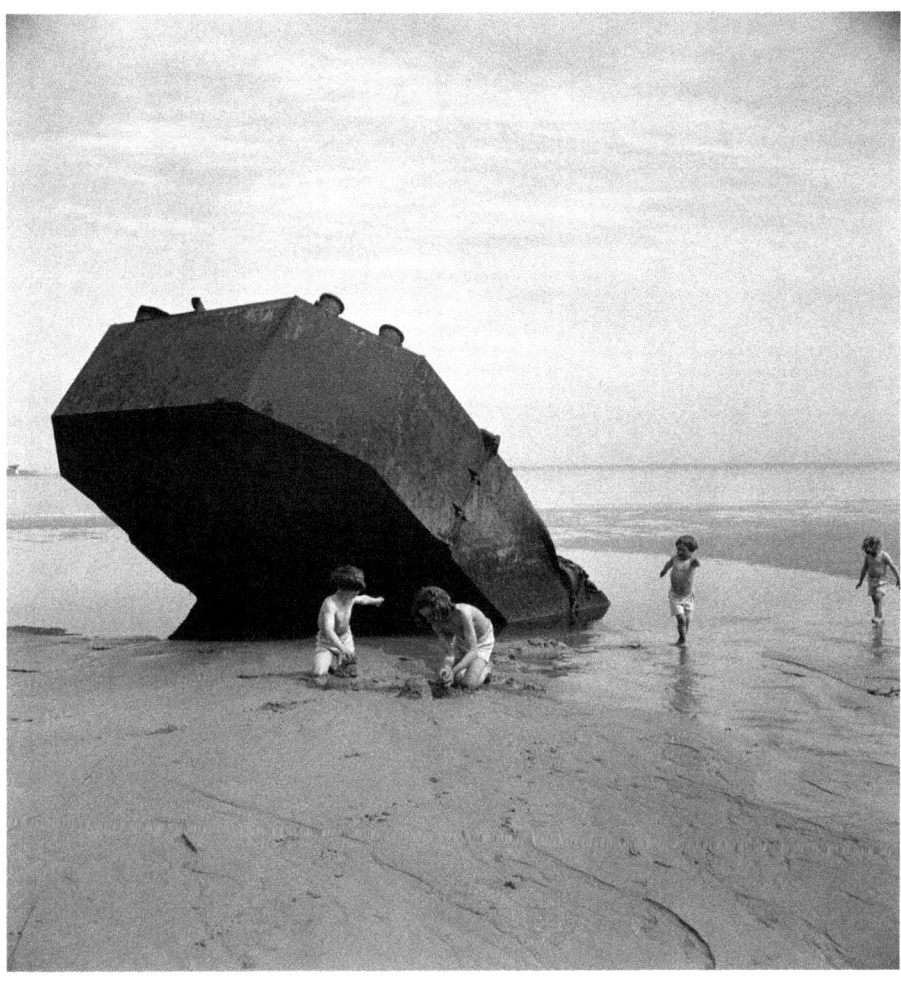

Fig. 63: Children play among the wreckage of D-Day Invasion. Omaha Beach, Normandy, 1947. © David Seymour-Magnum Photos.

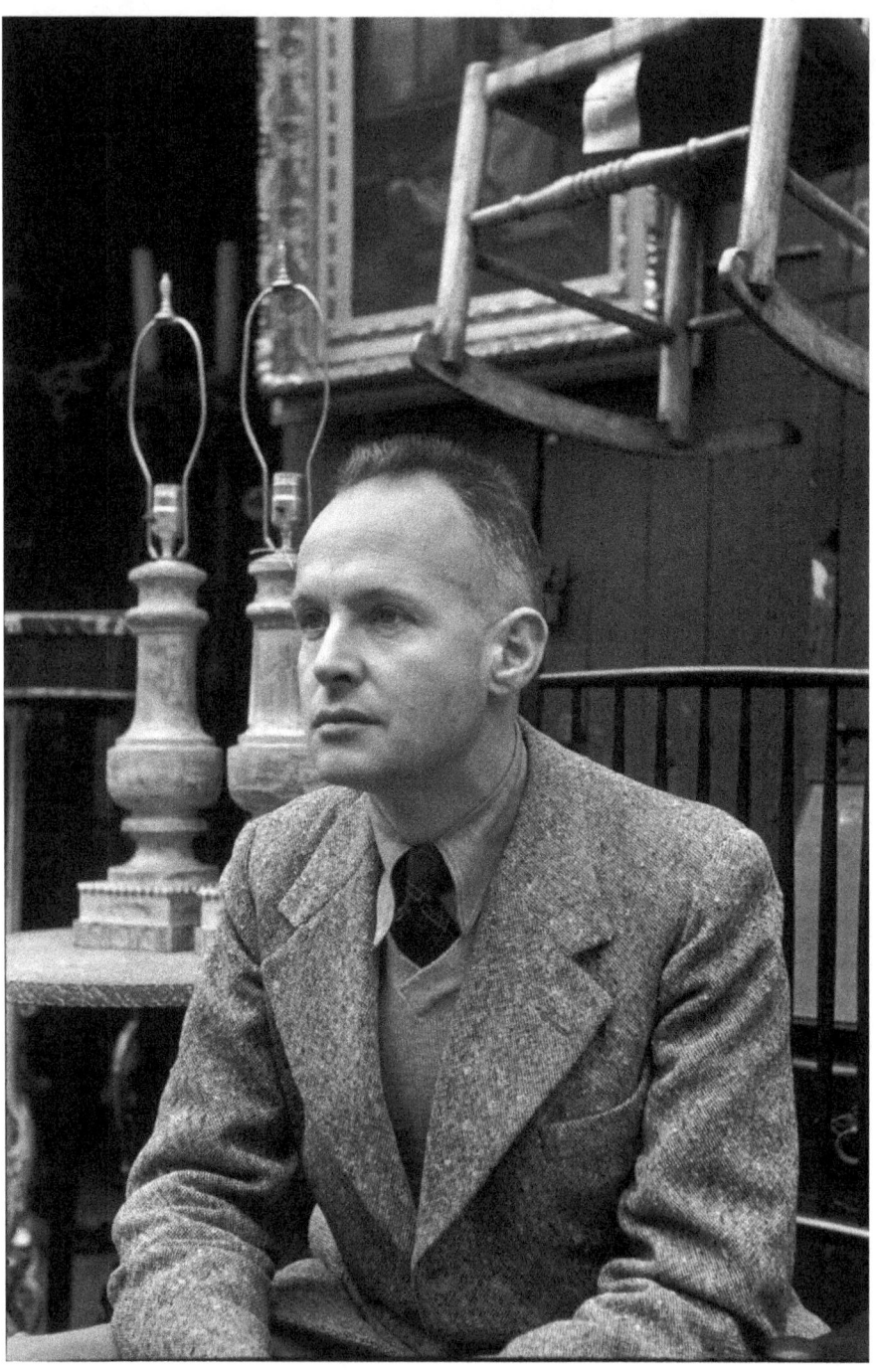

Fig. 64: Henri Cartier-Bresson photographed by Chim, New York City, 1947. © David Seymour-Magnum Photos.

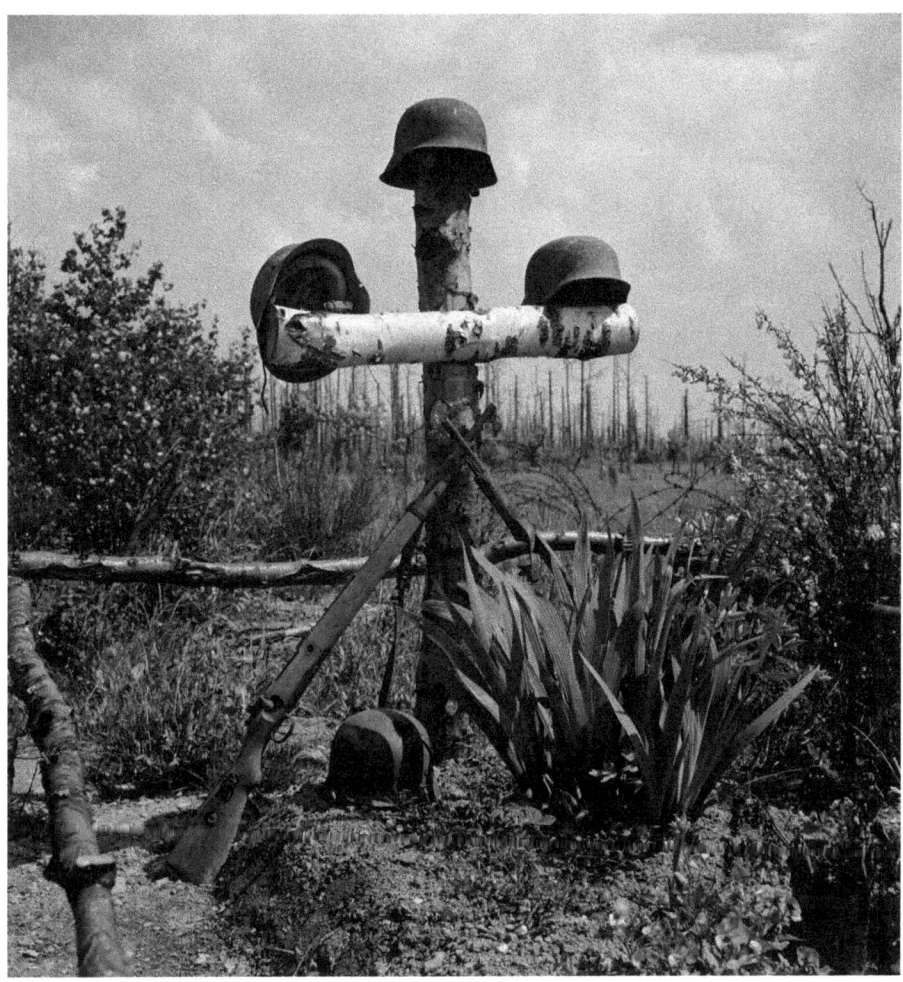

Fig. 65: Soldier's tomb near Huertgen Forest, German-Belgian Border, 1947. © David Seymour-Magnum Photos.

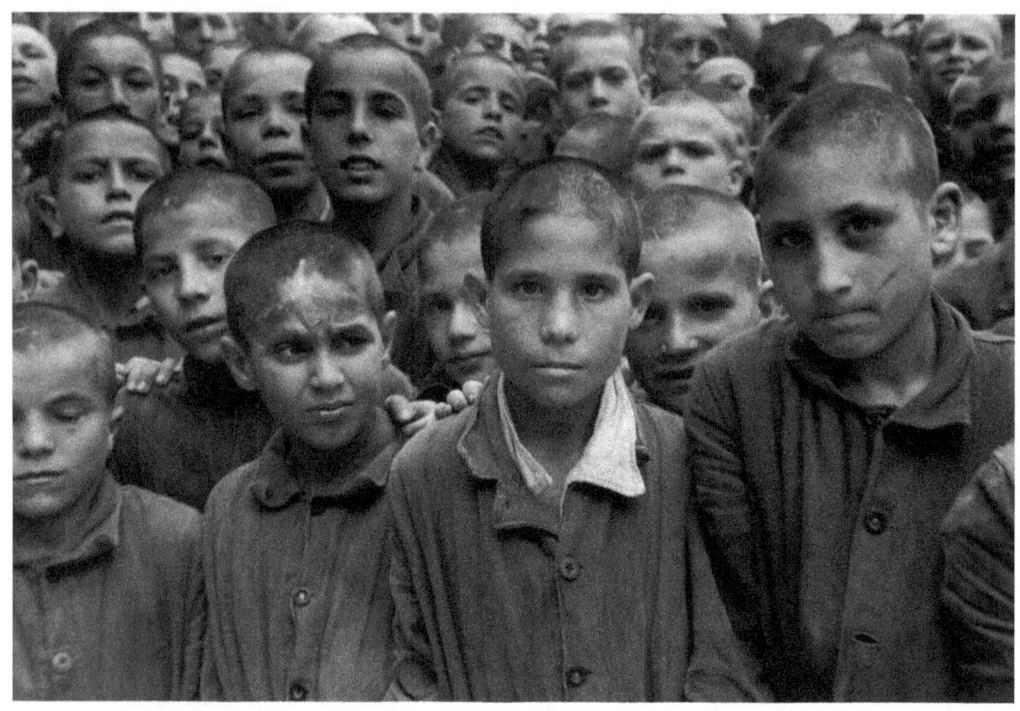

Fig. 66: Albergo dei Pobre Orphanage, Naples, Italy, 1948. © David Seymour-Magnum Photos.

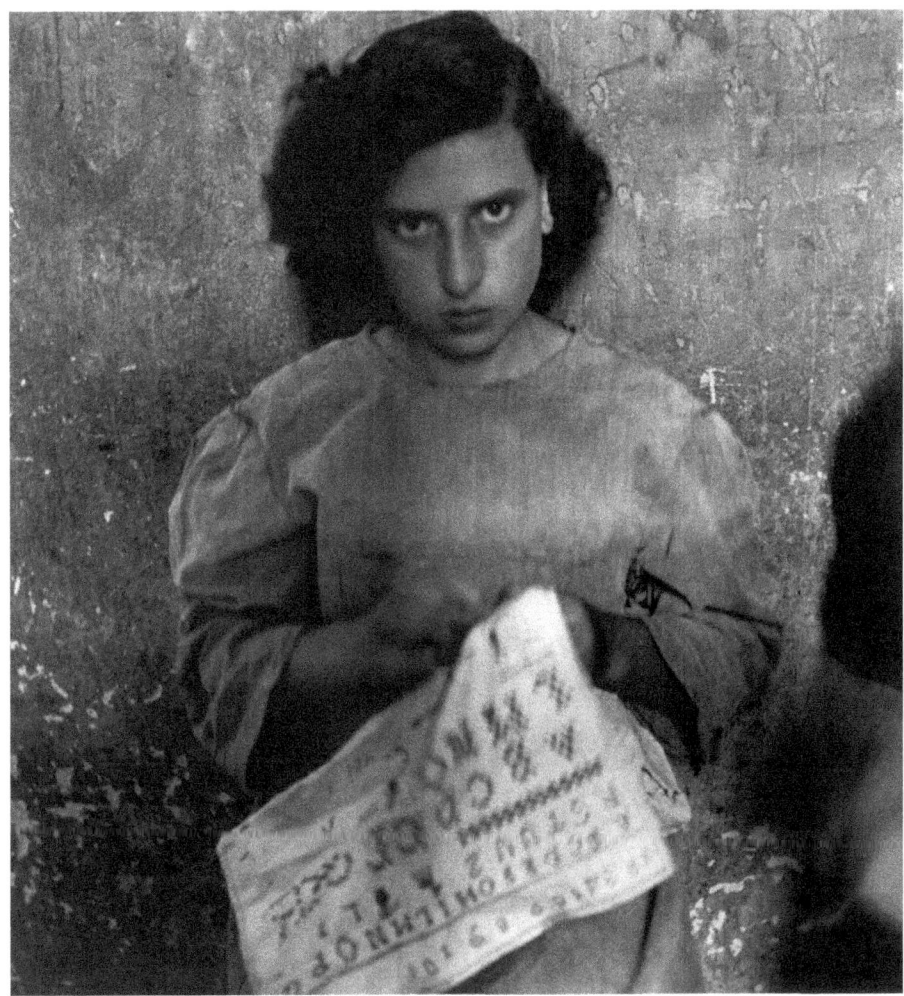

Fig. 67: Young woman who was raped during the war, Albergo dei Pobre Orphanage, Naples, Italy, 1948. © David Seymour-Magnum Photos.

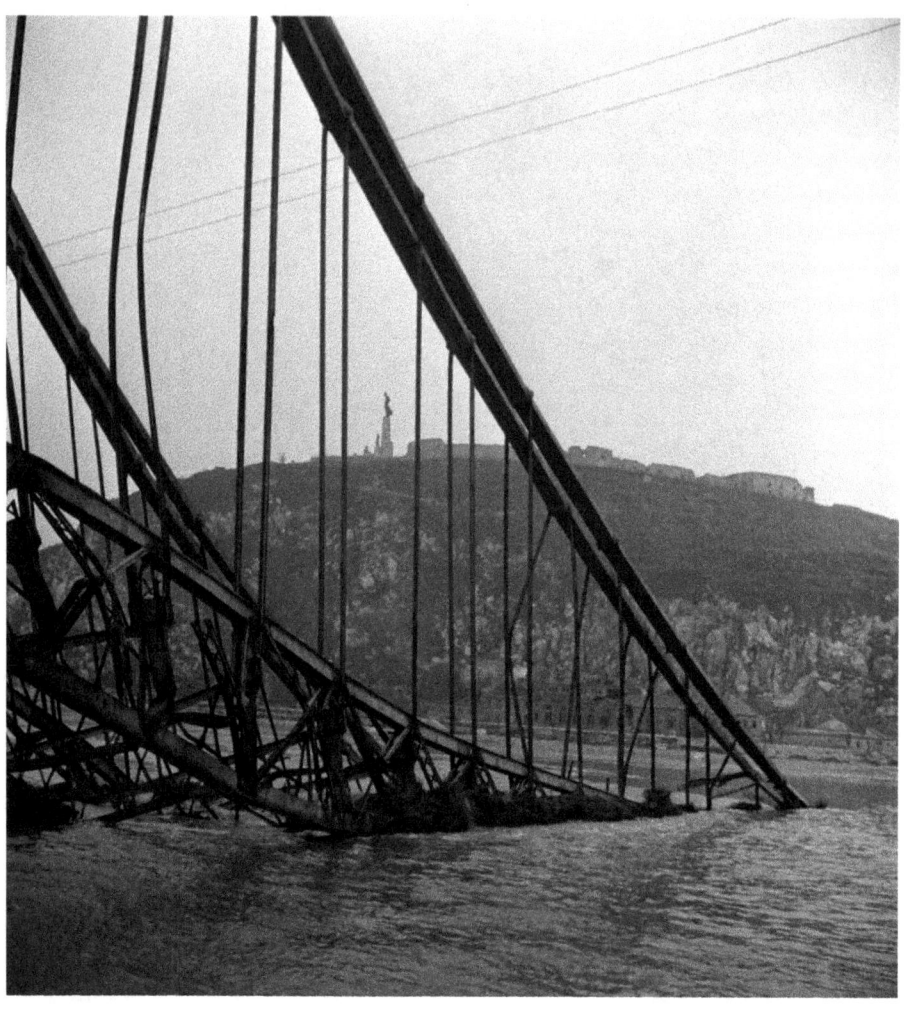
Fig. 68: Destroyed Elizabeth Bridge, Budapest, Hungary, 1948. © David Seymour-Magnum Photos.

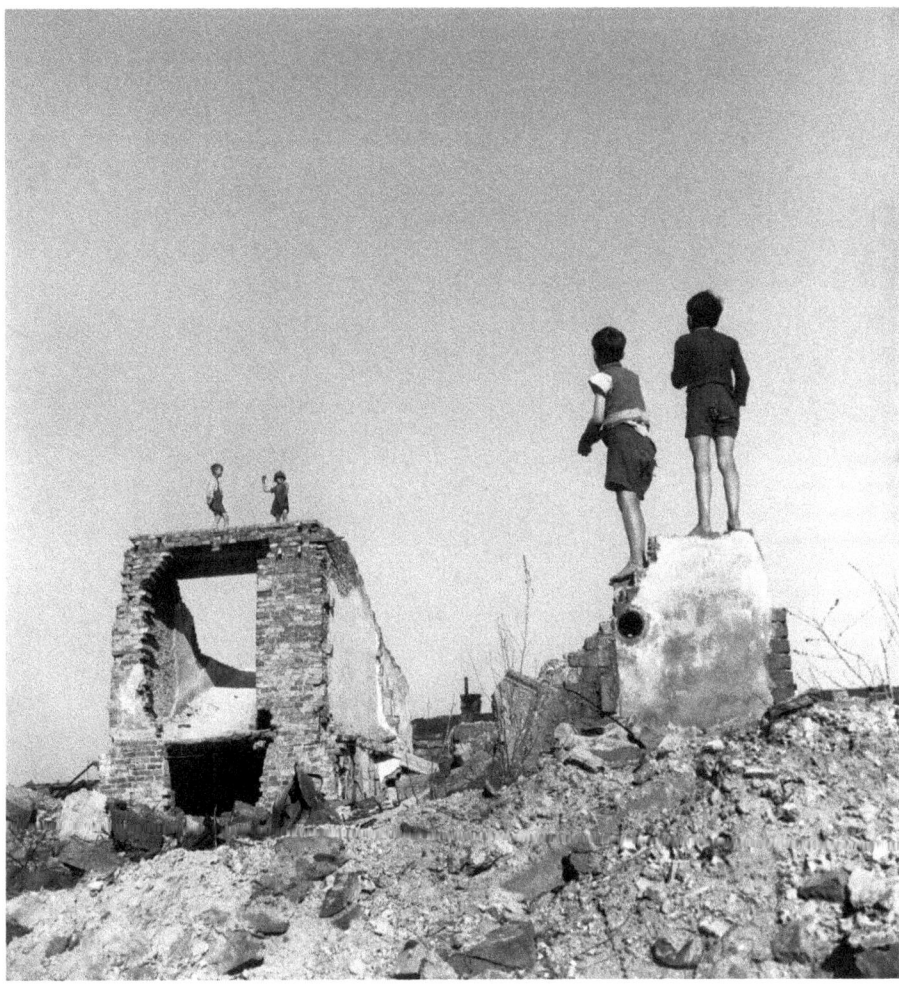

Fig. 69: Boys play in bombed-out buildings in the working-class district of Favoriten, Vienna, 1948. © David Seymour-Magnum Photos.

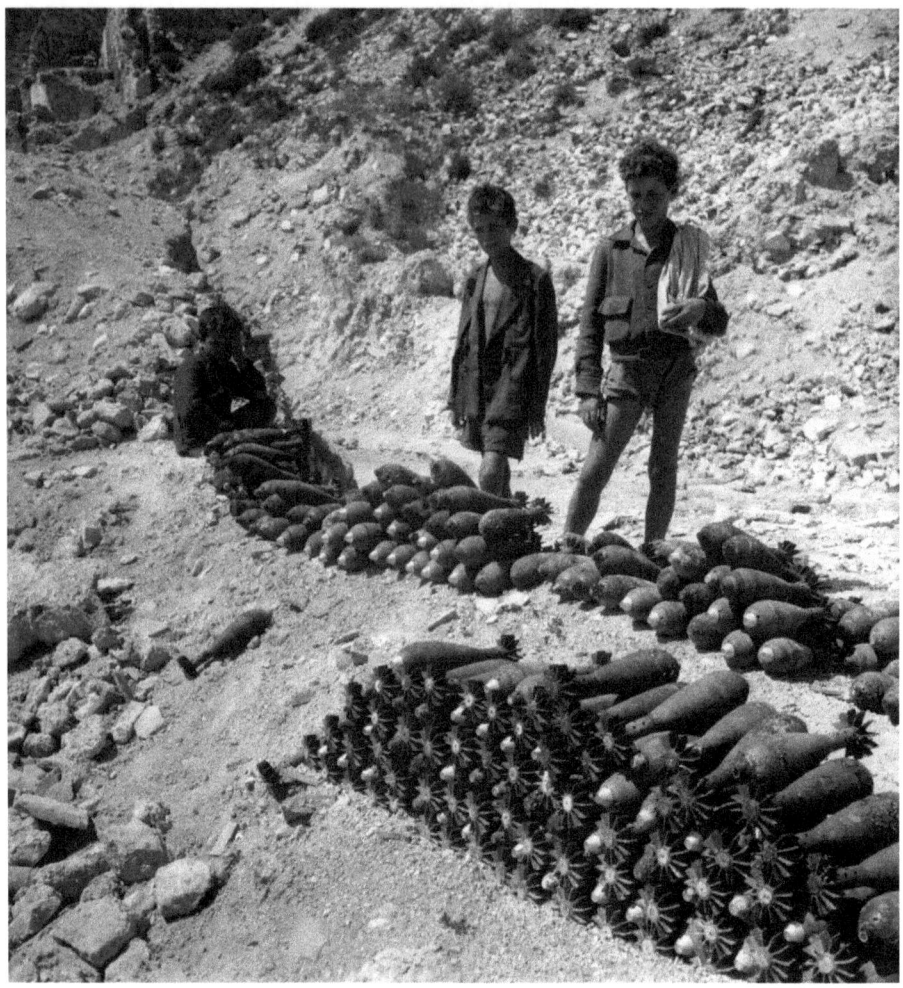

Fig. 70: Three urchins of Cassino with dud mortar shells they collect and sell to scrap merchants. Unexploded shells cause many grave injuries. Monte Cassino, Latium, Italy, 1948. © David Seymour-Magnum Photos.

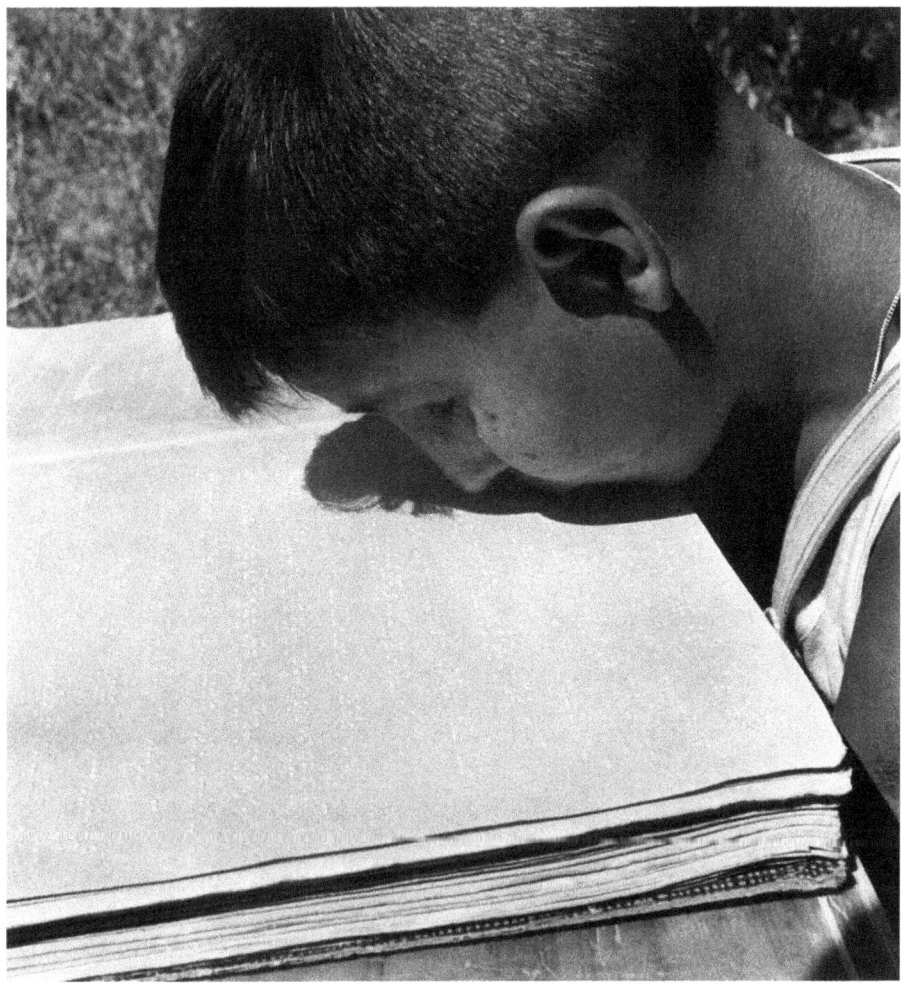

Fig. 71: Blind boy who lost his arms during the war has learnt to read with his lips. Rome, Villa Savoia, 1948. © David Seymour-Magnum Photos.

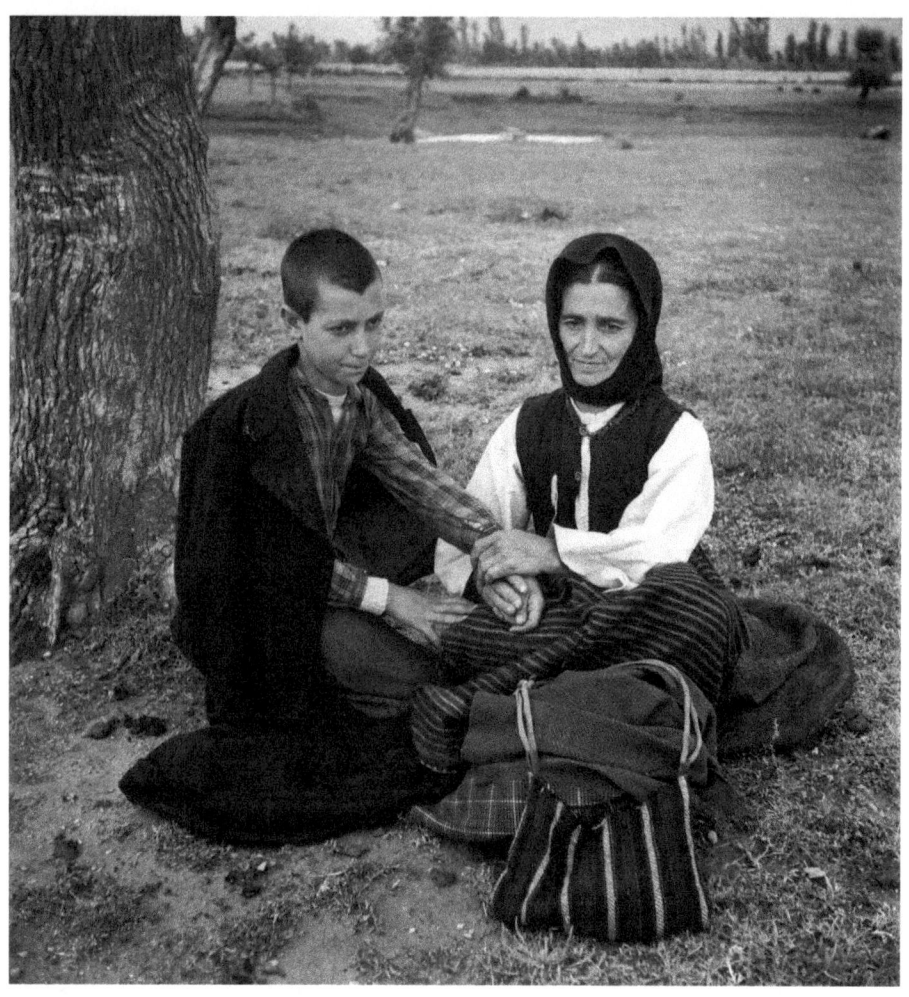
Fig. 72: Refugees from the Civil War Areas, Greece, 1948. © David Seymour-Magnum Photos.

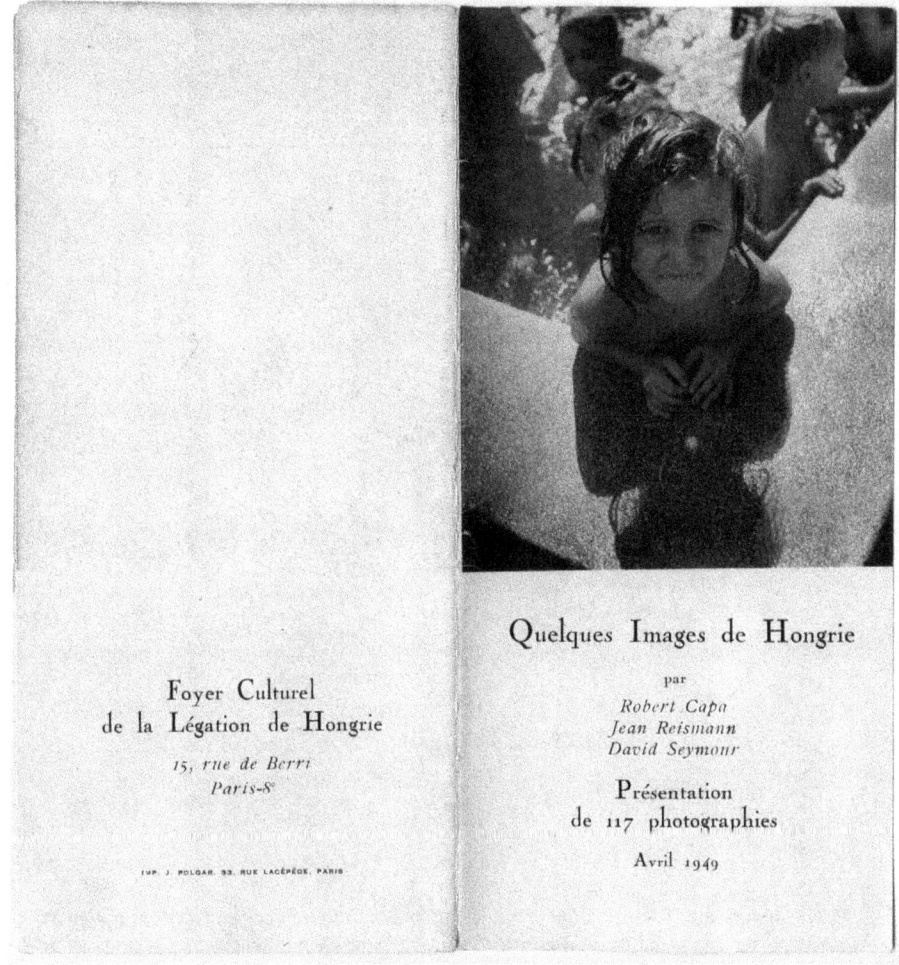

Fig. 73: Brochure for a group exhibition in Paris, "A Few Images from Hungary," 1949. © davidseymour.com online archive.

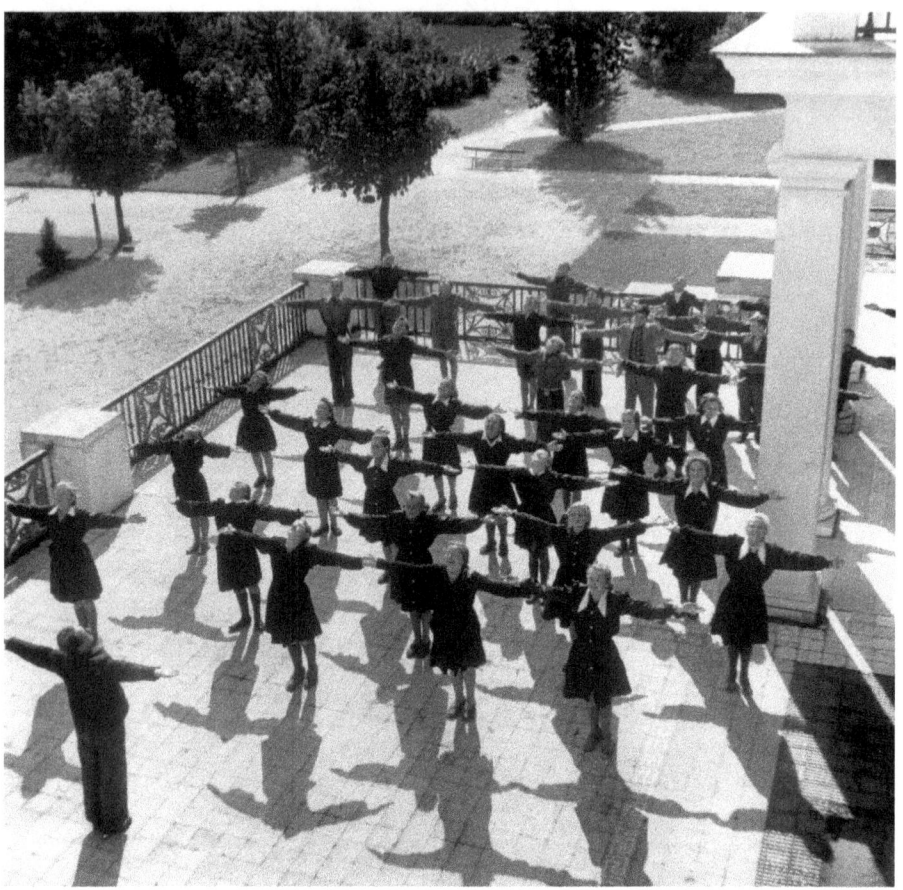

Fig. 74: Gymnastics at a sanatorium for Jewish children suffering from tuberculosis. About 70 patients are taken care of here by a Jewish health organization called T.O.Z. Otwock, Poland, 1948. © David Seymour-Magnum Photos.

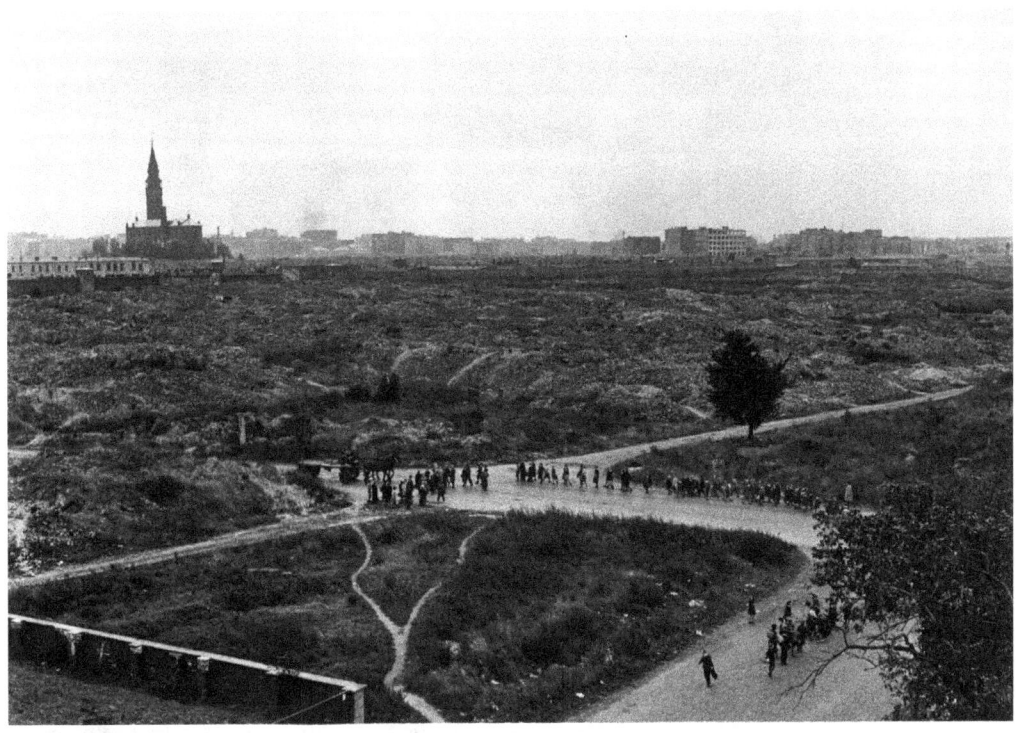

Fig. 75: Schoolchildren walking home through the ruins of the Warsaw Ghetto. The St. Augustin church in the background was the only building not destroyed in that neighborhood. Warsaw, 1948. © David Seymour-Magnum Photos.

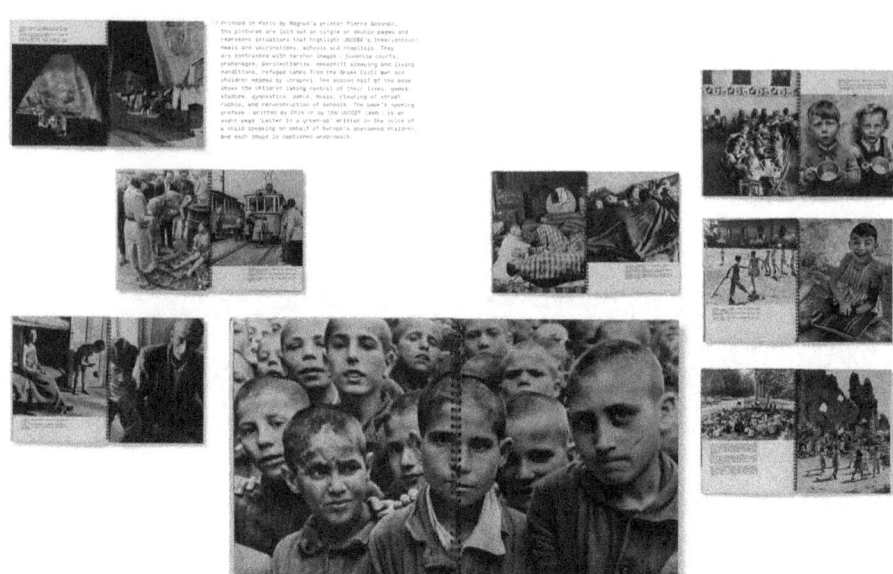

Fig. 76: Spreads from Chim's UNESCO book *Children of Europe*, 1949.

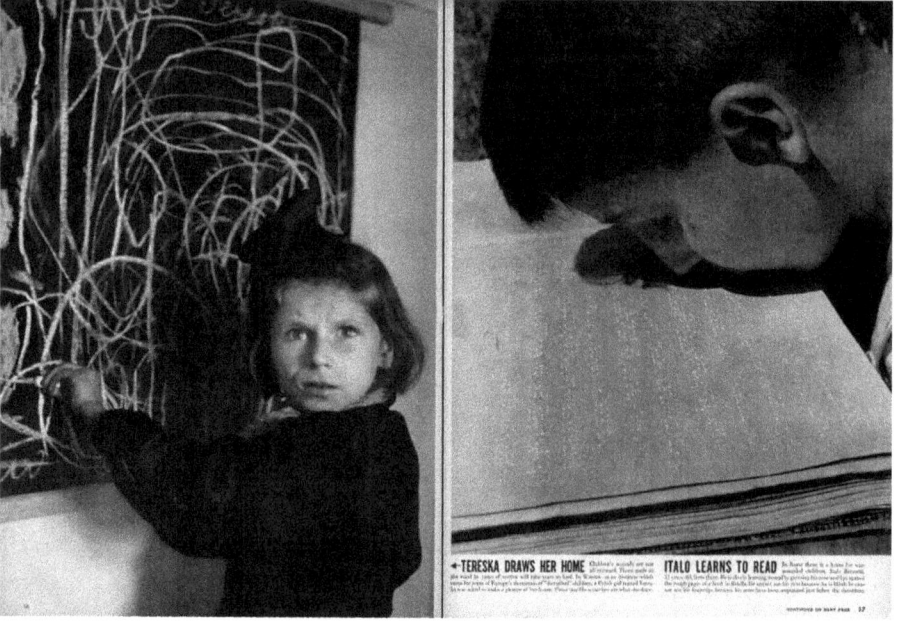

Fig. 77: Double page from publication of Chim's *Children of Europe* reportage in Life, December 21, 1948.

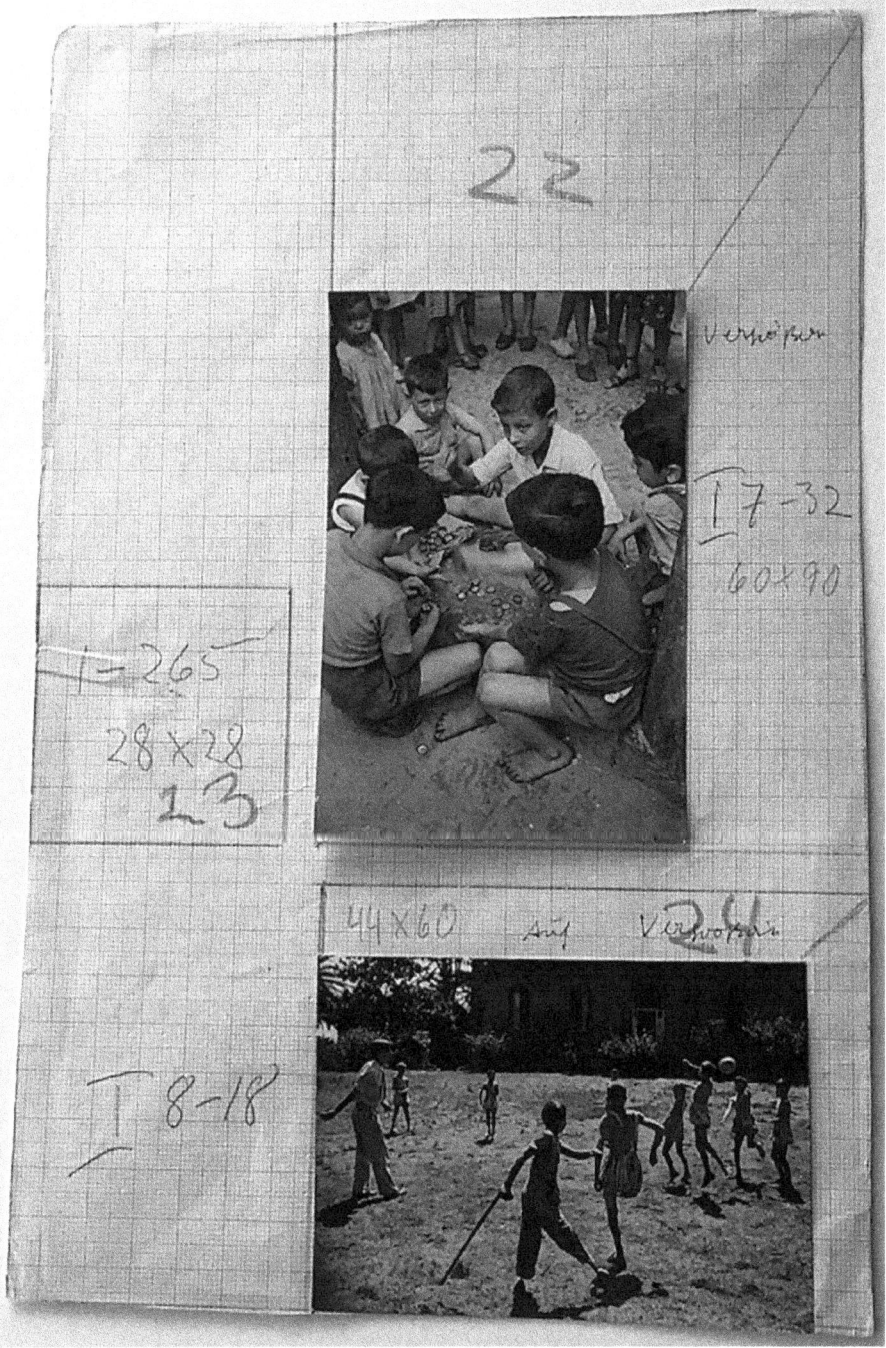

Fig. 78: Page of original layout by Chim for the book *Children of Europe*. Courtesy Howard Greenberg Gallery, New York.

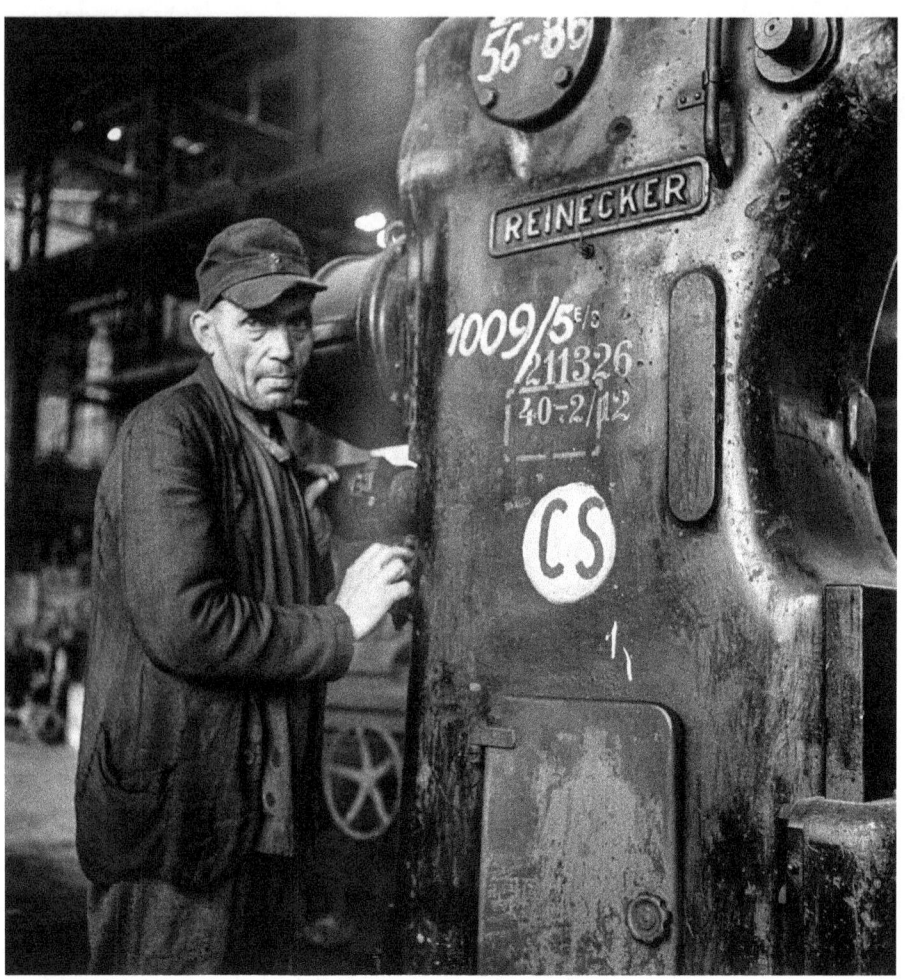

Fig. 79: Worker at the Krupp Steelworks in the Ruhr Valley, Essen, Germany, 1949. © David Seymour-Magnum Photos.

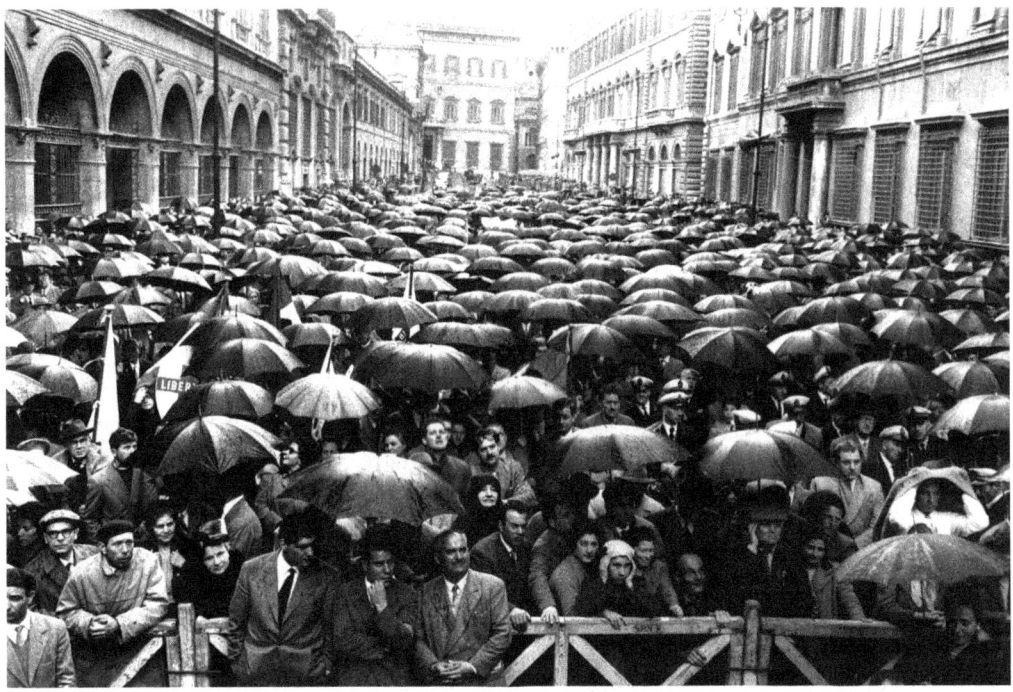

Fig. 80: Crowd listening to a speech by Socialist Pietro Nenni. Basilica di Massenzio, Rome, March 11, 1948.
© David Seymour-Magnum Photos.

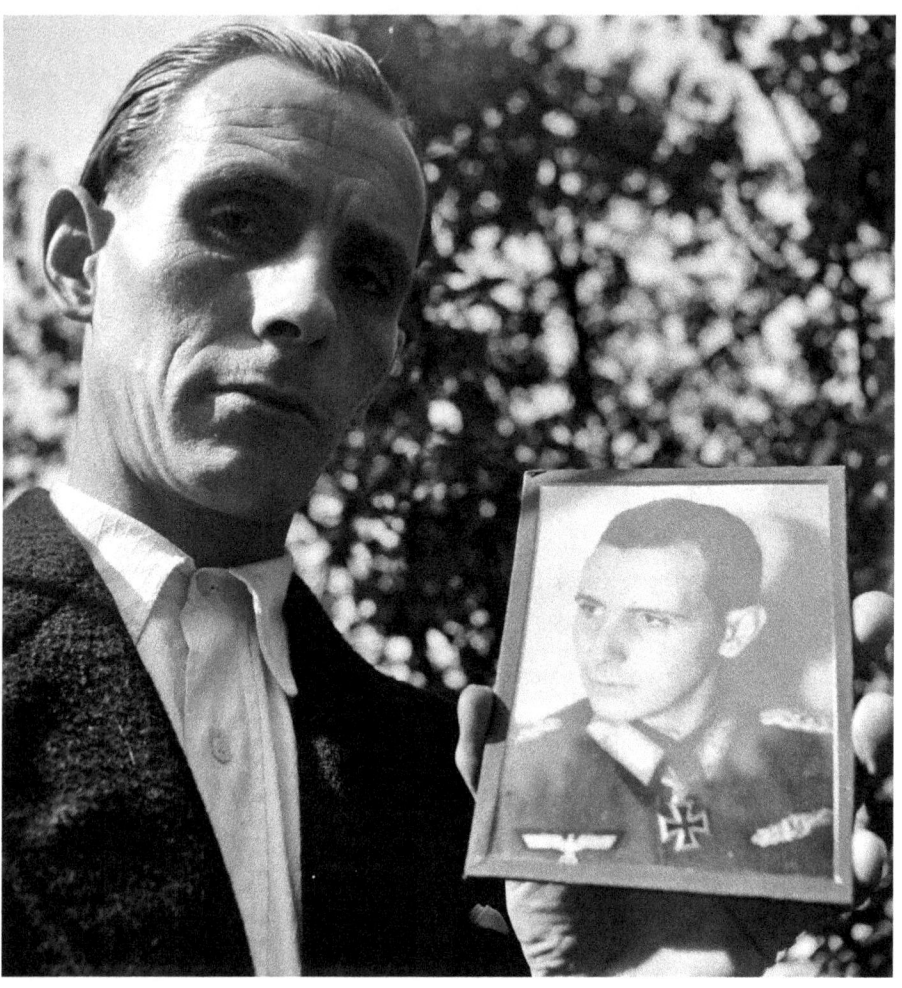

Fig. 81: Former Nazi General Otto Ernst Remer holding a portrait of himself as a young officer. Vavel, Germany, 1949. © David Seymour-Magnum Photos.

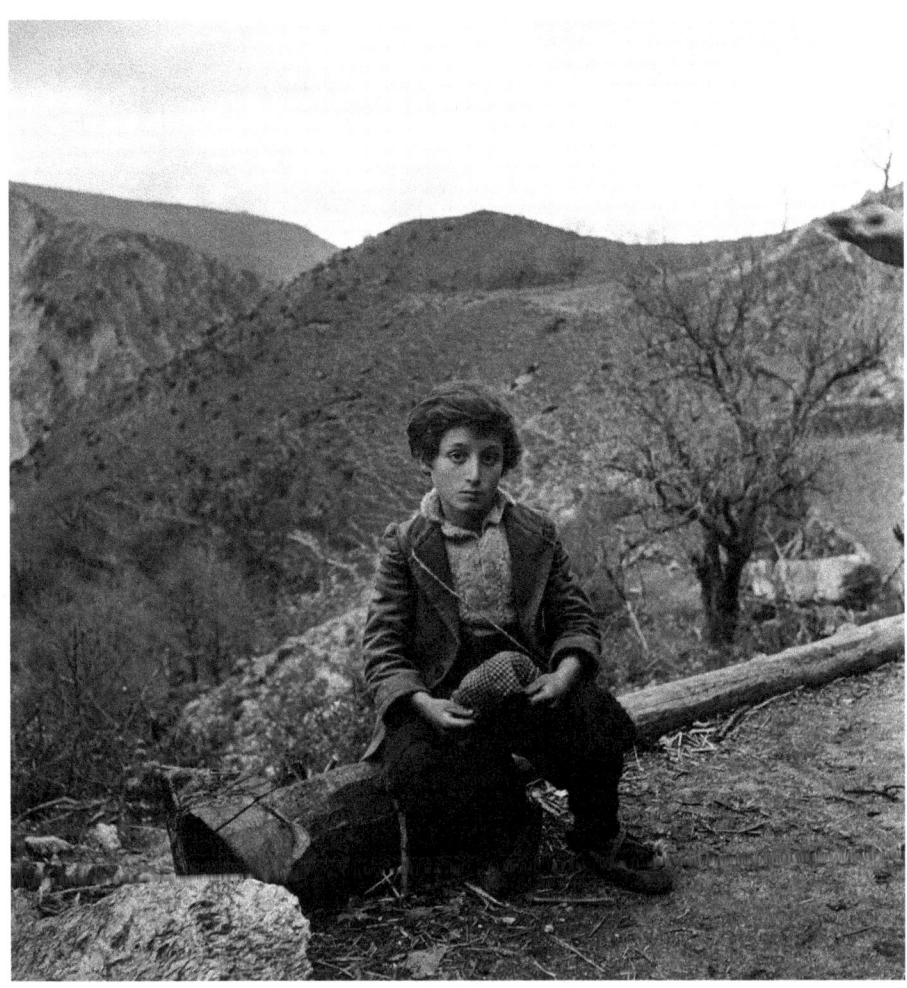

Fig. 82: Young Shepherd in Saucci, Southern Italy, 1950. From the *Fight Against Illiteracy* series. © David Seymour-Magnum Photos.

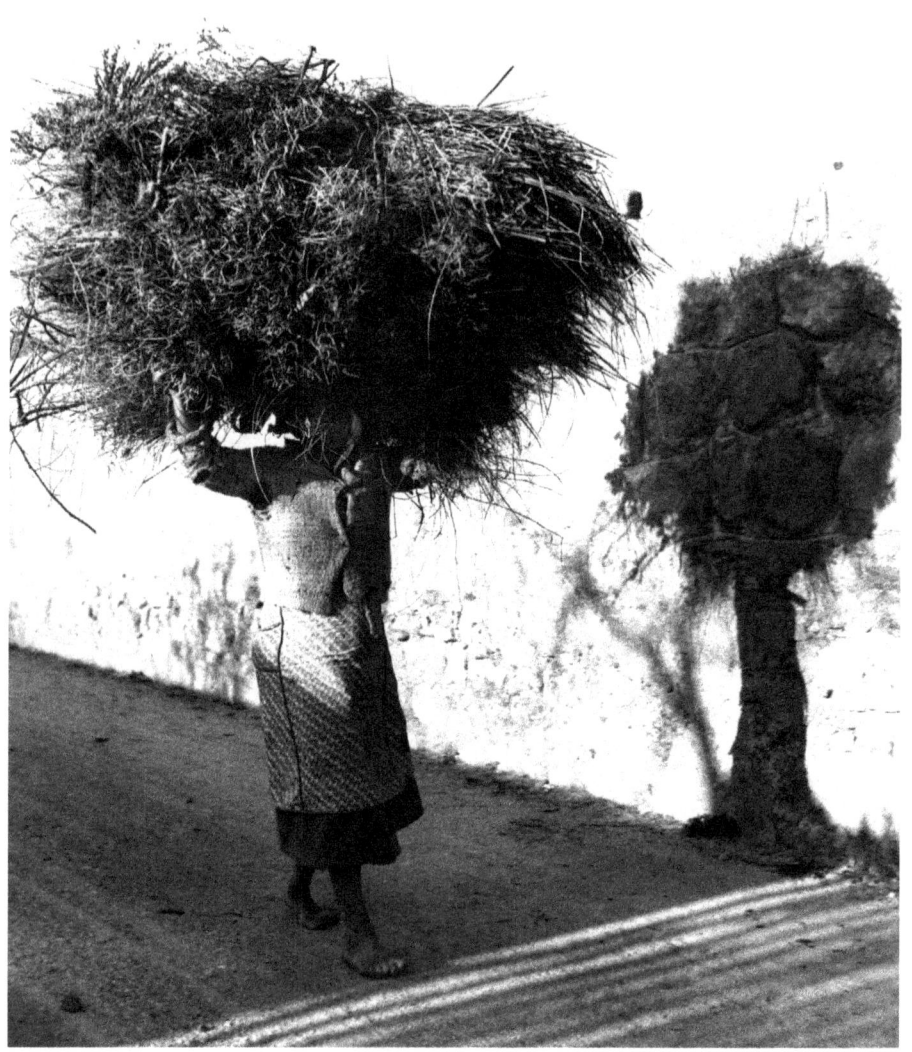

Fig. 83: Woman carrying a large bundle on her head. Calabria, Italy, 1950. From the *Fight Against Illiteracy* series. © David Seymour-Magnum Photos.

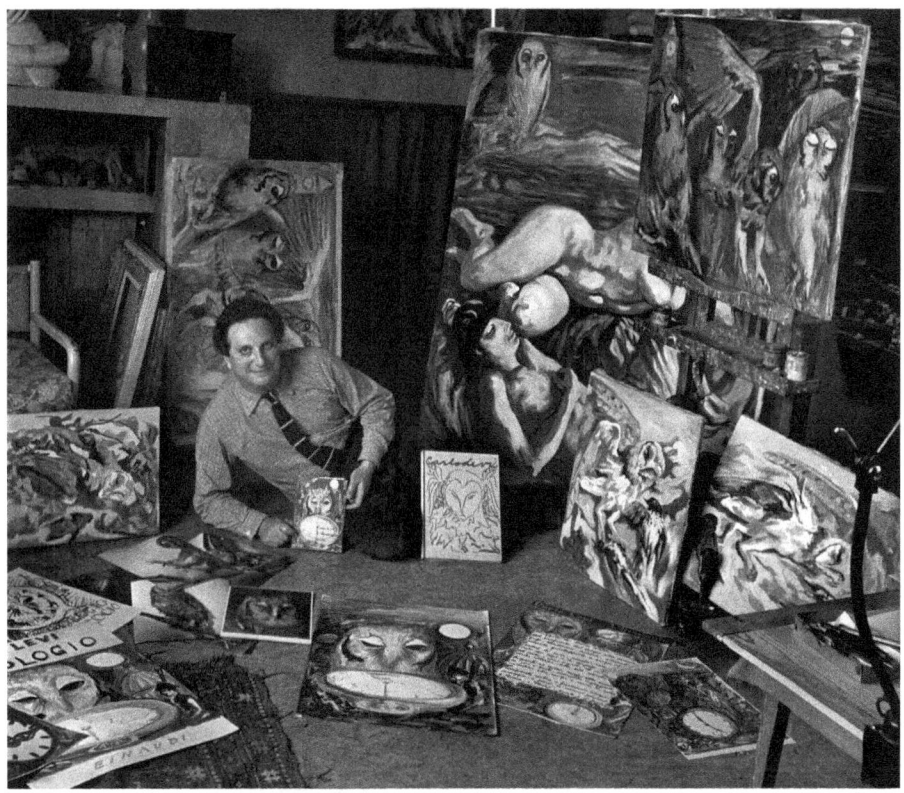

Fig. 84: Painter and writer Carlo Levi in his studio, Rome, 1950. © David Seymour-Magnum Photos.

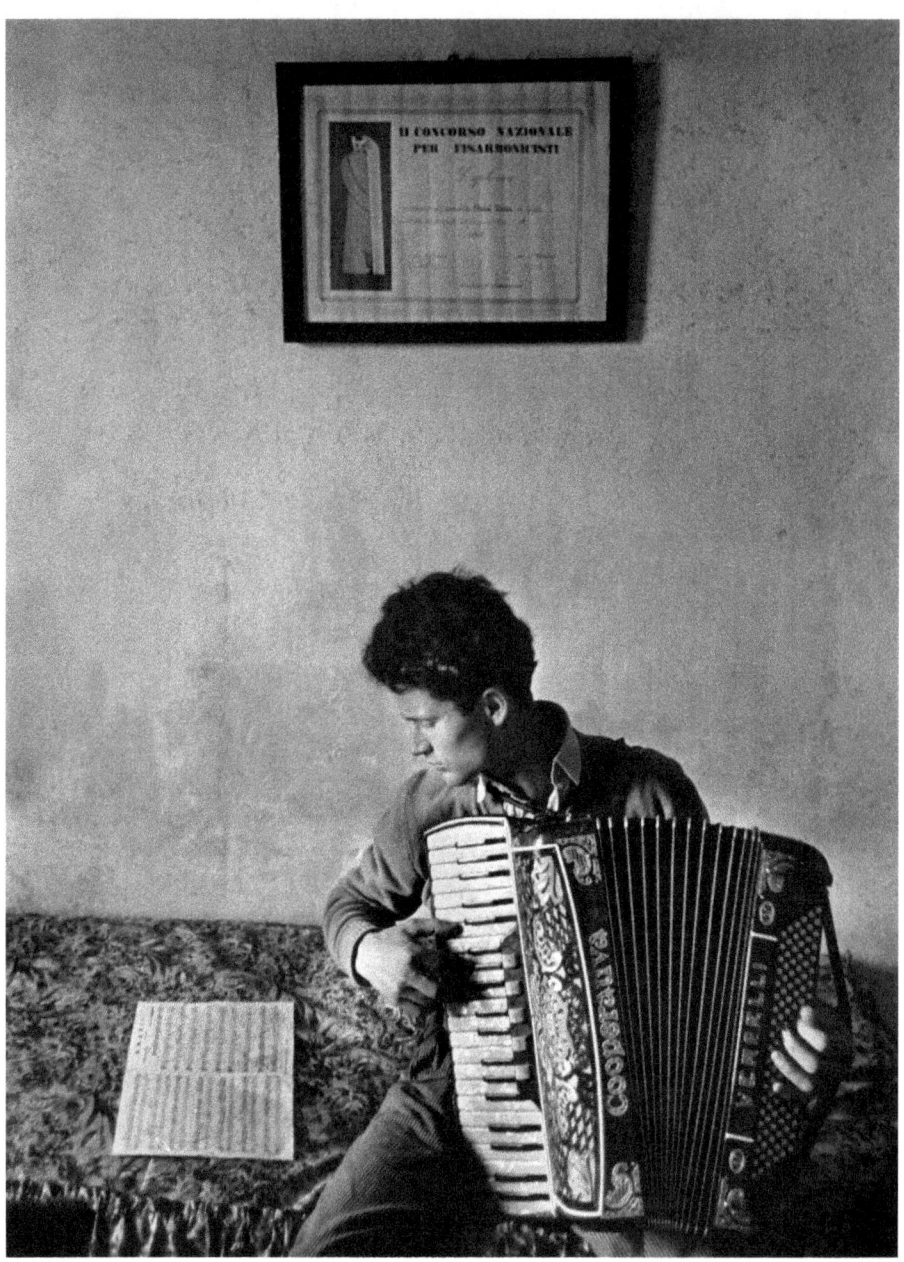

Fig. 85: Ubaldo playing his accordion, Umbria, Italy, 1951, from the series *Generation X*.© David Seymour-Magnum Photos.

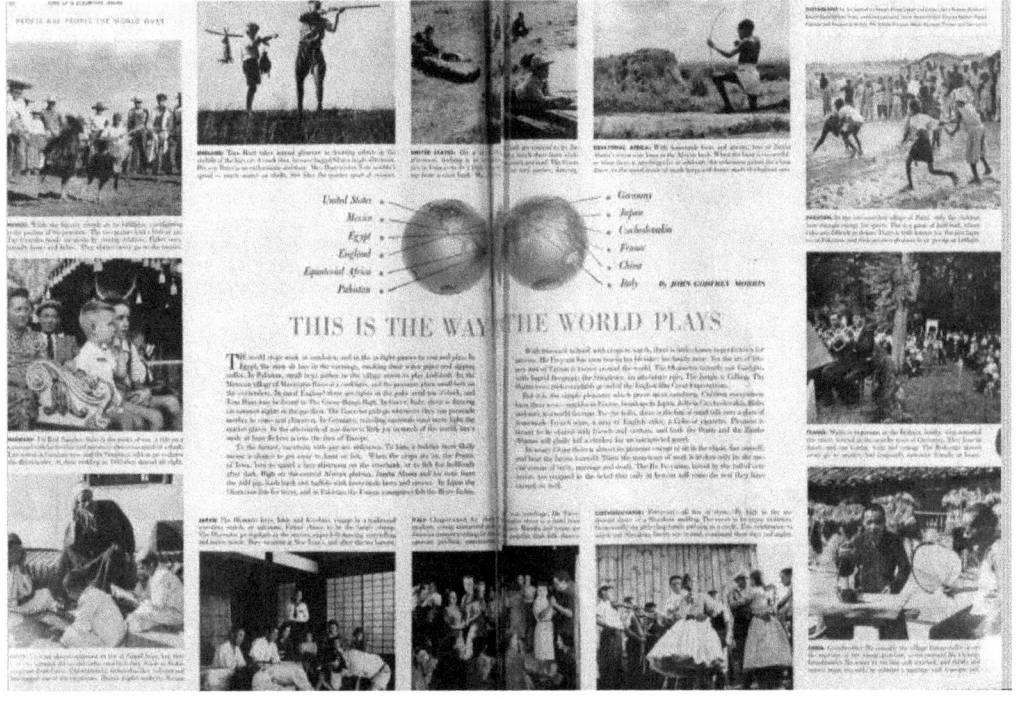

Fig. 86: "This is The Way The World Plays." A Spread from the project *People Are People the World Over*. Courtesy The Ladies Home Journal, 1948.

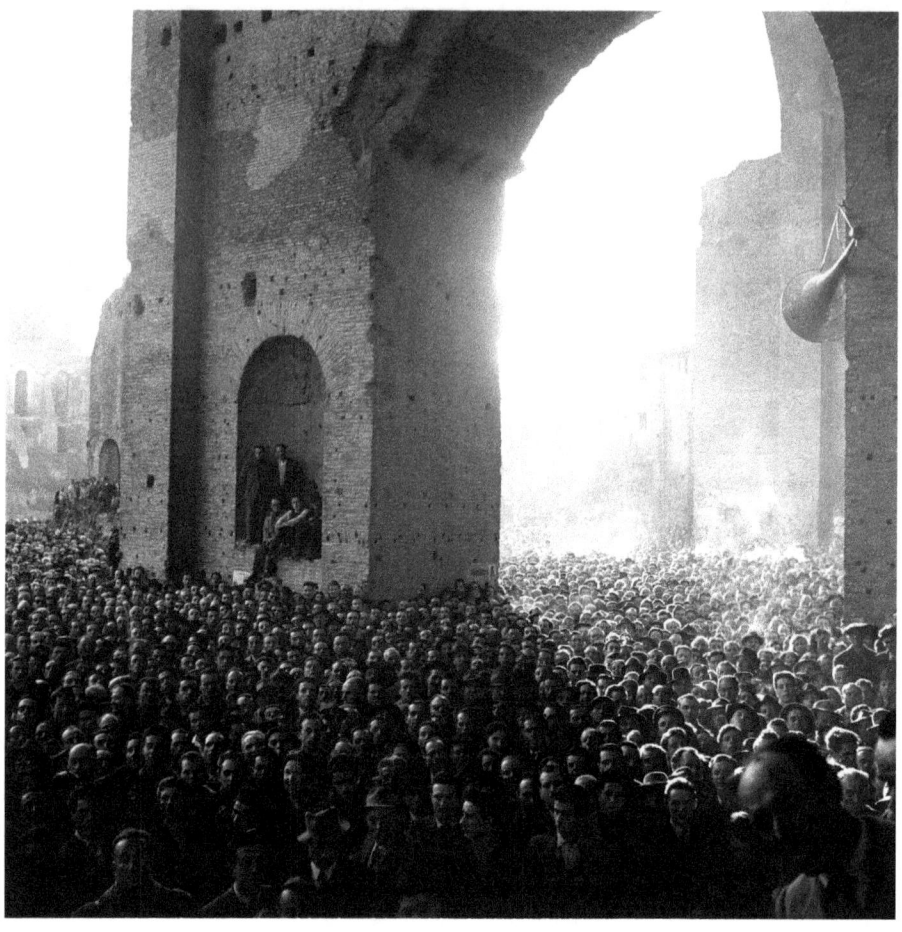

Fig. 87: Spectators listening to a political speech by Antonio Segni in the Piazza Santi Apostoli. Rome, May 1956. © David Seymour-Magnum Photos.

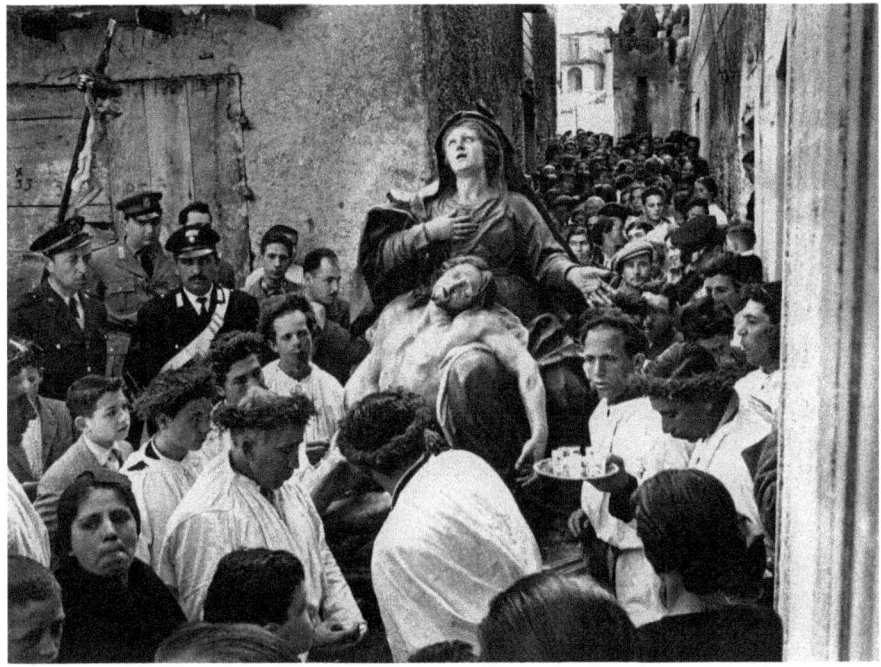

Fig. 88: Celebration of Good Friday. San Fratello, Sicily, 1955.© David Seymour-Magnum Photos.

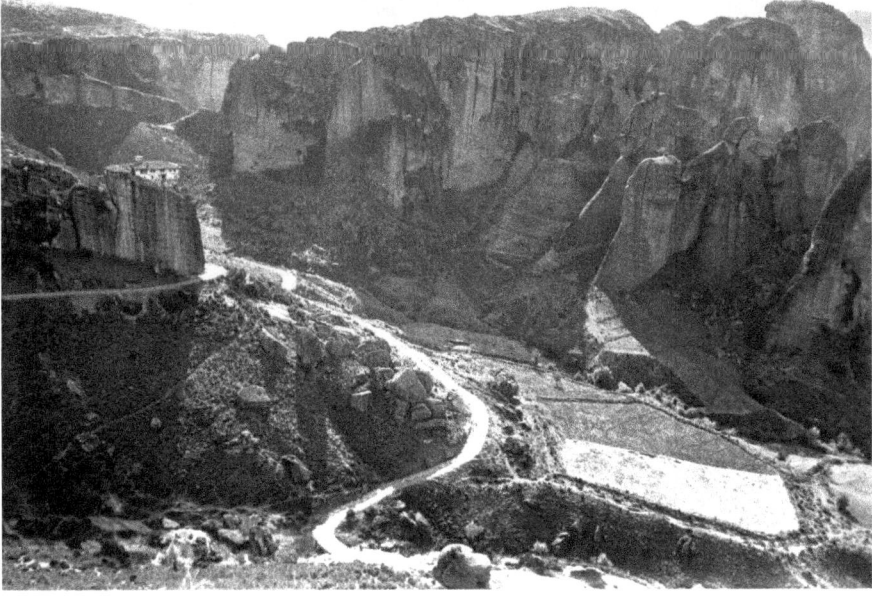

Fig. 89: Mountains near Meteoras Monasteries, Greece, 1954. © David Seymour-Magnum Photos.

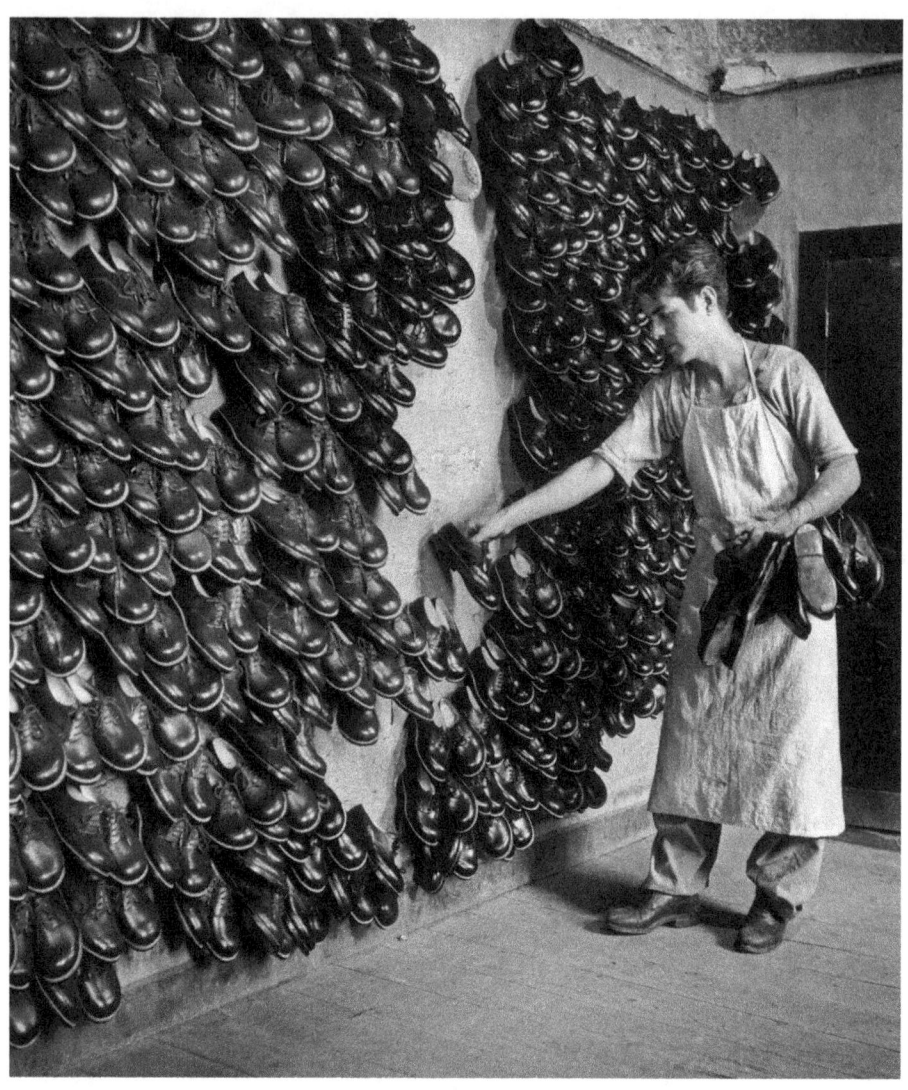

Fig. 90: Young shoemaker in a Greek island, 1951. © David Seymour-Magnum Photos.

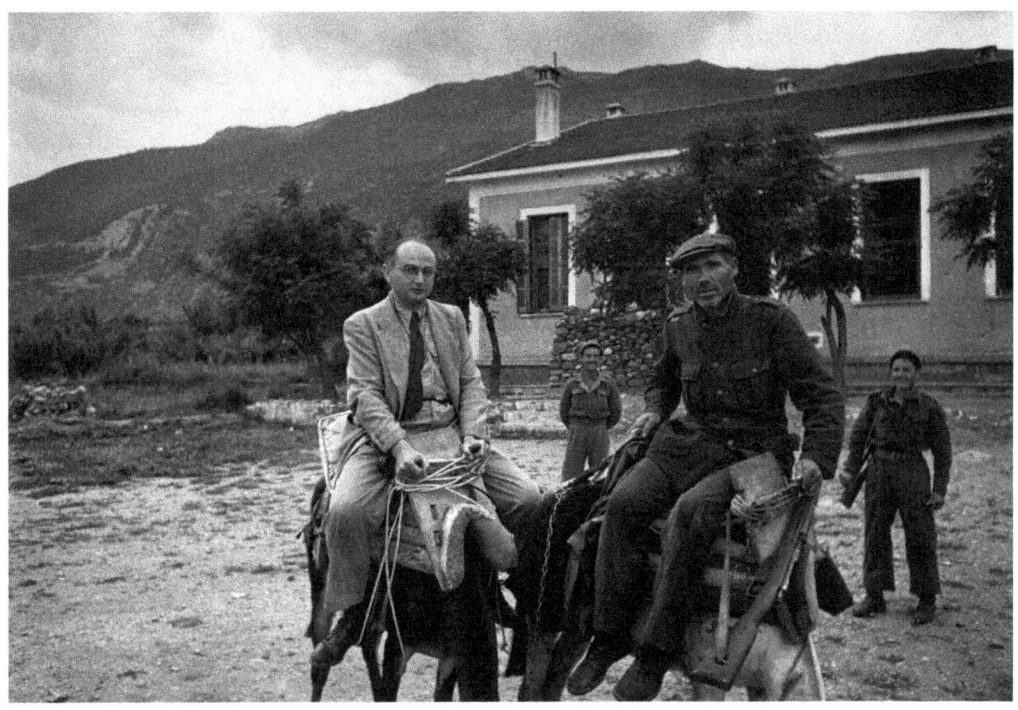

Fig. 91: Chim heading out to Oinoi, Greece, 1949. © David Seymour-Magnum Photos.

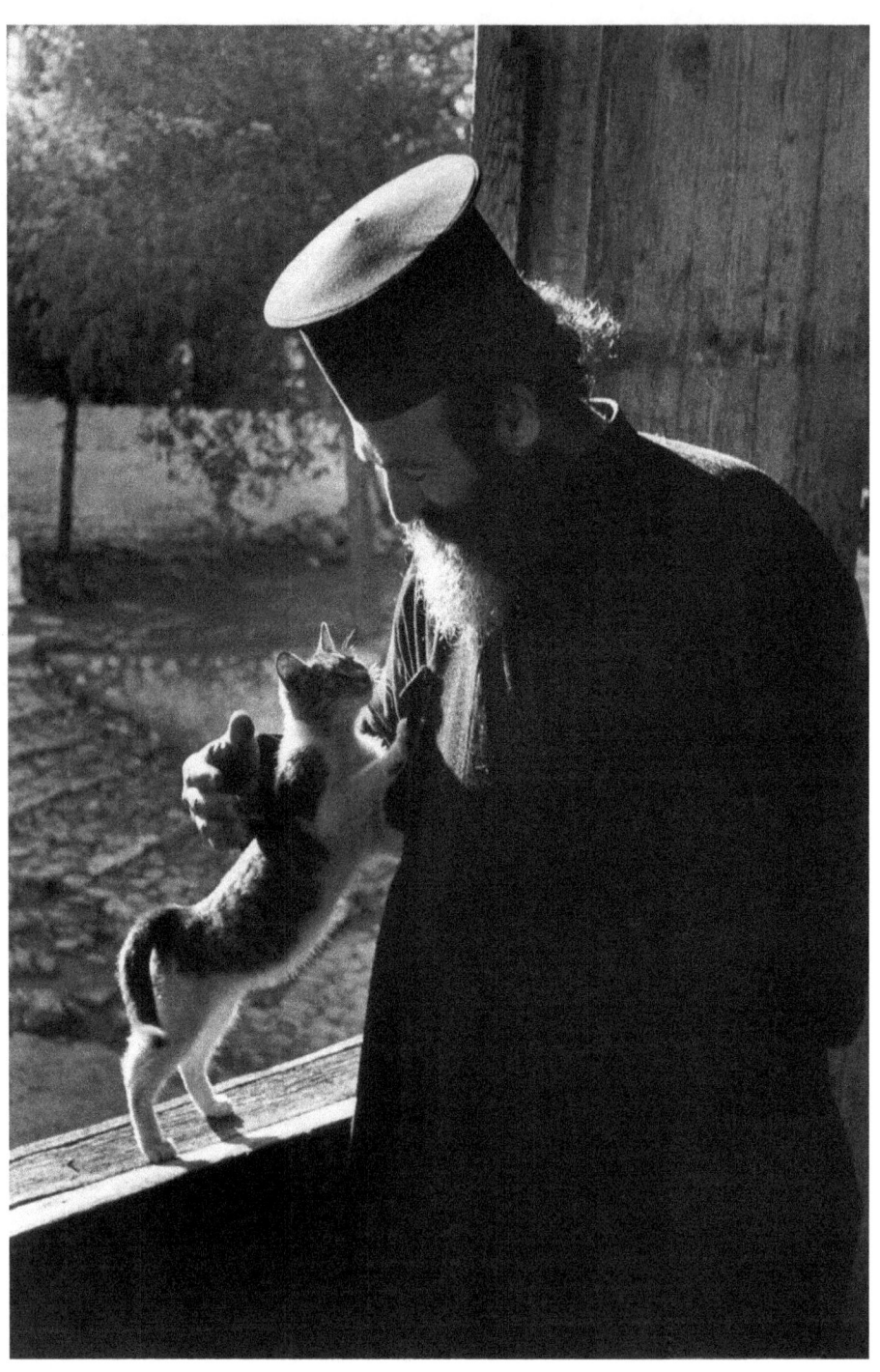

Fig. 92: Priest at Meteoras Monastery, Greece, 1954. © David Seymour-Magnum Photos.

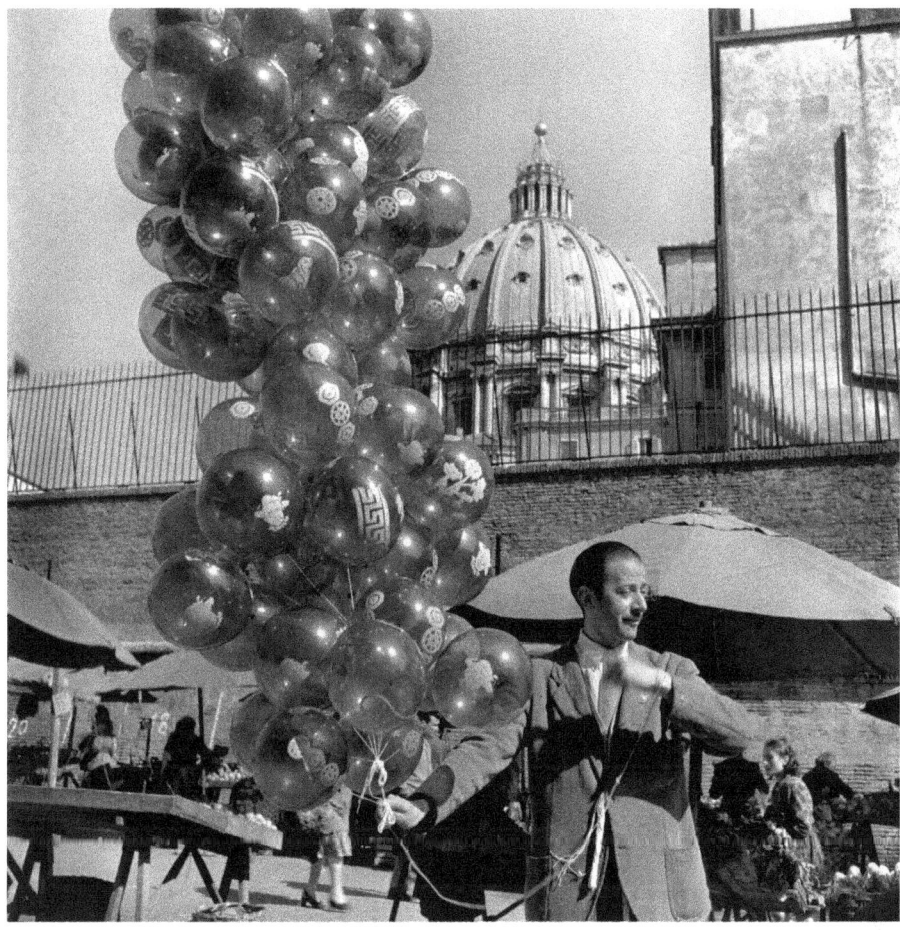

Fig. 93: Vatican City, Rome, 1949. Dome of St Peter's is visible in the background. © David Seymour-Magnum Photos.

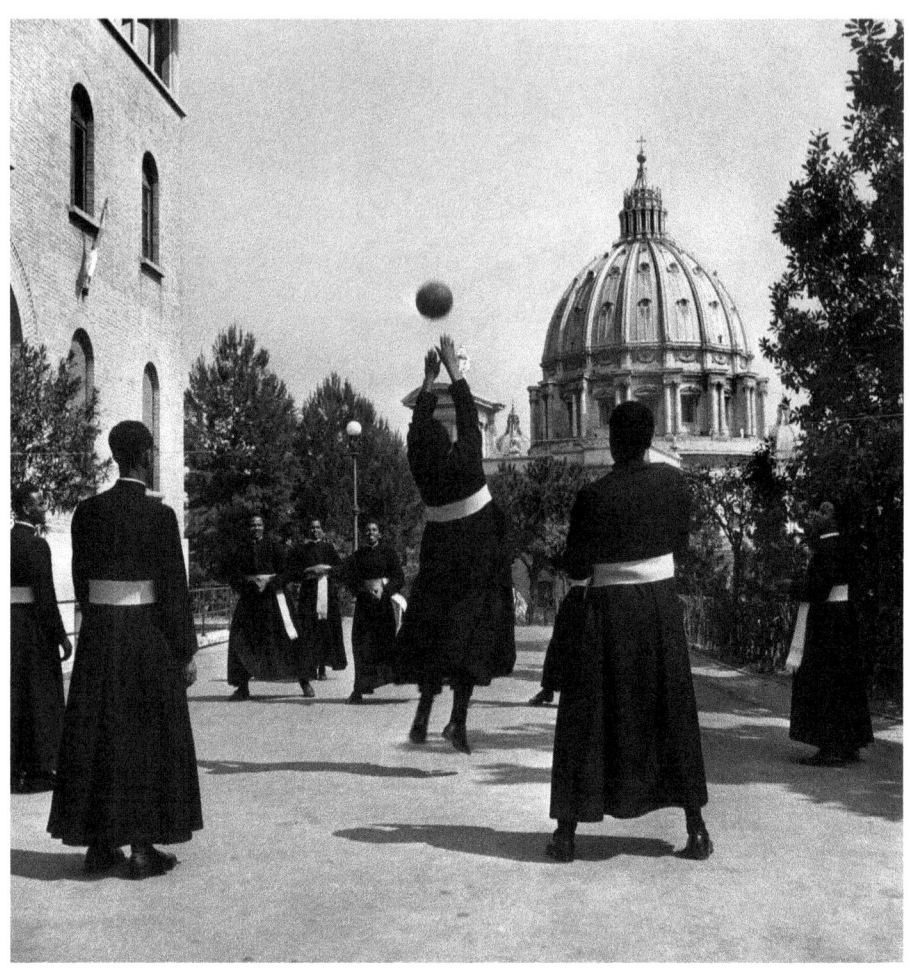

Fig. 94: Ethiopian Priests playing handball, Vatican, Rome, 1949. © David Seymour-Magnum Photos.

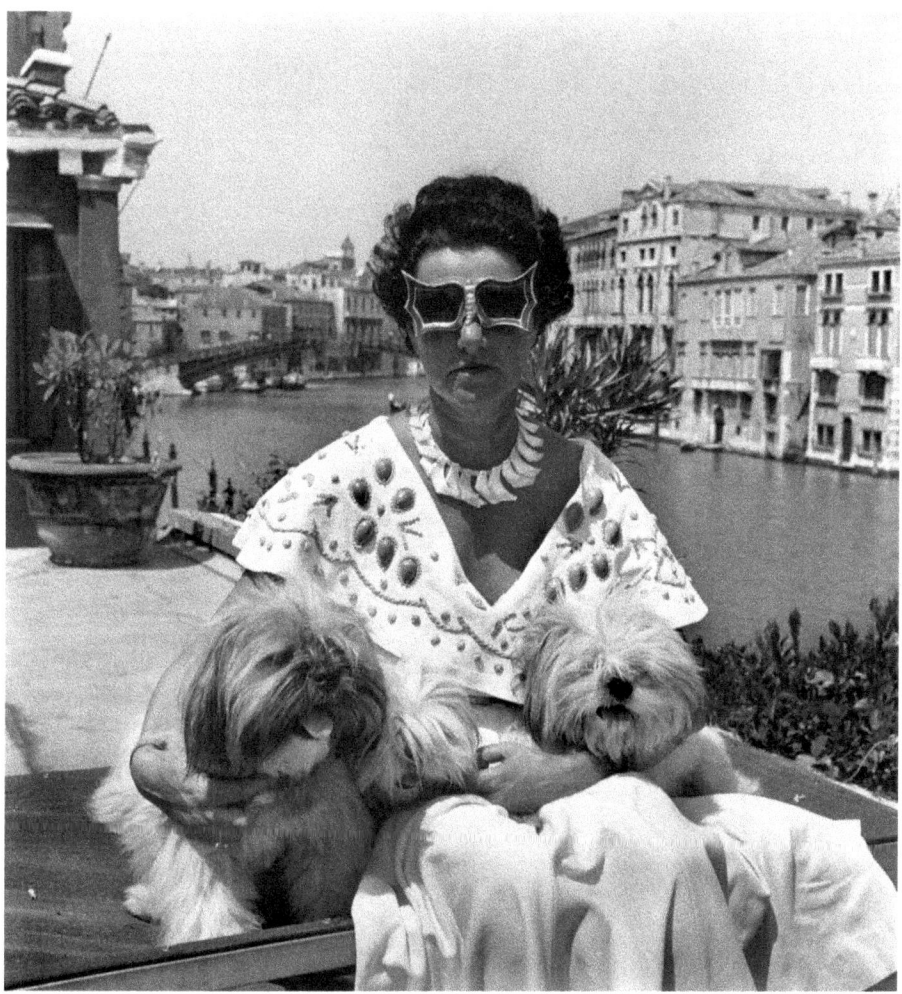

Fig. 95: Peggy Guggenheim on the terrace of Palazzo Venier dei Leoni on the Grand Canal, Venice, 1950. © David Seymour-Magnum Photos.

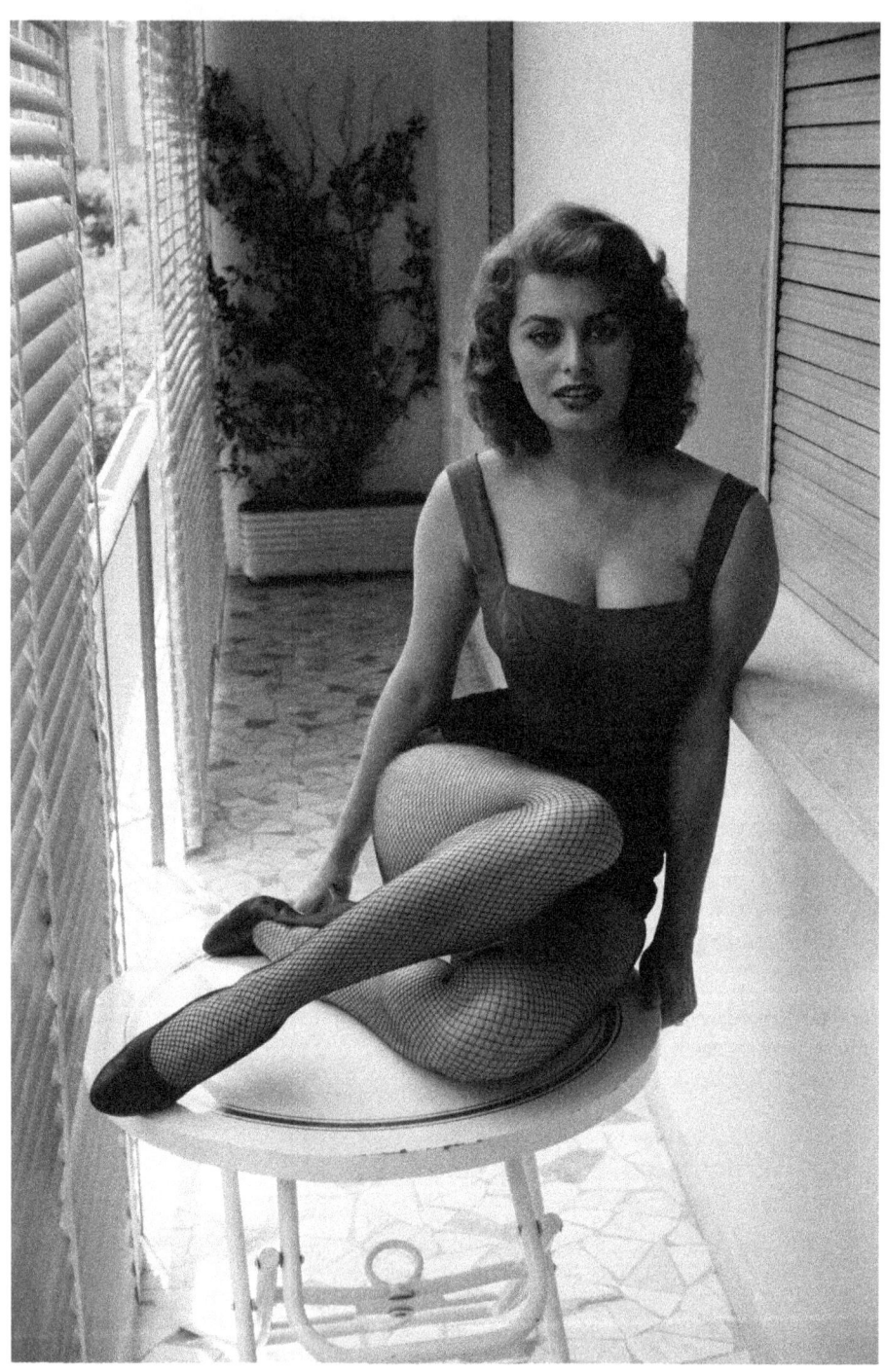

Fig. 96: Sophia Loren at home, Rome 1955. © David Seymour-Magnum Photos.

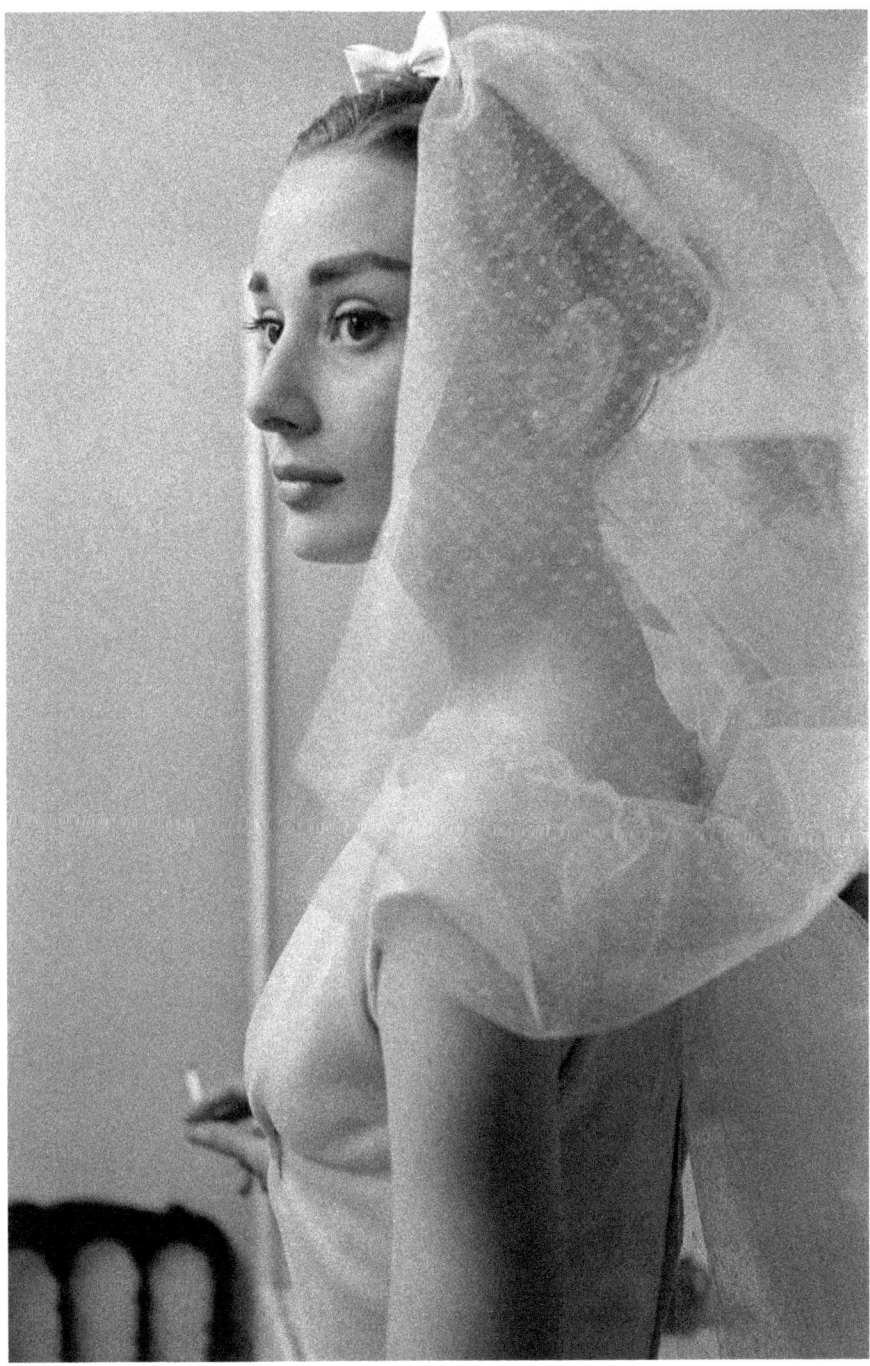

Fig. 97: Audrey Hepburn on the set of *Funny Face* by director Stanley Donen, Paris, 1956. © David Seymour-Magnum Photos.

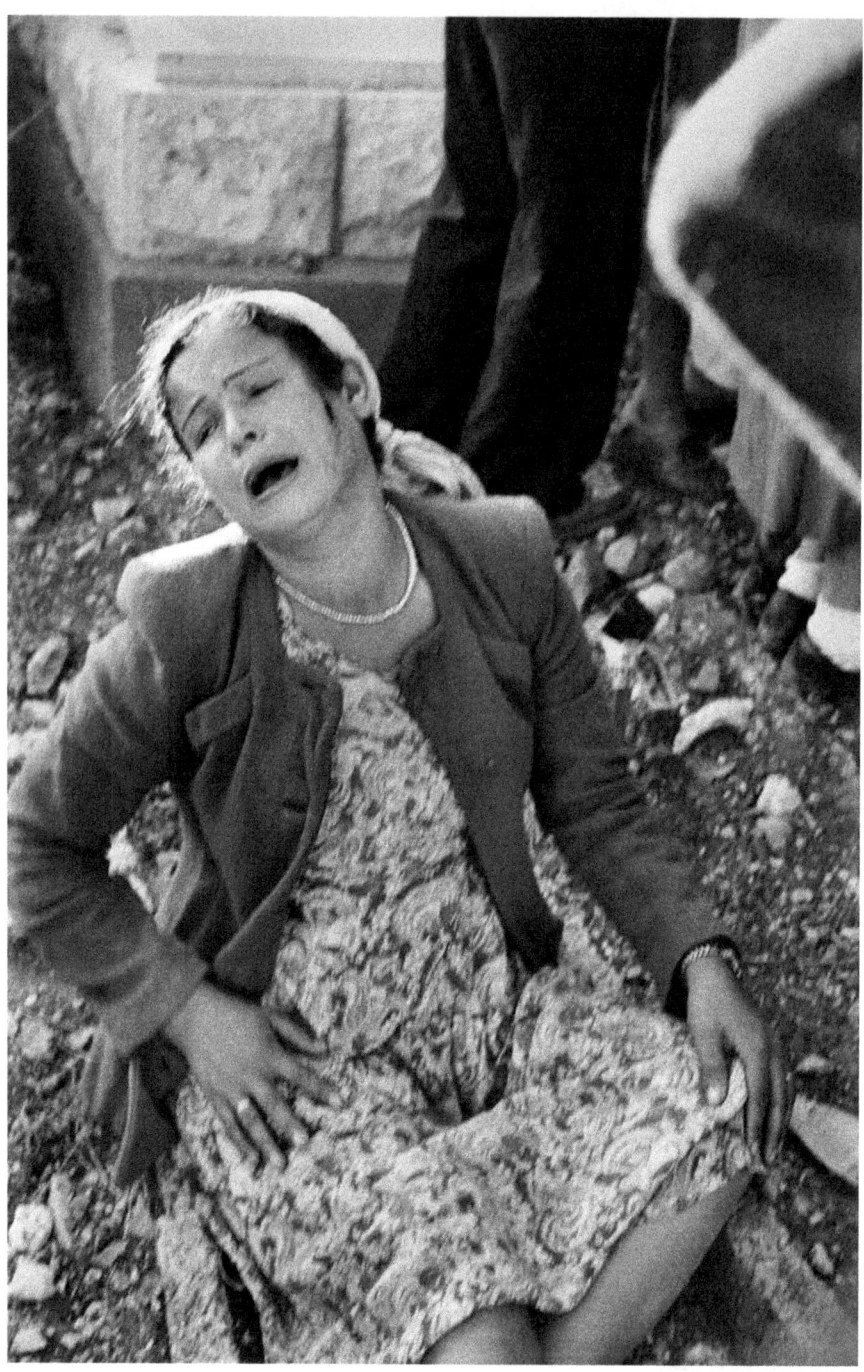

Fig. 98: A woman mourns at the funeral of an Israeli watchman slain during a border incident at Beth Hafafa. Jerusalem, 1953. © David Seymour-Magnum Photos.

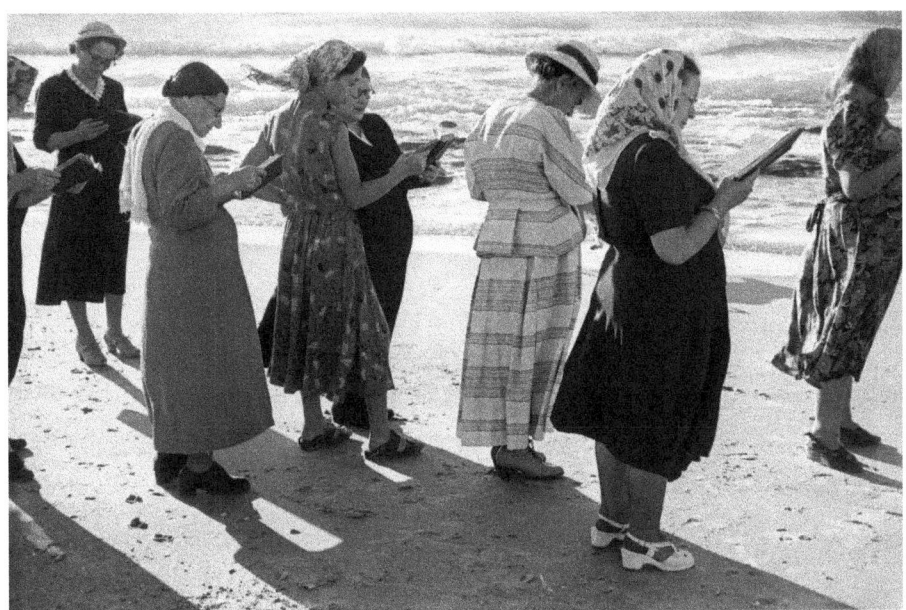

Fig. 99: On the first day of Rosh Hashanah, the Jewish New Year, participants throw crumbs into the sea, symbolizing sins of the past year. Tel Aviv, Israel, 1954. © David Seymour-Magnum Photos.

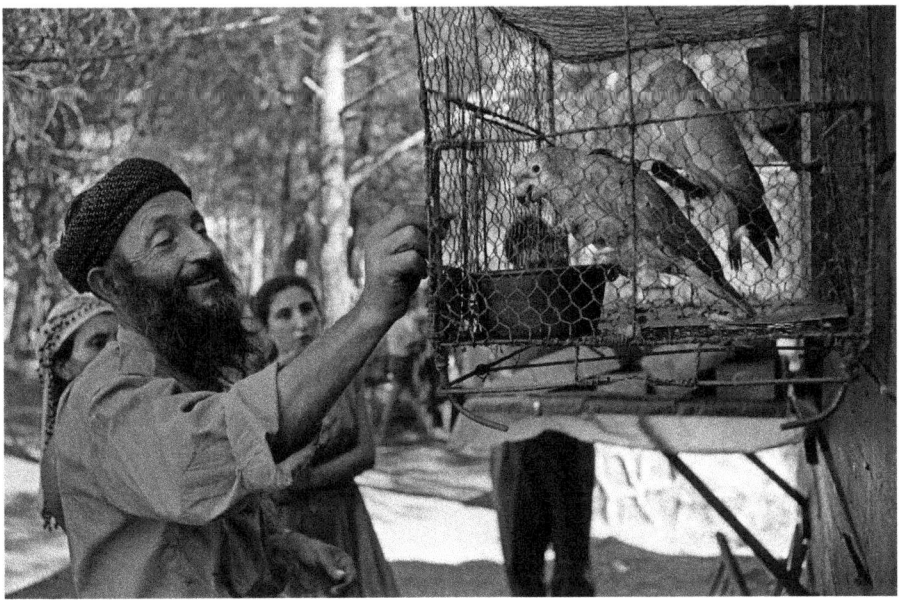

Fig. 100: Israel, 1954.

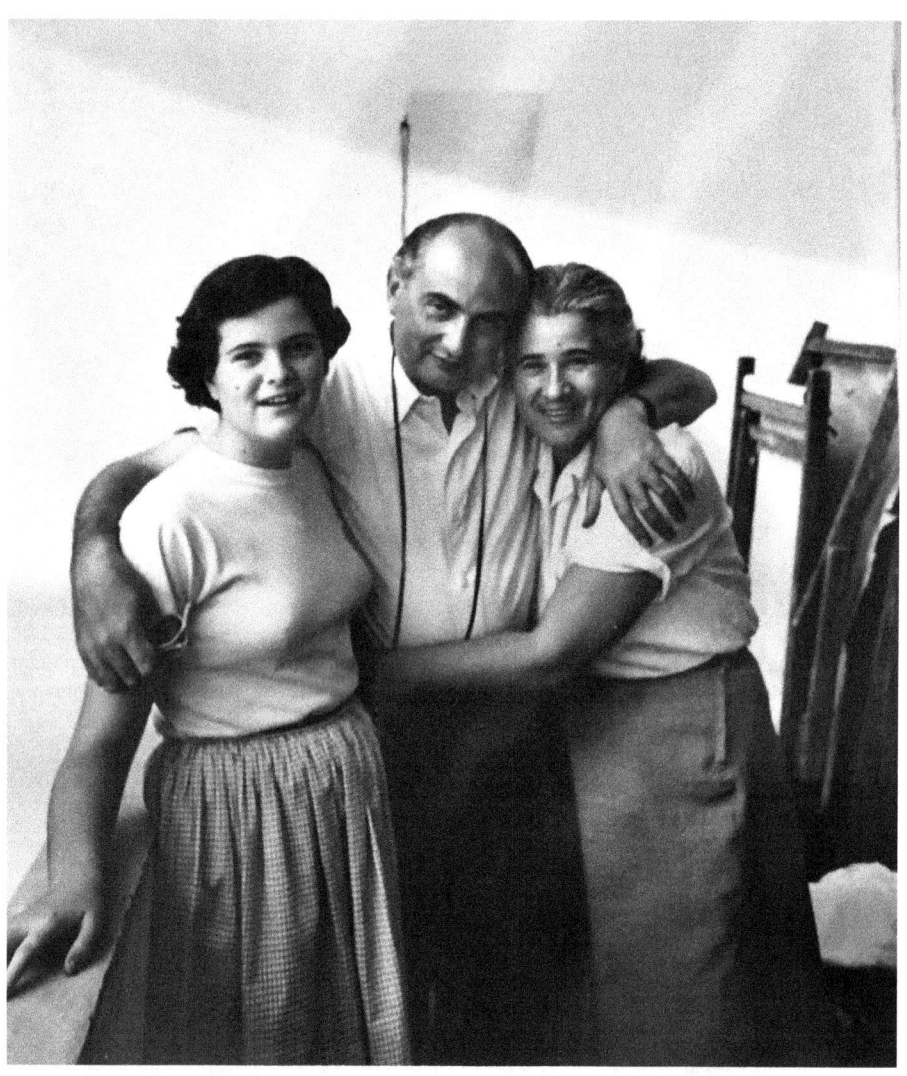

Fig. 101: Chim reunites with cousin Natcha and her daughter Varda. Tel Aviv, Israel, 1951. Courtesy Ben Shneiderman and Helen Sarid.

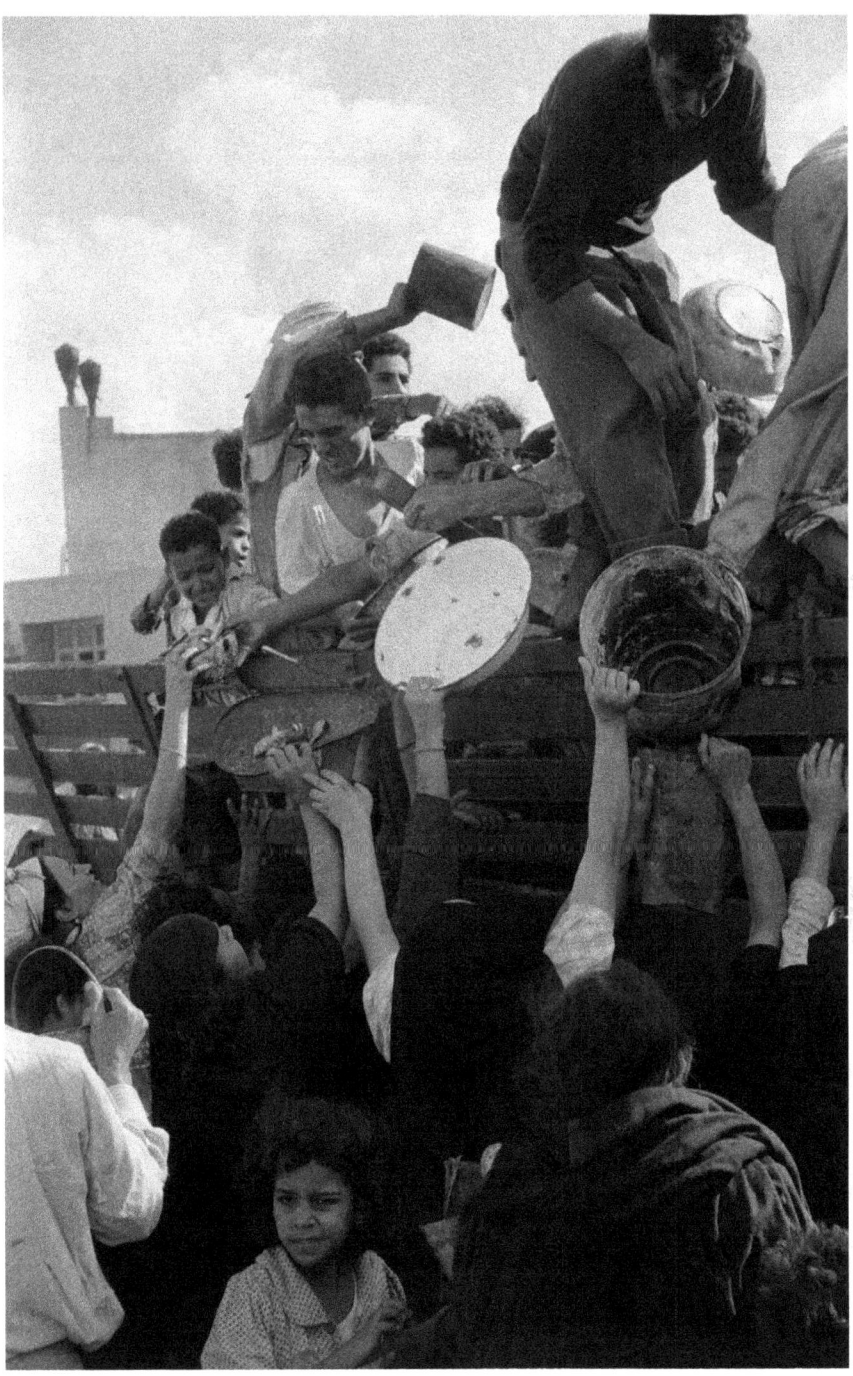

Fig. 102: Hungry crowd mobbing a truckload of fish, Port Said, Egypt, November 1956. © David Seymour-Magnum Photos.

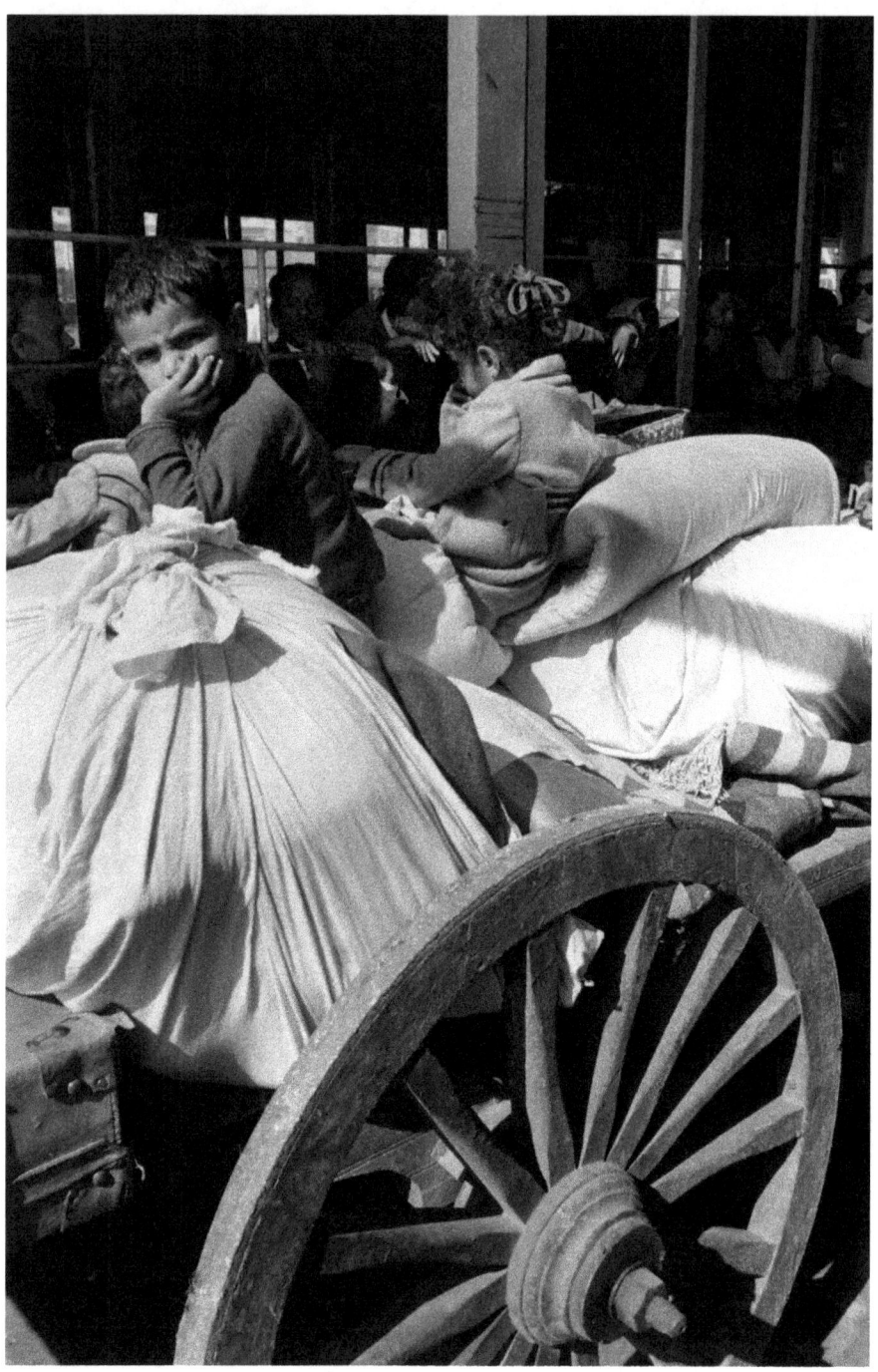
Fig. 103: Refugees waiting for evacuation on the ferryboat from Port Said to Port Fuad. 1956.© David Seymour-Magnum Photos.

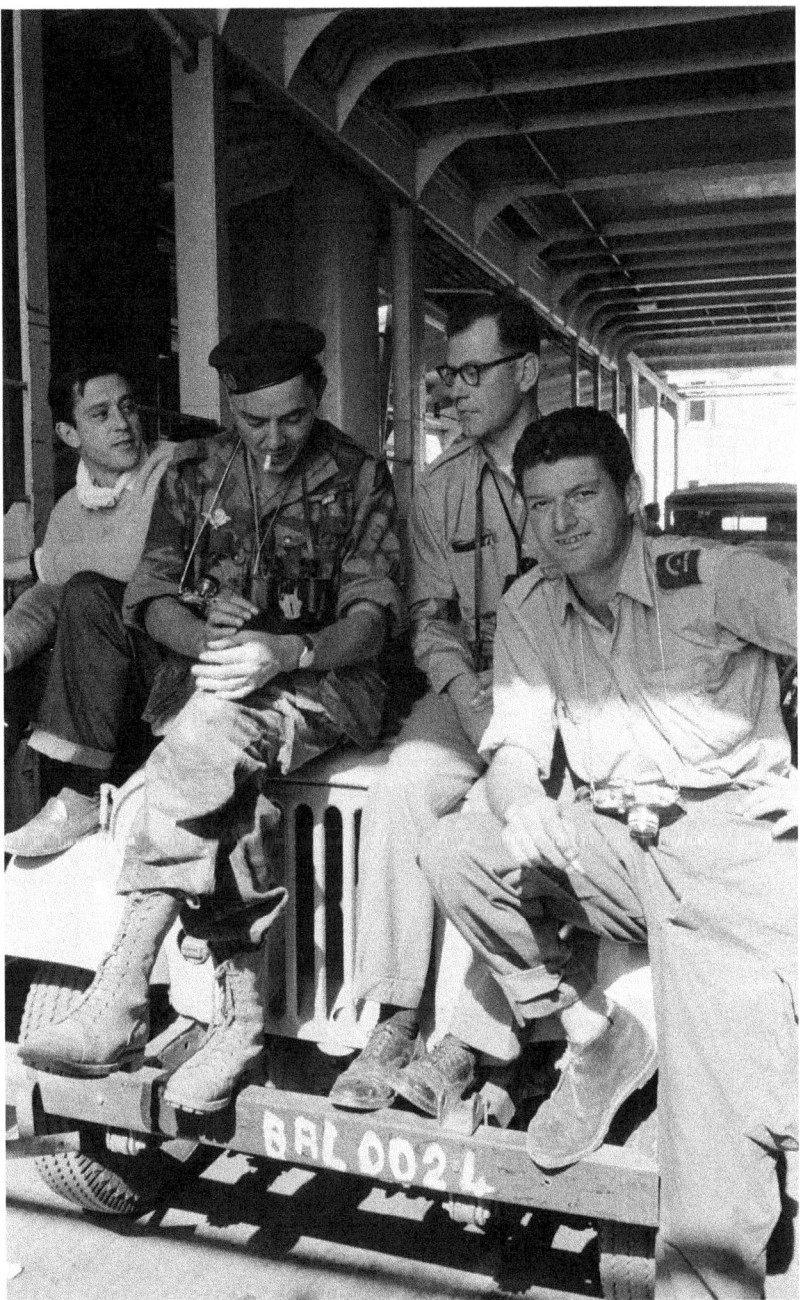

Fig. 104: On the ferry from Port Said to Port Fuad (left to right): Benjamin Bradlee, European correspondent for *Newsweek*; *Paris-Match* photographer Jean Roy; Frank White, Paris Bureau Chief for Time-Life; Paul Bonnecarrère, *Jours de France* combat photographer. November 1956.© David Seymour-Magnum Photos.

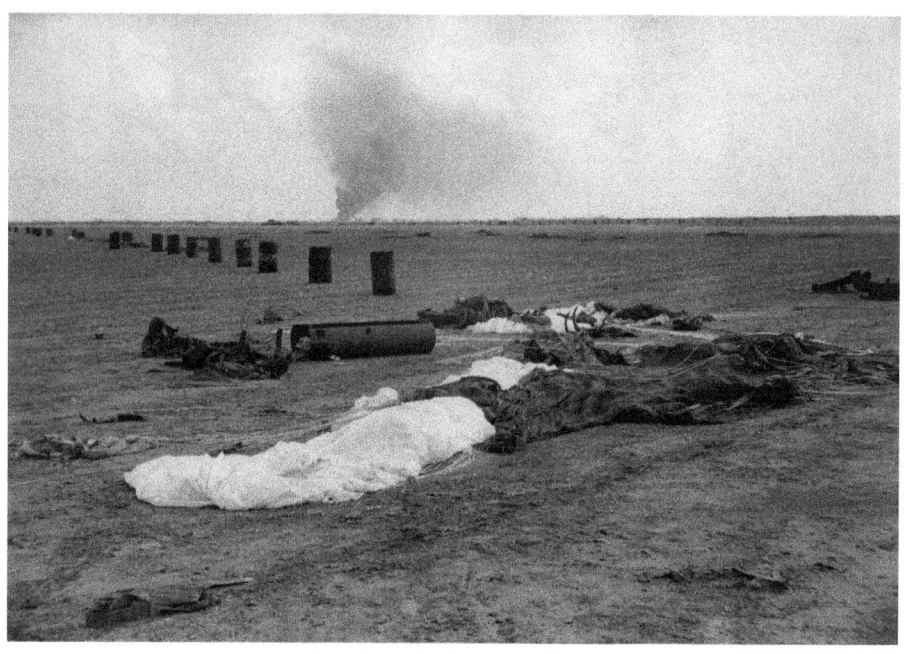

Fig. 105: The El Gamil airfield littered with parachutes and containers after the landing of French parachutists on November 8, Port Saïd, Egypt, 1956. © David Seymour-Magnum Photos.

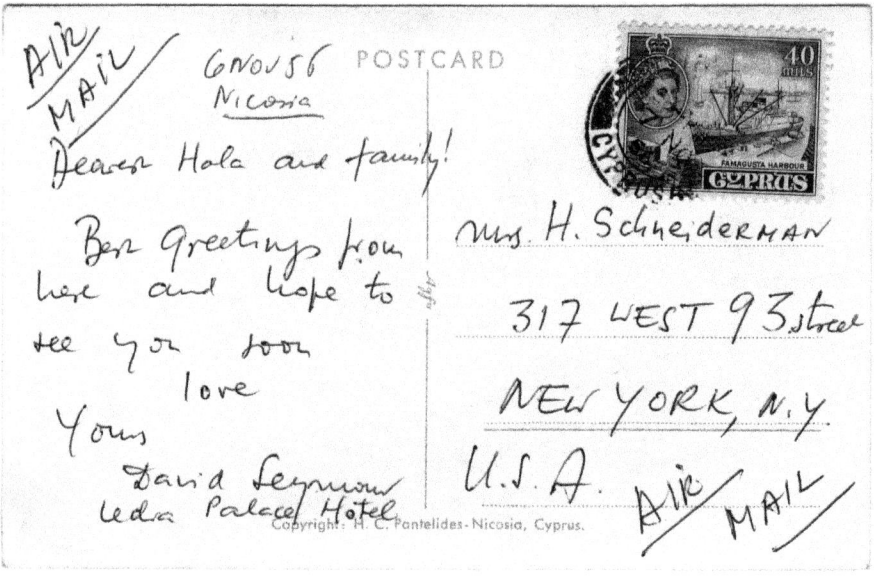

Fig. 106: Last postcard sent by Chim to his family from Nicosia, Cyprus, November 6, 1956. david-seymour.com online archive.

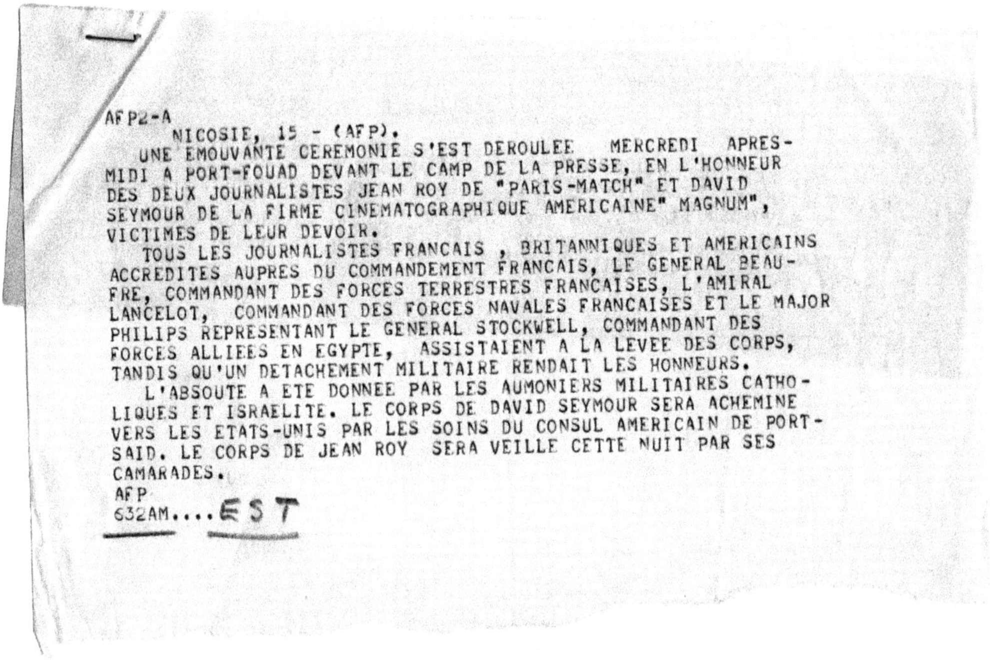

```
AFP2-A
    NICOSIE, 15 - (AFP).
    UNE EMOUVANTE CEREMONIE S'EST DEROULEE    MERCREDI   APRES-
MIDI A PORT-FOUAD DEVANT LE CAMP DE LA PRESSE, EN L'HONNEUR
DES DEUX JOURNALISTES JEAN ROY DE "PARIS-MATCH" ET DAVID
SEYMOUR DE LA FIRME CINEMATOGRAPHIQUE AMERICAINE" MAGNUM",
VICTIMES DE LEUR DEVOIR.
    TOUS LES JOURNALISTES FRANCAIS , BRITANNIQUES ET AMERICAINS
ACCREDITES AUPRES DU COMMANDEMENT FRANCAIS, LE GENERAL BEAU-
FRE, COMMANDANT DES FORCES TERRESTRES FRANCAISES, L'AMIRAL
LANCELOT,  COMMANDANT DES FORCES NAVALES FRANCAISES ET LE MAJOR
PHILIPS REPRESENTANT LE GENERAL STOCKWELL, COMMANDANT DES
FORCES ALLIEES EN EGYPTE,  ASSISTAIENT A LA LEVEE DES CORPS,
TANDIS QU'UN DETACHEMENT MILITAIRE RENDAIT LES HONNEURS.
    L'ABSOUTE A ETE DONNEE PAR LES AUMONIERS MILITAIRES CATHO-
LIQUES ET ISRAELITE. LE CORPS DE DAVID SEYMOUR SERA ACHEMINE
VERS LES ETATS-UNIS PAR LES SOINS DU CONSUL AMERICAIN DE PORT-
SAID. LE CORPS DE JEAN ROY  SERA VEILLE CETTE NUIT PAR SES
CAMARADES.
AFP
632AM....EST
```

Fig. 107: Agence France Press telegram announcing Chim and Jean Roy's death, November 1956. davidseymour.com online archive.

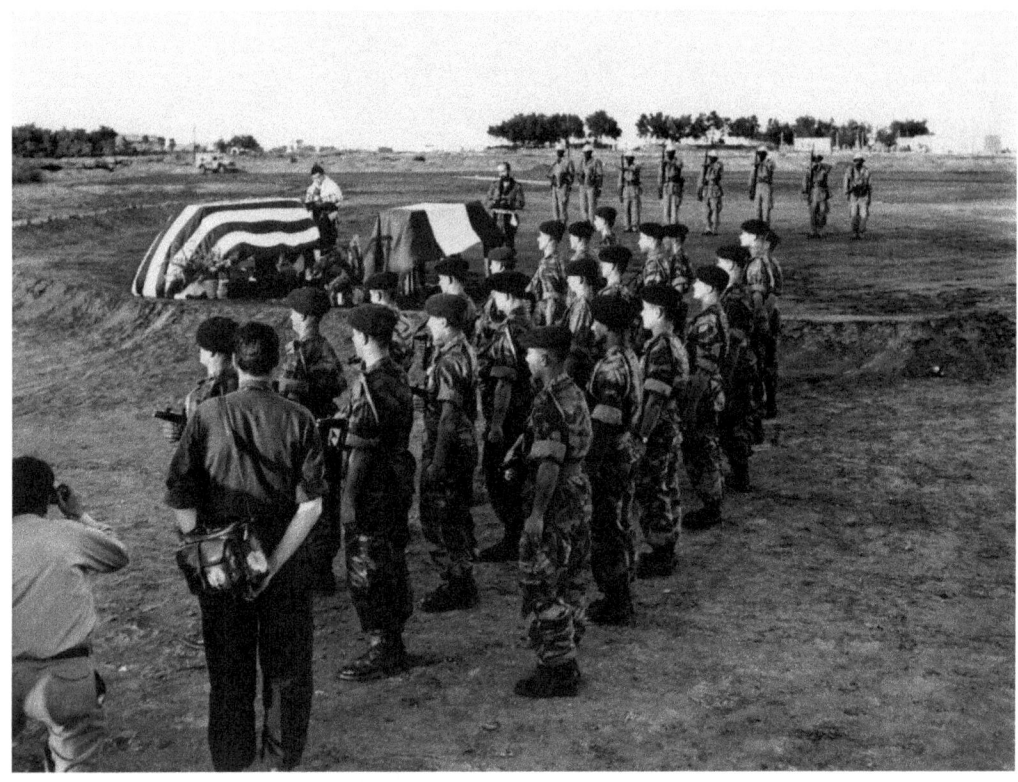

Fig. 108: Detachment of French Marine Commandos honor guard coffins of Jean Roy and David Seymour, attended by General Bauffre, General Stockwell and Admiral Lancelon. The coffins of David Seymour (US flag) and Jean Roy (French flag). Jewish and Catholic chaplains are praying in front of the coffins. Port Fuad, Egypt, 1956. © David Seymour-Magnum Photos.

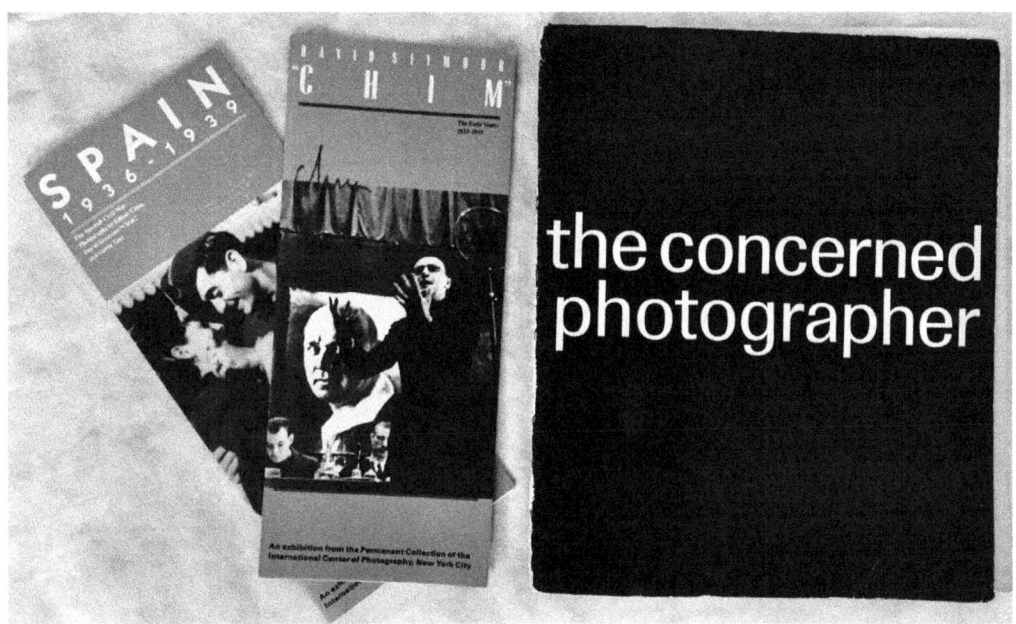

Fig. 109: Book "The Concerned Photographer" and ICP exhibition brochures: "Chim, The Early Years" and "Spain." © the author, 2021.

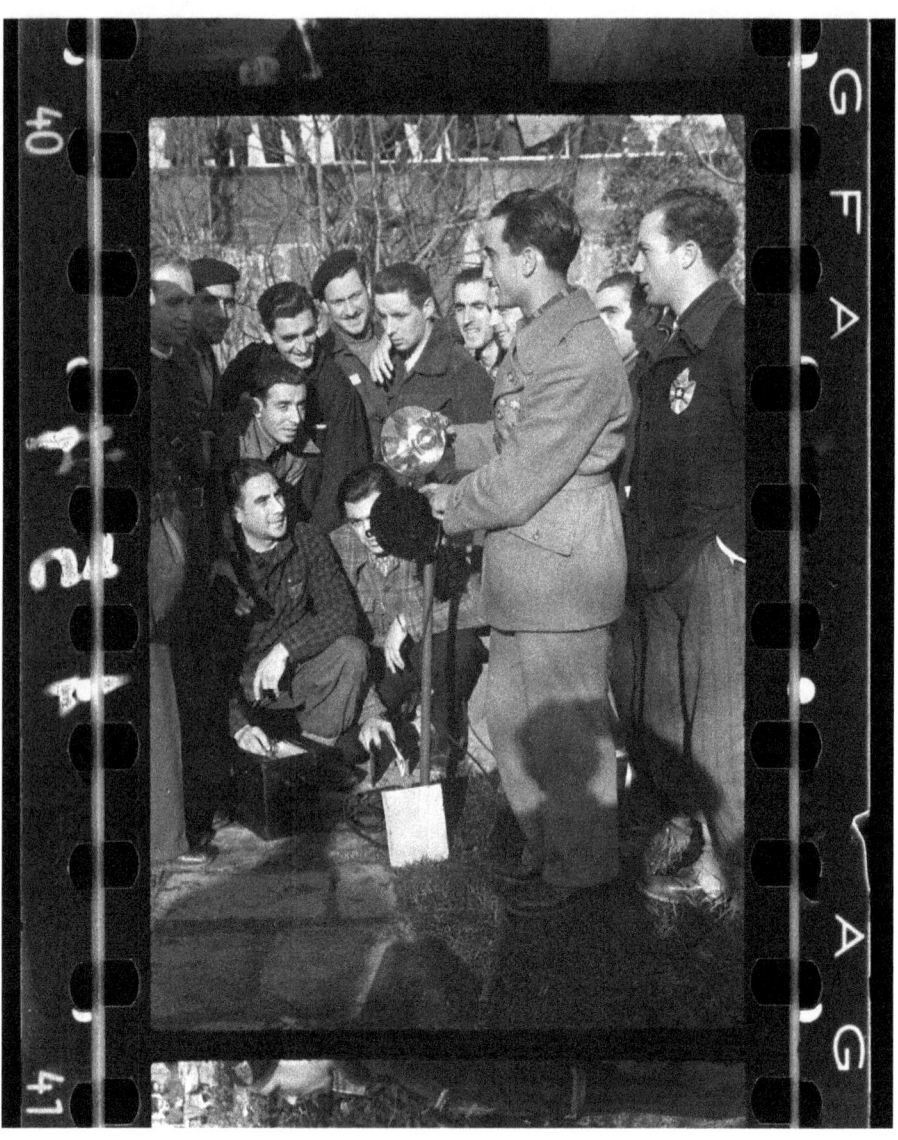

Fig. 110: Endpaper. Army Photographer at Amorebieta cloister, Basque country, Spain, January 1937. © David Seymour-Magnum Photos. From the Mexican Suitcase.

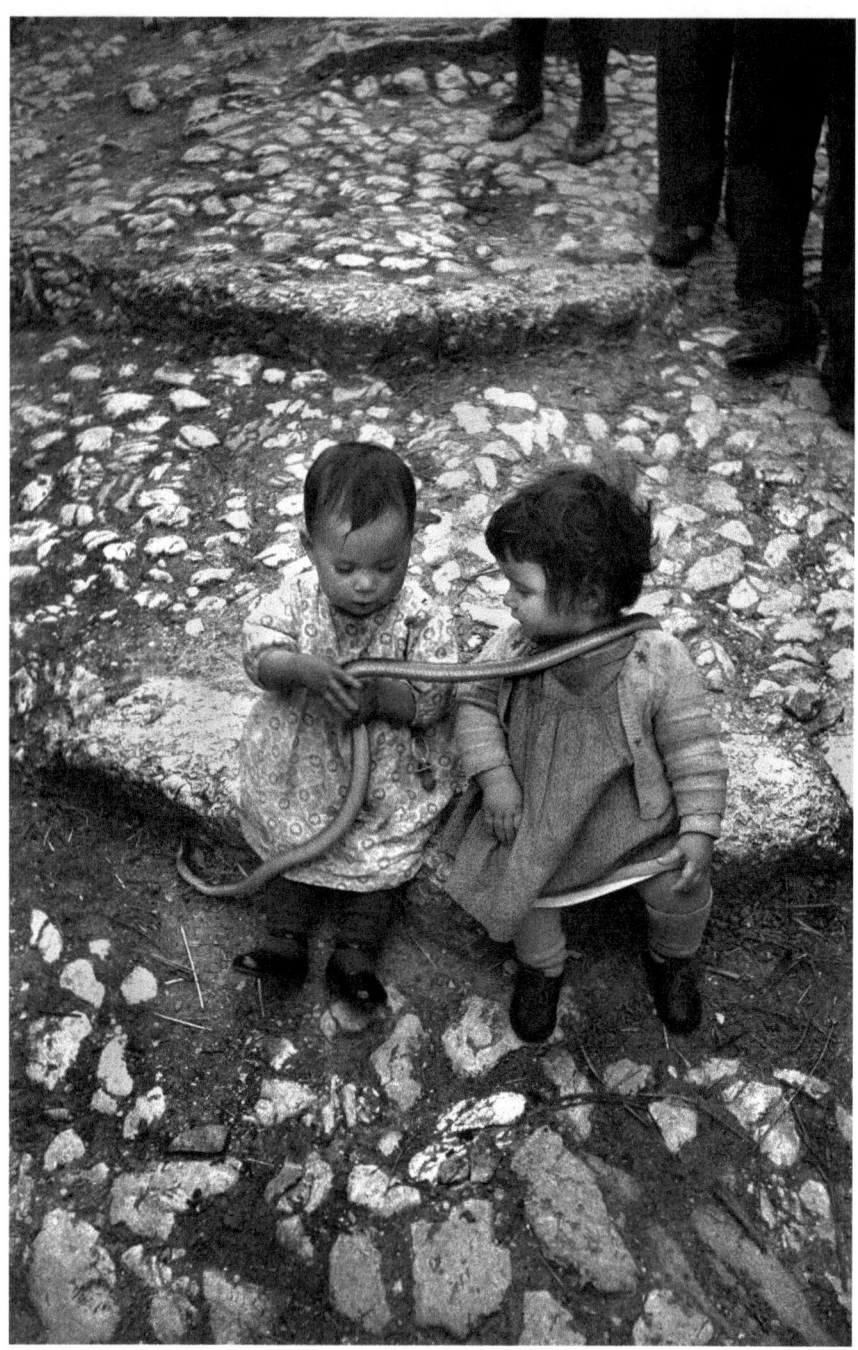

Fig. 15: The people of Cocullo capture snakes for a festival in honor of a Benedictine monk named San Domenico, believed to be a protector against snakebites, Sicily, 1951. © David Seymour-Magnum Photos.

Chapter 13: Of Saints, Snakes, and Angels. 1951–1955

In the late 1940s, after the publications of Carlo Levi's *Christ Stopped at Ebol*, with its striking scenes involving the village witch, and Gramsci's *Observations on Folklore*, there had been a revival of studies relating to popular religion in Southern Italy. The village witch is an important character in Levi's book: in a section of the book, the peasants wait for a procession bearing a statue of the Madonna. They carry baskets of wheat and throw handfuls of it at the statue, hoping to secure a good harvest. Levi writes: "The black-faced Madonna, between the wheat and the animals, the detonations and the trumpets, was not the merciful Mother of God but an underground deity that had drawn its blackness from the land of shadows in the earth's entrails, a peasant Persephone, an infernal goddess of harvests."[1]

While traveling in the South for his illiteracy project, Chim's curiosity was piqued; besides, he was greatly influenced by his new friendship with Levi: his contact sheets show that he visited Levi's painting studio in 1950 when they worked together on a story entitled *Il Gufo* (the Owl) about Levi's pet bird Graziadio, which he had acquired from a traveling zoo.[2] Chim wrote that "Graziadio became Carlo Levi's obsession and he painted, wrote and even composed poetry about him [The Owl]."[3]

The photographs from that studio session show Levi's paintings, some of which detail intricate scenes of the villages where he had been exiled, while others include the figure of his owl, flying around or perching on his shoulder.

While Chim himself was often compared to an owl, he thinks it is Levi "who looks like a human edition of an owl."[4]... Chim made several portraits of the bird, including one where it is a mysterious figure, shrouding its face with its wings, as if shying away from the photographer. In his text for the story, Chim wrote: "When the prints were ready, Carlo Levi was enthusiastic and said that I had helped him see Graziadio. A few months later, when I returned to Rome and visited him, I discovered his studio was filled with drawings, sketches and paintings of Graziadio and Carlo showed me a first print of his book "Orologio" [sic] and on the front cover there is a painting of Graziadio which reminded me faintly of one of my photographs."[5]

Published five years later together with Chim's photographs, Levi's text explains his fascination with the owl as a living creature and as a symbol: "I have always admired and perhaps even loved all kinds of night birds, those strange animals that are more than anything else reminiscent of the ancient gods. My feeling for, or pas-

---

1 Carlo Levi, *Christ Stopped at Eboli* (New York: FSG, 2006), 111.
2 MPNYA, ADS 1950–1951, story #50-9.
3 MPNYA, DST, *Carlo Levi and the Owl*, DSA 1950–1951.
4 Ibid.
5 Ibid.

sion, or love, or attraction to them is surely nothing strange, since the round eyes of the owl and her hooting, have from the earliest days moved the imagination of humanity and it has been like this for centuries, from the Athenian owl onwards to the death-bringing owls in the poetry of Cassian (...) she has always been to me a symbol of eternity, dating back to the beginning of the world." In the same text, Levi describes owls as "crossing the sky at twilight, like flying cats, witches surprised by the coming dawn."[6]

Chim shared Levi's fascination with myths, traditions, and history, and he had always seen the present as infused with layers of the past, expressing that awareness in the pictures he made in Greece and Italy. Now, after completing his Vatican piece, he was eager to photograph the religious rituals of Italy's South, which the church in Rome sometimes tolerated but generally sought to root out, believing that they emerged from ignorance and superstition, or were even demonic.

This curiosity and desire to document the peripheries of religion, a cultural phenomenon that had been mostly explored by anthropologists, is typical of Chim. In his agenda, he noted saints' days and the dates of upcoming religious festivals, and when he could find the time between assignments, he traveled by bus or train to remote villages, often sleeping in shabby inns or, if there was no alternative, on hard wooden station benches.

In the religious festivals and processions that he photographed, magical, pagan, and Christian elements converged to answer needs that official Catholicism could not fulfill. Many of the rituals were derived from the cults of ancient Greece; the Greeks referred to Southern Italy–present-day Campania, Apulia, Basilicata, Calabria, and Sicily–as Graecia Magna (Μεγάλη Ἑλλάς), regions that had been populated by Greek settlers who imported their culture, especially religious rites and traditions, and belonged to mystic cults such as Orphism and Pythagoreanism.

From 1951 to 1955, Chim documented the festivals of the South. In March 1951, on his way to shoot a story about Holy Week in Sicily, he stopped at the Villa Pelagonia near Palermo and photographed with his Rollei the grotesque statues of dwarfs or mythological creatures adorning niches and walls, making a surreal image of a small child standing in an alcove alongside a statue that was taller than him.[7] He continued on to several villages: Isnello, high up in the mountains, Piana dei Greci, an hour away from Palermo,[8] and Caltanissetta, overlooking the Salso Valley and surrounded by hills.

Caltanisetta was famous for its Holy Thursday Procession of the *Misteri*, during which 16 life-size groupings of wooden statues, each representing a moment of the Passion Play, were carried through tows. Taking place at night, it was illuminated

---

6 MPNYA, *The Owl*, Story 50-9, and *Unesco Courier*, August 1957, "Carlo Levi, artist by day, author by night."
7 MPNYA, ADS 1950–1951, picture in story #51-18-7.
8 MPNYA, ADS 1950–1951, story #51-18-7.

with acetylene lamps, candles, and Bengal flames that created a theatrical setup with deep shadows.[9]

Chim wrote a lengthy, well-documented text to accompany his story, which was shot in three different locations, both in black and white and in color:

> Each of the group [of statues] represents a moment out of the Passion play. They are immense, sometimes composed of twelve to fourteen statues each. They are richly colored and illuminated at night with acetylene lamps and Bengal flames. They are very heavy, and some are carried by over 30 men who, step by step, slowly drag them through the streets. Every statue is in custody of a trade group so that, for instance, the Last Supper is in charge [sic] of the Bakers; the butchers take care of the Crucifixion; the Deposition is in the custody of the Sulphur Miners, etc.[10]

The procession started in the dark, each group preceded by a band playing funeral marches and a chorus singing hymns, while prayers, hosannas, and fireworks greeted the parade. During Chim's visit, almost 100,000 people were present. The statues, lifted over the shoulders of the crowd, take on a life of their own as candlelight plays over their features, animating them. When the procession arrived in front of the Cathedral around two in the morning, a sharp whistle sounded and it disbanded. "Tradition also demands that the statues are carried away running," wrote Chim, "and it is an extraordinary sight to see the dead-tired men make a last sport of the finish."[11]

Traveling on to Isnello, he found the mountain village covered in snow. Since 1627 the villagers had performed the story of Christ in a play called *Casazza* and as he approached, Chim observed "the great movement converging into town. By truck, cart, mule, horse and on foot, thousands of people were streaming into the small town (...) the streets of Isnello were transformed into an enormous theater a couple of miles long, then the play started."[12]

Six hundred peasants participated in the 13-act performance. Starting with the Annunciation, they performed a Nativity scene, a Passion Play, and a Crucifixion, the actors moving along in procession, stopping and repeating scenes so that everyone could follow from up-close. Chim observed the crowd as much as the play: "It was very cold and the crowd huddled in blankets waiting for each scene to come along, tense and reacting to every word. Judas was booed and so were the Roman soldiers martyrizing Christ."[13]

That year, 1951, the Greek Orthodox and Catholic Easter fell on the same day, March 25. On Easter Sunday, Chim went to the village of Piana dei Greci, populated by people of Albanian descent who belonged to the Orthodox church. He made

---

9 MPPA, PAR116201, PAR116202, PAR116206,
10 MPNYA, ADS 1950–1951, story #51-18-1, "Holy Week in Sicily."
11 Ibid.
12 Ibid.
13 Ibid.

beautiful portraits of the crowd attending mass and individual portraits of the women proudly wearing centuries-old Albanian dresses, family heirlooms transmitted from mothers to daughters to be used only on that one day. In his color pictures (he also shot in black and white), their belts, called *breza*, made of silver hammered into the shape of the Madonna or St. George and the dragon, contrasted with their red skirts, and gleamed in the sun that greeted the special day.[14]

Chim's next story, called "The Snake Pit of Cocullo," was shot in the village of Cocullo, in the mountains of the Abruzzi, a central region of Italy. For the peasants who lived there, snakes, mostly harmless ones, were part of everyday life and not to be feared. Chim wrote: "Everybody believes in supernatural powers connected with the snakes. The snakes' fat is the base of almost all home medicines."[15]

The celebration of snakes originated with San Domenico, a Benedictine monk who had lived in these mountains a thousand years ago and was said to have protected the villagers from snake bites, attacks from rabid dogs, and toothaches. His molar, imbued with magical powers, was kept in the church as a powerful relic and it was believed to be a magical tool that could counter the maleficent fangs of the snake, which, in the Christian tradition had become the incarnation of evil, sin, and Satan.

This feast day is believed to have subsumed a more ancient celebration of the goddess. In pagan times, the people of Abruzzi had worshipped Angitia or Anagta, a Roman goddess of thaumaturgy who had the powers of witchcraft, magic, and medicine. Associated with the Greek sorceress Kirkè, she was proficient in the art of miraculous and herbal healing, especially when it came to snake bites. In those early days, the snakes were killed and eaten in a feast, but by the time Chim attended the festival, the peasants had substituted bread formed in a variety of snake shapes, some formed into rings, biting their tails in the uroboros shape, a symbol of eternity or the wholeness that could be regained by absorbing it.

On the day of the festival, the snake-catchers (*serpari*) went hunting in rock formations and scree slopes around the village, and, bare-handed, in a lightning flash of motion, grabbed the snakes from behind their heads. Thousands of people from the whole Abruzzi region congregated in the narrow streets. Though pagan in spirit, the festival started on the front steps of the Catholic church where a relic of the saint was kept.

Using both 35mm and his Rollei, Chim photographed the young snake hunters, and children playing with snakes (one boy had captured 67 of them!). The most desired species were the olive-colored grass snake, the whip snake, and the Aesculapian snake which was falsely believed to wrap itself around a cow's leg to drink its milk. "The people of Cocullo do not fear snakes", Chim wrote. "The small ones play with them like everywhere else a child plays with a cat or a dog."[16]

---

14 MPNYA, ADS 1950–1951, story #51-18-1.
15 MPNYA, ADS 1950–1951, DST, "The Snake Pit of Cocullo," for story #51-19.
16 MPNYA, ADS 1950–1951, text "The Snake Pit of Cocullo" for story #51-19.

One of Chim's most striking photographs depicts two toddlers sitting on village steps, with one of them, full of curiosity, playing with the snake draped around his friend's neck.[17] (figure 15) He made closeups of hands belonging to Francesco Jovine, the medicine man; snakes are rolled around his wrists like strange bracelets. In another image, Jovine takes a nap in the sun, his body covered with snakes that keep him company[18]. Chim also followed a street photographer who shot family portraits in front of a painted background, and he took a picture of a picture, a fragment of street view showing around the other photographer's frame.[19]

Then he followed the procession: two young girls in silk robes carried on their heads ornate baskets containing three round loaves of sweet bread, an offering to San Domenico. The statue of the saint had snakes draped around its shoulders and around the two angels below, and people were pinning lire bills to the ribbons hanging from it. "The miraculous statue of San Domenico is carried through the streets, adorned with live snakes, and all the *serpari* carrying snakes in their hands," Chim wrote.[20]

Two years later, Chim went to Sardinia to cover another important festival for a story entitled "The Journey of San Efisio."[21] San Efisio, the patron saint of Cagliari, Sardinia's capital city, is so important to worshipers that they postpone the Labor Day feast (May 1) for a few days in deference to the saint, to whom they made a promise in the seventeenth century. Efisio was a fourth-century Roman governor of the island who had been sent by Emperor Diocletian to suppress Christianity there. Instead, he experienced an epiphany, converted to Christianity, and was subsequently martyred. When the plague ravaged Cagliari, its citizens, remembering Efisio, asked him for his help and thanks to him the epidemic ended. Ever since, the citizens have carried his effigy to the shores of the island.

Reflecting the legacy of the seventeenth-century Spanish dominion of the island, the ceremony resonated with the traditions of southern Spain. The saint's statue was carried on a seventeenth-century gold-plated coach drawn by oxen from the church in Stampace where the saint was kept a prisoner—then beheaded. The coach was accompanied by the *Guardiana*, who wore black top hats and tails. Behind the saint walked the bishop and other members of the clergy, followed by penitents in embroidered costumes who had vowed to walk the entire distance of the pilgrimage[22]. A few miles outside the town, they stopped in a small church where they dressed the saint in an armor to protect him from the bandits who traditionally roam Sardinia. The procession then traveled around the Gulf of Cagliari and through its little towns until it reached the edge of the sea in Nora, where Efisio was killed. As

---

17 MPNYA, ADS 1950–1951, story #51-19-9.
18 MPNYA, NYC42636 and MPPA, PAR291507.
19 MPNYA, ADS 1950–1951, story #51-19-9.
20 Ibid.
21 MPNYA, ADS 1950–1951, text "The Snake Pit of Cocullo" for story #51–19.
22 MPNYA, NYC64585.

the pilgrims chanted, the image of the saint was silhouetted against the setting sun and the sea. Four days later after a ceremonial banquet, the statue, guided by the faithful carrying torches, started to make its way back to Cagliari.[23]

For Chim, history was being made visible through the unchanging rituals, and photography was his tool for uncovering these layers of memory and immortalizing traditions that might soon disappear. Thus he followed the procession for four days, photographing its extraordinary display of costumes and accessories—the ox-drawn carts carrying delegations from every village in Sardinia wearing medieval costumes of thick velvet and lace; the mayor with his coat, top hat and silver chain with a large silver medallion dating back from the time of the Spanish occupation; and the saint's fraternity on horseback with two brilliantly costumed flutists playing the traditional Sardinian pipes, the *laudennas*.[24]

On Good Friday of 1955, Chim set off for San Fratello, a Sicilian village high in the mountains between Messina and Palermo. He had heard about a strange ritual that had been performed there since the Middle Ages. "Good Friday is a day of mourning and is celebrated with great fervor and devotion all over Italy," he wrote. "The beautiful village of San Fratello in Sicily manages to combine the sorrow and joy, the tears and laughter, funeral marches and gay songs in one extraordinary celebration."[25] A statue of the Mater Dolorosa is carried by the crowd under the eyes of benevolent *carabinieri*. The mourning effigy, holding the dead Christ on its knees, is on the same scale as the people who carry it, wearing white robes and crowns of thorns. It is so life-like that it seems to blend with them.[26] (Figure 88).

Before setting out, Chim had consulted a professor of ethnography in Rome: "[He]was hesitant to give me any exact indications. He was bitter and sad about the vanishing traditions. He was disappointed because of the speed with which modern life penetrates the villages, the movies which provide the entertainment, the neon lights which change the piazzas. He could not tell me anything, afraid that when I reached the place, I would find nothing."[27]

Undeterred, Chim pursued his research and was referred to a San Fratello teacher, the daughter of a local blacksmith, who was writing her doctoral thesis on local traditions: "I was happy. I had a lead."[28] Around the dinner table, the teacher told Chim that the tradition went back to the Middle Ages when pilgrims from the Holy Land tried to educate the people in the mysteries of the Christian religion and, with the permission of the Church, did it through visual artifacts. The procession was made official in 1626.

---

23 MPPA, PAR158573 and PAR158574.
24 MPNYA, ADS 1954.
25 MPPA, ADS 1955, DST "Good Friday in San Fratello," story #55-12, January 26, 1955.
26 In *We Went Back, photographs from Europe 1933–1956 by Chim*, ed. Cynthia Young (ICP & Steidl, 2013), 224–25, fig. 130.
27 MPPA, story #55-12.
28 Ibid.

Fortunately, the professor's fear was unwarranted: the Good Friday pageant witnessed by Chim included striking scenes of flagellation; The *Flagellantes*' costumes had evolved through the years, gradually becoming carnival attire. The revelers competed over who could wear the most ornate costume, display the most rowdiness, blow trumpets the loudest. "The *Flagellantes* have the freedom of the village for almost two days," Chim wrote. "They climb balconies, make mock attacks on young girls and make noise day and night with the complete approval of the populace."[29]

In 1748 a local sculptor had designed iron frames that supported children who, anchored to the steel and wooden structures, seemed to float in the air. "The children are costumed colorfully," wrote Chim, "with the strong influence of Oriental style [sic]. This is partly due to the Moorish influence brought over by the Crusaders, especially strong in this Southern part of Italy, close to the Adriatic coast."[30] Each contraption was held on the shoulders of 12 men who marched from the church across the city center.

In color and black and white, Chim photographed the elaborate preparations for the festival as the children, dressed in vibrant costumes with wings, were carefully lifted onto pillows and strapped to the iron bars. In a tender picture, a little angel gets her first taste of pink lipstick.[31] Another of Chim's photographs shows the Holy Virgin rising to heaven, surrounded by angels holding a crown of stars. The Mystery of Abraham represents Abraham ready to strike Isaac but held back by the flying angel. Under the iron contraption, a boy walks with a live lamb across his shoulders.[32]

"The streets were jammed with people who came from far away to see the procession," Chim wrote. "The excitement was great and the kids were encouraged by shouts. Candy was thrown to them, water and ice cream given. The ordeal lasted for two hours, at the end of which the kids were exhausted. Then the procession returned to the school courtyard. Here the families were waiting again to take them down. Tired, red-faced, perspiring, the saints and angels went home for the traditional feast. The memory of the day will be lasting."[33]

The village's older women had baked special loaves of round bread as offerings, and they gathered around the statues to chant poetic prayers called "Lamentations." A penitent impersonating Christ, carrying a cross and stripped to the waist, walked through the streets followed by a group of boisterous masked and costumed *Flagellantes* who attacked and wounded him. "The *Flagellantes* are called 'Jews,'" wrote

---

29 Ibid.
30 MPPA, DSA 1954, DST "The Flying Angels of Campobasso," story #55-04.
31 MPNYA, images SED1955004K004, SED1955004W00004/34, SED1955004K001, SED1955004K002, and SED1955004K003.
32 MPMYA, SED1951018W00026/X1.
33 MPPA, DST 1955, "The Flying Angels of Campobasso," story #55-04.

Chim—surely conscious of the irony—"and they represent the joy of infidels celebrating the death of Christ."[34]

Chim's friend from Rome, editor Bill Pepper's wife, the sculptor Beverly Pepper, accompanied him on this expedition. She remembers:

> It was a kind of Easter Festival, and the pilgrims were rubbing glass into their arms and bleeding and whipping themselves. We had to walk up a hill. Chim walked up backwards and photographed everybody. He was so warm that everybody related to him. But he was also like Cartier-Bresson in the sense that he made himself invisible. I have seen him go up to people and photograph them right in their face, and they would never flinch. At the top of the hill there was a bar, with the only television for the whole town. 'Let's not just photograph the fiesta,' he said. 'Let's photograph the people looking at the fiesta.' It was like *Cinema Paradiso*.[35]

Through all the rituals Chim documented during these five years, it was as if history had been made visible to him—but the images also hold a sense of fragility. Because of his personal history, and the way history had impacted the Jews of Europe, annihilating their traditions and ways of life, he must have been acutely aware of the impermanence, the ephemeral quality of these rituals and customs. While he had uncovered layers of the region's shared memory through his work, he knew that the traditions he had recorded could soon disappear. He was planning a book on Italian religious festivals, but life did not give him time to put it together.

Early in 1955, Chim photographed a Roman story on the elections held by the Knights of Malta, a Catholic order of European aristocrats founded in 1099 in Jerusalem, and that story, too, reflects his enduring interest in religion, especially in its most obscure aspects. [36]The order was founded to nurture, witness, and protect the faith, and to serve the poor and the sick. In 1530, the Knights were given the island of Malta, and they have been called "the smallest sovereign state in the world." Long recognized as a lay religious order, they had, in the previous four years, run into problems with the Vatican. The upcoming election, which the Pope had approved, was a sign that a good relationship had resumed, a fact noted by Chim who read the Italian press every day and kept abreast of Vatican's inner workings, out of personal interest but also because he always hunted for good stories that Magnum could sell.

Given a rare invitation to witness the Knights' proceedings, Chim photographed them in the gardens of their villa on the Aventino hill near Rome. They were leaving church after a solemn mass, on their way to elect the new head of the order, wearing *manipolos*, heavily embroidered black stoles, over their bright red uniforms. As in a papal election, they used black or white balls to cast their votes into an ancient urn.

---

34 Ibid.
35 Interview of Bill and Beverly Pepper by the author, New York, January 2005.
36 MPNYA, NYC54187.

In one of Chim's captions, he comments: "One picture by a wide-angle lens covers the entire territory of the world's smallest sovereign state."[37]

Magnum's Paris office had built a solid European circuit for distribution of images in Europe. Its members had success at shooting stories for weekly magazines such as *Paris-Match*, *Jours de France*, *Epoca*, *Stern*, *Du*, *Panorama*, *Der Spiegel*, and *Katholieke Illustratie*. But soon the U.S. market became dominant in the field, with magazines including *Life*, *Holiday*, *Fortune*, *The New York Times Magazine*, *National Geographic*, *Vogue*, *Harper's Bazaar*, *Look*, and *Ladies Home Journal*, and they became the agency's main clients. Recognizing the significance of this shift, Robert Capa developed a new strategy for Magnum, leading it toward photography books and television, which were becoming increasingly important. In a December 2, 1953 memo to Morris and Bischof, Capa wrote: "Besides and beyond promotion, the exploration of new fields from unknown markets into books and television should have first priority; even if the present photography market has improved, not only its financial limits are obvious, but many of us have to aim to go beyond the frame of the magazines, as we grow older."[38] Capa was right about the rise of books and television, but he may have been ahead of the times. Even if the magazine market had its limits, it remained, for the next ten years, the main outlet for Magnum photographers, and, during the mid 1950s, the main distribution channel for Chim and other Magnum members became the US magazines.

Since the arrival of Kodachrome in the late 1930s, the quality of color reproduction had been greatly improving, and most magazines now dedicated several pages per issue to color. Color photographs commanded twice the rate of black-and-white, and photographers followed the money. Reluctantly at first (color was not yet considered "serious"), Magnum photographers started working in color to fill the magazines' needs. As traveling became more commonplace, lifestyle and tourism stories followed, then celebrity stories and reportages on the movie industry. As Nadya Blair, commenting on the "Generation X" project, writes in her recent book, "In less than a decade Magnum embraced the shift from editorial to travel photography and bridged these two modes in its work for *Holiday*."[39] In the ensuing years, the line between editorial and commercial agendas would become increasingly blurred and Chim, maybe reluctantly (as an author who remained extremely modest), maybe not (he had to earn a living and contribute to Magnum's support), followed the trend.

---

37 MPNYA DSC #55-1, Knights of Malta.
38 AJGMUC, document given by John Morris in Paris, 2010.
39 For an in-depth analysis of this transition, see Nadya Blair, *The Decisive Network* (Oakland: University of California Press, 2020), 127–139.

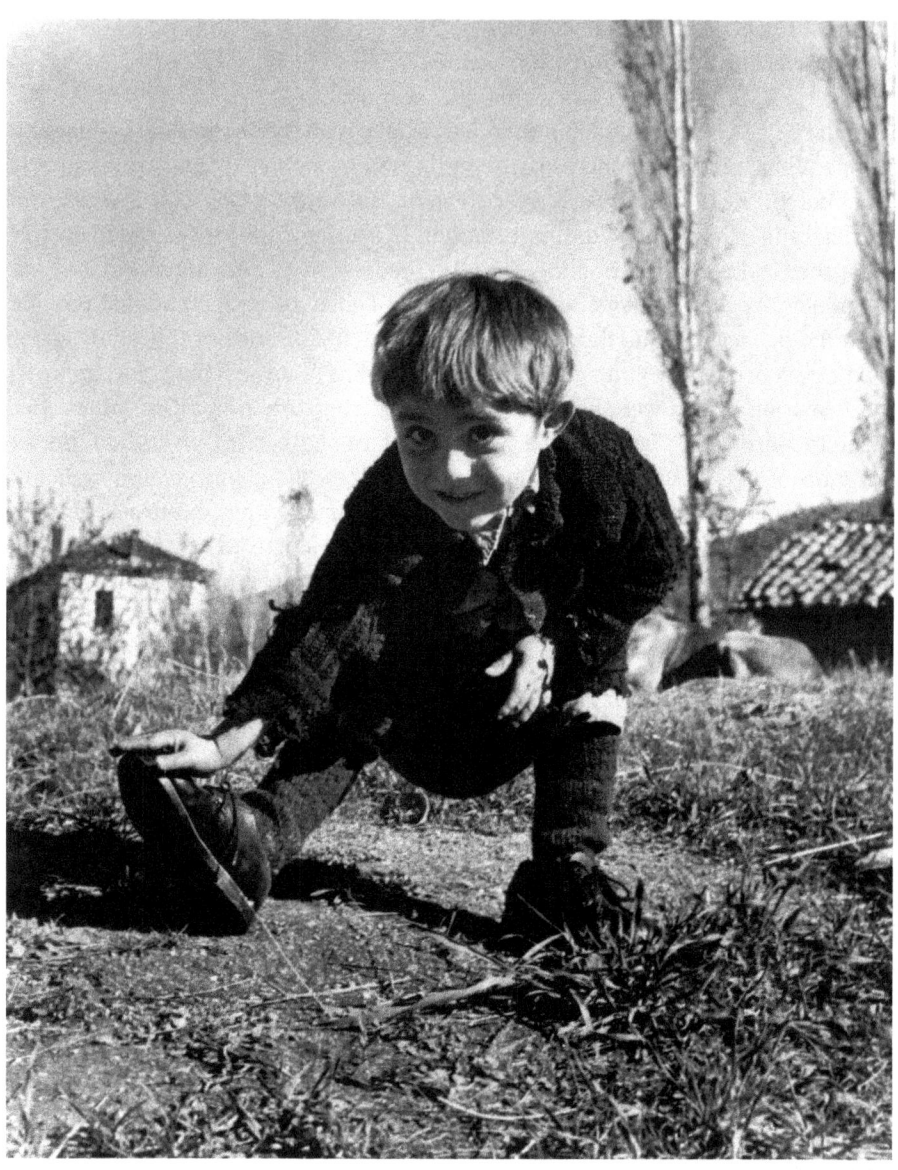

Fig. 16: Elefteria, the only child not evacuated from her remote village during the ravages of the civil war in Greece, receives her first pair of shoes from UNICEF. Oxia, Greece, 1949. © David Seymour-Magnum Photos.

Chapter 14: Under Greek Skies. 1951–1954

Given Chim's deep appreciation of history and his delight in declaring himself "a Mediterranean," it was no surprise that throughout the 1950s he often worked in Greece, relishing the clarity of the light. His friend Jinx Rodger, George Rodger's second wife, describes one of his departures for Greece in a letter from Paris to Morris: "Chim is in Greece. I'll never forget the day he took off, sad and pathetic, with his camera bag strapped onto his back, and his shoulders hunched—all alone Chim, going off into the great big world. We were all sitting around in the little bistro—and Cartier said, 'There is none in the world more happy than Chim when he looks so sad.'"[1]

His Greek reportages were mostly elegant and light-hearted, catering to the magazine editors' demand for lifestyle stories. In 1948, for instance, he had traveled from Naples to Salonika to photograph shoeshine boys and men, making close-ups of their elaborate shoeboxes that were covered with brass ornaments of Turkish inspiration—small mirrors, hearts, planes, boats, or birds—"each trying to outdo the next in the magnificence of the ornamentation."[2]

In 1951, he visited the Cyclades archipelago, photographing daily life for his story, "The White Islands of Greece."[3] These 24 islands off the Greek coast are rocky and arid, with fishing, olive-growing, and winemaking as the main occupations. In his series, shot in 35mm both in color and black and white, the sea, the architecture, and the landscape are ever-present. Chim worked in Delos, the "Holy Island" where, according to legend, Apollo was born, and in Mykonos and Santorini. In Mykonos he photographed a contemplative scene from above: a young woman plays her guitar on the quay, seemingly oblivious to the pile of dead black and white roosters at her feet. Following the division between stone and water, the image is built along a strong oblique line. A light wind lifts the woman's hair; her shadow and that of her instrument link her to the birds; her face remains hidden, adding to the image's mystery.[4]

Another image in a similar location plays with contrasts in scale, with the huge shape of a metal anchor in the foreground against a group of two men and a child who form a triangle. In the strong midday light, their bodies are only silhouettes, while in the background, a folded net and small boats in the harbor form another triangle.[5]

---

1 GRA, August 19, 1951.
2 MPNYA, DST, ADSS 1948-005-1948-010, story #48-9. MPNYA, NN11558446, NYC131488, NYC131489. MPPA, PAR168293.
3 MPNYA, ADSS 1950–1951, *The White Islands of Greece*, story #51-4.
4 MPPA, PAR116249.
5 MPNYA, ADSS 1950–1951, DSC for color pictures, *The White Islands of Greece*, story 51-4.

Tall windmills and 360 chapels with cupolas painted blue, red, magenta, or yellow dot the island. Chim wrote: "Houses, monasteries and chapels look more like sugar and marzipan confectionery."[6] Another Mykonos picture, this time taken from below, shows four children running up a steep, narrow cobblestoned street punctuated with huge marble blocks; the irregular paved steps are painted with white circle motifs. Far away, at the top of the stairs, a round windmill stands with its pointed roof and 12 triangular cotton wings, an iconic feature of the island and a reminder of a time when the Venetians ruled.[7] During a strong wind called a *melteno* that made fishing impossible, Chim photographed the fishermen repairing their nets on the quay.

Next, he went to Santorini, a crescent-shaped island enclosing a body of water that fills the crater of an ancient volcano, forming a natural harbor. On the path from a half-abandoned village to the capital, Phira, that nests on top of a volcanic cliff, Chim made a striking image of a woman carrying on her back two huge jute sacks of fodder for donkeys. Walking through the island's arid, rugged, stony landscape; the shape of her sack parallels that of the cone-shaped volcanic mountains in the background, and an immense sky stretches above.[8] With its empathetic interest in people's daily work—,a constant for Chim throughout his career—the image reverberates with those he did in Calabria during his reportage on illiteracy, showing women carrying heavy loads of furniture or firewood on their heads.

While some of Chim's pictures are specifically captioned as being taken in Mykonos or Santorini, some are only labeled "Cyclades Archipelago" and the locations are harder to pinpoint. A tiny child carrying a bucket almost as tall as he is silhouetted in a narrow, whitewashed village street where a perspective of successive arches draws the eye up to the cubic houses in the back of the image.[9] Four older women with alternating white and black head coverings turn away from the photographer as they sit in a row on a low wall facing the sea and a faraway coast. A chalk line drawn on the ground underlines the oblique perspective. Fishermen in a line fold their nets after a day's work; older men and an orthodox priest sit outside their houses on wooden chairs, absorbed in conversation. A striking image of a young shoemaker shows him in front of a vertical wall from which hundreds of pairs of identical shoes hang like grapes from a vine. He has culled a few pairs and suspended them from his left arm by their laces.[10] (Figure 90)

Chim sometimes does closeup portraits, such as that of a fisherman sitting with rolled-up pants, legs apart, mending his net, or a smiling woman at a fountain who pours water from a small bucket, but most of his Greek photographs inscribe the

---

6 MPNYA, SED1951004W00003/15 (PAR116250).
7 MPPA, PAR116257.
8 MPPA, PAR116257.
9 MPPA, PAR319987.
10 MPNYA, DST, *Greek Elections*, story #51-10.

people within their specific landscape. The photographer underlines the strong links connecting people, their way of life, and an environment that has known little change over the centuries. There is a sense of fascination and longing for a place where history seems to stand still, as it did not in his own life.

In the fall of 1951, Chim covered the Greek election campaign, which pitted Field Marshal Alexander Papagos, leader of the group Greek Rally, which was conservative but promised reform, against General Plastiras and Prime Minister Sophocles Venizelos.[11] It was a way for him to take the pulse of post-war politics: "Everybody agrees that a strong government will have to emerge from the elections which will be able to cope with the enormous problems of reconstruction and the post war economic crisis."[12]

His pictures shrewdly detail the different styles of the contenders: Papagos and Venizelos ran lavish, American-style campaigns. Riding a train with his entourage, Papagos stopped in small towns and villages to address delegations through a microphone and a makeshift loudspeaker. Venizelos arrived in Salonika and Kavalla by plane and spoke with politicians during organized banquets. More informal than both his rivals, Plastiras preferred to campaign in small bars and taverns where he engaged in conversations with supporters and opponents. The Greek Rally soon became the strongest political force in Greece, and Papagos would lead his party to victory in the November 1952 elections, becoming Greece's premier.[13]

Chim was happy to keep returning to Greece, and some smaller pieces, such as his story on the Olympic Games, combined the present and the past in the way that always appealed to him. As he saw it, Greece was the source of civilization, and many traces of the past were still visible there.

His text[14] traces the history of the Olympics from antiquity. The little town of Olympia, where it all started in 776 BC, held its own version of the games every year, featuring high jump, discus throwing, a 400-meter race, and a closing ceremony where the Nomarch (Governor) placed the traditional olive wreath on the victors' heads. The small Olympiad took place at the full moon in September, which was when the Olympic Games used to take place in ancient times. "To keep the tradition alive," Chim wrote,[15] "schoolboys of the neighboring villages stage a miniature Olympiad, complete with priestly invocation, Olympic oath and olive wreath," honoring the monument to the father of the modern Olympic games. Chim photographed young men running a 400-meter race on an improvised track while a crowd of spectators applauded, and another group preparing for a discus-throwing contest.

---

11 MPNYA, A.D.S.S. 1951, story #51-9.
12 MPPA, PAR319996.
13 MPNYA, *Greek Elections*, story #51-10.
14 MPNYA, DST, story # 51-10.
15 Ibid.

He was still in Olympia when, over two days, the small, sleepy town with whitewashed houses lining its only street woke up for a large country fair: "Thousands of peasants from all over Peloponnesus come to congregate in the village for the annual county fair, or *panegyrei*," Chim wrote. "For these two days the taverns are filled until late at night with people drinking and dancing. The shooting galleries are crowded, and the gambling tables have to refuse customers. Roasting pigs and lambs turn over open fires and amidst noise and music and smoke people eat, drink and sleep off their hangovers."[16] During that trip, he also photographed a story on Knossos Palace in Crete.[17]

In a letter to Hala, Chim commented on his Greek experience:

> My previous trips here were during the civil war and they were rather dramatic experiences. This time it was a classical tour—Delphi, Olympia and the Aegean Sea islands—and it was enchanting!
> It is really a sort of escape from the world we are living in now to wander through the ancient Greek ruins and sail around the islands. One gets philosophical looking at the remnants of great civilizations which disappeared and got preserved as ruins. (...) And there is another great advantage to being in Greece—there is no way to read the newspapers. So, outside from Athens where you get all the French and U.S. papers, the isolation is perfect and wonderful (...).[18]

Working with his Leica, Chim captured lively market scenes with older women, clad in black, selling colorful, hand-woven blankets. A group of young men examined handmade sieves used to separate grain from chaff. At the cattle market, men were discussing prices as they examined donkeys, while nearby, whole sheep and pigs roasted on giant skewers. In a daytime photograph taken at a tavern, groups of men are absorbed in a game of cards. Another image, shot at night with a single lamp as illumination, shows a crowd of attentive young men at a roulette table, one of the biggest attractions of the fairgrounds. Emerging from deep shadow, their faces are expressive and attentive as they play until late at night, often losing a lot of money.[19]

At a tavern where an orchestra played, Chim photographed a dancer and a Roma woman playing the tambourine, as well as men dancing between tables in their Sunday-best white shirts and black pants.[20]

In 1951 Chim worked for about three weeks for the UNESCO-UNICEF team again on an assignment of a more serious nature. "School feeding in Greece and Yugoslavia is still meeting an emergency situation," UNESCO had stated in a 1950 re-

---

16 Ibid.
17 A 1993 note, by a Magnum Photos archivist, states that the negatives were not found. There remains only a text by Chim tracing the history of the palace.
18 DSA, letter to Hala, September 19, 1951.
19 MPPA, PAR412222.
20 MPPA, PAR154525, PAR154527.

port.²¹ The U. N. Emergency Fund, in association with the non-profit *Aide Suisse à l'Europe*, was providing children with essential food rations, medical aid, and a vaccination program as well as clothing donations and mobile clinics that could be used in difficult-to-access areas.

Chim's story was called "Return to Oinoi." Situated in the northern Gramos mountain region, on the Greek-Albanian border, the village had for years been the scene of recurring battles and sieges, with the last attack in 1947 leaving it in ruins. After 17 battles between the Andarte rebels and the Greek army, the families had been forced to leave their village with their possessions and animals and settle in a refugee shelter camp near Kastoria while their houses were destroyed and set on fire.

In September 1949, the village was declared safe and army trucks brought the inhabitants back to their houses, where only broken walls and caved-in roofs remained. Most of their cattle had died or had been sold during the residents' two years in the refugee camp. With the teacher's help, they worked on reconstructing the old school while trying to prepare the land for future crops and repair their houses.

When Chim arrived, the rudimentary school building was almost finished (figure 91). "All the freshly rebuilt school of Oinoi can offer its 110 pupils are three rooms and two benches. So the children bring their own home-made and rough wooden stools along (…). Many a time, dictating must replace the lacking books. Children carefully and ambitiously try to copy what the teacher says. They practically must lay down on the floor to be able to write in their school without proper benches."²²

However, Chim remarked, although they had spent two years in refugee camps facing difficult conditions, the children were not discouraged. Their demeanor as they hunch over tiny tables seems joyful and intent on their work, and strikingly similar to that of the children featured in his previous series on illiteracy in Southern Italy.²³ Chim quotes the teacher, Vasikleos Hartides, as saying, "schooling is our children's only hope for a better life than this!" Photographing the children at mid-morning, when their cups were filled with milk or cocoa from UNICEF, Chim wrote: "Now the UNICEF milk and cocoa, cooked every day in two big kettles on a primitive brick-built fireplace, for many of them are still the best part of their daily meals."²⁴

On August 12, 1953, Chim was completing a mundane reportage on the Greek royal family, King Paul, Queen Frederika, and their three children on holiday in their summer palace of Tatoi, when they heard about a disastrous earthquake that had just happened in the Ionian islands.

---

21 In *First Executive Board Final Report*, 1950, UA, https://unesdoc.unesco.org/ark:/48223/pf0000114590, accessed August 16, 2020.
22 MPNYA, DST, ADSSA 1950–1951, *School Without Benches*, story #51-20. The contacts are marked "missing negatives—at UNICEF." MPNYA, NYC131518, NYC66801.
23 MPNYA, NYC131518.
24 DST, MPNYA, ADSS1951, story #20, 1951.

With more than a hundred tremors, it was the worst earthquake in Greece's history. Chim was soon on a ship bound for the main island of Zante, where he met Pericles Paraskevopoulos, an engineer who in 1932 had been responsible for writing building code guidelines for erecting earthquake-resistant buildings. Paraskevopoulos was to help with the island's reconstruction.

One of the buildings Paraskevopoulos had monitored was the Church of St Denis, housing the mummy of the saint who was the island's patron. "When the church remained intact [in the earthquake]," Chim wrote in a letter to Morris, "the people believed it a miracle. When a few days later the Saint's Day came, all the population turned out for the traditional procession in which the mummy is carried through the streets of the town. The religious fervor was running high. I landed in Zante with the professor just in time to see the procession."[25]

Chim's pictures show throngs of people paying respects to the saint, whose body was carried in a glass case by priests in festive robes with armed soldiers escorting them. In a display of public piety, the crowd was lighting candles, chanting prayers, and kissing the saint's gold embroidered slippers.

For three days and nights, 450 Israeli sailors, side by side with members of the American and British navies, struggled to provide relief to the residents of the Greek islands, saving hundreds from death, transporting 400 seriously wounded people to mainland hospitals, and providing medical assistance to 16,000 residents.

Yiftach Kozik, a member of the Israeli Navy at the time, wrote about his experience:

> Huge clods of earth were falling into the water at tremendous speeds, the summit of Mount Ainos on the island of Kefalonia looks as though it were split in two, pillars of smoke rising from cracks could be seen throughout the town, and fierce fires had broken out in the oil storerooms and were burning all that remained (...) in most of the island's villages not a building remained standing, and thousands were wounded in critical condition, among them pregnant women, old and young, people with amputated and crushed limbs, and all were in need of immediate help (...).[26]

Chim accompanied King Paul and Queen Frederika as they toured the islands to show their solidarity. For him, the earthquake summoned images of wartime: "It looks like a bombing raid, but it is not the same. It is less messy (...), a sudden collapse (...) one wall slipping, the nearest standing (...) and the people standing. If one believes in anything, it would be the solidity of the ground on which we stand, and if that starts to jump—what can be trusted?"[27] In a message to the Greek people, Queen Frederika said, "The catastrophe exceeds description. Rich and lovely towns

---

25 AJGMUC, letter to John G. Morris, August 27, 1953.
26 MPNY, DSA 1953005-19530016, story #51-10.
27 See Yiftach Kozik, blog Seven Seas—notes from the Great Blue, quoted in https://www.pappas-post.com/august-12-1953-great-ionian-earthquake/, accessed February 23, 2022, and Yiftach Kozik "Cephalonia Greece 1953 Operation 'Rescue'," *Jerusalem Post*, August 21, 1953.

lie in ruins. Survivors have no shelter. The wounded groan in tents. Bodies are hidden in the wreckage of homes."[28]

Chim photographed scenes of desolation. One of his strongest images show a woman with hands to her head, horrified at the destruction. Just behind her, a corpse lies under a destroyed tin roof while the background of the image is filled with an accumulation of debris, wood rafters snapped like matches.[29] Chim usually avoided photographing dead bodies. In this case, what drew his eye and strikes the viewer is that the dead woman whose body lies in the background was heavily pregnant. Another image, of a woman refugee under a tent holding her sleeping child, recalls the reportage Chim did in 1948 at the Ioannina camp. The expression of shock, and the numbness on her face, are the same as those he saw on the faces of earlier refugees.[30]

In Zakynthos, the island's capital, huge fires swept the ground as strong winds whipped the flames to oil depots and set them aflame. British and Israeli sailors, American marines, and Greek troops tended to the injured and started to clear roads blocked by hundreds of tons of earth and rocks. Aid promptly poured in from all over the world, bringing food and medical supplies by air and sea. Soon, news organizations followed. When he had started out for Athens, Chim could not have predicted how quickly the peaceful feeling of his Greek stay would be shattered.

In November 1954, Chim started on a very different story, on the Meteoras Eastern Orthodox monasteries. Shot with a book in mind, which for reasons unknown was never published, images in 35mm remain in both black and white and color, as do chapters written by the Greek author Mando Avarantinou describing their experiences.

After traveling about 200 miles northwest of Athens, Chim and Aravantinou arrived at Kalambaka in Thessaly, the central region of Greece that was home to the Meteoras monasteries. The name *Meteora* in Greek means "suspended in air," which perfectly described these fourteenth-century places of worship built as refuges from Ottoman invasions during wars between the Serbian and Byzantine empires. Because of the prevalence of brigands, the monks created inaccessible retreats for themselves, stone structures that seemed to float atop unusually shaped sandstone peaks—vertical cliffs that look like a giant's pleated vestments. Of the more than 20 original monasteries, only five remained at the time of Chim's expedition.

With letters of recommendation from the Orthodox bishop in their pockets, Chim and Aravantinou started their journey on a rainy November afternoon. Driving their old Ford down a potholed road, they arrived at the base of the rocks and the

---

[28] In Inge Bondi, *Chim – the photographs of David Seymour* (NY: Bulfinch Press, 1996), 166.
[29] MPPA, PAR116259.
[30] Yiftach Kozik, *Jerusalem Post*, August 21, 1953.

car refused to go any further. They proceeded on foot, with a biting wind blowing in their faces as they tried to avoid puddles and the sharp stones sliding underfoot.

About their approach to the first monastery, Aravantinou wrote: "The rocks lowered above our heads: all became united in one solid wall. Mist came low and hid all their bases. The rocks themselves looked like monsters without their feet, crippled yet terrifying (...) The path grew dangerously narrow (...). The climb did not end at the corner as I had thought; it still went on. Nobody spoke and Chim no longer asked about the road (...). I did not look into the ravine but around me. Heart and mind could not take in these forms; they were gray masses of solid rock, supernatural bodies broken up and cut about. Terrifyingly ill-assorted shapes, a furious outcrop of the outraged earth gave the place a quality of nightmare."[31]

Soon, the faint sound of a psalm came rolling down from the summit and they knew that they were approaching their destination.

In this series, Chim demonstrates that he could read landscapes as he did people. In the projected preface to the book, Aravantinou explains Chim's uncanny understanding of Greek landscape and myths, and how "someone who, having been brought up in another mythology, discovers it intact as soon as he comes in contact with a locality which is charged with it. Thus my companion on that journey, to Meteoras, David Seymour (...) responded to, and was quickened by these undefinable stimuli that afterwards achieved their most perfect expression in a chronicle of photographs."[32]

The images of the stone outcrops are charged with magic, an almost mystical and majestic emotion, as if the layers of the stone also represented layers of time. Many pictures were taken from below, as if we ourselves were ascending the outcrops, but one, taken from above, shows a winding river below, snaking through the fields in the valley.[33] (Figure 89). Chim also did several portraits of the monks—one older, with a frizzy white beard, arthritic hands and a vague gaze; the other, a tender image of a young, bearded monk sitting in the sunshine on a windowsill, caressing the cat that stretches up to his friendly hand. Behind him the landscape is bathed in fog from which mountain summits emerge like jagged teeth. The sun delineates the man's smiling profile and the cat's supple body.[34] (Figure 92).

---

31 MPNYA, ADS1954, no page ###.
32 MPNYA, PAR116259 and PAR319975.
33 MPNYA, PAR116253.
34 MPNYA, PAR26029.

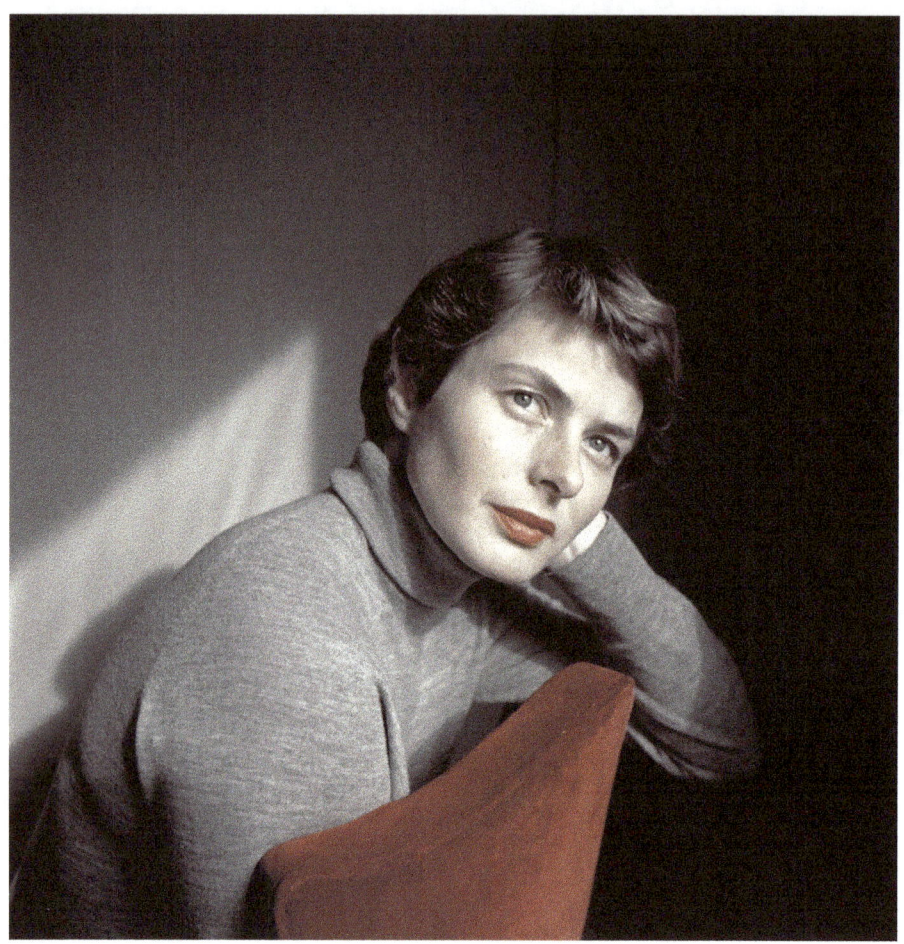

Fig. 17: Ingrid Bergman, Rome, Italy, 1953. © David Seymour-Magnum Photos.

Chapter 15: Pinups, Snails, Pigeons, and Spaghetti. 1950–1955

In the spring of 1950, Chim had to interrupt his photographic work for a while because Magnum members had called on him to help manage the Paris office which was experiencing organizational and financial trouble. He wrote to Hala:

> Life was quite hectic in the last few months. Not so much work with camera, but this time taking care of Magnum problems. (…) I never believed I had managerial talents, but I succeeded to reorganize our European setup. It sounds artificial the way I put it now—but it represented a good, solid month of office work—trips around Europe to see editors and completely new, unknown to me problems of "executive" work. I am happy it is over, and I am looking forward to photographing again.[1]

In October, he was able to return to work on the kind of human-interest assignment he liked best, a story on premature infants and their care in the *Centre des Prématurés*, headed by Dr Alfred Rossier, and the *Ecole de Puériculture*, headed by Alfred Lelong. Like his story on illiteracy in Southern Italy, it was done in collaboration with a humanitarian organization. This time it was WHO, the World Health Organization. Patricia Palmer, a public officer at UNICEF, wrote a text: "WHO is sponsoring a vast program of supplying equipment and technical assistance to various European countries wishing to improve their standard of premature care."[2]

Chim's story covers every stage of the infants' lives: the rushed transport by a nurse and a father from the birth center to the premature center in a portable incubator, with the taxi driver carrying an oxygen tank; the baby's arrival at the incubator ward; the nurses' work in the premature ward where they tend the incubators, feed the babies, and give them blood transfusions; the preparation of formula bottles for feeding; the return of the babies and mothers for a checkup, and the consultation with a doctor.

Though the story was an assignment, Chim's interest in the topic is palpable, and his photographs are intimate and empathetic. The sequence reads like a film, with an especially striking image showing a nurse's hands as they poke through the porthole of an incubator to clean a screaming baby's eyes with a cotton swab. The hands touching the baby's tiny face are bigger than it is and the disparity in scale is striking, emphasizing both the infant's fragility and the delicacy of the nurse's touch.[3]

Chim's story was meant to be the first in a Magnum series on the world's public health problems, but that did not materialize. However, his photographs were suc-

---

1 DSA, letter to Hala, April 23, 1950.
2 MPNYA, story #50-7-1.
3 MPNYA, Story 1952-01.

cessful, published in *Illustrated*, *Life* (May 7, 1951), in the WHO Newsletter,[4] *Réalités*, and *World Health*.

Recognizing Magnum's financial problems, Chim took on a good number of assignments to boost the agency's finances. Though he did them competently, he harbored no illusions about their significance, as revealed in his wry commentary to an editor on a typical 1951 United Nations assignment in Paris, a portrait gallery of chief delegates and their responses to a U. S. peace proposal: "These should serve to show as much visual reaction as we're going to get. Nobody expected to get the boys leaping or falling down or even grimacing much (...). Note last sheet. It's old Léon Jouhaux, listed as a French UN delegate, who turned up yesterday Wednesday at the UN looking mournful as a Saint Bernard. The day before he had won the Nobel Peace Prize for 1951."[5]

Chim's work in Italy during the 1950s was centered around three main themes, politics (figure 12), religion, and culture, including music, art, and food, an inescapable part of Italian life and one in which he had maybe too strong an interest, as his thickening waist attested.

Rather than fancy restaurants such as Osteria dell'Orso, Tre Scalini, and Tor Carbone, he preferred popular *trattorie*, which he recommended to his friends and where he had favorite dishes: spaghetti alle vongole and scampi in white wine at Gigitto, spaghetti alla carbonara at Al Moro, pollo all' diavolo at Pancrazo, spaghetti al carrettiere—a Sicilian style—and oxtail at Ceccho e carrettiere. He also liked to sit and people-watch at Pancrazo, a small, pretty restaurant near Campo di Fiore, where the food was good and unpretentious.[6]

In his stories centered on food and drink, he gave his whimsical side free play. His sense of humor and the absurd led him, for instance, to cover a 1951 spaghetti race in a little outdoor restaurant in the Roman suburb of Montemario, where a group of champions assembled to find out who would become Spaghetti King.[7] The contest was very popular, and a radio truck was broadcasting it:

> Sucking is the right word. The strict rules of this contest required the entrants to have both hands tied behind their back, so that the actual eating had to be performed with no external help but the sheer power of the lips and lungs. It took only 21 seconds for the *campionissimo* to lick his plate clean ahead of the others (...). The runner-up is already making plans for revenge.[8]

Four years later he was assigned to shoot spaghetti again, this time in Naples. After some research, he located a restaurant where Mount Vesuvius would be visible behind the spaghetti eaters: "Here is the spaghetti opus, which caused me quite a lot

---

4 *Illustrated*, February 10, 1951, text by Jack Ensoll; *LIFE*, May 7, 1951; W. H.O Newsletter, 1953.
5 MPNYA, letter from Chim to editor, November 8, 1951, and MPNYA, DST, ADSS 1951, story #1951, *United Nations of Paris*. MPPA, PAR116233 and PAR295707.
6 DSA, letter to Sono and Victor dated Hotel Inghilterra, Rome, August 8, 1955.
7 MPPA, PAR170112.
8 MPNYA, DST in ADSS, 1951, story # 51-11, "Spaghetti Race."

of trouble. I never thought that spaghetti eating was unphotogenic, and the victim's resistance was great. I was slightly swimming in the spaghetti sauce because I had no idea how *McCalls* visualized using it (...) Eventually I went overboard, or underboard. Time will show."[9] The "trouble" he was referring to is the fact that he had to go back to Naples for a re-shoot: after he had shipped his film, a cable came back from the editor: "Color fine but that mountain of spaghetti not high enough."[10]

While in Naples, where he watched "the world championship of Greco-Roman wrestling,"[11]—a surprise because Chim was never a sports aficionado—he visited d'Angelo, a popular restaurant where he made a portrait of Vincenzo d'Amorino, a popular singer who appears in Vittorio de Sica's film *L'Oro di Napoli* (Gold of Naples), and of a shellfish vendor who operated an ornate kiosk with seafood displayed on a bed of seaweed. He also went to the fish market at Porta Capuana and photographed children at a Punch and Judy puppet show. The Galleria Umberto, where, during his UNESCO-UNICEF trip of 1948, he had seen destitute children beg and sell contraband cigarettes, had been renovated and was now a prosperous center, full of cafés and stores bustling with tourists.

Covering a Burgundy gala in Beaune, France, Chim described a scene where 20 wines were sampled during the meal: "Our photographer, confronted by mountains of delectable food and floods of vintage wine, fought to finish his assignment before blissful sleepiness would overpower him (...). When faces became red, hands started to loll and hands moved amorously, he snapped a last sentimental shot—completely out of focus—and then passed out into the darkness."[12]

In 1953, *Holiday* devoted an entire issue to Paris. [13]The editors explained their decision by writing that the city "for years, has best represented the essential qualities of civilization in terms of culture and the attendant graces" and also because of "the logic, discipline and good taste which Paris offers to the writers, artists, photographers and editors who know her and love her passionately."[14]

One of the articles, Art Buchwald's "Paris! City of Night Life," featured *risqué* aspects of Parisian nightlife, including an image of scantily clothed women at a nightclub. Chim's piece, "Paris, City of Fine Food," was paired with a text by Silas Spitzer, a journalist who in 1971 would become food editor of *Travel & Leisure*.

After World War II, Paris was struggling. According to Margaret Nervik, author of *An American's Paris*, "Parisians in the aftermath of World War II dealt with lingering food shortages and the devaluation of the Franc in comparison with the U. S.

---

9 MPNYA, DST in ADSS, 1951, story # 51-11, "Spaghetti Race."
10 MPPA, note to John Morris and Inge Bondi April 29, 1955.
11 MPNYA, from McCalls' editor, no precise date, Spring 1953.
12 DSA, letter to Hala and Emil, Rome, Naples, April 19, 1953.
13 *Holiday*, April 1953, cover, 2, 36–47.
14 The Editors,Holiday 13,no4 (April 1953),33.

Dollar."[15] Because of this economic crisis, Parisians were particularly open to visitors from the United States, who were encouraged to visit by the strong dollar and a greater availability of flights. Consequently, the city had become a magnet for American tourists. Tourism became an industry and lifestyle topics such as restaurants, leisure, and nightlife became popular subjects for American and European magazines alike.

Shot in medium format and focused on gastronomy, Chim's piece, shot at the end of 1952, included a variety of pictures of high society, recalling Brassai's work. From a private box at Théâtre Marigny, he photographed a show of the *Revue Fantastique* that was followed by a supper at Laurent restaurant. In Neuilly sur Seine, a chic Paris suburb, he went to a Concours d'Elégance at the Pré Catelan restaurant and a garden party at the Polo grounds. He was present at the Bal de Versailles, a benefit for the Society for Cancer Prevention; a supper at Maxim's in honor of Benjamin Britten; an Opera gala opening with the ballet "Les Indes Galantes"; a lunch given by Prince Curnonsky, where Chim noted: "A great dish is served. The woman being served has a manner bordering on the devout as she waits."[16] He made close-up medium-format portraits of Paul Thély, a chef at L'Escargot,[17] notable for its Second Empire décor, preparing and serving his specialty of snails as well as plates of ducks and salmon; and of sommelier René Pierron proudly displaying precious, dusty bottles of 1865 cognac in his cellar.[18]

The film industry also focused on Paris, and filmmakers projected their fantasies on the French capital, recreating the bygone Belle Époque in several musicals, rescuing the cancan from oblivion, and reviving the Impressionists. Vincente Minelli's 1951 film *An American in Paris*, for instance, features a half hour of dancing with Impressionist backdrops in Technicolor. Several other films reflect a similar fascination with Paris, including John Huston's *Moulin Rouge* (1952), Howard Hawks' *Gentlemen Prefer Blondes* (1953), Billy Wilder's *Love in the Afternoon* (1957), and Stanley Donen's *Funny Face* (1957), featuring Audrey Hepburn, which Chim documented in 1956 in Paris.

In the same *Holiday* piece, Chim included photographs of Bastille Day, when crowds were dancing in the street and queuing for a free performance at the Opera. He caught a shot of two concierges joining the dancing. [19]The section of his piece entitled *Nuits de Montparnasse* featured girls posing in G-strings on the pretext of a competition of artists' models. Chim marked one of two successive images "Same as 29 but printable version."[20]

---

15 See Margaret Nervik, An American's Paris: tourism and theAmerican consumer, 1947-1961, 2015, 43. https://scholarworks.uni.edu/cgi/viewcontent.cgi?article=1146&context=etd, accessed September 1,2020.
16 MPNYA, DST, *Holiday*, story 52-6
17 MPNYA, DST, *Holiday*, story #52-6.
18 MPNYA,DST,Story #52-6
19 MPPA, PAR150910.
20 MPNYA, DST, *Holiday*, story #52-6.

In the spring of 1954, Chim found a way to return to his beloved Greece, photographing a light-hearted story about kite-flying called "Tadpoles in the Sky." Hundreds of people, taking advantage of the fine windy weather, had congregated on the hills around Athens, especially under the Acropolis temple, to launch kites they had made during the winter. With its mix of Greek antiquity as the background and joyful modern celebration as the focus, the story was a perfect match for Chim. He documented family picnics, children's games, a candy seller pushing his cart up the hill. "Kites could be elaborate or naïve," Chim wrote, "mature businessmen, fat children, and everyone in-between can be part of the kite democracy (...). At first sight, the sky looks like a huge aquarium filled with tadpoles (...). And for those who do not indulge in the active side of kite-flying, there is the fascination of lying on sun-warmed rocks and watching the bright bits of paper dodge each other or fight and tangle in the Grecian-blue bowl of the Acropolis."[21] Chim took pictures of the crowd from afar, then came closer in to photograph families, especially a mother and her young son. While the mother smiles, the boy sticks his tongue at the photographer.[22]

Back in his adopted country, Chim soon got to know Venice as well as he knew Rome and, based at the Hotel Danieli, started a story on the city. As he had done in Rome, he tried to avoid tourist spots in favor of scenes of everyday life. In his reportage he included only three well-known figures. One was the eccentric heiress Peggy Guggenheim, sitting on her Palazzo Venier dei Leoni roof overlooking the Grand Canal. While her accoutrements are exuberant–quirky sunglasses, chunky metal necklace, perhaps created by Calder, and an embroidered dress–her smile remains inscrutable as she clutches the three Lhasa Apso dogs that crowd her lap.[23] (figure 95).

The Countess Albrizzi represented old Venetian nobility and Chim photographed her from mid-distance. "She is over 70 and told me that in order to photograph her, I should have come 20 years earlier," Chim wrote.[24] She posed in her palace under Baroque ceilings and her collection of paintings by Pietro Longhi, many of which depicted members of her family. Finally, Chim photographed the British expatriate Victor Cunard, heir to the Cunard shipping fortune. The Rome correspondent for the *The Times* of London, he lived in the Foscarini palace, which had belonged to the last Doge of Venice.

Other photographs of everyday scenes hold a quiet and mysterious feeling. In one, water is at the front of the image, lapping at a staircase that ends in the canal. Under the arch of a narrow street, a ray of sunshine falls on the tiny silhouette of a girl who runs, arms extended like wings[25].[26] A man bends over to drink from a round

---

21 MPNYA, DSC, *Holiday*, story #52-6, picture #30. MPPA, PAR116247, PAR291504.
22 MPNYA, DSC, *Holiday*, story #52-6.
23 MPPA, PAR116247 & PAR291504.
24 MPPA, PAR311052.
25 MPPA, PAR114514
26 MPNYA, ADSS 1950–1951, DST, *Three Personalities of Venice*, story #50-1.

fountain as three pigeons look on. In another image, a child sits pensively on top of a metal mailbox.[27] A group of boys fight with wooden spears, their bodies hitched to their long shadows.[28] One boy, crouching in a gondola, has launched a tiny gondola-shaped toy which he directs with a length of string.[29] Chim comments: "Children of Venice have unusual games. The child's imagination is inspired by the ever-present gondola. Maybe he dreams of being a gondolier one day."[30]

A man whose identity remains unknown, probably art critic Bernard Berenson—only his ribboned white straw panama is visible over the striped deck chair—contemplates the canal and an approaching gondola. Next to him, an incongruous Esso gas station symbolizes the changes taking place as motorboats claim the canal, a move the *gondolieri* opposed because the boats created waves that disturbed their traditional boats' smooth gliding.[31]

Another example of modernity encroaching on Venice was the Bauer Hotel, a chunky metal and concrete structure that the locals despised because it was said to clash with the Baroque façade of the San Moise church located alongside it. Taking the long view, Chim thought that the new façade would soon blend with the older one. In another of his photographs that illustrated the clash between past and present, he showed a bottle depository from the Coca Cola Company that had taken over the ground floor of a storehouse on the Grand Canal. Crisscrossing the canals, gondolas painted with the Coca Cola logo would deliver bottles to distant neighborhoods.[32]

Focusing on the *gondolieri* Guild and the hardships of their everyday life, Chim photographed Angelo Madallena, the technical director of the Cooperative Gondolieri, "a winner for the great regatta in 1920 and 1923"—which still took place between Venice and Murano. He followed the funeral of 67-year-old Marco Vianello, who had spent his life as a *gondolier*: "Brought by a special funerary *gondola* decorated with flowers, the coffin is carried by old friends to the mortuary chapel."[33] Chim made a portrait of two representatives of the *gondolieri* guild leaving the church, their faces sad and solemn, carrying the guild's sculpted emblem.[34] The coffin was carried by the funerary black gondola, the *gondolieri* wearing mourning scarves and carrying the guild flag. They brought the coffin for burial to the Isla of San Michele's cemetery, just outside Venice. Circled with high walls, it was called the Island of Death. On the way back, as the sun set over the leafy island of Torcello,

---

27 MPPA, PAR11451.
28 MPPA, PAR158566 & MPNYA, NYC 131514.
29 MPPA, PAR154519. MPNYA, DST, Venice, story 50-1
30 MPPA, PAR154519 & MPNYA,DST,Venice, story #50-01
31 MPNYA, ADSS 1950–1951, DST *Venice*, story 50-1.
32 MPNYA, SED1950001W00039/37C.
33 MPPA, PAR154578.
34 MPNY, ADSS 1950–1951, DST *Venice*, story 50-1.

Chim photographed three robed priests backlit, silhouetted on a small arched stone bridge.[35]

He also caught happier scenes: diners enjoying the views near a canal; a wedding party leaving the church in a gondola; a first communion ceremony with girls happily dancing in a circle in their white dresses; a lively series unspooling like a film at the Rialto Bridge fish market, where he captured the strange pantomime of buyers examining the fish and whispering their offers into the sellers' ears.[36] The auction ended with the seller pointing to the buyer whose offer had been selected. "It is a very unusual sight," Chim wrote, "everything happens in silence."[37] He was probably remembering working at Les Halles in Paris in the early 1930s, where the haggling was hardly silent.

Taking a break from his magazine assignments, Chim invented a light-hearted story about a pigeon: "Arturo, Citizen of Piazza San Marco." Since Arturo was a celebrity, Chim needed to be formally introduced: he explains how he met him "through the good offices of a white-haired lady who sells corn for the pigeons."[38] The rest of the story unfolds like a La Fontaine fable, with the pigeon talking about his life and his problems, and providing a way for Chim to make fun of Italian bureaucracy: "We sort of feel that in winter they should increase the ration, as without us pigeons the Piazza San Marco wouldn't be the Piazza San Marco, and if they want us to survive from one tourist season to another, they should consider the slow winter months. But bureaucrats have their regulations."[39] Poking fun at close-mindedness and fear of the "outsider," Arturo complains about pigeons flying in from other neighborhoods ("Dorsoduro, Canareggio and even from Castello!") to eat their food: "All day long we strut around, creating the atmosphere of the Piazza, playing with the tourists, posing for pictures (,.,) and we feel that it is scandalous to have all these foreigners coming in to eat, and then flying off again."[40] The pigeon appears as rather vain, territorial, and imbued with its own importance—a humorous way of describing many an Italian male.

Crouching on Piazza San Marco's pavement, Chim photographed Arturo at his own height, with feathers fluffed and legs firmly planted, looking at the photographer with some impatience. The focus is on Arturo, and the rest of the image is intentionally blurry.[41] In another picture, a cloud of birds—the "foreigners?"—maybe

---

35 MPPA, PAR158567.
36 MPPA, PAR158563 & MPNYA,DST, Venice, story 50-1.
37 MPPA, SED1950001W00039/37C & MPNYA, DST, Venice, story #50-01.
38 MPNY, ADSS 1950–1951, DST *Arturo, Citizen of Piazza San Marco*. ADSS 1950–1951, Story #50-001.
39 MPNY, ADSS 1950–1951, DST *Arturo, Citizen of Piazza San Marco*. ADSS 1950–1951, Story #50-001.
40 MPNY, ADSS 1950–1951, DST *Arturo, Citizen of Piazza San Marco*. ADSS 1950–1951, Story #50-001.
41 MPPA, PAR210127.

frightened by the church bells, rise over the piazza. Behind them, the domes of San Marco Basilica and the silhouette of the Bell Tower are visible.[42]

In his captions to his story, Chim wittily describes the relationship between the pigeon and himself: "My friend the photographer allows me sometimes to eat out of the iron horn. It is extremely uncomfortable, but the corn is good. I like photography and I always go to the picture-board to see how I came out. It's fun to see the different expressions I can have. And this fellow Seymour I have seen photographing Venice for the last four weeks. He must have taken thousands of photographs, and I cannot wait till next week when his pictures will appear in ILLUSTRATED. Fortunately, they sell ILLUSTRATED in the newsstand here, and I will go and have a look."[43]

That summer, Chim also covered the twenty-fifth Venice Biennale, a huge affair with 34,000 works of art from 22 countries shown all over the city. The main exhibitions were in a hall in the public gardens across from the Lido. The international painting prize went to Matisse, and Zadkine received the first prize in sculpture. Chim noted that no Eastern countries took part, and that "the Mexican exhibit was sensation—the first time the great Mexican painters Rivera, Orozco, Tamayo and Siqueiros were shown in Europe."[44]

For a 1955 story for *Newsweek* entitled "Americans in Venice: Europe's Grand Tour in '55", Chim had to adopt a more conventional approach, but even so, his work did not satisfy the editor, Frank Gibney, whose telegram read in part: "Something like clean-limbed American girl in Gondola viewing San Marco and pigeons is what we are after Stop hope fullest you can solve problem in happy combination corn and culture stop can you proceed Venice Monday and ship us transparencies soonest query our need urgent."[45]

At that time, picture editors such as Gibney and *Life*'s Wilson Hicks were gaining more and more power, often imposing drastic scenarios and demands on the photographers, who had to fight for their independent point of view. It took Chim a return trip to Venice for a reshoot before his story could satisfy the editors and make the August 1 cover.

The last project that Capa conceived before his death was a group effort, to picture children all over the world. This sequel to "Generation X" and "Generation Women" was entitled "Children's World." Taconis documented the nomadic life of Isak Henryk Magga, a young Sami boy whose family followed the migration of their reindeer herd across Lapland's tundra. Two of the newcomers to Magnum—Inge Morath and Cornell Capa—chose Europe and South America, respectively. Morath photographed Ian MacPherson, a six-year-old English boy attending a privileged

---

42 MPPA, PAR291994.
43 MPNYA, ADSS 1950–1951, DSC, story #1950-001.
44 MPNYA, ADSS 1950–1951, DSC, story #50-5, *The 25th Venice Biennal*. MPPA, PAR118538
45 MPNYA, ADSS 1950–1951, telegram from Frank Gebney to Chim, July 1955, no exact date.

prep school. Cartier-Bresson photographed Arlette Rémy, a young *petit rat* (apprentice ballerina) with the Paris Opera. And Chim chose as his subject Roberto Moncelsi, a 12-year-old Italian boy whose parents owned a café in Orvieto that served modest meals.[46] The oldest of three children, Roberto had not endured malnutrition after the war, but he still remembered the misery and fear of that period when there was very little food and his parents had to struggle just to keep the family alive.

Roberto, who had picked up some French and English and a little German by listening to tourists and reading scientific brochures, acted as a guide and conducted his business in front of his parents' café, explaining to tourists and visitors the history, symbolism, and technical details of his city's Gothic *Duomo,* including details that were not included in guidebooks. A fan of football and bicycle races, Roberto had visited museums in Orvieto and Rome and he liked theater, music, and dance.

Chim obviously had deep sympathy for the boy and admired his courage and self-reliance. He photographed intimate scenes of family life and meals, or Roberto studying with a local priest and deciphering a music score. While guiding a group of robed monks, he gestures expressively, pointing to details in the *Duomo* façade's ornamentation (figure 14). In a rare relaxed moment, he laughs as he plays a game of checkers with a group of children his age. Chim stressed the child's seriousness and sense of responsibility: Roberto had worked since he was seven years old, and though he would have liked to study, he knew his family needed the extra income he brought. The war and the deprivations of postwar life had shaped him in profound ways, just as they had for the children in Chim's "Children of Europe" reportage.

For a story on English retirees in the ghost-town of Mentone, in the south of France, Chim teamed up with Australian journalist Gael Mayo, who was working with *Picture Post* and who had recently visited Magnum's Paris office. Mayo wrote "*Picture Post* was interested in Mentone as a strange phenomenon—a retreat for expatriates, mainly geriatric." Travelling from Paris' Gare de Lyon on the overnight Train Bleu, Mayo noted Chim's careful choice of claret in the restaurant. The two worked for three weeks in Mentone, photographing in the streets, and gaining access to peoples' homes, front lawns, and elaborate gardens to conduct their interviews. "The job was subtle, the work hard, and it took all the time we had. I suppose we must have slept, but the job seemed to take twenty-four hours a day—though we did not mind; we were absorbed."[47]

Since Victorian times, the English had been choosing Mentone as a retirement town, but as fixed incomes shrank and income taxes rose, the expats' living conditions deteriorated. Unable to afford heating bills and repairs, the 200 surviving residents mostly lived in tiny flats or in the wings of their half-closed grand homes. At

---

46 MPNYA, NN11488453.
47 Gael Mayo, The Mad Mosaic: A Life Story (Bookblast epublishing, 1983; third edition, 2007) no page #.

the end of her text, Mayo wrote: "They wait gallantly but eerily, cutoff in a world where shadows are lengthening across sad lawns where an exotic yet familiar smell of rosemary and buddleia, wisteria and mimosa still links England with the Mediterranean. We are at the end of a chapter. The way of life that was once Mentone has become an impossibility."[48]

Published in *Picture Post* as "City of the Unburied Dead," the story featured melancholy portraits: one of the retirees wears a beret and an old-fashioned frock coat with a fur collar, and clutches her tiny dog[49]; an antiques seller who had furnished the residents' villas when they were wealthy now buys back furniture while the residents leave one by one; a florist who used to supply Queen Victoria now barely survives; after an autumn rain, a sad landscape of wet palm trees is reflected in a street puddle, as the bench sits empty.

On May 29, back in Paris, Chim, Cartier-Bresson, and Charles Steinhammer, a Magnum stringer, rushed to the airport to welcome Rodger and his wife Jinx, just back from a long African trip. They helped the couple fill a cab with their luggage: spears, poison arrows, solar topees and walking sticks, plus 14 cases of photography equipment.[50]

Chim wrote to his sister:

> There is not much to report. The same old running around. My last card was I believe from Wiesbaden—where I did a very fine picture of Nefertiti, the famous Egyptian Queen head—it came out beautiful and you will see it soon in *This Week*. Then I went to Mentone, on the Rivieira, where it was raining all the time, I did a story on the dying British colony— the remnants of the past Victorian days. It came out to great satisfaction of mine and the editors of *Picture Post*.
>
> Now off to Italy for two months stay, very many assignments to do so that I had to postpone my Israel trip. But I will be there this year (...). What are your plans? Is Emil [Shneiderman, her husband] coming this way?[51]

The assignments Chim was alluding to were mostly portraits of film stars or future stars. Working in both color and black and white, Chim made many of these portraits at the *Cinecittà* studios or other film sets in Italy. Right after the war, money and equipment had been in short supply and Cinecittà, built by Mussolini as an expression of his belief in the affinity between fascism and film, had become a refugee camp. The studio complex had been revived and revitalized by the work of De Sica, Fellini, Rossellini, and Antonioni, it had become the cradle of neorealism. One of its hallmarks was using ordinary people rather than professional actors and actual locations rather than sets. American production companies in search of cheap facili-

---

48 MPNYA, Gael Mayo,"City of the Living Dead",text for story #1951-008
49 MPPA, PAR210132
50 GRA, George Rodger's diary, summer 1951
51 DSA,Letter to Hala,May 7, 1951.

ties soon arrived and the studios were nicknamed "Hollywood on the Tiber" for the number of lavishly financed historical epics made there, such as *Quo Vadis? Ben Hur, Cleopatra*, and *Land of the Pharaohs*.

As the film industry blossomed, Magnum took on the job of still photography, photographs made during filming that could be used for documentation and promotions. Stills had formerly been the domain of specialized photographers, but Magnum had realized that this type of work was more profitable than reportage: earnings could go up to $1,000 a week. Besides, while the movie studios used the images for promotion, they did not own their copyright, which meant that the photographers were free to resell their pictures to magazines. Consequently, Chim could sell his picture stories to *House and Garden, Holiday, Newsweek, Epoca, Harper's Bazaar, Look, Paris Match*, and many others.

With Rome as his base, Chim was ideally situated to photograph film sets and make portraits of the actors. His first work was on a British film, the 1949 *Glass Mountain*, which was shot in the Italian Dolomite mountains. A nostalgic and slow-paced movie based on a folkloric tale, it was not one for the ages, but some of Chim's humorous notes for his story are vivid: "Conditions alternated between blazing sunshine and frost; and cameramen sweltered and shivered in turn. An Olympic champion skier carried out a shuttle service between Giau, lonely location site, and Pocol, taking continuity sheets from one sector to another."

In 1950 he started covering Italian movies, photographing Anna Maria Pierangeli, an 18-year-old actress who starred in Fred Zinnerman's MGM film *Teresa*. The film was shot in the Apennine mountains, in Scascoli, a village on the road between Florence and Bologna where wartime battles had left their scars.[52]

Around the same time, Chim met Roberto Rossellini and worked on the set of his film *Onze fioretti de François d'Assise* (*The Flowers of St Francis*), which was shot in the countryside near Rome. Fellini co-wrote the film and Rossellini directed it. Following the neorealist credo, the actors (among them Franciscan monks) were not professional, except for Aldo Fabrizzi who had previously worked with Rossellini on the film *Roma, Citta Aperta* (*Rome, Open City*). Every morning, Rossellini drove to the shooting location near the Bracciano lake, and Chim photographed the groups of monks in sandals and homespun habits. He also made beautiful portraits of Rossellini himself, caught in action behind his oversize movie camera, instructing the actors, surrounded by extras dressed as peasants.[53]

Rossellini, while still married, had started an affair with Ingrid Bergman the previous year; during the shooting of the film on St Francis, their son Robertino was born on February 2, 1950. The affair caused an enormous public scandal in Catholic Italy. Chim wrote a text for his story explaining its context: "While bishops, public figures and catholic organizations were accusing Rossellini and Ingrid Bergman of

---

52 MPNYA, DST, story #48-4, *Glass Mountain*, contacts #48-4-1 through 48-4-14.
53 MPNYA,NYC135865 &MPPA,PAR32670.

moral turpitude (...) Roberto Rossellini is working on his new film with the Vatican's approval, the permission of the General of the Franciscan order, and using Franciscan monks as actors."

Chim had first become acquainted with Bergman through Capa, who had had an affair with her in the late 1940s, and she and Chim became good friends. He photographed her as she played Irina, the tragic heroine of the film *Europe 51*, who gets locked up in a mental institution after her son's death.

He recounted how he had stayed with the Rossellinis, who were besieged by journalists and photographers at the clinic where Bergman had given birth. The *paparazzi* profession was flourishing; in a letter to Hala, Chim talked about his experience: "An agency offered one million Lire for the baby's picture, and many attempts were made to introduce spy-cameras and use subterfuge to get the pictures (...). This is quite the moment to be with Roberto who is now the center of commotion here in Rome, and probably around the world. (...) Nobody till now could photograph the baby. I have the permission from Rossellini to be the first one to do it (...). The 'Scoop' would be sensational!"[54] He made the scoop.

Rossellini and Fellini had a rough screenplay for their movie, but, believing in improvisation, they wrote very little dialogue. Chim wrote: "Rossellini believes that this is the pure way of movie-making. The director keeps his imagination free and is not limited by a pre-arranged script."[55] This modern way of thinking prefigured French New Wave ideas, and filmmaker François Truffaut, one of the founders of the movement, called *The Flowers of St. Francis* "the most beautiful film in the world."[56]

In the spring of 1952, as the friendship between Chim, Bergman, and Rossellini became a close one, Chim did a story on Rossellini as he relaxed in Amalfi between takes, swimming, and deep-water fishing. A few months after the movie was finished, Ingrid's twins, Isotta and Isabella, were born and Chim joined the family in their country house in Santa Marinella, 60 kilometers from Rome. The white, modern house faced the sea and had a terrace overlooking a private pier: the perfect setting for the informal pictures Chim took. He was the only photographer to have access to their life, and his photographs have the feel of an intimate family album. In a tender image, he captures Bergman with her son Robertino on her lap as he strokes the head of their spaniel. He shows her sitting on the terrace, hands on her lap, tanned and radiant in a summer printed dress with the sun playing on her hair, and again, depicting her more serious side, as she types at a desk covered with piles of books and correspondence.[57] Another photograph shows her holding twin baby-carriers as she steps out on the terrace. The babies peer curiously over the edge.[58] A series of

---

54 DSA, letter from Chim to Hala, February 5, 1950
55 MPPA, DST, album 1950–1951, Story#1950-008, "Onze fioretti de François d'Assise".
56 Tag Gallagher, The Adventures of Roberto Rossellini (New York: Da Capo Press,1998), 350.
57 PAR347125
58 NYC58645

square Rollei images in closeup portray the expressive emotions on the little girls' faces. Chim saw them as real persons and was attuned to their emotions.[59] Bergman wrote to him: "You are a marvelous photographer and I am a marvelous baby maker! Of course I have 103 requests among friends for these photos!"[60]

The following year, Chim shot a more glamorous, beautiful color portrait of Bergman (figure 17). She wears a light gray sweater and sits in the natural light from a window. The deep velvety red of the chairback she leans on picks up the shade of her lipstick. She wears no other makeup and the expression in her blue eyes makes us feel as if we had surprised her in an unguarded moment, while she was gazing into a distant dream.[61]

Through this friendship, Chim gained access to many other stars or stars-in-the-making. His unobtrusive manner and sense of humor, and his ability to listen and be a confidant, resulted in portraits that went beyond the usual "glamour shots," conveying an air of ease and intimacy.

Early in 1952, Chim, who was working in Israel, photographed the filming of Wilhelm Dieterle's new film, *Salome Unveiled*, starring Rita Hayworth[62]. With now-forgotten films such as *Samson and Delilah* and *David and Bathsheba*, Hollywood had recently seen a revival of biblical subjects. During a location shoot in a Druze village, Chim photographed Dieterle filming, the local Druze Israeli-Arabs who contributed camels and extras for the crowd scenes, and the "Roman" soldiers recruited locally. For the dance scenes, he photographed Tamara Rappaport, a young Israeli stand-in for Hayworth.[63]

Next it was Gina Lollobrigida's turn. In 1953 she was a rising star, preparing for John Huston's comedy *Beat the Devil*, where she was playing Humphrey Bogart's wife. She had done several films in Italy, but this was her first widely distributed English language film. Chim also photographed her on the set of the 1954 Italian movie, *Pane Amore e Gelosia*, directed by Luigi Comencini, where she starred alongside Vittorio de Sica. Extending the story beyond her work, he photographed her at home with her husband in their garden, as well as alone in her room as she sat on

---

59 MPPA,PAR95015
60 DSA, letter from Ingrid Bergman, October 11, 1952.
61 MPNYA, ADSS 1951–1952, story #52-4 "Ingrid Rossellini 1952", contacts #52-4-9 and 52-4-10.
62 PAR32608
63 MPNYA, NYC58651. For more comments on the portraits, see Tom Beck, *David (Chim) Seymour* (London: Phaidon, 2006). See also Cynthia Young ed., *We Went Back, Photographs from Europe 1933–1956 by Chim* (NY: ICP & Göttingen: Steidl, 2013), fig. 138, 233.

her bed among piles of discarded clothing "In her dressing room," Chim wrote, "Gina said: I can pose also like Marilyn Monroe (...) and she did."[64]

Working in black and white and Kodachrome for a *Holiday* story, Chim continued his work with Gina as she prepared for her role in *The Woman of Rome*, a film adapted from a famous Moravia novel that takes place in Mussolini's Rome. [65]This was the first movie where she had the lead. In a letter to Morris, Chim wrote, "The basic idea of Gina's story is the transformation of the pin-up into a dramatic artist."[66] He photographed her lying on her bed, reading scripts; she selected the screenwriter for the film herself and discussed the script with everyone involved. "Before every scene," Chim wrote, "she reads the corresponding passage in the book in order to keep alive the extraordinary quality of the character created by Moravia. (...) She is proud that her position in the movies has changed: no longer merely an object to be photographed, she can now use the screen to display her acting qualities."[67]

Chim photographed Gina one last time in 1955, practicing ballet for the film *Lina Cavallieri* with a dancer of the Rome Opera Ballet and then working with a famous Hollywood stuntman, Eddie Ward, before she left for Paris to shoot *Trapeze* with costars Burt Lancaster and Vittorio Gassman. Ward rigged a trapeze on the terrace of Gina's house on Via Appia Antica in Rome and gave her lessons in acrobatics. Chim's portraits of Gina do not play down her playful sexiness—the tight, bright tee-shirts and pancake makeup—but they also speak of her ambition, strength, and determination to acquire the difficult new skills necessary for her developing career.[68] Predictably, however, the magazines did not follow Chim's lead, and focused more on Gina as "bombshell" than on her efforts at education.

Aside from his work on movie sets, Chim continued working on the smaller, somewhat eccentric stories that he always enjoyed. He explains in a letter to Hala: "After two weeks with John Huston movie in Ravello, I am spending a few days in Naples—watching the world championships in Greco-Roman wrestling. As you see there is a certain amount of variety. The occasion here is a great one with the Iron Curtain countries attending—with the Russians and the Turks being the champs."[69]

Sophia Loren turned out to be a favorite subject for Chim. When he met her, he was working for several magazines including *True*, "The Man's Magazine," which specialized in pinups. The editor, Bill Mason, did not find it problematic to make lurid suggestions to Chim and Loren,[70]—recommending, for example, fishnet stockings, tighter undergarments, and shaved underarms. Women thus packaged could

---

64 PAR32608
65 MPNYA, story #52-1, Salome Unveiled
66 MPNYA, DSC, story #54-001, *Speaking of Gina*.
67 MPPA, PAR32611, PAR32615
68 MPPA, DST, story #54-001; *Speaking of Gina*, MPNYA, NYC58652 in color and MPPA, PAR278162 in black and white.
69 DSA, letter to Hala, Naples, April 19, 1953.
70 MF, letter to Chim, June 21, 1955, MF 011-001-001/2.

excite a certain type of readership. Reflecting the editor's growing power, neither photographer nor model protested. However, it is remarkable that Loren, while she followed the instructions, does not look vulgar. What we see is a radiant woman, happy and sure of her sensual power, with a complex aura that is both demure (in her facial expression) and sexy (in her body language). [71] It is that mix that makes the picture (figure 96). However, an element of playfulness also shines through, as Chim observed:

> By now she knew that my pinup abilities are in dire need of development and volunteered to give me a hand. She changed costumes. She went to a covered balcony, and I had nothing to do but record a set of positions which somehow met my memory of wartime pinups. All this was done with a touch of irony and mischief—sort of "I can do it too" attitude. There was a running conversation about "Il Grande Marilyn," the Goddess of all this, who obviously inspired Sophia. I felt, however, that this was not just copying. The Neapolitan wit was making fun and enjoyed it. And strangely enough, from what I have seen, I liked it too.[72]

Among Chim's other subjects of 1954 was 22-year-old Joan Collins, whom he photographed on the set of Howard Hawk's *Land of the Pharaohs*, a fictional account of the building of the Great Pyramids. The film had an enormous cast (between three and 10,000 extras working every day) and was one of Hollywood's largest-scale, ancient-world epics, together with *Ben-Hur* and *The Ten Commandments*. Even though William Faulkner was one of the three screenwriters, the film was not a success. It did, however, launch Collins's career.

A British actress who had just been "discovered," she played Neliphar, second wife of the Pharaoh, who was played by Jack Hawkins. Chim focused on her, while on set in Egypt his Magnum colleague Haas mostly filmed the actors and the crowd of Egyptian extras. In his story, Chim wrote: "Joan Collins has taken to the disclosing manner of dress in which she is costumed for Land of the Pharaohs. Off the set, she lounges under a tree, wearing a minimum of confining garments."[73] Back in Italy, Chim photographed her in black and white and color posing on her balcony or in the street, followed by a crowd of Italian admirers.[74] "Although Joan is 'made in Britain', she has the savage spice of an Italian actress, and fits perfectly on Italian streets, as was attested by the behavior of the man on the streets. They accorded her the attention usually reserved for home-grown beauties." One of his color portraits made the cover and a black and white spread of *Picture Post*.[75]

Chim had a gift for friendship with these ambitious young women who were starting their careers. Another of his favorites was Irene Papas, whom he had met four years earlier when she was very young, modeling diadems and earrings for a

---

71 MPNYA, NYC40337, NYC40336, NYC58655. MPPA, PAR39419.
72 MPNYA, DSC, story #54-001.
73 Letter to John Morris, AJGMUC, 1954, no file ###.
74 MPNYA, NYC58654, PAR412004.
75 "Joan Collins, British for Glamour," *Picture Post*, September 1, 1954, cover, 16–17.

story he was shooting on ancient jewelry. He wrote, "After a long search for the classical Greek profile, the model was found. She is a talented young Athenian actress, Irene Papas, 22."[76]

The relationship was obviously important to Papas, who wrote to him in 1955, while she was on the set of *Tribute to a Bad Man* with James Cagney, acknowledging his importance to her life and career, and she evokes their past relationship:

> My dear dear Sim [sic],
> (...) I know you are my friend and I know also you are my first one. I did not have anybody when I met you and during those years—which by the way must be around 5—you held the claim of me and put together Greece and Italy. You saw me change, you insulted me, you loved me, you picked on me but always forgave me like a child—I am—Now you write more and often. Kiss Rome's air and embrace its beauty. Lots of love, Irene.[77]

By 1953, Chim had started to work with *Look*, which published his stories on Bergman and Rossellini, and his portraits of writers and intellectuals. One of his best was a profile of Arturo Toscanini[78] at home in Milan, on the occasion of his eighty-eighth birthday and his last concert.[79]

This was a difficult assignment. Chim wrote, "The Maestro has little sympathy for photographers and always refuses to see them (...). There are very few pictures which show Toscanini at home and this series is a rarity."[80] He tried to get close to the Maestro but it was not easy: "Often he gets involved in musical discussions and then, to illustrate his point, he might sing while he conducts an invisible orchestra."[81] He tried to mollify him by showing him pictures from his stories on the Meteoras monasteries and Arturo the pigeon. "He was amused that the pigeon had his name," Chim wrote to Morris.[82] With Toscanini refusing to pose again after the morning shoot, photographer and model played a game of cat-and-mouse during the session, facilitated by Toscanini's daughter, Wally.

Chim started photographing while Toscanini was listening to a recording:

> My first click startled me but there was no reaction from him. I went on until the moment when the Maestro dropped the remark, 'Some background violin doesn't come through perfectly.' This scared me and from then on I was waiting for percussion instruments or trumpets to cover up my click. (...) I tiptoed back into the music room and started working (...) I came closer and then I saw, on the Maestro's side, a wooden box with a glass top. Inside, on black velvet, there was a little collection of death masks of great composers who inspired Toscanini. There was the death mask of Beethoven, of Wagner, and of Verdi. The light was hard and at one moment,

---

76 MPNYA, DST, ADSS 1950–1951, Ancient Jewelry, story #51-16.
77 DSA, letter from Irene Papas, July 30, 1955.
78 *Look*, March 8, 1955, 30–31.
79 MPNYA, PAR26027, NYC41564
80 MPNYA, DST, ADSS 1954–1955, The Maestro at 88, story #54-001.
81 MPNYA, DST, ADSS 1954–1955, The Maestro at 88, story #54-001.
82 Letter to John Morris, in AJGMUC, Paris, no file ###.

Toscanini's head got a gypsum-like quality. This made the picture that I believe to be the key picture of the story.[83]

After that, Chim was not permitted to return. Wally reported the Maestro's comment: "I saw the photographer and I didn't want to stop him because he behaved. But I don't want him anymore."[84] Nevertheless, Chim had succeeded in his assignment. He had been attracted by the Maestro's mix of vitality and vulnerability and his photographs reflect this duality.

Among Chim's other famous subjects was the new Archbishop of Milan, Giovanni Battista Montini, the future Paul VI, whom he was photographing for *Newsweek*. During unusual preliminary discussions,[85] Gibney had asked Chim to write the text as well, even though Franz Spellman had been commissioned as the writer,[86] and Chim agreed:

> This thin-lipped, meticulous man with the quiet voice has serious enthusiasm for his mission and a background of experience in fighting totalitarianism. It is believed almost certain that Monsignor Montini will be given the red hat of a cardinal at the next Roman consistory, early this coming Spring. And already he has been referred to as a hard-to-best candidate for the Papal throne itself.[87]

Chim was a shrewd observer of Vatican politics, and his intuitions about Montini proved right. Just as with screen actors, Chim was a step ahead and photographed his subject as he was on the verge of greatness.

The shoot happened in a small town near Milan during a popular celebration: the four hundredth anniversary of the apparition of the Madonna of Corbetta.[88] In 1949, in the course of his Vatican story, Chim had taken a solemn portrait of Montini, but these new portraits were livelier and more dynamic, stressing the prelate's modern style in relating to the faithful. His story shows the archbishop's arrival as he greets the crowd, standing in a slick car, and shaking hands with the workers at the Pirelli rubber plant, where he inaugurated a kindergarten for workers' children.[89] "A few stood aloof," Chim wrote to Gibney. "For these ones Montini had a charming way of stretching out his hand and shaking the hands in the most civilian manner. This was irresistible and the response was tremendous. I feel this one picture you will find buried in the story should have a meaning and great impact."[90] As he would often do, Chim was discreetly suggesting his choice for the story's lead picture.

---

83 MPNYA, DST, *The Maestro at 88*, story #54-001.
84 DSA, letter from Frank Gebney, May 3, 1955.
85 MPPA, ADSS1955, story #55-3, *Cardinal Montini*.
86 MPPA, ADSS 1955, story #55-3, *Cardinal Montini*. MPNYA NYC93740.
87 Letter to Frank Gebney, dated Rome, May 26, 1955.
88 MPNYA, PAR288998, NYC54189.
89 MPNYA, NYC93740.
90 Letter to Frank Gebney, dated Rome, May 26, 1955.

Montini also celebrated an outdoor mass: "The ceremony took place in great splendor," Chim writes. "Little girls dressed as angels and little boys dressed as pages formed at the entrance of the church."[91] He did a closeup of two of these "angels" pouting, while a serious *carabiniere* in ceremonial nineteenth century-style uniform with silver braids, epaulets, and bicorne towers over them.[92] In another image, Montini's embroidered stole occupies the foreground, overpowering his face, which is close to that of the Madonna's statue. The scene is set on a balcony with a bird's-eye view over the crowd massed below.[93] This effect, blending the subject's face with that of the statue, recalls the Good Friday images he had made in Sicily earlier that year. Entitled "The Archbishop of Milan: the Pope's Man, the People's Power," Chim's story made the cover of *Newsweek* as well as five pages inside—substantial coverage for a magazine not primarily dedicated to photographs.[94]

The 1950s was a period of economic development and industrial progress for northern Italy, (mostly leaving the South behind) and Chim was assigned a *Fortune* story on Italian industry. The piece that he shot in black and white, and color, appears competent but not enthusiastic. Paired with *Fortune* editor Herbert Solow, he worked all over Italy, photographing gas and oil development, steel mills, pipe and car factories, and concentrating on "the point of view of use of natural gas (methane)."[95] He focused on industrial installations in northern Italy, and, to show progress in the South, the construction of an aqueduct in the Naples area, as well as a sorting and packing plant designed to ameliorate the problem of fruit and vegetable spoilage.

Other pictures taken at the Naval Meccanica Shipyards in Naples dramatize the unemployment situation. With a thousand workers laid off, the unions had organized a protest strike. Chim wrote: "It was very difficult to convince the management that I should be let in and allowed to photograph the laid-off workers in the old shipyards at Vigliena, Naples (...) wanting to keep their good will, I refrained from photographing the shipyards which were protected by strong detachments of police."[96] The next day, he found a way to photograph the laid-off men, "a group of idle workers in despairing, sad mood, and a few of them engaged in slow maintenance work, like the picture of 3 men working on nailing a few boards together."[97] His story got the cover and nine pages.[98]

---

91 MPNYA, DST, story #55-3.
92 MPPA, PAR122876.
93 MPPA, PAR47324.
94 *Newsweek*, June 13, 1955.
95 MPNYA, DST, *Italian Industry* story #55-20.
96 DSA, letter to Frank Gibney, May 26, 1955.
97 MPPA, May 5, 10, and 18 shipments, stories #54-13 & 54-15.
98 *Fortune*, July 1954.

Chapter 15: Pinups, Snails, Pigeons, and Spaghetti. 1950–1955 — **231**

During their extended collaboration, Chim and Gibney had grown close and Chim's frequent letters to Gibney often contained personal anecdotes: he wrote playfully, for instance, about the elevator in his Rome hotel:

> We had lots of trouble with our elevator. It did stop last week, and if its sickness would last longer, you can be sure that I wouldn't hesitate to cable you. But the technicians came, and they repaired him. They did it so thoroughly and so well that the little charming noise of tra-ta-tra-ta disappeared completely and one raises now in horrifying silence without soundtrack. I protested to the management and mentioned your name for additional importance. He promised me to call the technicians back and restore the noise. I will let you know what happens.[99]

In the summer of 1955, the American producer Mike Todd invited Chim to London and Madrid to photograph *Around the World in 80 Days*, a film inspired by Jules Verne's novel. [100] In a letter to Gibney, he explained: "Madrid will offer some bullfight scenes at Chinchon then we all go to London where Mike told me he took over the Royal Guards, a couple of streets, the Lloyds of London."[101]

Among the film's stars were David Niven, who played Phileas Fogg, Noel Coward, and the famous matador Luis Miguel Dominguin, who had retired in 1953 but returned to the arena for a scene he staged himself. Chim's intimate images of Dominguin being made up and costumed are especially beautiful—the matador had come up with eighteenth-century museum-piece costumes that he would be wearing on set. At the time he was married to Italian actress Lucia Bose and Chim photographed the couple at their Villa Paz ranch.[102]

Meanwhile, the *Family of Man*, a massive exhibition featuring the work of several Magnum photographers, opened at MoMA in New York. In 1954 Edward Steichen, the director of MoMA's photo department and his assistant, Wayne Miller (soon to become a member of Magnum), had come to Paris in 1954 to choose photos for the show, which would run from January 24 to May 8, 1955 and feature 553 images by 273 photographers from 68 countries. It would tour the world and be seen by millions. Steichen and Miller chose work by photographers from Magnum's first and second generation: Capa, Chim, Cartier-Bresson, Rodger, Arnold, Bischof, Erwitt, Glinn, Haas, Jean Marquis, and W. Eugene Smith (who was briefly a member).

With its giant, overlapping photographs mounted on panels, the *Family of Man* exhibition bears a striking resemblance to the 1937 Spanish Pavilion at the *Exposition Universelle* in Paris. Echoing the previous show's overtones of Soviet agit-prop (even though that political angle had lost its meaning), it also referenced the now-standard look of photo magazine layouts.

---

99 DSA, letter to Frank Gibney dated Rome, 6 August 1955.
100 MPPA, PAR291501, PAR274194, PAR218265.
101 Letter to Frank Gibney dated Rome, 6 August 1955.
102 MPPA, PAR218259 & PAR21823.

In June and July of 1955, Chim made portraits of art critic and Renaissance specialist Bernard Berenson, who had just celebrated his ninetieth birthday. He photographed the writer on a nostalgic round of Roman and Venetian museums, but at the Museo delle Terme, the guards refused to let him take pictures. With Berenson standing in a good spot, Chim became extremely frustrated, and this amused his subject. Commenting on Chim's obvious distress, he quipped, "Look at him! He's like an addict without his dope."[103]

Despite these limitations, Chim made several good portraits of Berenson, some in color, including one at the balustrade of his Villa Tatti near Florence, looking down at the gardens, shoulders wrapped in a shawl. The best-known portrait was taken at the Villa Borghese in Rome, where Berenson, dressed to the nines in a dark suit, tie, and light straw hat, examines a marble nude statue of Pauline Borghese by Canova; it looks as if a silent dialogue is taking place between man and statue. [104] The contrast between the well-dressed man and the sculpture of the nude woman recalls Manet's *Déjeuner sur l'herbe*.[105]

In the fall of 1955, Chim and Morris met in New York to discuss the idea of newspaper syndication, a way to break *Life*'s monopoly on the picture market. The plan met with opposition from Magnum members, and there were few takers in the newspaper world, so it did not work out. "Forget about newspapers," Morris wrote. "Chim knew what we really needed: a new office in New York. The 64th Street basement was bursting at the seams, and that summer we were flooded, although the files escaped damage. In October, I found a terrific space atop a building largely occupied by diamond merchants at 15 West 47th Street. It was close to our most important customers and had a view in four directions. Best of all, it had a kind of Magnum character—unpretentious, a little funky, wide open (...) We would open there for business, and a new chapter of Magnum history, on Friday November 11, 1955."[106]

In February of the following year, Chim started a story on Maria Callas, Renata Tebaldi's up-and-coming rival, who had a growing reputation as a soprano, with a repertoire ranging from classical opera to *bel canto*. She was slated to sing Rossini's *Il Barbiere di Seviglia* at La Scala, Milan, and was about to make her New York debut at the Metropolitan Opera in October with the leading role in *Norma*.

Newsweek seemed to have been disappointed by the intimate portraits in black and white and in color that Chim took of Callas in her dressing room of Opera San Carlo in Naples and rehearsing at the piano in her home in Milan with a manuscript page of Donizetti's *Lucia di Lammermoor*.[107] In a letter to Gibney, Chim noted: "Maria Callas (...) surely is not a beauty, but she is a great soprano and when she will hit

---

103 MPNYA, DST, story #1955-007.
104 MPNYA, NYC63837.
105 DSA, letter to Frank Gibney, August 13, 1956.
106 AGJMUC, Paris, communicated by John Morris, no reference number and John G.Morris, Get the Picture (NY:Random House, 2002),175-176.
107 MPPA, PAR47380, PAR80450.

New York, I can predict there will be some noise around it. This is said in all humility, not being an expert on it but somebody who hates opera and was convinced by Maria that there is something in it (...). I am sorry that you are disappointed, and I agree that a soundtrack would help. But for this we will have to wait until the 21st century *Newsweek*." As his friends and colleagues Jean and Susie Marquis explained: "Chim had the intuition for possible successes, like when he photographed Callas and Sophia Loren in their very beginnings."[108] And his remark prefigured the hybrid media that have become common nowadays.

Three months later, Chim was back in Rome, shooting one of his most powerful images of a political crowd, as they listened to a speech by Antonio Segni in the Piazza Santi Apostoli (Figure 87). The photograph has a strong, triangle-shaped composition with a classical perspective. The massive crowd fills the piazza with its stone arcades, sheltering under umbrellas that glisten from the rain. It is like a human tide of eager, attentive faces.[109]

Once again he visited Bergman, creating an intimate album of family scenes in color and black and white as she played with her son Robertino and cared for her twins. He also photographed her in her Cannes hotel room: in a dark suit and sunglasses, he makes an appearance in the mirror above her, snapping away on his Leica, as she looks up—one of the very rare images where he is more than a projected shadow in his own pictures.[110] Another image, taken on the set of Renoir's *Elena et les Hommes*, is centered on filmmaker Jean Renoir explaining a scene to Bergman, who is in an elaborate nineteenth-century costume, while her colleague, American actor Mel Ferrer, stands in the shadows.[111] William Atwood, editor of *Look*, wrote "Everyone here was most enthusiastic about your Ingrid pictures (...). We will certainly give it plenty of space."[112] In April, Chim wrote to Hala and family: "I am back with my cameras, around my favorite subject, Ingrid Bergman."[113]

He continued photographing Bergman, first on the train to Cannes and at the Cannes Festival, then in Paris on the set of Anatole Litvak's *Anastasia*. The film marked Bergman's return to a Hollywood role after several years of working in Italy with Rossellini. She would win the Academy Award for Best Actress for her role in the movie. Chim, however, was not happy with the job. In a memo to Morris, he explained: "The Litvak movie was one of the most difficult productions to photograph because of a lack of spectacular scenes. 95% of the movie was shot in a studio (...). The way the movie was treated precluded any interesting photographic work."[114] In spite of these difficulties, Chim succeeded in several beautiful, pensive, and lonely

---

[108] Interview of Jean and Susie Marquis by the author, Rambouillet, France, May 11, 2005.
[109] MPNYA, NYC131530.
[110] MPPA, PAR122884.
[111] MPPA, PAR32616.
[112] DSA, William Atwood, letter to Chim, June 22, 1956.
[113] DSA, letter to his family dated Rome, April 9, 1956.
[114] 1956, JGMAUC Paris, no ###.

nighttime portraits of Bergman, wrapped up in a coat and scarf, alone or with actor Yul Brenner in a night-time street scene with lights on a bridge gleaming in the background.[115]

Audrey Hepburn evoked a different kind of response from Chim. His 1956 pictures of her, unlike those of Lollobrigida and Loren, capture her more modern sort of beauty: athletic and slim, elegant, and spirited. Chim describes her in his text as "sylph-like in black tights" and writes:

> Although she studied ballet for much of her young life, Audrey felt she needed special lessons for her role, because her dancing partner in *Funny Face* will be the *maestro* Fred Astaire. In order to regain her old agility, Audrey spent a few months studying ballet under Lucien Legrand of the Paris Opera. Then she took singing lessons with Roger Edens, producer and composer of the film, and practiced the George Gershwin songs with Astaire and Kay Thompson, the night-club entertainer.[116]

During the production of Stanley Donen's *Funny Face*, Hepburn posed during a break in a beautiful tulle wedding dress by Givenchy, smiling softly, looking down. Half-hidden behind the dress, the tip of a cigarette protrudes from her right hand [117] (figure 97). In another image, taken at the Tuileries Gardens in Paris, she is wearing a chic black Givenchy dress and matching hat, and holds a bunch of balloons.[118] It has just rained, and a few puddles shine in the mud on the ground.[119] It was probably that day that Chim, prompted by *Harper's Bazaar*'s editor, shot the photographer Richard Avedon and Fred Astaire under a big umbrella. Like two schoolboys conspiring in a prank, they look happy and animated as Avedon advises Astaire on his role as a photographer in the film.[120]

While in France, Chim also did a portrait of the young Françoise Sagan, whose novel *Un Certain Sourire (A Certain Smile)* had just been translated into English. Brooding and dreamy, hand supporting her chin, she sits at her typewriter and seems to be miles away: she does not take in the photographer's presence.[121]

From the early 1950s on, Magnum progressively reinforced its copyright policy, demanding that the integrity of the frame, the caption, and the signature under each published photograph be protected. To protect copyrights further, each photograph was stamped on the verso with the inscription: "This photograph can be reproduced only with accompanying caption or text strictly in the spirit of its captions."[122] The agency established several types of relationship with newspapers and magazines:

---

115 MPPA, PAR32616.
116 MPNYA, DST *Funny Face*, Story #56-003.
117 MPPA, PAR153424.
118 MPPA, PAR82667.
119 MPNYA, Story#56-003.
120 MPNYA, NYC28006.
121 MPPA, PAR47397.
122 MFNY, Magnum meeting summary, July 23–24, 1954, #010-004-001.

sometimes it negotiated assignments, but in other instances it functioned with what was called a "guarantee," meaning that the magazine did not assign the story but had first exclusivity. In other instances, the magazine had only a first look, enabling it to look at photographs and buy them before the competition. More and more, Magnum photographers were taking the initiative and self-starting with their own story ideas, or that of the agency's staff, before negotiating with the press.

This was the case, for instance, with Chim's stories on religious festivals in Italy, which he hoped to put together in a book. In 1957, journalist Byron Dobell would write:

> Recently, the very close interdependence of the Magnum members so characteristic of its early years has given way to a more open kind of give and take with increased responsibility resting on the individual's shoulders (...). Morris is particularly happy to see the photographers latch onto pet ideas which can be developed into assignments. He knows that a photographer is always at his best shooting something that interests him. Approximately one half of Magnum's stories originate with members or from leads uncovered by the staff. The rest, of course, are straight editorial assignments (...). Magnum's basic policy is to keep its journalistic core from getting lost in the shuffle of purely commercial activities.[123]

---

[123] Byron Dobell, "The First Ten Years," *Popular Photography*, September 1957.

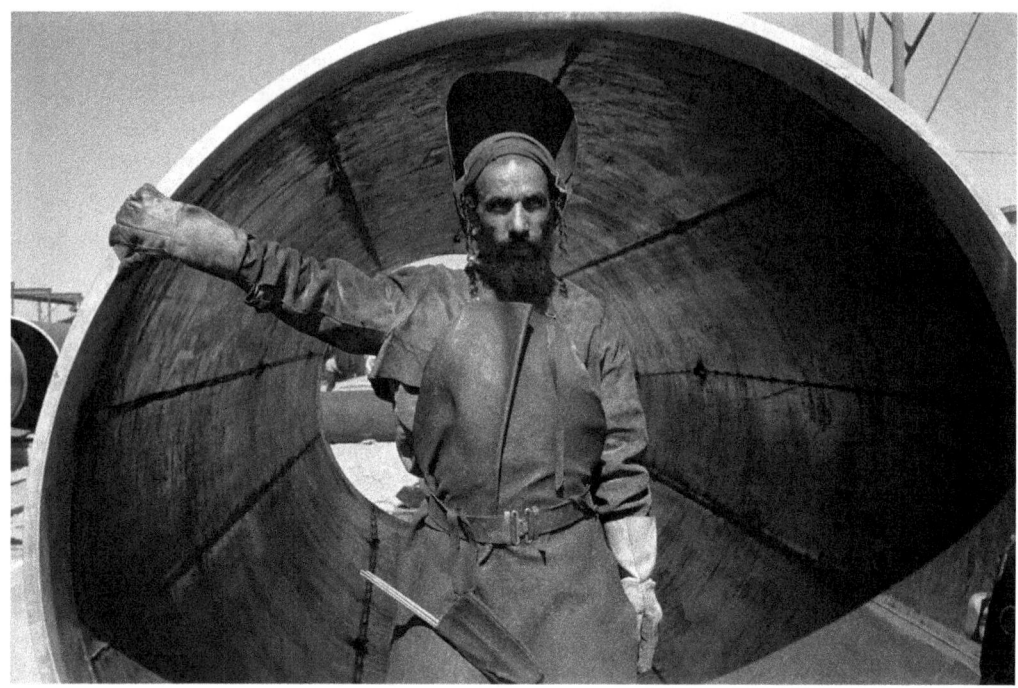

Fig. 18: Yemenite welder inside a large concrete pipe, part of the new Israeli water supply system, at a pipe factory near Migdal, Ashkalon, Israel, 1954. © David Seymour-Magnum Photos.

Chapter 16: I Found a Home: Israel. 1951–1955

Three of the four Magnum founders—Capa, Rodger, and Chim—visited Israel in the late 1940s and early 1950s. They brought back very different stories, but for all three men, the photographs were personal and imbued with strong emotion.

On November 29, 1947, the United Nations had decided to divide Palestine and create two new states—Arab and Jewish—but Egypt, Transjordan, Syria, Iraq, and Lebanon rejected the partition and war broke out. Six months later, as the hostilities began, Capa arrived in the country to photograph the ceremony for the declaration of the State of Israel at the Tel Aviv Museum.

As the Hebrew poet Haim Gouri later commented: "The photographs of the Israeli war recall the pictures of the Spanish Civil War: sandbags against a wall, rifle slits, someone scampering across an area under fire, volunteer units, a soldier at rest reading a newspaper in the shade of a tree, the ubiquitous stocking cap, a meal eaten against a wall pitted with bullet holes."[1]

Haim Gouri's intuition (it was also Inge Bondi's opinion in her book about Chim) rings true. In Capa's photographs as well as in those that Chim would make a little later, the style and spirit of the 1930s work is clearly recognizable. As in the Spanish Civil War, both Capa and Chim would take a side: Israel was a cause. As they had supported the Spanish Republic, they now supported Israel.

When Capa spoke with Eugen Kolb of the Hebrew daily *Al Ha-mishmar*, he declared: "I was never a Zionist, and I'm not one now either, but in any event, I have changed my view about Israel: I am now convinced that for most of the world's Jews there is no other solution except Israel. And those who deny this rely on reasons that are immoral. Yes, I am a friend of this land and its people."[2]

As a result of his conviction, while Capa notes in a *Look* story[3] that new immigrants are boarding a truck for resettlement in "an abandoned Arab village, where they must first rebuild the houses"; he does not question the fact that those settlements are "abandoned" because they have been taken over by the Israeli settlers. For Chim, the same point of view stands. In a reportage about Italian Catholic peasants who had converted to Judaism and moved to Israel, he writes that the immigrants' first settlement is in Ras el Ahamar, "a formerly Arab village",[4] without questioning why the village had been emptied. In a 1950s context, after the news of the destruction of European Jews reached a larger public, and just two years after the creation of Israel, this was a largely shared opinion.

---

1 In catalogue of the exhibition, *Robert Capa: Photographs from Israel, 1948–1950*, 1988, as quoted in Andrew L. Mendelson and C. Zoe Smith's thoughtful article "Vision of a New State, Israel Mythologized by Robert Capa," *Journalism Studies* 7, no. 2 (2006), 210.
2 Interview by Eugene Kolb, *Al Ha-Mishmar*, June 21, 1948. The daily was published 1943–1995.
3 "Israel Reborn," *Look*, November 8, 1949.
4 MPNYA, DST, "Israel's New Jews," story #51-2.

For George Rodger, a devout Church of England follower and one of the four Magnum cofounders, there was an evolution of a different sort. He flew to Jerusalem to photograph a Christmas story for the *Illustrated*, "Jerusalem Anno 1951". Its concept was: what would Christ find if he returned to the Holy Land today?

It was meant to be a joyful piece with coverage of all the sites that had become important symbols to Christians around the world: the Via Dolorosa, the Gardens of Gethsemane, the Basilica, the Russian Church of St Mary Magdalene. However, Rodger could not come up with a postcard-happy vision of Jerusalem. Eight and a half years after the "peace agreement" between Arabs and Jews, conflicts over the capital had hardly been resolved. In the center of the Old City, a road divided Jews from Arabs. Jews could not pray at the Wailing Wall, and Arabs had no access to Nazareth.

Rodger's visit to photograph Palestinian refugees in Beet Jibreen, near Jerusalem, had a profound impact on him. All the inhabitants of a village near Jaffa had fled from their homes and taken refuge in a camp for the previous four years, during which time the camp's population had swelled from 1,500 to 80,000. Rodger, a long-time sympathizer of the Arab cause (he had traveled extensively in the Middle East) became a strong advocate of the Palestinians, even though, to do so, he ignored some aspects of the 1950s political situation.

In April 1945, he had been traumatized when he was the first photographer to enter Bergen-Belsen; but when he went to Israel shortly after, he probably did not understand, or chose to ignore, their massive impact, and the result: a massive, sudden emigration *(alyah)* of the Jewish survivors to Israel. Instead, he took sides, seeing Palestinians as victims, and focused only on the awful situation in the makeshift Palestinian camps.

His facts were often skewed, his figures inflated. He decried American politics and the loans extended to Israel by America's "Jewish financiers"—without acknowledging that American Jews (and others) were simply trying to help Holocaust survivors; neither did he acknowledge that the Palestinians' confinement to camps suited most of the region's Arab governments, who had no interest in welcoming them.

After Rodger sent his story "The Damned Can Be Dangerous" to Magnum, he received a long letter from Capa, the bulk of which was a stark criticism of his work in the Middle East:

The *Christmas in Bethlehem* story had arrived too late and was too literary. *Life*'s editor, Ed Thompson, had already rejected Rodger's story on the Palestinians, but, Capa argued, it was not turned down on political grounds: "The text piece, not because I am not in agreement with it, is the best example of what you should not do. No magazine will print editorial conclusions instead of reporting. (…) The worst part of it is that where your text is full of misery and drama, your pictures showed a peaceful and nearly contented camp. So the two of them did not go together at all."

Capa then tried to steer Rodger toward breaking news: "When Suez and Teheran are burning, the quiet middle between the two is not going to excite editors."[5]

Capa's business-like perspective on Magnum and his desire for scoops also clashed sharply with Rodger's preference for covering everyday life in-depth. Capa had a very clear sense of what New York editors wanted, and he was aware that Magnum needed those editors as clients more than ever; the European magazines were seriously short of both paper and funds and were assigning far fewer stories than before. Therefore, he said, Rodger should take the initiative and find subjects himself. That perspective echoes exactly what Maria Eisner had told Chim a few years before.

As for Chim, in 1947 he had told his sister, "The next trip I would like to do is Palestine. A book about it before partition and edited at the moment of it would not be a bad idea".[6] When other assignments intervened, Chim was unable to make his trip to Israel, and the moment was lost. But in October 1951, he finally arrived, and he found ways to keep returning every year until his death five years later, sometimes on his own, sometimes with magazine assignments.

In many ways, Israel, and the communal life of the kibbutz, embodied Chim's ideal of a political utopia, fusing solidarity, a melding of nationalities, a pioneering spirit, and fervent idealism. It also represented his fervent hope of healing his life after the Shoah. As he wrote to his sister, "It was like coming home again. It was like picking up the living threads of my life, for which I had been searching in vain on the heaps of rubble and ash in the ruins of Warsaw."[7]

First, Chim wanted to find any family members who had survived (figure 101). Hala had given him addresses for several cousins who had emigrated before the war. Asked about those visits recently, Chim's niece Lenka, now Helen Sarid wrote:

> When Chim came to Israel, he knew that he and my mother had cousins in Israel who came before the war—Heniek Flint and 2 other cousins—a brother and sister both married with children (...). He took many pictures of the Flint family—their new apartment—and lovely little Yaakov. (...) My second cousin Varda gave me the following information: her mother Natka Okuniev-Pintel was my mother's first cousin married to Heniek Pintel. Natka's brother Shimek Okuniev was also in Tel-Aviv, married with a son, so there were many cousins here. Varda remembers a visit from Chim during Succoth—sitting in the succah—speaking Polish with her parents—her father explaining the role of the succah in Jewish tradition. I wonder if the family had a succah in Poland???? There is no one left to ask (...). So—my grandfather Benjamin Szymin was a brother to Natka's mother. So (...) Chim—everyone called him Didek (...) had 3 first cousins here in Tel Aviv.[8]

---

5 GRA, letter from Robert Capa to George Rodger, January 16, 1952.
6 DSA, undated letter to Hala, 1947.
7 DSA, undated letter to Hala, circa 1950.
8 Email from Helen Sarid, Chim's niece, to the author, May 11, 2020.

As described by Helen Sarid, Chim's niece, several family photographs, hidden on a top shelf and recently rediscovered in the archives of Magnum New York office, are also in the respective archives of Helen Sarid and Ben Shneiderman. They show a beaming Chim standing on a Tel Aviv balcony with his arms around family members with whom he had just reconnected.

Newly arrived immigrants were an obvious subject for Chim to document, but, as a journalist, he knew that other photographers—including Capa in his 1949 reportage on the immigrants' arrival to the Haifa port—had already covered that story. He needed a new slant, and he found it when he discovered the Jews of San Nicandro. Their story seemed perfect for him: it was offbeat and linked his interest in Italy and the Catholic religion with his new interest in Israel.

Led by the sayings of a local "prophet", a cobbler named Donato Manduzio, the inhabitants of the small Italian village of San Nicandro Garganico in southeastern Italy had decided to follow the writings of the Old Testament and convert to Judaism. Early in 1948, the 80 people in this community immigrated to Israel and sought to transform themselves, choosing new biblical names. After they settled in Ras el Ahamar near the Syrian border, one of their most influential members "heard voices proclaiming this new place [the Alma settlement] as the right spot for the San Nicandro community."[9]

Chim shot his in-depth story—16 rolls of black and white film with Rollei and Leica cameras—in their chosen settlement. Alma was an unpromising spot, a dry valley without water or trees: "The unfertile, stony land requires hard labor to clear and prepare it for cultivation. Slowly roads are being built and improved (...). They have confidence in the future; they are sure they can make the desert bloom."[10]

Chim loved the spirit of this pioneering frontier town. He photographed the barren landscape of northern Galilea, with the Syrian frontier visible on the horizon. Covering the new immigrants' everyday life, he recorded the men at the improvised synagogue where they congregated every morning; they are wearing prayer shawls and the service is presided over by a local rabbi who stands in the center of Chim's picture while a toddler dressed in a sailor suit, incongruous in scale with the rest of the group, is at their feet.[11] Since they do not know Hebrew, the immigrants read the Old Testament chapters in Italian and "sing the religious hymns written by Manduzo with their own musical accompaniment, strangely reminiscent of Italian church singing."[12]

Another image, taken in a home, is much more intimate and shows a group of men, women, and children singing while a young man plays an ornate mandolin. The image recalls Chim's portrait of Ubaldo, the young accordion player from Um-

---
9 MPNYA, DST, "Israel's New Jews," story #51-2.
10 MPNYA, DST, "Israel's New Jews," story #51-2.
11 MPPA, PAR116142.
12 MPNYA, DST, "Israel's New Jews," story #51-2.

bria in the "Generation X" story. Even though the wall ornaments are Israeli (a Middle Eastern carpet, the star of David), the look of the people and their clothing, the way an older woman wears her printed kerchief knotted on her head, are very Italian. It is as if the image was taken in a strange land somewhere between Italy and Israel.[13] The same is true of another picture, of a hatted peasant stroking his horse's head[14]: the horse wears an ornate headgear with a star of David ornament, but the image is strongly reminiscent of Chim's reportage from Southern Italy in the previous year. So is a picture of women standing in a field with the buckets they use for clearing the land of stones before water pipelines are laid.[15]

In the most famous picture from this series, a proud and beaming father, Eliezer Trito, holds up his daughter, Miriam Trito, the first child born in the Alma settlement. The tiny baby seems lost in the long, white, embroidered baptismal dress that her parents brought with them from Italy.[16] In another image, taken from above, the newborn, this time held by her mother, almost as an offering, has the central focus while a large group bends over her admiringly. Chim also photographed the small school where the children, seated at wooden desks, were learning the basics of Hebrew under the supervision of a Tripolitan Jew.[17]

In 1951, Chim shot a story on Haifa's oil. During World War II, Haifa had provided fuel for the Allied Mediterranean fleet but by 1951 the port was working at only 20 percent of its capacity because Egypt and Iraq had embargoed it after the armistice ending the war. Storage tanks were empty, and pipelines closed. Chim's story represented a forceful advocacy for Haifa's possible future role in the Israeli economy.

Back in Paris in November, Chim wrote to his friend Carlo Levi:

> Dear Carlo, just came back from Israel where I spent two weeks and where I deeply regret not having you with me. I went to Alma to visit the San Nicandro converted peasants, and, believe me, it was a great experience. The story is amazing, more amazing than I expected. They live now near the Syrian border in a new settlement, together with Tripolitan Jews, extremely Arab-looking, and are still in a state of spiritual fulfillment and excitement. I really believe that it would be a great story for you. (...) My pix are fine and we could complete the story going later on to San Nicandro. Please let me know what you intend to do because I would withhold distribution till I hear from you.[18]

Levi never joined Chim, who wrote his own text for the San Nicandro story.

---

13 MPNYA, NYC13151.
14 MPPA, PAR188546.
15 MPPA, PAR153422.
16 MPNYA, NYC63835.
17 MPPA, PAR127415.
18 Letter to Carlo Levi, November 1, 1951. Courtesy Fondazione Carlo Levi and Archivio Centrale dello Stato, Rome.

In 1952, Chim returned to Israel, and started using color in a story on King Solomon's mines, which would be published in the Dutch magazine *Panorama*[19] with a text by Ruth Cale.

The idea behind the story was to cover a new industry based on the famous Biblical tale. Copper deposits had recently been found in the Negev, not far from Eilat, and it was thought that mines had already existed at the time of the Old Testament: archaeologists had discovered ancient furnaces, caves, and inscribed clay tablets there.

Chim photographed the magnificent landscape of multicolored sandstone and black granite, and some of the 100 men who worked in the mines, leading a well-paid but difficult and monotonous life. He made close-ups of the men drilling the rocks. Some of them have a heroic style, close to the Soviet images of the 1920s and 30s, such as a portrait of a guard, oxygen mask dangling from his neck, holding a machine-gun.[20] "The world will learn that Israel does not have only oranges for sale," Ruth Cale wrote in her text.[21]

When Chim returned to Paris in early 1952 for discussions with the other Magnum founders, he once again faced, in George Rodger's words, "a feeling of crisis in the organization": Capa and Chim were working every night until dawn to stabilize the agency's finances, and ultimately succeeded, as the Paris and New York offices started supporting themselves on their own incomes. But in April, Capa, who felt he had too many administrative tasks and not enough time to take pictures, stepped down from his post. Rodger continued, "This resulted in Capa's resignation from the Presidency in April, my own appointment as stockholders' representative, and a tremendous exchange of letters in all directions."[22] Rodger became a coordinator and was also responsible for the agency's finances. One of Magnum's problems was that they had taken on too many contributors, or "stringers", which took up an enormous amount of office time and resources while contributing little.

By the end of the year, Chim (also representing Cartier-Bresson by proxy), Capa, Haas, and Rodger had solved part of Magnum's problems by accepting the resignations of contributors Fenno Jacobs, Homer Page, and Carl Perutz, and had voted that the agency should be run by a board of directors consisting of the four original stockholders. Capa was reelected as president with the understanding that he would travel once a year to New York to supervise and coordinate the New York production, three times to London, and once to other European markets and agents. As president, he received a salary for the first time.[23]

---

19 "Konig Solomons Minjnen," *Panorama*, September 12, 1952.
20 MPNYA, NYC46048.
21 MPNYA, Ruth Cale, story #52-003, "King Solomon's Mines."
22 GRA, Interim Report to Stockholders, June 7, 1952, signed George Rodger.
23 JGMAUC, "Report on the Conference of the Stockholders of Magnum on December 15, 1952." Capa was given a $10,000 a year salary.

Back in Israel, Chim reported a story about the Israeli Army, called "Youth with Scythe and Sword."[24] His point of view, shared by many at the time, was that the state needed continual vigilance in order to survive, which made the young army an obvious choice to cover and so he went to photograph the *Nahal*, a special branch of the army where young Israeli girls and boys served for a year. Their badge was a sword and a scythe, symbolizing a dual purpose of training for defense and helping in the country's development. After three months of intensive military service, the soldiers were posted in an agricultural settlement where their lives were divided between military training and agricultural work.

The Nahal kibbutz that Chim visited was "on the foot of a barren hill at the Eastern shore of Lake Huyleh near the Syrian border, overlooked by majestic Mount Hermon—so near and yet so far—in enemy territory. About 100 boys and girls, originating from 14 different countries, live, train and work together."[25] The young soldiers were encouraged to settle permanently in the kibbutz after their service.

In this context, Chim's photographs are relaxed and intimate. He caught joyful scenes of a group holding hands in a circle as they dance the traditional Israeli *hora*. In the dining room he noted the easy camaraderie between boys and girls, the rudimentary wooden benches and tables, a girl in shorts leaning on a table in conversation.[26] He made a portrait of a young woman ready for sentry duty with her gun on her shoulder, focusing on her lively expression and soft smile as a light wind blows her hair.[27]

This is where Chim found Cori, his subject for the "Generation X" story, and photographed her in the nursery, bottle-feeding a baby while a toddler looks at her from his crib.[28] Heavy on symbolism, one of his better-known images shows an outdoor wedding where bride and groom stand under the traditional tent, or "huppah," held up by improvised poles of guns and pitchforks.[29] Another lively image shows two men and a woman dancing after the wedding, while in the back a young man plays the accordion. His story was published in *Holiday* with the title "Youth and the World: Israel, the World of the Kibbutz."[30]

Just one of Chim's stories from Israel deals with conflict. For "Israeli Border," he spent three weeks documenting one of the world's great trouble-spots, the Israeli-Jordan border. "For most of its length in open country," wrote Chim, "the Israeli frontier is indicated only by an occasional marker and the landscape looks decep-

---

[24] MPPA, DST for "Youth with Scythe and Sword—The Boy and Girl Army of Young Israel," story # 52-2.
[25] MPNYA, NYC131517.
[26] MPPA, PAR116144.
[27] MPPA, PAR125252.
[28] MPNYA, NN11501043. See Chapter 12.
[29] MPNYA, PAR116146. It must be noted that the use of pitchfork and gun for the huppah was not fabricated for the picture. See *Holiday*, January 1953.
[30] MPNYA, ADSS1952, DST for story #52-01.

tively peaceful."³¹ But it was an armed truce. All along the border, settlers were taking precautionary measures against attacks, strengthening barbed wire enclosures around the settlements, installing searchlights, increasing patrols, and sending agricultural workers into the fields under armed guard.

As the number of incidents at the border increased, roads that could have linked Israel and its neighbor were blocked with obstacles or rendered impassable by large ditches dug across them at the border. The border's only crossing point was the Mandelbaum Gate in Jerusalem, where Chim photographed warning signposts in five languages and a narrow no-man's land filled with barbed wire.³² He documented the settlers along the frontier taking precautions against attacks, installing barbed wire or patrolling with searchlights, and, in one of his only pictures featuring an Arab, he photographed an Arab-Israeli citizen from the village of Tayaba plowing the land: "The vagaries of the border leave Arabs living on both sides of the frontier", he commented.³³

Chim covered the aftermath of the death of Zion Manton, an Israeli watchman who had been killed in a frontier incident while guarding Arab Israeli women as they picked olives a hundred yards inside the Israeli border. One of his most dramatic pictures was taken at the Jerusalem cemetery on the day of Manton's funeral. Sitting near her husband's grave, Manton's wife, her head thrown back in deep grief, closes her eyes.³⁴ (figure 98).

For his story "Water for the Desert". (1953), Chim covered Israel's new irrigation scheme, a pipeline that would channel water from the river to the Negev desert. Coaxing the desert into fruit-bearing would become one of the Israel's best-known achievements. "Reservoirs are being built, pipelines laid, and pumping stations installed," he wrote.³⁵ He photographed, among other topics, the irrigation ditches that were being dug to prepare the fields for a new olive grove.

Shooting with Leica in black and white and Rollei in color, he often duplicated the shots for safety and resale reasons.

Chim's story has a heroic tone and again uses tropes that recall Soviet 1920s and 30s propaganda, for instance, in one of the best-known photographs in the series: the portrait of a Yemenite welder, a recent immigrant, standing inside a large concrete pipe, one of the last sections of the Yarkon Negev pipeline he has helped build (figure 18). His stern expression, his gloved arms set at a 90-degree angle, the strong sunlight striking his nose and brow, seem to transform him into a bronze Soviet worker statue as he proudly poses for the photographer.³⁶

---

31 MPNYA, ADSS1952, DST for story #52-01.
32 NN11503529.
33 DST for story#52-01.
34 MPPA, DST, "Water for the Desert," story SED # 53-4.
35 MPPA, PAR122760 in black and white and NYC64582 in color.
36 MPPA, NN11468232.

As usual, Chim was interested in the creative culture of the countries where he worked. He used color in a series of artists' portraits taken in Ein Hod, a colony of 65 artists established in an abandoned Arab village (the colony still exists today). Many of the artists were part of the *Ofakim Hadashim* (New Horizons) movement that had started in 1948 around the time of Israel's independence, when a positive spirit prevailed and they had been influenced by the European modernism of the 1910s.

One of Chim's portraits is of the painter Moshe Mokadi, one of the colony's founders, who had been chosen to represent his country in the 1952 Venice Biennale. He is shown in his studio, pondering an abstract painting that is influenced by the light and colors of the Israeli landscape. Chim also made a portrait of Shulamit Branitzky, a painter and Holocaust survivor whom, according to her daughter Diana Dolev, he first met in 1950, while she was in a relationship with Capa. Dolev remembers Chim's visit in May 1954, shortly after Capa's death: "We all drove together to Tantura, where he took photos of my mother, Ilana [Dolev's sister] and me. Tantura was a Palestinian Arab village on the coast, not far from Binyamina; its inhabitants had been driven out and dispersed during the 1948 war. My mother and her spouse, Naaman Stavy, whom she'd married in 1956, turned one of the emptied houses there into a summer retreat.". Then Dolev contrasts Capa's more distanced style with Chim's approach: "In Chim's photos we are not only aware of his presence, but also interacting with him. So Chim's photos are not simply depictions of us but also of the communication between us."[37]. These portraits of artists, musicians, and dancers show the link between Chim's work in Israel and the artists'portraits he did, in Rome and wherever he lived or traveled.[38]

The United Nations decision to divide Palestine and create two new states had an immediate and terrible impact on the Jewish populations of the Middle East. They may not have realized right away that the founding of Israel was, for them, the beginning of the end, that living in countries with a Muslim majority would become impossible, even though their roots there might have been established two or three thousand years earlier—but the politicians were all too aware of the trouble ahead.

On November 24, 1947, the head of the Egyptian delegation to the General Assembly, Muhammad Hussein Heykal Pasha, declared that "the lives of a million Jews in Muslim countries would be endangered by the creation of a Jewish state." The next day, in a speech to the General Assembly Hall in Flushing Meadows, New York, Iraqi Foreign Minister Fadel Jamall said: "Partition imposed against the will of the majority of the people will jeopardize the peace, security and harmony in the Middle East. Not only is an Arab uprising in Palestine to be expected, but the masses

---

[37] For the complete story written by Dolev, see https://www.magnumphotos.com/arts-culture/society-arts-culture/my-private-capa-and-chim-unknown-records-from-a-family-archive/, accessed February 23, 2022.
[38] MPPA, DST, story SED #54.

in the Arab world cannot be restrained. Relations between Jews and Arabs around the world will deteriorate dramatically."[39]

When these warnings fell on deaf ears, the partition of Palestine was declared. Thus Israel, after welcoming Holocaust survivors early on, was required to accommodate a new, large wave of immigrants fleeing from Algeria, Egypt, Iraq, Morocco, and Tunisia.

In Haifa, on assignment for *Holiday*, Chim photographed the ship *Golden Isles* as it arrived with 600 Moroccan newcomers on board. He wrote "Recent events there and the anti-Jewish riots have led thousands of Moroccan Jews to leave their country and settle in Israel, which after a lull has opened up her doors again (...) all formalities are accomplished during the trip, and within a half-hour upon disembarking the immigrants were on trucks on their way to an assigned village where a home was waiting for them."[40]

As the immigrants disembarked, Chim focused on a young Moroccan mother holding her baby and walking down the gangplank with a slightly apprehensive smile.[41] Following the immigrants to their new homes in the village of Achusam, Chim photographed a little boy in a sailor's suit as he lights the four candles of a menorah; the village children sit in a circle in the back, welcoming him.[42]

One of his strongest photographs[43] from this series shows a group of religious Jews praying on the beach. They will perform Tash'lich, a Rosh Hashana ritual, casting breadcrumbs into the waters to symbolically dispose of their sins for the New Year (figure 99). Although Chim's family was not particularly religious, he was always moved by these shared traditions that expressed hope and the desire to go forward, maybe wishing he could be a part of them and shed his heavy past.

Understandably, given that past, Chim's view of Israel was lyrical and romantic. Arabs almost never appeared in his stories, a striking omission when compared to his later coverage of the Suez war, when he unequivocally took the Egyptians' side. In his photographs, the *sabra* appeared hard-working, noble, intimately connected to the land, capable of coaxing trees, fruit, flowers, and vegetables out of the desert and turning a desolate, unpopulated strip of land into an oasis.

Chim's work helped to substantiate the myth that the settlers believed in: the land was rightfully theirs, a land to which they had a spiritual connection. They would be heroic pioneers, new, strong Jews, different from the suffering and victimized Jews of Europe(sometimes, myth hold a grain of truth). Chim at the time seemed unaware of a bitter irony of history: many of the Jewish refuges relocated in Israel wound up occupying villages and neighborhoods that had recently belonged to

---

39 MPPA, PAR124391.
40 MPPA, PAR124391.
41 MPNYA, PAR116147.
42 MPNYA, PAR122769.
43 MPPA, PAR116147.

Palestinian Arabs. In 1948 those Arabs themselves became refugees and were parked in refugee camps such as the one that Rodger photographed.

As was true of his work for *Vu* and *Regards* in the 1930s, Chim's Israel photographs are full of hope and belief; they are photographs for a cause and possess a kind of demonstrativeness, even triumphalism. He was seeking a way to reconnect with his own youth, his life as it had been before World War II, a way to try and heal what had been shattered. That is why, in his eyes, Israel could do no wrong. Nowadays it would be easy to dismiss such a point of view but in the 1950s, for many like him whose families had been killed in the Holocaust, Israel offered hope.

Because Chim's vision was somewhat distorted by strong repressed emotions, which he finally was able to free, and because he wanted to help create support for the fledging state, darker aspects of Israel found little to no place in his images—for example, the extreme food shortages that the country was experiencing. By 1949, Israel's population had doubled, with 700,000 new immigrants, and the country was struggling to accommodate them. Israel was living through a period of austerity, the *mishtar ha-tzena*, which lasted until 1959. Food was scarce and unemployment was high. Each month, every citizen would get food coupons for six Israeli foods and each family was limited to a diet of about 1,600 calories a day. Capa, unlike Chin, had photographed people staring grimly at grocery store windows that were mostly empty.

Chim also overlooked the violence that was necessary to establish and defend the Jewish State. He presented Israel as a vulnerable country that had no choice but to shore up its defenses against its powerful Arab neighbors. As a result, his vision of the Israeli army is idealized, for instance, in his reportage on the youths of Nahal. Often portraying smiling young people, Chim downplays the soldiers' fierceness and their use of force against Palestinian Arabs.

Chim's bias was perhaps inevitable, given his circumstances, and the fresh memory of the destruction of his family and that of the Jews of Europe. His images, with their quasi-mythical quality, were probably the only ones he could have made at the time. Anything more skeptical could have felt like treason. However, 70 years on, the passage of time and the reality of Israel's current politics as opposed to the immense hopes raised by the country's creation have cast doubt on Chim's utopian view.

Chim's photographs from Israel raise an all-important question: what is a witness? As art historian Georges Didi-Huberman wrote, "Isn't [a photograph] contact and distance at the same time?"[44]

Maybe being a witness is a bit like tightrope-walking; it implies a difficult balance, where the concerned photographer is both on the inside and the outside.

---

[44] Georges Didi-Huberman in *Eparses, Voyage dans les papiers du ghetto de Varsovie* (Paris: Éditions de Minuit, 2020), 110. Quote translated from the French by the author.

In Chim's case, Israel, in filling the void of his lost family, must have become so close, so intimate, that he lost his usual sense of nuanced distance. His photographs became almost like a family album, where smiles and happy moments are emphasized, and shadows unconsciously pushed aside.

But, in the process of writing this book, a small discovery upended these assertions, suggesting that when Chim revisited his contact sheets after his assignments were done, possibly in early 1956, he wished to put forward a more nuanced, more personal point of view than the one emphasized in his publications.

A small envelope titled "Israel Book," possibly dating from the end of 1955 or the beginnings of 1956, containing the few contact prints that constitute the very early stages of Chim's edit, interrupted by his death:

The prints numbered on verso in his hand, hold no images from the main body of his magazine assignments. Instead, the photographs he chose are joyful, but much more subtle and discreet: a young worker drinking water from a metal container; attendees at the edge of a funeral, not in the center; a man teaching two children, recent immigrants, to read Hebrew; three small Orthodox boys in *kippas* and long *payes* (sideburns) on a bench, reading what looks like cartoons; two smiling miners, faces smudged with dust; a cheerful young family behind ropes at what looks like a fair; two boys playing in mounds of cotton in a field; kibbutz dwellers dancing wildly; a man talking to his caged bird (figure 100). These images are vintage Chim, more intimate than heroic.

In the Spring of 1954, Chim's focus was harshly drawn back to other questions. With the almost simultaneous deaths of Capa and Bischof, that year became, for Magnum, the end of an era.

That May, Jinx and George Rodger were on the other side of the world in the southern Sudan, photographing wildlife, then following the White Nile towards Uganda. After being completely out of touch with the outside world for several weeks, the travelers reached Shellal, where the Nile meets the rail line to Cairo.

Rodger recounts the wrenching moment when he learned the news about Robert Capa. "An Egyptian news vendor walked the hot sand beside the [railway] line and I bought a month-old copy of *Time*. I opened it at random, too hot to take an immediate interest. Then, suddenly, the world stood still. I couldn't believe the cruel outcry of the print—Indochina, Dien Bien Phu—Bob Capa was dead. As though it was not shock enough, I read in the same issue of *Time* that our gentle, talented, sensitive Werner was dead also—killed during the same week but on the other side of the world on assignment in Peru."[45]

On his way to Saigon on a *Life* assignment, Capa, while waiting for a change of planes, had as usual written notes to all Magnum members; these would be his last communications with them. Working on a story in Vietnam, he stepped on a landmine. Within hours, word of his death reached Paris and New York. Robert Capa's

---

45 GRA, George Rodger, 20,000 Days, Unfinished autobiography, no page #.

younger brother Cornell, decided to join Magnum, and all members were called to convene at the Paris office by the end of June. As for Bischof, he died with his chauffeur when their truck tumbled off a narrow, winding road and into a gorge.

On May 27, Chim wrote an emotional but resolute letter to all Magnum members, which reads in part:

> My dear Magnum family: the lump is still in the throat, the dust not settled yet. The blow is hard, and the reaction slow to come. Somewhere, however, there is a faint reasonableness coming, and the realization that the reality has to be faced.
> If we are all numb at present, it looks like soon enough we will have to face it. So we have to go on, keep together, and avoid the stunning effects of our sorrow. Maybe through this we will help ourselves and find strength to keep and develop Magnum—a home for all of us.[46]

Marc Riboud, a young photographer who was close to Chim and Cartier-Bresson and had recently joined Magnum, remembers that period well: "In spite of all these successive deaths," he said, "these were the most beautiful years of my life, everything took on extraordinary intensity."[47]

Chim returned to New York for the memorial services and was immediately asked to take on the role of treasurer and bring order to the organization. At the beginning of July, an emergency meeting took place, attended by Cornell Capa, Chim, Rodger, Cartier-Bresson, Haas, and Morris. The priority was finding a new president to replace Capa.

No one was eager for the job but Chim was *de facto* the only choice because of his skill as an organizer and manager. In a letter to Cartier-Bresson, Rodger describes Chim's Talmudic-like approach to discussions. His fond, humorous letter about his friend and colleague reads in part:

> I had a very nice letter from Chim which made me happy. I learned that his silence, which had worried me, was due only to the fact that my letters to him addressed to Israel were so long delayed. I hope you will be able to work together with him happily in the building of the new Magnum and remember that with Chim the direct approach always works if you want to get your point across. He himself, in his arguments, deviates, wanders around the side and then comes in from the back. If you hit out in a straight line, straight at him, you will be able to put across your points with less argument. At the same time, you will save thousands of words and hours of time.[48]

Chim tried to keep the agency on track, forcing through an often-unpopular program of austerity. In a letter from Tel-Aviv to Cartier-Bresson and Rodger, he explained:

> I would like you to realize that our decision (Cornell and mine with Haas present) to cut staff in the future if the perspective will not change—is related to our present Paris deficit and reduced distribution. George in conversation with me agreed this should be done. Now I feel it

---

46 DSA, letter from Chim to Magnum, May 27, 1954.
47 GRA, Letter from George Rodger to Henri Cartier-Bresson, Beirut, Lebanon, November 20, 1954.
48 GRA, letter to the cofounders, June 19, 1954.

will help all of us to have your opinions on this subject (...). The deficit is something which we all have to deal with. I believe that one of my functions is to keep balance between expenses and income. (...) So please—analyze the situation and make your proposals. (...) However, you have to realize that eventually we will be <u>forced</u> to reduce the budget.[49]

The agency needed new blood: by the end of 1954, Magnum Photos had 24 new members and associates. After a mid-September meeting of the stockholders and the board in Paris, Chim, Cornell Capa, Cartier-Bresson, and Morris were appointed to the Executive Committee for a year; Elliott Erwitt became a member of the Board of Directors. The members' roster included Eve Arnold, Inge Bondi, Burt Glinn, Erich Hartmann, Erich Lessing, Wayne Miller, Inge Morath, Marc Riboud, Dennis Stock, and Kryn Taconis. After Capa and Bischof's deaths, it was a whole new generation.

Amazingly, Chim's output as a photographer did not suffer during his two years as president. Although Magnum was going through growing pains, Rodger helped him keep the organization afloat through changes of staff in Paris and reorganizations in New York. Using his skill as a conciliator and diplomat, Chim worked to quell internal dissension, and in September 1954 he wrote in a circular to all members:

At first, we behaved magnificently—but inevitably there came a letdown—when the body refused to work more hours and the spirit flagged with bitterness. So now there are some signs that we are tearing ourselves apart, in jealousy and mistrust. We must not let this happen. We have come through too much together. We cannot falter now, when we have already proved to the outside that the principles of Magnum survive (...). Let patience and humor replace irritation and anger. Let us share the problems of our future rather than dwell on misfortunes and the past. Magnum is something of a miracle by its very existence. And miracles require continued faith.[50]

By the Spring of 1955, Chim was back in Rome, and for the first time in his life, decided to settle down: he needed a place for his growing collection of books, antique maps, globes, and the other objects he had started to collect. His May 27 lease, signed by his friend Thomas Sterling, describes the rental in Palazzo Orsini as "an apartment consisting of one room, kitchen and bath (furnished) at Via degli Orsini 34, Rome, Italy, beginning August 1st, 1955."[51] He wrote to Hala: "It looks like I will soon have a place for myself. Friends of mine are occupying the top floor of Palazzo Orsini—an old Roman palace—full of history—the present Pope was born there. They have a separate small apartment, and their tenant is moving out. I will move in mid-July and will have a little place for my old books."[52] As he explains in a later letter to friends, he soon added to its decoration: "The latest addition is the top of a cardinal's chair which decorates my bedstead and an old Sicilian gilded wood crown

---

49 Ibid.
50 MPPA, letter dated September 1954.
51 DSA, Lease document.
52 DSA, Letter to Hala dated 7 June 55, Rome.

which I use as a bed lamp. Beverly [Pepper] lent me a few of her paintings so that my place looks lived in and pleasant."[53]

In Paris that fall, Chim wrote Magnum's bylaws, which are still in effect today: a new charter with 22 clauses outlining a three-tier system. Each newcomer should be a "nominee" for two years before becoming an "associate" for a further two years; then, if his or her work received peer approval, that person would become a member for life.[54]

Magnum once again enlarged its list: the new associates were Brian Brake, Jean Marquis, and Ernst Scheidegger; contributing photographers included Philippe Halsman, Dorothea Lange, Russell Lee, and Herbert List. Trudy Feliu was heading the Paris office, and Inge Bondi was secretary-treasurer in New York. Chim was still president. Cornell Capa was vice-president of American operations and Cartier-Bresson vice-president of European operations. Morris was executive editor, and in that role was trying to extract the agency from its financial problems.

The photographers had to find new ideas for work because the magazine market had peaked in the 1940s and early 1950s, and now freewheeling assignments were more difficult to come by and to finance. Accepting industrial reports and even commercial shoots would become a necessity for most members.

Soon Morris and Chim were at loggerheads: Morris wanted Magnum to expand and market photographs through syndication around the world, and he was frustrated by what he saw as Chim's excessive caution. In August 1955, he had circulated to board members a proposal to greatly increase the size and scope of the agency, and Chim replied with a cable asking him to "soft pedal everything."[55] Rodger agreed, and, worried about Morris's plans for the agency, wrote to him, saying: "I do think that you are trying to do too much and Magnum itself seems to be growing into a great beautiful thing that, as far as I know, none of us on this side [meaning Cartier-Bresson and Chim] particularly want."[56]

Since June 1954, during his tenure as an executive editor for Magnum's New York office, Morris had been circulating once-a-month newsletters, and he had also created "Where's Magnum?," an information sheet that circulated among the members, listing where each photographer was working that month.[57] In the December 7, 1955 Magnum newsletter, Morris listed trips by Haas, Rodger, Cornell Capa, and Taconis, and wrote that "David Seymour rented an apartment in Rome but has since spent so much time away (in Paris, London, Vienna, Zurich, Salzburg and New York) that he has yet to sleep in it."[58]

---

53 DSA, Letter to Irene and Henry dated 13 August 1956.
54 Philippe Séclier, *Magnum Photos, 60 Years* (FOT Lyon, 2007), no page #, Charter, 1955.
55 AJGMUC, Paris, unnumbered document.
56 GRA, letter to John Morris, September 5, 1955.
57 DSA, Letter from Frank Gibney to Chim dated Munich, August 4, 1955.
58 Copies of the newsletters can be found at AJGMUC or MFNY.

The April 1955 sheet showed the same number of photographers as the previous year, working mostly in Europe and in the U.S., with a few "elsewhere": Port-au-Prince, Singapore and Jakarta, Ankara, Beirut, Calcutta and Bombay, Bogota. The small percentage of these photographers working "elsewhere"—which was most of the world!—clearly demonstrates how geo-political news coverage would evolve to a completely different perspective, one that Magnum did not anticipate: in today's world, most Magnum photographers can be found working "elsewhere" rather than in Europe and the U.S.

In addition to the recently added members, Magnum had brought in several contributors whose presence in the group would not last, such as Herbert List, Max Scheler, James Whitmore, Hans Wild, Ansel Adams, Ted Castle, W. Eugene Smith, Roger Coster, Ernst Scheidegger, and Ray Witlin. Working alongside Morris and Bondi, the New York office now employed June Torrey and Dan Dixon; Michelle Vignes became a photo editor, joining Trudi Feliu in Paris. In a touching note, the newsletter states, "The picture files of the late Robert Capa and Werner Bischof are available in the Paris and New York offices."

In the mid 1950s, magazine editors were gaining more and more power. However, in the power struggle between photographers and editors, Chim did not give up: his captions often contain commentaries and thoughts, almost like short letters inserted among factual information. They also contain pointers for editors as to how to use the pictures (i.e. size and placement)—since pictures for the same story might be in different batches—and in what context.

By this point, Chim and *Newsweek's* Gibney had established such a strong rapport that Gibney sent Chim a list of potential topics for his consideration. He needed portraits and cover stories on famous writers such as Thomas Mann, Agatha Christie, François Mauriac; artists such as sculptor Jacob Epstein; musician Jan Sibelius; dignitaries such as the Archbishop of Canterbury and the Patriarch of Constantinople. Other ideas concerned human interest stories such as European car racing, The Comédie Française, the U.S. Consulate in Naples (the starting point of most immigration to the U.S.), Interpol, a comparison between East and West Berlin, Jews in Germany, and the Vienna Opera.[59] While Chim did not cover all of these, he became well-known for his expressive portraits of Jacob Epstein, Tennessee Williams, Berenson, Toscanini and more, which were highly praised, and his story on the rebirth of the Vienna Opera made *Newsweek's* October 31 cover. A Magnum index kept in the Paris office lists almost 300 of his portraits of notable personalities.

---

59 DSA, Letter from Frank Gibney to Chim dated Munich, August 4, 1955.

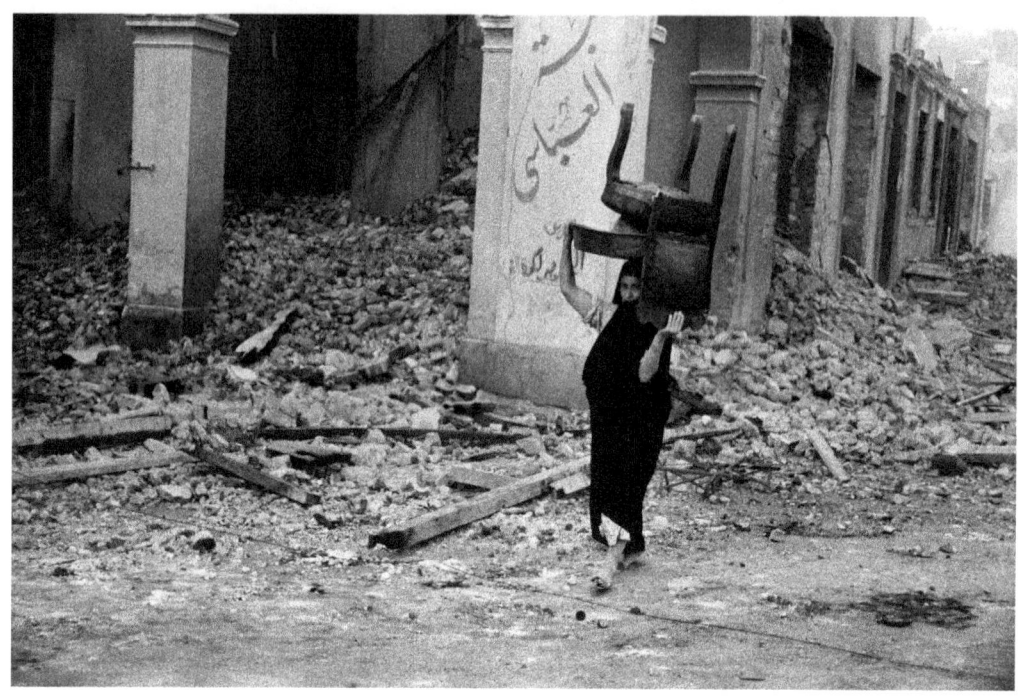

Fig. 19: A woman in the ruins of Port Said after its destruction by Israeli bombing. Egypt, October 29th, 1956.

Chapter 17: I Want to be into Things. November 10, 1956

Chim spent a good part of October 1956 in Rome and Sicily, then in Greece. For the first time, he was settling down and able to spend about a third of his time in his Palazzo Farnese apartment. He wrote to Morris, "Rome is still my sentimental base, and my apartment has grown in comfort and is almost a menace to freedom",[1] and to producer and director Marshall Jamison, a friend: "I had the courage to move out of the Inghilterra. (…) It is a most wonderful way of being. I have a view of the roofs of all Rome, I have my books around me, and I have an old Ines who is taking care of me, fighting for my trousers to be pressed."[2] On September 29 he went to Cologne to represent Magnum, which had been invited to participate in a group show by Fritz Gruber, director of exhibitions at the Photokina. He attended the opening, escorting Theodor Heuss, the first president of the German Federal Republic.

Established in 1950, the same year as the FIAP (Fédération Internationale de l'Art Photographique), Photokina was both an annual trade fair and a photo exhibition complex. That year the cultural aspect had included retrospectives of Erich Solomon and Ansel Adams, group exhibitions organized by the American magazines *Modern Photography* and *Popular Photography*, and a Magnum exhibit showcasing Bischof, Cartier-Bresson, Capa, Haas, Rodger, and Smith.[3] Apart from the first Magnum group show—the 1950 *Face of Time*,[4] which toured five Austrian cities and featured 83 black-and-white prints by Bischof, Capa, Cartier-Bresson, Haas, Lessing, Marquis, Inge Morath, and Riboud—this was the group's most important exhibition to date, and an occasion to network, meet new clients, and check in on the latest technical progress in photography.

The Magnum exhibit, printed by Picto, the Montparnasse lab with which the agency had been working for two decades, displayed enlargements of various sizes arranged on free-standing panels.

Chim was very happy with the exhibition and, back at the Hotel Inghilterra, wrote to his family:

"We had a most impressive exhibition in Cologne at the Photokina Photographic Trade Fair. And it was a tremendous success. Suddenly Germany discovered Mag-

---

[1] DSA, letter to John Morris, no precise date, October 1956.
[2] DSA, letter to Jamison dated October 9, 1956.
[3] Photokina 1956 Catalogue, quoted by Alise Tifentale *in Photokina 1956: A Revolt Against the Universal Language of Photography* (The Graduate Center, City University of New York, 2018), https://static1.squarespace.com/static/5623280de4b08ff533eaa145/t/5a5d0bfe4192027c066beda9/1516047359028/Tifentale_Alise_Photokina_01_15_2018_final.pdf, accessed August 18, 2020.
[4] At the time of this writing, the original set of the *Gesicht der Zeit* exhibition is stored in the Paris offices of Magnum Photos and considered too fragile to be circulated.

num in a big way, and we were front-page news. The visit to Germany was most instructive, especially North, and it is a miracle of reconstruction".[5]

In a letter to Rodger, Chim confided about the toll his role as a president had taken on him

> My executive functions were more involving in the past year than you could realize from the outside. Also they were more frustrating than you imagine. But there is no doubt that we are coming to a meeting in a good, healthy state, without crises which usually took all our time and attention in past meetings. (...) I wouldn't say that Magnum is a European conception. I truly believe it is pretty universal and is suited for a selected group which has a certain amount of unity in its aspirations. (...) The problem of new members is less acute now, because after the growing-up period, having reached a level of organizational importance which makes our global operation possible, we can be extremely selective and slow in accepting new members.[5]

During his tenure as president, Chim had succeeded in stabilizing Magnum's finances, as evidenced by a memo he wrote in October 1956: "This past year has been one of consolidation. We have lost almost no photographers and there has been very little staff change since the New York reduction of last fall. A year ago we had a substantial deficit; now there is a small surplus (on paper) and prospects are good for profitable future operations."[6]

In July 1956, Egyptian leader Colonel Gamal Abdel Nasser seized control of the Suez Canal, declared it nationalized, and imposed dues on all shipping in the canal. A third of this shipping was British—which prompted Prime Minister Anthony Eden's public declaration: "The Egyptian has his thumb on our windpipe!"[7]

Three months later, Chim was in Olympia, Greece, photographing the excavation of the ancient Olympic stadium, when he got the news that Israeli forces had invaded Egypt (figure 106). He immediately wrote to Trudy Feliu in Paris that in view of the crisis he had decided to postpone an upcoming meeting:

> I did not hear the news about Israel until four in the afternoon. My little Olympia story that I found as a lovely excuse to come to Greece suddenly meant nothing. It was clear to me as soon as I had heard the news that I was to return to some basic center of operations (...) [Athens] is full of frustrated correspondents trying to get to Israel. I have run into many old friends as soon as I arrived, and we were all plotting together (...) I would like to be into things (...) At first sight I feel we cannot stay out of world events if we are to grow as a group in world photography.[8]

Although he had not worked as a war correspondent since 1939, Chim was adamant: he needed to cover the conflict. His strong emotional attachment to Israel had clearly

---

5 GRA, letter to George Rodger, October 22, 1956.
6 MPNYA, Memo in ADSS 1956.
7 Quoted by numerous sources, for instance https://anglotopia.net/british-history/british-empire/british-history-showdown-at-suez-eden-nasser-and-the-end-of-empire-long-read/, accessed March 24, 2020.
8 AJGMUC, letter to Trudy Feliu, October 31, 1956.

motivated a decision which seemed in other ways completely out of character. Although his friends and colleagues tried their best to dissuade him, it was to no avail.

On October 14, Nasser had made clear his intention to attack Israel. With the backing of Britain and France, Israel launched a war against Egypt on October 29. Within 72 hours, the Israeli air force was operational, and 100,000 soldiers had been mobilized. By November 5, the entire Sinai had been captured. That same day, British and French paratroopers landed near Port Said to join the Israelis, and amphibious ships dropped commandos ashore.

Chim, traveling with Ben Bradlee, the chief European correspondent of *Newsweek*, and Frank White, Paris bureau chief for Time-Life, was not with the original invasion forces but, thanks to Chim's diplomatic talents, the three scooped most war correspondents, landing in Port Said on November 7. Operation Musketeer, which was intended to topple Nasser and control the Suez waterway, had begun two days earlier, and met disorganized, impulsive, but fierce Egyptian resistance. As the British fought house-to-house battles, that resistance became desperate. Two oil tank containers erupted into flames, blanketing the town with greasy black smoke that lingered for days. Soon French *paras* and a British commando unit linked up at Raswa Bridge. Allied victory was close.

However, the war was unexpectedly cut short: the United States was applying intense political and economic pressure on London and Paris to pull out of Egypt. The "ceasefire at midnight" order reached General Stockwell, commander of the Anglo-French ground forces, at 7.30 on the evening of November 7. Aghast at being, in Stockwell's words, "thwarted in the middle of success," the English and French nevertheless had to comply. Soon after, the first elements of a newly created, blue-helmeted United Nations Emergency Force consisting of soldiers from half a dozen neutral countries reached the Canal Zone, driving Land Rovers with white flags.

The scenes that Chim documented after the ceasefire in what would be his last reportage reflected the havoc this short-lived war had wreaked on Port Saïd's citizens: homes and infrastructure destroyed, acute hunger, thousands of dead or wounded. His images are a stark testimony to the toll that war takes on civilians.

Bradlee, White, Chim, and Jean Roy, a courageous *Paris-Match* photographer who had been helping Egyptian civilians for several days in Port Said and was wearing the full camouflage uniform of the French *para*, went to El Gamil airport, where French paratroopers were assembled, waiting to take off for neighboring Port Fuad. Chim photographed Egyptian prisoners, who were being kept in a garage and then ordered to do clearance work.[9] The field was still littered with parachutes and containers after the landing of the French parachutists (figure 105). Chim proved especially adept at evoking war through its landscape. In a beautifully composed image, crumpled parachutes occupy the foreground, and a line of metal canisters marks an

---

9 MPPA, PAR127070.

oblique perspective under the gray, snow-punctuated sky. The picture evokes Roger Fenton's nineteenth century views of the Crimean War.[10]

The group proceeded to the Egyptian General Hospital, where there were so many wounded that there were not enough beds for them all, and many people were lying on the tiled floor, wrapped in thin blankets.[11] The electric lines were down. By the end of the conflict, Egyptian casualties would amount to 1,650 dead and 4,900 wounded. Ben Bradlee described the scene: "On the ground floor, the wounded were lying all over the place. There was no morphine. Chim walked around photographing. An Egyptian female doctor, Dr. Elezdeine Hosny, operated with an acetylene torch."[12]

Chim photographed refugees being evacuated on the ferry linking Port Said and Port Fuad, including two small boys sitting on a cart among their few possessions which were wrapped in large bundles[13] (figure 103). One of his shots shows Bradlee, Roy, White, and Paul Bonnecarrère, a combat photographer for the French weekly *Jours de France*, sitting on the hood of a Jeep on the ferry. As a photograph by Daniel Camus shows,[14] Roy had painted over the jeep's plate in large white letters the phone number of *Paris Match*: BAL 00 24 (figure 104). It was in that Jeep that Chim and Roy would meet their death.

For two days, Roy drove the group rather recklessly through the streets of Port Said, which were littered with bodies. Allied tanks prowled the streets while patrols tried to contain groups of starving, angry Egyptians. "Port Said was complete chaos," Bradlee recalled. "People had had nothing to eat for three days and were rioting for food, searching through garbage. The city was in ruins. Electric lines down, streets flooded, rubble, dead animals, and sewers broken. There was no police. There must have been thousands of dead and wounded, but the English generals and the French were both lying about it, giving a figure of one hundred dead." He further described the city as "an ugly, festering sore on the mouth of the Suez Canal," with a "choking, inescapable smell of death, smoke, and sewage."[15]

We can only guess at Chim's emotions while he was taking these pictures. Was he feeling torn between his loyalties to Israel, which had won the war, and his empathy for the Egyptians? The people of Port Said and Port Fuad had suffered the brunt of the war, not only their armed forces but also civilians. As Chim knew from his previous experiences in the Spanish Civil War, this was always the case, but it still felt unacceptable.

---

10 MPPA, PAR127042.
11 MPPA, PAR127077.
12 CNA, interview of Ben Bradlee by the author, Washington, D. C., November 9, 2005.
13 MPNYA, NYC1311531.
14 JFAP, *Paris Match* archive, Levallois-Perret, Daniel Camus negative # OR 56/3, communicated by James Fox.
15 CNA, interview of Ben Bradlee by the author, Washington, D. C., November 9, 2005.

Glistening and wet, like a small pond in the sunlight, a French flag spread on the ground marked a friendly area.[16] The city streets were a tangle of powdered brick, collapsed electric cables, and debris, and water-main explosions had turned some into lakes. Jumping out of the jeep into ashes and rubble that crunched under foot, Chim photographed the scenes of desolation through sheets of smoke. A strong sequence of images depicts the ruined city, tanks rolling through the streets, stunned men and women trying to salvage a few possessions[17] (figure 19). He made a striking portrait of an elderly man looking at the wreckage, hands pulled to his mouth in shock and disbelief.[18]

Bradlee vividly remembered a specific scene of looting:

> When I think of Chim, I think of the flour (...). In the center of town, we came upon a flour depot guarded by British soldiers. The crowd broke in. They were carrying huge sacks of flour away, but as soon as they left, others attacked them. The soldiers finally slashed the sacks open and everybody ran, with baskets, pans, any sort of containers they could put their hands on. (...)
> Men, women, and children were walking around powdered with flour like so many ghosts, up to their ankles in spilled white. I did not see Chim jump very fast out of the jeep. Then I saw him—he was very small, walking slowly with his camera, chaos all around him (...) a lone figure, completely calm, clicking away. It was almost in slow motion. He looked at the scene and raised his camera and took these pictures very slowly.

In Chim's images, we see the scenes of looting and images of children scraping the ground in that frantic effort to get spilled flour (figure 102); a British soldier stands guard at the already-looted flour depot; and, in a further scene of pillage, Chim photographed from below a desperate human column of people as they climbed a fish truck as if they were assaulting it.[19]

White remembers that Chim was fearless, taking more and more risks. In a letter to Feliu at Magnum-Paris written just four days after the events, he remembered:

> Dave must have known what he was letting himself in for. Ben Bradlee and I made no secret of the fact we were scared to death. But David, the quiet rational man, the intellectual, the man whose family was wiped out in Warsaw, said nothing. He just kept making pictures. I remember many occasions when we had driven up to particularly nasty food riots, areas where the French and British troops had not yet been but where we had been warned that everybody still had arms. Dave would have already made two, three or a dozen pictures of the scenes, but in each case David kept shooting in spite of our entreaties to leave. When making pictures, he seemed to be an entirely different man. He kept saying, "this is a great story". I got the impression that he felt this made him somehow impervious to the risk.[20]

---

16 PAR127065.
17 MPNYA, SED1956014W00007/36.
18 See for instance MPNYA, SED1956014W00001/34C, SED1956014W00008/19.
19 MPPA, PAR127048 & PAR127049.
20 JFAP, letter from Frank White to Trudy Feliu, November 14, 1956, communicated by James Fox.

Those words from Bradlee and White convey Chim's surreal detachment, as if he was moving in an alternate reality, oblivious to the violence of the scenes he was documenting. This sense of being dazed, detached, is one that many war photographers would no doubt recognize as a tool to cope with reality in moments where they would otherwise be overwhelmed. In these high-risk situations, they often feel that their camera protects them, almost like armor, and it's only later, when they look at their contact sheets, that they realize what they have been through—a perception that resembles a time-bomb. This kind of eerie detachment was the way Chim had always dealt with the trauma of the Holocaust. Since the 1950s, and presumably at some personal cost, this safety reflex had enabled him to lock his emotions away and continue functioning as a photographer.

On the evening of Thursday, November 9, Bradlee and White left for Cyprus in time to file their stories, and Bradlee later delivered Chim's first rolls of film to the Magnum Paris office. Meanwhile, Roy had received a tip from an informer about an exchange of Egyptian prisoners that would take place at Al Qantara, the last post before the Egyptian front lines. As White remembers it, Chim and Roy had started talking earlier that evening about going down to the Canal the next day to witness the exchange.

A little after noon on Friday, Chim and Roy headed for the outpost, about 50 miles away. The narrow road paralleled the canal and from the jeep they could see the brownish-green waters flowing between steep banks. Stopping at the last outpost of French soldiers, they received stern warnings about what lay ahead. "Be careful," the *legionnaires* said. "With the other Egyptian soldiers, we drank coffee and smoked cigarettes, but those are not the same as before. With them we have no contact, and they are more nervous."[21] A British lieutenant was quoted as saying: "We tried to stop them, but they were driving hell-for-leather and they crashed right by us. Then we heard shots from the Egyptian side and the two men did not come back."[22]

Some other British soldiers watching with binoculars saw the Jeep zigzag and topple into the canal. A photograph sent over the wire by United Press shows it half-submerged, with many bullet holes, being checked by two Egyptian soldiers.[23] Another grim, unpublished photograph shows Chim's body riddled with bullets. Three days after the ceasefire, Chim and Roy were dead. Just ten days later, Chim would have turned 45.

A cable published in the French daily *France-Soir* describes a religious ceremony that was conducted a day or two after the two men died:

---

21 Telephone interview with Jean-Pierre Biot, April 14, 2005.
22 Ibid.
23 United Press Radio Photo/Caire/Paris, November 13, 1956. JFAP, communicated by James Fox who found it in *Paris-Match* archives.

> A moving ceremony took place yesterday afternoon in Port Fouad in the presence of all the French and English special correspondents in memory of Jean Roy and David Seymour, whose bodies were returned yesterday morning to the cemetery of El-Gamil, by the Egyptians. The absolution was given to Jean Roy and David Seymour at the end of the afternoon in the presence of Generals Beauffre and Stockwell, very close to the shore where the French commandos landed ten days ago. Two coffins covered with national flags, two sections of paratroopers and naval commandos presenting the arms, the chants of the Catholic and Israelite chaplains carried by the breeze, before us this mound of ocher and arid land from which rose the "Last Post", further still this rough sea where the silhouettes of the warships loomed, such is the scene where we said our goodbyes to our two comrades.[24] (figures 107, 108).

After the Port Fuad ceremony, Chim's body was flown through Nicosia, Cyprus, to New York, where he was buried at Cedar Park and Beth El Cemeteries, Paramus, New Jersey, on November 26, after a remembrance at Riverside Chapel, conducted by Rabbi Louis J. Newman. Members of Chim's family and his colleagues took turns speaking, and his brother-in-law, Samuel "Emil" Shneiderman, said Kaddish, the Jewish prayer for the dead.

Letters and telegrams poured in from all over the world. Articles about his death appeared in the international press, many of them featuring his most famous photographs of the Spanish Civil War or the children of Europe.

"I would like to be into things," Chim had written in his last letter to Magnum. In these words, we may read a certain wistfulness, but also a passionate desire to belong, like his friends Capa and Rodger, to the select group of war photographers that his association with Roy, physically and emotionally his opposite, may well have symbolized. "He went off of his own free will," wrote Judy Friedberg.

> He was a newsman, this was news. Moreover, his beloved Israel was involved (...) we did agree that the most exciting stories of the fifties were starting in Central and Eastern Europe. Chim's last words to me were to get my bags packed and head east to Budapest, Warsaw. 'Go,' he said, 'where I should go and can't bring myself to do it yet.' (...) Somehow, I was sure that wise little Chim would know better than to break the first precept of war photography—never be first down an empty road. Sadly, he either didn't or didn't care.[25]

The sun was setting through the window of the Riverside Drive apartment with its views of the Hudson river. Or maybe it was after dinner? Helen 'Lenka' Sarid, Hala's daughter and Chim's niece, was 19, and listening to the wireless with her mother and young brother Ben when they heard a communiqué about Jean Roy, a *Paris Match* photographer whom they did not know, and their uncle Didek—Chim. He had just been killed in Suez by Egyptian machine-gun, three days after the cease-fire.

---

24 *France-Soir*, November 15, 1956, communicated by James Fox.
25 Letter from Judy Friedberg to Inge Bondi, December 1, 1956, MFNY, MF 011-001-001/2.

Twenty years later, Sarid wrote a poem about her beloved uncle:[26]

My uncle CHIM left no children
When he was killed in a jeep in Port Said
His cameras stilled.
They called him the Owl
And owl-like he loved me.

So many children caught in a flick of light
In some millisecond of recorded time,
Shimmered through celluloid
Turned dark to light,
Washed by those solutions
That could not solve the world
In their incredible eyes.

Chim's children
Dragging oversized shoes
Or limbless
Hugging rag dolls.

And in Alma,
A treeless settlement,
White-washed pre-fabs
Reflect the almighty sun and
A proud father lifts his first born
To the Owl.

Just a few days earlier, in Cyprus, Morris had sent Chim a telegram listing Magnum's receipts for October. He had added: "Take it easy—we don't need the money."[27]

---

26 Email from Helen Sarid to the author, September 22, 2021.
27 Telegram in AJGMUC.

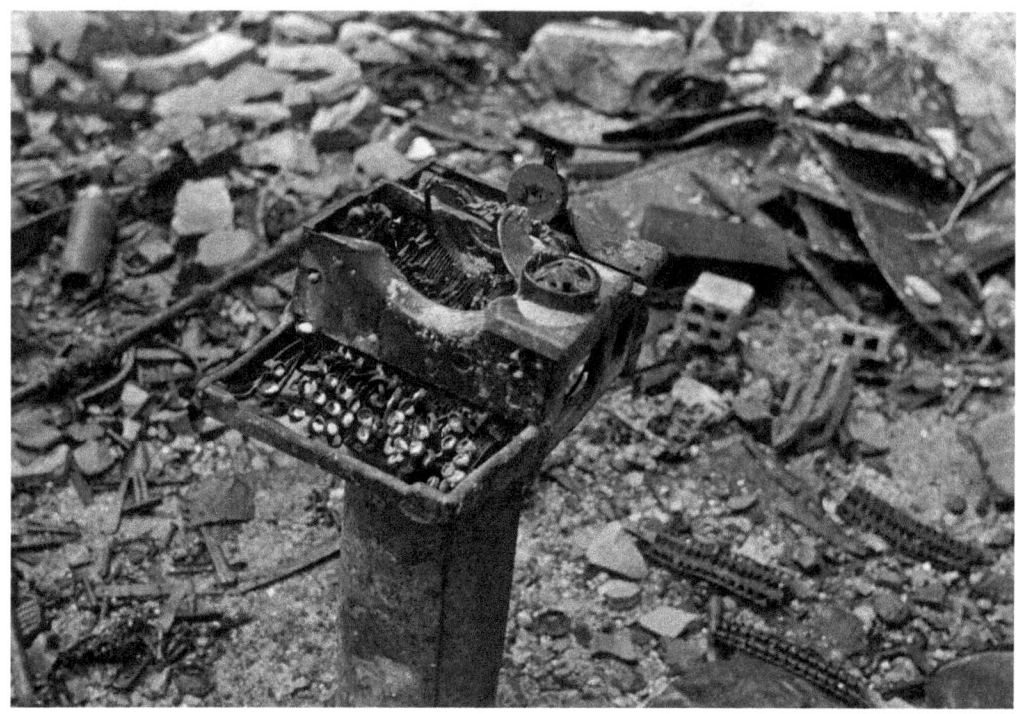

Fig. 20: Destroyed typewriter after bombing , Gijon, Asturias, Spain, January, 1937. © David Seymour-Magnum Photos. From the Mexican Suitcase.

Epilogue: His Name Opened Doors. Chim's Legacy

Henri Cartier-Bresson once described his Magnum community to several witnesses: "When we were together, we did not speak about photography. We spoke about the world."[1] Chim shared his opinion, writing, "We're only trying to tell a story. Let the 17th-century painters worry about the effects. We've got to tell it now, let the news in, show the hungry face, the broken land, anything so that those who are comfortable may be moved a little."[2]

As many people noted, Chim remained modest, despite the acknowledged brilliance of his work. In her testimony, *A Man of Peace,* Judy Friedberg wrote:

> Though he was a true professional photographer and a painstaking one (…), Chim would often smile at the pretensions of some of his colleagues. He decried visual gimmicks in photography and delusions of grandeur on the part of photographers. When someone talked on for hours about his "art", Chim grew bored. If the talk grew too high flown, he was apt to deflate it. 'All you need' he once said as a noted photographer orated on the psychology behind one of his pictures, 'is a little bit of luck and enough muscle to push the shutter.'[3]

During his lifetime, Chim was too busy working to produce books of his photographs. An exception was the 1949 *Children of Europe,* for which he did the layout.[4] However, it was published in haste, with somewhat grayish reproduction, and its aim was political: UNESCO needed it as a propaganda tool to publicize the work of UNICEF, its new children's department. As in Therese Bonney's book, *Europe's Children 1939–1943,*[5] the photographs were paired with demonstrative or descriptive sentences that called attention to the particulars of children's lives. Later, Chim did not have the time to make his own edit of his work on children for a book that might have reflected his taste more than UNICEF's desires and the necessities of fundraising did. His one other book was the 1950 *Vatican* with writer Ann Carnahan,[6] but the photographs are used as illustrations to the text, without much presence of their own. Again, the reproduction is mediocre.[7]

---

1 CNA, interview of Henri Cartier-Bresson by the author, Paris, January 4, 1998, in davidseymour.com/writingson-cn-friends-and-colleagues.
2 Bob Considine, "Snapshot of a Gentle Photographer," *New York Journal,* February 18, 1957.
3 Judy Friedberg "Chim, a Man of Peace," 3/28/66. MPNYA, ADSS,1956.
4 Some pages of Chim's original rough draft are in the collection of the Howard Greenberg Gallery, New York.
5 Thérèse Bonney, *Europe's Children 1939–1943* (New York: Plantain Press, 1943).
6 See Chapter 15.
7 See Chapter 10.

In 1938 the book *Krieg in Spanien* (War in Spain) was published in Warsaw. It credits only S. L. Shneiderman as an author, but it contains ten of Chim's photos of the Spanish conflict. [8]

The book's most striking aspect is its poster-like red, black and white cover, featuring a cut-out of a Chim photograph of a Republican soldier cuddling a child, overlaid by part of the title, then traversed by a red, flag-like band bearing the rest of the book's title in Yiddish. The text is a compilation of various, seemingly random journalistic pieces by Shneiderman, ranging from the description of a bullfight to that of a speech by President Manual Azaña. However, the text and photographs do not relate, the photographs seem inserted randomly into the articles, and Shneiderman never mentions Chim in his text. We have to assume that Chim just gave or sent his brother-in-law a sheaf of pictures, letting him use them as he wished. Another volume by S. L. Shneiderman, *Reportaze Hiszpanskie*, published in Warsaw in 1939, has been lost.[9]

Several of Chim's projects did not see the light of day: one on the Meteoras monasteries and landscapes, in black and white and color, with Greek writer Mano Aravantinou; another on religious festivals in Southern Italy; and his "Israel Book" selection of photographs. In 1957, the book *Little Ones* was published in Tokyo.[10] Chim himself had not conceived it and the inclusion of texts from some of his colleagues suggests that Magnum put it together after his death, as an homage. While the book's copyright mentions an English-language Magnum edition, that edition, as far as I could find, never materialized.

Published in a small format, the Japanese edition of *Little Ones* is more arresting than *Children of Europe* because it is better printed. The general mood of the book is more tender than tragic, and we are left with a familiar, touching awareness of children as a constant presence in Chim's career and his sensibility.

Including images from Chim's 1948 story, it also contains some lesser-known images from that series and the second half of the book features pictures from other reportages: a young boy running with a hoop in a Naples street; two children playing with a snake in Cocullo, from his work in the Abruzzi; children playing in a Venetian plaza; a boy carrying a pail in a white-vaulted street from the story on the Cyclades Archipelago; a shoeshine boy in Greece in 1948; a woman nursing her baby at a land reform meeting in Extremadura in 1936; an Egyptian refugee boy perched on a cart

---

8 Book in the S. L. and Eileen Shneiderman Collection of Yiddish Books, The University of Maryland, https://www.lib.umd.edu/slses, accessed February 23, 2022.

9 At the time of this writing, *Krieg in Shpanien* is being translated from Yiddish as *War in Spain* by Deborah Green, who also communicated me the details about the first tome of Shneiderman's writings (Warsaw: Yiddish Universal Library, 1939). There is currently no information on *Reportaze Hiszpanskie* (Spanish Reportage), published in Warsaw just before war was declared. So far no copy has been located and we don't know if any photographs by Chim are in that volume. Presumably it was destroyed, either by Polish censors or the Nazis.

10 *Little Ones* (Tokyo: Heibonsha, 1957).

on the Port Said ferry, from Chim's last reportage in Suez; three Orthodox Jewish boys on a bench and a boy reading a prayer book, both in Israel.

Since the 1980s, the rise of the photobook as a genre and the growing number of photography exhibitions have encouraged the public to think of photographs as beautiful objects, focusing on their style rather than the content of the story. And notwithstanding Chim's declared emphasis on content over style, we have come to see how well composed and beautiful his pictures were. Although he was an understated personality who did not have a big ego, his photographs slowly came to be rightly appreciated in their "second life" for their strong structure and subtle composition as much as for their empathetic spirit.

In 1957, just a few months after Chim's death, Peter Pollack curated the 40-photograph exhibition, *Chim's Children*, at the Art Institute in Chicago (where the false narrative of Tereska as a concentration camp survivor began).[11] The exhibition, printed in two editions, toured 20 venues, mostly college museums, over 16 years.

One year later, Cornell Capa established a foundation in memory of his brother Robert, Bischof, and Chim, and, in a partnership with Chim's sister and Robert and Capa's mother Julia, he created the Robert Capa-David Seymour Foundation in Israel. The idea was to present the two photographers' work to the public and give awards to promising young Israeli photographers working in their tradition. Magnum set aside funds for a Robert Capa-David Seymour picture library with help from a librarian, from Bischof's widow, Rosellina, and Hala, Chim's sister. They created about a hundred master prints and sets of contacts for both Magnum offices and started looking for the best ways of using their large archive in books and exhibitions.[12]

Cornell Capa chose the phrase "concerned photographer" to describe these brilliant photographers whose work had demonstrated a humanitarian impulse to use pictures to educate and change the world, not just record it, and in 1966, he established the International Fund for Concerned Photography. From 1966 to 1974 it operated out of the Riverside Museum in New York, which in 1967 hosted the exhibition *The Concerned Photographer* featuring, besides Capa, Chim, and Bischof, photographs by Dan Weiner, André Kertész, and Leonard Freed and a companion book.[13] In 1974, the fund established the International Center of Photography (ICP), an organization in New York dedicated to the support of photography as a means of communication and creative expression, and to the preservation of photographic archives as a vital component of twentieth century history. Robert and Cornell Ca-

---

[11] A list of colleges and universities in the tour, a brochure, and typed captions can all be found in MPNYA, ADS 1956–1957.
[12] For detailed accounts, see Nadya Blair, *The Decisive Network* (University of California Press, 2020), 216; AJGM, Memos April 18, 1959, May 16, 1959; Magnum Board Meeting Minutes, September 29, 1959, as quoted in her notes.
[13] *The Concerned Photographer*, Vol. 1 (New York: Grossman, 1967).

pa's photographs, as well as Chim's, are permanently stored in the ICP archive (figure 109)

Cornell Capa was a major force in promoting Chim's work. He curated several exhibitions dedicated to him or featuring his photographs: one celebrating the opening of ICP's collections (1981); another displaying the Spanish Civil War[14] photographs by Chim, Capa, and Taro. In 1974 he also published Chim's work[15] in the first volume of *The Concerned Photographer* series and in *Photographers at War*.[16] And in 1996, Inge Bondi, who had worked as an editor at Magnum New York for a long time and was a close friend of Chim, was the first to publish an illustrated biography,[17] which was followed by numerous books and catalogs.

Since the early 2000s, several exhibitions have featured Chim's work—for instance at the Jewish Museum, Brussels[18]; ICP, New York[19]; D17 Gallery, Budapest[20]; The Jewish Historical Museum, Amsterdam[21]; and Beit Hatfusot Museum, Tel Aviv.[22] The 2010–2011 *Mexican Suitcase* exhibition at ICP[23] contained a strong selection of his photographs with many of his magazine pieces from the Spanish Civil War. By carefully analyzing the content of the Mexican Suitcase, curators Cynthia Young and Brian Wallis were able to separate out Chim's photographs from Capa's and correct wrong attributions (including the poster announcing Robert Capa's retrospective at the Jewish Museum in Brussels in 2009, which featured Chim's photograph of a young Republican boy).

During his lifetime and after his death, Chim's colleagues at Magnum and a larger circle of photographers acknowledged his great influence. Erich Hartmann, for instance, who was the secretary-treasurer of Chim's estate, wrote, "As the pain of realizing the untimely deaths of Chim, and of Bob and Werner, has been absorbed in Magnum and in every member, the magnitude of the work these great and gifted men have left us becomes increasingly clearer and continues to have influence over

---

14 Spanish Civil War, photographs by Robert Capa, David Seymour (Chim), and Gerda Taro, January 9, 1987–February 22, 1987.
15 *David 'Chim' Seymour* (New York: Grossman Publishers, January 1974).
16 *12 at War: Great Photographers Under Fire* (New York: JP Putnam's Sons, 1967).
17 Inge Bondi, *Chim: The Photographs of David Seymour* (New York: Bulfinch Press, 1996).
18 October 29, 2010–February 27, 2011.
19 We Went Back: Photographs from Europe 1933–1956 by Chim, International Center of Photography, New York, curated by Cynthia Young, January 18, 2013–May 5, 2013.
20 *Children of War*, Hungary and Poland, curated by Carole Naggar, October 14–29, 2016.
21 Chim (David Seymour), Legendary Photojournalist, October 19, 2018–March 10, 2019.
22 Capturing History: The Photography of Chim, Beit Hafusot Museum, Tel Aviv, Israel, curated by Asaf Galay, March 29, 2017–January 10, 2018.
23 The Mexican Suitcase, ICP New York, curated by Cynthia Young, September 24, 2010–January 9, 2011.

us and over our work. Anyone who comes into contact with Chim's work is moved, impressed and inspired."[24]

Inge Morath remembers what a powerful effect Chim's work had on her. "I was pretty new at Magnum when he arrived with the pictures of children from the UNICEF story. They left a deep impression. I still see them in front of my eyes: the little Greek girl holding up a pair of shoes, the girl in front of the blackboard. That was the spirit in which we wanted to work, show the world how to make things better by showing them what happened, moving them to help."[25]

René Burri said: "It is Chim who launched me into photography. He was my *padrino* (...) Chim sent me to Czechoslovakia. Contrary to many of his colleagues, he was not competitive. He was generous, he helped young photographers. For instance, he gave me a letter of recommendation to Bernie Quinn of LIFE magazine. He had a magnificent heart (...). After Capa's death, he became the heart and soul of Magnum. When he died it was among the deaths in the family, that golden triangle. Everything changed because Chim's warmth was not there anymore. Trudi [Feliu], who was close to Chim, left. (...) In the sixties, I arrived in Rome with the idea of photographing the Pope. I met with Vatican's chief of photography. He said: 'Magnum? Chim.' And immediately he gave me exclusivity inside the Vatican (...). Even years after, his name evoked a power, opened doors (...)."[26]

Nowadays, photographers tend to specialize in only one area of work but, like other photographers of his generation, Chim was adept at many kinds of photography, from reportage to architecture, landscape to portraits or celebrity portraits, black and white to color.

However, he is probably best remembered for his empathy and his special relationship with children as the most vulnerable victims of wars and social upheaval. His photograph of Tereska, a child he met only briefly in 1948, motivated philanthropist Gregory Siebenkotten to create the Tereska Foundation[27] to help children suffering from profound mental, physical, or economic difficulties. And as a symbol of children's suffering in war, that photograph has been an enduring source of inspiration for painters and photographers over the years.

Historian Simone Gigliotti writes: "His focus on the psychological, learning and health needs of children in Europe provided a foundation for portraying vulnerable children across generations and countries. Alone in the world, without parents, friends or foster families, the projection of children's scars and disabilities aided the post-war mission of UNICEF and UNESCO to educate, fundraise, and disperse a por-

---

24 davidseymour.com, "Chim Seen by his friends and colleagues," Erich Hartmann, letter to Ms Eileen Shneiderman, February 26, 1962.
25 Inge Bondi, *Chim: The Photographs of David Seymour* (New York: Bullfinch, 1996), 115.
26 Interview by Carole Naggar, Paris, May 2005, in davidseymour.com.
27 https://www.tereska.de/en/about/tereska/.

traiture of displacement that future photographers inherited and deployed in visual awareness campaigns."[28]

Chim was truly one of the first human rights photographer, who, in the tradition of Lewis Hine, Jacob Riis and the FSA photographers, practiced advocacy as a vehicle of social change. His photography, in particular his work on children for UNICEF, was groundbreaking, and it inaugurated a tradition of photographers working with human rights organizations. Among those who have followed in his footsteps are Magnum photographers René Burri, Bruce Davidson, Thomas Dworzak, Martine Franck (who often worked with children and senior citizens), Paul Fusco, Mary Ellen Mark, Susan Meiselas, Marc Riboud, Sebastião Salgado, Fazal Sheikh, Chris Steele-Perkins, Larry Towers, and others.

Today, the situation has shifted. Instead of a large organization such as UNESCO operating from the top down, numerous smaller human rights organizations have taken a moral stance, shaping the public discourse and humanitarian initiatives. Today's NGOs communicate directly with the public and often put pressure on governments and international organizations such as the United Nations. And in this new context, Chim's work with children still influences the younger generations of photojournalists. As the world witnesses the largest number of displaced people since the Second World War, there is a natural connection to be made with his most memorable photography.

Chim's photographs initiated a type of storytelling that is still used in reportage on refugee crises and to that end they are often showcased in online platforms and in exhibitions. The 2015 UNICEF exhibition "Refugees in Europe: Then and Now", which toured France and Germany in 2016–2017[29] paired post-World-War-II photographs with contemporary ones. For example, Chim's image of children with disabilities playing football at a Rome orphanage was shown alongside a 2015 color photograph of teenagers, also playing football, at a refugee and migrant reception center in the former Yugoslav Republic of Macedonia. The comparison was intended to stress the unchanging need for children to have safe places where they can receive emotional support.

Similarly, the 2016 exhibition and catalog of Magnum's *Odyssey Europe* project showed 50 pictures curated from the Magnum archive on the subject of escape and refuge. The timeline began in Germany in March 1945, including Chim's "Children of Europe" photographs, and shows stark parallels with the situation of today's war refugees in Syria, Iraq, and Ukraine.[30]

---

28 See Simone Gigliotti, "Patterns of Prejudice," *Displaced children of Europe, then and now: photographed, itinerant and obstructed witnesses*, 52, no. 2–3 (2018), 149–171, https://doi.org/10.1080/0031322X.2018.1433010, accessed December 1, 2020.
29 *Medium: Photography and Social Change*, https://medium.com/photography-and-social-change/refugees-in-europe-then-and-now-1f71790c8d83#.qux6s836i, accessed December 1, 2020.
30 http://pro.magnumphotos.com/C.aspx?VP3=SearchResult&ALID=24PV7C0WHQL, accessed December 1, 2020.

As part of the 2017 *Magnum Retold* series which celebrated the agency's seventieth anniversary, contemporary Magnum photographers took as their inspiration some of the most resonant stories in the agency's history as well as Olivia Arthur's work with the Scottish charity *Positive Action in Housing* to document the contemporary lives of child refugees.[31]

Cultural historian Tom Allbeson has stated that "the children captured by Seymour as published in 'Children of Europe' have become symbols rather than citizens. They are symbolic of a need; they are a means to elicit funds; they facilitate the performance of the concerned gaze of UNESCO. But they are not themselves."[32] However, this statement overlooks the fact that the way Chim chose and photographed the children was very different from the way UNESCO editors used the images. For UNESCO, these images were a means to elicit compassion and funds, but for Chim, each and every child he photographed was, above all, an individual.

It would be a mistake to assess Chim's work and his influence on other photographers only in terms of his work on children. The power of his images strikes deeper. What publisher Robert Delpire wrote about Marc Riboud, a Magnum photographer whom Chim nurtured,—"he conveys the horrors of war without dipping his camera in blood"—helps us to better understand Chim's images, especially the many that are related to war, pain, exile, and conflict, all events he knew intimately from his life experience. The images of the destroyed typewriter on its pedestal in the ruins of Gijon; of Republican soldiers on the attack, their bodies reduced by their speed to clouds of atoms; of Tereska's haunted gaze and the maelstrom of chalk lines she drew; of a young blind boy reading a book with his lips, his severed arms absent from the picture—all these convey immediate emotion but also work to build meaning indirectly, allusively. Their strength is metaphoric as well as descriptive (figure 71).

Chim's images are profoundly different from Cartier-Bresson's decisive moment, Rodger's elegant documents, or Capa's raw slashes of the instant. They are layered, poetic, and complex, like magnets attracting shards of space-time within their careful frame. In his work as a photographer, Chim was profoundly shaped by the intellectual milieu of his youth, his enduring connection to books and reading. That reflective stance, that desire to tell the story differently, is characteristic of younger, educated Magnum photographers such as Thomas Dworzak in his series on war games and Chechenya's Russian occupation, or Peter Van Agtmael in *Disco Night September 11* and *Buzzing at the Sill*.

In 2017, Magnum created the Magnum Foundation which has already helped more than 500 photographers all over the world, especially in non-Western develop-

---

31 https://www.magnumphotos.com/events/event/magnum-retold-exhibition/, accessed December 1, 2020.
32 Tom Albeson, *Photographic Diplomacy in the Postwar World* (Cambridge University Press, 2015), 30.

ing countries.[33] If Chim was alive, he would undoubtedly have sympathized with the foundation's ethics, its low profile, and its methods, including grant-making, training, workshops, mentoring, and collaborations. The foundation's small team remains faithful to the ideals of the four men who created Magnum.

Meanwhile, with offices in London, New York, Paris, and Tokyo, its 89 members and its million-image archive at the time of this writing, Magnum itself has become a sprawling international organization, very different from the small, family-like cooperative that Chim knew and in which he thrived for ten years.

In his preface to the 1956 Magnum Photokina exhibition, Chim wrote:

> The Magnum group cannot be considered a homogeneous school of photography. It includes all varieties of individual talent, different technical approaches, creative interests. There is, however, some unity, difficult to define but still existing. There is a great affinity among Magnum photographers in terms of their photographic integrity and respect for reality, their approach to human interests and search for emotional impact, their preoccupation with composition and layout, and their awareness of narrative continuity.

That description still stands.

---

[33] https://www.magnumfoundation.org/, accessed February 23, 2022.

Timeline

November 20, 1911: Born Dawid Szymin in Warsaw, then part of Russia.
1911: Founding of Central publishing house with Dawid's father, Benjamin, as co-founder.
1914: Benjamin and Rivka, Dawid's parents, move the family to Minsk, Ukraine.
1916: The Szymin family escapes to Odessa.
November 1, 1918: Poland regains independence and the Szymins return to Warsaw.
January 5, 1920: Dawid starts studies at Ascolah Boys Gymnasium.
1929–1931: He studies book art and techniques at the Stäatl Akademie für Graphische Kunst und Buchgewerbe in Leipzig and graduates on March 9, 1931.
1931–Spring 1932: Szymin goes back to Warsaw.
Spring 1932: Moves to Paris and registers at the Faculty of Science of the Sorbonne in Paris. Starts episodic collaboration with *Ruan* photo agency.
1933: Joins *Agence Rap* photo as photojournalist and starts selling pictures to illustrated magazines. Joins the AEAR (Association des artistes et écrivains révolutionnaires). Meets Cartier-Bresson and Robert Capa. Chooses the name *Chim* as byline.
February 1934: Is hired full time by weekly illustrated *Regards*. Covers social unrest, working class, demonstrations, politics, and culture in France.
1934–1935: Meets Maria Eisner, who has just founded *Alliance Photo* and will later become head of *Magnum Photos* Paris office. His sister Hala marries journalist S. L. (Later Emil) Shneiderman and they move to Paris.
June 1935: Attends the International Congress for the Defense of Culture.
1936: Covers demonstrations and strikes in Paris.
March 1936–December 1938: Is sent to Spain to cover the Civil War as Special Correspondent to *Regards*. Comes back briefly to Paris in May 1936. In the course of three years, shoots 1,500 images and produces 30 stories all over Spain, including Tetuan, Estramadura, Seville, Abdalusia, Barcelona, Madrid, Saragossa, Basque country, the Catalan Pyrenees, the Asturias, and Ebro.
Back in France in 1936 reports on the first paid holidays (Congés payés).
Summer 1938: Reportage on Tunisia for *Ce Soir*.
Winter 1938–39: Reportage on Minorca for *Regards, Weekly Illustrated*, and *Ce Soir*.
January–February 1939: Photographs the Spanish *Retirada* crossing over to France in Le Perthus. February: Photographs in Madrid.
May 24, 1939: Sails on the S. S. Sinaia bound for Veracruz with 1,620 Spanish refugees, arriving on June 12.
Summer 1939: Covers Mexican industry and agrarian reform for President Lazaro Cardenas.
September 3, 1939: World War II is declared. Chim crosses into the United States at Laredo, Texas, and arrives in New York.
Early 1940: Starts working for Leco labs and becomes an associate on August 22, 1942.
October 26, 1942: Is inducted into U. S. Army and sent to Fort Dix, then Camp Edison, N. J.
May 1943: Becomes an American citizen and takes on the name David Robert Seymour.
November 1, 1943: Transferred to Camp Richie, trains as interpreter of aerial photographs.
March 25, 1944: Is promoted to sergeant and leaves for Europe. Is appointed as photography interpreter at the ACIU in Medmenham near London.
1944: Is promoted to Lieutenant and receives Bronze Star for his work as interpreter.
September 1945: Returns to New York as a courier and resumes work for Leco.
April 1947: Receives *We Went Back* assignment from *This Week* magazine; ends partnership with Leco and travels back to Europe on April 25. Reports on Great Britain, Normandy, Belgium, the Netherlands, and Germany.

May 22, 1947: Receives telegram from Maria Eisner informing him he is president of the newly founded *Magnum Photos*. Completes *We Went Back* assignment in mid-June.

July 1947: Photographs Frédéric and Irène Joliot-Curie, Nobel prize winners.

September–October 1947: Photographs French elections. Assignments on Trieste, on CARE package distribution, on Monte Cassino after the war, on the rehabilitation of the Corinth Canal in Greece. Covers C. I. A. M. Architects Congress and meets UNESCO representative. Photographs French elections.

Spring 1948: Covers Italian pre-elections. Meets writer Carlo Levi in Rome. Documents poverty in Naples. Works on *Magnum*'s first group project, *People Are People the World Over*, contributing essays on a French family and a German family.

Spring–Fall 1948: UNESCO Reportage on Children of Europe. Travels to Greece, Italy, Austria, Hungary, and Poland, where he confirms his parents' death at the hand of the Nazis. Reportage on shoe-shine boys in Naples and Salonika.

1949: Reportages on Germany, on the Vatican (with writer Ann Carnahan), on Rome neighborhoods. Story on Elefteria's first pair of shoes in Oxia, Greece. Starts work for the film industry with reportage on film set of *Glass Mountain*.

Spring 1950: Reportage on illiteracy in Southern Italy for UNESCO. Works on "Il Gufo" story about Carlo Levi's owl. Story on Oinoi school for UNICEF. Story on premature infants in Paris in collaboration with W. H. O. Reportage on Venice neighborhoods and on expatriates. Stories on Venice gondoliers and on Arturo the pigeon. Coverage of the 25th Venice Biennal. Stories on actress Pierangeli, Rossellini's film on St Francis of Assisi. Befriends Rossellini and Bergman and does several stories on their family.

1951: Participates on Magnum's group project *Generation X* with stories on Italian boy, Italian girl, German girl, and Israeli girl. First trip to Israel. Starts series on Italian religious festivals in Italy with story on Holy Week in Sicily (Spring) and Cocullo's snakes (Abruzzi). Reportage on the Greek Cyclades islands. Coverage of the Greek elections and the Olympic games. Story on United Nations delegates. Stories on spaghetti race in Montemario and wine gala in Beaune, France. Story on Mentone on the French Riviera with writer Gael Mayo.

1952: Photographs on set of film *Salome Unveiled* starring Rita Hayworth.

1953: Story on Zante earthquake, Greece.

1953–1995: Several stories on Gina Lollobrigida.

1954: Story on the journey of San Efisio in Cagliari, Sardinia. Story on the Meteoras monasteries with Greek writer Mando Aravantinou. Story on Greek kites, *Tadpoles in the Sky*. Participates in Magnum group project *Children's World* with a story on an Italian boy, Roberto. Photographs actresses Joan Collins and Irene Papas. Portrait of conductor Arturo Toscanini. Portrait of Giovanni Battista Montini, the future Paul VI. Story on Italian Industry.

May 1954: Deaths of Robert Capa and Werner Bischof. Chim becomes Magnum Photos president.

1955: Stories on Good Friday in San Fratello, Sicily, and the Flying Angels of Campobasso. Story on the Catholic order of the Knights of Malta. Story on Americans in Venice. Photographs Sophia Loren. Photographs on the set of *Around the World in 80 Days*. Portrait of art historian Bernard Berenson. Is part of Edward Steichen's *Family of Man* exhibition at the MoMA, New York.

1956: Travels in Italy, Greece, and France. Story on Maria Callas. Photographs Ingrid Bergman in Cannes and on the set of *Anastasia*, and Audrey Hepburn on the set of Stanley Donen's *Funny Face* in Paris. Photographs Richard Avedon and Fred Astaire on the same set. Documents Ava Gardner and David Niven during the filming of *Little Hut*. Makes portraits of French writer Françoise Sagan. The first *Magnum Photos* group exhibition, *Gesicht der Zeit* (Face of Time), opens in Vienna and circulates in five cities of Europe. On September 29 Chim goes to Cologne to represent *Magnum Photos*, invited for a group show by Fritz Gruber, director of exhibitions at the Photokina. End of Chim's tenure as a *Magnum Photos* President. In October, reportage on Olympia, Greece. On November 7, lands in Port Saïd at the end of the Israel-Egypt war. Dies under Egyptian fire with *Paris-Match* photographer Jean Roy on November 10, 1956.

Appendix

The Magnum Photos Archive, an important European Historical Archive.

I received the following precisions about the Magnum Photos Archive from Ana Cruz Yaybar, Global Head of Heritage and Archives:

In 1991, Anne Crémieux, Director of the Magnum Archives in Paris, proposed a new strategy to adapt the archiving system used at Magnum to the needs of the imminent computerization. Until then, photographers (except a few) assigned only a "story number" to these black and white reports, indicating the year they were taken and the chronology of the story. for the current year: "69-13". The new system is intended to be appropriate and efficient for the management of physical and digital archives, and is based on the introduction of a unique identification number for archives ('Unique numbering system'):

This number consists of the photographer's initials—the first two letters of the photographer's name followed by the first letter of his first name -, then the year of the shooting, the report number, a letter corresponding to the nature of the photo. photograph (black and white, color, color negative, duplicate, digital file, etc.), followed by the position of the image in the report. Ex: SED1951004W00001 / 18. On a computer screen, the letter C for "Color" could be mistaken for an O and the letter B for "Black" could be mistaken for an 8, the letters W and the letter K respectively were adopted as substitutes.

This unique number, which is still used today, is a code that allows the exact location of the original source within the archives of photographers.

Matt Murphy, Archive Director and Licensing Manager, Magnum Photos New York office, added the following precisions to the Abbreviations page of the book:

"... Images made with Rollei are sometimes unnumbered."

I do know that a lot of 120mm/6x6 negatives we have stored in our cold room have hand-written frame numbers on them. Regardless, it is certainly true that at least some of Chim's 120mm/6x6 film have no frame numbers at all.

"... Ex: #54-2-1, for instance, designates the first contact sheet in a 1954 story, the second story covered by Chim that year."

MM: For most cases, this would be true though for Chim (and some other photographers), stories were created at later dates to better divide his 1930s subjects which hadn't originally been divided by story number. As you'll recall, most of Chim's 1930 contact sheets don't have story numbers on them, and are simply numbered with consecutive roll numbers.

"Ex: PAR116249: additionally, pictures have in parenthesis an inventory number with a reference to either New York (NYC) or Paris (PAR) archives."

MM: The Cortex digital database assigns these system-generated "short numbers" consecutively. When Magnum used to rely on an older version of the Cortex database, which existed on local servers in each office, the database would assign

https://doi.org/10.1515/9783110706345-021

the next available short number for that office (PAR for Paris, LON for London, NYC, for New York). The only conclusion that could be made by looking at the office-codes in these older short numbers is that the corresponding office was the first to create an entry for this record in the database (this would include many instances from the earliest days of the database when some staff were creating empty metadata records for keeping track of physical assets, such as prints, and/or there were plans to upload an image file over the blank record in the future even if not by the office who created that blank entry). Also, it should be mentioned that you'll find a lot of older, iconic images with PAR short numbers on them even though the images had not been scanned at that office. The reason for this is because Cortex's software company (Orange Logic) used to be based in France and as such, when Magnum first uploaded batches of the highest priority images to digitize during the early set-up of the database, Orange Logic uploaded the collected files through the Paris office's local Cortex server.

Note that short numbers that begin with "NN" or "MG" were generated after Magnum began uploading new image files directly to the online Cortex server instead of the local Cortex servers.

In brief: "long numbers" are used for archiving and indexing with the database whereas short numbers are the primary client reference code (when we deliver image files, they use short numbers as file names and invoices reference short numbers). Also, while it is possible to alter a long number in the database (say, for instance, we realize a frame # is inaccurate) but the short number could never be changed.

Selected Bibliography

Books by Chim or containing his photographs

Beck, Tom. *David Seymour (Chim)*. London: Phaidon, 2005.
Bondi, Inge. *Chim: The Photographs of David Seymour*. Bullfinch Press, 1996.
Capa, Cornell. *The Concerned Photographer*. New York: Grossman Publishers, 1968.
Capa, Cornell, and Karia Bhupendra. *David Seymour-Chim*. New York: Grossman, 1974.
Capa, Robert. *Death in the Making*. New York: Covici-Fried, 1938. Photographs by Capa, Chim, and Taro. Republished and reedited by Cynthia Young. New York: Damiani/ICP, 2020.
Capturing History: The Photography of Chim. Catalogue for retrospective at Beit Hatfusot Museum, Tel Aviv, Israel. Beit Hatfusot Museum, 2017.
Chiisana Inochi/Little Ones texts by Natsuya Mitsuyoshi, John Morris, and Frank White. Tokyo: Heibonsha, 1957.
Children of Europe. UNESCO publication no. 403, January 1949. Other editions in French and Spanish.
David Seymour, Chim. Valencia: IVAM Institut Valencià d'Art Modern, 2003.
Hendel, Giovanna, Carole Naggar, and Karin Priem, eds. *They Did Not Stop at Eboli. UNESCO and the Campaign against Illiteracy in a Reportage by David "Chim" Seymour and texts by Carlo Levi (1950)*. Contributions by Giovanna Handel, Juri Meda, Carole Naggar, and Karin Priem. Berlin: De Gruyter; and Paris: UNESCO, 2019.
Hood, Robert. *12 at War: Great Photographers Under Fire*. New York: Putnam's Sons, 1967.
Krig in Shpanyen. S. L. Shneiderman. Warsaw: Yidisch-Universal Bibliotek, 1938.
Madrid. Barcelona Generalitat de Catalunya, February 1937. Photographs by Capa, Chim, and Taro (cover by Chim).
Mauro, Alessandra, ed. *David Seymour*. Milan: Hachette, 2004.
Naggar, Carole. *David Seymour*. Photo Poche/Actes Sud, 2011.
Naggar, Carole. *Chim's Children of War*. New York: Umbrage, 2013.
Naggar, Carole. *David Seymour: Vies de Chim*. Biarritz: Contrejour, 2014.
No Pasaran. Brussels: Propaganda Bureau, Belgian Workers Party, 1937. Photographs by Capa, Chim, and Taro.
Tereska and Her Photographer. By Carole Naggar. New York: Russet Lederman; Paris: The Eyes, 2019.
David Seymour, (New York: Paragraphic Books, 1966), edited by Cornell Capa and Sam Holmes.
David Seymour "Chim", 1911–1956. (New York: Grossman Publishers, ICP library of photographers,1974).
The Crimes of Francisco Franco: Murder, Pillage, Ruin, Fire. New York: North American Committee to Aid Spanish Democracy, 1936. Photographs by Capa and Chim.
The Spanish People's Fight for Liberty/La lucha del pueblo espanol por su libertad. London: London Press Department of the Spanish Embassy, 1937. Photographs by Capa, Chim, and Taro.
The Vatican: Behind the Scenes in the Holy City, text by Ann Carnahan. New York: Farrar, Straus, 1949.
Young, Cynthia, ed. *The Mexican Suitcase: The rediscovered Spanish Civil War Negatives of Capa, Chim and Taro*. ICP/Steidl, 2010.
Young, Cynthia, ed. *We Went Back. Photographs from Europe by Chim 1933–1956*. Contributions by Roger Cohen, Carole Naggar, and Cynthia Young. New York: Prestel/ICP, 2013.

For a complete bibliography of periodicals in which Chim's reportages were published, compiled by Cynthia Young, see: *We Went Back. Photographs from Europe by Chim 1933–1956*. New York: Prestel/ICP, 2013.

Books and Periodicals

Abramowicz, Hirz. *Profiles of a Lost World: Memoirs of East European Jewish Life before World War II*. Detroit, 1999.
Agusti Centelles 1909–1985. Arles: Actes Sud, 2009.
Albeson, Tom. *Photographic Diplomacy in the Postwar World*. Cambridge University Press, 2015.
Alun, Kenwood. *The Spanish Civil War: A Cultural and Historical Reader*. Providence, RI: Berg Press, 1993.
Amao, Damarice, and Christian Jochske, eds. *Photographie, arme de classe*. Paris: Centre Pompidou, 2018.
Arnold, Eve, and Martine Franck. *Magna Brava: Magnum's Women Photographers*. New York: Prestel, 1999.
Babington Smith, Constance. *Evidence in Camera: The Story of Photographic Intelligence in the Second World War*. Phoenix Mill: Sutton Publishers, 2004.
Bashevis Singer, Isaac. *Lost in America*. NY: Doubleday & Company, 1981.
Baynes, N. H., ed. *The Speeches of Adolf Hitler*, I. London: Howard Fertig, 2012.
Berger, John. *Ways of Seeing*. New York: Penguin Books, 1973.
Blackwell, Basil. *The Jews in Warsaw*. Oxford, 1991.
Beck, Tom. *David Seymour (Chim)*. London: Phaidon, 2005.
Beckett, Samuel. *The Complete Short Prose of Samuel Beckett*. New York: Grove Press, 2020.
Benjamin, Walter. *Illuminations*. HarperCollins Publishers, 1981.
Bienczyk, Marek. *Tworki, writings from an Unbound Europe*. Evanston, Ill.: Northwestern University Press, 2008.
Blair, Nadya. *The Decisive Network*. University of California Press, 2020.
Böll, Heinrich. *The Silent Angel*. London: Cassell Military Paperback, 2002.
Bondi, Inge. *Chim: The Photographs of David Seymour*. Boston: Bullfinch Press, 1996.
Bondi, Inge. *Ernst Haas*. New York: Delmonico, 2021.
Bonney, Thérèsè. *Europe's Children 1939–1943*. New York: Rhode Publishing, 1943.
Boot, Chris, ed. *Magnum Stories*. London: Phaidon, 2004.
Bouqueret, Christian. *La Nouvelle Objectivité*. Paris: Marval, 2003.
Bouveresse, Clara. *Histoire de l'Agence Magnum: L'art d'être photographe*. Paris: Flammarion, 2017, based on her more complete Phd. Thesis, Paris 1 Panthéon. Sorbonne U University, 2016
Bouveresse. Clara. Israël et Palestine dans l'objectif des photographes de Magnum: les espoirs déçus? (1948–2014). Le Temps des médias. Revue d'histoire, Nouveau Monde Editions, 2020, n°35 (2), pp. 156. ⟨10.3917/tdm.035.0156⟩. ⟨hal-03162616⟩
Bouveresse, Clara. L'agence Magnum en ligne Photothèque et numérisation des images. Transbordeur. Photographie histoire société, Edition MACULA 2019, pp. 136–145. ⟨hal-02011479⟩
Bouveresse, Clara. Du fonds commercial à la patrimonialisation. Conservation et valorisation des archives de l'agence Magnum Photos. In Situ: Revue des patrimoines, Ministère de la Culture et de la Communication, Direction de l'architecture et du patrimoine, [Sous-direction des études, de la documentation et de l'Inventaire], 2018, 36, pp. 18394. ⟨10.4000/insitu.18394⟩. ⟨hal-01995086⟩
Brassai, *Secret Paris of the 1930s*, 1976, reedition. London: Thames & Hudson, 2001.

Brugioni, Dino. *Military Intelligence*, vol. 9, #1, Jan.-Mar. 1983.
Buffet, Alexis, ed. *Vladimir Pozner, Un Pays de barbelés dans les camps de réfugiés espagnols en France, 1939*. Paris: Claire Paulhan, 2020.
Capa, Cornell, ed. *The Concerned Photographer*, vol. 1. New York: Grossman Publishers, 1967.
Capa, Cornell, ed. *The Concerned Photographer*. New York: Grossman Publishers, 1968.
Capa, Cornell, ed. *The Concerned Photographer*, vol. 2. New York: Grossman Publishers, 1972.
Capa, Cornell, and Karia Bhupendra. *David Seymour-Chim*. New York: Grossman, 1974.
Capa, Robert. *Death in the Making*. New York: Covici-Fried, 1938. Republished and reedited by Cynthia Young. New York: Damiani/ICP, 2020.
Capa, Robert, and Chim. *The Crimes of Francisco Franco: Murder, Pillage, Ruin, Fire*. New York: North American Committee to Aid Spanish Democracy, 1936.
Capa, Robert, Gerda Taro, and Chim. *No Pasaran*. Brussels: Propaganda Bureau, Belgian Workers Party, 1937.
Capa, Robert, Gerda Taro, and Chim. *The Spanish People's Fight for Liberty/La lucha del pueblo espanol por su libertad*. London: London Press Department of the Spanish Embassy, 1937.
Capa, Robert, Gerda Taro, and Chim. *Madrid*. Barcelona Generalitat de Catalunya, February 1937.
Capturing History: The Photography of Chim. Catalogue for retrospective at Beit Hatfusot Museum, Tel Aviv, Israel. Beit Hatfusot Museum, 2017.
Carmaux, André. *L'action se passe en France*. Paris: *Les Volontaires* #8, July 1939.
Carnahan, Anne, and David Seymour. *The Vatican: Behind the Scenes in the Holy City*. New York: Farrar, Straus, 1949.
Cartier-Bresson, Henri. *The Decisive Moment*. New York: Simon & Schuster, 1952.
Caruso, Martina. *Italian Humanist Photography from Fascism to the Cold War*. London: Bloomsbury, 2016.
Chapnick, Howard. *Truth Needs No Ally: Inside Photojournalism*. Columbia: University of Missouri Press, 1994.
Children of Europe. Paris: UNESCO, publ. No. 403, January 1949. Other editions in French and Spanish.
Chiisana Inochi/Little Ones texts by Natsuya Mitsuyoshi, John G. Morris, and Frank White. Tokyo: Heibonsha, 1957.
Cookman, Claude H. *American Photojournalism: Motivations and Meanings*. Evanston, IL: Northwestern University Press, 2009.
Daix, Pierre. *Picasso the creator*. New York: Somogy Publishers, 1964.
Das Deutsche Lichtbild, Jahresschau. The German Annual of Photography. Berlin: Verlag Robert & Bruno Schultz, 1926.
David Seymour Chim. Valencia: IVAM Institut Valencià d'Art Modern, 2003.
de Donato, Gigliola, and Sergio d'Amaro. *Un torinese del Sud: Carlo Levi: Una biografia*. Milan: Baldini & Castoldi, 2001.
de Martino, Ernesto. *Panorama e spedizioni: le trasmissioni radiofoniche 1953–1954*. Torino: Bollati Borighieri, 2002.
Denoyelle, Françoise. *La lumière de Paris*. T.1: *Le marché de la photographie*. T.2: *Les usages de la photographie 1919–1939*. Paris: L'Harmattan, 1997.
Didi-Huberman, Georges. *Eparses, Voyage dans les papiers du ghetto de Varsovie*. Paris: Editions de Minuit, 2020.
Dobell, Bryon. "The First Ten Years." *Popular Photography*. September 1957.
Downs, Bill. "The Battle of Nijmegen Bridge." London: *The Listener* magazine, BBC, September 28, 1944.
Downs, Bill. *The Men in Germany's Future*. London: *This Week*, October 5, 1947.
Film Und Foto. New York: Arno Press, 1979.

Faeta, Francisco, *"There are many roads to Italy". David 'Chim' Seymour in Calabria*, in *Vi sono molte strade per l'Italia. Ricercatori e e fotografi americani nel Mezzogiorno*, Soveria Mannelli (CZ),
Friedberg, Judy. "Chim, a Man of Peace." In *David Seymour Chim*. New York: Grossman publishers, 1974.
Frizot, Michel, and Cédric de Veigy. *Vu: The Story of a Magazine*. London: Thames & Hudson, 2009.
Gallagher, Tag. *The Adventures of Roberto Rossellini*. New York: Da Capo Press. 1998.
Gellhorn, Martha. *The Face of War*. London: Granta Books, 1993.
Gellhorn, Martha. *Till Death Us Do Part*. New York: Simon & Schuster, 1958; and NY: Vintage Books, 1994.
Gidall, Tim. *Modern Photojournalism: Origin and Evolution, 1910–1933*. New York: MacMillan, 1972.
Gigliotti, Simone. "Displaced children of Europe, then and now: photographed, itinerant and obstructed witnesses." *Patterns of Prejudice* 52, nos. 2–3 (2018).
Graham, Helen. *The Spanish Civil War: A Very Short Introduction*. Oxford University Press, 2005.
Gries, Zeev. "The Revolution in the World of Hebrew Books at the Start of the Twentieth Century." In *The Book in the Jewish World, 1700–1900*. Oxford, 2007.
Hendel, Giovanna, Naggar, Carole and Priem, Karin *They Did Not Stop at Eboli. UNESCO and the Campaign against Illiteracy in a Reportage by David "Chim" Seymour*. Berlin: DeGruyter, 2020.
Hicks, Wilson. *Words and Pictures: an Introduction to Photojournalism*. New York: Harper & Brothers, 1952.
Hitler, Adolf. Speech of August 1, 1944. In *Zbrodnie okupanta w czasie Powstania Warszawskiego w 1944 roku (w dokumentach)*, edited by S. Datner and K. Leszczyński. Warsaw, 1969.
Hood, Robert. *12 at War: Great Photographers Under Fire*. New York: Putnam's Sons, 1967.
Ignatieff, Michael. *Magnum Degrees*. London: Phaidon, 2004.
In Our Time: The World as Seen by Magnum Photographers. Contributions by Jean Lacouture, William Manchester, and Fred Ritchin. New York: Norton, 1989.
Jackson, Gabriel. *A Concise History of the Spanish Civil War*. New York: John Day, 1974.
Jochske, Christian. "Presse communiste et correspondants ouvriers: Allemagne, France, URSS." in catalogue *Photographie, arme de classe*. Paris: Centre Pompidou, 2018.
Joseph, Gilbert M., Timothy J. Henderson, Orin Starn, and Robin Kirk, eds. *The Mexico Reader: History, Culture, Politics*. N. C.: Duke University Press, 2003.
Kaplan, Louis. *Moholy Nagy: Biographical Witings*, 36. Duke University Press, 1995.
Kershaw, Alex. *Blood and Champagne: The Life and Times of Robert Capa*. New York: St. Martin's Press, 2003.
Kirshenblatt-Gimblett, Barbara, and Lucjan Dobroszycki. *Image Before my Eyes, a photographic history of Jewish life in Poland 1864–1939*. NY: Knopf, 1987.
Knightley, Philip. *The First Casualty. The War Correspondent as Hero and Myth-Maker from the Crimea to Iraq*. Baltimore: Prion Books, 2004.
Kolb, Eugene Kolb. *Al Ha-Mishmar*. Jerusalem, June 21, 1948.
Kozik, Yiftach. *Cephalonia Greece 1953 Operation "Rescue"*. Jerusalem Post, August 21, 1953.
Lavrentiev, Alexander. *Varvara Stepanova: The Complete Works*. Boston: MIT Press, 1991.
Lebrun, Bernard. *Une rencontre à Budapest, 1948*. Rochefort: Les petites Allées, 2022.
Lebrun, Bernard, and Michel Lefebvre. *Robert Capa, The Paris Years 1933–1954*. New York: Harry Abrams, 2012.
Lefebvre, Michel. *Paul Senn, Un photographe Suisse dans la Guerre d'Espagne et dans les camps français*. Rivesaltes: Tohu-Bohu, ed., 2019.
Levi, Carlo. *Christ Stopped at Eboli*. New York: Penguin Books, 2000.
Levi, Carlo. *The Watch*. New York: Farrar Straus & Young, 1951.
Levi, Carlo. "Eboli Revisited: New Life Stirs." *New York Times*, March 13, 1949.

Levi, Carlo. "Italy Fights the Battle of Illiteracy." *New York Times*, April 4, 1950.
Levi, Carlo. "Peasants Stir in Groping Italy." *New York Times*, September 14, 1947.
Levi, Carlo. "Is Europe Through? A Decided 'No.'" *New York Times*, December 7, 1947.
Levi, Carlo. "For Freedom We Must Conquer Fear." *New York Times*, October 3, 1948.
Levi, Carlo. "Italy's Peasants Look at Land Reform." *New York Times*, May 17, 1953.
Lorentz, William, and Marc Crawford. *The Lincoln Brigade—A Picture History*. The Apex Press, 2013.
Lubben, Kristen, ed. *Magnum Contact Sheets*. London: Thames & Hudson, 2017.
Molderings, Herbert. *La seconde découverte de la photographie*, in Paris-Berlin catalogue. Paris: Centre Pompidou, 1978.
Lubow, Arthur. *The New Leipzig School*. The New York Times, January 8, 2006.
Mauro, Alessandra, ed. *David Seymour*. Milan: Hachette, 2004.
Mayo, Gael Elton. *The Mad Mosaic: a Life Story*. New York: BookBlast, 2017.
Mendelson, Andrew L., and C. Zoe Smith. "Vision of a New State as Mythologized by Robert Capa." *Journalism Studies* 7, no 2 (2006): 187–211.
Mendelson, Jordana. *Modernity and War 1936–1939*. Madrid: Museo] Natcional Centro de Arte Reine Sofia, 2007.
Miller, Russell. *Magnum: Fifty Years at the Frontline of History*. New York: Grove Press, 1997.
Morris, John G. *Get the Picture: A Personal History of Photojournalism*. University of Chicago Press, 1998.
Mircevska, Katerina. "The Children evacuated from Greece in 1948: to the Eastern European countries and Yugoslavia." *Politeja #30*, "Macedonia in the 20th and 21st century". Prague: Księgarnia Akademicka, 2014.
Molderings, Herbert. *La seconde découverte de la photographie* (The Second Discovery of Photography), in Paris-Berlin catalogue. Paris: Centre Georges Pompidou, Paris, 1978.
Morris, John G. *International Herald Tribune*. November 18, 1989.
Morris, John G. *Get The Picture, A Personal History of Photojournalism*. University of Chicago Press, 2002.
Naggar, Carole, and Fred Ritchin. *Magnum Photobooks: A Catalogue Raisonné*. London: Phaidon, 2016.
Naggar, Carole. *Chim's Children of War*. New York: Umbrage, 2013.
Naggar, Carole. *David Seymour*. Paris: Photo Poche/Actes Sud, 2011.
Naggar, Carole. *Tereska and Her Photographer*. New York: Russet Lederman; Paris: The Eyes, 2019.
Naggar, Carole. *George Rodger, An Adventure in Photography 1908–1995*. Syracuse University Press, 2003.
Naggar, Carole. *David Seymour: Vies de Chim*. Biarritz: Contrejour, 2014.
Nasierowski, Teresa. "The extermination of the mentally ill in Poland during the Second World War." *International Journal of Mental Health* 35 (2006): 50–61.
Nervig, Margaret. *An American's Paris: tourism and the American consumer, 1947–1961*. UNI Scholar Works, University of Iowa, 2015.
Payne, Robert, ed. *The Civil War in Spain*. New York: Putnam & Sons, 1962.
Preston, Paul. *We Saw Spain Die-Foreign Correspondents in the Spanish Civil War*. London: Constable, 2008.
Priem, Karin "Visual Presence and Interpretation: Two Dimensions of the Fight Against Illiteracy in Texts by Carlo Levi and Photographs by David Seymour (1950)," *Appearances: Studies in Visual Research*, Vol. 3, (2021): 189.
Priem, Karin and Herman, Frederik "Humanitarian Photography Beyond the Picture: David 'CHIM' Seymour's Children of Europe,". *Appearances – Studies in Visual Research*, Vol. 2 (2021): 181.
Ringelblum, Emmanuel. *Notes from the Warsaw Ghetto*. New York: Ibooks Inc., 2006.

Roh, Franz, and Jan Tschichold. *Foto Auge, 76 fotos der zeit zusammengestellt*. Stuttgart: Akademischer Verlag dr. Fritz Wedekind & Co., 1929.

Rosenhaft, Eve. Beating the Fascists: The German Communists and Political Violence, 1929–1933. Cambridge University Press, 1983.

Sanchez-Vasquez, Adolfo, ed. *Sinaia: diario e la primera expedicion de republicanos españoles à México*. Mexico: *Coordinacion de difusion cultural*, UNAM, 1989.

Schaber, Irme. *Gerda Taro: With Robert Capa as Photojournalist in the Spanish Civil War*. Göttingen: Steidl, 2007.

Scott Brown, Timothy. *Weimar Radicals: Nazis and Communists between Authenticity and Performance*. New York: Berghahn Books, 2016.

Sebald, W. G. *On the natural history of destruction*. New York: Random House, 2003.

Segel, Harold B. *Egon Ewin Kisch, the Raging Reporter*. Indiana: Purdue University Press, 1997.

Seymour, David. "Somewhere in Europe: A Photographer Highlights the Drama of Post-War Youngsters." *UNESCO Courier* 2, no. 1 (1949).

Shneiderman, S. L., and Chim. *Krieg in Shpanyen*. Warsaw: Yidisch-Universal Bibliotek, 1938.

Shneiderman, S. L. *Notes for an Autobiography*, translated by Fannie Peczenik. University of Maryland Library, 2001.

Sontag, Susan. *On Photography*. New York: Farrar, Straus, Giroux, 1989.

Sontag, Susan. The New Yorker, December 9, 2002.

Steinhorth, Karl, ed. *Film und Foto. Internationale Ausstellung des Deutschland Werkbunds*. Stuttgart: Deutsche Verlags-Anstalt, 1979.

Strand, Paul, and Cesare Zavattini. *Un Paese*. Milan: Einaudi, 1955 (English edition, *Un Paese: Portrait of an Italian Village*, NY: Aperture, 1997).

Sutton, Horace. *Magnum Opus*. In The Saturday Review, December 1, 1956.

Szurek, Jean-Charles. *Juifs et Polonais (1918–1939)*. In *Les Cahiers de la Shoah* #1. Paris: Editions Liana Levi, 1994.

Taslitzky, Boris. *La Nouvelle Critique*. Editions du Parti Communiste français, Paris, December 1955.

Thompson, Larry V. "Lebensborn and the eugenics policy of the Reichsführer-SS." *Central European History* 4, no. 1 (1971).

Tifendale, Alise. *Photokina 1956: A Revolt Against the Universal Language of Photography*. The Graduate Center, City University of New York, 2018.

Tuban, Gregory. *La Retirada dans l'objectf de Manuel Moros*. Perpignan: Mare Nostrum, ed., 2009.

Vigano, Erica, ed. *NeoRealismo: The New Image in Italy 1932–1960*. Milan: Admira Edizioni; Munich: Prestel; London; and New York: Delmonico Books, 2018.

Viollis, Andrée. *Notre Tunisie*. Paris: Gallimard, 1939.

Vittorini, Elio, ed. *Americana*. Milan: Bompiani, 2015.

Vittorini, Elio. *Conversazione in Sicilia*. Milan: Bompiani, 1953.

Vox, Maximilien, and Carlo Rim. *Tout est foutu*, in catalogue *Photographie, arme de classe*. Paris: Centre Pompidou, 2018.

Whelan, Richard. *Robert Capa: A Biography*. University of Nebraska Press, 1994.

Weil, Simone. *Révolution Prolétarienne*, June 10, 1936.

Young, Cynthia, ed. *The Mexican Suitcase: The rediscovered Spanish Civil War Negatives of Capa, Chim and Taro*. ICP/Steidl, 2010.

Young, Cynthia, ed. *Death in the Making*. New York: Damiani and ICP, 2020 (original edition: New York: Covioci-Friede, 1938).

Young, Cynthia, ed. *We Went Back. Photographs from Europe by Chim 1933–1956*. Roger Cohen, Carole Naggar, and Cynthia Young, contributors. New York: Prestel/ICP, 2013.

Zelizer, Barbie. *Remembering to Forget: Holocaust Memories Through the Camera Eye*. Chicago: University of Chicago Press, 1998.

Periodicals Consulted

Ce Soir
Epoca
Fortune
France-Soir
Harper's Bazaar
Heute
Holiday
Illustrated
Ladies Home Journal
Life
Look
Match
National Geographic
Newsweek
New York Times
Panorama
Paris-Match
Picture Post
Regards
Science Illustrated
Sie Und Er
Vendredi
Vogue
Vu

Archives and Collections Consulted

Archive of George and Jinx Rodger, Smarden, U.K.
Archives Nationales, Paris
Archivio Centrale dello Stato, Rome
Beinecke Rare Books and Manuscript Library, Yale University, New Haven
Ben Shneiderman Collection, Bethesda, Maryland
Biblioteca Nazionale Centrale, Roma (Carlo Levi Fund)
Bibliothèque Nationale, Periodicals Collection, Paris
Fondation Henri Cartier-Bresson, Paris
Fondazione Carlo Levi, Rome
Helen Sarid Collection, Tel Aviv
Inge Bondi Collection, Princeton, New Jersey
Inge Morath photographs and Papers, Beinecke Library, Yale University, New Haven.
International Center for Photography, New York and ICP Archive, Mana, New Jersey
James Fox Archive, Paris
John G. Morris Archive, Paris and University of Chicago
Magnum Foundation Archive, New York
Magnum Photos Collection, New York, London, and Paris
Marc Riboud Archive, Paris

Photography Archive, United States Memorial Holocaust Museum, New York
Paris-Match Archive, Paris
Robert Delpire Archive, Paris
S. L. and Eileen Shneiderman Collection, University of Maryland Library
UNESCO Archive, Paris
Werner Bischof Estate Papers, courtesy of Marco Bischof, Zurich

Acknowledgements

I would like to thank first of all Karin Priem, with whom I have previously worked as a coeditor on the De Gruyter-UNESCO volume "They did not stop at Eboli" and who enthusiastically accepted and backed my proposal for Chim's biography in the collection she codirects, *Appearances: Studies in Visual Research*.

Ben Shneiderman and Helen Sarid, Chim's nephew and nieces who have encouraged my research on Chim since the early 2000s. Nelly and Gilbert Leonardt, Chim's Paris family.

Inge Bondi, a colleague and friend who wrote Chim's first illustrated biography.

Kristen Lubben and Susan Meiselas, whose Magnum Foundation gave me a researcher's grant.

The team at De Gruyter, and especially Jana Fritsche, Evelyn Klehr, Rabea Rittgerodt, John Ryan, Waldemar Isak and Monika Pfleghar.

Fred Ritchin, whose research on Magnum Photos inspired me.

Claude Nori, who published my book "Vies de Chim"

My clever editor, Helen Rogan, who asked the right questions and made tailored cuts and changes to this book.

The teams of *Magnum Photos* in New York and Paris, especially Clarisse Bourgeois, Andrea Holzherr, Naïma Kaddour, Matthew Murphy, Michael Shulman, and Pauline Vermare.

With a special thanks to the brilliant Magnum Photos archivists. In New York: Matthew Murphy, Archive Director and Licensing Manager. In Paris: Ana Cruz Yábar, Global Head of Heritage and Archives.

Rachel Stirberg, who while interning at *Magnum Photos* New York in 2020 helped me discover unknown documents about Israel by Chim.

My former assistant Lola Reboud for scanning several hundred documents relating to Chim for the site www.davidseymour.com.

Nelly and Gilbert Leonhardt for their encouragements and for the early photograph of Nelly's father, Moshe Shajderman, taken by Chim, that they gave me.

Helen Graham, author of a book which is an excellent introduction to the Spanish Civil War, for her careful rereading of the chapter on the War.

Julia Blume, Historian of the Staatliche Akademie für Graphische Kunst und Buchgewerbe (State Academy of Graphic Arts and Book Trade) in Leipzig where Chim studied, for her information about his studies and lodgings, and journalist Britta Veltzke, who connected us.

Zoe Freilich, for her tremendous help in editing the notes, and for her montage of photographs from Chim's World War II handmade album.

Jane H. Pierce, for her research on Chim and her work on his site.

Asano Kinuko and Takemori Tsuyoshi for their help in translating from the Japanese Kimura Ihei's 1955 article on Magnum Photos.

The writers, filmmakers, researchers and publishers whose work has inspired me: Tom Beck, Inge Bondi, Christian Bouqueret, Clara Bouveresse, Marco Bischof, Martina Caruso, Clément Chéroux, Roger Cohen, Robert Delpire†, Françoise Denoyelle, Sebastiaan Faber, Joanna Fikus, Judy Friedberg†, Simone Gigliotti, Linda Gordon, Helen Graham, Giovanna Hendel, Gabriel Jackson, Bernard Lebrun, Michel Lefebvre, Hervé Le Goff, François Maspéro†, Andrew L. Mendelson, Russell Miller, John G. Morris†, Claire Paulhan, Vladimir Pozner†, André Pozner, Paul Preston, Emmanuel Ringelblum†, Fred Ritchin, Irme Schaber, S. L. Shneiderman†, Zoe Smith, Ellen Tolmie, Richard Whelan†, Brian Wallis, and Cynthia Young.

Chim's friends and colleagues who gave me interviews: Jean-Pierre Biot, Marco Bischof, Benjamin Bradlee†, René Burri†, Joan Bush, Henri Cartier-Bresson†, Elliott Erwitt, James A. Fox, Georges Fèvre†, Trudy Feliu†, Lucy Frucht†, Pierre Gassmann†, Burt Glinn†, Erich Hartmann†, Ruth Hartmann, Erich Lessing†, Trudl Lessing†, Jean Marquis†, Susie Marquis, John G. Morris†, Marc Riboud†, William Richardson†, George Rodger†, Jinx Rodger, Willy Ronis†, and Dave Schoenbrun†.

Special thanks to my friends Marie Céhère and Bernard Lebrun† for helping with long-distance research during the epidemic—one time in a Sherlock- Dr Watson style.

And a big thank you to my readers: Melissa Harris, Russet Lederman, Sarah Putnam, Fred Ritchin, and Pauline Vermare, whose suggestions helped deepen and refine my writing.

For their financial help, which cleared time for a part of the writing of a book that stretched over fifteen years, my heartfelt thanks go to:

The Magnum Foundation, New York

The Andrew and Marina Lewin Family Foundation.

Also by Carole Naggar (selection)

What They Saw: Historical Photobooks by Women 1843–1999, 10 x 10, New York: 2021 (contributor: chapter The "New Woman" 1920–1935 and 10 historical notices)
Inge Morath: An Illustrated biography, Series Editor. Text by Linda Gordon, preface by Andrew Lewin. NY: Magnum Foundation/Prestel, 2018
Bruce Davidson, An Illustrated Biography. Series Editor. 2017. NY: Magnum Foundation/Prestel, 2017
Eve Arnold, An Illustrated Biography, Series Editor. NY: Magnum Foundation/Prestel 2015
Bruno Barbey, Passages. Paris: La Martinière, 2015 (in English and French).
Chim's Children of War. New York: Umbrage editions, 2013.
Christer Stromhölm: Passages and Metamorphoses. In "Postcriptum". Stockholm: Max Strom, 2013.
David Seymour. Paris: Photopoche, Actes Sud, 2011.
Dennis Stock: Time is on Our Side. Munich: Prestel, 2015.
Egypte Retour, a memoir with photographs. Paris: Nahar Misraim ed., 2007.
Eve Arnold, An Illustrated Biography. 2015.
Exils, poems. Décharge/Gros Textes ed., 2021.
George Rodger: An Adventure in Photography 1908–1995. Syracuse University Press, 2003.
Giocometti à la Fenêtre. Rochefort: Les Petites Allées, 2019.
Magnum Photobooks. London: Phaidon, 2017 (with Fred Ritchin).
Récits instantanés, memoir. Atelier de l'Agneau, 2019.
Saul Leiter: In My Room. Göttingen: Steidl, 2018 (English and French version).
Tereska and Her Photographer, fiction. New York: Russet Lederman; and Paris: The Eyes, 2019.
They Did Not Stop at Eboli—A 1950 reportage by Chim and Carlo Levi on illiteracy in Italy. UNESCO & De Gruyter, December 2019 (in English and French). Co-editing and contribution.
Werner Bischof: Carnets de Route. Editions Delpire, collection Textis/ Des Images et des Mots, Paris, November 2008.

Index

Adenauer, Konrad 166, 168
AEAR 31–35, 41, 48
Aguilar, Francisco 67, 96
AIZ 19–20, 36, 66
Al Qantara 260
Alba, Duke of 62, 76
Albergo dei Pobre 140, 150
Albeson, Tom 271
Alliance Photo 34, 47, 63
Anita 188–189
APO 35, 37
Aravantinou, Mando 209–210, 266
Archives Nationales 85–86
Arnold, Eve 19, 187, 231, 250
Arthur, Olivia 20, 37, 113, 271
Arts et Métiers Graphiques 29, 48
Arturo 219, 228
Auschwitz-Birkenau 150
Austria 10–11, 18, 42, 86, 102, 136, 143–144, 179
Azana, Manuel 63, 65, 91
Baldo 189 *see also* Ubaldo
Barbusse, Henri 31, 37, 52–53
Barcelona 66, 68–70, 76, 89–91, 99, 101
Basque country 70, 73, 77–78, 85
Bastille 53, 56–57, 216
Bauhaus 17, 19–23, 31, 35, 76, 159
Beckett, Samuel 114
Beit Hatfusot Museum 268
Belgium 111, 121, 187
Belzec 150
Bénès, Edvard 87
Benjamin 10, 67, 216
Berenson, Bernhard 218, 232, 252
Bergen-Belsen 153, 238
Bergman, Ingrid 143, 223–225, 228, 233
Bianka 34
Billed-Bladet 98
Bischof, Werner 5, 135, 145, 181, 187, 201, 231, 248–250, 252, 255, 267, 287
Bochot, Pierre 29, 43–46, 48, 51
Bogart, Humphrey 225
Bondi, Inge 104, 108, 119–120, 164, 209, 215, 237, 250–252, 261, 268–269, 286–287
Bonney, Thérèse 135, 265
Bouveresse, Clara 119, 191, 287
Bradlee, Benjamin 257–260, 287

Brake, Brian 251
Brassai 29, 32, 37, 51, 106, 216
Brecht, Bertolt 22–23, 52
Bristol, Horace 126
Brugioni, Dino 104–105
Brunete 64, 81–82
Buchwald, Art 215
Budapest 32, 146–147, 261, 268
Burger, Dina 123–124
Burri, René 169, 269–270, 287
Cale, Ruth 242
Callas, Maria 232
Camp Ritchie 102–103
Capa, Cornell 67, 116, 220, 249–251, 267–268
Capa, Robert 4–6, 17, 31–32, 34–35, 37, 47–48, 56, 62, 64, 66–67, 69–70, 73, 80–86, 91, 96, 103–104, 106, 111, 114–120, 124–126, 130, 147, 163–165, 172, 185–188, 191, 201, 220, 224, 231, 237–240, 242, 245, 247–250, 252, 255, 261, 267–269, 271
Caption 21, 58, 66, 71, 76, 85, 89, 91, 105, 118, 126–127, 135, 140, 142, 150, 152, 154–155, 172, 191, 201, 220, 234, 252, 267
CARE 130
Cari 190
Carnahan, Ann 169–170, 265
Cartier-Bresson, Henri 5–6, 17, 30–32, 34, 37, 48, 58, 62, 79, 83, 86, 106–107, 114, 116, 118, 124, 126, 164–165, 186–187, 200, 221–222, 231, 242, 249–251, 255, 265, 271, 287
Caruso, Martina 181, 287
Catholic Church 27, 61, 77, 169–170, 196
CBS 111–112, 127
Ce Soir 29, 31, 36, 49, 58, 63, 79, 82, 85–91, 95, 98
Centelles, Agusti 62, 96
Central Publishing 153
Cerbère 95
Chelmno 150
Children of Europe 70, 126, 135, 137–139, 161, 170, 180, 221, 265–266, 270–271
Chim 3–7, 11–13, 17, 20, 23, 30, 32–34, 36–38, 41, 43–58, 62–92, 95–108, 111–116, 118–132, 135–147, 149–161, 163–174, 177–182, 185–190, 193–201, 203–210, 213–235, 237, 239–252, 255–262, 265–272, 276, 286–287 *see* Seymour, David

Clair, René 28, 74
Cocullo 182, 196–197, 266
Collins, Joan 181, 227
Comintern 69
Concerned Photographer 247, 267–268
Contact sheet 5, 30, 41, 52–53, 65, 67, 78, 86, 105, 113, 115, 119, 122, 124, 129, 141, 153, 160, 170, 178, 180, 193, 248, 260, 276
Copyright 117–118, 191, 223, 234, 266
Cyclades 203–204, 266
David *see* Seymour, David
Davidson, Bruce 270
De Gaulle 106, 128–129
De Martino, Ernesto 181
De Sica, Vittorio 143, 173, 215, 222, 225
Death in the Making 83
Denise 32, 107, 163, 208
Der Spiegel 201
Didi-Huberman, George 247
Dinamitero 70, 79
Dobell, Byron 235
Dom Diecka 159–160
Donen, Stanley 216, 234
Downs, Bill 111–112, 115, 121–123
Du 187, 201
Duffort, François 80, 161
Dworzak, Thomas, 270–271
Ehrenburg, Ilya 29, 37, 52, 65–66, 74
Eisner, Maria 5, 47–48, 63, 74, 112, 116, 118, 124–125, 127, 185, 239
Elefteria 174
Elisofon, Eliot 101
Emma 28, 30, 34
Epoca 164, 185, 187, 190, 201, 223
Essen 18, 121–122, 168
Evans, Walker 180
Ewa 33, 46–47
Exile 3, 17, 90–92, 97, 99, 178, 271
Exposition Internationale 21, 29, 79–80
Family of Man 127, 231
Fascism 16, 27, 31, 33, 45, 52, 61, 72, 77, 89–90, 178, 181–182, 222
Feliu, Trudi 3, 170, 251–252, 256, 259, 269, 287
Fellini, Federico 222–224
Fenton, Roger 258
Fernworth, Lawrence 69
FIAP 255
Film und Foto 21–22, 36, 41
Fort Dix 102

Fortune 118–119, 125, 129, 187, 201, 230
Foto Auge 22
France Illustration 161
France-Soir 260–261
Franck, Martine 270
Franco, Francisco 63, 68, 74–77, 79, 84–85, 87, 89–91, 95–96
Francoist 71–72, 78, 84–85, 89, 91, 95
Freed, Leonard 187, 267
Friedberg, Judy 3, 160, 163, 261, 265, 287
Front Populaire 36, 46, 54–55, 81
Frucht, Lucy 101–102, 287
Fusco, Paul 270
Gamboa, Fernando 97–99
Garcia Lorca, Federico 81
Gassmann, Pierre 31, 80, 161, 287
Gellhorn, Martha 4, 61, 85
Generation Children 188
Generation Women 188, 220
Generation X 186–191, 201, 220, 241, 243
Germany 10–11, 16–17, 19–20, 22–23, 29, 31, 42, 47, 49, 61, 68–69, 71–72, 86–87, 95, 102, 106–108, 111, 116, 121–123, 126, 136, 143, 145, 158, 166–168, 187, 189–190, 252, 255, 270
Gestapo 107, 144, 156
Ghetto 27, 72, 100, 136–137, 150–154, 156, 158–161, 247
Gijon 71–72, 114, 145, 271
Glinn, Burt 6, 36, 164, 169, 186, 231, 250, 287
Good Friday 198–199, 230
Gouri, Haim 237
Graziadio 178, 193
Greece 3, 136–138, 194, 203, 205–206, 208–209, 217, 228, 255–256, 266
Grierson, John 125, 135
Guernica 79–80, 101
Guggenheim, Peggy 217
Gwaltney, Corbin 164, 172
Haas, Ernst 119, 181, 187, 227, 231, 242, 249, 251, 255
Hala 9–13, 15, 52–53, 84, 95, 99–103, 106–108, 118, 157, 160–161, 163, 166, 169, 182, 206, 213, 215, 226, 233, 239, 250, 261, 267
Halsman, Philip 251
Harper's Bazaar 161, 164, 201, 223, 234
Hayworth, Rita 225
Heartfield, John 19, 37
Helsinki 174

Hemingway, Ernest 4, 28, 103–104
Hepburn, Audrey 216, 234
Heute 166, 170, 185, 187
Hicks, Winston 191, 220
Hitler 16, 31, 37, 42, 52, 58, 62, 69, 77, 86–87, 91, 95, 103, 123, 161, 167, 190
Holiday 118, 147, 164, 166, 185–186, 188, 190, 201, 215–217, 223, 226, 243, 246
Hollywood 6, 117, 143, 223, 225–227, 233
Hotel Inghilterra 164, 214, 255
Hungary 11, 16, 52, 136, 142, 145, 147, 150, 179, 268
Huston, John 216, 225–226
ICP 38, 41, 66–67, 83, 92, 111–112, 161, 166, 198, 225, 231, 267–268
Illiteracy 126, 132, 177–180, 182, 193, 204, 207, 213
Illustrated, The 29
Israel 3, 9, 187, 190, 222, 225, 237–249, 256–258, 261, 266–268, 286
Italy 3, 61, 69, 78, 83, 89, 126, 129–132, 136, 140–141, 143, 164–165, 177–179, 181–182, 187–190, 193–194, 196, 198–199, 207, 213–214, 222–223, 225, 227–228, 230, 233, 235, 240–241, 250, 266
Jacobs, Fenno 187, 242
Joliot-Curie, Frédéric and Irène 127–128
Joschke, Christian 20, 37
Jours de France 201, 258
Katholieke Illustratie 170, 180, 187, 201
Katyn Forest 149
Kertész, André 18, 22, 32, 83, 101, 267
Kibbutz 6, 190, 239, 243, 248
Kisch, Egon Erwin 29, 37, 44, 81, 98
Kites 217
Knights of Malta 200–201
Kollar, François 81
Korczak, Janusz 150
Korda, Alexander 28
Krull, Germaine 22, 29, 32, 107
Krupp 121–123, 168
L'Humanité 35, 41, 79, 82
Ladies Home Journal 125, 127, 172–173, 191, 201
Lange, Dorothea 251
Le Perthus 84, 90, 95–96
Leco 101–102, 104, 111
Lee, Russell 71, 251

Leica 19–20, 29–31, 62, 101, 105–106, 111, 132, 137, 140, 143, 147, 170, 189, 206, 233, 240, 244
Leipzig 13, 15–20, 22–23, 27, 30, 35, 45, 76, 286
Lengrand, Paul 177
Les Halles 30, 32, 43, 47, 51, 219
Lessing, Erich 187, 250, 255, 287
Levi, Carlo 27, 131–132, 164–165, 177–182, 193–194, 241
Lifar, Serge 28
Life 9, 53, 56, 62–63, 82–83, 91, 98, 104, 106, 116–117, 126, 136, 159, 161, 164, 166, 178, 186, 190–191, 201, 213–215, 220, 232, 238, 248, 257, 269
Lincoln Brigades 62
Lissitzky, El 29
List, Herbert 22, 252
Litvak, Anatol 10, 233
Lollobrigida, Gina 225, 234
Look 124, 170, 178, 201, 223, 228, 232, 237
Loren, Sophia 226, 233–234
Lotar, Eli 22, 31–32, 48
Lucania 141, 177, 181–182
Luftwaffe 156
Maar, Dora 80
Mac Orlan, Pierre 29
Macedonia 138, 174, 270
Madrid 66, 68–70, 72, 74–76, 79, 81–82, 84–85, 90–91, 95, 97, 231
Magnum Foundation 271, 286–287
Magnum Photos 3, 30, 48, 58, 112, 116, 118–119, 154, 170, 206, 250–251, 255, 276, 286
Majdanek 150
Malraux, André 28, 33, 37, 46, 52–54
Manos, Constantine 187
Marquis, Jean 4–5, 30, 231, 251, 255, 287
Marquis, Susie 5, 163, 233, 287
Marty, André 57
Mason, Jerry 124, 164, 226
Match 43, 46, 48, 79, 91–92, 96, 98, 146, 209, 223, 258, 261
Mayo, Gael 62, 91, 98, 186, 221–222
McCalls 186, 215
Medmenham 103–104
Meiselas, Susan 270, 286
Meteoras 209–210, 228, 266
Mexican Suitcase, the 66–67, 71, 74, 83, 85, 92, 96, 268

Mezzogiorno 131–132, 177–179
Miller, Wayne 71, 231, 250, 287
Minelli, Vincente 216
Minorca 89, 99
Moholy-Nagy, Lazlo 18–21, 36, 41, 45, 56, 159
MoMA 118, 127, 231
Moncelsi, Roberto 221
Monte Cassino 130, 137, 142
Montebourg 116
Montini, Signor 171, 229–230
Morath, Inge 107, 220, 250, 255, 269
Morocco 63, 246
Moros, Manuel 96
Morris, John G. 4, 104, 106, 116, 125–127, 164, 171–172, 186, 190–191, 201, 203, 208, 215, 226–228, 232–233, 235, 249–252, 255, 262, 287
Mussolini 42, 52, 58, 62, 69, 79, 87, 130–131, 165, 177, 222, 226
Mykonos 203–204
Nahal 243, 247
Namuth, Hans 62, 68
Nasser, President 167, 256–257
National Geographic 181, 201
National Socialism 19–20
Nazism 170
Negrin, Juan 84, 91
Nenni, Pietro 131
Nervik, Margaret 215
Netherlands, the 52, 121
New York Times, The 20, 166, 178, 180, 201
Nijmegen 121
Nowolipki street 10, 153
Oinoi 207
Oliwa, Franciszca 159–160
Olympic Games 68, 205
Omaha Beach 114–115, 121
Operation Musketeer 257
Operation Pluto 113
Otwock 9, 13, 100, 149, 157–161
Oviedo 63, 68, 70, 72, 75, 79
Oyneg Shabbos 153
Page, Homer 187
Palazzo Farnese 255
Panorama 180–181, 185, 187, 201, 242
Papas, Ireni or Irene 163, 227–228
Paris-Match 201, 257, 260
Pearl Harbor 102
Peignot, Jérôme 29, 48

Pensjonat Zacheta 157, 160
People Are People The World Over 125, 127
Pepper, Beverly 6, 164, 200, 251
Pepper, Bill 6, 200
Père Lachaise 53, 55–56, 82
Perutz, Carl 172, 242
Pétain 128
Photokina 107, 255, 272
Picasso 28, 71, 79–81
Picto 30, 161, 165, 255
Picture Post 29, 187, 221–222, 227
Pignon, Edouard 41
Point de Vue–Images du Monde 187
Poland 3, 9, 11, 13, 16, 18, 27, 33, 43, 49, 52, 56, 63, 95, 102, 136, 145, 147, 149–150, 152, 155–158, 160, 179, 239, 268
Port Fuad 257–258, 261
Port Said 257–258, 262, 267
Prebezac, Earl 103
Prieto, Indalecio 91
Queen Frederika 207–208
Quinn, Bernie 269
Rap 30, 33, 38
Ray, Man 18, 22, 32
Réalités 214
Red Cross 114, 157
Refugees 9, 47, 53, 67, 70, 72, 76, 84, 90, 92, 95–98, 102, 120, 139, 174, 209, 238, 247, 258, 270–271
Regards 29, 35–38, 41–48, 50–52, 54–55, 57–58, 63–65, 67, 69–70, 72–74, 76–86, 89–91, 98, 113, 247
Regina 9, 53 *see also* Rivka
Regulares Indigenas 74
Remer, Otto Ernst 167
Renau, Josep 79–81
Renault 30, 44, 57
Renger-Patzsch, Albert 21–22
Renoir, Jean 28, 83, 106, 233
Republican 61–63, 67, 69, 71–76, 78–81, 83–87, 89–92, 95–97, 99, 169, 266, 268, 271
Riboud, Marc 4–5, 164–165, 249–250, 255, 270–271, 284, 287
Ringelblum, Emmanuel 153, 287
Rodger, George 5, 58, 103, 106, 116–119, 124, 126, 130, 153, 187, 203, 222, 231, 237–239, 242, 247–251, 255–256, 261, 271, 287
Rodtchenko, Alexander 22

Rollei 101, 111, 132, 137, 140, 143, 170, 173, 189, 194, 196, 225, 240, 244, 276
Ronis, Willy 56, 106, 287
Rosemary 189, 222
Rossellini, Roberto 140, 143, 173, 189, 222–224, 228, 233
Roy, Jean 257–258, 260–261
Rulfo, Juan 98
Sagan, Françoise 234
Salgado, Sebastiao 270
San Domenico 196–197
San Efisio 197
San Fratello 182, 198
Santorini 203–204
Sarid, Helen 13, 52–53, 63, 84, 101, 158, 239–240, 261–262, 286
Savoia, Villa 141
Schaber, Irme 17, 34, 48, 287
Scheidegger, Ernst 251–252
Schoenbrun, David 6, 107, 127–128, 164, 287
Science Illustrated 128
Sebald, W.G. 113, 124
Segni, Antonio 233
Senn, Paul 96
Serpari 196–197
Serrano, Carlos 86
Sète 97
Seymour, David 3–4, 9, 34, 66, 102, 104–105, 108, 112, 136, 165, 179, 209–210, 220, 225, 251, 261, 267–269, 271
SHAEF 106
Sheikh, Fazal 270
Shneiderman, Ben 29, 33, 52–53, 158, 240, 286
Shneiderman, Eileen, *see* Hala 163, 269
Shneiderman, family 22, 53
Shneiderman, Samuel Leib [later Emil] 11–12, 15, 63, 149, 151, 160–161, 222, 266, 287
Sie und Er 161
Siebenkotten, Gregory 155, 269
Singer, Isaac Bashevis 10, 149, 157
Snakes 57, 196–197
Sobibor 150
Sontag, Susan 61
Sorbonne 27, 83
Soria, George 54, 64–65, 67–69, 92, 96–98 *see also* Ribécourt
Sotelo, Calvo 63

Spanish Civil War 4, 6, 17, 35, 48, 58, 61–63, 67, 69, 80, 87, 89, 92, 105, 118, 136, 159, 169, 180, 237, 258, 261, 268, 286
Spooner, Lens 119
St Augustine 152–153
St Lô 114
Stawki street 152
Steele-Perkins, Chris 270
Steichen, Edward 21, 127, 231
Stendhal 107, 164, 172
Stern 166, 201
Stock, Dennis 90, 187, 250
Stockwell, General 257, 261
Stotz, Gustav 18, 21–22
Suez 3, 239, 246, 256–257, 261, 267
Suez Canal 256, 258
Szymin *see* Seymour, David
Szymin, Benjamin 9–11, 13, 15, 35, 100, 239
Tabard, Maurice 22
Taconis, Kris 187, 220, 250–251
Taro, Gerda 17, 34, 37, 48, 62, 64, 66, 69, 73, 80–83, 85–86, 96, 268
Tash'lich 246
Tereska 155–156, 267, 269, 271
Tereska Foundation 155, 269
This Week 111–112, 114–115, 122, 124, 126, 128, 161, 164, 166, 170, 185, 222
Thorez, Maurice 42, 57
Todd, Mike 164, 231
Tomatsu, Shomei 71
Toscanini, Arturo 228, 252
Toulouse-Lautrec 28
Towers, Larry 113, 230, 270
TOZ 159
Treblinka 100, 150, 152, 158
Trieste 129, 131
Tschichold, Jan 18, 22
Tunisia 87–88, 246
UNESCO 70, 125, 135–146, 150, 152–153, 155, 161, 177, 179–180, 206, 215, 265, 269–271, 286
UNESCO Courier 136, 154, 161, 179, 194
UNICEF 122, 135–136, 139, 144, 146, 149, 157, 165, 174, 206–207, 213, 215, 265, 269–270
United Nations 129, 135, 214, 237, 245, 257, 270
UNLA 177
Vaillant-Couturier, Paul 31, 54
Valencia 68, 76, 81, 84, 97
Van Doesburg, Theo 28

Vandivert, Rita 112, 116, 118–119, 125, 127
Vatican 6, 78, 169–172, 194, 200, 224, 229, 265, 269
Vendredi 63, 86
Venice 51, 177, 217–218, 220
Venice Biennal 28, 220, 245
Veracruz 98
Viollis, Andrée 29, 86–90, 107
Vittorini, Elio 180
Vogue 201
Voilà 29, 36, 47–48, 63, 72
Vu 29–30, 35, 37, 48–49, 53, 58, 62–63, 76, 189, 247
Wallis, Brian 268, 287
Warsaw 3, 9–13, 15, 21, 23–24, 27–29, 32–33, 36, 46, 52–53, 72, 99–101, 136–137, 149–152, 154, 156–157, 159–160, 163, 239, 259, 261, 266

Warsaw ghetto 151–153
Weiss, Ciki 66, 96
Whelan, Richard 64, 82, 120, 287
White, Frank 257–260
WHO 213–214
Witherspoon, Jinx 119
World Health 213–214
Young, Cynthia 83, 85–86, 92, 111–112, 166, 198, 225, 268, 287
Yugoslavia 51, 129, 137, 174, 187, 190, 206
Ziff, Trisha 67, 99
Zionist 237
Zofiowka Sanatorium 158
Zozaya, Antonio 97

Printed in the USA
CPSIA information can be obtained
at www.ICGtesting.com
JSHW051435030624
64243JS00006B/195